Sustainable Business Development

In today's turbulent business environment, leaders must begin to think more broadly about what a corporation is, and how it can create a richer future. With the globalization of the world's economies, the intensification of competition, and recent quantum leaps in technological development, the insular and static strategic thinking of many global corporations has become inadequate for understanding the business environment and determining strategic direction. This book provides comprehensive and practical analysis of what sustainable business development (SBD) is, and how companies can use it to make a significant difference. Case studies of companies in the United States, Europe, the Pacific Rim, and South America demonstrate that achieving innovation and integration depends on a comprehensive understanding of all of the forces which drive change and responding to them with new ways of strategic thinking. The book will be compulsory reading for MBA students and executives as well as professional readers.

David L. Rainey is Professor of Management at the Lally School of Management and Technology, Rensselaer Polytechnic Institute, New York. He is an internationally recognized authority in sustainable business development, product innovation, technological entrepreneurship, and strategic enterprise management. He is the author of *Product Innovation: Leading Change through Integrated Product Development* (Cambridge University Press, 2005).

Dr. Rainey has over thirty years' experience and leadership in industry and academia. He is a Professor of Management and Chair of the Hartford Department of the Lally School of Management and Technology at Rensselaer Polytechnic Institute. He is also a Visiting Professor at the Technical University of Munich and an Associate of "The Center for the Study of Corporate Sustainability", Instituto de Estudios para la Excelencia Competitiva, Buenos Aires. He is also a member of the Board of Directors of the National Association of EHS Management.

Sustainable Business Development

Inventing the Future through Strategy, Innovation, and Leadership

David L. Rainey

CAMBRIDGE UNIVERSITY PRESS
Cambridge, New York, Melbourne, Madrid, Cape Town, Singapore, São Paulo

Cambridge University Press
The Edinburgh Building, Cambridge CB2 2RU, UK

Published in the United States of America by Cambridge University Press, New York

www.cambridge.org
Information on this title: www.cambridge.org/9780521862783

First published 2006

Printed in the United Kingdom at the University Press, Cambridge

A catalogue record for this publication is available from the British Library

ISBN-13 978-0-521-86278-3 hardback
ISBN-10 0-521-86278-7 hardback

I would like to dedicate this book to my deceased parents, Raymond and Helen Rainey, for their love and dedication to my upbringing, to my brothers, Raymond and Richard, and my sister, Deborah, for their love and support during my whole life, to my wife, Liz, for her endless love and sharing, and to my children, Jonathan, Christopher, and Timothy, for their love and encouragement. It is fitting that the previous generation ensures that the present generation is morally prepared and intellectually equipped to take on the opportunities and challenges to make the world a better place. Likewise, it is the obligation of the present generation to pass on to the next generation a more sustainable and fruitful world that has more opportunities and fewer problems for everyone.

Contents

Part I   Enterprise thinking, the driving forces of change, and leadership

Part II   Innovation management, life cycle considerations, and insights

Figures

Tables

Boxes

Abbreviations

3P	Pollution Prevention Pays (3M)
ACARE	Advisory Council for Aeronautical Research in Europe (EU)
ACEA	European Automobile Manufacturers Association
AIMS	Alcan Integrated Management System
ANSI	American National Standards Institute
ARTE21	Aeronautical Research and Technology for Europe in the Twenty-First Century (EU)
ATV	all-terrain vehicle
B2B	business-to-business
BCSD	Business Council for Sustainable Development
BSI	British Standards Institution
CAD	computer-aided design
CAFE	corporate average fleet efficiency
CAM	computer-aided manufacture
CARB	Californian Air Resources Board
CCA	copper, chromate, and arsenic
CEFIC	European Chemical Industry Council
CEO	chief executive officer
CERES	Coalition of Environmentally Responsible Economies
CFC	chlorofluorocarbon
CIA	Central Intelligence Agency (US)
CLM	Council of Logistics Management
CMA	Chemical Manufacturers' Association
CRT	cathode ray tube
CTQ	critical-to-quality (GE)
db	decibels
dba	decibels absolute
DCF	discounted cash flow
DDT	dichlorodiphenyltrichloroethane

DEHS	Design for the Environment, Health, and Safety (DMAIC)
DFE	Design for the Environment
DFS	Design for Sustainability
DFSS	Design for Six-Sigma
DJSGI	Dow Jones Sustainability Group Index
DJSI	Dow Jones Sustainability Index
DJSTOXX	Dow Jones STOXX Sustainability Index
DJSWI	Dow Jones Sustainability World Index
DMADV	define, measure, analyse, design, and verify
DMAIC	define, measure, analyze, improve, and control
DMWO	Designing Management Waste Out (P&G)
DoD	Department of Defense (US)
DOE	Department of Energy (US)
DRAM	dynamic random-access memory (Intel/Honeywell)
ECRA	Emergency Planning and Community Right-to-Know Act (US)
EDF	Environmental Defense Fund (US)
EEC	European Economic Community
EH&S	health, safety, and environmental (protection) (Dow Chemical Company)
EHS	environment, health, and safety (Alcan)
EI	environmental indicator (Repsol YPF)
EIA	environmental impact assessment
EMAS	European Union Eco-Management and Audit Scheme
EMF	electromagnetic force
EMM	enterprise management model
EMS	enterprise management system
EMS	environmental management system
EoL	end-of-life
EPA	Environmental Protection Agency (US)
EQCD	environmental, quality, cost, and delivery (Canon)
ESAP	Environmental Self-Assessment Program (GEMI)
ESTC	Environmental and Safety Technical Committee (Repsol YTF)
EU	European Union
EV'21	Ecovalue'21 rating (Innovest)
FDA	Food and Drug Administration (US)
FP5	5th Framework Program (EU)
FP6	6th Framework Program (EU)
FTC	Fair Trade Commission (US)

GATT	General Agreement on Tariffs and Trade
GBP	General Business Principles (Philips)
GBU	global business unit (P&G)
GDP	gross domestic product
GE	General Electric
GEMI	Global Environmental Management Initiative
GM	General Motors
GoP	Group of Personalities (EU)
GRI	Global Reporting Initiative
HR	human resources
ICAO	International Civil Aviation Organization
ICC	International Chamber of Commerce
ICLOP	Industry Coalition of the Reduction of Ozone Depleting Materials
ICT	information and communications technology
IISD	International Institute for Sustainable Development
IP	International Paper
IPD	integrated product development
IPP	integrated product polices (BMW)
IRR	internal rate of return
ISO	International Organization for Standardization
IT	information technology
IVA	Intangible Value Assessment rating (Innovest)
JV	joint venture
LCA	life cycle assessment
LCD	liquid crystal display
LCT	life cycle thinking
LEV	low-emission vehicle
LPG	liquified petroleum gas
MITI	Ministry of International Trade and Industry (Japan)
MOS	metal-oxide semiconductor (Intel)
NAFTA	North American Free Trade Agreement
NGO	nongovernmental organization
NPD	new product development
NPERT	New Product Requirements Tracking (Eli Lilly Company)
NPV	net present value
NRA	National Rife Association (US)
NTA	sodium nitrilotriacetate
OAAT	Office of Advanced Automotive Technologies (US)

OECD	Organization for Economic Cooperation and Development
OEM	original equipment manufacturer
OM	operations management
P&G	Procter & Gamble
PC	personal computer
PCB	polychlorinated biphenyl
PEP	product evolution process (BMW)
PERI	Public Environmental Reporting Initiative
PNGV	Partnership for a New Generation of Vehicles (Union Carbide)
ppm	parts per million
PPP	Polluter Pays Principles
PRM	product recovery management (US)
PwC	PriceWaterhouseCoopers
R&D	research and development
R&TD	research and technology development
RARCO	Reynolds Aluminum Recycling Company
RC	Responsible Care (CMA)
SBD	sustainable business development
SBU	strategic business unit
SCA	Corporate Sustainability Assessment (SAM Research)
SEC	Securities and Exchange Commission (US)
SETAC	Society of Environmental Toxicology and Chemistry
SIGMA	EMS of Repsol YPF
SLCA	streamlined life cycle assessment
SMS	strategic management system
SPE	Strategic Plan for the Environment (Repsol YPF)
SRA	Strategic Research Agenda (EU)
SRAM	static, random-access memory
SRI	socially responsible investing
SUV	sport utility vehicle
TMESC	Top Management Environmental and Safety Committee (Repsol YTF)
TQEM	total quality environmental management (P&G)
TQM	total quality management
TRIZ	Theory of Inventive Problem Solving
ULEV	ultra low-emission vehicle
UNEP	United Nations Environmental Program
URS	United Research Services
UTC	United Technologies Corporation

VC	value creation
VCR	video cassette recorder
VOC	volatile organic compound
WBCSD	World Business Council for Sustainable Development
WCED	World Commission on Environment and Development (UN)
WEEE	Waste Electrical and Electronic Equipment (Directive, EU)
WEF	World Economic Forum
WICE	World Industry Council for the Environment
WRAP	Waste Reduction Always Pays (Dow Chemical Company)
WRI	World Resources Institute
WTO	World Trade Organization
WWI	Watchworld Institute

Acknowledgments

I would like to express my sincere appreciation to Dixie Yonkers who edited the initial manuscipt and Barbara Docherty, copy editor, who edited the final document for their outstanding contributions to the success of this book. I would also like to personally thank Jayne Aldhouse, Production Editor, and Katy Plowright and Chris Harrison, Commissioning Editors. Their professional and personal contributions have made this book possible.

Introduction

The coming of age of sustainable business development

At the dawn of the twenty-first century, **sustainable business development (SBD)** is coming of age. Leading global corporations are embracing SBD as a strategic framework for integrating their business enterprises, creating innovative solutions to the complex needs and requirements of the business environment, and thinking strategically about leading change. SBD takes a comprehensive perspective of the corporation and its business environment that includes direct relationships with suppliers, distributors, customers, partners, employees, and shareholders and indirect linkages with stakeholders, competitors, related industries, and the natural environment (the eco-systems).

SBD may be perceived as a subset of the broader concepts of **sustainability** and **sustainable development** as defined by the international community of nations and the United Nations. Sustainable development involves articulating, integrating, and achieving social, economic, and environmental objectives and initiatives to protect humankind and the natural world. The formal legal underpinnings of sustainable development were developed during the United Nations Conference on Environment and Development at the Rio Earth Summit in June 1992. At the Rio Earth Summit, *Agenda 21: Earth's Action Plan* was prepared and presented as "a set of integrated strategies and detailed programs to halt and reverse the effects of environmental degradation and to promote environmentally sound and sustainable development in all countries."[1] The Rio Conference and the subsequent World Summit on Sustainable Development in Johannesburg in August 2002 laid out the principles and proposed action plans but did not reach consensus on how to implement the initiatives. Agenda 21 specifies objectives for governments, **nongovernmental organizations (NGOs)**, businesses, workers and trade unions, and many other groups and individuals relating to concerns such as poverty and promoting human health.

Corporations today face the daunting challenges of achieving superior business performance as well as meeting the expectations of the social, economic, and environmental dimensions articulated in Agenda 21. This book examines how global corporations are integrating SBD into the mainstream of strategic thinking and management.[2] The discussions in the book include the basic foundation of Agenda 21, but they also reach into the corporate world to identify, describe, and analyze the principles, strategies, processes, and practices used to achieve sustainable success. The text describes innovative techniques for leading change and dealing with the complexities of managing in the twenty-first century. SBD involves high-level corporate strategy and executive leadership that is mindful of business, social, economic, and environmental forces. It is the convergence of externally driven conventional processes and practices with evolving strategic management constructs that expand the roles and responsibilities of corporations engaging in SBD in the twenty-first century.

SBD is a holistic management construct that includes the entire value system from the origins of the raw materials to production processes and customer applications to end-of-life (EoL) solutions. It encompasses the full scope of relationships with supply networks, customers and stakeholders, and support service providers for providing business solutions and also handling wastes, residuals, and impacts. It does this through the management concepts of enterprise management and **life cycle thinking** (LCT), building an organization's awareness, and strategic management to encompass the appropriate mindset well beyond its direct actions.

Sustainable outcomes are those that balance the performance objectives of the present with the needs and expectations of the future. Among global corporations today, these kinds of outcomes result from profound changes in strategic thinking, leadership, and management of businesses, some of which include:

- *Enterprise thinking* Shifting from managing the internal aspects and direct linkages of the corporation to assuming broader responsibilities for the entire enterprise – i.e. the practices of suppliers and their suppliers, customers and their customers, stakeholders, and those who dispose of or recycle/refurbish a product at the end of its useful life.
- *Visionary leadership* Having visionary and principled leaders with the knowledge, analytical skill, creativity, and inspiration to craft preemptive strategies and initiatives, lead change, and create breakthrough solutions to meet the needs of the global business environment, both today and tomorrow.

- *Strategic thinking*   Transforming the **strategic management system (SMS)** from one that is focused on producing products and services, satisfying customers, and generating profits to a richer framework that connects all constituents via an interactive system focused on creating value through sustainable solutions and total satisfaction.

- *Product and technological innovation*   Developing new technologies and products that create solutions depends on the intellectual capital of the organization and its systems and processes for turning opportunities and challenges into sustainable success.

Enterprise thinking integrates the full spectrum of social, economic, environmental, market, technological, and management responsibilities and realities into a global **corporate management system** and organizational structure. This holistic perspective transforms "supply and demand" management systems into sophisticated frameworks focused more on value creation, social responsibility, principles, ethics, and total satisfaction. The focus shifts from short-term financial benefits to a more balanced perspective that includes both short-term and long-term views of visionary leadership, strategic thinking, and product and technological innovation.

Visionary leadership guides the organization. It links the business enterprise with humanity and the natural world and connects the present with the future. Visionary leadership provides the insight for creating sustainable competitive advantages. This high-level strategic guidance is the primary responsibility of the executive leadership of the corporation and the senior management of the strategic business units (SBUs). Corporate leadership continually reaffirms the vision and direction of the organization, making it understandable and attainable in the hearts and minds of the people who work for it. People are the essence of a corporation and its ability to achieve sustainable success.

Strategic thinking and business integration allow a corporation to create solutions that are based on the whole enterprise and not just focused on products and customers. **Business integration** redefines the purview of executive management and leadership, expanding it to include parties once considered far outside a corporation's concern. It is at the heart of enterprise thinking and is becoming a mainstream management consideration as corporations depend increasingly on "outside" resources and capabilities for solving problems and exploiting opportunities. The ability to integrate far-flung organizational resources, strategic partners, and enterprise linkages is an essential requirement for effective management performance.

Innovation is the link to the future through new technological solutions and new and improved products and processes. Driven by a dramatic increase in the variety of products and the shortening of product life cycles, product innovation has evolved since the 1980s from slow and simple, uncoordinated new product development (NPD) programs to highly integrated management processes using sophisticated methods and techniques that focus on speed, quality, performance, reliability, and cost effectiveness. Technological innovation focuses on creating new technologies that provide better solutions and eliminate past difficulties and negative impacts. The ability to innovate faster than the competition or the expectations of customers and stakeholders is a key factor in achieving and maintaining a sustainable competitive advantage.

The rapid spread of information and knowledge, the increasing expectations of customers and stakeholders, hyper-competition, the dramatically increased dependence on supply networks, and the breathtaking speed of change are making SBD a critical management concept. The implications of change are forcing corporate leaders to think more broadly about their roles and responsibilities. Corporations are becoming more connected with their customers, stakeholders, suppliers, distributors, and other partners. They are moving from owning and managing physical resources within the corporate umbrella to developing capabilities across the whole enterprise and motivating people engaged in any way with the corporation's strategies and operations to be creative and innovative, and to produce superior and sustainable performance.

Leading global corporations are moving away from just managing within the confines of customers, markets, competitors, and industry structure to a richer landscape of creating exciting solutions to the social, economic, ecological, technological, and business problems associated with past and existing practices and inventing future opportunities and solutions. While the change mechanisms are more evolutionary than revolutionary, the transformation of how management thinks about the implications and impacts of the corporation's decisions represents a paradigm shift centered on the principles of SBD. While most global corporations are in the early stages of adapting the philosophies, principles, and management constructs of SBD, many have committed their enterprises to the long journey toward a more sustainable world. The main theories, concepts, philosophies, and approaches are generally less than ten years old. The methods and techniques for analyzing and developing sustainable business practices are still evolving and may require decades to come to full fruition.

Philosophy and purpose of the book

This book is about how corporations can use enterprise thinking, visionary leadership, strategies, and product and technological innovation to embark on a path toward SBD and sustainable success. It examines the principles, strategies, methods, and practices of SBD. It focuses on the important roles of enterprise thinking and product and technological innovation because of their broad reach across the corporation including customers and stakeholders. Its main premise is that SBD as a management construct can, and should, enhance corporate leadership and strategic management. It is not a radical concept; it involves mainstream strategic development and growth and continuous improvement at the highest level of the corporation.

The book examines the role that global corporations play in developing a more sustainable business environment in the future. The focus is on the strategic management aspects of SBD in relation to the forces driving change. The book includes examples of how leading global corporations are leading change using the principles, strategies, processes, and practices of SBD. The examples highlight innovative approaches for achieving sustainable success.

The book is intended to assist executives, managers, and professionals in formulating, implementing, and evaluating business strategies and decision-making processes concerning SBD. It provides insights into what leading global corporations have done and are doing to create extraordinary value and provide benefits for their customers, stakeholders, and constituents. It studies the implications of these changes for executives, managers, and professionals and explores the next generation of strategic, technological, and environmental management methodologies.

This book does not examine the broader aspects of sustainable development and the related social, political, and economic perspectives, nor does it get into the debate about what "sustainability" means or what the prescribed solutions should be. It examines sustainable development strictly from a business perspective. The discussions in the book focus instead on what is practical and achievable during the early part of the twenty-first century, without suggesting that certain solutions are superior or that selected problems are the most profound. For instance, it avoids the political questions pertaining to the importance of certain issues over others (climate change versus air pollution) or whether renewable energy sources are superior to nonrenewable resources (biomass versus petroleum). While these are important discussions and debates, the theoretical and practical perspectives outlined and discussed in the book pertain to the strategies, initiatives, and actions of global corporations. The book focuses on the development and implementation of corporate strategies, processes, and practices in general rather than prescribing precisely what should be. The intent is to provide the reader with insights about enterprise thinking, visionary leadership, strategies and business integration, and product and technological innovation from some of the most innovative global corporations and from recognized experts in the field.

The twelve chapters define and analyze management constructs, strategies, methods, and practices for creating sustainable technologies, products, and services in the complexities of the twenty-first century. They also examine selected examples and vignettes of corporations that have made significant contributions to the understanding and application of SBD. The examples reveal common elements and patterns that shed light on SBD's meaning and applications.

The book is divided into two parts:

- *Part I*   Introduction to SBD, enterprise thinking, the forces driving change in the business environment, and the power of leadership.
- *Part II*   The strategic management of product and technological innovation, program management, LCT and LCA, and analytical techniques for managing sustainable development programs.

Part I provides an overview of SBD and the implications of strategy and business integration, innovations, and leadership. It describes enterprise thinking, its fit with SBD, the formulation and implementation of related strategies, and how integration plays a significant role in developing solutions. It reviews the social, economic, environmental, and market forces in the business environment and how they provide opportunities and challenges. Most importantly, it discusses the power of visionary leadership.

Part II explores the importance of technological innovation and new product development constructs for creating sustainable solutions. It also examines LCT and management approaches. It provides an overview of **life cycle assessment (LCA)** without getting overwhelmed with quantitative methods.

SBD represents a change in strategic thinking because it expands the traditional boundaries of management systems and focuses corporate strategists on the dynamics of change itself. It invokes proactive thinking about the present and future. This change challenges corporations to manage the whole of the enterprise, including all of the external relationships, and to understand the depth of all of the processes in sufficient detail to ensure that positive contributions are enhanced and negative effects and their impacts are reduced or eliminated.

But SBD also implies preempting expectations and leading change through innovation and leadership. It focuses on what the enterprise must become instead of what it currently is. The overarching objective is to transform the corporation into a richer, more valuable, all-encompassing enterprise that creates incredible value for all constituencies.

Such a challenge as this depends on people who have the intellectual capacity to think "outside-of-the-box" and create new knowledge and capabilities that truly enrich the world. SBD must be grounded in strategies and objectives that are achievable. It must exist in the real business world and lead to real improvements.

The discussions and suggestions in this book are based on what real corporations have done, and are doing (box I.1). To date, there are no corporations that might serve as the perfect model of what SBD means in a corporate setting. Nonetheless, the aggregate experiences of select leading global corporations provide valuable insights and lessons about both SBD and its evolution during the twenty-first century.

Box I.1 Vignettes, case studies, and quantitative methods

This book presents the principles and framework for integrating SBD with strategic management. The case studies and examples of leading corporations provide specific insights about both constructs and management practices, serving as evidence, but not proof, of the SBD phenomenon. They provide an understanding of the dynamics involved in SBD and identify principles, processes, and practices that can be used by others. For reasons of space, the case studies are provided in summary form.

There is no attempt to suggest that the selected vignettes and case studies depict perfection, nor that the corporations themselves have fully implemented the principles and constructs of SBD. Each of the corporations is in transition toward SBD, and it may take many years for them to achieve their ultimate objectives. This is to be expected: SBD is a long-term venture.

Case study methodology is not only appropriate in discovering and understanding the methods and implications of SBD, it is also necessary since the research is on a leading edge, practitioner-oriented phenomenon that is not fully developed in the mainstream of business management. In dealing with complex, diverse, and innovative situations, theories must be derived from real world examples.

SBD is still in its infancy. It will continue to evolve throughout the twenty-first century. As more corporations become part of the paradigm, a richer and more productive world will emerge as the theoretical underpinnings come to full fruition.

NOTES

1. Nicholas Robinson, *Agenda 21: Earth's Action Plan* (New York: Oceana Publications, 1993), p. i. The United Nations Conference on Environment and Development was held in Rio de Janeiro, Brazil on June 1–12, 1992.
2. *Agenda 21*, pp. 525–532.

REFERENCES

Robinson, Nicholas (1993) *Agenda 21: Earth's Action Plan.* New York: Oceana Publications

Part I

Enterprise thinking, the driving forces of change, and leadership

SBD is a strategic management framework for leading change using enterprise thinking, visionary leadership, strategy and business integration, and innovation. It requires a holistic view of the business environment taking in social, economic, and environmental considerations as well as the more conventional concerns of customers, markets, and competition. SBD involves defining, assessing, and improving the whole business enterprise to achieve superior and sustainable performance that exceeds the challenges of the present and the expectations for the future. It integrates business strategies, organizational leadership and capabilities, and needs and expectations into an effective management system for creating innovative solutions for customers, stakeholders, and shareholders of global corporations. SBD is a way for corporations to improve the present and create a better future.

A commitment to pursue SBD places corporations on the leading edge of proactive changes to business strategies, manufacturing and marketing methods, operational and organizational practices, and financial and business performance measures. It engages them in dealing with the impacts and consequences of technologies, products, and processes from cradle-to-grave, and inventing significant improvements from within every facet of the enterprise. By doing so, SBD provides exciting opportunities to change the world through improved systems, technologies, products, and processes that have greater benefits with reduced negative consequences. World-class corporations are indeed reinventing themselves in this way to create a more sustainable future.

SBD depends on the leadership of executive management and its vision of harmony between the enterprise, human activities, and the natural world. SBD and **enterprise thinking** are naturally linked, since both focus on the whole system as their platform for making dramatic improvements to the quality of life, the business and natural environments, and social, economic, and environmental concerns. Enterprise thinking allows leaders to successfully integrate the corporate and strategic management systems of the corporation, including activities related to customers, stakeholders, supply networks, strategic partners, and related industries.

Part I provides an overview of SBD and its essential elements, including enterprise thinking. It examines the critical forces driving changes in the business environment, forces that provide the context for SBD. It examines the importance of understanding the needs and wants of customers, stakeholders, shareholders, and employees, the desires and expectations of society, the directives and mandates of political and regulatory entities, and the implications of knowledge and learning within organizations. It also discusses the importance of communicating openly with constituencies across the world.

Part I includes six chapters:

- Chapter 1   Sustainable business development: overview and guiding principles
- Chapter 2   Enterprise thinking and the strategic logic of strategic business development
- Chapter 3   Crafting sustainable business strategies and solutions
- Chapter 4   The driving forces of social-, economic-, and environmental-related change
- Chapter 5   The driving forces of markets and stakeholders' connectedness
- Chapter 6   Crafting a sustainable enterprise through leadership and capabilities

Chapter 1 examines the evolution of strategic and environmental management frameworks for exploring and satisfying customer and stakeholder needs and wants and the underlying social, economic, and environmental drivers and issues. Corporations across the world are engaged in a relentless struggle to keep pace with dramatic and accelerating changes. Globalization, demanding expectations from customers and stakeholders, hyper-competition, the rapid spread of information and knowledge, shrinking product life cycles, the dependence on supply networks, and the breathtaking speed of change pressure producers and service providers to dramatically improve the quality, performance, and environmental impacts of their technologies, products, processes, and services. Leading corporations are examining their concepts, strategies, and processes as they seek improvements, and it is becoming clear that strategic management thinking must include the whole business environment to invent solutions that are sustainable across time. They must create better technologies, products, and processes that offer customers and society extraordinary value and total satisfaction.

Chapter 2 discusses two of the most powerful management constructs of the twenty-first century: SBD and enterprise thinking. SBD is a vision, an overarching philosophy, and a grand strategy. The vision is to create a business world that incorporates sustainable solutions for meeting the needs of humankind and the natural world and to fulfill those needs without significant negative impacts and burdens. The overarching philosophy of SBD promotes solutions that are positive and sustainable from social, economic, environmental, technological, and business perspectives. This philosophy guides corporations as they select the most appropriate initiatives and development programs. Enterprise thinking calls leadership to consider the entire enterprise as it determines high-level corporate strategies and objectives. It requires that leaders take a global view of the business environment with all of its customers, stakeholders, partners, suppliers, competitors, related industries, employees, shareholders, and agents. It encompasses both internal and external facets, the past, the present, and the future.

Chapter 3 provides an integrated perspective on how corporations can craft corporate strategies for creating sustainable business solutions. The analysis and selection of effective strategies are based on the capabilities, knowledge, intellectual capital, and relationships of the organization and the business environment. The basic approach for building a sustainable management system is to create value streams for the customers, stakeholders, and organization that exceed social, economic, and environmental requirements. Value streams and processes must delight customers and provide solutions for all constituents. These outcomes will dramatically improve performance while reducing the drain on resources and minimizing negative effects.

Chapter 4 discusses how social, economic, and environmental considerations provide opportunities for corporations to develop and enhance customer and stakeholder value, solutions, linkages – and ultimately, corporate reputation and image. By building key stakeholder relationships among government, NGOs, and other constituents, corporations can anticipate and manage issues and concerns that, unrecognized, could develop into major problems. Building relationships requires being in sync with constituencies and creating trust within the business environment. The chapter examines the social, economic, and environmental forces that affect the business environment.

Chapter 5 discusses how social, economic, and environmental considerations can provide exciting market opportunities and challenges for innovative organizations. These concerns can spur corporations to find ways to exceed customer and stakeholder expectations using leading edge product innovation and **lean production**, and to differentiate their corporate image and build a sustainable position for the future with green marketing. Transparency and open communications provides information that includes the positive benefits of products along with the negative impacts and their consequences. Such disclosures examine the whole truth about the products, processes, and operations so that customers and stakeholders can make informed decisions. This chapter also explores how green marketing and environmentally conscious communications can play a vital role in achieving SBD.

Chapter 6 focuses on building awareness, knowledge, and performance throughout the organization. Effective leadership encourages cultural changes through cross-functional integration and investments in building new capabilities. The gap between planning and action in most management systems is often wide and fraught with obstacles. Many corporations have committed to protecting social and environmental considerations, but very few have made this commitment meaningful throughout the entire organization. Successful firms focus on creating a corporate-wide culture for ensuring the necessary awareness, knowledge, learning, and actions across and among business units, functions, and external relationships. The elements that leaders use to hone an organization's culture or "the way they do things around here" include education, accountability, and performance evaluation metrics.

1 Sustainable business development: overview and guiding principles

Introduction

Overview

Leading business corporations in the industrialized world are changing their SMSs to incorporate the principles, strategies, processes, and practices of SBD. They are moving from the company-centric structures of the twentieth century to highly interactive management constructs framed in the global context of the social, political, economic, environmental, market, and technological realities of the twenty-first century. The transformation process is subtle and involves evolutionary changes that have been dramatically reshaping the business world since the 1970s. With globalization, technological changes, economic drivers, and social and environmental mandates, the global business environment is less predictable and more challenging than it was even a decade ago. Customers, stakeholders, and society expect and demand superior products, services, and operations with less waste, reduced impacts on health, safety, and the environment, and enhanced corporate responsibilities for the decisions, technologies, products, processes, and activities of every facet of the business enterprise. Moreover, these expectations also apply to the operations, actions, and contributions of supply networks, partners, allies, and others that are directly and indirectly linked to the corporation.

The implications of such expectations and demands are profound. Leading and managing a large corporation has become more complex and challenging, yet also more exciting and rewarding. Corporations have broadened the scope of their thinking and include many more considerations in their decision-making. They have moved beyond concentrating on core competencies in order to satisfy customers with high-quality products: that thinking characterized the 1990s. Today, businesses must thoroughly analyze the global business environment to gain a firm understanding of the opportunities and challenges it presents, and develop aggressive strategies for improving every aspect of their enterprises.

To do this, corporations must have in place a comprehensive and integrated **strategic management framework** for formulating and implementing business strategies, programs, and actions based on considerations that include the entire business environment. Such a framework requires the capability to integrate both internal systems and processes and those of external business entities, including customers, stakeholders, and supply networks. It must encompass all of the corporation's relationships and actions that occur from a product's very beginning to its final end, from "cradle-to-grave." This includes the recovery of valuable resources at the end that can be reused and recycled into future products. Having distinct management systems for quality, environmental management, product delivery, customer relationships, supply networks, and technology and product development are commonplace today, but result in complicated and difficult interactions between the various management systems, leaders, managers, and professionals. They can make integration of these concerns and considerations difficult, if not impossible. Outcomes are often compromised, and internal consistency and fluidity are lost.

As a result, leading global corporations are transforming conventional management approaches into robust, fully integrated management systems that engage customers and stakeholders, and involve technologies, innovation, and management processes, both internally and externally. Such corporations are creating highly capable and responsive systems for achieving positive results in the present, correcting defects and burdens from past practices, and inventing powerful future positions. They are doing this through enterprise thinking, strategy development, business integration, visionary leadership and innovation as the principal means and mechanisms for achieving strategic objectives, enduring competitive advantages, and sustainable success. For example, Siemens AG, a global corporation engaged in the fast-paced world of electronics headquartered in Berlin and Munich, Germany, is a leader in SBD as well as corporate social responsibility, environmental stewardship, corporate citizenship, and business excellence. It advocates "Inventing the Future"[1] through visionary leadership and innovation. Siemens knows the power of SBD:[2]

Sustainable success is our number one priority. Our activities focus on meeting the needs of customers and creating value for our shareholders and employees. Our innovations – generated through our own laboratories and in cooperation with customers, business partners and universities – are our greatest strengths. Siemens' Global Network of Innovation is developing new products and services for a world that – while limited in resources – is boundless in possibilities.

SBD involves the total integration of the enterprise and the deliberate linking of its SMSs and the product delivery systems with all of the value networks, strategic partners, and constituencies. This connectedness works to further the overarching objective of the enterprise: *to create value and sustain the benefits of investments, contributions, and achievements over the long term for customers, stakeholders, value networks, employees, and shareholders.* Siemens suggests that long-term success is sustainable success.[3]

SBD, then, involves the convergence of separate management systems that focus on specific opportunities and challenges into an enterprise-wide management framework that can respond to the business environment and create sustainable success through effective strategies and exceptional leadership. Its centerpiece is the integration of all of the internal capabilities and resources of the corporation with all of the external contributors to exceed the needs, requirements, and mandates of the external business environment. Attaining this integration depends on a comprehensive understanding of all of the forces (internal and external) that drive change and responding to them in ways that enhance the positive attributes of the enterprise and mitigate the negative impacts and consequences. Visionary leadership, technological and product innovation, and organizational capabilities are critical to this task.

The four primary elements of SBD are:

- *Enterprise thinking* A means of examining the whole business world and its context. This includes being thoroughly inclusive and open with all customers, stakeholders, and constituents.

- *Strategic thinking and business integration* Involves crafting strategies and linking all of the essential elements into a comprehensive system. This includes being connected with all constituents.

- *Visionary, exceptional leadership* Involves having the knowledge, analytical skills, creativity, and learning to think strategically and lead change that exceeds the requirements and mandates of the present, and achieves sustainable competitive advantages and success in the future.

- *Leading change through innovation* Involves creating new solutions that create extraordinary value and are sustainable from social, economic, and environmental perspectives.

Enterprise thinking involves integrating the whole business environment into the strategic landscape of the corporation. It is an inclusive perspective of the domain and responsibilities of the corporation and its leadership. As the world continues to shrink and the pressures of the human condition are felt everywhere, corporations have to think about the entire macro-environment and consider the corporation's impacts on people, societies, economies, health and safety, and the natural world. Enterprise thinking focuses on laying the foundation for the vision, objectives, strategies and behaviors in the context of the business environment and strategic direction. Global corporations are extending their reach and thought processes beyond customers and markets. For instance, in the past suppliers were not deemed to be part of the enterprise but necessary support entities that had to be carefully controlled, if not exploited. Likewise **customers** were viewed as buyers of products and services and the sources of cash flow, but their satisfaction was often viewed to be tangential if they could be induced to continue buying even if the products and services were inferior and failed to meet their needs and expectations. While there were many exceptions, most corporations were narrowly defined and focused on direct relationships and their internally driven objectives. Today, many global corporations are linking with customers and stakeholders and providing opportunities for all their support entities, including strategic partners, suppliers, distributors, etc. to contribute to sustainable success and enjoy present and future rewards. Global corporations are changing their management frameworks to be broader and more inclusive of the business environment. Such frameworks are based on the entire external context and what it means to the corporation. The overarching objectives are to create value streams, processes, and solutions based on the needs and expectations of the customers, stakeholders, and other constituents that exceed the social, economic, environmental, and business requirements. These constructs are developed further in chapter 2.

Strategic thinking and business integration involve connecting all facets of the enterprise, not just within the corporation itself. They take into account the entire scope of strategic plans, programs, responsibilities, and actions of every entity, from the partners, alliances, suppliers, distributors, and business units to customers, stakeholders, governments, and society. The ability to integrate such diverse organizational resources and linkages is at the core of business integration, enterprise thinking – and, ultimately, SBD. These constructs are further developed in chapters 2–5.

Visionary leadership means inspiring people within and outside the corporation to contribute to creating value and achieving sustainable success. It places corporations on the cutting edge of change and innovation. The rapidity of change today has moved corporations away from owning and managing capital assets and physical resources to developing the capabilities of an integrated enterprise and motivating that enterprise to be creative, to create sustainable positions, and develop enduring outcomes. The focus has changed from managing resources to leading change and people. Leadership must use business integration to allow the corporation to strategically select and develop principles, processes, practices, and techniques that obtain superior results. These constructs are developed further in chapter 6.

Innovations are changes and improvements that have positive outcomes with respect to customers, stakeholders, the organization, and other constituents. Such changes can be pivotal to the prosperity and longevity of an organization. A corporation's ability to innovate can allow it to manage its destiny instead of reacting to the pressures of the markets and the business environment.

Innovation requires strategic and operational management that is willing to take the initiative to make incremental and even radical improvements to the existing technology and product portfolios, to replace current products and processes with new ones, and/or develop new-to-the-world technologies and products for the benefit of existing or new customers, stakeholders, and society. Innovation management must lead this kind of change in order to satisfy customers and stakeholders in the fast-paced world of technological change and globalization. These constructs are developed further in chapters 7 and 8.

When employed together, enterprise thinking, strategic thinking and business integration, innovation management, and visionary leadership provide a sophisticated management model for achieving success in the long term. They launch an organization on the path of SBD, promising an exciting, fast-paced quest to make significant improvements. Life cycle thinking and LCA are discussed in chapters 9–11; chapter 12 provides some concluding insights.

Focus

This book focuses on the principles, theories, strategies, processes, and practices of SBD in concert with enterprise thinking as the means for corporations to create innovative solutions to social, economic, environmental, and business challenges. It introduces the concept of **enterprise management** and explores the other essential aspects of SBD examining, from a strategic perspective, the essential concepts, methods, techniques, processes, and practices necessary for achieving sustainable success. The theories and perspectives are grounded on the principles, processes, and practices of leading global corporations who are already employing SBD as their framework for inventing the future. The book is intended to provide a strategic view of what is needed to formulate and implement corporate strategies for leading profound change.

The premise of the book is that global corporations can achieve SBD through enterprise thinking, strategic thinking and business integration, innovation management, and visionary leadership. This premise holds that sustainable success is achieved by creating outstanding solutions and providing total satisfaction, and that such performance can be derived only from a comprehensive understanding of the underlying needs, wants, and expectations of all of the customers, stakeholders, and constituents.

The book examines how SBD and enterprise thinking, business integration, technological and product innovation, and visionary leadership can create sustainable solutions to the social, political, economic, environmental, and market imperatives of the twenty-first century. Global corporations are reinventing themselves to ensure their future success. Doing so gives them an exciting opportunity to change the world through improved systems, technologies, products, and processes, and to possibly even achieve harmony between business endeavors, human activities, and the natural world.

The book examines the strategic importance that technological innovation and **product development** play in achieving the objectives of SBD. Mapping and assessing customer and stakeholder needs and expectations, benchmarking alternatives, developing gap analyses, and other analytical tools are explored and discussed. The book also provides an overview of LCT and management, LCA, and the associated tools and techniques.

Chapter 12 examines the future directions of enterprise thinking and SBD. The strategic implications for building a sustainable enterprise include creating environmentally sound value streams, products, and processes that are based on the strategic needs of the business and society. The principles of SBD hold that the primary goal of a corporation is to maximize the value derived by every member and every entity of the enterprise and not simply to maximize profits or shareholder value. Such thinking builds a solid foundation for long-term sustainable success that also enhances shareholder wealth.

The framework of the book

Global corporations seeking to implement SBD as the means for leading change and inventing the future must understand and deploy SBD principles when formulating and implementing strategies, developing new technologies, products, and processes, and improving their businesses.

SBD is predicated on the premise that there can be a convergence of internal and external objectives for the purpose of creating an improved future for everyone. It implies that corporations can achieve their business and financial objectives as well as meet their social, economic, and environmental goals and mandates. The great challenge is to transform corporations from narrowly focused organizations concentrating on markets, customers, products, production, revenues, and profits to inclusive enterprises that provide total satisfaction for customers, stakeholders, and society. Rising expectations and improved connectedness around the world are making the integration of the business enterprise imperative in the twenty-first century.

Figure 1.1 depicts a general framework for understanding and managing SBD. The chapters of the book correspond to this framework. As discussed in the introduction to part I, chapters 1–6 define the principles of SBD, examine the strategic of enterprise thinking, explore the driving forces of change, and discuss visionary leadership. Part II involves sustainable technology management and development, crafting SBD programs, and LCT and LCA that provide the analytical and support mechanisms that facilitate decision-making and continuous improvement.

A brief history of environmental management

The business perspective

SBD has its roots in environmental management and the concepts of pollution prevention and waste minimization. Driven by a dramatic increase in the number of environmental laws and regulations, environmental management has evolved since the mid-1970s from dealing with compliance issues and waste problems to sophisticated management systems focusing on external drivers and internal capabilities. The maturation process has been difficult as corporations learned how to respond to the ever-changing landscape of laws, regulations, and directives.

Prior to the enactment and promulgation of environmental laws and regulations, most corporations focused on market and economic considerations and paid little attention to the broader social and environmental concerns.

With the advent of government mandates effecting environmental protection during the 1970s, most corporations either resisted government

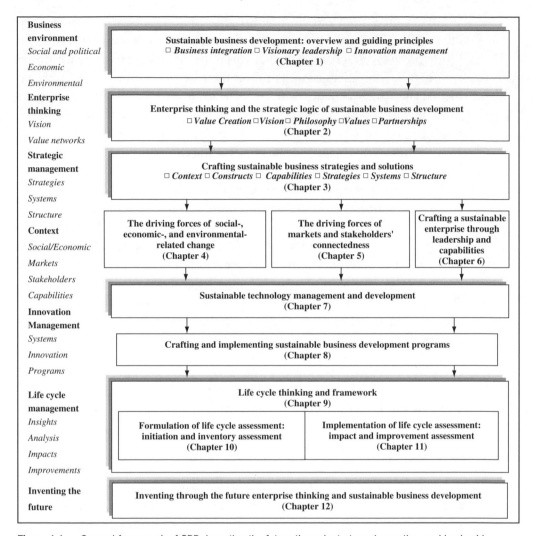

Business environment	Sustainable business development: overview and guiding principles

Figure 1.1   General framework of SBD: inventing the future through strategy, innovation, and leadership

encroachment into their domain or simply followed the laws and regulations while trying to minimize the impact of them on their businesses and operations. Changes were made, but often unwillingly. Even leading corporations that tried to comply with the government regulations and directives rarely considered going beyond compliance.[4] Most corporations desperately tried to stay abreast of the mandates for reducing air emissions, improving water effluents, managing and reducing hazardous waste, preventing spills and accidents, and managing the cleanups of improperly disposed wastes. These challenges required significant investments in improving operations, processes, and practices, buying pollution abatement equipment and managing remediation programs. The prevailing philosophy was to comply with the laws and regulations, to do what had to be done. Environmental management was in its infancy and the focus was on compliance. Moreover, environmental management was not considered an essential part of the business strategy during the early years. Traditional environmental management was largely reactive, often fragmented and ill defined. It was viewed as a necessary, but an unwanted, aside.

The 1980s was a period of growth and learning in Canada, Japan, the United States, Western Europe, and other developed countries. Environmental requirements were becoming more challenging, management methods more sophisticated. For example, with the enactment of the US Emergency Planning and Community Right-to-Know Act (ECRA) in 1986, businesses were forced to disclose information about their operations and the waste streams they generated. ECRA began to change how businesses viewed their environmental and social responsibilities. As stakeholders' rights to information expanded, business objectives pertaining to social and environmental consequences began to move from simple compliance to waste minimization. Laws and mandates such as ECRA sowed the seeds for more inclusiveness, openness, innovativeness, and effectiveness regarding environmental considerations. Environmental management became a two-dimensional undertaking, dealing with laws and regulations and managing customer and stakeholder expectations. Although this represented a significant philosophical change in management thinking, corporations were still slow to change from viewing environmental mandates as business threats to discovering in them opportunities to excell.

During the 1980s and 1990s as the public, customers, and stakeholder groups became more aware and involved in reducing pollution, the paradigm changed again. The advent of the Internet further advanced corporate openness during these years. Information and data about the social, economic, and environmental impacts of business operations and activities and the corporations themselves became widely available and more broadly distributed. People could easily obtain information about the products, processes, and operations of global corporations and other firms.

Corporations became interested in preventing and/or reducing the quantities of waste they produced. **Pollution prevention (P2)** rather than waste management became the way to solve environmental problems, and environmental management advanced again. P2 represents the "second generation" of environmental management that focused on creating **environmental**

management systems (EMSs) to systematically deal with environmental laws and regulations and attempt to prevent pollution and waste problems before they became significant. P2 focused on pollution reduction at the source, reuse, recycling, and proper disposal of residuals and wastes. For example, through pollution prevention initiatives, United Technologies Corporation reduced many of its waste streams by 80 percent during the 1990s.

Concurrent with the developments of pollution prevention, Dow Chemical and several other corporations introduced product stewardship as an approach to inform their customers about the safe use of their products and to proactively minimize misuse.[5] Pollution prevention and product stewardship both focus on exceeding government mandates and meeting customer and stakeholder expectations.

Moreover, during the 1990s, the International Organization for Standardization (ISO) developed the **ISO 14000** family of environmental management standards to provide a framework and guidance for EMSs, environmental auditing, environmental labeling, environmental performance evaluation, and LCA.[6] Many global corporations adapted the ISO 14001 EMS standard or created their own version to provide a systematic approach for managing environmental issues and structuring management initiatives for solving related problems. However, difficulties persisted. The basic problem was that environmental management strategies were not integrated with the mainstream corporate strategies. They were tangential. Environmental management was still a specialty. While environmental managers were in the know, the rest of the corporate professionals tended to operate independently if they could get the environmental specialist to manage regulatory compliance and EMS aspects.

Today, in the early years of the twenty-first century, the paradigm is again shifting, this time to SBD. The focus is now on creating business value and discovering opportunities within the social, economic, environmental, and market dimensions and integrating them into systematic solutions rather than thinking just about the costs and inconveniences of managing environmental issues or complying with environmental laws and regulations. SBD aims to create new solutions that eliminate the defects, burdens, and impacts associated with many of today's technologies, products, and processes.

Figure 1.2 depicts the fundamental changes that have occurred in environmental management since the mid-1970s. Most global companies have initiated an EMS construct to meet the mandates and expectations and have made significant improvements in achieving compliance and pollution prevention initiatives.

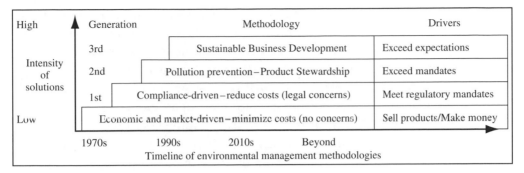

Figure 1.2   A simplified pathway to SBD

Today, environmental management and SBD examine the effects, implications, and impacts of business decisions and provide more balanced solutions for businesses, customers, and stakeholders. According to Robert Kaplan and David Norton (1996), an organization must use what they call a "balanced scorecard" when making decisions.[7] They suggest that business organizations balance their objectives by including in them financial considerations, customer satisfaction, organizational learning, and internal business improvement.

Clearly, their concept is relevant to environmental management and SBD. Balanced solutions – that is, a balanced scorecard – are discovered, formulated, and implemented through innovative strategies, business integration, and sound decision-making that are based on broad considerations and visionary leadership. Corporations must build balanced objectives into every product and service, every process and every operation. This perspective is the next logical step in the maturation of environmental management. It allows corporations to solve problems using environmental and business metrics while fostering development programs and initiatives that not only exceed compliance, but create sustainable competitive advantages through reduced impacts and costs, increased benefits and outcomes, improved brand images, improved market positions, and enhanced corporate reputations. It requires corporations to expand the scope of environmental management from the domain of operations management (OM) and environmental professionals to a broader array of business leaders, managers, and specialists including research and development (R&D) professionals, product designers, marketing and sales executives, public relations experts, supply chain specialists, accountants, and corporate lawyers.

The maturation of environmental management may be viewed as the genesis of SBD in the corporate world. It involves the integration of environmental as well as social and economic considerations with mainstream strategic thinking and management. With visionary leadership and innovation, environmental management in the context of SBD can move the solution process from the present or the past to the future through both mainstream strategies and "out-of-the-box" creativity. The focus of SBD is on preemptive strategies and initiatives that proactively address and solve problems before they deteriorate into catastrophic consequences. Although this transition is difficult to prove, many corporate examples provide evidence of innovative and successful business strategies and management approaches that are resulting from this new multifaceted view of corporate environmental management. They demonstrate that SBD is a viable business concept to improve outcomes, mitigate negative impacts, reduce risks, and achieve balanced solutions.

SBD implies that strategic management will drive change in order to enhance business value and create exciting new opportunities. The challenges are no longer as simple as responding to government mandates or simply meeting customer needs. While most environmental and business professionals would argue that achieving compliance with laws and regulations is not easy, and even regulators would agree, compliance-driven approaches are prescriptive. The corporation's task is simply to do what is required.

SBD, however, moves corporations away from responding solely to the dictates of governments and markets and toward preemptive strategies developed by their leadership. But generating and sustaining business value is much more complicated than compliance. The focus is on the future, on creating opportunities. That requires moving social, economic, and environmental issues, concerns, and challenges toward the apex of business activities and away from being tangential to the central mission of the corporation. It also requires a thorough understanding of present and future expectations and a strategic perspective on how best to exceed those expectations. It connects and integrates the external and internal dimensions in the most comprehensive way possible. It addresses the following four pivotal questions:

- What social, economic and environmental issues require new solutions?
- How can the external and internal dimensions be positively linked?
- What are the most appropriate strategies for meeting/exceeding all expectations?
- What are the long-term strategic implications on sustainable success, and how should the change mechanism be managed?

Clearly, social, economic, and environmental challenges are crucial business issues that invoke high-level thinking, strategizing, and action. SBD presents opportunities for corporations to better differentiate their businesses, their products, and their reputations by creating new offensive strategies for serving and satisfying markets, customers, and stakeholders in exciting new ways. It reaffirms the philosophical and strategic intent of the organization, making it understandable and attainable in the hearts and minds of the people. It creates a new mindset that focuses on being the best and achieving extraordinary results. It focuses on the pursuit of excellence in every facet of the business.

The management challenge then becomes figuring out what to do next as the expectations of customers, stakeholders, and other constituents continue to rise. The dramatic improvement in product quality since the mid-1980s provides an analogous situation. Over several decades, companies such as General Electric, Honeywell, Motorola, Siemens, and Toyota have improved their quality from one defect per hundred opportunities for defects to less than ten defects per million opportunities.[8] Still, as quality has improved, customers have become less impressed with the improvements and expect even more. In fact, customers continue to pressure companies to make ever-greater improvements. The same is true for all categories of improvements: social, economic, and environmental. As improvements are made, more improvements are expected. However, business leaders then have the opportunity to differentiate their corporations, products, and processes by developing superior solutions for stakeholders and customers. It also puts pressures on competitors and peers to keep pace.

The scholarly and academic perspective

Environmental management has evolved and improved significantly as leading corporations and scholars have contributed to its principles, processes, and practices. The first generation of environmental management was based on laws and regulations. Numerous lawyers and legal scholars have captured and examined this history in many books. Their most profound insights, and those of scholars studying the later subtopics of environmental management – such as design for the environment, LCA, recycling, pollution prevention, and ISO 14000 – are summarized in such works.

Frank B. Friedman wrote the *Practical Guide to Environmental Management* in 1988.[9] He was an environmental lawyer who worked for the US Department of Justice, Atlantic Richfield, Occidental Petroleum Corporation, and Elf Aquitaine, among others. As head of a number of environmental, health, and safety departments, Friedman had first-hand experience in infiltrating environmental management into the operating levels of businesses. He helped engineers, operating personnel, and business managers understand environmental management. The book also helped move businesses from compliance thinking to environmental management.

In *Environmental Politics and Policy* (1991), Walter A. Rosenbaum discussed the "Second Environmental Era."[10] His book examined environmental issues that were critical during the early 1990s and described how the focus was shifting to policy-making. Rosenbaum suggested that a paradigm shift was under way and described a broader social, economic, and environmental framework for solving problems.

Frances Cairncross wrote *Costing the Earth: The Challenge for Governments/ The Opportunities for Business* in 1991.[11] Cairncross encouraged "industry to use its inventive power" to solve environmental problems. Her book proposed that sustainable development principles such as environmental equity, making polluters pay, and cleaner processes and products were some of the most important concepts of the day.

In 1992, Bruce Smart wrote *Beyond Compliance: A New Industry View of the Environment.*[12] His book covered the fundamentals of environmental management across many sectors. Smart used real world corporate examples of practical solutions.

Stephan Schmidheiny, the founder of the World Business Council for Sustainable Development, was instrumental in moving environmental management from solving environmental problems to incorporating sustainable development into mainstream business management. His book, *Changing Course: A Global Business Perspective on Development and the Environment* (1992),[13] discussed the benefits of a more comprehensive view of the social, economic, and environmental considerations and how more than thirty businesses around the world were already taking steps toward sustainable development. His work opened the door to the more inclusive world of sustainability.

Paul Hawken became one of the leaders of SBD with the publication of *The Ecology of Commerce: A Declaration of Sustainability* in 1993.[14] He helped change the agenda from a focus on pollution prevention to the more comprehensive topics of sustainability. His contribution was more visionary than substantive, articulating the environmental challenges facing businesses and stimulating more thinking about SBD.

In 1996, Joseph Fiksel helped to expand the concepts of sustainable development into the world of product development with the publication of *Design for Environment: Creating Eco-Efficient Products and Processes.*[15] The book provided an overview of design for the environment and how it relates to business practices.

Livio D. DeSimone and Frank Popoff wrote *Eco-Efficiency: The Business Link to Sustainable Development* in 1997 as a guide for business leaders who wanted to understand the practical side of sustainable development.[16] DeSimone and Popoff were the chief executive officers (CEOs) of 3M and Dow Chemical, respectively. They offered real world insights about SBD. Their book focused on eco-efficiency, its meaning, uses, and measurements, and was supported by the World Business Council for Sustainable Development.

In 1998, Hens B. L. Nath, and D. Devuyst wrote *Sustainable Development*, a textbook that provided a solid foundation about the conceptual background of sustainable development.[17] It described in detail the international conferences and the political side of sustainable development.

Paul Weaver, Leo Jansen, Geert van Grootveld, Egbert van Spiegel, and Philip Vergragt wrote *Sustainable Technology Development* in 2000.[18] Their book included seven cases portraying analysis of issues, technologies, and methods pertaining the sustainable development and LCT.

In 2003, Bob Doppelt wrote *Leading Change toward Sustainability: A Change-Management Guide for Business, Government and Civil Society*. The book provides techniques for understanding the applications of sustainability.[19]

All of these books together represent just a fraction of the contributions made by scholars since the 1980s. The focus of this book is on SBD and not the broader topics of sustainability and sustainable development from a political, social or government perspective. In addition to these books, there are many articles in the literature that described leading edge SBD concepts. Among the most important are:[20]

- Stuart L. Hart's *Beyond Greening: Strategies for a Sustainable World*
- John Elkington's *The Triple Bottom Line for Twenty-first Century Business*
- Forest Reinhardt's *Bring the Environment Down to Earth*
- Michael Porter and Claas Van Der Linde's *Green and Competitive: Ending the Stalemate.*

Hart is a leading SBD scholar who discussed the integration of strategic management and sustainable development. Elkington introduced the concept of the "triple bottom line," which ties the social, economic, and environmental objectives to the mainstream financial objectives of the corporations. Reinhardt discussed how to manage environmental risks and find practical solutions to environmental questions. Porter and Van Der Linde focused on innovating to be competitive and leading change. Moreover, there are numerous other contributors to the theoretical underpinning discussed throughout the book. There are also many strategic management, environmental management, and operations professionals working for the global corporations discussed in the book who have contributed to the practical concepts and approaches.

The references used in this book provide the theoretical and practical foundations for formulating and implementing management constructs pertaining to SBD and the related strategies, systems, technologies, products, and processes. Given that global corporations are just starting to pursue SBD as a strategic management construct, it is hard to prove the validity of all of the concepts, principles, processes, and practices. However, the approaches are fundamentally sound and represent the next wave in the ongoing sophistication of strategic business management.

The underpinnings of SBD

Perspectives of leading organizations

SBD and sustainability are relatively new concepts. There are many perspectives and definitions for the related terms, and numerous interpretations as well. Stakeholders in the global business environment typically view sustainable development and sustainability in the context of the social, political, economic, technological, and ecological implications of governmental laws, regulations, and actions, and in terms of business operations, activities, and outcomes. The perspectives are often based on what the governments and businesses should be, rather than what they are, doing. The views are also based on how they should interact with the business environment and the natural world. While there may be precise definitions in the minds of various stakeholders and constituents, the concepts tend to have more of a relative than an absolute connotation. Still, that, too, is changing. A global view of SBD typically focuses on three main dimensions: social, economic, and environmental. The precise definition continues to evolve.

There are many sources of perspectives and definitions for sustainable development and sustainability. Table 1.1 lists some of the leading organizations that endorse and subscribe to sustainability, sustainable development, and/or SBD, and identifies their working perspectives and/or definitions.

SBD involves formulating and implementing business strategies, innovations, and initiatives to help create a more sustainable world. It is a philosophical perspective that permeates every aspect of what a corporation is, and

Table 1.1. Perspectives of selected leading international organizations relating to sustainable development

Organization	Perspectives	Background
United Nations Environmental Program (UNEP)	UNEP's mission is to provide leadership and encourage partnership in caring for the environment by inspiring, informing, and enabling nations and people to improve the quality of life without compromising that of future generations It promotes the application of assessment techniques	UNEP's Industry and Environment was established in 1972 Its offices develop policies and practices for mitigating the risk of degradation It issues a biennial *Global Environment Outlook* to provide an overview of the world-wide environment assessment process
Coalition of Environmentally Responsible Economies (CERES)[a]	Champions ten official CERES principles pertaining to the protection of the biosphere; sustainable use of natural resources; reduction and disposal of wastes; energy conservation; risk reduction; safe products and services; environmental restoration; informing the public; management commitment; and audits and reports	Established in 1989, CERES is a not-for-profit organization dedicated to helping investors and the general public to understand the environmental performance of companies It is a coalition of investors, public pension funds, foundations, labor unions, and environmental, religious, and public interest groups
International Chamber of Commerce (ICC)	The ICC is an international NGO established in 1919 to promote trade, investment, and the market economy It promotes business interests with governments and international entities	The ICC Commission on Environment was created in 1978 to lobby governments to endorse business positions ICC formulated its Business Charter for Sustainable Development in 1990
International Organization for Standards (ISO)	The ISO standards are voluntary ISO 14031 covers environmental performance evaluation and ISO 14040–43 cover LCA They are the most critical from a sustainable development perspective	The ISO is an international standard setting organization that has crafted ISO 9000 and ISO 14000 quality standards ISO 14000 relates to EMSs
World Commission on Environment and Development (WCED)	The WCED views sustainability as the principle of ensuring that actions today do not limit the range of economic, social, and environmental options open to future generations	The WCED is an international commission started in 1987 to study the connection between economics and the environment The commission wrote *Our Common Future* (the Brundtland Report)

Table 1.1. (cont.)

Organization	Perspectives	Background
World Business Council for Sustainable Development[b] (WBCSD)	The WBCSD is committed to sustainable development via the three pillars of economic growth, environmental protection, and social equity It believes that sustainable development is best achieved through open, competitive international markets that honor legitimate comparative advantage Such markets encourage efficiency and innovation, both necessities for human progress[c] (See also WICE in table 1.3)	The WBCSD was formed in 1995 through a merger of the Business Council for Sustainable Development (BCSD) and the World Industry Council for the Environment (WICE) The WBCSD is a coalition of 150 international companies providing business leadership for change toward sustainable development and promoting eco-efficiency, innovation, and corporate social responsibility It is located in Geneva
World Economic Forum (WEF)	The World Economic Forum includes sustainable development on its agenda It discusses environmental issues as related to economic performance	The World Economic Forum is an annual meeting in Switzerland at which political leaders and business executives discuss economic issues
Watchworld Institute (WWI)	The WWI publishes the *State of the World* on an annual basis It is committed to sustainable society	The WWI is a NGO established in 1974 to collect, analyze, and distribute information relating to global environmental issues
World Resources Institute (WRI)	The WRI works in fifty countries to provide insights on scientific research, economic analyses, and practical experience to political and business organizations and NGOs	The WRI was founded in 1982 It is an independent, Washington-based research organization focusing on sustainable development

[a] CERES Help Guide, *Instructions for Companies* (1997).

[b] World Business Council for Sustainable Development (WBCSD), "The base case for sustainable development" (September 2001).

[c] *Ibid.*

what it does. It forms the basis for a corporation's vision of the future and how senior management and the professional brains trust (the intellectual capital) plan to invent and build that future.

Executive leadership has to champion SBD as the way to sustainable success and the most appropriate framework for decision-making. Dr. W. Edward Deming, the guru of **total quality management (TQM)**, said in 1986 that:

"the job of management is not supervision, but leadership."[21] He maintained that "the performance of management should be measured by the potential to stay in business, to protect investment, to ensure future dividends and jobs through improvement of product and service for the future, and not the quarterly dividend."[22] His views ring as true today as the challenges to sustain growth and development become more difficult due to the complexities of the business environment and the demanding expectations of customers, stakeholders, and society.

The transformational process

One of the most significant difficulties in attempting to advance SBD during the first decade of the twenty-first century is the legacy of past technologies, products, production systems, and processes, and their associated waste streams and impacts. Many were created in an era when strategic management focused first and foremost on markets, economics, and technological and product considerations. They represent an enormous investment, and it is understandable that senior management views suggestions to radically and rapidly change these existing systems, technologies, and products as disruptive.

For this reason, the process of implementing SBD and the related innovative solutions must evolve in an orderly fashion from the existing business structure to more sustainable positions. The time frame is unclear, but the process can be specified. History is replete with stories of such conversions. The adoption of new technologies generally follows a predictable transition from the old to the new. For example, digital cameras have slowly replaced film-based cameras as the new technology equals and then exceeds the benefits of the old in terms of quality, convenience, and affordability. The new technology also provides additional benefits such as instantaneous gratification and digital storage and eliminates many of the environmental problems associated with film processing chemicals. Moreover, its potential increases as related products like photo-quality printers become available at reasonable prices. Such transformations usually take several iterations and many years to come to full fruition.

Figure 1.3 provides a hypothetical view of the transformation to SBD. The numbers of years are provided to give a sense of the time span and are not intended to be a prediction of how long the transformation will take for SBD to become the mainstream.

The transformation process requires integration, imagination, and innovation. Integration implies viewing the whole rather than just the pieces and

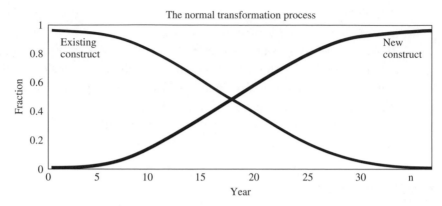

Figure 1.3   A hypothetical view of the transformation to SBD[a]

Note: [a] The fraction is the percentage of corporations or the percentage of the aggregate activities that are deploying a specific construct. The model depicts a standard case where one construct (paradigm) is the dominant and the other is just developing. The transformation process evolves over time and eventually in those cases where the transformation is a success, the new replaces the old. However, there are many variations on the hypothetical model. There may be three or more other constructs operating at the same time. The old construct (paradigm) may evolve and successfully maintain its dominance. The new construct may quickly be replaced by another alternative that assumes the role of the high-potential replacement. In the automobile industry, the internal combustion engine technology is currently the dominant form of power. The prevailing technology might be challenged by new technologies such as the hybrid internal combustion engine combined with an electric motor. However, the two options might in the future be replaced by fuel cells.

conceiving options that lead to improvements and ultimately to outcomes that are closer to the ideal. With unifying approaches, corporations can align people, capabilities, and resources into viable management constructs. They can link all constituents in order to formulate and implement new courses of actions for obtaining sustainable results for everyone.

Imagination involves creative thinking about potential solutions and all of their ramifications. It is through imagination that new opportunities are created and old problems are solved. Imagination is expressed through management's vision for the future when the corporation focuses on what should be, instead of what is. Imagination transcends the prevailing paradigm of fixing problems and dreams freely about new solutions that eliminate the problems. Imagination involves thinking "out-of-the box" about what the best solution might be, and contemplating how to create the means and mechanisms to obtain the solution. For example, it is easy to describe what the ideal automobile might be like – its fuel efficiency, emissions profile, size, weight, and performance. However, it is an enormous challenge to actually design such a vehicle.

Innovation links the wants and needs of customers and stakeholders with the creative processes within an organization necessary for realizing them. It turns strategies, objectives, and plans into development programs and desired outcomes. Through innovation, dramatic improvements are realized – improvements such as discovering, developing, and deploying new and superior technologies.

The triad of integration, imagination, and innovation provides a sophisticated management perspective for achieving SBD in the long term. It links people, data, information, technology development, product creation, process improvement, and decision-making into a seamless model for inventing solutions, eliminating defects and impacts, and building a better business environment and natural world. It abides in an exciting, fast-paced reality, offering enormous opportunities for creative corporations that want to change the world.

Linking SBD with sustainability

The stability of today's economic, social, and political systems depends upon complex arrays of interfaces and actions. Instantaneous conversion to a world based on the concept of "sustainability" is virtually impossible. The notion of "sustainability" usually implies that all human and business activities are carried out at rates equal to or less than the Earth's natural carrying capacity to renew the resources used and naturally mitigate the waste streams generated. Such moves would require wholesale replacement of almost every product and process in use.

The automobile industry best exemplifies the scale of change this transformation would entail. The automobile industry and all of its related parts and support industries (petroleum, road construction and maintenance, repair services, etc.) typically produce between 10 and 20 percent of the total output of the economies in the developed countries. Radical change or eliminating the automobile altogether would result in a significant economic gap and social and political problems of the highest magnitude. Moreover, it would be difficult to quickly convert the large fleets of conventional automobiles built with twentieth-century technologies (internal combustion engines) to new technologies like hydrogen-based fuel cells. Even with all of the promise that the newer technologies have for reducing air emissions, improving efficiencies, and eliminating the burdens and dangers associated with gasoline and other fuels, it is not possible to create the systems and infrastructure for producing and distributing hydrogen and converting the enormous number of conventional vehicles around the world in a relatively short time frame (say, less than five years): witness the number of pre-1972 cars that are still on the highways in California. With all of the new legislation and regulations to significantly reduce automobile emissions on a federal and state level in the United States since the 1970s, there are still millions of clunkers (or cherished antiques) registered and presumably being used for transportation. It often takes decades to fully implement new solutions, especially when the implications are as far-reaching as converting the prevailing automobile technology to another form.

The movement toward sustainability has to be orchestrated in manageable steps. Solutions have to be feasible and achievable within a reasonable time horizon. There has to be commitment to change and everyone involved has to understand and believe that the vision, strategies, objectives, and means are sound and doable. Even getting to that commitment can take time. Motorola's transformation from a standard-quality manufacturer in the early 1980s to a world-class, high-quality producer of pagers and cellular telephones in the mid-1990s is an illustrative example of the time frame involved in making such profound changes. It took Motorola approximately fifteen years in three stages to move from producing products with about 10,000 defects per million opportunities for defects to less than 4 defects per million.[23] The company had a well-established plan subdivided into reasonable stages, and it maintained a vigilant and dedicated approach over the years to ensure continuous improvement and ongoing success. The lesson learned is that such outcomes are achievable through commitment, tenacity, investments, and time. With such bold strategies and objectives, patience and perseverance are the glue that holds the strategies and initiatives together over the long term.

Significant achievements in SBD can be realized through the strategies and initiatives of corporations if there is a long-term commitment to change. The long road toward sustainability involves incorporating SBD principles into the design and development of new technologies and new products over time. The management construct of SBD and its subset **Design for Sustainability (DFS)** are the logical progressions to the ultimate goal. Figure 1.4 provides an overview of this perspective.

The notion of sustainable development originated in the Brundtland Report entitled *Our Common Future*, prepared in 1987 by the World Commission on Environment and Development (WCED).[24] The WCED was established as an independent organization in 1983 by the General Assembly of the United Nations "to re-examine the critical environment and development issues and to formulate realistic proposals for dealing

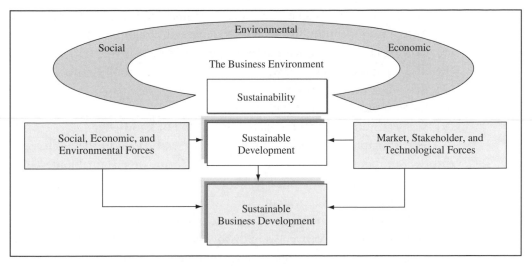

Figure 1.4   An overview of the linkages between SBD and sustainability

Note: The shaded areas involve topics discussed in this book.

with them; to propose new forms of international co-operation on these issues that will influence policies and events in the direction of needed changes; and to raise the levels of understanding and commitment."[25] The report defined sustainable development as that which "meets the needs of the present without compromising the ability of future generations to meet their own needs."[26] It suggested that new development programs should follow the precepts of sustainability. Whether the business environment is sustainable today is not as relevant as the question about the direction and imperatives of future development programs. Sustainable development inherently means working to create a future that minimizes the depletion of resources, eliminates environmental degradation from the impacts of pollution and waste streams, avoids disruptive and destructive behaviors, and builds longevity into the solutions.

The most important characteristics of sustainable development are the principles upon which it is based. Professor William McDonough of the Darden School of the University of Virginia is one of the foremost authorities on sustainable development. He developed the "Hannover Principles" which articulate the basis for integrating business management with the realities of humanity and nature.

The nine Hannover principles are:[27]

(1) Insist on the rights of humanity and nature to co-exist

(2) Recognize interdependence

(3) Respect relationships between spirit and matter
(4) Accept responsibility for the consequences of design
(5) Create safe objects of long-term value
(6) Eliminate the concept of waste
(7) Rely on natural energy flows
(8) Understand the limitations of design
(9) Seek constant improvements by the sharing of knowledge.

These principles and derivatives of them are embedded in the discussions throughout this book. While there are many forms of sustainable development and SBD principles, most forms have a similar flavor. Table 1.2 summarizes the most critical principles.

The overarching principles of SBD include inclusiveness in analysis and decision-making, innovativeness in discovering and implementing new solutions, value creation in the short term and the long term, and openness in managing the social, economic, and environmental dimensions. These four overarching principles are integrated into the enterprise through leadership and management commitment.

Sustainable development is a far-reaching construct that cuts across many sectors: global communities of nations and governments, NGOs, markets, customer groups, and other constituencies. While each sector has its own perspective, there are many shared ideas that provide a common ground for establishing agreements on future direction.

The crux of SBD is to focus on future technologies and products that are developed using criteria specifying outcomes that are balanced in terms of business objectives and the needs of all of the constituents, internal and external, in the present and the future. This means that technology and product development programs have to be based on a broader array of considerations and consequences, and that the analysis used for making decisions has to include inputs and outputs from cradle-to-grave. The focus has changed from managing resources to leading people and change.

But the change envisioned requires a long-term commitment of continuous improvement. The ultimate success will not be achieved in one day, one month, one year, or even one decade. It may well require many decades. However, every contribution builds upon the foundation for a more sustainable future and a better world.

Reynolds Metals Company's initiative and commitment to aluminum can recycling during the 1960s and 1970s is an excellent example of how "outside-the-box" thinking can create a more sustainable solution and contribute to a more sustainable future (box 1.1).

Table 1.2. Overarching principles of SBD

SD principles	SBD construct	Context
Right to co-exist	**Enterprise thinking** Cradle-to-grave thinking Balanced objectives	The recognition of the rights of humanity and nature to coexist implies that businesses must use a broader context for assessing, understanding, and dealing with their business environments and the natural world
Recognize interdependence	**Inclusiveness** Business integration Linkages and relationships	The interrelationships between the social, economic, and environmental underpinnings of a corporation are complex, and it is difficult to understand causes and effects without analyzing the whole system
Respect relationships	**Value networks** Business environment Natural world	The opportunities and challenges of the world can be sustained through the effective use of all of the capabilities and resources of the corporations and their linkages Good solutions meet the full spectrum of expectations
Accept responsibility	**Social responsibility** Integrity Honesty Enterprise management	Good decisions are based on the broad analysis of the business environment and the natural world Great leaders accept the implications and consequences of their decisions and do everything possible to enhance the positives and mitigate the negative impacts
Create long-term value	**Value creation** Value proposition Balance	The overarching goal of a corporation is to create and sustain value over time Value is built upon the knowledge and capabilities of the enterprise It includes designing new products and creating new technologies
Eliminate wastes	**Innovativeness** LCT Sustainable technologies and products	Ideal solutions eliminate the production of waste streams and increase the value created Total satisfaction means that all criteria are achieved, not just business objectives Ideal solutions are derived from a comprehensive understanding of expectations
Rely on balanced solutions	**Openness** Transparency Balanced Scorecard thinking	Sustainable solutions meet all of the objectives of the social, economic, and environmental considerations They are inclusive and innovative They also meet the short-term and long-term objectives for the application of the world's mass and energy They are open to scrutiny

Table 1.2. (cont.)

SD principles	SBD construct	Context
Design limitations	**Risk mitigation** LCA Risk assessment	All technologies, products, and processes have positive and negative aspects The long-term goal of sustainable development is to enhance the positives and reduce the negatives
Continuous improvement	**Leadership** Short-term/long-term plans	Sustainable development is manifested through the compounding effects of continuous improvements Great outcomes derive from inspired people and dedicated leaders

Box 1.1 Reynolds Metals Company and its radical innovation for recycling aluminum

On March 21, 1968, Reynolds Metals Company (hereafter, Reynolds), a fully integrated aluminum producer, opened the industry's first consumer recycling center in Los Angeles, California.[1] The recycling program had a modest beginning, reclaiming less than 1 million lb (453,720 kg) during the first year. Many industry executives had doubts about the viability of the concept, but Reynolds succeeded, and within two years it had opened five more centers.

At the beginning of the venture, Reynolds found that the collection costs for used beverage cans significantly contributed to the high cost of recycled aluminum.[2] In 1972, Richard Bolling, Manager of Reynolds' Recycling Plan, realized that the way to make recycling pay was to turn it into an independent business with its own set of values and culture.[3] Economics and social responsibility drove the recycling plan. Reynolds created an opportunity to produce metal from alternate means. Society enjoyed the benefits of a reduced litter problem, and social groups discovered a means to generate cash by collecting used cans.[4] Without the community efforts, the cost of recycling post-consumer scrap would have been prohibitively expensive.

By the early 1990s Reynolds collected and processed an estimated 530 million lb of recycled aluminum.[5] Within two decades it had converted an impossible dream into a successful money-making venture that created value for the company, its stakeholders, and shareholders. The net effect of its recycling effort was equivalent to the construction of a fully integrated primary production plant, which at the time of the investment would have cost approximately $1 billion.[6] The capital cost avoidance was overwhelming. Moreover, recycling capacity could be added in small increments instead of a large-scale plant. The recycling operation required a massive reverse logistical infrastructure.

As an innovator of aluminum recycling, Reynolds realized that reaching the consumer was the most critical requirement. To deal with the market, the company established the Reynolds Aluminum Recycling Company (RARCO) to implement the operational interface requirements. Reynolds targeted the ordinary citizen and developed the system around the private consumer. It established a customer service organization that provided educational service and customer support. Reynolds had changed the culture of the company. Its business philosophy pertaining to recycling operations was to provide customer satisfaction by allocating the margins made available by the new value of recycling aluminum. (The cost to buy and reprocess scrap aluminum was approximately $0.55 versus $0.65 per lb for virgin aluminum.) Without a continuous commitment to the customer, it would be impossible to maintain the flow of scrap.

From inception, Reynolds' recycling strategy can be characterized as a preemptive move to reshape its organization and to create an infrastructure for achieving its goals. Reynolds was clearly a pioneer in recycling. It turned the problem of littering into a competitive advantage.

David Reynolds, who was instrumental in formulating the strategy, had the vision to not only solve a problem but to create an opportunity. His leadership gave the company, its customers, and society an economical and environmental solution. He and his colleagues had the courage to invest in a business plan that was not profitable during the early years. The cornerstone of the strategy was the leadership exhibited by management and the integration of the company's resources and those of its outside partners.

In a dynamic business environment, continuous change is expected. Executives and company professionals moved beyond the traditional "profit and loss" mentality and took financial risks to invent a new solution. Given that Reynolds had to compete against giants like Alcoa and Alcan, it had to be creative and to take risks. It had to build an infrastructure to realize the opportunity. It had to change the fundamentals of the business and change the culture of its organization. Its strategy paid off by providing a source of low-cost metal. The solution started with 1 can, then 1,000, a million, and now billions of cans are recycled each year.

The Reynolds story is relatively old but, nevertheless, still significant. The company started to recycle aluminum cans before the government initiated any actions to force the industry to do something. Although environmental concerns were important in 1968, aluminum recycling was thought to be technologically impractical. Reynolds didn't accept this external dictate, but rather chose to lead change. Senior executives turned a threat into an incredible opportunity; they understood what environment leadership really meant and created a new organizational structure and culture to take advantage of the situation. The people involved embraced change and took on the challenge.

Although Reynolds merged with Alcoa in 2000, and is no longer the leader in aluminum recycling, its reputation as a leader endures.

Notes:
1. Reynolds Metals Company brochure, p. 1. Its recycling efforts were a precursor to the pollution prevention thinking of the 1980s and 1990s. Reynolds' program can be viewed as an example of early initiatives to move beyond compliance and solve prevailing problems before the government became a player.
2. Dana Milbank, "Aluminum's envious rivals turn green, rush to show they too are recyclable," *Wall Street Journal*, September 18, 1991, p. B6. The total cost for recycled aluminum was $1.25 per lb or $1.00 more than the cost for virgin metal in 1968.
3. *Ibid.*
4. Bill Leonard, "Businesses discover aluminum recycling," *HR Magazine*, March 1991, p. 31.
5. Reynolds Metals Company, *Annual Report*, 1991, pp. 6, 11.
6. During the early 1990s, Alcan built a new smelter having a capacity of 215,000 metric tons per year in Laterrierre, Quebec that reportedly cost $1.1 billion.

Markets', customers', and stakeholders' perspectives

In the light of dramatic changes in the business environment and significant pressures for increasingly better performance and more openness, management approaches have evolved from tightly held constructs with limited disclosures to the public to more open-ended models with extensive communications and reporting. Communications with markets, customers, and stakeholders about social, economic, and environmental performance have become just as important as the mandatory requirements for financial reporting. Leading corporations have created communications vehicles that extend well beyond the regulatory requirements to provide detailed information about operations, technologies, products, services, processes, and their impacts. Environmental leadership now means not only reducing the environmental footprint of various products and operations, but also providing these extensive disclosures to outside entities.

Empowering the constituencies with information and knowledge builds connectedness and opens the door to further dialog. It is better to disclose problems and suggest solutions than it is for others to discover the difficulties and interpret the motives and causes on their own. Moreover, the complexities of government mandates often make it very difficult to comply absolutely with laws and regulations and very easy to fail to disclose everything that is required. The simple solution is to have a philosophy of open disclosure on all items that are not deemed to be confidential from a competitive perspective. Knowing that there is a high likelihood that outsiders will scrutinize one's actions encourages proper conduct.

During the 1990s there was a global trend to expand corporate reporting on social and environmental considerations. Multinationals and global corporations were encouraged to voluntarily publish annual environmental reports. Table 1.3 lists a number of the well-known global institutions that provide guidelines for preparing environmental and/or sustainable development reports for public disclosure.

Open communications extend beyond the statutory or regulatory requirements to provide additional information about the corporation and its operations and transactions. Corporations must become transparent, open and forthright about their actions. In an era colored by the negative experiences of Enron, Global Crossing, Tyco, and WorldCom, openness and transparency are important for improving corporate reputations and images with customers, governments, NGOs, and the public. In the United States, the Sarbanes–Oxley Act of 2002 requires executives to be more diligent in

Table 1.3. Select environmental reporting schemes and their sponsors[a]

Entity	Focus	Comments
AccountAbility: Institute of Social and Ethical Accountability	Its AA1000 Framework: Standard, Guidelines and Professional Qualifications provides stakeholder-based approaches and methods for enhancing accountability AA1000 includes corporate responsibility policies, stakeholder dialog programs, and auditing of reports	The new series AA1000S describes the roles of stakeholders, organizational learning, and innovation It provides modules for social and ethical, economic, environmental, and sustainability performance
Agenda 21: *Earth's Action Plan*, Charter 30, Business and Industry	Chapter 30 of Agenda 21 focuses on the role of business and industry in sustainable development It encourages corporations to communicate performance through annual reports	Agenda 21 is the "Earth's Action Plan" for sustainable development[b] The participants at the Rio Conference in June 1992 formulated and adopted it
European Chemical Industry Council (CEFIC)	CEFIC has adopted its own environmental reporting guidelines, focusing on the chemical industry	Established in 1993, CEFIC implements the Chemical Manufacturers' Responsible Care Program It focuses on EMSs, including human resources (HR), environmental impact assessment (EIA), auditing, and emergency preparedness
European Union Eco-Management and Audit Scheme (EMAS)	Requires that environmental statements be published They must be designed for the public and written in a comprehensive form EMAS was revised in 2001	EC Directive 90/313 concerning Freedom of Access to Information on the Environment led to this audit scheme Over 300 sites have registered using EMAS
Global Environmental Charter	Focuses on technology transfer and corporate involvement in environmental and development problems	Established in1993 by the Japanese *Keidanren* industry association
Global Environmental Management Initiative (GEMI)[c]	GEMI developed an Environmental Self-Assessment Program (ESAP) in 1992 based on the ICC's Business Charter for Sustainable Development Its focus is on (1) compliance; (2) systems development and implementation; (3) integration into general business functions; and (4) total quality	Established in April 1990 by a group of twenty-one leading US multinational corporations, GEMI is a nonprofit organization dedicated to helping business achieve EH&S excellence GEMI is located in Washington, DC

Table 1.3. (cont.)

Global Reporting Initiative (GRI) – Sustainability Reporting Guidelines	Global guidelines for preparing enterprise-wide sustainability reports describing economic, environmental, and social performance GRI published guidelines in 2001	Established by CERES in 1997 GRI is a multi-stakeholder initiative based on input from corporations, business associations, NGOs, universities, and other organizations
International Chamber of Commerce (ICC)	Point 16 of the ICC Business Charter for Sustainable Development details "Reporting and Compliance – To Measure Environmental Reporting"	Established in 1990 The Charter for Sustainable Development supports 1,200 companies
Public Environmental Reporting Initiative (PERI)	PERI guidelines identify ten components for comprehensive reporting on environmental performance: organizational profile; environmental policy; environmental management; environmental releases; resource conservation; environmental risk; management; environmental compliance; product stewardship; employee recognition; and stakeholder involvement	PERI guidelines were developed during 1992–3 The Business Council for Sustainable Development contributed, and CERES and GEMI helped
Responsible Care (RC)	Responsible Care is an industry-wide initiative to improve the performance of chemical companies It is based on six codes: community awareness and response; pollution prevention; process safety; distribution; environment health and safety, and Product Stewardship	Established in 1988 by the Chemical Manufacturers' Association It was originally formulated and implemented by the Canadian Chemical Manufacturers
World Industry Council for the Environment (WICE)	WICE is a task force that reviews industry initiatives on environmental reporting and develops guidelines	Formed in 1995 as joint program of the International Environment Bureau and ICC, WICE became WBCSD following its merger with the Business Council for Sustainable Development

[a] http://cei.sund.ac.uk/envrep/erepgui.htm.
[b] Nicholas Robinson, *Agenda 21: Earth's Action Plan* (New York: Oceana Publications, Inc., 1993).
[c] Global Environmental Management Initiative (GEMI), *Environmental Self-Assessment Program* (Washington, DC: GEMI, September 1992).

reviewing corporate disclosures and ensuring that there is proper corporate governance and reporting.

Michael Parker, President and CEO of Dow Chemical, stated that "In light of the current crisis in corporate credibility, it is worth noting that Integrity is first in our list of Values, because integrity is first."[28] His comments provide a sense of the logic for improving corporate communications. Dow realizes the criticality of openness as evidenced by the statements contained in its 2001 *Public Report*:[29]

We realize that making known our positions is a prerequisite to engaging in a meaningful dialog. As part of our commitment to this dialog with our stakeholders, we will make public Dow's opinions on key topics. We will also develop a set of Internet-based communication tools that will be used for meaningful discussion between Dow and stakeholders whenever possible.

But the benefits of establishing a dialog go beyond reputation and image. Communications make products and services more valuable to customers and users. Dow's dedication to Product Stewardship provides customers with the salient information they need to effectively use Dow products and avoid problems (box 1.2). Customers can use the products more efficiently and effectively. While such methods may reduce sales in the short term because there is less product waste by the customer, in the long term they create more value. Product Stewardship is a transitional step between pollution prevention and SBD.

Developing an SBD program

SBD provides management and practitioners with a clear understanding for the reasons and needs for the changes, innovations, and development programs that are necessary for making progress toward sustainable success. It is based on the premise that long-term success is achieved through a systematic process of business, technology, and product development programs that are formulated and implemented through a seamless and holistic strategic management system.

From a corporate perspective, the overarching direction for SBD can be defined in the narrow context of the EMS and in the broad arena of the entire business enterprise and the SMS. While there are many ways to define and develop business, technology, and new product development (NPD) programs, the two generic approaches are "top-down" (transformational)

Box 1.2 Dow Chemical Company and Product Stewardship

Dow Chemical Company (hereafter, Dow) with headquarters in Midland, Michigan, is the fifth largest chemical company in the world. Its revenues and net income in 2004 were $40 billion and $2.8 billion, respectively. Dow operates 115 manufacturing sites in thirty-seven countries. More than half of its sales are generated outside the United States. Dow produces primarily commodity-type chemicals like chlorinated compounds. Unfortunately, many of its products are toxic substances subject to regulation.

Dow has been an environmental leader since the 1930s. During the 1950s, Dow performed industrial hygiene surveys for customers and provided safety data with its products. In 1972, Ben Branch, the then President, introduced the concept of "Product Stewardship" to mitigate the risks associated with the use of chemicals. His initiative created a mindset and a culture that would endure for decades.

However, during the late 1960s the company was engaged in bitter litigation pertaining to its production of Agent Orange for the US government during the Vietnam War. It also became embroiled in a debate with the US Environmental Protection Agency (EPA) about providing access to Dow operating facilities. In 1983, Congressional hearings related to dioxin damaged Dow's image.

In an effort to overcome these negative impacts, Dow took actions in 1985 to reinforce Product Stewardship. It emphasized more open communications. With the establishment of its ChemWare Program, Dow actively enhanced its product information to move beyond simply providing the required information like material data safety sheets to providing additional product literature, videotapes, and technical data regarding the safe handling and use of its products. In the same year, the company introduced its waste reduction initiative called WRAP (Waste Reduction Always Pays).

In 1989, Dow joined the Chemical Manufacturers' Association's (CMA) Responsible Care (RC) Initiative. Responsible Care was a good fit for Dow's community outreach and its goals of preventing and eliminating adverse environmental and health impacts, waste streams, and emissions. These were precursors to SBD concepts. The CMA Codes of Management Practices include: (1) Community Awareness and Emergency Response; (2) Process Safety; (3) Employee Health and Safety; (4) Product Stewardship; (5) Distribution; and (6) Pollution Prevention.

Product Stewardship was the last code added in 1992 in order to "make health, safety, and environmental (EH&S) protection an integral part of designing, manufacturing, distributing, using, recycling, and disposing of chemical products."[1] Today, every Dow product has a product steward who is responsible for ensuring regulatory compliance, evaluating customer uses and practices, communicating information, investigating incidents, and taking corrective actions.[2] Every three years, Dow reviews its Product Stewardship within each business unit using life cycle analysis (LCA). The reviews are used to identify and mitigate serious adverse impacts.

Product Stewardship was an important element in Dow's transformation to "cradle-to-grave" thinking. It is how Dow assumed responsibility for all of the implications and impacts of its products, including how customers used them.

Dow continues to update its environmental management philosophies and programs. Many programs like ChemWare have been assimilated into Responsible Care and its current focus on sustainable development. Dow's 12-Point Sustainable Development Operating Plan includes: (1) People; (2) Brand; (3) Transparency; (4) Integration; (5) Dialog; (6) Advocacy; (7) Globalization; (8) Solutions Development; (9) Community; (10) Six Sigma; (11) EH&S; (12) Industry Alignment. The corporation represents an excellent example of the meaning of business integration and environmental leadership. Dow has articulated eight guiding principles for SBD: Product Stewardship, Eco-efficiency, Eco-systems Integrity, Transparency, Stakeholder Partnerships, Local and Dow Standards, Equity and the Quality of Life, and Employee and Public Outreach.[3]

The *Dow Global Public Report*, which basically follows the Global Reporting Initiative (GRI) guidelines, provides a link to all of its stakeholders and the means to articulate its fulfillment of sustainable development principles.

Notes:
1. Dow Chemical, "Continuing the Responsible Care Journey," Principles, Objectives and Goals for 2005, Form 162-01296-395F-P&E.
2. Dow Chemical, 1996 EH&S Report, *Environment, Health and Safety, Responsibility and Accountability*.
3. Dow Chemical, web pages, www.dow.com.publicreport/2001/twelvepoint/principles.htm.

Source: Dow Chemical Company, *Annual Report*, 2004.

and "bottom-up" (transitional). The former addresses the entire SMS through high-level thinking and formal criteria that are formulated at the executive management level and implemented uniformly across the business units and subsets of them. The latter generally entails a more flexible approach in which the business units create individual programs or projects at the grass-roots level and fit them into an overall corporate program. Each has advantages and disadvantages. Table 1.4 provides some insights about the salient points of each.

The selection of which approach to take is rarely an "either/or" proposition. There are many choices in between. The selected approach is usually based on the advantages and disadvantages of the existing portfolios of SBUs, technologies, product lines, and products, and the underlying nature and purpose of the enterprise.

Determining the program methodology is a strategic decision. Often the existing situation determines the choice. If the current technologies and products are powerful, with many strengths and only a few weaknesses, and the defective aspects can be corrected over time using incremental innovation, then the "bottom-up" approach may be the most viable and cost effective. However, if there are mostly weaknesses, the current situation may be unsustainable in the long term, requiring dramatic innovations to create a more viable position; therefore, a more systematic approach might be

Table 1.4. Differences between a large-scale, top-down SBD program approach and the more ad hoc, bottom-up project approach

	EMS – Transitional (Bottom-up)	SMS – Transformational (Top-down)
Primary objective	Move the business units to a richer, more sustainable reality with incremental or radical improvements in performance and significant reductions in impacts It involves the elimination of negative impacts and their consequences	Convert the entire enterprise to a new reality for all the SBUs, technologies, products, and services It involves radically changing the underpinnings of the corporation based on the principles, processes, and practices of SBD and enterprise thinking
Scope	Cradle-to-grave assessment and improvement of products, processes, and services based on the best development programs using a project-by-project basis	An enterprise-wide roll-out of programs that may be divided into stages The formulation and implementation covers the whole system It takes a cradle-to-grave view of the enterprise and aligns the various entities into an effective system for creating sustainable success
Structure	Less formal structure using criteria that are established during the execution of the program The methodology evolves as experience is gained and individual projects are completed Lessons learned from one project are transferred to the following ones	More formal structure using well-defined criteria, standards, and guidelines during the development and implementation of the program The methods are constructed during the early stages and are shared with all the business units There tends to be less flexibility and it may be difficult to share lessons learned across SBUs
Time horizon	Relatively short startup period since the roll-out can proceed one project at a time However, the whole program may take longer to complete, especially if the projects are implemented sequentially	Long startup stage since the whole program has to be articulated, documented, and communicated before launch Each stage may take years to accomplish However, the entire program may gain momentum as successes fuel the expansion
Direction	Bottom-up, driven by individuals or lower-level management	Top-down, driven by senior management with well-defined approaches requiring formal authorization
Risks	Modest investments requiring critical mass to make significant improvements	Large investment commitments with high level of uncertainty

the most feasible and have the greatest return. Such thinking is based on the philosophy that it is a waste of resources to invest into seriously flawed technologies, products, processes, and operations.

Enterprise thinking, as detailed in chapter 2, lays the foundation for making this determination. While there may be materials and components that are naturally sustainable, most corporations are involved in businesses that are not. Even those enterprises having naturally renewable resources have to have programs that reduce, mitigate or eliminate their negative impacts on the natural environment and the human condition. SBD necessitates, first, an enterprise-wide understanding of the businesses and operations and their impacts, and then a grand strategy for moving the corporation from what it is to what it would like to be, transforming or moving the enterprise into a new reality via strategies, investments, and improvements.

The "top-down" or transformational approach primarily considers the total business environment. Large-scale business management systems that produce commodity-type products usually have top-down management constructs because they require high-level decision-making for effecting SBD. Petroleum-related products, paper and forest products, chemicals, and food products are a few examples of this type of business system. Large global corporations with far-flung operations, such as in the petroleum industry, tend to have centralized approaches since it is difficult for a single business unit to set direction or to have an influence on outcomes. Likewise, many high-tech businesses often need more centralized management systems because of the inherent risks involved in developing new technologies and new products or adding to capital assets. Boeing and Airbus are corporations that produce complex products that require very stringent controls for ensuring safety, reliability, and economic viability. Centralized constructs are often the only viable option for such companies.

International Paper's (IP) sustainable forestry initiative is an example of the complexities involved in changing the nature of core business philosophies and activities (box 1.3). It has the advantage of using raw materials that are inherently renewable and arguably sustainable. However, SBD at IP is not as easy to implement as it might appear.

At the other extreme, SBD programs may be based on a transitional or "bottom-up" approach for moving the product delivery system or just the EMS toward SBD rather than having a grand strategy that engages the entire enterprise. Such a scheme involves evolutionary changes to the business units and their technologies and products rather than revolutionary changes to the entire enterprise. While there is a lack of evidence to suggest one approach is

Box 1.3 International Paper and its conversion to a sustainable future

International Paper (hereafter, IP) is the world's largest paper and forest products company with revenues of approximately $26 billion in 2004.[1] Its primary resources are renewable materials (trees) that have mostly positive characteristics.

John Dillion, Chairman and CEO, states that IP has "three equally important sustainability goals: to be financially successful, socially responsible, and environmentally excellent." He says "our business is grounded, quite literally, in sustainability of our primary raw material – wood fiber. We manufacture the products our customers want and need using the only natural resources that perpetually regenerates itself in harmony with the environment – trees."[2]

However, the challenge to create a sustainable future is daunting. IP has approximately 20 million acres of forests that it owns or manages. It typically harvests about 2 percent of the trees per year to fulfill its needs for wood fiber. The management process includes ensuring the long-term viability of the natural resources through proper cutting techniques, the replanting of seedlings, the protection of wildlife, plants, soil, air, and water quality. IP's Sustainable Forestry Initiative® is an ambitious program that includes providing training in best forestry practices to more than 80,000 loggers and other harvesting professionals.[3] Given the magnitude of the resources and the participants involved in the program, it is unlikely that individual business units could manage such a program without significant direction and support from corporate management.

IP operates over 200 manufacturing plants.[4] These include 34 pulp, paper and packaging mills; 145 converting and packaging plants; 26 wood products facilities; 2 specialty panel and laminated products plants; and 13 chemical specialty plants in Asia, Canada, Europe, South America, and the United States. IP uses approximately 70 million tons of raw materials including harvested wood, purchased pulp, chemicals and supplementary primary materials not including fuels and water in 2003.[5] These operations produce hazardous waste, solid waste, air emissions, greenhouse gas emissions, and toxins. These waste streams represent challenges that will require a SBD program that addresses each challenge at each location.

IP reported that 95 percent of the chemicals used in its operations are recycled.[6] It also produces paper with 30 percent recycled content. These efforts have a positive effect on the environmental side of the ledger and provide powerful economic benefits as well. The use, reuse, and recycling of raw materials and energy resources reduces the costs of the product by maximizing the benefits of the input resources and minimizing the costly waste streams.

The company also examines the life cycle implications of its products and processes. It uses the GRI indicators in disclosing essential environmental information and data to its constituencies. IP makes strong statements that it has an inherent advantage in moving toward sustainability because its primary raw material comes from trees. However, because of the size of its global operations and supply networks, which include chemical companies, loggers, equipment manufactures, and many others, IP has to integrate both internal and external resources as part of its sustainable development program. Senior management has to provide the direction to ensure that every part of the enterprise is moving in the right direction.

Notes:
1. *Annual Report*, 2004.
2. *Ibid.*
3. *International Paper and Sustainable Forestry: Sustaining Forests – Sustaining the Future*, p. 12.
4. *Annual Report*, 2004, p. 19.
5. *Ibid.*
6. *Ibid.*

superior to the other, most of the current applications of SBD fit into the category of evolutionary change rather than radical change. These change mechanisms allow corporations to be guided by business performance and financial outcomes as well as by SBD philosophies and corporate strategies. They allow the time necessary to arrive at a consensus and to build capabilities, knowledge, and confidence for going forward. Previous successes can fuel the passion for making further gains, and difficulties or failures can provide insights for further changes and improvements.

The transitional approach is also clearly easier to articulate and facilitate in the normal context of managing a business. The strategic implications are more closely aligned with the existing business situation, and are, accordingly, less profound and less threatening. However, it is important to remember the seemingly lower inherent risks often result in lower rewards. Regardless, the essential conditions for developing and implementing of programs include:

- A firm understanding of the business environment and the significant issues affecting the markets, customers, stakeholders, and other constituents.
- A philosophical perspective on SBD that provides guidance for establishing strategies, objectives, and evaluation criteria.
- Strong corporate policies clearly guiding program selection and change.
- A management construct for developing new technologies and new products that is based on the total requirements of customers, markets, stakeholders, governments, value networks, and significant related industries. Also a well-established management process that provides a framework for the integration of all business units and operations.
- LCT for analyzing and improving every facet of the impacts of resource use, technologies, and products.

Box 1.4 3M's evolution from "pollution prevention pays" to sustainable development

3M is organized into more than forty business units in six markets with revenues of $20 billion, net income of $2.99 billion and R&D expenditures of $1 billion.[1] It has over 70,000 employees, in over sixty countries, split about evenly between US and international locations.

Five businessmen who wanted to exploit the mining of what they believed to be corundum deposits began the Minnesota Mining and Manufacturing Company (3M) in 1902. While that venture failed, their subsequent manufacturing of sandpaper was very successful. Thereafter, 3M's innovative capacity produced many successes including waterproof sandpaper, masking tape, Scotch-brand Cellophane tape, Post-it Notes, and more than 50,000 other new products over its history.

In 3M's case, the company created the products, and customers discovered the applications. 3M's innovative capabilities derive from its corporate culture and management philosophy that rely on customer input and employee contributions. Historically, 3M promoted creativity and decentralized thinking. William McKnight, the Chairman between 1949 and 1966, encouraged delegating responsibility and taking initiative.[2] He was credited with 3M's famous "15 percent rule" that permeates the culture today, allowing its technical employees the flexibility to use 15 percent of their time at work on their own projects. In this way, 3M empowers its employees to seek quality and sustainable growth.

3M's very successful Post-it Notes were developed under the 15 percent rule. Researcher Art Fry used an adhesive that had previously failed because of its inability to attach permanently. From this "failure," Fry created the Post-It, meeting people's needs for short-term notes.

3M believes that the risks inherent in developing new products are mitigated by its diversity. It does not expect that every new product will be successful. The company promotes being on the leading edge of innovation and creativity. Its vision is to be the most innovative company in the world.[3]

In 1975 the company adopted its Environmental Policy and created the voluntary Pollution Prevention Pays (3P) Program. The program has been an outstanding success as suggested in the following statement from 3M's *Environmental, Health and Safety Progress Report*: "In just over two decades, more than 4,600 3P projects initiated by employees worldwide have produced total savings of $810 million while eliminating 1.6 million pounds of releases to the air, water, and land."[4]

The company led the way for the pollution prevention thinking of the 1990s. It continues to capture economic benefits from the savings, enhance environmental performance by reducing waste streams, and improve its corporate image by exhibiting environmental leadership. As the 3P program has evolved into 3P Plus, employees have sought new initiatives to continue the long tradition of research and innovation. While it takes management commitment to support the initiatives, employees at every level understand that pollution prevention is everyone's responsibility.

"3M's process for moving toward SBD is called eco-efficiency, as defined by the World Business Council for Sustainable Development."[5] In 2001, it combined its EMS and the Global Heath and Safety Plan into an integrated Environmental, Health and Safety Management System. While it still focuses on pollution prevention, 3M's three environmental strategies focus on continual improvement of its compliance assurance system, the use of life cycle management to ensure that opportunities and issues are considered through all stages of a product's life, and meeting environmental, health and safety goals.

Notes:
1. http://www.mmm.com/about3m/facts/3Mfacts.jhmtl.
2. Ernest Gundling, *The 3M Way to Innovation: Balancing People and Profit* (Tokyo: Kodansha International, 2000), p. 58.
3. Rosabeth Kanter, John Kao, and Fred Wiersema, *Innovation Breakthrough Thinking at 3M, DuPont, GE, Pfizer, and Rubbermaid* (New York: Harper Business, 1997), pp. 54–59.
4. 3M, *Environmental, Health and Safety Progress Report.*
5. *Ibid.*, p. 2.

SBD is relatively new for most corporations, executives, managers, professionals, and practitioners. The experience base for establishing a program exists only within a relatively small number of leading corporations. Moreover, most of the information and data pertains to insights and lessons learned rather than a fully articulated framework describing how to develop and implement SBD.

3M is one such global corporation that is moving from its very successful approaches for pollution prevention to more sophisticated SBD constructs (box 1.4). It is building on its long-standing foundation in business integration and innovation to establish a new management system and processes for developing sustainable technologies and products. 3M typifies how to succeed via the "bottom-up" approach and incremental innovation.

An SBD perspective on innovation management

Leading change through innovation theory and reality

Change is one of the most discussed and intensely debated topics dating back to famous Greek philosophers over two thousand years ago. Arguments varied from the changeless, immutable view of the world of Parmenides and Zeno to Heraclitus' dynamic unity of process in which each momentary phase was continuously transformed into a subsequent qualitatively different phase.[30] In the context of business over most of the last two centuries, changes have been ever-present but occurring at relatively slow and manageable rates.

During the nineteenth century, technological changes created opportunities to improve business processes and operations as well as new devices for consumers, agriculture, industry, transportation, and communications. Steam engines, steamships, railroads, telegraphs, telephones, reapers, and sewing machines, among thousands of other devices, changed how fast businesses and people could produce goods, travel, communicate, harvest food, and make clothes. Most of the changes were driven by inventions and innovations by creative inventors like Cyrus McCormick (the reaper), Werner Siemens (dynamos), Thomas Edison (lighting) and Otto Benz (cars), who used their ingenuity and talents to develop new technologies and new products as well as new business enterprises for the commercialization of their technologies. During the early twentieth century, executives and innovators in industries such as steel, petroleum, automobiles, aircraft, food processing, chemicals, household goods, and numerous others managed change by managing the life cycle of their technologies and products and keeping the rate of change at a comfortable pace. Moreover, it could be argued that the rate of change was slow because the capabilities of most business organizations were relatively weak in managing change and in developing new technologies and products. Moreover, the slow almost controlled rate of change allowed senior management in most corporations to have the time to make adjustments and maintain their strategic positions with relatively low risks. While this is a broad-brush view of a complex historical situation, there is evidence that most executives preferred stability and tried to reduce disruptive actions due to technological change. For instance, the US automobile industry during most of the 1930s–1970s had an oligarchic industry structure that was dominated by General Motors (GM). Most of the executives believed that it was in everyone's best interest if the industry maintained economic stability through the prevailing industry structure.[31]

During the second half of the twentieth century change became more commonplace and a much more critical topic, especially with the turbulence of the 1970s. With the oil crises of 1973 and 1979, economic stability was severely challenged and inflation, stagnation, and high interest rates had devastating effects on businesses, consumers, stakeholders, and society. The late Peter Drucker, in *Managing in Turbulent Times*, characterized the prevailing situation as fraught with uncertainty and risks. He described his expectations for the future as "a period of structural change rather than one of modification, of extension, or of exploitation. The period ahead [the 1980s] will shift technological change to new realm ... One of these areas of structural change ahead is electronics."[32] While Drucker was not the only management guru who initiated the discussions about structural change his insights provide a sense that fundamental changes were occurring in the business environment of the 1980s. Among the many changes, leading edge corporations in many industries converted their quality methods to the precepts of TQM and improved the quality of their products dramatically. Customers demanded quality products and made purchase decisions based on perceived value, cost effectiveness, and responsiveness. Technological change shifted into a higher gear as electronics, personal computers, software, and communications technologies became driving forces of change. Change was driven by external forces, especially social, political, economic, technological, environmental, and market ones, as well as the internal technology and product development initiatives and strategies.

Structural change involves the transformation of the organization, operations, programs, processes, and/or activities from the prevailing paradigm to a whole new way of achieving positive outcomes and sustainable success. Unlike evolutionary change or cyclical changes that are extremely small or temporary ups and downs, respectively, structural changes are significant permanent transformations that revolutionize the underpinnings of business and performance. For example, PCs not only impacted the market potential for electronic typewriters but they transformed the work place and how people prepared documents. Gone are the "typists." The average "white-collar" worker now acts as her own secretary. Structural changes include the impacts of innovative technologies and how customers and stakeholders buy and use products. For instance, the Internet provides opportunities for Amazon.com to sell products directly to customers using personal computers, servers, and software augmented by a logistical support for companies such as FedEx and UPS.

The rapid changes in the driving forces and the more turbulent business conditions of the late 1970s, 1980s, and early 1990s meant that management had to preempt change or at least stay abreast of it if the organization was to maintain currency with the business environment and achieve a reasonable level of performance and success. The rapidity of change in the business environment was the death knell of the "do nothing" strategy or its co-equal strategy of "maintaining the status quo." Persistent change necessitates leading change through strategic actions.

At the end of the 1980s, reengineering became a prevailing management approach for managing change. The original intent of reengineering, which was made popular by Michael Hammer and James Champy via their book, *Reengineering the Corporation*, was to make quantum leaps in improving performance through innovative processes and structures. Hammer and Champy defined reengineering as:[33]

The fundamental rethinking and radical redesign of business processes to achieve dramatic improvements in critical, contemporary measures of performance, such as cost, quality, service, and speed.

The authors clearly had a modern sense of what was required to manage or even lead change. "Dramatic improvements" meant factors of two or ten times or more improvements over the previous outcomes. "Radical" meant rethinking every process and making them efficient and effective. Unfortunately many business leaders viewed reengineering as a way to eliminate middle management and downsize their organization. Rather than focusing on radical and systematic changes and improvements, most corporations and their leaders thought in terms of cost reductions and improving share price (market capitalization). While many such corporations did make short-term gains, most of them failed to achieve substantial improvements in their organizations.

During the early 1990s with the fall of the Soviet Union, the rise of globalization, the integration of the European Union, the rapid changes in technological innovations, and the intensity of competition, leading change was recognized as a critical consideration in managing large corporations. While external change has always been a key factor in strategic thinking, the rate and number of significant changes in the business environment during the mid-1990s necessitated a change in management philosophy. The concept of managing change gave way to the notion of leading change.

John P. Kotter of the Harvard Business School was one of the advocates for leading change. His "eight-stage process of creating major change" provided executives, managers, and professionals with the fundamentals for leading change and transforming their organizations. In *Leading Change*, Kotter outlined the eight major stages as:[34]

(1) Establishing a sense of urgency
(2) Creating a guiding coalition
(3) Developing a strategic vision
(4) Communicating the change vision
(5) Empowering broad-based action
(6) Generating short-term wins
(7) Consolidating gains and producing more change
(8) Anchoring new approaches in the culture.

Kotter believed that changes should follow the suggested sequence. Each of his stages fits into the context of strategic thinking and leading change, and the constructs of SBD. Establishing a sense of urgency is one of the most important aspects of moving toward SBD. Corporations have to preempt changes in the business environment and become the architects of the future. They can not rest on their laurels and expect that their competitive advantages will last forever. In a fast-moving business environment, competitive advantages are very transient.

Daryl R. Conner, author of *Managing at the Speed of Change*, discussed a fundamental axiom: "Our lives are most effective and efficient when we are moving at the speed that allows us to appropriately assimilate the changes we face."[35] Moreover, he suggested that "As the world grows more complex, the pressures mount for us to manage more change at increasing speed."[36]

Kotter's strategic vision is a critical stage for inventing the future. It is pivotal in differentiating leading change from managing change. It is the vision for the future that provides the strategic direction and belief that sustainable success can be achieved. Communicating the vision is an imperative if leaders, professionals, practitioners, partners and other constituencies are going to accept and believe in it. Empowering people across the enterprise brings the power for leading change. Quantum improvements can not be realized if only a few people participate in the change process. However, if everyone participates, the energy and people power can be enormous.

The notion of achieving short-term wins is especially important for long-term initiatives that may take decades to accomplish. The people engaged in the change processes need to gain recognition and rewards along the path to the vision for the future and the ultimate sustainable success. Moreover, recognition and reward provide the means to leverage past achievements and maintain the process toward the ongoing objectives of creating extraordinary value and a better world in the future. Anchoring change in the culture of the organization makes the process self-sustaining. People have to believe in the benefits of change and accept the reality of making changes to achieve a richer and more fruitful world for all.

Innovation is a change or improvement that has a positive outcome(s) with respect to customers, stakeholders, and the organization. It is an essential management construct for leading change. While the process depends on the type of innovation (business, technological, product, or process), most innovations have common characteristics.

Most innovations start with the imagination or insights of the innovator(s). Both involve mental images or mental models of what is or what could be. Peter Senge, in *The Fifth Discipline*, defined mental models as "deeply ingrained assumptions, generalizations, or even pictures of images that influence how we understand the world and how we take action."[37] Whether mental models are assumptions or generalizations is not critical, they influence how someone perceives the world or understands reality. Imagination and insights are mental models of what could be, or what is.

Imagination is a high level of thinking about the world and how to create possible solutions for making dramatic and even quantum improvements. Imagination involves thinking based on what could be, rather than what is currently happening. It is usually based on out-of-the-box thinking about the way the world could be, or even should be. The challenge with innovation using imagination is that it requires perception and theoretical constructs since it is impossible in most cases to use analysis because the data does not exist. For example, Henry Ford created the opportunities for developing, producing and marketing the Model T Car. The US market in 1903 was approximately 11,000 cars.[38] The perceived automobile market was based on the concept of chauffer-driven luxury vehicles costing several thousand dollars or more. Ford imagined what the market could be if he produced a cost effective (less than $500) automobile using advanced manufacturing methods (mass production) that he gleaned for the meat packaging houses in Chicago and sold at an affordable price to the large demographic groups of lower income people. Another more recent example is how eBay created online auctioning by linking millions of its clients to create business opportunities for everyone. The power of eBay is its software and management system that connects millions of traders in a convenient and cost effective business model that allows effective and efficient person-to-person exchange of information, goods, and money. With safe and secure transaction supported by eBay's business model and augmented by logistical support from UPS, USPS and over 250 strategic alliances, eBay's clients and business associates can leverage the benefits of eBay for achieving their objectives and making transactions that would be impossible on an individual basis. eBay makes only a small fee on each transaction, but with millions of transactions per year its revenues and profits in 2003 were $2.165 billion and $447 million, respectively.

On the academic side, Stuart Hart, one of the world's top authorities on sustainable development and Chair of Cornell University's Sustainable Global Enterprise, discusses "the great leap downward" and how businesses can expand their opportunities by "driving innovation from the base of the pyramid (potential customers with low incomes)."[39] Hart's perspective fits perfectly into what imagination means in the context of innovation. While many corporations are engaged in highly competitive markets, imagine the opportunities that could be developed if those corporations expanded their marketing to people further down the economic pyramid. Most corporations focus their efforts only on the top of the economic pyramid which includes approximately 1 billion people: those with purchasing power parity (PPP) in US dollars of more than $15,000.[40] With imagination, business leaders can discover how to visualize solutions to overcome the "most difficult problems" and create new opportunities for people and corporations.

Insights involve understanding reality or discovering the true nature of a situation. This usually requires an in-depth assessment of reality and the ability to discern the essence of the conditions and trends in the business environment or a subset of it. Insights are often based on analyses of reality using intuition, scientific methods, and prevailing business constructs. One of the most intriguing stories of how insights resulted in changing strategic direction involved Sears, Roebuck and Company and the development of its innovation of mall-type stores in the suburbs. General Wood, Sears' CEO during the early 1950s, was a very competent leader and administrator, who depended on "a steady flow of accurate figures on which to base his action."[41] After the Second World War there were concerns among the leading US retailers that the Depression would return. Wood was an accomplished statistician who studied retail sales and trends in the regional markets. At the time the major retailers concentrated their resources (stores) in the centers of the large cities. In studying market data, Wood realized that people were moving to the suburbs and that while the cities were still dominant, the growth potential was in the suburbs. Sears created the mall-type store and built extensively in the suburbs instead of the city centers. Wood outsmarted his principal competitors, J. C. Penney and Montgomery Ward, because his analysis of market statistics provided insights about the future opportunities. Sears took advantage of those opportunities years before it became apparent that the major retailers should be building stores near where the population was moving.

Another example is how Bill Gates and Paul Allen understood the power of software during the early days of Microsoft. When they obtained a contract to develop an operating system for IBM, they negotiated to retain ownership of the intellectual property. IBM at the time was concentrating on the hardware and seemingly did not understand the full value of software. Microsoft's intellectual property became one of the company's most valuable assets. A more recent example involves Toyota's investment into the Prius, a fuel-efficient hybrid car with an internal combustion engine and an electric motor, during the 1990s when fuel prices were low (petroleum was only

$10 per barrel in the late 1990s). Toyota's foresight and investment paid huge rewards five years later. Business executives and strategists at Toyota knew that the constraints on the supply and production of gasoline would result ultimately in higher prices. It was just a matter of time.

On the academic side, C. K. Prahalad in his book, *The Fortune at the Bottom of the Pyramid*, provides insights about how to expand business opportunities around the world through innovation.[42] Both Prahalad and Hart offer ways in which social and economic problems can be solved using innovative business approaches to expand markets and opportunities.

Imagination and insights are essential for developing new ideas and creating new opportunities. They may act independently or interdependently. John Kotter's book, *The Heart of Change*, discusses two models for change: The "See–Feel–Change" model and the "Analysis–Think–Change" model.[43] The former involves emotionally derived change based on what could be or should be. It fits the discussions about imagination. The latter involves a more rationally based approach using data and information from the business environment. It fits the discussions about insights. While there are numerous "schools of thought" about which is the preferred or best approach, both have advantages and disadvantages. Imagination allows for unconstrained thinking about the future and what kinds of solutions may be possible. Its main disadvantage is that it can be based on emotional perspectives that are difficult to articulate and validate. On the other hand insights, if based on analysis, tend to be rational and scientific and, therefore, easier in most cases to verify. Thus, the resultant ideas and opportunities are usually viewed as being more realistic and less theoretical. The disadvantages of extensive analysis are that it takes time and is often limited by what is instead of what could be. It is also more costly. There is no perfect answer. Moreover, imagination and insights can be used in combination to develop and validate ideas and concepts pertaining to opportunities for innovations.

Imagination and insights have to be translated into ideas on how corporations can take advantage of opportunities. An idea is simply the possibility of a new technology, product, or process that requires further definition and detail before it can be converted into a business opportunity. Ideas lead to change. However, ideas have be defined and articulated before the organization can appreciate their value and potential. They have to be assessed and screened to determine which fit the organization and will lead to important contributions for sustainable success.

Leading change requires processes that take ideas and turn them into well-honed concepts and then fully articulated candidates that can be evaluated with respect to predetermined criteria that include business, market, financial, stakeholder, and competitive considerations. Concepts become the candidates for further development into initiatives and action programs. Ultimately, leading change in most organizations involves selecting the best opportunities from a myriad of candidates.

Using Kotter's views on leading change involves both short-term initiatives to move the organization to make improvements and achieve "short-term wins" and long-term programs that transform the corporation into a more sustainable and successful enterprise. Most of the prevailing management constructs focus on moving the businesses, technologies, products, operations, processes, and people through incremental change and/or continuous improvement. While the logic of such thinking is sound, evolutionary change may not be sufficient in a dynamic business environment where change is accelerating. Transformation of the corporation through quantum or radical change may become imperative if the corporation is to excel and preempt the needs of customers and stakeholders, and outperform competitors and those challenging its existence. This is especially that case if the business environment is turbulent and unstable. Moreover, it is more than competitors that challenge corporations' ability to survive. Technological change and obsolescence are factors in causing the decline of some of the most successful companies. For example, Polaroid and even Kodak are having trouble finding their way in the complex world of digital photography. The history of business enterprises is replete with great corporations failing to keep pace with the requirements of the future and fading into oblivion. RCA was one of the most technology-rich corporations of the twentieth century, but all of their successes did not save them from being acquired by General Electric (GE) and then being dismantled and sold off in pieces.

Leading change and innovation are really parallel constructs. They are essential for SBD.

Technological innovation for SBD

Technological innovation includes **R&D** activities associated with creating and developing innovative technologies, improving existing technological assets, discovering ways to improve existing products and processes, and finding new opportunities to exploit the technical capabilities and resources of the organization. Technological innovation generates business opportunities by dramatically modifying the underlying technological resources and capabilities.[44] It sets the stage for product and process innovation, translating inventions and new technologies into the means and mechanisms to design, produce, and market new products for a better world.

Historically, environmental technologies meant selected technologies that were developed or enhanced to solve specific environmental problems. Most environmental technologies addressed regulatory requirements and were designed as control technology for cleaning up waste streams after they had been generated or to prevent or recycle the burdens associated with products and production processes. Such technologies included the catalytic converter used on automobiles, an outcome of the US Clean Air Act Amendments of 1970 and similar laws across the world. Other examples included flue gas "desulfurization" equipment used to abate sulfur dioxide emissions from industrial processes, the recycling of aluminum, water purification equipment, and wastewater treatment processes.

Effective technological innovation from a SBD perspective involves improving the benefits and cost effectiveness of the technologies and the related new products and processes (more for less), reducing the impacts, consequences, and risks associated with the applications of technologies and products (making them cleaner and safer), and enhancing the quality, reliability, and longevity of technologies and products (making them more useful for longer periods). This concept of technological innovation applies to improved hardware, software, process knowledge, systems, and services.

The many technological developments during the twentieth century both contributed to the problems, and provided solutions.[45] For instance, the extensive use of "convenience" products that are immediately discarded after a single use contribute significantly to solid waste problems in most developed countries. Increased waste generation accompanies increases in real gross domestic product (GDP), population growth, affluence, demand for more convenient products and attractive packaging, and the use of nonsustainable technologies. On the other hand, technologies such as the microprocessor have made significant contributions to improving many aspects of other product and process technologies. PCs have evolved since the 1980s, becoming smaller and more powerful. The PCs of today weigh significantly less and contain fewer toxic substances than the original devices, are much more capable, and significantly less expensive. While there are still many concerns associated with PC technologies, their negative footprint has diminished over the years. Most importantly, PCs have replaced many technologies that had much greater environmental impacts.

Technological innovation for SBD involves assessing the prevailing technologies and products and selecting development programs that lead to improvements from every perspective. Such improvements are based on input from and consideration of many perspectives, including societal, political, economic, technological, and environmental. The desire to create a better future through innovation instead of responses to government mandates, social pressures, and unfavorable economics drives SBD.

Incremental product innovation and radical technological innovation

With the dramatic upsurge in the development of new technologies and the rapid changes in the global business environment, technology and product life cycles have significantly diminished since the 1990s. This quicker product life turnover has, in turn, pressured companies to create new products and technologies even faster. The business environment and its broad constituents expect solutions and improvements. The challenge is to determine the right mechanisms for delivering on those expectations. The answers depend on the requirements of the business environment, the core capabilities of the organization and its resources, and the need for addressing social, economic, and environmental concerns.

The typical investment model involves a portfolio approach allocating money and resources between evolutionary and revolutionary innovations. This approach indicates that investments should be made in various categories to obtain a balanced or diversified portfolio of new solutions.

Evolutionary development focuses on making incremental improvements to existing products to enhance their value (improve benefits, diminish defects, reduce burdens, and improve cost effectiveness). This is the general approach that 3M follows as it continuously examines its product portfolios for ways to improve outcomes (see box 1.4, p. 50). The logic is to stay ahead of the expectations of customers, stakeholders, society, governments, and the pressures of competitors. Incremental improvements typically address the concerns of external entities which are usually familiar to management. The changes are easier to identify and track because they are related to the present situation and may already have a natural "fit" within the management system.

The normal reaction to changes in the business environment is to respond with incremental improvements. These provide good answers as long as the dominant technologies and design characteristics do not change significantly or such technologies do not have overwhelming environmental impacts and negative consequences. Moreover, as environmental laws and regulations become more stringent, the EMS for responding to the mandates becomes more complex and expensive. The solution for dealing with the winds of change in this arena may be to incrementally eliminate all the technologies and products that trigger regulatory responses.

However, if the business environment is changing dramatically, radical change may be required. For example, producers of tobacco products and firearms have not quelled the debates about their products even though innovations have been made. In these cases, incremental change does not provide the right answer.

Radical technological innovation is a more far-reaching and difficult phenomenon to understand and manage and, for this reason, is much less prevalent. Changing the very nature of the corporation and its technologies and products requires wholesale changes to the organizational structure, the capabilities of management and employees, the value networks, and many other elements. Radical innovation is usually invoked when the business environment becomes unstable due to social, political, economic, and/or technological forces. For example, the political and economic uncertainties associated with the petroleum industry are driving some in the industry like BP plc (formerly BP Amoco or British Petroleum) to think about transforming resources, capabilities, and operations to a more balanced portfolio of renewable energy resources and traditional petroleum-based assets and product delivery systems.

Radical technological change focuses on developing or improving the underlying technology and knowledge base. SBD can involve either evolutionary or revolutionary changes. The choice depends on the situation and the expected outcomes. In either case, the basic construct is to use technological innovation and product innovation as a means to create better solutions and invent a better future. Chapters 7 and 8 cover these aspects in much more detail.

Overview of LCT and LCA

LCT is an inclusive, intellectual methodology for examining and improving technologies, products, and processes. It consists of "cradle-to-grave" evaluation of: (1) raw material acquisition and distribution through the supply networks; (2) materials handling, processing, fabrication, and assembly; (3) distribution; (4) sale, use, and service of the product, including secondary and tertiary applications; (5) recycling, retirement, and disposal. It includes analysis of the operations of upstream and downstream entities within the enterprise.

The use of LCT for reducing environmental impacts, improving economics, and enhancing social dimensions requires analyses of product requirements and selection of the most economically, technically and environmentally conscious approaches. Appropriate strategies must satisfy the entire set of product specifications, thus creating a sustainable design from every perspective. LCT and management is covered in chapter 9.

LCA is a systematic methodology used to identify and evaluate the environmental impacts and burdens associated with products, their related processes, supply and distribution requirements, and applications. LCA uses scientific principles and technical rigor to ensure the validity of the assessments and the appropriateness of the steps taken to make improvements.

LCA is a multistage, input/output model that analyzes all of the inputs and outputs, their impacts, including materials, products, wastes, and emissions, and the possible options for improving the value proposition of products and processes. LCA examines the existing situation and explores the possibilities for systematic improvements through product design, development, and deployment.

The basic purposes of LCA are to create more value for the organization, its customers and stakeholders, to make dramatic improvement, and to mitigate risks. More value derives from increasing benefits and decreasing defects and burdens, including environmental and social burdens and costs. Burdens increase cost, decrease quality, reduce flexibility, or increase time, all of which lowers customer satisfaction. LCA is covered in chapters 10 and 11.

Performance evaluation is the systematic examination of the technological and product innovation and LCA over time, examining the achievements in terms of the targets and criteria established by management. It is used to determine the extent to which the corporation is meeting the objectives and targets and managing the risks and consequences of sustainable development. It measures performance against the needs, wants, and expectations of customers and stakeholders. Performance criteria and metrics are used to determine the likelihood of success. Performance evaluation must have a flexible framework in order to respond to the changing business conditions and new expectations of the numerous constituents.

Performance evaluation is designed to provide a consistent format for an authoritative overview of performance. It enables the organization to determine performance and take corrective actions to get back on track if necessary. It is ultimately concerned with improvement and the prevention, detection, and correction of difficulties and problems.

Summary

For decades, environmental management was relegated to the bottom of the management structure. It was the purview of the operating system at the grass-roots level, viewed as a necessary requirement, but not a central means for achieving business success. However, the dramatic increase in public awareness and understanding of environmental issues during the 1990s forced business executives to elevate the importance of environmental management within their SMS and organizational structure.

SBD embodies the need to reinvent and reinvigorate the corporation and its enterprise through strategies, innovation, and leadership. It includes dealing with the legacy of past events and practices and determining the proper course for future development and ongoing success. SBD involves appreciating the past, understanding the present, and inventing the future. It represents a shift in thinking from making trade-offs and compromises to considering how to achieve ideal solutions for maximizing value and benefits. It is the systematic approach to realizing opportunities for creating a better business environment and a much more innovative, effective, productive, and leaner enterprise.

The history of business management is replete with stories of leaders seeking better solutions to the prevailing problems and more effective ways to exploit emerging opportunities. It is that ongoing quest to explore, exploit, and expand that drives the improvement process and ultimately satisfies the social, economic, environmental, and business forces. Successful corporations are the ones that find the best solutions and are adept at implementing those solutions. SBD is the all-encompassing mantra that guides decision-making toward this end.

Philosophies, principles, and beliefs are directly linked to the overarching goal of creating value in a sustainable way. Enterprise thinking and SBD tie all of the business forces together and define what good solutions are. For instance, management at companies such as Enron and WorldCom would not have had to struggle with many of their decisions if they had had well-articulated views of acceptable ethical beliefs, values, principles, and practices.

Leadership is pivotal. It transforms the broad constructs (vision, philosophies, and values) of the intellectual foundation of a corporation into dynamic interactions that create exciting possibilities for changing the world. Effective leadership is about sustaining improvements and success over many decades.

Innovation deals with enhancing the corporation's capabilities for satisfying demand in the most suitable fashion. It focuses on the traditional concepts of efficiency (doing more with less), effectiveness (doing the right things), and environmental consciousness (eliminating waste). Doing more with less reduces costs, saves resources, and thereby mitigates environmental burdens. Effectiveness improves performance, reduces defects, and enhances environmental benefits. Environmental consciousness also saves money by reducing resource utilization, lessening environmental impacts by eliminating waste streams, and by making outcomes more sustainable because they are more valuable.

SBD involves moving from the older paradigms of compliance-driven mandates and pollution prevention thinking into a new world of preemptive business strategies for creating value, developing solutions, and providing total satisfaction. It forms the basis for a unified approach for dealing with social, economic, and environmental problems through a comprehensive analysis of the business environment and systematic improvements to the underpinnings of the corporation. The move toward SBD requires senior management commitment and the ongoing support of intellectual capabilities and financial capital.

SBD has embedded within it the constructs of the previous methodologies and approaches. It incorporates the lessons from the past into a comprehensive strategic management framework for inventing the future. The focus is on the global enterprise and its long-term viability. Success is achieved in the long term and sustainable success is what is critical. Figure 1.5 depicts the simplified view of these relationships.

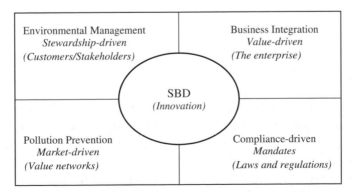

Figure 1.5   A simplified view of SBD and its precursors and embedded constructs

Survivability and sustainability are the fundamental objectives of corporations. The long-term goal of SBD is to make environmental laws and regulations and other mandates irrelevant because the very causes for their existence have been eliminated. It is to provide the best solutions that provide total satisfaction. The strategic objective is to reach a higher level of reality where environmental management as we know it today no longer exists and environmental considerations are instead embedded within the SMS.

Supplementary material

Learning objectives

Chapter 1 has the following learning objectives that are intended to guide and support students and practitioners:
- Understanding the meaning and purposes of SBD and the underlying principles, philosophies, and methods.
- Appreciating the historical development of environmental management and SBD.
- Exploring the underpinnings and overarching driving forces for transitioning or transforming global corporations to achieve sustainable success.
- Understanding the means of enterprise and enterprise management and the importance of enterprise thinking.
- Linking the corporation and its enterprise with the business environment for formulating and implementing SBD strategies.
- Identifying and assessing the main management constructs for adapting SBD.
- Identifying and assessing the main types of SBD innovation programs.
- Describing the fundamentals of SBD.

Research questions

The following are questions related to SBD in order to facilitate learning and ongoing discussion and analysis of the main topics covered in the chapter:
- What are the philosophical underpinnings and essential principles of SBD being used by large corporations?
- What are the overarching objectives of global corporations that would warrant adapting SBD?

- Why have SBD principles, constructs, strategies, processes, and practices evolved from the simpler constructs of environmental management?
- How do global corporations view the distinctions between sustainability, sustainable development, and SBD?
- What are the major business management constructs for developing and implementing SBD programs in large corporations?
- How do global corporations deploy innovation in adapting SBD?
- How do global corporations view the difference between incremental innovation and radical innovation?
- How would large corporations use LCT and management to contribute to SBD?
- Why should a corporation adapt SBD?

NOTES

1. *Siemens Corporate Social Responsibility Report 2002*, Berlin and Munich: Siemens AG, 2002, p. 24.
2. *Ibid.*, p. 16.
3. *Ibid.*, p. 21.
4. The focus of the book is on the global business environment and the implications of managing social, economic, and environmental challenges, and leading change. Therefore, specific laws and regulations are not discussed other than as specific examples of driving forces and mandates for change. There are many similarities between the environmental laws of the leading industrial countries in the world.
5. Product Stewardship is explained and assessed in box 1.2 about Dow Chemical.
6. Tom Tibor and Ira Feldman, *Implementing ISO 14000* (New York: McGraw-Hill, 1997, pp. 15–32). The ISO 14001 Standard is a voluntary guideline for developing an EMS. It was based on British Standard BS 7750. It was published in 1996.
7. Robert Kaplan and David Norton, *The Balanced Scorecard: Translating Strategy into Action* (Boston, MA: Harvard Business School Press, 1996), pp. 7–18.
8. Six Sigma means 3.4 defects per million opportunities. Motorola is a Six-Sigma company in many of its product lines.
9. Frank B Friedman, *Practical Guide to Environmental Management* (Washington, DC: Environmental Law Institute, 1988), pp. 1–10.
10. Walter A. Rosenbaum, *Environmental Politics and Policy*, 2nd edn. (Washington, DC: CQ Press, 1991).
11. Frances Cairncross, *Costing the Earth: The Challenge for Governments/The Opportunities for Business* (Boston, MA: Harvard Business School Press, 1991).
12. Bruce Smart, *Beyond Compliance: A New Industry View of the Environment* (Washington, DC: World Resources Institute, 1992).

13. Stephan Schmidheiny, *Changing Course: A Global Business Perspective on Development and the Environment* (Cambridge, MA: MIT Press, 1992).

14. Paul Hawken, *The Ecology of Commerce: A Declaration of Sustainability* (New York: Harper Business, 1993).

15. Joseph Fiksel, *Design for Environment: Creating Eco-Efficient Products and Processes* (New York: McGraw-Hill, 1996).

16. Livio D. DeSimone and Frank Popoff, *Eco-Efficiency: The Business Link to Sustainable Development* (Cambridge, MA: MIT Press, 1997).

17. Hens B. L. Nath and D. Devuyst, *Sustainable Development* (Brussels: VUB University Press, 1998).

18. Paul Weaver, Leo Jansen, Geert van Grootveld, Egbert van Spiegel, and Philip Vergragt, *Sustainable Technology Development* (Sheffield: Greenleaf Publishing, 2000).

19. Bob Doppelt, *Leading Change toward Sustainability: A Change-Management Guide for Business, Government and Civil Society* (Sheffield: Greenleaf Publishing, 2003).

20. *Harvard Business Review on Business and the Environment* (Boston, MA: Harvard Business School Press, 2000).

21. W. Edward Deming, *Out of the Crisis* (Cambridge, MA: MIT Center for Advanced Engineering Study, 1986).

22. *Ibid.*, p. ix.

23. Gregory Bounds, *Cases in Quality* (New York: Irwin, 1996), p. 229.

24. The World Commission of Environment and Development (WCED) for the General Assembly of the United Nations, *Our Common Future: The Brundtland Report* (Oxford: Oxford University Press, 1987), p. 8. WCED was under the direction of G. H. Brundtland, the then Prime Minister of Norway.

25. *Ibid.*, p. 3.

26. *Ibid.*

27. William McDonough, "The Hannover Principles: design for sustainability" (1992), p. 5. He also prepared guidelines for the World's Fair in Hannover in 2000.

28. http://www.dow.com/publicreport/2001/mpletter/index.htm, p. 1 of 3.

29. http://www.dow.com/publicreport/2001/todo/new/trans.htm, p. 1 of 1.

30. Paul Edwards, *The Encyclopedia of Philosophy, Volume Two* (New York: Macmillan and The Free Press, 1967), p. 75.

31. "Everyone" includes producers, consumers, employees, labor unions, society, governments, and whole economies. Charles E. Wilson, President of General Motors in 1953, during confirmation hearings before the US Senate to become Secretary of Defense, when asked about any possible conflict of interest stated that "I cannot conceive of one because for years I thought that what was good for our country was good for General Motors, and vice versa." *Source*: http://www.gm.com/company/corp_info/history/gmhis1950.html.

32. Peter Drucker, *Managing in Turbulent Times* (New York: Harper & Row, 1980), p. 51.

33. Michael Hammer and James Champy, *Reengineering the Corporation: A Manifesto for Business Revolution* (New York: Harper Business, 1993), p. 32.

34. John P. Kotter, *Leading Change* (Boston, MA: Harvard Business School Press, 1996), p. 21.

35. Daryl R. Conner, *Managing at the Speed of Change: How Resilient Managers Succeed and Prosper Where Others Fail* (New York: Villard Books, 1992), p. 12.

36. *Ibid.*, p. 13.

37. Peter M. Senge, *The Fifth Discipline: The Art and Practice of the Learning Organization* (New York: Currency/Doubleday, 1990), p. 8.

38. The MIT Commission on Industrial Productivity, *The Working Papers of the MIT Commission on Industrial Productivity* (Cambridge, MA: MIT Press, 1989), p. 13.

39. Stuart Hart, *Capitalism at the Crossroads: The Unlimited Business Opportunities in Solving the World's Most Difficult Problems* (Pearson Education, Inc./Wharton School Publishing, 2005), pp. 107–133.

40. *Ibid.*, p. 111.

41. Alfred D. Chandler, Jr., *Strategy and Structure: Chapters in the History of the American Industrial Enterprise* (Cambridge, MA: MIT Press, 1962), p. 282.

42. C. K. Prahalad, *The Fortune at the Bottom of the Pyramid: Eradicating Poverty Through Profits* (Pearson Education, Inc./Wharton School Publishing, 2005), pp. 25–28.

43. John P. Kotter, *The Heart of Change: Real Stories of How People Change Their Organizations* (Boston, MA: Harvard Business School Press, 2002), p. 11.

44. David L. Rainey, *Product Innovation: Leading Change through Integrated Product Development* (Cambridge: Cambridge University Press, 2005).

45. Paul Ehrlich and Anne H. Ehrlich, *Population, Resources, Environment: Issues in Human Ecology*, 2nd edn. (San Francisco: W. H. Freeman, 1972), p. 145. While the list of similar books is long and additional sources could have been cited, the notion that technology is to blame is an old one. Many social scientists attribute environmental problems to population growth, industrialization, and technological development. While it is not the purpose of this book to explore the historical record to discover who is at fault, the defects, burdens, and impacts of technologies are far-reaching and causality is usually a function of many variables and not a single cause.

REFERENCES

Bounds, Gregory (1996) *Cases in Quality.* New York: Irwin

Cairncross, Frances (1991) *Costing the Earth: The Challenge for Governments/The Opportunities for Business.* Boston, MA: Harvard Business School Press

CERES Help Guide (1997) *Instructions for Companies*

Chandler, Jr., Alfred D. (1962) *Strategy and Structure: Chapters in the History of the American Industrial Enterprise.* Cambridge, MA: MIT Press

Conner, Daryl R. (1992) *Managing at the Speed of Change: How Resilient Managers Succeed and Prosper Where Others Fail.* New York: Villard Books

Deming, W. Edward (1986) *Out of the Crisis.* Cambridge, MA: MIT Center for Advanced Engineering Study

DeSimone, Livio D. and Frank Popoff (1997) *Eco-Efficiency: The Business Link to Sustainable Development.* Cambridge, MA: MIT Press

Doppelt, Bob (2003) *Leading Change toward Sustainability: A Change-Management Guide for Business, Government and Civil Society.* Sheffield: Greenleaf Publishing

Drucker, Peter (1980) *Managing in Turbulent Times.* New York: Harper & Row

Edwards, Paul (1967) *The Encyclopedia of Philosophy, Volume Two*. New York: Macmillan/Free Press

Ehrlich, Paul and Anne H. Ehrlich (1972) *Population, Resources, Environment: Issues in Human Ecology*, 2nd edn. San Francisco: W. H. Freeman

Elkington, John (2001) "The triple bottom line for twenty-first-century business," chapter 2 in Richard S. Starkey and Richard Welford (eds.), *The Earthscan Reader in Business & Sustainable Development*. London: Earthscan Publications, pp. 20–34

Fiksel, Joseph (1996) *Design for Environment: Creating Eco-Efficient Products and Processes*. New York: McGraw-Hill

Friedman, Frank B. (1988) *Practical Guide to Environmental Management*. Washington, DC: Environmental Law Institute

Global Environmental Management Initiative (GEMI) (1992) *Environmental Self-Assessment Program*, Washington, DC: GEMI, September

Hammer, Michael and James Champy (1993) *Reengineering the Corporation: A Manifesto for Business Revolution*. New York: Harper Business

Hart, Stuart (1997) "Beyond greening strategies for a sustainable world," *Harvard Business Review*, January–February, pp. 66–76

Hart, Stuart (2005) Capitalism at the Crossroads: *The Unlimited Business Opportunities in Solving the World's Most Difficult Problems*. New York: Pearson Education, Inc./Wharton School Publishing

Harvard Business Review on Business and the Environment (2000). Boston, MA: Harvard Business School Press

Hawken, Paul (1993) *The Ecology of Commerce: A Declaration of Sustainability*. New York: Harper Business

Kaplan, Robert and David Norton (1996) *The Balanced Scorecard: Translating Strategy into Action*. Boston, MA: Harvard Business School Press

Kotter, John P. (1996) *Leading Change*. Boston, MA: Harvard Business School Press

Kotter, John P. (2002) *The Heart of Change: Real Stories of How People Change Their Organizations*. Boston, MA: Harvard Business School Press

McDonough, William (1992) "*The Hannover Principles: design for sustainability*". Hannover: William McDonough & Partners

The MIT Commission on Industrial Productivity (1989) *The Working Papers of the MIT Commission on Industrial Productivity*. Cambridge, MA: MIT Press

Nath, Hens B. L. and D. Devuyst (1998) *Sustainable Development*. Brussels: VUB University Press

Porter, Michael and Claas Van Der Linde (1995) "Green and competitive: ending the stalemate," *Harvard Business Review*, September–October, pp. 120–134

Prahalad, C. K. (2005) *The Fortune at the Bottom of the Pyramid: Eradicating Poverty Through Profits*. New York: Pearson Education, Inc./Wharton School Publishing

Rainey, David L. (2005) *Product Innovation: Leading Change through Integrated Product Development*. Cambridge: Cambridge University Press

Reinhardt, Forest L. (1999) "Bring the earth down to earth," *Harvard Business Review*, July–August, pp. 149–157

Robinson, Nicholas (1993) *Agenda 21: Earth's Action Plan*. New York: Oceana Publications, Inc.

Rosenbaum, Walter A. (1991) *Environmental Politics and Policy*, 2nd edn. Washington, DC: CQ Press

Schmidheiny, Stephan (1992) *Changing Course: A Global Business Perspective on Development and the Environment*. Cambridge, MA: MIT Press

Senge, Peter (1990) *The Fifth Discipline: The Art and Practice of the Learning Organization*. New York: Currency/Doubleday

Smart, Bruce (1992) *Beyond Compliance: A New Industry View of the Environment*. Washington, DC: World Resource Institute

Tibor, Tom and Ira Feldman (1997) *Implementing ISO 14000: A Practical and Comprehensive Guide to the ISO Environmental Management Standards*. New York: McGraw-Hill

Weaver, Paul, Leo Jansen, Geert van Grootveld, Egbert van Spiegel, and Philip Vergragt (2000) *Sustainable Technology Development*. Sheffield: Greenleaf Publishing

World Business Council for Sustainable Development (WBCSD) (2001) "The base case for sustainable development," September

The World Commission of Environment and Development (WCED), for the General Assembly of the United Nations (1987) *Our Common Future: The Brundtland Report*. Oxford: Oxford University Press

2 Enterprise thinking and the strategic logic of strategic business development

Introduction

With the expanded globalization of the world's economies, the intensification of competition, and the quantum leaps in technological development during the latter part of the twentieth century, the insular strategic management of many global corporations has become inadequate for understanding the business environment and determining strategic direction. Global corporations require a higher level of sophistication for responding to all of the forces impinging upon them – their supply networks, allies, partners, stakeholders, and customers. They must think more broadly about what a global corporation is. Today, a corporation has to consider all of the effects, implications, and impacts of its businesses, operations, resources, and capabilities and those of its customers, stakeholders, and supporting entities from cradle-to-grave, including the sources of raw materials and EoL considerations. This more inclusive perspective involves enterprise thinking. An enterprise view of a global corporation encompasses all of the entities, organizations, and relationships that are required to formulate and implement strategies and to achieve the objectives of the corporation in the present and future and to mitigate the internal and external negative impacts of decisions and actions.

Enterprise thinking takes a holistic view of the corporation and its business environment. It involves recognizing and managing the full reach of the corporation across space and time, all of the actions and transgressions of all of the direct and supporting players, even those many levels deep in the supply networks or customer applications. An enterprise perspective is pivotal for leading change today as corporations increasingly depend on supply networks, partners, strategic alliances, and external relationships for sustaining their vision and mission and achieving positive outcomes. This broader, more inclusive perspective is even more crucial as more and more of the global corporations outsource parts and components, noncritical processes, and even complete operations to supply networks around the world. While outsourcing may provide benefits to producers, customers, and stakeholders, especially through more cost effective solutions, there is always the concern and danger that the selected suppliers, distributors, and related entities are not competent and/or diligent in meeting their responsibilities to the social, economic, and environmental requirements and mandates.

In *Leading the Revolution*, Gary Hamel describes the future of strategic management as the "age of revolution." He suggests that "it is not knowledge that produces wealth, but *insights* into opportunities for discontinuous innovation."[1] He also suggests that a business model has to be dynamic, and it must focus on how to get people to adapt to change. Hamel has it right; it is all about insights and people. People lead change! When management inspires people, an organization can actively create a more productive, exciting, and sustainable future. But, it is also about knowledge and how to use the knowledge to sustain performance.

Enterprise thinking focuses a corporation on strategy, integration, innovation, and visionary leadership. It engages a corporation in integrating its high-level corporate management, its SBUs and their product delivery systems, and all of its relationships with supply networks, partners, allies, and other value networks. Enterprise thinking includes all the people, processes, practices, and programs, both internal and external, within a fully integrated corporate/SMS that forms the basis for analysis, understanding, decision-making, and continuous improvements, as well as revolutionary change. Enterprise thinking is a unifying approach essential for laying the foundation for SBD. It forms the architectural foundation for inclusiveness, connectedness, innovativeness, openness, and effectiveness within the strategic leadership of a corporation. It requires corporate and business leaders of the corporation to think about the whole and to ensure that all the responsibilities of the enterprise are carried out to the fullest extent possible given the realities of the world and the limitations of knowledge and resources.

This chapter describes and evaluates enterprise thinking and the strategic logic of SBD. The chapter considers the following topics:
- Enterprise thinking and management
- A business model of enterprise management
- The value proposition
- The strategic process for inventing the future
- The strategic logic of SBD.

Enterprise thinking and management

Historical circumstances

People have been producing and selling products and services from time immemorial. During the nineteenth and twentieth centuries, corporations became the prime institutions for managing the commercial activities associated with products and services. Producers focused on production and selling, using a "make and sell" strategy.[2] Very little regard was given to depletion of resources, waste generation, the impacts associated with products and processes, or the disposal of the products at the end of their life. Successful corporations explored the prevailing conditions and satisfied the existing needs in the most efficient way possible. Economics drove production; producing products at low costs and high margins allowed companies to generate excellent profits. Although this logic was rational, it was limited in scope and neglected social and environmental considerations. Businesses generated significant waste streams that had to be addressed at a later date, elsewhere, or by others. If the scope of the pollution was small or if someone else (governments or society) paid the price for the cleanups, these problems could be managed with "end-of-pipe" treatment. In essence, companies typically did not worry about waste problems during production or application, but rather transferred these concerns to downstream entities or future management that bore their costs and burdens.

Such logic become uneconomical as the scope and costs associated with environmental problems increased dramatically during the last quarter of the twentieth century. In order to combat such negatives, corporations used remediation technologies to cleanup old problems and adapted pollution prevention and waste minimization programs to mitigate the negative effects and impacts of their products and processes. While these innovative methods were significant improvements, the corporate mindset was still based on the old patterns of having both abundant resources to draw upon and low-cost means to handle and dispose of the waste streams. Corporations continued to rely on the prevailing ways of designing, developing, producing, distributing, selling, and using products and services. Management thinking generally included only direct considerations and primary effects. The basic framework focused on the direct suppliers, distributors, and customers. Moreover, corporate responsibilities for products and processes were viewed as those linked directly to the product itself. After all, these were the legal and contractual responsibilities of the producer.

The changing landscape of twenty-first-century enterprise thinking

With this history of social, economic, and environmental problems, global corporations today are changing their strategic perspectives. Leading global corporations are taking an enterprise-wide view (enterprise thinking) of their responsibilities and looking to technological and product innovation to solve the inherent and structural problems associated with their products and processes.

The "enterprise" is a more comprehensive management construct than the simple perspective of the corporation. The narrow view of an enterprise focuses on the corporation and its undertaking and initiatives. The broader view focuses on the extended corporation, including all of the appropriate and necessary external relationships that are part of the value system and are required to provide sustainable solutions for customers, stakeholders, and other constituencies. The extended corporation is often referred to as the "extended enterprise," especially in managing the flow of information and transactions. In the book, *Lean Enterprise Value*, members of MIT's Lean Aerospace Initiative, provide an innovative and inclusive definition of an enterprise:[3]

The *enterprise* perspective we bring makes it possible to see entire 'value systems' as well as the interconnected levels of activity that reach across national and international boundaries. That perspective stands in sharp contrast to 'lean' as narrow change efforts in only one part of an organization, such as manufacturing or supply network.

The extended enterprise redefines the corporation and its management systems in their broadest terms, from cradle-to-grave, including every supplier, distributor, customer, stakeholder, and all of the entities providing support. The enterprise view of the scope of management responsibilities is also expanding to include the future expectations of customers and stakeholders. This means the corporate/SMSs have to extend beyond the boundaries of the corporation and include the effects of the customers, stakeholders, supply networks, and others who provide resources or who are impacted by the products and operations. The extended enterprise must involve the suppliers of suppliers, all of the entities in the distribution channels, the logistical support units, and all of the users, reusers and EoL implications of the products and waste streams.

An enterprise view is more complex than just examining the direct production and consumption linkages, processes, and activities. It requires thinking about all of the relationships, actions, and inter-temporal causes and effects, especially those that have long-term consequences.

Using traditional economic perspectives, corporations focus on the relationships between buyers and sellers (customers and producers). Customers want to satisfy their needs and meet their expectations. Producers want to design, produce, and market their products and services to derive revenues and profits. Market demand for existing products and services drives producers to seek cost effective, market-related solutions. Supply and demand determine price levels and production volumes. The quantity demanded is a function of the benefits obtained and the prices paid. These supply and demand models typically focus on the primary considerations such as resources, products, channels of distribution, and markets. Suppliers provide inputs to the producers who create and produce products that flow through distributors to customers. Customers buy and use the products during their useful life and are responsible for the applications, use, ownership, maintenance, and ultimate disposal aspects. The producer's responsibilities are typically limited to the upstream actions, the contractual transactions, and product liabilities.

Today, however, the scope of the corporation and its systems, processes, activities, and flows of goods and services must include all of the social, economic, environmental, political, technological, and market-related perspectives. Moreover, such views must include not only the primary considerations (products and services) but also the secondary effects, such as the residuals of production and use (pollution, discards, and other waste streams). Residuals are important consideration in determining the social and economic viability of products, services, and processes.

The simple economic models that examined supply, production, demand, and applications are being transformed into more comprehensive (holistic) frameworks including the design and development processes, cradle-to-grave implications of inputs and outputs, supply and delivery considerations, consumption and applications, and EoL considerations (reuse, refurbishment, recycling, and/or proper disposal of residuals). EoL considerations are becoming increasingly significant factors.

The concept of the "extended enterprise" is based on the recognition that corporations are no longer self-sufficient in meeting the needs and expectations of markets, customers, and stakeholders and depend on a vast array of networks from suppliers to customer service providers and waste management entities. Corporations have become large combinations of internal and external operations and support networks that are interconnected and interdependent. The concept of the "extended enterprise" evolved over the 1990s in response to the expansion of e-business and information technologies (ITs). While most of the current uses of the extended enterprise focus on the relationships with supply networks and the information systems that facilitate process development, transactional exchanges, and decision-making, the extended enterprise is becoming a strategic framework for assessing, understanding, and managing the complexities of the business environment through strategic integration and innovative strategies. In their book, *Enterprise Business Architecture*, Ralph Whittle and Conrad Myrick provide their version of an extended enterprise.[4] Their enterprise entity model is similar in intent to the concept of extended enterprise. They define the enterprise entity model as follows:[5]

The enterprise entity represents the highest-level model of the enterprise. It illustrates the relationships between all external entities such as its customers, suppliers, stakeholders, service providers, regulatory agencies, and infrastructure providers. It identifies all external inputs and outputs with their respective sources and destinations.

Executives, managers, and senior professionals have to understand and manage the whole extended enterprise and not just the strategic and functional areas of the corporation. They must possess broad knowledge about every facet of the global business environment and understand the underlying context of the whole, including the natural world and the social (man-made) world. They must be able to integrate corporate and business strategies and operations, processes, and practices, and make effective decisions that improve the prospects of the enterprise and the corporation at rates greater than the general improvements in the mainstream business environment. While the traditional management focus has been on strategic direction and financial outcomes, business leaders must also focus on discovering and exploiting opportunities to create extraordinary value, integrate all of the extended entities in the business environment, achieve sustainable competitive advantages, and ensure future success. This requires outstanding management skills, competencies, and knowledge, and exceptional strategic leadership that can handle complexity and an extended scope of the enterprise. Successful leadership and management achieve extraordinary results in both the short term and the long term.

Strategic enterprise integration is essential for linking all of the entities of the extended enterprise into the corporation's business model for assessing, strategizing, leading, and managing across the broad horizons of the business environment. This is akin to planning the development and growth of a city or even a nation.[6] It requires thinking about the natural environment of land, water, and air, the social considerations of households, transportation, employment, and quality of life, among numerous others, and the physical structures of buildings, roads, communications, water and sanitation, and others, and the management systems required to provide essential human services, systems management, and emergency responses. The requirements are complex and extend beyond the scope of the governments involved and include all of the directly and indirectly related entities such as corporations and infrastructure providers. Strategic leaders of extended enterprises, typically the executives and strategic management of global corporations, are responsible for the whole enterprise, and an economic output that is larger than many of the countries in the world. Of the hundred largest economies in the world either based on corporate revenues or GDP, more than half are global corporations with revenues of more than $50 billion.[7] Wal-Mart and Exxon Mobil have revenues that are larger than the GDPs of 180 countries.[8]

Figure 2.1 depicts a simplified view of the extended enterprise. It depicts how the extended enterprise fits into its business environment, the ecosystems, and the social world. In this book, the term "extended enterprise" is simply called "the enterprise" since it is simpler than constantly stating "extended enterprise" and it also connotes what an enterprise truly is. An enterprise is a large commercial undertaking or business organization of substantial scope and complexity involving risks for the purpose of creating innovative solutions for customers, stakeholders, and society, achieving sustainable positions and competitive advantages, and obtaining significant financial and market-based rewards in the short term and long term.

The concept of the enterprise in the context of the whole business environment is still in its infancy. It is a historic term with important modern connotations. Enterprise thinking and management are also evolving constructs that are in the early stage of development.

Enterprise thinking and management involves a multidimensional view of the business environment, including all customers, stakeholders, supply networks, strategic partners, related industries, competition, and infrastructure providers. Enterprise management is a dynamic general management construct characterized by broad social, economic, environmental, and organizational perspectives and initiatives that are integrated into a holistic framework for understanding, assessing, strategizing, and achieving strategic objectives and desired outcomes. Enterprise management is characterized by

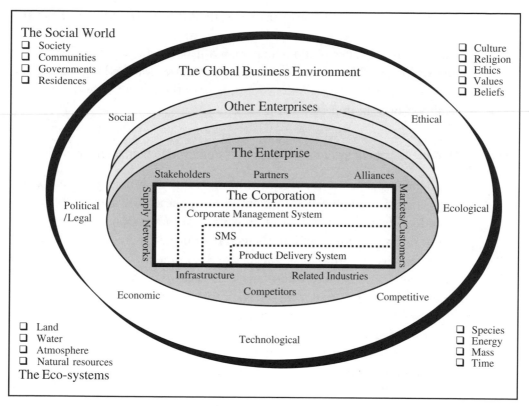

Figure 2.1   A simplified view of the extended enterprise

imagination, innovation, creativity, agility, and risk mitigation. It is predicated on creative thinking about future possibilities rather than just on present capabilities. It focuses on what the corporation and its business units and their relationships with external entities should be, instead of what they are. It includes the corporate management system (the entire corporation), SMSs of the business units, and all of the product delivery systems in each of them. Enterprise management provides a framework for ensuring that all of the essential dimensions and elements of the enterprise are covered in the analyses of the business environment, and that they become part of the solution matrix. It sets the stage for a descriptive, analytical, and structural understanding of the needs, opportunities, challenges, requirements, and specifications, and the strategies and action plans.

A fully articulated enterprise management system may take several decades to realize. It is a broad mental model of the potential solutions for producing extraordinary value, exceeding customer and stakeholder needs and expectations, and achieving sustainable success in the future. The power of the enterprise management perspective is that it provides a comprehensive framework for executives and business leaders to think "out-of-the-box" and to contemplate solutions that may not be doable or even practical in the short term but present exciting opportunities for the long term. Plato discussed ideas in the context of a dream of the perfect answer, of which reality is only an imperfect copy.

The embedded management systems of sustainable enterprise management

Sustainable enterprise management has three internal management systems (levels): the corporate management system, the SMSs, and the operating (product delivery) management systems. Corporate management concentrates on the corporate vision, the grand strategies and competitive advantages relative to the global business environment, and the creation of sustainable success. Strategic management involves assessing, developing, and implementing business strategies and initiatives for leading changes that facilitate the strategic transformation to a richer existence. Operating (product delivery) management addresses near-term goals and the related activities to ensure superior performance and exceptional results. It involves the day-to-day execution of the mission.

Figure 2.2 depicts in simple terms the primary considerations of the main levels of sustainable enterprise management. It depends on leading change through business integration, innovation, and leadership, and creating harmony between business endeavors, human activities, and the natural world through enterprise thinking and management. The most significant underpinnings include inclusiveness in management constructs and analysis, connectedness with customers, stakeholders, and contributors, innovativeness in design and development of new technologies and products, and openness in governance and communications. The critical philosophy is to create value for all based on social, economic, environmental, technological, and market considerations.

It is critical to understand that each level is related to the others, but typically involves its own roles and responsibilities. If the corporation is highly centralized to the point where the levels lose their autonomy, there may be just a single level. The organizational structure may be the dominant form of management control and governance. It is difficult to imagine leading a large, global organization from a centralized perspective. However, there are still business models that mimic the old vertical approaches rather than the horizontal forms of the late twentieth century. Sustainable enterprise management is preferred,

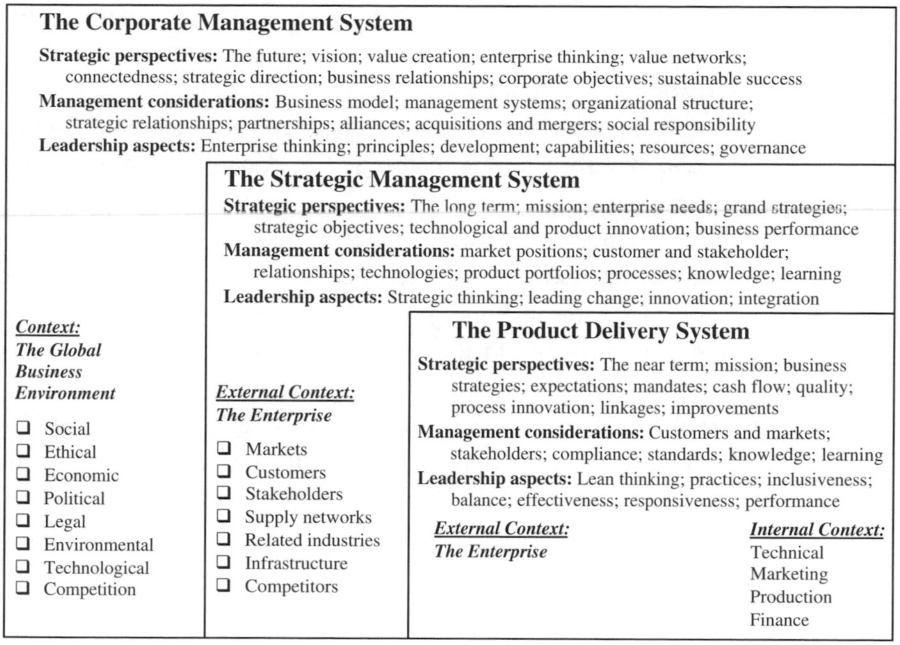

The Corporate Management System

Strategic perspectives: The future; vision; value creation; enterprise thinking; value networks; connectedness; strategic direction; business relationships; corporate objectives; sustainable success

Management considerations: Business model; management systems; organizational structure; strategic relationships; partnerships; alliances; acquisitions and mergers; social responsibility

Leadership aspects: Enterprise thinking; principles; development; capabilities; resources; governance

The Strategic Management System

Strategic perspectives: The long term; mission; enterprise needs; grand strategies; strategic objectives; technological and product innovation; business performance

Management considerations: market positions; customer and stakeholder; relationships; technologies; product portfolios; processes; knowledge; learning

Leadership aspects: Strategic thinking; leading change; innovation; integration

Context:
The Global Business Environment

❑ Social
❑ Ethical
❑ Economic
❑ Political
❑ Legal
❑ Environmental
❑ Technological
❑ Competition

External Context:
The Enterprise

❑ Markets
❑ Customers
❑ Stakeholders
❑ Supply networks
❑ Related industries
❑ Infrastructure
❑ Competitors

The Product Delivery System

Strategic perspectives: The near term; mission; business strategies; expectations; mandates; cash flow; quality; process innovation; linkages; improvements

Management considerations: Customers and markets; stakeholders; compliance; standards; knowledge; learning

Leadership aspects: Lean thinking; practices; inclusiveness; balance; effectiveness; responsiveness; performance

External Context:
The Enterprise

Internal Context:
Technical
Marketing
Production
Finance

Figure 2.2   The embedded management systems of sustainable enterprise management

however, because it is difficult to include external participants and impacts with a vertical structure. Enterprise management cuts across each level of management from the corporate and strategic to the operating and functional. It implies that leaders at every level are thinking and managing from an enterprise perspective. Enterprise thinking and management are based on the recognition that corporations at every level are dependent on the contributions of other entities (suppliers, their suppliers, distributors, partners, financial institutions, governments, etc.) for ensuring that the quality, performance, time, responsiveness, learning, and financial objectives are met and that all of the direct and indirect responsibilities of the enterprise are fulfilled.

The corporate management system focuses on the strategic context of the global business environment and provides high-level analysis and decision-making for the corporation. The chief executive officer (CEO) or equivalent is the senior individual responsible for the overall vision, direction, and performance of the enterprise. The *primary considerations* of the CEO or the executive management team include:

(1) establishing a vision
(2) identifying and managing the needs and requirements of the business environment
(3) inspiring people and leading change

(4) positioning and directing the corporation on its path to the future
(5) formulating and implementing corporate strategies, action plans, and programs
(6) creating and managing the embedded management systems
(7) reinvigorating and expanding the capabilities and resources of the organization
(8) connecting the enterprise with its supply networks, partners, and alliances
(9) acquiring new knowledge, capabilities, resources, technologies, and businesses through mergers, acquisitions, and other forms of development
(10) ensuring that performance and communications meet the expectations of all constituencies.

While the list is extensive, it is not exhaustive of the responsibilities of high-level executives in global corporations. It does, however, provide a sense of the scope and range of senior executive concerns.

The corporate management system is responsible for the embedded management systems related to strategic direction and product delivery. Its aim is to create extraordinary value for the enterprise, to provide proper governance, and to ensure sustainable success. Creating a sophisticated business model that provides proper strategic direction, control, and governance, and guides the strategic and operating actions of the corporation is a fundamental responsibility of executives. It is through the business model that the other levels come to understand their roles and responsibilities. This is especially critical for inspiring people and leading change. The vision and strategic direction should inspire people within the organization to take charge, build relationships, acquire new knowledge and capabilities, and achieve superior performance.

Corporate executives responsible for enterprise management are generally concerned about the complexity of the global business environment and the corporate vision of the future. Enterprise thinking provides the basis for determining what the future positions will need to be in light of the business environment. This high-level thinking is the primary responsibility of executive management and epitomizes what SBD really is: looking at the whole picture to see what it should be, instead of what it is. It is about discovering opportunities instead of discussing the limitations and barriers. It is about inventing the desired future through insights and leadership rather than being stymied by the prevailing conditions and trends.

Executive leadership continually reaffirms the vision and direction of the organization, making it understandable and attainable in the hearts and minds of people throughout the corporation. Leadership necessitates an interactive relationship between management and the organization. The relationship is built on respect, trust, communication, cooperation, and coordination. The intent is the creation of a cohesive, strategically aligned organizational force that is fully integrated and moving in the same direction and it is in concert with the realities and requirements of the business environment.

The SMSs focus on the strategic logic of the business units and their mission. They connect their core operating units at the base of the corporation with the global view of the entire enterprise. They integrate the objectives, strategies, concerns, and directives of the corporate executives with the management of operations. The general managers at this level are also responsible for linking their management systems with the business environment, thinking about innovation, and providing strategic leadership for the organization. They examine and analyze the business environment to discover opportunities and understand challenges. Strategic management leadership is rather more than simply satisfying current business and customer needs. It requires a broad mindset about the future.

The product delivery systems are the core operating level. They concentrate on the existing conditions and meeting the market, production, technical, and financial requirements of the organization. They are typically supported by incremental product and process innovations. Operations management uses well-defined systems and processes for producing outcomes and results. Historically, product delivery has focused on the resources deployed within the system and the organizational elements engaged in production and marketing. The new perspective, however, also includes inspiring people to achieve outstanding performance, building new capabilities, and improving processes and outcomes. The product delivery level may have several subsystems, such as quality management and environmental management, to address the specific needs of customers and other outside entities.

The power and problems associated with enterprise thinking and management

Enterprise thinking and management involve both revolutionary and evolutionary changes to the management mindset required for managing complex organizations. Stefano Tonchia and Andrea Tramontano, in *Process Management for the Extended Enterprise*, identify two main factors that have lead to the concept of the extended enterprise:[9]

(1) increasingly specialized enterprises focus on core competencies, outsourcing all other activities
(2) globalization, brought about through new technologies, has intensified the range of choice among collaborating enterprises.

The focus on core competencies enhances the internal organizations' strategic focus and concentrates investments on the strengths of the organization. Outsourcing reduces the scope of the corporation's operating system but expands the external contributions and their implications. It typically improves resource utilization and the internal investment portfolio by leveraging the assets of suppliers and partners. However, it increases the complexity of the management systems because there is less information and management control over the operations and activities of external entities. Globalization involves rapid changes in the business environment and much broader scope of customers, competitors, stakeholders, partners, and technological changes. All of these factors make leading and managing global corporations more difficult.

The radical changes of e-business have fueled many of the driving forces in the business environment. There are many new cost effective ways that corporations can provide products and services to customers and link with their supply networks. Information and communication technologies and the Internet provide informational and transactional capabilities and access to external entities that did not exist a generation ago. However, technologies alone do not provide solutions. Solutions require the technologies to be integrated into the management systems and to be deployed for the benefits of all constituencies.

eBay is an example of exploiting the power of sophisticated technologies and advance management approaches. It links millions of clients in its business environment to create an enterprise that provides effective and efficient person-to-person exchange of information, goods, and money. Its system is supported by logistical services from UPS, USPS and over 250 strategic alliances, customers, clients, and other businesses. The power of eBay lies in its management system that is expandable to accommodate significant increase in business transactions without a linear increase in investment.

As the new technological capabilities become available in the mainstream, corporations have to develop the means and mechanisms to incorporate the approaches in their management systems. Enterprise thinking and management embraces the technologies to expand the mindset of what makes the system. It is part of the evolutionary changes in systems thinking. Peter Senge, in *The Fifth Discipline*, identified "systems thinking" as one of the critical disciplines of a learning organization. He defines system thinking as:[10]

A conceptual framework, a body of knowledge and tools that have been developed over the past fifty years, to make full patterns clearer, and to help us see how to change them effectively.

In Senge's context, enterprise thinking and management are a natural extension in viewing the management systems. They are simply the "next wave" in management approaches for managing business complexities.

The power of enterprise thinking and management on a macro-environment basis is that they provide a management framework that mirrors the complexities of the real world. The underlying philosophy is to be as inclusive of the forces of changes and the essential considerations and factors in the business environment as possible so that corporate leaders are not caught off guard by unexpected situations or by hidden issues and difficulties. It is also based on the philosophy that it is better to manage complexities on a strategic level with all of the power of the intellectual capital of the corporation than it is to manage problems at the operating or functional levels where resources are scarcer and the expertise is limited. Simply stated, it is easier to handle complexities and challenges in strategic formulation rather than during implementation.

Enterprise thinking and management provide the following advantages in managing the business environment:

- Improved understanding and "connectedness" with the external entities
- Enhanced responsiveness to change and complexity and the needs and expectations of customers, stakeholders, and other constituencies
- Increased effectiveness and productiveness of the whole system because it is integrated
- Reduced economic and environmental wastes across the whole since the objective is to improve the whole and not just the individual parts
- Improved openness through the integration of the essential relationships and the disclosure of information.

Inclusiveness is a pivotal concept. Enterprise thinking is based on ensuring that all entities and considerations are part of the business framework. While this means handling more information and data about the variables involved, modern information and communications technologies (ICTs) make such tasks possible, if not relatively easy. For instance, Bank of America processes over 11 billion checks per year, a feat that would have been impossible a decade ago. Responsiveness to customers and stakeholders is also pivotal. But it goes beyond meeting contractual obligations. It involves being ahead of the needs and requirements and providing solutions before they are mandated. Moreover, it involves knowing what is happening in the business environment and discovering opportunities and threats before they become apparent. It is about gaining insights from all of the relevant entities, not just customers.

Daryl Conner's *Leading at the Edge of Chaos* believes that most leaders are unprepared for turbulent conditions because they do not appreciation the demands for moving businesses to more sophisticated levels and the impacts such changes have on the resources and capabilities of the organizations.[11] Conner suggests that three factors explain why most executives, managers, and employees are inundated with change:[12]

(1) *Volume*   Every year, organizations report dealing with a greater number of significant disruptions in people's lives

(2) *Momentum*   Organizations demand an accelerated speed when people engage change today, and people are given less time to execute these initiatives

(3) *Complexity*   The projects taken on today are much more sophisticated and involved than those assigned a few years ago.

Simply stated, the business world is much more complex and demanding, and leaders have to have a more sophisticated management framework for leading change.

Enterprise management focuses on the effectiveness and competitiveness of the extended system. Suppliers and distributors have an increasingly important role in obtaining high-quality outcomes. Producers recognize that their deliveries are dependent of the capabilities of the whole system, not just their manufacturing facilities or internal operations.

Enterprise thinking and management, especially through LCA, address pollution and waste generation, and attempt to find improved solutions through cleaner technologies and leaner operations. While such detailed analysis is often thought of as excessive, the ability to discovery hidden defects is critical for mitigating business risks and preventing problems in the future. The concepts also apply to economic waste that exacerbates resource scarcity and reduces the viability and sustainability of the management system.

The most critical yet problematic advantage is openness to discovery and disclosure of information, problems, and solutions. Enterprise thinking involves collaboration across the enterprise, cooperation among all of the participants, and communications between companies, customers, stakeholders, advocates, and opponents.

Enterprise thinking and management also provides significant organizational advantages. The most important reason is increasing management confidence that appropriate forces and factors have been included in the assessment of the business environment and that the most advantageous decisions have been made. While it is always difficult to know how much analysis is necessary, the more insights that leaders have about their enterprise, the more likely they are to understand what has to be done to sustain success.

Reducing uncertainty and mitigating risks are fundamental in improving management's ability to achieve excellent performance and exceed external and internal expectations. Moreover, mitigating risks and liabilities protects the reputation and market capitalization of the corporation. While there are numerous advantages pertaining to learning and knowledge and preparing the organization for the future, enterprise thinking allows management to appreciate the strengths and weaknesses of the whole enterprise, not just the organization. It focuses attention on where attention is needed, internally or externally. Many corporations have tried to optimize their operating systems and improve quality only to discover significant problems in the supply networks that negate the competitive advantages of the organization. For example, Nestlé has been severely criticized for the labor standards and practices of its suppliers.

Enterprise thinking and management using a cradle-to-grave perspective does have its detractors. The most significant difficulty that is often raised is the complexities involved in trying to obtain information about the whole business environment and to conduct the required assessments of all of the entities involved. The high cost of obtaining and processing the information and doing the analyses without having knowledge of the potential benefits to be derived is also cited. It is not only difficult to determine the precise value of examining the details of the whole enterprise; it is equally difficult to identify the future value of making better-informed decisions.

The perceived disadvantages of enterprise thinking and management include:

- The lack of cost/benefit justification threatens the profit maximization objectives of the corporation and may reduce shareholder value
- It is difficult to obtain the necessary information to determine the strengths, weaknesses, opportunities, and threats facing the enterprise
- Practitioners may find hidden problems that cannot be cured causing ethical, legal, and market-related difficulties.

The list is not comprehensive. Moreover, many business professionals believe that the corporation's business responsibilities are restricted only to direct responsibilities and not those beyond its borders or those that are not part of its system. Ultimately the discussions boil down to the question of value versus costs. Opponents believe that the broader scope of understanding and management influence and the knowledge gained are not worth the investment. Proponents argue that knowledge is intrinsically worth the investment and that the evolutionary and revolutionary improvements provide opportunities for a richer and more sustainable future. Moreover, the risks associated with the lack of understanding are higher than what would be deemed acceptable. Using the precautionary principle, they would rather err on the side of safety: they believe that corporations have an inherent responsibility to improve all aspects of their enterprises. As per W. Edwards Deming's assertions in the field of quality management, quality initiatives do not require justification. Deming believed that most defects are attributable to the management system and the failure of the system to detect defects and problems. Deming was a strong proponent of management's responsibility to ensure quality and continuous improvement and initiate process analysis for problem-solving and decision-making. Improving the management system is inherently valuable.

The discussion about the advantages and disadvantages of enterprise thinking will continue throughout the book. While the intent of the discussions in the book is to be balanced, SBD provides a framework that is more inclusive than most of the existing business models. In the final analysis, it is the adaptation of enterprise thinking and management, or derivative constructs, that will determine its usefulness.

An enterprise management model[13]

The **enterprise management model (EMM)** is a holistic management construct, which provides an understanding of the needs, expectations, and forces defining the business environment and their relationships with the enterprise. EMM outlines the means by which all of the implications of the technologies, products, and processes can be examined and evaluated. It is inclusive of the product life cycle, from the extraction of raw materials to EoL and the impacts and their consequences thereafter. It can be used at each level: EMM is necessary for discovering and exploiting opportunities and challenges, and hence, is a powerful mechanism for enterprise thinking and SBD.

EMM is a multidimensional perspective of the business environment that includes the assessment, discernment, and assimilation of the social, economic, political, technological, and environmental climate to assure that decisions are well thought out and balanced. It is used to examine the external dimensions of customers and markets, stakeholders, supply networks, related industries, infrastructure, and competition and the interfaces

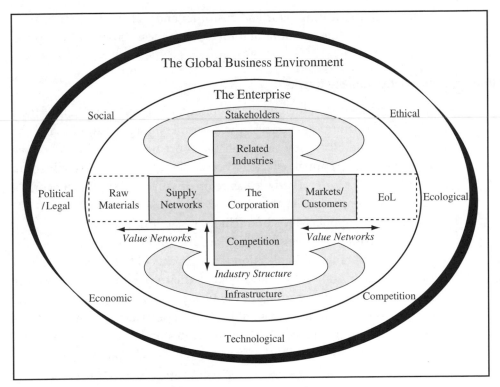

Figure 2.3   The enterprise management model

between them in sufficient detail to provide management with a comprehensive picture of reality from which to formulate and implement business strategies.

EMM is more complex than standard approaches to management due to the number of dimensions and elements, but it is absolutely necessary for establishing the principles, systems, and processes of SBD and setting the stage for enterprise thinking and life cycle management. It provides the structure for analysis and decision-making. The most critical aspect of EMM is its inclusion of all of the relationships involved in product applications and EoL considerations. This is an essential requirement for using LCA.

Figure 2.3 provides a model of the dimensions of the EMM model.

The strategic alignment of the dimensions requires the coordination of capabilities and relationships. This includes defining the roles and responsibilities of the internal participants and external constituents, collecting information about the opportunities and challenges, developing a vision about the future, understanding the processes, and managing change over time. EMM integrates the elements of the management systems with the resources used for creating value and customer and stakeholder satisfaction. It focuses on providing solutions and total satisfaction across the enterprise.

The primary dimensions: value networks

The primary dimensions include the producer, its suppliers and all of their suppliers, the distribution channels, the customers, their customers and the tertiary users, and all those engaged in the retirement and disposal of the products and the residual effects. Michael Porter called this construct the value system. More recently it has referred to as the supply network.[14] EMM is more comprehensive than Porter's value system since it reaches out beyond first-tier suppliers and also includes EoL considerations.

The most profound aspects of EMM are the implicit responsibilities for managing the full range of implications and impacts of the value system and beyond: the inputs and outputs of suppliers, their operations, and all of the suppliers from the very beginning of the flow process. Raw materials, fabricated parts and components, assemblies, and goods flow from all of the upstream suppliers to the producer who creates and delivers value-added products and services through the distribution channels to customers.

The impacts and consequences of upstream suppliers are critical inputs in LCAs. Improving just the internal aspects of the management system does little to reduce the footprints if most of the difficulties in the value networks are within the suppliers' domain. For instance, no longer is it a benefit to "unload" processes with negative environmental impacts to suppliers or their suppliers and then claim that the corporation has improved its operations. With life cycle management and assessment, negative impacts count against the producer regardless of their origin.

EMM defines and links the internal and external elements of the enterprise. The critical internal elements include the policies, strategies, selected programs, new and existing technologies, products and services, business processes, and the prevailing practices of the organization. They are linked internally and externally by knowledge and information flow.

Figure 2.4 shows the essential elements of the primary dimensions.

The producer's view of the market includes the selected market segment(s), targeted customers, and their applications. It also includes the secondary markets, including the customers' customers, their applications, the reuse of the products, the recycling potential, and EoL considerations. In many cases, products flow through a distribution channel to the ultimate customers. For example, Procter & Gamble (P&G) sells most of its products

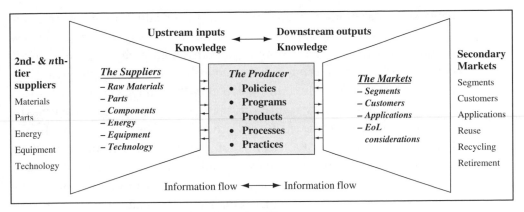

Figure 2.4   The primary dimensions: the value system plus

to retail outlets, which then sell the products to consumers. (Box 5.2, p. 309 provides details on the relationships between P&G and its constituents.)

EMM goes beyond the primary applications of the product and examines secondary customers and their uses of it. It explores how all of the market participants, including those engaged in the repair, reuse, and recycling of the product, can promote its social, economic, and environmental viability. The prime objective is to maximize value creation and retention by discovering as many secondary applications as possible for the products or the materials. This is not a radical concept; the secondary market for used automobiles has for decades helped the primary market sell new cars by creating outlets for the older vehicles.

The secondary dimensions: external structure

The secondary dimensions include stakeholders and the external infrastructure. From an enterprise perspective, stakeholders and the infrastructure are critical external dimensions that warrant significant consideration. Stakeholders are the supporting, challenging, confronting, and/or controlling entities that influence the life cycle of products, from their development to application and beyond. Stakeholders include the local community, consumers, interest groups, environmental activists, governments, regulatory agencies, the international community, and all other entities that play significant roles in the business environment.

Stakeholders can support and facilitate SBD: for example, society may welcome and endorse new products that reduce or eliminate the hazards associated with toxic substances such as lead and cadmium. On the other hand, some stakeholder groups may resist the introduction of new technologies and products, making it more difficult and costly to pursue the new product opportunity. For example, certain environmental groups create barriers for products using chlorinated solvents or ones producing by-products that theoretically contribute to global warming. Government agencies may promulgate new regulations that have a significant impact on the time and investment needed to get products to the marketplace. In the European Union, The Restrictions of the Use of Certain Hazardous Substances in Electrical and Electronic Equipment Directive bans the sale of devices using lead, cadmium, mercury, hexavalent chromium, polybrominated diphenyls and polybrominated biphenyl ethers after July 1, 2006.[15]

Customer satisfaction is often touted as the primary marketing objective, but the EMM suggests that stakeholder satisfaction is also a primary objective. It is too simplistic to only satisfy the customer. Intel worked closely with the local communities and government agencies to obtain their approvals during the development of the Pentium 4 processor. The effort allowed the company to obtain the necessary permits in just a few months.

The external infrastructure includes the Internet communications, telecommunications, energy systems, the airways, the roads, the waterways, atmosphere, etc. These networks and resources add value that facilitates the movement of goods, information, data, waste, and energy to and from the supply networks. The infrastructure provides logistical support for the flow of products to customers. In every product category, the external infrastructure plays an important supporting role that sustains the viability of products and services. Figure 2.5 provides a view of the critical elements of the external structure.

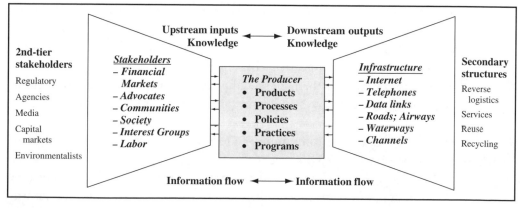

Figure 2.5   The secondary dimensions: external structure

The infrastructure makes SBD possible by providing the means for delivering the product or by reducing the costs of production or delivery. For example, e-commerce increases the speed at which information, data, and transactions are performed. It reduces both the fixed costs of the **product delivery system** and the variable costs of transactions. Communications integration via the Internet provides an enterprise-based system of carrying out activities regardless of where the participants are located.

The infrastructure also provides the means to eliminate the waste generated during production. It provides solutions to EoL issues and disposal problems. Reverse logistics provides a means to recycle or reuse used products and materials. The infrastructure improves producers and customers' ability to communicate with each other, transport goods and services, and solve problems, thereby reducing the cost of ownership, increasing speed and reliability of the systems, products and processes, and enhancing overall quality and performance.

The infrastructure supports the activities of the value system and provides the mechanisms to link key players. A closed-loop system integrates all of the mechanisms to move products and processes forward and by-products and residuals backward as quickly as possible. Just as companies can use their inventories of materials and goods in a manufacturing facility to improve performance by reducing assets, infrastructure provides ways to improve performance and reduces the need for new resources. For example, aluminum cans have the potential to be produced, filled, used, and remanufactured within a ninety-day period. The infrastructure of redemption facilities, highways, and communications contribute to a low cycle time, allowing not only the reuse of the metal, but a significant reduction in the amount of aluminum in use.

The industry dimensions: industry structure

The industry dimensions include the producer, its competitors, and related industries. These dimensions represent the industry structure from an economic perspective. The industry supports customers with additional product and service choices needed for making purchase decisions, for supporting product applications, and/or for managing the implications of the product. Figure 2.6 provides the key elements of the industry dimension.

In twenty-first-century thinking competitors are not always the adversaries; competitors may form an alliance to solve a problem. During the early 1990s, Union Carbide and other chemical companies along the upper

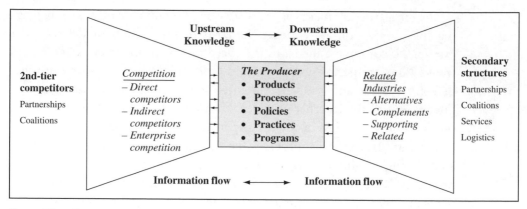

Figure 2.6   The industry dimension: industry structure

Potomac River in West Virginia worked together on improving the quality of the river's water by enhancing the wastewater treatment processes. Union Carbide executives realized that no single entity could solve the problem; only the combined efforts of the industry participants could successfully reduce the impacts. In addition, while the Partnership for a New Generation of Vehicles (PNGV), which focused on designing high fuel-efficiency vehicles, may not be the perfect example, the collaborative program between General Motors, Ford Motor Company, and Daimler–Chrysler provides evidence that global corporations who are competitors can work toward a common goal.[16]

Related industries provide additional resources and means to improve solutions. They offer complementary or supporting products and services that may complete the requirements for sustainable development.

SBD centers on a multifaceted understanding of the global business environment, a commitment to meeting the expectations of all constituents, and a broad-based framework for achieving outstanding results. EMM is more inclusive than the twentieth-century management models that focused on customer expectations and satisfaction. While a market/customer-centered approach makes intuitive sense, the narrow scope of such management frameworks leaves out too many important considerations (social, economic, and environmental).

Enterprise thinking, as described earlier, provides a higher level of sophistication by incorporating all of the forces impinging on the corporation and its suppliers, partners, stakeholders, and customers. This construct is increasingly critical for long-term success as more corporations come to depend on supply networks, strategic alliances, and external relationships for sustaining their vision and mission and achieving results (box 2.1).

Box 2.1 Nokia's development of a framework for sustainable development

Nokia Corporation is a relative newcomer to the ranks of the leading global corporations. Formed in 1967 through the merger of three Finnish companies, in the 1990s, Nokia made a strategic decision to concentrate on telecommunications and become a leading supplier of mobile telephone technology and networks. Nokia is a world leader in mobile telecommunications. Its net sales in 2004 were €29.3.0 billion with net profit of €4.3 billion. It has seventeen production facilities in nine countries.[1] Nokia consists of four business groups: Mobile Phones; Multimedia; Networks; and Enterprise Solutions. The structure also includes three horizontal groups: Customer and Market Operations; Technology Platforms; and Research, Venturing and Business Infrastructure (figure 2B.1).[2]

Nokia is engaged in continuous dialog with its external stakeholders to stay abreast of issues they see as important now and in the future and to better understand what is expected of Nokia and how this can be achieved. These stakeholders include private customers, corporate customers, investors, NGOs, governments and authorities, industry cooperation, and legislators.[3]

Nokia's vision is to be a leading, global provider of communications products and services. It developed the "Nokia Way," a principle of its environmental policy, as an active, open and ethically sound approach to environmental protection. The company's strategy for sustainable development extends to all of its supply networks and includes: (1) Environmental Management Systems; (2) Supplier Network Management; (3) Design for the Environment; and (4) EoL practices.[4] The scheme runs the gamut from improving the operating system and eliminating risks to gaining stakeholder acceptance and increasing profits in the long term.[5] Nokia's goal is to "develop advanced technology, products, and services that have no undue environmental impact, conserve energy efficiently, and can be appropriately reused, recycled, or disposed of."[6] Product LCA are essential tools in Nokia's implementation of sustainable development: the company requires suppliers to follow the principles and objectives of the Nokia Way.

The company's strategy of covering the entire enterprise in the analyses of its environmental impact is a crucial step toward using EMM concepts to deploy SBD. The company uses **Design for the Environment (DFE)** methods to "design in" solutions to environmental

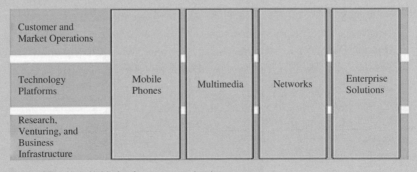

Figure 2B.1 New Nokia business group structure

impacts and make products more environmentally efficient. Production plants and service facilities have integrated environmental matters into business management. The extension of LCT into the supply networks and the inclusion of stakeholder requirements into the strategic thinking of the company are solid indications that Nokia is in the process of moving toward a broader view of its business environment and incorporating the essential external dimensions. It considers the mitigation of the environmental impacts of its suppliers as an important Nokia "supply network management" responsibility. Moreover, it expects its suppliers to apply the same standards to their suppliers. Likewise, EoL practices involve activities that reuse and recover materials and energy and assure the proper disposal of harmful substances. The following quote by Jorma Ollila, Chairman and CEO, Nokia in April 2003 provides a sense of Nokia's commitment to sustainable development.[7]

> Sustainability is about the future, and it is about us. Our way of doing business is sustainable when it takes into account the needs of future generations. The drive for sustainability becomes effective when it is a shared global pursuit enlightened by the best available understanding of the constraints set by nature, the silent partner in all our undertakings.
>
> It is our mission to drive a profitable and growing business, but that does not mean business at any cost. Our products and operations have an impact on two global environmental issues in particular, climate change and the depletion of natural resources. We consider these issues primarily in the forward-looking design of our products as well as in our procurement, assembly, and logistics operations.
>
> Our product designers consistently strive to reduce the life-cycle energy consumption of our products while at the same time working to increase the recyclability of the materials used in them. We do not see carbon dioxide emissions and the consumption of nonrenewable resources as separate environmental issues. They are increasingly influencing the value chains of our business. By accepting responsibility for the future we can add value to our customers, our shareholders, our employees and the global community . . .
>
> As market leader and a global company, Nokia takes its responsibilities seriously. Sound environmental principles make business sense by helping minimize risk, ensuring legal compliance, and building reputation among stakeholders. By conducting business in a responsible way, Nokia can make a significant contribution to sustainable development, at the same time building a strong foundation for economic growth.

Nokia appears to be on the path to SBD. Most importantly, it has extended the normal reach of a corporation into the realm of the full value chain, and it is assuming the responsibility for more of its enterprise. Like most corporations, its pathway to success depends on evolutionary changes that become significant improvements in the long term.

Notes:
1. www.nokia.com, "the Nokia Group."
2. *Ibid.*
3. *Ibid.*, "Nokia and the Environment."
4. *Nokia Environmental Report*, 2002, p. 10.
5. *Ibid.*
6. *Ibid.*
7. *Nokia Environmental Report*, 2002, p. 5.

The value proposition: the essence of SBD

Philosophical perspectives

The purposes of a corporation are to increase shareholder wealth, to satisfy the needs of customers and stakeholders, to create extraordinary value for civil society, and to protect human health and safety and the natural environment. The overarching purpose is to maximize value creation for everyone. This implies that new solutions are based on creating more value than the previous solutions did. It implies that solutions are not optimizations of one factor and the suboptimization of the others. Rather, when solutions satisfy the needs and expectations of all the constituents, not just customers and shareholders, SBD is realized. Value maximization is an enlightened view, but nonetheless, in 1974, Peter Drucker was already talking about social impacts and responsibilities and how to achieve the theoretical optimum.[17] His focus was then on what inhibits attainment of the full return on the resources and efforts of corporate strategies.

Value maximization is a powerful guiding philosophy for decision-making in the context of the global business environment and SBD. Simply put, sustainable solutions create more value than the alternatives. They produce stability within the business environment, provide corporations with effective use of resources and capabilities and outstanding performance, have real world logic, and meet the needs and wants of constituents. While these requirements may seem to be impossible to obtain simultaneously, the principles and philosophies of SBD maintain that they represent the path to the greatest results in the long term. These become criteria for testing options and selecting the best solutions. Specifically, value maximization integrates the following principles into cohesive and sustainable outcomes:

- *Value creation*   Value creation involves moving toward more ideal solutions with greater benefits, fewer deficiencies, and reduced impacts. The objective is to create the best possible solutions for customers, stakeholders, and society, solutions that maximize gains and minimize losses. Such solutions are sustainable solutions.
- *Insightfulness*   Information, data, and analysis drive solutions. Solutions originate in the real world of the twenty-first century and are not just hypothetical or theoretical constructs. Insights gleaned from analogous solutions set the stage for improvements in the future. Most importantly,

initiatives and programs of other global corporations serve as evidence of what is doable and advantageous.

- *Equity*   Good solutions are not compromises where one group wins and another loses. The social, economic, and environmental factors have to be part of all outcomes. Compliance with laws and regulations, pollution prevention, stewardship, and enterprise thinking are inherent elements within any satisfactory solution. Equitable consideration of all impacts on all parties is critical in achieving balanced and sustainable outcomes.
- *Effectiveness*   The transition from current processes and practices to more sustainable ones has to be orchestrated within a framework that achieves the social, economic, and environmental goals in concert with business objectives and realities. Solutions have to be based on the needs and desires of the business environment and the corporate structure and have to be constructed in ways that are achievable and sustainable.
- *Stability*   SBD involves systematically creating a better future through evolutionary and even revolutionary changes that produce stable and sustainable outcomes. In essence, if solutions are totally disruptive, gains in one arena may be losses in another. For example, a wholesale change of conventional automobile technologies to fuel cell-based automobiles within a short time frame would have dramatic impacts on the viability of the automobile industry and related industries.

Sustainable value creation is the most crucial criterion for decision-making. Insightfulness, equity, effectiveness, and stability provide parameters for the discovery and development of appropriate and sustainable solutions.

Value creation defines and provides the underpinnings of SBD. The presumption that one product is automatically better than another is unacceptable. Such presumptive statements have to be examined in terms of the value created. For example, in the P&G disposable diaper debate of the 1980s, its detractors believed that cloth diapers were superior (fewer environmental impacts) and, therefore, consumers should use the more sustainable cloth diaper. However, a study conducted by Arthur D. Little, Inc. indicated that the impacts, though different, were approximately equal in magnitude. The superiority of one technology or product over another has to be established based on evidence and analysis, not presumption or belief.

Opinion-makers around the world have differing notions about what sustainable development is or should be. However, insights, knowledge, and evidence provide the rational basis for decision-making. Moreover, corporations have to create sustainable solutions that are based on the realities of their existence (the business environment and corporate capabilities). They have to develop strategies and courses of actions that are feasible, practical, and make sense from every perspective. They cannot risk "trial and error" or "hypothetical" approaches. Insights are often based on past successes of other corporations as a guide or a benchmark for measuring and managing one's own strategic direction.

Equity encompasses the human side of the equation and the social implications of corporate responsibilities. There are always many stakeholders involved within the business environment, and their needs and expectations are important considerations in decision-making. Equity can be divided into four categories: the "must do" (laws and regulations), "should do" (social norms and expectations), "may decide to do" (logic and fit), and "would like to do" (philanthropy). The first category is mandatory and usually well defined. The second category is often based on the context and setting of the corporation. For instance, most corporations provide benefits to their employees and support community initiatives. An objective of the Chemical Manufacturers' Association's (CMA) Responsible Care (RC) initiatives is to provide information to the community about the operations within the chemical plant (Community Awareness Initiative). The "may decide to do" category is the most difficult to determine. It is based on objectives, strategies, analyses, resources, and decision-making. The actions include initiatives to improve technologies, products, and processes so that defects, burdens, and impacts are significantly reduced, if not eliminated. Making decisions pertaining to the third category is difficult because the logic is not based on mandates or norms. The choices are more open-ended and require strategic thinking and choices. The "would like to do" category is based on a corporation's philosophical perspective and the availability of resources, usually money. A preset amount of money is often budgeted each year for work for charities and other philanthropic purposes.

Effectiveness involves selecting the right programs to investigate, analyze, and implement, allocating the appropriate resources to achieve the desired results, and leading the proper change mechanisms in the right direction. It is about discovering opportunities for leading change and creating solutions that eliminate underlying problems and impacts. Effectiveness is critical in producing the right improvements.[18] The late Peter Drucker defines the term accordingly:[19]

Effectiveness is the foundation for success – efficiency is a minimum condition for survival after success has been achieved. Efficiency is concerned with doing things right. Effectiveness is doing the right things.

Too often, the solution to a problem becomes a problem in the future. Drucker implied that even the best solutions have to be reinvented or reinvigorated to match the needs of the times. Yesterday's solutions are often today's problems and tomorrow's opportunities.

Stability involves balancing the needs of present customers and constituents, meeting the goals for the future, and ensuring continuity over time. Stability is central to the effective flow of goods and services in the global economy. Corporations invest in capital assets, programs, and people because there is evidence and a belief that the anticipated returns justify the commitments to the future. If the business environment is unstable, corporations are less likely to make investments because they are unsure about the viability of the investments and the ability to earn an adequate return.

Stability is therefore pivotal when analyzing and determining the implications of proposed solutions. While there are many potential solutions for most situations, solutions that mitigate problems in the short term, but create other problems in the long term tend to be undesirable and unstable. For example, eliminating the automobile without a phased approach for dealing with the social, economic, and technological issues would wreak havoc with the economies of the developed world. It could also exacerbate environmental problems. Without mobility, people would not be as productive, which could lead to many suboptimal approaches.

In *Breaking the Impasse*, Lawrence Susskind and Jeffrey Cruikshank discussed the four characteristics of a good negotiated settlement: fairness, efficiency, wisdom, and stability.[20] Some of their suggestions about dispute resolution apply to value creation and SBD. Fairness is akin to equity. The authors stated that settlements should be judged in terms of the fairness of the process used to reach the resolution. They suggested that the process should be open to public scrutiny and that all parties be given access to the technical information.[21] Disclosures through environmental reporting initiatives fit that characteristic and support the notion of openness. Openly reporting on the social, economic, and environmental consequences of a corporation's products, operations, and activities is an effective way to move toward better balance and fairness across the business environment. Efficiency and wisdom are also critical criteria for making choices about the utilization of resources and the avoidance of wastes and pollution. Effective resource utilization helps realize conservation and promotes the ongoing success of processes. Good solutions meet the needs and expectations of customer and constituents and are based on the efficient and wise deployment of capital, resources, and people.

Perhaps most important are Susskind and Cruikshank's compelling statements about stability. Unless an agreement meets the test of time, the value derived by the resolution of the problem or the launch of an initiative is significantly diminished. The authors also emphasize the importance of the feasibility of the agreements. They must be doable, based on realistic timetables.[22] These same points apply to SBD. The initiatives and programs must be realistic and achievable within the time frame established. They must be stable and enduring over time.

The value proposition

The value proposition defines the worthiness of a purchase, investment, or program. The traditional value proposition was a **cost/benefit (C/B) analysis**. The value derived from investing in a product, program, or activity was measured against the cost of obtaining the benefits. The analysis was based on the ratio of outputs to inputs in very simple terms. It provided an answer relative to prevailing conditions rather than a more precise view of the value derived over time. The result of the "C/B" analyses of multiple options could be compared and the investment with the best ratio selected. This methodology was practiced for most of the twentieth century and is still prevalent today. Most product improvements followed the simplified view of improving the sum of the benefits (ΣBenefits) in relation to the increase in related costs (ΣCosts). For example, a machine that could carry one unit of weight costing one unit of money could be improved and made more valuable by increasing its capabilities to two units of weight with a cost of 1.5 units of money. The "C/B" ratio would be improved. The PC and microprocessor are good examples of improving the benefits without increasing the costs, thus making the products significantly more valuable and even more environmentally conscious. Moore's Law (coined by Intel's founder) suggested that microprocessor technology doubles in performance every eighteen months, while the costs stay relatively the same.

However, in today's complex business environment, "C/B" analysis is too simplistic to assess and understand the implications of strategic and operating decisions as they relate to customers, stakeholders, other constituents, and the future of the corporation. This is especially true when examining the social and environmental impacts. The value proposition provides a more complex and thorough perspective. SBD involves enhancing the value proposition of strategies, actions plans, and innovations which provide positive contributions and mitigate negative impacts and their consequences.

Table 2.1. A simplified view of the positive and negative effects of an automobile

Effects	Category	Positive	Negative
Tangible	Physical	Hardware, software, utility	Fuel consumption, emissions, disposal problem
	Financial	Transportation, mobility	Taxes, insurance, accidents, theft
Intangible	Psychological	Good feeling	Fear of loss, risk of damage
	Perceptual	Status, style, appearance	Envy, contempt
	Temporal	Enjoyment	Nervousness

Figure 2.7   The value equation from an enterprise perspective

Every technology, product, process, and operation has positive and negative effects (attributes) and impacts. Moreover, these effects and impacts can be categorized as tangible or intangible. Table 2.1 depicts a simplified view of the positive and negative effects of a typical automobile.

The value equation provides a visual understanding of the main elements of the value proposition. It takes the form of a ratio, with positive aspects in the numerator and negative aspects in the denominator. The value proposition examines all of the benefits, positive effects, and knowledge gained in terms of the investments made by all of the constituents – and, similarly, all of the costs, defects, and burdens associated with the situation. Figure 2.7 depicts the general form of the value equation from an enterprise perspective.

The prevailing view of what "value" is in most situations constitutes the key effects: it is the benefits or performance relative to the cost or price. It is simple **benefit/cost (B/C) analysis** or the more contemporary version, "performance/price" ratio. Most corporations subscribe to this simplified version wherein value is improved by increasing performance or decreasing price or both.

A more sophisticated approach looks at improving the sum of the benefits (performance) by enhancing the tangible and intangible aspects. The value of the benefits is established by the investment of time and money to acquire the benefits. Money might be viewed as the tangible aspect, since it represents the ability to acquire actual resources, property, or physical goods. Time might be seen as intangible, since it cannot be captured or stored. Still, time may be as critical as money in the calculation of the investment, given that time can never be recovered.

The value equation (value ratio) is divided into three categories of effects: leading effects, lagging effects, and limiting effects. The leading effects are usually apparent when determining whether programs, technologies, products, or processes are worthwhile.

Lagging effects and defects are a little more difficult to ascertain. A lagging effect is actually a benefit or benefits that were not contemplated during design, development, and early commercialization. They are often discovered after customers start enjoying the results. For example, the automobile has provided greater mobility, allowing the development of the suburbs and enriching the quality of life. The tangible aspects include larger homes, more real estate, and more options for employment. The intangible aspects include greater educational opportunities for the children, the flexibility to change employment, and the freedom to decouple one's life style from the work environment.

Lagging defects include quality defects in production or design. Lagging defects in quality are the obvious concerns that reduce the utility and effectiveness of products and processes. Defects require additional time and effort to correct or resolve, thereby reducing the value generated. Certain defects are inherent, but not obvious during the initial development and deployment period. Such defects may only show up at a later time. Many environmental problems are lagging defects caused by the expansion of a situation to new applications. DDT is a good example. It was originally developed as an agent to protect American soldiers against disease-carrying insects during the Second World War.[23] It was the expanded use of the product in agriculture after the war that created the concerns that Rachael Carson addressed in her pivotal book, *Silent Spring*.[24] As with DDT, such defects can become liabilities and burdens.

Defects are not only problems that have to be managed and resolved. They also add costs to the denominator, reducing value and driving the equation toward a less favorable position. There are many examples of such defects becoming incredible liabilities. The defects in the Exxon management system and personnel contributed to the *Exxon Valdez* disaster in 1989. These relatively simple defects turned into liabilities, costing the corporation billions of dollars.

Similarly, corporations often create liabilities without realizing it. Polychlorinated biphenyls (PCBs) were excellent heat transfer materials used in electrical transformers and capacitors beginning in the late 1920s and early 1930s. When PCBs were classified as suspected human carcinogens, however, PCB inventories and applications changed from assets to liabilities.[25]

Liabilities are also often created because a company wants to save money. For example, during the 1970s, Hooker Chemical Company disposed of certain hazardous wastes in its own landfill. On-site disposal was less costly than transporting the wastes to a certified treatment facility. Unfortunately, the short-term cost reductions were extremely expensive in the long run. Hooker sold the site and its landfill, and eventually developers built residential housing on it. The Love Canal incident that resulted became one of the worse environmental disasters in our time, costing Hooker Chemical Company hundreds of millions of dollars.[26]

Limiting effects are barriers to the expansion of value. If the systems become constrained, for instance, the ability to enhance and improve slows dramatically. Most importantly, if unresolved, such effects can cause the value to start declining rather than improving. For example, manufacturing plants are often restricted from generating more than a certain quantity of air emissions, water effluent or solid waste. Such restrictions, which are typically stipulated in the environmental permits for the facility, create barriers to expansion and have a limiting effect on the business opportunity.

Burdens at any point in the equation become a significant consideration when calculating the value of a product, process, or transaction. This recognition is crucial to the process of creating true value. Burdens reduce the benefits to customers, have negative impacts on stakeholders, and often impose a cleanup cost on society. They affect the enterprise and its constituents, reducing their long-term potential. However, burdens are often not apparent at the inception of the product, process, or business. For example, the effects of the first lb of wastewater dumped into a river are impossible to detect, and the consequences are minuscule. But, after many years of pouring one lb of effluent per hour into the same river, the impacts of the pollution are clearly dramatic. In the same way, the long-term effects of automobile traffic and congestion can be viewed as burdens making travel more difficult and ambient air quality less acceptable. While burdens may be difficult to determine during the early stage of an endeavor, it is imperative that a continuous evaluation be made to discover and mitigate such impacts over time.

Eliminating the causes of burdens and their implications therefore generates value for the corporation and its constituents. Doing so can generate a

Table 2.2. Examples of burdens and their implications

Example	Burdens	Implications	Solutions
Wastewater	The quantity of wastewater generated during a manufacturing process requires filtering, treatment, and disposal	The more water used on the input side, the more wastewater that has to be processed Each step in the process costs money and represents a loss of valuable resources	Minimize the amount of water required for production Reuse or recycle lightly contaminated water for processes that do not need ultra-clean water The potential capacity of the plant is expandable
Air emissions	Combustion processes to produce energy (electricity) or heat require air that provides the oxygen to burn the fuel The combustion process produces various products of combustion that require treatment and/or are emitted to the atmosphere	The products of combustion require expensive pollution abatement equipment The emissions from such facilities necessitate permits and ongoing monitoring The emissions affect local communities and have negative consequences on the quality of the ambient air	Explore new fuels that have fewer negative constituents (reduced sulfur) Use more efficient process equipment to reduce the amount of air required Find alternative technologies that rely on solar energy instead of fossil fuels

positive intangible effect by enhancing the public's perception that an environmentally conscious solution has mitigated concerns. People like to buy products that are solving problems rather than creating them.

Table 2.2 provides some examples of burden reduction.

LCT is a good way to reveal defects and burdens and assess their impacts and implications. It goes beyond conventional thinking and attempts to include additional ways to increase value. Such thinking moves SBD beyond the considerations of social responsibilities, environmental impacts, and economic considerations, to providing sustainable competitive advantages. If defects and burdens are eliminated from the bottom of the equation, value increases, and system complexity decreases.

Finally, knowledge is one of the most powerful components of the value equation. Knowledge of the systems and its effects is critical for improving and expanding. Knowledge is a limiting effect, given that the knowledge about a system or situation is never perfect. Epistemology and theories of knowledge suggest that there are limits to what is known; there are always missing elements within the information system that can lead to potential difficulties. For example, gasoline is an inherently dangerous product, but the petroleum industry, the distributors, retailers, and consumers have learned how to safely use it as a fuel for automobiles. On the other hand, the infrastructure for a hydrogen-based fuel system is in its infancy. The lack of knowledge about its safe and effective use is a limiting factor in the short term. The limitations can be reduced or eliminated with more information, knowledge, and learning about the effective handling, distribution, and use of hydrogen. LCT, life cycle management, and LCA can help improve the requisite knowledge.

Knowledge allows improvements in the quality of life, protection of the environment, and enhancement of economic output. Improving knowledge, therefore, is an essential part of enhancing the value proposition. The underlying premise of product stewardship is that providing customers and stakeholders with more information about products will allow them to make informed decisions about appropriate applications. Such knowledge can help mitigate the dangers associated with the products and reduce potential impacts. The simple act of labeling products can provide the information consumers need to make good decisions about the effective and safe use of those products.

Knowledge is also essential for leading the SMS, managing the product delivery system, and ensuring that compliance, prevention, and other corrective actions are mitigating the short-term and long-term defects and burdens (i.e. costs and liabilities). Moreover, knowledge is crucial for innovation. SBD is built on the foundation that knowledge and learning facilitate effective decision-making for minimizing future difficulties and maximizing positive effects.

LCT and LCA provide the means to advance knowledge and can lead to improvements in technologies, products, and processes. Such improvements contribute to better products and improved outcomes. LCT and LCA are covered in detail in part II.

The value equation is intended to provide a more comprehensive perspective on managing an enterprise. The historic focus has been on the benefits side of the equation. While the logic of such approaches makes intuitive sense, focusing only on creating more benefits and improving performance misses many other opportunities for improvements. The value proposition of the twenty-first century focuses on maximizing benefits, reducing investment, minimizing defects and burdens – and, most importantly, on expanding knowledge. It provides a strategic perspective for creating the organization's vision, developing objectives, and selecting the metrics for decision-making.

The ultimate objective of the enterprise is to maximize value – that is, to maximize positive outcomes for customers, stakeholders, suppliers, and related industries, and wealth for shareholders. This can occur when an enterprise creates relationships that support each other. While it is impossible to prescribe the actual flow of value to every constituent, a balanced approach means that each receives its expected benefits and that the negative implications to each are minimal.

SBD focuses on providing customers with superior products at very low costs, minimizing stakeholder concerns about negative consequences, and reducing the burdens of these operations to society. This means creating value by simultaneously improving the top of the equation (the benefits) and the bottom (eliminating costs and problems). Value creation includes the present and the future consequences of decision-making. It also explores the burdens that limit the potential and identifies the knowledge necessary to move beyond the present.

The paradigm shift to SBD is already in motion, with many of the leading global corporations using it as a construct for leading change within their organizations. Like most change mechanisms, the move toward SBD often occurs in a circuitous manner. Indeed, global corporations are using SBD as both a strategic management construct for managing technological and product innovations and as a means to invent a new reality (box 2.2).

Box 2.2 Intel Corporation: leading change through enterprise thinking and enhancing the value proposition

The microprocessor technology of the twentieth century owes its origin and sustenance to its developer, the Intel Corporation. Intel reigns as the dominant producer of the microprocessors used in PCs and electronic devices world-wide. The microprocessor and all of the related products define the digital age of the Internet, networking, telecommunications, and computing. Moreover, the microprocessor has brought rapid change to the technologies used by industries ranging from the automobile to food processing. It has improved the social, economic, and environmental viability of almost everything it has touched. The high growth rates and the quality of life improvements in developed countries during the 1990s are related to the contributions of the microprocessor.

Intel is the industry leader from every perspective. It leads the world in the design, development, production, and marketing of microprocessors. Intel has managed innovation by being a proactive change agent. Its business strategies reinforce the public perception that Intel is an innovative company keenly aware of the social, economic, technological, and environmental implications of its products and processes.

Robert Noyce and Gordon Moore founded Intel in 1968. They were also co-founders of Fairchild Semiconductor, where Noyce was one of the creators of the integrated circuit. Moore was an outstanding chemical engineer with a doctorate from California Institute of Technology. When they founded Intel Corporation, they were already successful, well-known industry players with vision, determination, and a keen sense of what they wanted to accomplish.

One of their first moves that proved to be a brilliant strategy was to select Andy Grove as director of operations, responsible for product development and manufacturing. Grove had been an assistant to Moore at Fairchild where he was responsible for process development. He had a PhD in chemical engineering from the University of California at Berkeley. Grove's personal philosophy helped Intel define the company during the early years and set the stage for the development of its management system. Grove did everything possible to stay ahead of the competition and confront problems as soon as they arose. He instilled a philosophy of using rational analysis in solving management issues and tackling potentially long-term difficulties early.

In 1969, Intel introduced its first product: a bipolar, static, random-access memory (SRAM) chip. Intel wanted to replace magnetic core memories, which comprised 60 percent of the cost of a computer, with a powerful, yet cost effective device that would improve the ratio of performance to price for computer memory by ten-fold. Intel's new process technology, the metal-oxide semiconductor (MOS), increased transistor density and reduced the number of steps in the fabrication process. Intel's first memory chip was a 256-bit MOS SRAM "1101" device.

In 1970, Intel, in conjunction with Honeywell, developed the first dynamic random-access memory (DRAM) chip. With the 1-kilobit MOS DRAM "1103," which was more powerful than the conventional magnetic core technology, Intel technology first established its dominance. By 1972, the "1103" was the largest selling integrated circuit in the world, accounting for more than 90 percent of Intel's $23 million in revenue.

In 1981, the PC industry exploded with the introduction of the IBM PC based on the Intel 8088 or 8086 computer chip. IBM adopted an open architecture to facilitate software development of the many potential applications. In February 1982, Intel introduced the 286 chip. At the end of 1984, IBM introduced the AT personal computer using Intel's 286 microprocessor, which was significantly faster than the older 8088 or 8086 chips.

In October 1985, Intel introduced the 386. On September 9, 1986, Compaq unveiled the Deskpro 386, the first computer based on Intel's 386 chips. In April 1987, IBM introduced four models of the new PS/2 system, containing 3.5 disk drives and proprietary technology. In August 1989, Intel introduced the 486 microprocessor. In March 1993, Intel introduced the Pentium chip. The Pentium II was born in 1997; the III in 1999; and the 4 in 2000. To minimize competition from other chip manufacturers, Intel had successfully increased its new product introductions, thus shortening the product life cycle of microprocessors. It had branded its products with the Pentium name, and promoted the "Intel Inside" logo. These technological and product innovations and the integrative capability of PCs had an incredible impact on producers, users, and society.

Rapid changes in the world of computing, information processing, and IT have profoundly affected the value proposition of PCs and Intel's position in microprocessor technology. In a business environment characterized by shrinking product life cycles and rapid change, customers seek innovative ways to acquire the knowledge and resources to stay competitive. PC product life cycles shrank from five years in 1981 to eighteen months in 2000. The rapid development of new products continues to be an important means for Intel to maintain its competitive advantage in a dynamic market environment.

Source: www.intel.com/reseach/silicon/morreslaw.htm.

The strategic process for inventing the future

SBD involves connecting the corporate vision for the future with the realities of the existing business environment and capabilities of the corporation. Enterprise management means having an embedded, integrated system for managing the business, the social, economic, and environmental aspects, innovation, and the organization. From a strategic perspective, an integrated management system means everything is linked within and outside the corporation. It means that alliances, partnerships, and relationships, wherever they may be, are part of the system and are linked strategically and tactically.

Strategic management in the twenty-first century is complex. Senior management must monitor the needs and wants of customers, the capabilities of suppliers, as well as the actions of competitors. It must examine and assess "leading edge" corporations and innovative entrepreneurial organizations and their policies, principles, processes, practices, and performance. To lead change, management must also possess a comprehensive knowledge and understanding of future opportunities, challenges, and constraints. Senior management is expected to provide the direction and the commitment to this broader awareness. Figure 2.8 depicts a simplified flow diagram of the essential elements of the strategic process for leading change using SBD. The actual requirements in a given situation may be even more complicated, and the appropriate flow may take a different course.

The "Circle for inventing the future" is a high-level process dedicated to exploring the business environment for innovative ways to enrich the opportunities of the corporation and for assessing the best approaches for leading change. A strategic analysis of the business environment includes not only the primary constituents of the enterprise (stakeholders, customers, suppliers, distributors, related industries, and competitors) but other corporations who are initiating innovative processes and practices to improve outcomes and mitigate defects and burdens. It is a form of benchmarking that examines the global trends and innovations that are moving toward a more sustainable future. The goal is to discover new ways to create and/or enhance value.

Inventing the future is an ongoing process that expands as improvements are realized. The first segment involves scanning the external business environment and the forces driving change. The process for discovering opportunities requires inputs from all facets of the enterprise, including its

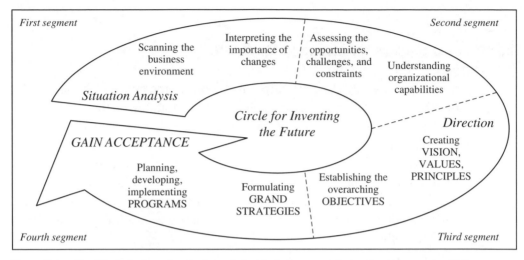

Figure 2.8   The "Circle for inventing the future": the strategic process for leading change using SBD

partnerships, alliances, and other key relationships. The first segment feeds the second. The second segment involves understanding how the present reality translates into opportunities and constraints and how the organization can respond to those realities to lead change. The third segment involves establishing a vision of the future, and setting the enterprise on a path of SBD. The fourth segment involves selecting the grand strategies and the development programs that will get the organization to its vision. Gaining acceptance within and outside the corporation is an essential part of the process.

The Circle for inventing the future: situation analysis

Scanning the business environment

The purpose of scanning the business environment is to diagnose potential and actual turbulence in the business environment in order to determine how to best respond to it. During the last half of the twentieth century, new technologies and innovations played greater roles in the dynamics of the business environment. By studying those dynamics, corporations can determine "who" and "what" is needed to create an improved future. Scanning is also useful for ascertaining shifts in customer and stakeholder perceptions.

Change-makers are directly and indirectly leading the transformation toward SBD. For example, Intel is a leader in monitoring corporations' standards setting initiatives around the world and is actively engaged in leading change through this process.[27] Chapter 4 expands on concept.

Interpreting the importance of change

The difficulty with any change phenomenon during its infancy is that evidence supporting the importance and viability of the various mechanisms and techniques is scant. There are many issues that warrant attention and require a response. Interpreting the importance of change means that one can understand its implications. A single stakeholder group may not suggest a trend, but many such groups indicate a powerful force for change. Listening and learning about the needs and wants of customers and stakeholders provide the inputs necessary for determining how to deal with forces of change within the business environment. It can establish the underlying conditions, trends, patterns, and related consequences.

Environmental management was relatively easy to interpret during the early years of compliance-driven approaches. The strategy was simply to follow the mandates and comply with the laws, regulations, and required permits. Public policy in each country drove the requirements and methodologies. When the focus moved to pollution prevention, methodologies shifted toward market-driven approaches aimed at impressing customers and stakeholders. In reality, the two approaches (pollution prevention and compliance) coexisted during the 1990s. Today, however, solutions have to be framed in the context of the social, economic, political, environmental, and technological structures as well as the legal and regulatory ones. Interpreting the mechanisms of change within the complexity of this more holistic view requires an enormous amount of information from a multiplicity of sources. Some of the most important considerations are:

- Who are the change agents?
- What are the requirements for change?
- What is the speed of change?
- What are the most compelling opportunities for effecting improvements?
- What are the required means and mechanisms to achieve sustainable competitive advantages?

The most crucial steps in interpreting changes are identifying the forces driving the changes and providing guidelines for establishing a general construct for managing change. It can be helpful to view SBD as a generalized theoretical and practical framework. The framework must be useful for a range of situations or for the various business units within a corporation, even if they are diverse.

Senior management today has become accustomed to selecting and investing in new technologies, new products and new processes. They have recognized that many product life cycles have shrunk to less than five years.

In some industries, such as electronics, life cycles are measured in months. Speed to the market is, in many instances, the driving criterion. Corporations accept the fact that competitive advantages are fleeting and that staying ahead means investing ahead. Intel is an outstanding example of a corporation that has "pushed the envelope" in order to remain in front of the pack. Intel recognizes that the next breakthrough innovation – or catastrophic challenge – could be just around the corner. For Intel and other corporations on the leading edge, change is the elixir of life. It provides the opportunities and challenges that engage leaders in pursuing that elusive ideal.

Assessing the opportunities, challenges, and constraints

Rapid change challenges the weak and ill prepared, but provides opportunities for the capable and strong. Change is the means for attaining power positions and differentiation. With a high-level, strategic assessment as outlined in this section (figure 2.8), corporations can understand the forces of change, ascertain the best future direction, and use the change mechanisms to their benefit. This is a precursor to strategic analysis and planning. Assessing the opportunities, challenges, and constraints is the highest level of strategic positioning. It guides the responses to opportunities, challenges, and constraints as well as the management of technologies, products, processes, capital assets, and intellectual capital.

Almost everything in the business environment is relative. Opportunities are defined according to how they fit into the corporation's grand scheme for the future. Problems and issues too are exacerbated or extinguished by that same vision of the future. For example, Exxon Mobil spends approximately $4 billion per year exploring and drilling for new petroleum reserves and new capacity. It may believe that the potential oil fields in Alaska and off the coast of California represent opportunities for sustaining its businesses. It understands the challenges that such locations present in terms of environmental issues and concerns and expects strong opposition from stakeholder groups and the state and federal governments.

US-based petroleum companies may view certain laws and regulations as infringements on their property rights or on the legitimate constitutional protections under the Commerce Clause of the US Constitution. However, the situation would be dramatically different if such companies viewed renewable energy sources as their primary focus for the future and petroleum-based assets as secondary. The opportunities would become the possibility of inventing new technologies, such as fuel cells, photovoltaic, or other solar-based methods. Finding the right perspective, however, requires strategic thinking, analysis, and a fundamental understanding of the long-term benefits of the alternatives. Indeed, the best solution may be a combination of approaches and often depends on the mindset of the innovators. Some of the social, economic, and environmental issues would be resolved if management thinking changed. Exploration issues would evaporate if future investments focused on renewable energy or hydrogen fuel. However, a hydrogen-based economy might present new opportunities, challenges, and constraints.

The bottom line is: opportunities are invented. They are not simply discovered. They are determined in large part by the pathway taken by the corporation, its ability to shape the future, and its willingness to create new directions and solutions to challenges and problems. The challenges hold opportunities for or constraints to future growth.

Understanding organizational capabilities

The organizational structure of the corporation is usually based on the existing mission, strategies, and objectives. It is typically not in sync with the vision for the future, nor well tuned for making dramatic changes. The main difficulty in changing the mission to be aligned with a new vision is instilling the proper management mindset and building the core capabilities that are necessary for moving in a new direction. The core competencies and capabilities of most organizations evolve over many years and take considerable time and investment before providing the company with truly competitive advantages. Intel is an excellent example of a corporation that has managed to have a solid base of core competencies and capabilities to achieve superior performance in the present while, at the same time, implanting new competencies and capabilities for future generations of technologies and products. It has been able to balance its short-term and long-term positions. It does not maximize the present at the expense of its next generation of technologies and products. However, Intel has to constantly reevaluate its strategic positions and development programs to ensure that they are in alignment with global realities. Past successes do not guarantee future positions.

The corporate management-level assessment of organizational capabilities examines the advantages and disadvantages of capabilities in light of the opportunities and challenges that might come to fruition given the strategic direction of the organization. The traditional approach for examining capabilities is to focus on the prevailing business situation. The answers that are provided from such analysis might be significantly different from those obtained from a more open-ended view. A static analysis of core capabilities might indicate sufficient strengths in critical areas. However, those critical areas may become unimportant in a different reality. Change creates new realities.

Organizational capabilities and resources provide the means to be successful within management system(s) and are the fundamental strengths that an organization enjoys. The capabilities and resource assessment, as an integral part of the "Circle for inventing the future," determines the capabilities for long-term change and what is needed in order to move in the new direction. The following are some of the questions at the heart of such an assessment:

- Does the leadership have the mindset for leading change and being at the forefront of new ways for achieving sustainable success?
- Does the organization have the knowledge, capabilities, and skills necessary for moving toward the corporate vision and strategic direction, especially if they are based on SBD?
- What organizational capabilities have to be added, modified, transformed, or eliminated over time to effect the new direction?
- What are the organizational and resource limitations that will have a profound impact on the ability to change?
- Does the organization have the capacity to learn quickly the new skills and capabilities necessary for achieving profound change?
- How does the organization move or transform to a more sustainable corporation?

The questions are important to the transformation or transition process. The specific answers evolve over time after the corporation has set its vision and agenda for the future. SBD is a long-term proposition that will take decades to implement. In order to make the change, it is crucial that the organization start adding the people, skills, capabilities, knowledge, and resources for transitioning from the old world of twentieth-century thinking to the new world of SBD and enterprise thinking. Table 2.3 suggests some important considerations for leading that change. In chapter 6, organizational capabilities are explored in more detail.

The assessment of high-level "organizational capabilities and potential" focuses on how to translate value creation into a vision for the organization's future. It provides strategic input for setting long-term direction, defining the "why," the "what," and the "how," including the required investments in people, knowledge, networks, and assets.

Similar questions arise for the value networks of the corporation (customers, markets, supplier networks, related industries, and infrastructure).

Table 2.3. Key organizational attributes relating to SBD

Area	Direction	Value networks	Social	Economic	Environmental
Level					
Corporate	Value creation	Insights	Equity	Stability	Effectiveness
Strategic	Vision	Inclusiveness	Openness	Innovativeness	Mitigation
Operating	Mission	Connectedness	Fairness	Development	Risk reduction
Organization	Knowledge	Capabilities	Learning	Equilibrium	Health and Safety
Leadership	Visionary	Strategic	Responsibilities	Responsiveness	Accountability
Integration	Strategic alignment	Linkages	Relationships	Solutions	Transparency
Innovation	Investment	Creativity	Dialog	Innovativeness	Improvements

In each of these paths, too, the assessment must go beyond the traditional market and financial aspects and include the social, economic, and environmental considerations.

The Circle for inventing the future: direction

Constructing the vision statement

The most important element pertaining to future strategic direction is the articulated Vision of the corporation. The vision statement should describe strategic direction and encompass the external constituencies and social, economic, and environmental factors. Because SBD is a holistic approach, it is critical to have a unifying vision for the entire enterprise.

Vision is the high-level perspective that encapsulates the desired translation of external forces, opportunities, challenges, and internal capabilities into a new reality for the enterprise. It should describe how a sustainable entity meets the needs of the present and the future. It is generally assumed that the vision may take years, even decades to realize. Vision is "what the enterprise can be or wants to be" rather than "what it is." It can be stated in terms of the ideal instead of the practical, although it should be logical and achievable if it is to be effective. Vision guides the people within the organization as well as customers, stakeholders, shareholders, and other constituents, clearly stating for them why the organization exists, and what it seeks to do to create an improved future.

The vision defines opportunities and challenges and provides strategic thrust for transforming the organization and its resources. The vision statement should be expressed in very positive terms that are meaningful and verifiable. Too many vision statements are simply great-sounding words that are so nebulous that they fail to convey meaning. The vision should be couched in the value proposition of the enterprise: indeed, the value equation is useful for providing the critical elements of the vision, for it details the essential elements needed to propel strategic change toward the new, more ideal, reality.

Table 2.4 lists the important factors to consider when composing a vision statement for SBD.

Each corporation faces a different set of opportunities, challenges, and constraints. Corporations have to select the most relevant factors and be as inclusive as possible without overwhelming the vision with so much specificity that it loses meaning. The application of the matrix involves selecting the appropriate elements that fit the corporation's situation, prioritizing them, and communicating them as effectively as possible to enterprise participants and external constituencies.

Vision statements serve to inspire people and facilitate leading change. They are not intended to serve as marketing devices for impressing customers with exemplary messages and wonderful slogans full of good intentions. They are not simply hollow thoughts without substance. Such insincere visions are ineffective, if not worthless. Moreover, they may be damaging in the long term if there are few accomplishments, and people come to realize that the vision is a sham. Instead, vision statements have to be built on the philosophies, principles, and beliefs of management and the organization (people) as it commits to leading change and inventing the future.

In building the business case for sustainable development, the World Business Council for Sustainable Development (WBCSD) asserts a principle that focuses on "learning to change." It holds that widespread change is necessary and that a unified corporate vision is an important goal. The WBCSD suggests that a corporation's vision "requires hard looks at such corporate basics as the product portfolio and relations with suppliers and customers." Unified vision is maintained by: "public reporting of announced goals, accountability, corporate transparency and stakeholder dialogs."[28]

There is growing support for having a comprehensive vision statement that includes facets of SBD. The elements identified in table 2.4 reinforce the concept that SBD is a broad construct that goes beyond the environmental arena. The GRI's 2002 *Sustainability Reporting Guidelines* indicate that the statement of an organization's vision should address the following questions:[29]

- What are the main issues for the organization related to the major themes of sustainable development?
- How are stakeholders included in identifying these issues?

Table 2.4. Essential elements of vision statements for SBD

Area	Value networks	Social	Economic	Environmental
The aspiration *Achieve sustainable success that creates value and rewards*	Exceeding the expectations of customers and markets with products and service that provide superior value; creating value networks that are sustainable and beneficial for the participants; creating new capabilities for solving all problems	Creating equitable solutions, including considerations for all constituencies in formulating and implementing strategies, policies, processes, and practices; Being socially responsible; improving the human condition and quality of life; Creating knowledge and learning for a sustainable future; Instilling a sense of fairness in decision-making	Developing solutions before the needs outstrip capabilities; Producing economic stability that includes the global communities and the local citizens; Being responsive to mandates and requirements; Reducing costs and wastes; Minimizing liabilities	Moving toward sustainable development; Achieving effectiveness and efficiencies; Developing and using cradle-to-grave thinking; Reducing impacts and depletion; Mitigating risks
The dream *Create perfectly sustainable products, processes, and services, and eliminate all negative impacts*	Creating products and services that are sustainable and provide outstanding value over time; eliminating defects and burdens and reducing investments; using knowledge and resources to eliminate risks and impacts	Creating management systems that are inclusive; Creating a business environment that satisfies all needs and wants; Minimizing the negative effects of pollution and waste streams on society; Ensuring that no one and nothing is excluded from the solutions	Creating economic growth and resources that sustain humankind; Assuring that the world communities share in the benefits of sustainable development; Ensuring accountability for decisions and actions across the enterprise	Developing environmentally conscious technologies, products, and processes; Achieving zero defects, burdens, and impacts; Achieving perfect transparency; Being in perfect balance with nature

- For each issue, which stakeholders are the most affected by the organization?
- How are these issues reflected in the organization's values and integrated into its business strategies?
- What are the organization's objectives and actions on these issues?

It is very difficult to include every essential issue in a vision statement. The first three questions pertain to vision. The latter two link vision to the strategies and objectives for realizing the vision.

Instilling corporate values pertaining to SBD

Instilling new values or changing old ones is a difficult proposition. Most executives and practitioners were educated and learned their "trade" using values, concepts, principles, and practices that were based on the strategic management and product delivery constructs of the twentieth century. They concentrated on profits, cash flows, customer satisfaction, core competencies, business strategies, marketing, production, and finance. They focused their attention on the present and/or near term and on products and customers. While it is an overstatement to suggest that the future was not an important consideration, it is clear that the short term took precedence.

Creating a more balanced approach between the short term and the long term requires education and learning. Management has to instill new values and beliefs and provide the means and mechanisms to achieve the appropriate balance. It is ultimately management's responsibility to create a system and belief structure within the enterprise that encourages and rewards the new values. Some corporations, such as 3M and Dow Chemical, have invested heavily in this type of innovation and change.

Selecting principles for decision-making

Corporate principles reduce the "fuzziness" associated with complicated issues, making things easier for decision-makers who must determine the proper course of action for resolving difficulties. While principles were always important and fundamental to good management, they are elevated to a higher role in SBD because the vision and corporate strategies and objectives have many more elements than just the strategic or financial considerations. For corporations using "profit maximization" as the focus, for example, the overarching goal is simply "to make money." As corporations move toward more sophisticated strategic management constructs, like SBD, with many overarching goals, including social, economic, and environmental goals, as well as the traditional strategic and financial ones, discerning the interrelationships between the goals becomes difficult. Principles can provide the guidance necessary to avoid potential inconsistency and lack of strategic alignment among executives, managers, professionals, and decision-makers.

Principles can be viewed as links between the vision and the objectives and strategies of the corporation. They help to provide an understanding of SBD and how professionals and practitioners within the strategic and operating management systems should respond to situations. They are intended to provide decision-makers with the means to make effective decisions and balance the competing objectives of the enterprise.

Principles are often called "codes of conduct." In 1991, the International Chamber of Commerce (ICC) launched its Business Charter for Sustainable Development, which included sixteen principles addressing corporate policy formation, systems and procedures, integration, risk management, education, implementation, and monitoring and reporting. The Business Charter was intended to provide guidance to management and practitioners.[30] Table 2.5 provides examples of the principles promoted and followed by several corporations.

In 1999, the Secretary-General of the United Nations formulated the Global Compact, which is a set of principles to guide and integrate business, labor, and society in the quest toward corporate social responsibility. While there are debates about the rationale behind the UN Global Compact, the principles are similar to other multinational agreements. The Principles of the Global Compact are:[31]

- *Human rights*
  - Principle 1: The support and respect of the protection of international human rights
  - Principle 2: The refusal to participate or condone human rights abuses.
- *Labor*
  - Principle 3: The support of freedom of association and the recognition of the right to collective bargaining
  - Principle 4: The abolition of compulsory labor
  - Principle 5: The abolition of child labor
  - Principle 6: The elimination of discrimination in employment and occupation.
- *Environment*
  - Principle 7: The implementation of a precautionary and effective program on environmental issues
  - Principle 8: Initiatives that demonstrate environmental responsibility
  - Principle 9: The promotion of the diffusion of environmentally friendly technologies.

Table 2.5. Main categories and examples of principles and codes

Main category	Key principles	Approaches	Targets (examples)
External			
Social responsibility	Inclusiveness	Enterprise thinking	100% participation
	Honesty	Ethical behavior	Zero exceptions
	Integrity	Codes of conduct	0 complaints (defects)
	Equity, fairness, and human rights	Corporate social responsibility	100% satisfaction
Economic stability	Value creation	LCT	Best-in-class performance/ price
	Responsiveness	Business integration	100% involvement
	Efficiency and effectiveness	Balanced solutions	Minimization of resources
	Polluter pays and user pays	Sustainable economics	Full inclusion of externalities
Environmental stewardship	Openness	Environmental reporting	Full transparency
	Preparedness	Education and training	100% of work force trained
	Precautionary approach	Stewardship and mitigation	100% contingency plans
	Waste minimization	Pollution prevention	50% reduction in 5 years
Internal			
Business strategy and integration	Vision	Visionary leadership	Sustainable success
	Good governance	Strategic thinking	Best practices
	Strategic alignment	Value networks	100% collaboration
	Participation	Networking	100% networked
	Accountability	Activity-based accounting	100% (full) accountability
Innovation	Innovativeness	Technological innovation	Number of new technologies
	Environmental compatibility	Product/Process innovation	Number of conforming products
	Continuous improvement	LCT/Life cycle management	Number of LCAs per year
Environmental leadership	Trust	Environmental quality	Six-Sigma quality
	Prevention	Pollution prevention plans	10% reduction in wastes per year
	Compliance	Waste management/ minimization	100% in compliance

- *Anti-corruption*
  - Principle 10: The promotion and adoption of initiatives to counter all forms of corruption, including extortion and bribery.

The principles are a mix of codes of conduct and statements of intent, but there are common themes. The principles within the "Environment" portion of the UN Global Compact resonate throughout this book. The Global Compact includes initiatives for sustainable investment, sustainable entrepreneurship, corporate management and sustainability, and investors and sustainability.[32] These programs relate to business and sustainable development.

The European Union includes good governance, participation, accountability, effectiveness, and coherence as its key principles.[33] The concept of good governance is central to leadership, business integration and decision-making. Outstanding business leaders are connected to their business environment and formulate and implement strategies and policies that are based on best practices across the world (box 2.3).

Overarching objectives of SBD

The overarching objectives of the enterprise articulate the direction of the corporation as it moves in space and time. They define the specific outcomes required for inventing the desired future and provide the criteria for selecting development programs, making investments, and measuring progress. Objectives are formulated based on vision, strategic direction, the needs of customers, stakeholders and other constituents, and the opportunities and challenges of the business environment. Objectives concerning SBD also include those related to pollution prevention, product stewardship, waste minimization, and compliance.

According to Robert Kaplan and David Norton, the well-known authors of the Balanced Scorecard, a corporation should have a balanced set of objectives that include the fundamental requirements for achieving long-term success.[34] They suggest that corporate objectives need to be based on more than just financial reward. The Balanced Scorecard approach for formulating objectives includes customer satisfaction, organizational learning, and internal capabilities, as well as financial requirements. The construct is a natural fit with SBD and enterprise thinking.

Objectives should be stated in definitive terms. For instance, it is useful to stipulate objectives that are intended to cover a number of years in terms of both the total amount and the per annum amount. An objective of achieving by 2015 (a ten-year period) a 50 percent reduction in off-site hazardous waste disposal could also be defined as 5 percent reduction of the original amount

Box 2.3 Eli Lilly and Company: values and principles

Eli Lilly and Company (hereafter, Lilly) is a leading pharmaceutical corporation headquartered in Indianapolis, Indiana. In 2002, Lilly had world-wide revenues and net income of $11.1 billion and $2.7 billion, respectively. The company has operations and R&D centers in nine countries and markets its products world-wide; 41 percent of its revenues were obtained from sales outside the United States. The company has enjoyed many blockbuster drug discoveries over the last several decades, including Prozac (for depression), Gemzar (for lung cancer), Evista (for osteoporosis), Humulin (insulin), and Hmatrope (a growth hormone).

Since its inception in 1876, Lilly has focused on innovation and research. In 2003, Lilly led the industry in R&D by investing 19 percent of its revenue in development programs. Total R&D expenditures were $2,149 million.

The company's mission statement focuses on being the best, and improving its strategic position by using research from its world-wide laboratories and from collaborating with scientific and academic organizations. The company's value statements embrace high standards, quality, continuous innovation and improvement, and a profound sense of including all stakeholders and participants. Its "Answers That Matter" philosophy is built on the perspective that "listening to and understanding our customers' needs" provides unparalleled value.[1] The core values include:[2]

- *Integrity*   We conduct our business consistent with all applicable laws and are honest in our dealings with our customers, employees, shareholders, partners, suppliers, competitors, and the community.
- *Excellence*   We pursue pharmaceutical innovation, provide high-quality products, and strive to achieve superior business results. We continually search for new ways to improve everything we do.
- *Respect for people*   We maintain an environment built on mutual respect, openness, and individual integrity. Respect for people includes our concern for all people who touch or are touched by our company: customers, employees, shareholders, partners, suppliers, and communities.

Most importantly, Lilly is governed by its core values and principles. Lilly's basic *principles of corporate governance* are stated as:[3]

> The company believes that a strong system of corporate governance is critical to creating long-term shareholder value. In pursuit of this objective, the interests of the corporation's principal constituents are considered: shareholders, employees, customers, partners and suppliers, and local communities. It is important to balance the interests of the corporation's many divergent constituents, as there can be no long-term shareholder value creation without fair treatment of all of those who touch or are touched by the corporation.

When Lilly began to move to sustainable development it moved cautiously. Like most large corporations, the company had instituted an EMS that provided the basic framework for ensuring regulatory compliance and meeting the expectations of stakeholders as articulated in the company's principles. While the company had a long history of focusing on social responsibility, it also had a legacy of many environmental problems over the last several decades.[4] The company has followed the management principles of Responsible Care and it is working on ISO 14001 certification. In 1997, Lilly implemented a New Product Requirements Tracking (NPERT) program to identify and quantify the quality and environmental considerations of the raw material and chemicals used in its product and manufacturing processes. The new product development team must now examine the waste stream implications of the selections that it makes during the discovery, development, and delivery processes used to create new products.

Lilly is instituting the philosophical underpinnings and creating the SBD management framework for leading change. It is working on mechanisms such as NPERT that allow practitioners to understand the implications of their selection decisions. Lilly's 2003 *Corporate Sustainability Report* is the first that focused on sustainable development instead of on the historical perspective of environmental management. The report was based on the GRI guidelines and is pivotal in the company's quest to be responsive. Lilly has an open dialog with stakeholders and provides information and answers to public sector needs and inquiries. Lilly is transforming its EMS into a broader perspective of corporate social responsibility that integrates the management system with social, economic and environmental performance.

Source: http://www.lilly.com/about/hightlights.html.

Notes:
1. Lilly, *Corporate Sustainability Report*, "Vision and Strategy," 2003.
2. http://investor.lilly.com/corp-gov.cfm.
3. http://investor.lilly.com/guidelines.cfm.
4. In its *Annual Report*, 2002, Lilly reported environmental liabilities of $267 million.

every year. This approach recognizes the need to achieve results continuously and provides targets for both the short term and long term. Alternatively, objectives can be defined using a half-life concept. The objective could be to cut the waste stream in half during the first period and in half again during the second period with the sequence continuing until the burden is reduced to approximately zero. (Note that "approximately zero" is hard to define.)

Table 2.6 provides a matrix of objective categories based on the key elements of the value equation and the principles of SBD. It suggests categories that could be used to identify and select objectives, but does not imply that an objective has to be identified for each category.

Objectives have to be balanced in terms of categories and time. The time dimension must be identified properly and articulated clearly. There is often a tendency to bias the selection of objectives to the extremes – i.e. focusing on the long term – which may mean that the objectives are challenging and substantial, but lack near-term relevancy sufficient to merit high priority. Conversely, they could focus primarily on the short term, which may result in

Table 2.6. Selected categories for determining SBD objectives based on the value equation

Area	Enterprise *Insightfulness*	Social *Equity*	Economic *Stability*	Environmental *Effectiveness*
Value creation **Top side**				
ΣBenefits – *Tangible*	– High-level performance	– Add value to society	– Lower operating costs	– Eco-efficiency
	– High quality	– Improve quality of life	– Durability	– Minimum resources
– *Intangible*	– Reliability	– Corporate citizenship	– Affordability	– Safety
	– Aesthetics	– Longevity	– High collateral value	– Healthful
ΣEffects – *Tangible*	– Enhanced capabilities	– Social responsibility	– Long life cycle	– More output per input
	– Secondary applications	– Indirect benefits	– Enhanced value	– Enhanced disposal
– *Intangible*	– Customer satisfaction	– Stakeholder satisfaction	– Residual value	– Enhanced image
ΣKnowledge	– Learning	– Public reporting	– Predictable demand	– Product stewardship
	– Confidence of success	– Full disclosure	– Stable costs	– Training & education
Bottom side				
ΣInvestments – *Money*	– High returns/rewards	– Enhanced value proposition	– Lower costs	– Reduced wastes
	– Cost effective solution	– Socially compatible	– Fewer hidden costs	– Reduced risks
– *Time*	– Ease of use and disposal	– Ease of use	– High compatibility	– Eliminate constraints
	– Degree of learning	– Positive esteem	– Long product life	– Easily retired
ΣDefects – *Quality*	– Zero defects	– Enhanced image	– Lower risks	– Pollution prevention
	– Low maintenance	– Lower effects	– Energy efficient	– Full compliance
– *Liability*	– Low risks	– Reduced injury/death	– Reduced litigation	– Reduced footprints
	– High level of safety	– Less destruction	– Lower risks	– Reduced impacts
ΣBurdens	– Low probability of negative events	– Less disruption	– Less remediation	– Lower pollution
			– Lower closure costs	– Reduced degradation

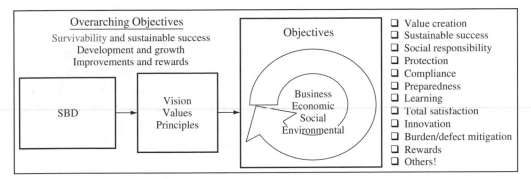

Figure 2.9   Integrated perspective for SBD objectives

easy victories, but may lead to inadequate progress toward long-term sustainable improvements. It is preferable to have a set of objectives that are distributed across space and time, combining all aspects of **global enterprise management**.

If objectives are defined correctly, failure to achieve one or more of the main elements of the value equation might be mitigated to some extent by successes with other elements. For instance, if benefits are not significantly enhanced, but organizational learning is improved dramatically and the knowledge base is more capable of achieving future initiatives, the overall objectives will be improved. This phenomenon is especially important for environmental initiatives involving life cycle management and assessment. Often the first stage in the improvement process is acquiring the knowledge necessary for understanding the defects, burdens, and impacts. Organizational learning is a primary objective, especially if the subsequent initiatives can result in significant rewards.

The long-term dream is to have a fully integrated management system without the separate categories of objectives. Such a system would be balanced and comprehensive. SBD derives from holistic constructs with multifaceted inputs, parallel processing, and solutions for satisfying all constituents. Figure 2.9 provides a sense of such as integrated perspective.

The design and selection of a balanced set of objectives are crucial to long-term success in the quest for SBD. The objectives establish the direction of product and technological innovation, LCT and assessment, and performance evaluation.

Formulating grand strategies and gaining acceptance

SBD represents a paradigm change for most organizations. It involves radical shifts in thinking, leadership, management, and program design, development and implementation. Reaching consensus within the organization and with the external entities about SBD is a pivotal point.

The grand strategy of SBD is to preempt the needs and expectations of the business environment and provide enhanced solutions before being required to do so and to outperform peers and competitors in all ways. To do so involves a specific balancing of the corporation's objectives with the demands of the business environment. Each corporation has to articulate its own grand strategy for pursuing SBD. The concept of "grand strategy" is explained in more detail in chapter 3.

Gaining acceptance of SBD is a crucial point in the process whereby success or failure may be determined. Without understanding and support for the tenets of SBD, progress is negated. Management may be committed and provide leadership, but it also must inspire in order to engender internal and external participation. Acceptance is the willingness to embrace change and fully integrate the methodology throughout the organization for every level and individual. It occurs when customers and stakeholders appreciate the larger context of the future enterprise and the benefits of more sustainable products and services. Gaining acceptance typically follows the "S" curve phenomenon: it takes time and effort to obtain acceptance.

For most change processes, there is usually a relatively long period of slow growth during the introduction and early achievements stage. It takes time for people to acquire the knowledge they need to perform and to accept the benefits of the change mechanisms. If the early initiatives are successful, further gains are possible as people recognize the value of investing their time, effort, and personal reputations. Acceptance continues to grow during the development stage, as more people become familiar with the methods and benefits, especially as significant improvements are realized.

The most important reason for gaining acceptance during the early stages is to discover ways to overcome the barriers to success. The initial step is to identify and describe the key barriers. Often there are several crucial areas that, if resolved, would clear the way for success. The following questions will help reveal the barriers:

- Why lead change?
- What are the most significant issues relating to SBD?
- What are the short-term benefits and long-term rewards?
- What are the expectations?
- How does the organization acquire the knowledge needed for changing its paradigm?

- What are necessary strategic assets, resources, and capabilities?
- Who are the strategic partners? What are their relationships?

Answering these key questions provides insights and direction for leading change and obtaining acceptance across the organization and the enterprise.

Planning, developing, and implementing programs for SBD

SBD necessitates a critical examination of capabilities, resources, and portfolios in order to move beyond compliance and pollution prevention and expand enterprise thinking beyond core competencies and customer satisfaction. Restructuring capabilities and resources are an inherent part of this process. The core capabilities of the organization are often structured for meeting past or present needs. The resources are typically skewed toward producing and delivering the current portfolio of products and services. While such a focus makes strategic sense in the short term, it can result in an unbalanced situation from a long-term perspective.

The portfolio of existing products typically has a powerful influence over the quest for improvements. It is typically the basis for the organization's core capabilities and resources, defining its strengths and its weaknesses. The prevailing approach for identifying and selecting new programs is to formulate derivatives and enhancements to existing platforms of technologies and products. While this approach fits within the SBD construct, it tends to result in evolutionary improvements only, rather than the recommendations that might result from a more comprehensive analysis of what the situation should be or could be. The selection, design, evaluation, and implementation of programs for SBD are discussed in detail in chapter 7.

Siemens AG, headquartered in Berlin and Munich, is an outstanding example of a global corporation whose business model is similar to the EMM. Siemens considers itself to be the leading knowledge management company in Europe[35] fully engaged in SBD (box 2.4).

Box 2.4 Siemens AG: achieving business excellence through vision, value, principles, and people

Siemens is a global corporation with over 416,000 employees in 190 countries. It had sales of €75.2 billion in 2003, with a net income of €3.4 billion.[1] The company has six major lines of business, including information and communications, automation and control, power, transportation, medical, and lighting. It also has two major affiliates, BSH Borchund Siemens Hausgerate GmbH (appliances) and Fujitsu–Siemens BV (computers).

Werner Siemens founded the company in 1847 as a producer of telegraph and electrical equipment. Siemens grew significantly during the nineteenth century based on the discovery

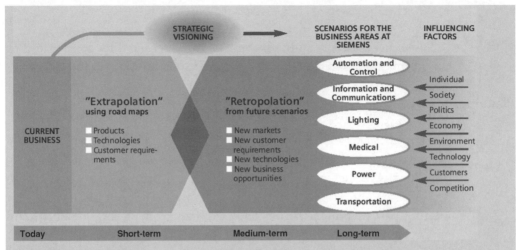

Figure 2B.2 Siemens and innovation

of the dynamo-electric principle and machinery. The two world wars of the twentieth century wreaked havoc on the assets and intellectual property of the company, but through its technical capabilities, innovative skills, and competent management, the company overcame the difficulties.

Siemens' R&D strengths lie at the center of its success. It has 53,000 researchers in 150 centers in over thirty countries world-wide. The total R&D budget for 2003 was over €5 billion. Innovation is among the foremost activities within the corporation. The various R&D centers created more than 7,000 inventions and produced 4,500 patent applications during 2002.[2]

CEO Dr. Heinrich Von Pierer stated that the "surest way to predict the future is to create and shape it yourself."[3] For Siemens, inventing the future means identifying customer needs, developing new technologies, recognizing technological breakthroughs, and creating new business opportunities, products, and solutions.[4] Siemens' corporate model provides management and researchers with a clear understanding of this underlying perspective for managing change. Figure 2B.2 depicts the essence of Siemens' "Pictures of the Future" that guide innovation.

Siemens' model is an excellent example of enterprise management as a construct for SBD. The model uses two complementary perspectives for determining the vision for the future. "One is obtained using extrapolations into the future based on the world of today; the other is obtained through retropolation or thinking about the desired future state and working back to the present, starting from the world of tomorrow. Extrapolation involves looking at today's known technologies and projecting them into the future. Retropolation involves envisioning possible scenarios in the future and drawing consequences from them for today."[5] Siemens follows this dual approach for examining and selecting opportunities.

Siemens leverages its knowledge management expertise to become the leader of innovations and change. Claus Weyrich, head of the Corporate Technology Group, stated that "we will continue to set the pace in technological progress, and have accepted the challenges of the future. A rising share of our sales is based on products that didn't even exist five years ago. Our vision, which goes by the name of 'Network of Competencies – Partners for Innovations,' is oriented toward the development of the company in the direction of knowledge-based products and customer oriented solutions. For us, the future has already begun."[6]

Siemens' management and employees are the guided by the following principles:[7]

- We strengthen our **CUSTOMERS** – to keep them competitive. Our success depends on the success of our customers. We provide our customers with our comprehensive experience and solutions so they can achieve their objectives fast and effectively.
- We push **INNOVATION** – to shape the future. Innovation is our lifeblood around the globe and around the clock. We turn our people's imagination and best practices into successful technologies and products. Creativity and experience keeps us on the cutting edge.
- We enhance company **VALUE** – to open up new opportunities. We generate profitable growth to ensure sustainable success. We leverage our balanced business portfolio, our business excellence and synergies across all segments and regions. This makes us a premium investment for our shareholders.
- We empower our **PEOPLE** – to achieve world-class performance. Our employees are the key to our success. We work together as a global network of knowledge and learning. Our corporate culture is defined by diversity, by open dialog and mutual respect, and by clear goals and decisive leadership.
- We embrace corporate **RESPONSIBILITY** – to advance society. Our ideas, technologies and activities help create a better world. We are committed to universal values, good corporate citizenship and a healthy environment. Integrity guides our conduct toward our employees, business partners and shareholders.

Siemens' primary mechanisms for meeting its principles and vision are business excellence and corporate citizenship. Business excellence involves supporting customers with "right-fit" solutions and environmentally compatible products. It also means "innovating for tomorrow" by turning ideas into innovation programs that are based on "clear goals, concrete measures, and rigorous consequences." Corporate responsibility helps build trust with stakeholders, government agencies, and society. The bottom line is to create value and share it broadly across the business environment and with shareholders.[8] Siemens works with 7,500 strategic partners and suppliers world-wide. It chooses the best and ensures consistent quality based on long-term relationships.[9] It requires suppliers to "do business in accordance with the fundamental laws and principles of the international community."[10] It expects them "to compete fairly and with integrity and also to protect the environment, to be socially responsible, and to have appropriate employee-oriented policies."[11]

Siemens' business conduct guidelines include: (1) mutual respect, honesty, and integrity; (2) behavior which abides with the law; (3) abiding by fair competition and anti-trust legislation; (4) rules against corruption; (5) rules for awarding contracts; (6) donations; (7) confidentiality and insider trading rules; (8) data protection and data security; (9) policies for protecting environment, health, and safety; (10) complaints and comments; (11) implementing and controlling.[12]

Siemens' corporate citizenship is expressed through open dialog with all constituencies and special relationships with the interested public, political leaders, and other associations. Business excellence and corporate citizenship are directly related to the corporation's environmental policy.

Siemens' Environmental Mission Statement is:[13]

Our knowledge and our solutions are helping to create a better world. We have the responsibility to a wider community and we are committed to environmental protection. In our global operations, featuring a great diversity of processes, products, and services, our company is concerned with sustaining the natural resources essential to life. We view the economy, environmental protection, and social responsibility as three key factors carrying equal weight in a liberal world market. We support the dissemination of knowledge needed for sustainable development through the transfer of knowledge in the fields of management and technology, wherever we operate as a company. For us, sustainable development means the careful use of natural resources, which is why we assess possible environmental impacts in the early stages of product and process development. It is our aim to avoid pollution altogether or to reduce it to a minimum, above and beyond statutory requirements.

Siemens integrates environmental protection and the associated management system into its overall perspective of corporate responsibility. Its EMS uses best practices for its world-wide operations and is aligned with ISO 14001 and the European Union's environmental management and audit scheme. The system has a strong health and safety component as well. The company's environmental protection foundation forms the basis for its initiatives in sustainable development.

The company is a leader in developing new technologies to conserve natural resources and habitats. It uses an integrated, "end-to-end" view of the environment that spans the whole product life cycle. This includes planning, development and production, packaging and logistics, utilization, recycling and reprocessing, and environmentally compatible disposal. CEO von Pierer helped found EconSense – A Forum For Sustainable Development, a German organization dedicated to integrating sustainable development in corporate strategies.

The most important factor in the company's transition to SBD is its management leadership and organizational structure. While the Three-Level Mode of Siemens' EMS does not perfectly mimic the embedded structure of the Enterprise Management System, it does have a similar logic. The levels are as in table 2B.1.

The Three-Level Mode defines responsibilities at corporate (global), group, and operating levels. Group and corporate executives support officers at the operating level. This model, with its vision, principles, and values, supports the practical side of the value proposition and provides a sense of doability. The focus on corporate citizenship and responsibility reinforces the importance of people.

Table 2B.1. The Three-Level Mode

	Supervisory responsibility	Technical responsibility
● Level 1	Members of the Managing Board of Siemens AG	Corporate Offices for Environmental Protection and Technical Safety
● Level 2	Members of Group Executive Management	Group Offices for Environmental and Technical Safety
● Level 3	Plant and Facility Management	Officers for Environmental Protection

Source: Siemens discloses details about the corporate, its social responsibilities and environmental protection in its *Annual Report*, *Corporate Citizenship Report*, and *Environmental Report*, respectively.

Notes:
1. www.siemens.com, "Key Figures."
2. *Ibid.*, "Patents."
3. *Ibid.*
4. *Ibid.*
5. *Ibid.*, "Technologies."
6. Corporate Brochure ZT MuK 04/2000, p. 3.
7. www.siemens.com, "Our Principles."
8. *Ibid.*, "Business Excellence Programs."
9. *Ibid.*
10. *Ibid.*
11. *Ibid.*
12. *Ibid.*
13. *Ibid.*, "Environmental Mission Statement."

The strategic logic for SBD

The most important reasons for adapting the principles, processes, and practices of SBD are to better respond to the increasing complexities in the business world and the growing challenges to corporate governance. Traditionally, governance has meant protecting the assets and well-being of the corporation. As the roles and responsibilities of corporations have become more difficult to define and measure, however, executives and managers have had to provide leadership and guidance to the organization and its related parties on proper behaviors and acceptable approaches. Corporate governance has also become protecting the enterprise and its capacity to create value. From a corporation's perspective, it is self-preservation, protecting the capabilities to generate revenues, earn income streams, enhance shareholder equity, and avoid mistakes that tarnish or destroy wealth and reputation.

Andrew Savitz, Partner of PriceWaterhouseCoopers (PwC), states that responsible corporate behavior is a significant reason for embracing more effective corporate governance. In PwC's 2000 *Sustainability Survey Report*, Savitz said:[36]

Responsible corporate behavior – whether defined to include sustainability or not – is based on effective corporate governance. A company cannot hope to behave responsibly, or sustainably, if it does not have effective internal controls – programs and processes, checks and balances – to identify and systematically achieve responsible, sustainable outcomes.

PwC's report was based on a survey of executives of 140 US-based companies. The major findings indicated that 52 percent of the companies had initiatives pertaining to sustainability and 17 percent were planning to have initiatives within three years.[37] Most importantly, the three main reasons for adopting sustainability were: (1) enhanced reputation – 90 percent; (2) competitive advantages – 75 percent; and (3) cost saving – 73 percent.[38] While there are other reasons including risk reduction, industry trends and competitive pressures, customer requests, and board of directors' requirements, the direct connection to business strategies and operations are still fuzzy. Nevertheless, the survey indicated that a significant number of companies are pursuing SBD for a combination of business-related (mainstream) reasons.

Automobile manufacturers have engaged in SBD to minimize the adverse effects of vehicle use on the environment and society.[39] This is an act of self-preservation. The industry's initiatives to enhance fuel efficiency, reduce emissions and noise, and improve safety are geared toward protecting the value of the automobile as the prime means of mobility.

The 2002 KPMG *International Survey of Corporate Sustainability Reporting* indicated that 45 percent of the top 250 corporations of *Global Fortune 500* (GFT250) have not only embraced SBD, but have committed to some form of sustainability reporting.[40] The survey indicated that companies were embracing sustainability to enhance business performance, including:[41]

- Reducing operating costs and improving efficiency
- Developing innovative products and services for access to new markets
- Improving reputation and brand value through integrity management
- Recruiting and retaining excellent people
- Gaining better access to investors' capital
- Adding to the stock value of the company through the financial market's appreciation of good sustainability performance
- Reducing a company's liabilities through integrated risk management.

While there may be many other reasons for employing SBD, the KPMG report summarizes the strategic logic in succinct terms. It involves fairly traditional strategic thinking: reduce costs and save money, leverage new innovations, enhance reputation and brands, gain access to capital, improve share price, and reduce risks. Such reasons suggest that SBD involves mainstream considerations and is central to the strategic success of global corporations. Those who appreciate this can enjoy an enhanced corporate reputation and image as a leader for positive change, sustainable competitive advantages, reduced risks and uncertainties, and an improved economic structure.

Enhancing corporate reputation

Strategic thinking, leading change, business integration, and innovation are among the hottest topics in the corporate world. The global business environment is changing at a tremendous speed, becoming more dynamic and exciting as new systems, technologies, and products replace the obsolete twentieth-century approaches. Corporate leaders are being pressured to produce outstanding financial results in the short term, as well as to create new capabilities and approaches for the future.

The market capitalization of a corporation represents the value of the corporate name and reputation, of its brands, assets, intellectual capital, and ability to generate revenues, cash flows, and profits in the future. Most global corporations would have significantly lower market capitalization if the streams of future cash flows and profits were not included in the calculation of present value, or limited to just the next few years. One of the most important reasons that corporations are embracing SBD is to protect the future value of the corporation. While most definitions of SBD focus on the social, economic, and environmental considerations pertaining to the external business environment, the logic for SBD also lies in the self-interest of corporate leadership, employees, and shareholders, in their desire to ensure that opportunities and corporate value are sustained and enhanced over time.

Trust and integrity are pivotal to this objective. People buy and use products from a given producer because they trust the company and its brands to provide the best solution and value. Customers are also becoming more sophisticated and making decisions based on numerous criteria, including the quality, ethics, and responsiveness of management and the corporation. Trust, reliability, and dependability can distinguish the capable, willing, honest, and committed from those who simply want to sell products and make profits.

Even some of the most highly regarded and successful corporations have been thinking about their businesses from the wrong direction. They view profits as the most important internal element in decision-making. However, from a business environment perspective, corporate image, reputation, values, integrity, and trust are among the most important factors in achieving sustainable success. They take time and effort to build, but can be easily damaged through even a single failure. For example, Merck has been ranked as one of the most admired corporations for many years, but its problems with Vioxx had an immediate impact on its reputation among customers, stakeholders, and investors. On November 18, 2004, Raymond V. Gilmartin, Merck's Chairman and CEO, had to testify before Congress to explain Merck's failure to disclose information about the problems with Vioxx.[42] While the case is in the early stage, the consequences have already been dramatic. *USA Today* published the following report:[43]

For Merck, the legal stakes are high. The company's stock has lost nearly 40 percent of its value since it closed at $45.07 a share the day before the Vioxx withdrawal. It closed Wednesday [November 17, 2004] at $27.34. Earlier this month, the Food and Drug Administration released details from an agency memorandum that said Vioxx might have played a role in more than 27,785 heart attacks and deaths from 1999 to 2003. In a November 3 report, Merrill Lynch estimated the company's potential legal liability could run as high as $18 million.

The story will take many months, even years, to unfold. It is nonetheless clear that Merck is engaged in a long and costly process to recover the strength of its name and the goodwill that it enjoyed. At this point in time, executives are on the defensive, customers are concerned, employees are worried, and shareholders have already lost a significant amount of money.

Corporate leadership has to ensure that success and performance is sustainable. There are many examples of leading corporations that were at the pinnacle of success in their industry, only to shrink into oblivion because they failed to provide total satisfaction. The scandals at companies such as Enron and WorldCom often get the headlines, but there are many stories about corporate failures to comply with government mandates, meet social expectations, or fully consider environmental issues that have led to significant problems or even the demise of corporations. AT&T was once one of the largest corporations in the world. Its difficulties with the US Justice Department ultimately resulted in its breakup in 1984. US Steel was the largest industrial US corporation at the beginning of the twentieth century. Its position declined over the decades due to its difficulties with its labor unions and global technological changes. The Johns–Manville Corporation was successfully selling products and generating profits when it filed for bankruptcy because of health-related issues and litigation over asbestos claims.

SBD focuses a corporation on protecting value and assets and ensuring that neither action nor inaction will lead to negative social, economic, and environmental consequences and severe financial impacts. Executive leadership and corporate governance must "provide for the needs of the present without compromising the ability to meet the needs of the future."[44] SBD is not a new theoretical approach or fad about managing corporations based on environmental considerations. Rather, it is simply a more comprehensive view of the business environment, the management system(s), and management responsibilities. This broader view affects everything that a corporation does, including its operations, attitude, and all of its external relationships.

Obtaining sustainable competitive advantages

For decades, global corporations have been on a quest to find and secure unique competitive advantages that will set them apart from their competition. While there are many examples of great successes in this, in most cases the results have been fleeting. Even when competitive advantages have endured for more than a decade, the most competent competitors generally catch up and become a threat to the leader. For instance, Canon became a major threat to Xerox during the 1980s even though Xerox had a ten-year lead on its competitor. More recently, AMD has been forcing Intel to rethink its "Pentium" platform in order to determine the next microprocessor innovations that will allow it to maintain its leadership.

In simple terms, competitive advantages are often based on outstanding strategic positions that depend on tangible aspects such as processes, products and services, technologies, and/or systems. In certain cases, they are based on a combination of two or more of these capabilities. The following are selected examples of each.

- *Process* Process advantages include efficiency, cost effectiveness, speed, lean management, information flow, and know-how. Fedex has created a world-class process for handling the informational requirements for shipping packages and documents that are inherent in everything that is shipped through its system. In many cases, the information about the package is just as important as the item itself. The efficiency and effectiveness of the whole process is what makes Fedex a powerhouse in the industry.
- *Product* Product advantages include innovative designs with special features and functions, high quality, low cost, unique benefits for customers, and effective support mechanisms. Toyota has many products in its portfolio that are leaders in their categories. Its products have numerous advantages that make copying them difficult even in an industry where "commoditization" is prevalent. The Toyota Camry offers customers a

cost effective, reliable, and technologically sophisticated product. Competitors can copy it, but they have to duplicate every aspect of the product and the related system to compete.

- *Service* Service advantages include unique relationships, low-cost support, efficient delivery, accurate information flow, and superior customer relations. Dell Computer retails its products directly to the customers. Its service capabilities to inform, package, deliver, and support are the essence of its success in the PC industry. Its competitive advantage is based on the total service provided to customers. While one aspect may be easily copied, competitors have to have the complete capability in order to outperform Dell.

- *Technology* Technology advantages include advanced technical capabilities, radical improvements, unique benefits, new-to-the-world products, and superior outcomes. Intel has been a leader in technology since the early 1990s. While there have been many competitors over time, the dynamic aspects of Intel's technological innovations have kept the development of new generations of microprocessors challenging and costly. The status quo is not a viable option.

- *System* System advantages include total integration, outstanding information flow, low-cost operations, minimal waste, lean management, and total effectiveness. Wal-Mart is an industry leader with a cost effective system that tries to optimize every facet of the procurement, processing, delivery, and sale of products and services to consumers. Its low-price strategy is based on the competencies and capabilities of the entire system. Such advantages are difficult to duplicate unless the competitor can effectively match the capabilities of the whole system.

In each category, there are numerous other advantages that companies may enjoy and use to achieve a differential advantage over others. Competitive advantages are difficult to achieve and even more difficult to maintain. However, they generally become more complicated and harder to duplicate as the focus moves from process and product to technology and system. The more complex the requirements, the more time and effort are needed to obtain the competitive advantages, and to keep them. Nonetheless, as global corporations become more sophisticated, competitors have to have the capacity to design, develop and launch high-quality, high-power processes, products, services, technologies, and systems. It requires a significant effort just to stay abreast of change.

The intangible competitive advantages are much broader than their tangible counterparts and, though more difficult to define and emulate, they are becoming more important. While additional complexity has a price in terms of learning, knowledge, and investment, some of the most important intangible competitive advantages stem from a corporation's uniqueness, depth of position, and its ability to manage complexity. The more complex the source of the advantage, the more difficult it is to duplicate. The most powerful intangible competitive advantages fit into the following categories:

- *Value creation* Value creation includes providing effective and eco-efficient outcomes for customers, stakeholders, and partners that improve their health, wealth, welfare, and pleasure; building brand identity for sustainable success; generating cash flow, profits, and shareholder equity; and ensuring rewards for management and employees. Coca-Cola, for instance, focuses on sustainable success that enriches suppliers, distributors, customers, stakeholders, and shareholders. It focuses on mutually beneficial outcomes, minimizing its impacts on the business environment and the natural world.

- *Total solution*   The total solution is the integrated contributions of those within the corporation and its support team (supply networks, partners, etc.). It includes excellence in design, superior product and service applications and benefits, waste minimization, pollution prevention, EoL answers, ongoing support, longevity, and value. IBM is world-renowned for its solution focus that provides customers and stakeholders with every part of the solution set rather than just the product or service.

- *Total satisfaction*   Total satisfaction is a complement to the total solution. It includes ensuring compliance with laws and regulations and other external standards, eliminating external impacts through effective management, providing supporting entities with the proper information, direction, development, and integration, and closing the loop on every question, concern, or problem. P&G recognizes that it needs repeat sales of its products over the long term if it is going to sustain success. Its customers must be delighted with the products and services and trust the people involved, otherwise they will switch to a competitor's products.

- *Total integration*   Total integration includes connecting the entire system and all of its participants into a cohesive and high-performance enterprise and ensuring that the system functions properly and meets all expectations. Total integration involves effective communications, building relationships and capabilities, and linking the present with the future. Siemens is an example of a leading edge global corporation that integrates its system and decision-making with customers and stakeholders as well as partners.

Sustainable competitive advantages are critical for enduring success. They are the principal means for differentiating a corporation from its competitors. Whether through tangible or intangible mechanisms, SBD focuses on securing competitive advantages: indeed, it provides the ability to achieve the more complicated and more enduring intangible advantages. It supports the development of truly extraordinary advantages that few are able to follow. Because of the inclusiveness and far-reaching influences of SBD, competitors who want to emulate the successes will have to improve their entire enterprise, use LCT to improve technologies, products, and services, and achieve a balanced perspective for managing the social, economic, and environmental considerations. Unlike simpler constructs, SBD is about achieving value creation, total solutions, total satisfaction, and total integration. These are highly prized outcomes in a world of intense competition and the "commoditization" of products, services, and technologies. Not only are such differential advantages more sustainable, they raise the bar of competition to a much higher level. The strong and capable will prosper, and the weak and incapable will find little space in a demanding world.

Risk mitigation

Addressing risks and reducing liabilities are critical management approaches for ensuring sustainable success. SBD and enterprise thinking offer an integrated way to gain insight about system-wide risk and use it to build corporate reputation, improve financial conditions, and protect shareholder value. While much of the discussion about SBD involves social, economic, and environmental risks, the strategic objectives include protecting share price, reducing product liabilities, avoiding litigation, and ensuring that every action is initiated and completed on a timely basis.

Risk mitigation is, in fact, one of the prime motivations for SBD. Many of the historical problems of businesses were a result of a lack of perspective. Business leaders simply did not think about social and environmental requirements unless they were required to do so by laws and regulations. Such failures often resulted in a single event or product failure that had a catastrophic effect on the corporation. Examples include the *Exxon Valdez* oil spill, the release of toxic gases at Bhopal in India, and the Firestone/Ford Explorer tire problem.

Reducing costs and saving money

Businesses' quest to reduce costs and save money is centuries old and is responsible for some of the most basic initiatives employed by corporations today. While the logic is obvious, the outcomes are not always predictable. For instance, lowering quality to reduce costs may have negative effects on market share in the long term as customers realize that overall value has been compromised. Moreover, executives might cut R&D expenditures to save money in the short term only to find themselves in highly competitive market conditions with declining prospects because their products and services lack distinctiveness.

SBD is occasionally viewed negatively because executives and practitioners believe that it will increase costs. While increasing complexity often results in short-term increases in operating expenses, the benefits derived from a more comprehensive understanding of the business environment and more inclusiveness in strategic thinking have the potential to save money in the long term. Investing in more thorough assessments of supply network implications and customer and stakeholder expectations, or in the search for hidden defects in new products, may increase costs in the present, but may avoid the extraordinary expenses of future accidents or liabilities. Through fine-tuning operations, improving quality, and driving out costs, corporations may have fewer short-term opportunities for additional improvements, there are always long-term opportunities to improve transactional activities and reduce costs across the entire value system, not just within internal operations and first-tier suppliers and distributors.

Furthermore, innovative clean technologies and products have the potential to reduce raw material needs, drive down the costs of procurement and production, and minimize the costs associated with handling waste streams and pollution. Such technologies and products typically have fewer compliance mandates and fewer defects and burdens. Collectively, such actions reduce costs and save money across the entire system.

SBD uncovers opportunities to reduce the costs of producing, using, and retiring products. It engages corporations in discovering and curing problems, all of which eventually would cost the corporation's bottom line and future. This nontraditional view of how to cut costs and save money may be the greatest opportunity for enhancing competitive positions in today's complex world of intense competition.

Economic structures are always critical factors for achieving enduring success. SBD activities improve operating costs by:
- Reducing wastes and residuals
- Enhancing resource utilization rates and efficiencies
- Making process capabilities leaner and more effective
- Developing new products and processes with fewer inherent difficulties

- Linking the enterprise to improve efficiency and effectiveness
- Avoiding future costs associated with remediation, liabilities, and insurance.

There are many other costs that can be reduced or eliminated and result in gains across the social, economic, environmental, and business dimensions.

Sustainability rating and tracking of global corporations

Socially responsible investing (SRI) is a recent trend among larger investment organizations that desire better-than-average returns from socially responsible investments. Fund managers and other fiduciaries assess the underlying quality of the corporations in their investment portfolios using social, economic, and environmental performance criteria. Studies have shown that there is a positive correlation between stock appreciation and social, economic, and environmental performance. It is a function of corporate leadership and the capability of the organization to manage complexity and lead change. Excellence in sustainability often translates into extraordinary strengths in managing business strategies and operations.

Innovest Strategic Value Advisors (Innovest) is a leading research firm focusing on the environmental and social performance of major corporations around the world. It was founded in 1995 and is headquartered in New York with offices in London, Paris, and Toronto. It produces reports on more than 1,700 global companies providing clients with insight into the quality of these companies' management, environmental and stock performance, risks, and related topics. Innovest prepares two main reports:[45]

- *EcoValue'21 Rating (EV'21)*   EV'21 provides a comparative rating of the corporation with others in their sector and assesses environmental and management performance. Assessment categories include environmental strategy and management, risk factors, eco-efficiency initiatives, strategic profit opportunities, and contingent liabilities.
- *Intangible Value Assessment Rating (IVA)*   IVA provides a comparative rating of the corporation with others in its sector and assesses social performance. Assessment categories include social strategy and policy, products and services, supply chain, international, stakeholder capital, and human development capital.

Innovest uses Product Stewardship, LCA, social impact assessment, corporate governance, stakeholder relations, and other criteria in making its determinations. Its methods and the reports it produces have a profound effect on the rating of corporations and how potential investors perceive the value of the corporations and the opportunities and risks that lie in their future.

The Dow Jones Sustainability Group Index (DJSGI) ranks and tracks the leading SBD corporations in the Dow Jones Group Index to provide investors and other related parties with an independent, comprehensive, and transparent measurement of sustainability performance relative to peers and competitors. DJSGI is based on the Corporate Sustainability Assessment (SCA) of SAM Research that is validated by PwC.[46] Corporations are assessed and selected based on their "triple bottom line," corporate citizenship, and the opportunities and risks associated with social, economic, and environmental performance. Criteria include corporate governance, customer relationship management, stakeholder engagement, investor relations, strategic planning, risk and crisis management, environmental reporting, environmental performance, corporate citizenship, human capital development, knowledge management, standards for suppliers, and other industry-specific measures.

The DJSGI consists of two main components:[47]

- *Dow Jones Sustainability Group Index World (DJSI World)*   DJSI World includes 300 companies selected from the top 10 percent of the leading corporations ranked in terms of SBD. It evaluates corporate governance, codes of conduct, environmental policies and reporting, attraction and retention, and stakeholder engagement.
- *Dow Jones STOXX Sustainability Index (DJSTOXX)*   DJSTOXX includes 151 companies selected from the top 20 percent of the Dow Jones STOXX600 index.

Other indexes include the Financial Times Stock Exchange Index series (FTSE4Good) and the Ethibel Sustainability Index (Ethibel). FTSE4Good is an index of the FTSE Group, which is an independent company formed as a joint venture of the *Financial Times* and the London Stock Exchange.[48] It uses criteria relating to sustainability, corporate citizenship, stakeholder relations, and human rights. Ethibel is a European-based index dedicated to advancing socially responsible investing.[49]

Investors and portfolio managers are paying increasing attention to such indexes. The indexes provide evidence that certain corporations are sound investments with low risk of having undiscovered problems. Likewise, customers and stakeholders chart corporations using the indexes to provide indications of how well they are being managed.

Even for those corporations that believe that social responsibility is not the duty of business executives, there are lessons to be learned. Leading edge corporations are assuming responsibilities for their actions and are achieving significant outcomes. People are seeking information about the quality of management and corporate performance. They are using the indexes like DJSI World to help them make decisions to buy stocks, purchase products, partner with the corporation, and/or to challenge the suitability of operations and management.

Summary

Business integration and leading change are two of the most important perspectives of strategic management. They necessitate a comprehensive framework for ensuring inclusiveness and innovativeness throughout the whole enterprise. Enterprise thinking provides a strategic framework for integrating the external dimensions from cradle-to-grave with the internal dimensions and resources. It focuses on the future in the full context of the business environment. Enterprise thinking includes assessing and developing strategic perspectives on global enterprise management, from the corporate level through the strategic management level to the product delivery level.

One of the most important means for obtaining an integrated view is the EMM. It involves a fully integrated framework for understanding opportunities and challenges and for inventing the sustainable future. EMM presents a holistic, multidimensional view of the business environment and facilitates a descriptive, analytical, and structural understanding of the needs, opportunities, challenges, requirements, specifications, and the flow of the new product development process. The EMM encompasses customers, stakeholders, supply networks, related industries, infrastructure, and competition.

The overarching goal of SBD is the creation of value, and the value proposition is a powerful mechanism for making strategic decisions, formulating strategies, and implementing action plans. The value proposition provides a comprehensive view of what the corporation delivers to its customers and constituents, both good and bad. Most professionals and managers operate according to the simplified version of performance (ΣBenefits) to price (ΣInvestments or ΣCosts) that holds that value is improved by increasing performance, or decreasing price, or both. Corporations pursuing SBD, however, know that enhancing the benefits, both the tangible and intangible ones, and reducing the negatives is what improves value.

The "Circle for inventing the future" is a high-level process of exploring the business environment for innovative ways to enrich the opportunities to lead change. It involves strategic analysis of the business environment and of the core strengths and weaknesses of the corporation. Based on the understanding gained, senior management then selects or reaffirms the vision, values, principles, objectives, and grand strategy of the enterprise. The goal is to invent a new future through innovative strategies and actions.

Enterprise thinking and leading change require expanding management approaches from just thinking about customers, markets, and competitors to more elegant constructs which examine all of the implications and impacts of business decisions to provide more balanced solutions for all customers, stakeholders, and related constituents. This kind of strategic integration produces objectives, strategies, and principles that are based on the full range of market, economic, technical, societal, and environmental, health, and safety considerations. It requires problem-solving and decision-making to be based on ethical, social, political, economic, legal, environmental, technological, and market perspectives.

Linking inclusiveness in business strategies with innovativeness through technological and product innovation is the critical step in improving technologies, products, and processes for meeting the expectations of the twenty-first century. Business leaders can differentiate their corporations, technologies, brands, products, and processes by offering balanced solutions to stakeholders and customers alike. In a world of high-quality, commodity-like products and services, the critical strategic management aspects are:

- *Enterprise thinking and business integration*
  - Understanding the global landscape
  - Discerning opportunities and challenges
  - Formulating and implementing strategies and action plans
  - Building capabilities and leadership
  - Integrating external and internal dimensions into an enterprise management system.
- *Strategic thinking and leading change*
  - Understanding the need for change
  - Creating new technologies, products, processes, and solutions
  - Developing new means and mechanisms for change
  - Leading change through innovation and entrepreneurship
  - Creating new paradigms.

These elements of strategic management for SBD are explored in subsequent chapters. SBD engages corporations in the quest for significant improvements and even radical changes in performance that benefit the market situation, customer needs and wants, stakeholder mandates and expectations, competitive advantages, core capabilities, core technologies, development capabilities, organizational skills and knowledge, and strategic position. The strategic logic is to improve the business environment and the prospects of the corporation. How SBD can do this is self-evident to some and impossible to articulate to others. Many scholars believe that businesses are social institutions and as such have broad responsibilities to ensure the health, safety and well-being of humankind and the natural world. Others believe that the roles and responsibilities of corporations are narrow and should focus only on maximizing shareholder wealth. The debates will go on.

During a speech at the Society for Organizational Learning's Sustainability Consortium on December 2, 2003, George David, Chairman and CEO of United Technologies Corporation (UTC), articulated a succinct message of the strategic logic of SBD (UTC has a number one ranking in the DJSI):[50]

There were 11 companies in the Dow Jones Industrial Average in 1896 when it was formed. More than a century later, one remains. Over the last 10 years alone, 211 companies have merged or otherwise left the Fortune 500. The goal of organizations in the first instance is survival and beyond this, growth and prosperity. We achieve this in countless ways, and the short-term profitability may not be one of them. The greatest force in the longest term is undoubtedly sustainability . . .

I'd like to leave you with three conclusions. First is that sustainability is broad scoped and appropriately so . . . The second conclusion is that best sustainability efforts, like everything else in human endeavor, are those coming from marketplaces not mandates . . . Third is that companies worldwide are getting started with sustainability and future gains are huge . . . It is UTC's firm goal always to be at the top of sustainability rankings and judgments.

The strategic logic for SBD also includes self-preservation. It is simply about *business*, achieving excellence and long-term success, about *development*, creating innovative solutions for the future that provide total satisfaction, and about *sustainable success*, creating value for all, mitigating risks, and obtaining truly distinctive competitive advantages through integration, innovation, and leadership. SBD focuses on achieving outstanding performance across the board.

Supplementary material

Learning objectives

Chapter 2 has the following learning objectives that are intended to guide and support students and practitioners:
- Understanding the meaning of enterprise and enterprise thinking and management, SBD, and its underlying principles.

- Appreciating how the corporation and its enterprise contribute to the business environment and the broader social and natural worlds.
- Exploring the underpinnings of the embedded management systems of sustainable enterprise management.
- Understanding how the EMM facilitates adapting SBD.
- Exploring the value proposition and how it contributes to developing strategic direction.
- Understanding the strategic process for inventing the future and developing SBD objectives.
- Examining the strategic logic of SBD and why global corporations are transiting or transforming their management constructs.
- Linking SBD to mainstream leadership and management.

Research questions

The following are questions related to SBD in order to facilitate learning and ongoing discussion and analysis of the main topics covered in the chapter:

- How do global corporations define the scope of their extended enterprises?
- What are the explicit and implicit roles and responsibilities of executives and senior management in global corporations that depend on extensive contributions of external supply networks, partners, and allies?
- What should be included in the management constructs related to SBD frameworks for global corporations?
- What are the critical dimensions of the EMM that global corporations should include in the scope of their business models?
- How do executives and strategic management select the right management constructs and frameworks for understanding the business environment and determining strategic direction?
- What are the critical elements of the value proposition? Do large corporations actually use the value proposition in decision-making?
- How do executives and senior management select the proper objectives for the corporations?
- What are the short-term benefits and long-term rewards of SBD?

NOTES

1. Gary Hamel, *Leading the Revolution* (Boston, MA: Harvard Business School Press, 2002), p. 13.

2. Selling the product(s) was the prime focus. Only during the latter part of the twentieth century did marketing become the more important perspective in dealing with customers. Read Theodore Levitt's famous *Harvard Business Review* article, "Marketing myopia," *Harvard Business Review on Management*, July–August, 1960, p. 176.

3. Earll Murman, Thomas Allen, Kirkor Bozdogan, Joel Cutcher-Gershenfeld, Hugh McManus, Deborah Nightingale, Eric Rebentisch, Tom Shields, Fred Stahl, Myles Walton, Joyce Warmkessel, Stanley Weiss, and Shelia Widnall, *Lean Enterprise Value: Insights from MIT's Lean Aerospace Initiative* (New York: Palgrave, 2002), p. 3.

4. Ralph Whittle and Conrad Myrick, *Enterprise Business Architecture* (Boca Raton, FL: Auerbach/CRC Press LLC, 2005), p. 68.

5. *Ibid.*

6. Beth Gold-Bernstein and William Ruh, *Enterprise Integration: The Essential Guide to Integration Solutions* (Boston, MA: Addison-Wesley, 2005), p. 65.

7. Medard Gabel and Henry Bruner, *Global Inc.: An Atlas of the Multinational Corporation* (New York: The New Press, 2003), p. 2.

8. *Ibid.*

9. Stefano Tonchia and Andrea Tramontano, *Process Management for the Extended Enterprise* (Berlin: Springer-Verlag, 2004), p. 64.

10. Peter Senge, *The Fifth Discipline: The Art and Practice of the Learning Organization* (New York: Currency/Doubleday, 1990), p. 7.

11. Daryl Conner, *Leading at the Edge of Chaos: How to Create the Nimble Organization* (New York: John Wiley, 1998), p. 13.

12. *Ibid.*

13. David L. Rainey, *Product Innovation: Leading Change through Integrated Product Development* (Cambridge: Cambridge University Press, 2005), pp. 53–64. This section is a derivative of chapter 2 in the author's book.

14. Michael Porter, *Competitive Advantage: Creating and Sustaining Superior Performance* (New York: Free Press, 1985), pp. 33–61. Porter's value system includes suppliers, the firm's value chain, the distribution channel, and the buyers. His generic value chain depicted inbound logistics, operations, outbound logistics, marketing and sales, and service as the primary internal activities. The primary dimensions of the EMM are essentially the same construct as Porter's model.

15. European Union Directive 2002/95 on the Restriction of Use of Certain Hazardous Substances in Electrical and Electronic Equipment, *OJL* 19 (January 27, 2003).

16. Office of Advanced Automotive Technologies (OAAT), Office of Transportation Technologies, Office of Energy Efficiency and Renewable Energy, US Department of Energy, "Government and Industry: Partnering for Success, February 1998." OAAT provides two-thirds of the funding for the development of new technologies. The results have been mixed, but the program indicates that companies have an interest in working together to solve common problems, especially ones that impact the social and economic arenas.

17. Peter Drucker, *Management Tasks, Responsibilities, Practices* (New York: Harper & Row, 1973), pp. 43–46.

18. *Ibid.* Drucker suggested that the optimizing approach should focus on effectiveness. It focuses on opportunities to produce revenues, to create markets, and to change the economic characteristics.

19. *Ibid.*, p. 45.
20. Lawrence Susskind and Jeffrey Cruikshank, *Breaking the Impasse* (New York: Basic Books, 1987), p. 21. Their four characteristics are similar to the four characteristics discussed in this book.
21. *Ibid.*
22. *Ibid.*, p. 31.
23. *Ibid.*, p. 33.
24. Rachael Carson, *Silent Spring* (Boston, MA: Houghton-Mifflin, 1962).
25. Richard Lewis, Jr., *Hazardous Chemical Desk Reference*, 2nd edn. (New York: Van Nostrand Reinhold, 1991), p. 966.
26. The intent of the discussion is not to cover the Love Canal story but to examine how saving costs can translate into a very expensive reality. Hooker Chemical used the remains of an unfinished canal begun by William Love in the 1890s as a disposal site for its hazardous wastes (1946–1953). The site was later used for a school and surrounding housing, but in the mid-1970s health problems led to the closure of the school and the buyout of the residents. Hooker Chemical ultimately paid out hundreds of million dollars its fees and remedies.
27. *Intel Global Citizenship Report*, 2001, p. 5. The comments were made by Craig Barrett, CEO, as part of question and answer sessions.
28. World Business Council for Sustainable Development, "The Business Case for Sustainable Development: Making a Difference toward the Johannesburg Summit 2002 and Beyond," 2002, p. 7.
29. The Global Reporting Initiative (GRI) (2002), *2002 Sustainability Reporting Guidelines*, p. 38.
30. Sven-Olof Ryding, *Environmental Management Handbook: The Holistic Approach – from Problems to Strategies* (Amsterdam: IOS Press, 1992), pp. 528–529. The sixteen principles are: corporate priority setting; integrated management; processes for improvement; employee education; prior assessment of risk; products and services; customer advise; facilities and operations; research; precautionary approaches; contractors and suppliers; emergency preparedness; transfer of technology; contributions to the common effort; openness to concerns; compliance and reporting. Whereas the principles listed would not all be viewed as such today, they did form the basis for thinking about codes of conduct for SBD.
31. www.un.org/Depts/ptd/global.htm.
32. *The Global Compact: Report on Progress and Activities*, Global Compact Office, UN, July 2002, p. 32.
33. *European Governance: A White Paper* Brussels: Commission of the European Union (2001).
34. Robert Kaplan and David Norton, *The Balanced Scorecard: Translating Strategy into Action* (Boston, MA: Harvard Business School Press, 1996), p. 9. The Balanced Scorecard is perfect fit for new product development (NPD). Most organizations focus on multiple objectives during the NPD process. Financial goals are important, but there are many other reasons why new products have to be developed. Moreover, the realization of financial goals is often the result of satisfying customers and stakeholders.
35. Thomas Davenport and Gilbert Probst, *Knowledge Management Case Book*, 2nd edn. (Munich: John Wiley, 2002), p. 6.

36. PriceWaterhouseCoopers, *2002 Sustainability Report*, August 2002, p. 2.

37. *Ibid.*, p. 6.

38. *Ibid.*, p. 7.

39. *UNEP Report on the Automobile Industry as a Partner for Sustainable Development* (Boston: Beacon Press, 2002), back cover.

40. *KPMG International Survey of Corporate Sustainability Reporting 2002* (Amsterdam: KPMG Global Sustainability Services, 2002), p. 6.

41. *Ibid.*

42. Alex Berenson, "For Merck chief, credibility at the capitol," *New York Times*, November 19, 2004, www.nytimes.com/2004/11/19/business/19merck.html.

43. Kevin McCoy, "Merck faces first hearing on Vioxx as lawsuits mount," *USA Today*, November 17, 2004, www.usatoday.com/money/industries/health/drugs/2004-11-17-merck-vioxx-hearing.

44. This statement is a derivative of the definition used in the World Commission on Environment and Development (WCED) for the General Assembly of the United Nations, *Our Common Future* (The Brundtland Report) (Oxford: Oxford University Press, 1987).

45. www.innovestgroup.com.

46. www.sustainability-indexes.com/htmle/assessment/overview.html.

47. www.sustainability-index.com.

48. www.FTSE4good.com.

49. www.ethibel.org. Ethibel is an independent advisory and research organization for SRI.

50. Remarks of George David, Society for Organizational Learning's Sustainability Consortium Luncheon, East Hartford, CT, December 2, 2003, p. 3.

REFERENCES

Carson, Rachael (1962) *Silent Spring*. Boston, MA: Houghton-Mifflin

Commission of the European Union (2001) *European Governance: A White Paper*. Brussels

Conner, Daryl (1998) *Leading at the Edge of Chaos: How to Create the Nimble Organization*. New York: John Wiley

Davenport, Thomas and Gilbert Probst (2002) *Knowledge Management Case Book*, 2nd edn. Munich: John Wiley

Drucker, Peter (1973) *Management Tasks, Responsibilities, Practices*. New York: Harper & Row

European Governance: A White Paper (2001). Brussels: Commission of the European Union

Gabel, Medard and Henry Bruner (2003) *Global, Inc.: An Atlas of the Multinational Corporation*. New York: The New Press

The Global Compact: Report on Progress and Activities (2002). Global Compact Office, UN, July

The Global Reporting Initiative (GRI) (2002) *2002 Sustainability Reporting Guidelines*

Gold-Bernstein, Beth and William Ruh (2005) *Enterprise Integration: The Essential Guide to Integration Solutions*. Boston, MA: Addison-Wesley

Hamel, Gary (2002) *Leading the Revolution*. Boston, MA: Harvard Business School Press

Kaplan, Robert and David Norton (1996) *The Balanced Scorecard: Translating Strategy into Action*. Boston, MA: Harvard Business School Press

KPMG (2002) *KPMG International Survey of Corporate Sustainability Reporting 2002*. Amsterdam: KPMG Global Sustainability Services

Levitt, Theodore (1960) "Marketing myopia," *Harvard Business Review on Management*, July–August

Lewis, Jr., Richard (1991) *Hazardous Chemical Desk Reference*, 2nd edn. New York: Van Nostrand Reinhold

Murman, Earll, Thomas Allen, Kirkor Bozdogan, Joel Cutner-Gershenfeld, Hugh McManus, Deborah Nightingale, Eric Rebentisch, Tom Shields, Fred Stahl, Myles Walton, Joyce Warmkessel, Stanley Weiss, and Shelia Widnall (2002) *Lean Enterprise Value: Insights from MIT's Lean Aerospace Initiative*. New York: Palgrave

Porter, Michael (1985) *Competitive Advantage: Creating and Sustaining Superior Performance*. New York: Free Press

Rainey, David L. (2005) *Product Innovation: Leading Change through Integrated Product Development*. Cambridge: Cambridge University Press

Ryding, Sven-Olof (1992) *Environmental Management Handbook: The Holistic Approach – From Problems to Strategies*. Amsterdam: IOS Press

Senge, Peter (1999) *The Fifth Discipline: The Art and Practice of the Learning Organization*. New York: Currency/Doubleday

Susskind, Lawrence and Jeffrey Cruikshank (1987) *Breaking the Impasse*. New York: Basic Books

Tonchia, Stefano and Andrea Tramontano (2004) *Process Management for the Extended Enterprise*. Berlin: Springer-Verlag

UNEP (2002) *UNEP Report on the Automobile Industry as a Partner for Sustainable Development*. Boston, MA: Beacon Press

Whittle, Ralph and Conrad Myrick (2005) *Enterprise Business Architecture*. Boca Raton, FL: Auerbach/CRC Press LLC

World Commission on Environment and Development (WCED) for the General Assembly of the United Nations (1987) *Our Common Future: The Brundtland Report*. Oxford: Oxford University Press

3 Crafting sustainable business strategies and solutions

Introduction

Understanding the business environment and formulating and implementing strategies for sustainable success are two of the most critical responsibilities of corporate management and strategic leadership. Regardless of the corporation's strategic position, its technologies and products, the forces of change in the global business environment require that a corporation has to continuously make dramatic improvements in order to stay on the leading edge. The rapidly changing life cycle of technologies and products suggests that maturity and decline are inevitable and that reinventing the corporation and its product portfolios and capabilities is an ongoing process. Even the most powerful strategic positions and competitive advantages erode over time.

Strategic leadership must integrate enterprise thinking and SBD throughout the corporation. Corporate leaders have to weave them into the decision-making processes. Strategic leadership involves making decisions about space (positions and movements), time (the present and future), mass (capabilities, resources, and money), and energy (knowledge, learning, and action). It must be dynamic and focused on the future "space–time" dimensions and the corporation's movements across those dimensions. Strategic management must integrate people, capabilities, resources, and relationships across the entire enterprise and all it touches. It must assure that the business constructs are analyzed, selected, and adapted sufficiently in advance to meet the needs of the future and address the challenges of the changing business landscape.

The process of crafting sustainable business strategies involves making judgments about the future business environment and shaping a new reality of five, ten, or even twenty years into the future. Corporations must understand the pathways to those futures and envision the necessary solutions, initiatives, programs, and actions to invent them.

SBD as a management construct includes a set of strategic initiatives of short-term programs for improving existing technologies, products, and processes and long-term programs for inventing the future. As one might guess, such strategic initiatives are based on technological and product innovations and related development strategies. But innovation is difficult to dictate. It springs from dedicated and enthusiastic people applying their imagination, creativity, productivity, and agility to discover new ways of thinking and solving problems. Indeed, one of the most powerful aspects of SBD is that the solution matrix is determined by understanding and facilitating the future instead of just solving existing or past problems. This concept is a radical change from the early days of environmental management or even traditional strategic management.

Figure 3.1 shows a general schematic of the external forces and their strategic implications for the corporation.

The framework depicted in Figure 3.1 provides an overview of the strategic implications of the global business context and, though entitled "simplified," shows how complicated the strategic decision-making process really is. The business environment is the context, and corporations determine their business strategies by analyzing the driving forces within that context – in particular, their effects on the near-term and long-term prospects for change

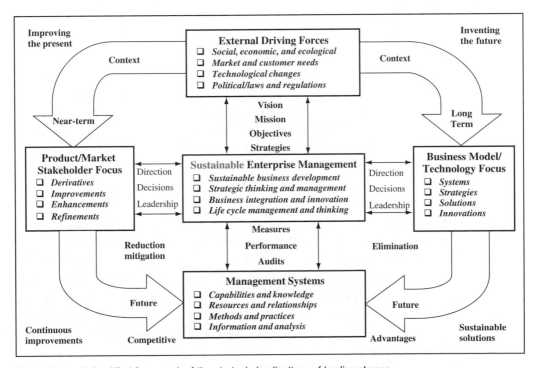

Figure 3.1   A simplified framework of the strategic implications of leading change

and improvements. Corporations must develop both short-term and long-term programs that involve, respectively, continuous improvements and sustainable solutions.

Determining the framework for analyzing the business environment is a significant decision that has to be made at the corporate management level. It includes defining the scope of the analysis and establishing the time horizon. It is impossible to establish a generalized or prescriptive approach for doing this since a primary premise of SBD is that the scope and time horizon should be as broad as possible. The simple answer is to say that enterprise and LCT and the related management approaches should be used in order to understand the effects and impacts of the enterprise on a global basis and its technologies, products, and processes on a cradle-to-grave basis.

The EMM, as defined in chapter 2, provides an overarching construct for strategic direction, business integration, innovation, leadership, and decision-making. The model facilitates and supports management decision-making at the strategic and operating levels of the corporation, including the product delivery systems, functional areas, and support mechanisms. It provides guidance and establishes metrics for the effective and responsible formulation and implementation of strategies and action plans.

Executive leadership formulates the corporate strategies that respond to the external driving forces and reflect the principles of SBD. The two main categories of strategic positioning are product/market and stakeholder strategies for improving the near-term business prospects and business model/technology strategies for capturing long-term opportunities. While there is some overlap, the former concentrates on improving the core strategic position of the corporation by exploiting capabilities, resources, products, and processes. The latter concentrates on creating new opportunities and capabilities to reinvent the corporation and improve its long-term strategic position.

The product/market and stakeholder strategy formulation and implementation are discussed in chapter 8. These methods typically enhance the positive aspects and reduce the negative implications and impacts. Gains should be robust, representing permanent changes to the operating systems that advance core capabilities and the knowledge base of the corporation. Improved methods and practices often translate into better strategic positions and/or competitive advantages for the corporation and its strategic relationships. The critical elements for making such improvements are information, strategic analysis, and continuous improvement initiatives.

Business model/technology approaches (systems and technology development) are discussed in chapter 7. They often result in dramatic, if not radical, changes that eliminate negative implications and impacts. Sustainable solutions affect the entire fabric of the corporation and provide new competitive advantages. The enterprise becomes richer and more capable of achieving even higher levels of improvements. It can redeploy resources and assets or dispose of them in an orderly fashion. New capabilities, approaches, methods, and practices create new opportunities and realities.

This chapter examines the identification, selection, planning, and integration of SBD strategies and initiatives. The discussion examines the roles of strategic thinking, SBD, innovation management, and life cycle management. The chapter includes the following sections:

- Defining the linkages between analytical models and business models
- Formulating strategies at intersections of space, time, mass, and energy
- Establishing high-level performance measures for decision-making.

The linkages between analytical models and business models

Creating a conceptual framework for strategic analysis and systems integration

Opportunities to achieve superior outcomes derive from enterprise and strategic thinking, visionary leadership, a solid understanding of the global business environment, knowledge of the internal organization, innovation, and integration, and insights and creativity. Figure 3.2 is a simplified model of a conceptual framework for determining the strategic perspective of the corporation, formulating and implementing strategies, developing the management systems, enhancing the corporation's organizational structure and governance, and assuring that solutions are sustainable.

Strategic management is the "art and science" of leading change and transforming a corporation seamlessly into the architecture of its own vision of the future. It is a complex process with many variables. Strategic management ensures ongoing improvements and constructive changes are aimed at exceeding expectations and outpacing the demands and challenges of the future business environment.

The strategic management process is an ongoing dynamic wherein corporate leaders formulate, implement, manage, and evaluate the expectations and outcomes that continuously affect the strategic position and direction of the corporation. It is a high-level responsibility of management, especially senior executives. Their ultimate responsibility is to ensure that the future is brighter than the present. The strategic management process incorporates the

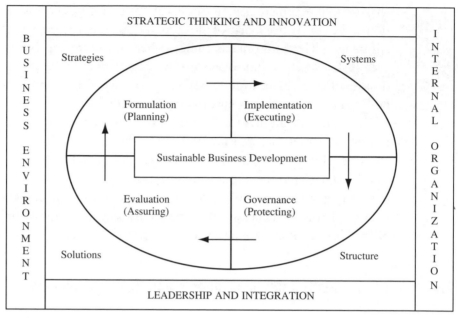

Figure 3.2   The four main elements of the strategic management process

analysis of the business environment, an evaluation of the prevailing strategies and strategic positions, the formulation and implementation of revised and new strategies, the development of initiatives and programs, and the governance of the corporation and its management systems.

The analysis of the business environment is often complex and fraught with many challenges and unforeseen difficulties. It requires comprehensive and ongoing efforts to appreciate the opportunities and requirements of the markets, customers, stakeholders, and all of the other constituencies. Strategic analysis requires computational models for obtaining insights and understanding and for selecting the most appropriate business strategies. LCT and management help corporations in understanding the business environment and determining new solutions for an improved future. The tools and techniques for assessing the business environment and discovering those solutions, especially LCA, are covered in part II.

Strategy formulation is based on the strategic assessment of the business environment and the existing capabilities and strategies of the corporation. Strategy formulation can be managed by a relatively small number of key people in the organization at the highest levels. Support professionals schooled in strategic planning provide the quantitative and qualitative analysis and strategic insights to define and articulate the strategic positions and movements. Examination of prevailing strategies is an ongoing process. While it is difficult to prescribe how often corporations should change their corporate strategies, the dynamics of the global business environment necessitate continuous reinvigoration that may be evolutionary or even revolutionary. Strategies that are based on SBD are more complex and broader than the generic strategies of a decade ago. The essential under-pinnings involve the balance necessary to achieve exceptional results in the present, to position the corporation for obtaining even better outcomes in the future, and to sustain the success of the corporation over an extended time horizon. SBD involves theoretical, practical, strategic, and analytical approaches in order to obtain significant positions and outcomes in the future without sacrificing near-term business performance or achievements.

Strategy implementation is often the least sophisticated element of strategic management. It usually takes the entire organization to execute corporate and business strategies. Historically, most managers and professionals in large corporations were not sufficiently schooled in strategic management to effectively lead the implementation of the strategies. The trend over the 1990s toward more sophisticated management systems has reduced the negative implications of this lack of strategic management training; many systems now facilitate strategy implementation. These points are examined in more detail in the next section.

Governance is a topic of growing importance. It traditionally involved management control, which meant ensuring compliance with laws and regulations, having control mechanisms, and managing the proper implementation of strategic initiatives. But governance is truly a much more powerful perspective on leading and managing change to achieve positive outcomes. It means that senior management must ensure that management systems are functioning properly, that all compliance requirements are understood and met, and that business units and product delivery systems are appropriate and effective. Governance means managing change and directing integration and innovation. It also includes the Board of Directors' and corporate officers' fulfillment of their fiduciary responsibilities to protect intellectual capital, corporate assets, and the interests of share-holders, society, customers, stakeholders, employees, partners, and all constituents. It means that the structure of the corporation – in particular, its high-level management – is sufficient for managing all potential outcomes, whether they are normal expectations or the most unlikely scenarios. Clearly, specific business situations and the culture, capabilities, and resources of the organization determine a corporation's governance.

Achieving effective governance is a continuous and increasingly difficult challenge. While it is relatively easy to define what the board of directors and senior management should be responsible for in the context of the corporation, it is another thing entirely to spell out precise rules and criteria for the entire enterprise. This is a huge challenge in the face of unexpected events and situations. Rigorous policies and procedures are becoming increasingly hard to define and develop and are even more challenging to implement. Such approaches may have worked adequately when the rate of change in the business environment was less rapid and the trends were more predictable. Today, flexibility in theory and practice is essential.

Governance includes self-directed approaches in which the participants set the rules and guidelines of their specific area of responsibilities and perform in accordance with overall corporate directives. The actual specifications depend on the nature of the business and the vision and mission of the corporation. If the demands are modest and the inherent risks are low, a more open-ended approach may provide the flexibility necessary to generate creative solutions to the challenges of the business environment. Conversely, if the situation is fraught with uncertainties and high risks, the approach may have to be prescribed with greater specificity.

Evaluation is the pivotal link that ties strategies and actions together in a systematic fashion. Evaluation is the ongoing examination of outcomes and business performance from the start of the strategic management process to the execution of initiatives and back to the beginning. It ensures that objectives and targets are achieved and highlights what adjustments have to be made.

Performance evaluation includes an assessment of the organization's performance against the needs and wants of customers and stakeholders and their expectations. The purpose is to reduce the variability within the process and to serve as an integrating mechanism for ensuring that there is consistency, balance, flexibility, and control. Performance evaluation needs to be dynamic and flexible in order to respond to changing business conditions. It should reflect the realities of the various participants. The following are its primary intended purposes:

- Guiding the strategic management process to ensure success, to keep pace with changing conditions and requirements, and facilitate decision-making
- Mapping developments with respect to customers' and stakeholders' expectations
- Benchmarking performance with respect to competitors, peers, or others in related areas.

Performance management is a process of assessing – both qualitatively and quantitatively – the organization's achievements with respect to the plans and objectives. An effective performance management process allows management to share the information with the participants and to initiate corrective actions expeditiously. Performance management is designed to provide a consistent format for an authoritative review of performance; the output is designed to enable the organization to determine performance and how to take corrective actions to get on track. Performance management is also concerned with the prevention, detection, and correction of the difficulties and problems that adversely affect the success of the corporation.

A framework for connecting analytical models with strategic thinking and management

Strategic management depends on a clear understanding of the distinction between the analytical models that explain what is happening in space and time and the business models that provide the means and mechanisms for effecting change and outcomes. The two broad types of models are inextricably linked and feed each other. The analytical models form the foundation for strategic thinking and policy formulation. The business models provide frameworks for helping management, professionals, and practitioners create real outcomes from conceptual models. The realities of implementation, governance, and evaluation then feed important information back to the analytical models to help further hone management's understanding of its strategies. Ongoing iterations continue to improve and correct the models.

Figure 3.3 portrays how the four elements of strategy development fit within the analytical and business models. The formulation of strategies is based on the conceptual and analytical methods used to discover and assess opportunities. Strategic formulation responds to context (the business environment) and crafts constructs (models) to create plausible and effective solutions (strategies). Implementation translates strategies into outcomes.

Analytical models: context, capabilities, constructs, and computations

Context

The question of **context** plagued the study of management for most of the twentieth century. Reductionism was the prevailing approach; it focused on narrowly defined parts of the business environment and took only a very

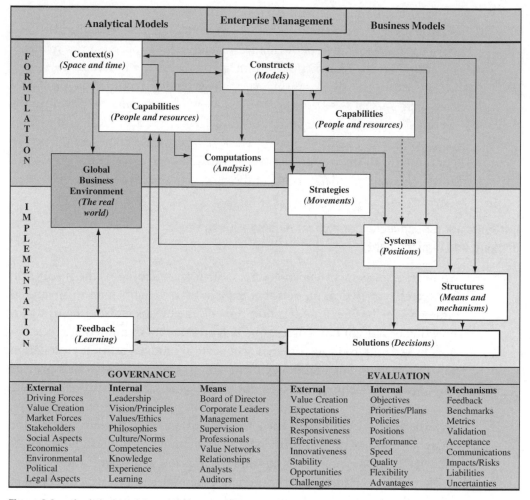

Figure 3.3   Analytical models and business models

limited view of external forces and other business entities. The basic philosophy was to facilitate the understanding of the essential few rather than the broader, more complicated, and multifaceted whole.

This approach defined the business environment in a way that eliminated many of the phenomena not directly related to the principal – usually the known – concerns. For example, industry analysis often focused on customers, markets, suppliers, and the competition – all factors that are critical for understanding and analyzing the economic and market forces. However, this limited view of the real world downplays other key considerations such as stakeholder perspectives, social issues, and environmental impacts.

Despite the significant drawbacks and limitations of reductionism, the related methodologies generally met management expectations during the early twentieth century because the business environments were changing relatively slowly. Moreover, most markets were national or regional instead of global. Customers had limited options that were constrained by the lack of information or effective logistical systems. In many cases, it was simply too expensive to move products beyond a certain distance. For example, breweries were often limited to serving customers within several hundred km of their production facilities because of the high costs associated with the transportation of products that had a high weight/price (value) ratio. Other variables were seemingly insignificant. For instance, management often failed to comprehend the necessity of controlling waste streams as part of managing product delivery and manufacturing or to think about the disposal of the products at the end of their useful life.

The selection of the context (the scope of the business environment under consideration) is an important determinant affecting the downstream elements and management decision-making. The preferred context is the whole of the global business environment, with all of its dimensions and variables. The trend for many global corporations is to include as broad a perspective as possible so that there is a thorough understanding of reality. This is an evolutionary change from the more restrictive view that included only industry structure and analysis. That type of context worked well when most of the changes in the business environment occurred within the given industry. For example, the automobile industry and the steel industry were for most of the twentieth century characterized by well-established industry structures and operating parameters that were easy to define and understand. As new forms of competition, new technologies, material substitutes, and component alternatives came on the scene during the 1980s and 1990s, however, the business environment became more dynamic and more complicated. The context for understanding and analyzing the business environment required a multidimensional, multifaceted global context. It included customers, markets, competitors, supply networks, related industries, the technology infrastructure, and all the relevant social, economic, and environmental considerations. Many innovations and changes were driven by entities outside the normal context of the industry. Indeed, the structure of the industry often changed to include these other participants.

Historically, industries tended to change slowly, in an evolutionary manner. With the rise of globalization and the rapidity of change in technologies, however, global corporations as well as smaller, more entrepreneurial

Table 3.1. Examples of contextual changes within the automobile and the steel industries between the 1970s and the present

Effects	Technology		Markets		Competitors	
	(1970s)	(Present)	(1970s)	(Present)	(1970s)	(Present)
Automobile industry	Dominant engine	Robotics	Performance	Quality and price	Vertical	Horizontal
	Mechanical	Electronic	Mass markets	Customization	US Big Three	Global giants
	Analog	Digital	Dealer-based	Internet-based	Foreign majors	Niche players
Steel industry	Integrated mills	Mini-mills	Supply-driven	Value-driven	National giants	Global giants
	Blast furnaces	Continuous casting	Auto-makers	Fragmented	US Steel	Nucor Steel
	Basic oxygen		Construction	Specialization		NNK-Nippon

organizations are now constantly involved in changing the basis for competition. Competitive advantages are obtained through new technologies, products, and innovative ways of conducting business. For example, the Internet, digital technologies, and wireless communications have profoundly affected most traditional industries. In some cases, these technologies have changed the essence of the industry. The Internet allows consumers to obtain information about products and shop online. An individual who plans to buy an automobile can obtain the relevant product and pricing information as well as make the actual purchase directly from the supplier without human interaction. Table 3.1 highlights a few significant effects of such change within the automobile and steel industries since the 1970s.

The context must include both time and space considerations and enterprise and LCT in order to provide a comprehensive and inclusive basis for decisions. The pivotal management perspective is inclusion.

Capabilities

The internal context includes the capabilities of the organization, and how it is able to meet and exceed the demands of the business environment and execute the selected strategies for achieving sustainable solutions. The power and position of an enterprise are defined to a large extent by the capabilities and resources of the corporation and its strategic partners, alliances, and supply networks. The strengths and limitations of the entire enterprise determine what is theoretically possible, and what the strategic direction should be.

But the analysis of capabilities is not just to examine strengths and weaknesses, because such assessments focus on what is. It must also examine the relevance of the capabilities to the business environment. For example, IBM's core capabilities in mainframe computers were still very powerful in the late 1980s and early 1990s. However, changes in computing technologies and market dynamics made those strengths less important. Even if IBM had invested heavily in improving its core capabilities in the mainframe computer segment, the result would probably have been the same: declining strategic importance and financial performance. Strengths and weaknesses are meaningful only in relation to the business environment. Capabilities are important only if there are opportunities to be exploited or value to be created. Therefore, they have to be continuously reinvigorated and refined to stay ahead of the needs of the business environment. Moreover, capabilities have to be nurtured and developed on an ongoing basis.

Capabilities are the strategic assets (people and resources) that translate the objectives and strategies into realities. They are the means for crafting strategies, effecting solutions, and sustaining them in the future. The analysis of capabilities determines the probabilities of carrying out the strategies and the articulation of what is needed to enhance the strategic position. Managing capabilities and understanding their importance are dynamic requirements. Concentrating on core competencies is a static proposition that eventually leaves the organization with antiquated, ineffective attributes.

Knowledge and the capacity to learn are essential ingredients in the capability profile of a corporation. Knowledge represents the present; learning is the future. While capabilities include the physical resources, financial assets, and intellectual properties of the corporation, the essence of a corporation's or enterprise's capabilities lies within its people. It is the innovative abilities that transform the core capabilities of the present into superior positions in the future.

Constructs

Constructs are the theoretical frameworks (models) used to analyze and determine strategies, systems, structures, and solutions. The concept of a construct is relatively new. Based on knowledge and understanding, a construct is intended to be a representation of the dimensions and elements of business situations. It combines information, data, and experience with theoretical thinking about how to view the corporation in the light of its opportunities, challenges, and constraints. A construct is simply a way of articulating the dimensions of the corporation, both internal and external.

Management and practitioners use constructs to depict their view of reality and their understanding of the full scope of the enterprise in order to make better decisions and create better solutions.

Historically, the basic constructs were organizational structures depicting the hierarchy of the reporting relationships within the organization and the roles and responsibilities of each level of management. During the early part of the twentieth century most global corporations were vertically integrated. The organizational pyramid, with executive management at the top and supervisors and employees at the bottom, was the prevailing means for formulating strategies, making decisions, and executing action plans and initiatives. Such constructs were based on simple notions about the flow of activities within an organization. They prescribed the relationships and the flow of information and decisions, top to bottom. The approach was effective for conveying information and decisions downward. However, the communications mechanisms were slow and fraught with problems. The most significant weakness was the arduous and slow **feedback mechanisms** for senior management to gain insights about the implications and impacts of their decisions and actions.

The idea of developing a more direct management construct for understanding the forces impinging on a corporation gained prominence during the 1970s and 1980s. As vertical structures were replaced with horizontal ones, the necessity to map out the essential elements of the construct and explain how they related to each other became critical in analyzing the business environment and determining the need for new strategies. For instance, Michael Porter's Value System and Value Chain are constructs that played important roles in helping executives, managers, and professionals understand, assess, and manage their businesses. A comprehensive list of the most significant constructs might include thousands of analytical and business models, running the gamut from a simple two-dimensional matrix such as the conventional price–performance concepts to more sophisticated models like enterprise management. *Business models are simply management constructs that have been validated through actual use over time.* They are often generalized approaches that are broadly used by many corporations. For instance, integrated product development is a framework (model) that most leading corporations have adapted for developing new products.[1]

The pressing need to make informed and well-thought-out decisions has existed throughout history, and it has not diminished. There is always a healthy tension between having constructs that are comprehensive and thorough and having constructs that are simple and easy to understand.

The simple ones are often inadequate for truly depicting the business environment. Simplicity and ease of use dominated management thought for most of the twentieth century. However, globalization, increased technological sophistication, shortened product life cycles and other changes in the business environment have dramatically increased the need for more comprehensive models. Today, senior management cannot afford to simply make trade-offs between accuracy and timeliness. They must do both. The demands and challenges are great, but those who can exceed expectations are in a position to outperform their peers.

SBD necessitates sophisticated constructs that examine the opportunities, challenges, strategies, systems, structures, and solutions in depth. In developing or improving technologies, products, and processes, the analyses and decision-making processes have to proceed beyond the fundamentals and primary considerations and attempt to discover all facets of a situation, including the hidden defects and burdens.

Constructs lay out the framework for the analyses that are needed to discover opportunities, understand challenges, manage constraints, mitigate concerns, and reduce or eliminate impacts and consequences. Sustainable solutions are derived from constructs that encompass the dynamics of the business world and "cradle-to-grave" and LCT.

Computations

Analytical models depend on computations for understanding information and data pertaining to the selected context of the business environment. Processes typically define computations. From a strategic perspective, a computational model has to include all or most of the elements of the business environment, the enterprise, and the natural world that it is representing. The computational model should support the EMM and its subsets at the strategic management and the product delivery levels. These should be linked to the broad economic systems, environmental aspects, and the social structures of the business environment. While reductionism focused the analysis on the part, SBD, being a holistic methodology, focuses on the entire system. Determining and defining the computational model is one of the most important parts of strategic analysis and policy formulation. If the analytical model is too narrow in scope, essential parts of the system may be excluded from it. This limited analysis may result in faulty conclusions.

The initial step in defining a computational model is to determine the purpose, objectives, and criteria (benchmarks) of the analysis and how various computational models fit those requirements. Benchmarks are performance criteria derived from the principles of SBD or the best practices used by leading corporations, peers, and competitors.

The second step involves selecting the scope of the analysis and the boundaries of the system. Selecting the scope includes determining the spatial and temporal dimensions of the construct for analysis. While the choice depends on the situation and the time and resources available for conducting the analysis, the general approaches are: (1) broad in scope with limited depth to save time and money and to quickly gain insights and knowledge about the total business environment; (2) broad in scope and extensive in depth to gain a comprehensive understanding of the construct in order to solve known difficulties and discover hidden defects and burdens; (3) narrow in scope with limited depth to improve a facet of the system; or (4) narrow in scope and extensive in depth to gain a comprehensive understanding of only a part of the total system in order to make significant improvements to it. While the second choice is deemed to be the best from an overall SBD perspective, the selected approach is dependent on the prevailing strategic position, the capabilities and resources available, and the linked needs of the present and the future.

The scope of the analysis depends on the strategic objectives and purpose of the analysis. The principles of SBD would suggest a comprehensive approach, analyzing the entire system or a significant portion thereof in depth. The more traditional approach may result in a narrower scope with less depth due to the constraints of the business environment and the realities of the corporate situation. The scope can vary considerably.

The third step is to map out the process(es) and detail the elements of the computational model. Figure 3.4 offers a generalized model, depicting some of the most salient elements of process analysis.

The fourth step is to state explicitly the criteria used so that the basis of comparison between the elements of the model and the benchmarks are clearly understood. The benchmark may be a leader in the industry, the world, or the hypothetical ideal case. The choice of the benchmark depends on the objectives and the needs of the system and its constituencies. The selection of metrics is explained in more detail in chapter 11.

Strategic analysis based on enterprise thinking and life cycle management is a comprehensive framework that uses rigorous methods and techniques. The computations are based on input/output equations and process management techniques. LCT, management, and assessment fit perfectly with SBD approaches that use process management techniques as the main construct or as a subset within a system. These topics are covered in depth in chapters 9–11.

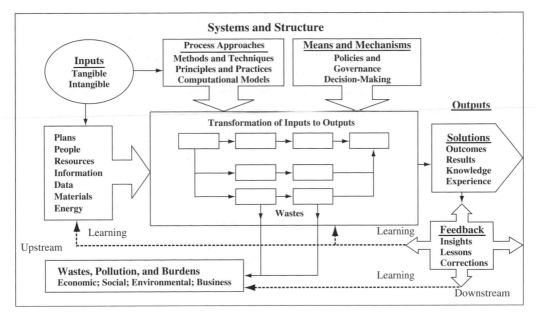

Figure 3.4   Computational framework for process analysis

Business models: strategies, systems, structure, and solutions

Strategy is one of the most pivotal constructs in business management. Kenneth Andrews defined it thus:[2]

Corporate strategy is the pattern of decisions in a company that determines and reveals its objectives, purposes, or goals, produces the principal policies and plans for achieving those goals, and defines the range of businesses the company is to pursue, the kind of economic and human organization it is or intends to be, and the nature of the economic and noneconomic contribution it intends to make to its shareholders, employees, customers, and *communities*. In an organization of any size or diversity, "corporate strategy" usually applies to the *whole enterprise* while "business strategy," less comprehensively defines the choices of product or service and market of individual businesses within the firm. Business strategy, that is, is the determination of how a company will compete in a given business and position itself among its competitors. Corporate strategy defines the businesses in which a company will compete preferably in a way that focuses resources to convert distinctive competence into competitive advantages. (Emphases added)

Andrews was one of the first scholars to articulate the meaning of corporate strategy, but his statements are still relevant today. Perhaps most importantly, Andrews makes a distinction between *business strategy*, which deals with the business units and their products and processes, and *corporate strategy* which focuses on the entire enterprise. These distinctions are often not articulated very succinctly by business scholars and professionals of today, as the concept of strategic management has blurred the differences. In most cases, the strategic management constructs explore business strategies and action plans, but corporate strategy remains fragmented, based on specific areas of interest such as acquisitions and mergers or building strategic alliances.

The inclusion of communities in the definition illustrates that corporate strategy is broader than the realm of customers, suppliers, and competitors. Scholars recognized decades ago that the context for decision-making and strategy formulation should include communities of stakeholders and other constituencies. Bernard Taylor and Keith MacMillan in their book, *Business Policy*, published in 1973, suggested the following:[3]

In the literature on planning, policy and strategy there appears to be common agreement that the environment must be monitored. Innumerable examples can be given, but most can be categorized into:
(a) Scientific and technical environment [product life cycle, etc.]
(b) Life style and life space environment
(c) Ethical, legal, and social environment
(d) Economic and political environment.

These categories also fit the concepts of SBD. The development of corporate strategy depends on how senior management interprets the needs, events, conditions, and trends in the business environment. Often these are viewed as opportunities, challenges, or even threats. The difference between an opportunity and a threat may depend on how and when the underlying implications are dealt with. Threats can be opportunities if management understands the potential effects, impacts, and consequences and takes positive actions to create solutions that are favorable to the corporation.

Management determines corporate strategy by analyzing the corporation's position and capabilities with regard to the context of its business environment. The computational models provide the logic and evidence for establishing direction and making decisions. The construct of SBD offers an integrated approach for developing a concise methodology for formulating and implementing **corporate strategy**. Corporate strategy links the theoretical and analytical world with the practical business world of implementation and achievement.

The renowned business scholar and historian, Alfred Chandler, Jr., stated that strategy precedes structure. His statement is articulated in the form of a theoretical construct:[4]

The thesis deduced from these several propositions is then that structure follows strategy and that the most complex type of structure is the result of the concatenation of several basic strategies ... This theoretical discussion can be carried a step further by asking two questions: (1) If structure does follow strategy, why should there be delay in developing the new organization needed to meet the administrative demands of the new strategy? (2) Why did the new strategy, which called for a change in structure, come in the first place?

That strategy sets the direction and that structure must be adapted to implement the strategic direction is an accepted principle of strategic management. But structure tends to be a static construct, requiring significant time and effort to change. There are delays in moving organizations from one position to another, and it takes time for people to adjust to new requirements and relationships. During the relatively slow changes of the 1960s, the construct of a vertically integrated corporation with its hierarchical organizational structure for command and control made sense and functioned reasonably well. Structure followed strategy. Change was slow, and there was time to make changes without necessarily losing competitive advantage. Also, moving slowly often allowed a corporation to avoid making inappropriate or incorrect moves.

In the fast-paced global business world of the twenty-first century, however, corporate- and business-level strategies evolve quickly and have to be implemented instantaneously. The time horizon for many opportunities, new technologies, and new products is measured in terms of months. Corporations cannot afford to waste time and effort.

The **management system** is the modern platform for translating strategies into the structure of the organization and for developing initiatives and action plans. The management system is generally a horizontal construct that relies on the capabilities of the organization to implement the strategies and to perform the work. The management system is a flexible construct that can be changed to meet the needs of the business environment; it is configured to capitalize on linkages, processes, and capabilities.

Gary Hamel in his book, *Leading the Revolution*, discusses the construct of configuration in terms of linkages between competencies, assets, and processes.[5] The horizontal construct allows management to create mechanisms to affect certain strategies, and then to reconfigure the linkages in a short time frame to affect other solutions as necessary. The management system can also be changed on an evolutionary basis and improved as new experiences and insights are realized; they are often continually adjusted as new strategies are developed and deployed. The power of a system is its relative flexibility to change related to the historical difficulties in changing organizational structure.

Strategies

The ultimate purpose of corporate and business strategies is to create value for everyone engaged in the enterprise, including stakeholders and other constituencies. Strategies based on the theories and constructs of SBD focus on finding enduring solutions for existing and future opportunities, challenges, and concerns. SBD strategies propose to eliminate difficulties and problems, to provide solutions in the present without negatively affecting the future, and to discover and exploit opportunities ahead of the competition and before they become obvious or mandated. Formulating new strategies is essential for reinventing the corporation to meet and sustain future needs. It is a response to the ongoing challenge of reaffirming the corporation's right to exist and prosper. Most importantly, sustainable corporations contribute to society, the economies they serve, and the natural world, and meet the needs and expectations of their external and internal relationships, their customers, their partners, their stakeholders, their employees, and shareholders.

Grand strategies are linked to the vision and the long-term objectives of the enterprise. They direct the corporation toward its desired future, at times even prescribing what the corporation is expected to become based on external conditions and the expectations of the business environment. While it can be argued that a corporation chooses its destiny, the evolution of the business environment and the thoughts and expectations of society, markets, customers, stakeholders, shareholders, and other constituents suggest that choices are constrained by the needs, requirements, and constraints. The changing attitudes about the use of tobacco products illustrate how such constraints can evolve. For most of the twentieth century, society tolerated smoking as an individual right to pursue one's chosen life style. However, over the 1990s, the negative effects of smoking caused public demand for laws restricting smoking to designated areas or times. The restrictions continue to become more stringent as public and political attitudes change.

The grand strategies for SBD focus on responding to opportunities and challenges to benefit the strategic position and direction of the corporation. They depend on building superior capabilities for meeting expectations, creating clean technologies and products, maximizing benefits, and minimizing problems. Grand strategies define a distinctive scheme for establishing business unit and product delivery strategies that set direction, speed, and movements, and define the required capabilities, systems, and structures.

Grand strategies are dynamic constructs that help direct the underlying business units and product delivery strategies. They prescribe the logic of the plans for growth and development and the aspirations to achieve harmony and consistency in thoughts and actions. Table 3.2 identifies some of the general categories of broad strategies based on SBD principles. The strategies listed are the main approaches that can be used to create a sustainable future and more powerful competitive advantages. These overarching, or grand, strategies tie SBD to the management of the enterprise.

The grand strategies are categorized according to the levels of the enterprise they affect and their emphasis on space, time, mass, or energy. Space refers to the position and movement of the corporation in a certain direction. Time relates to changes that occur and the speed at which they occur. Mass and energy pertains to the availability of resources and assets, and capabilities of people, especially their imagination, creativity, knowledge, inspiration, and motivation. Table 3.2 depicts distinct categories that, when combined, create an overarching strategy for SBD. The grand strategy crosses the enterprise horizontally and vertically.

In traditional terms, the grand strategy defines "the business the corporation intends to be in and the kind of economic and human organization it intends to be, along with the nature of the economic and noneconomic contributions it intends to make to its shareholders, employees, customers, and communities."[6] SBD depends on establishing the proper framework for formulating and implementing strategies and accomplishing the intended outcomes. The grand strategy, then, focuses on how to establish that framework. It must take a multidimensional approach, linking corporate-level considerations with strategic and product delivery-level considerations over space, time, mass, and energy. The grand strategies for SBD are dynamic constructs that focus on *integrating* the enterprise, *leading* change through innovation, and *transforming* and/or *moving* capabilities to meet the realities of the future.

At the corporate level, the spatial dimensions include the synergistic integration of all of the constituents into an effective system for creating value and achieving competitive advantages in the business environment. While reductionism suggested concentrating on the parts, the holistic approaches of SBD require taking the broadest view possible for strategy formulation and implementation. The temporal dimension finds corporations seeking continuous innovation, both evolutionary and revolutionary. Steady transformation of organizational capabilities is crucial for SBD, especially when it is impossible to make radical changes to the capabilities of the enterprise in a short time frame.[7]

Table 3.2. Selected overarching or grand strategies of SBD

Construct	Spatial strategies	Temporal strategies	Mass and energy strategies
Corporate management system (level)	**Synergistic networks** Providing a complete solution for all constituencies by integrating all facets of the value networks into a multidimensional force for satisfying needs and mitigating negative consequences and impacts	**Sustainable technological advantage** Using innovation and knowledge creation to initiate, develop, and implement future-focused solutions that exceed expectations and requirements and form the foundations for SBD and corporate advantage; preempting the competition and peers with innovative solutions and clean technologies	**Steady transformations** Transforming the knowledge and experiential base of the enterprise through learning; creating new capabilities, resources, and assets and building them into new, more powerful and energetic positions; providing dynamic leadership and the energy and resources for inventing a more sustainable future
Strategic management system (level)	**Systems integration** Integrating the entire system from the depths of the supply chain to the far reaches of customers and secondary markets; linking the afterlife of products and material recovery to the product delivery system	**Systematic change** Reinvigorating the SMS with new or improved clean technologies, products, and processes; leading change through innovation and integration of the value system across time to meet future needs and achieve sustained competitive advantage	**Substantial transitions** Adapting new ways of achieving positive outcomes; reinventing capabilities and resources to meet the future and not just exploiting the prevailing situation; ensuring that social, economic, and environmental factors are considered; being socially responsible
Product delivery system (level)	**Synthesis** Integrating the product delivery system with suppliers and customers to minimize disruptions and negative consequences, reduce losses, and improve effectiveness and efficiency	**Synchronization** Linking capabilities, resources, outcomes, and strategic direction with the needs and expectations of constituencies over the life cycle of products and processes Enhancing responsiveness over life cycles	**Superior satisfaction** Creating distinction and uniqueness that support viability and long-term success; satisfying constituencies with positive outcomes; providing total satisfaction to society, customers, stakeholders, employees, and shareholders

Corporate-level thinking considers the desired future of the corporation and what is required to move the enterprise towards it. However, the future is a moving target, itself a continuum of never-ending change. Moreover, getting there is not an ends–means equation. Rather, it is about vision, capabilities, achievements, and ongoing innovations and successes. The process is analogous to one's professional life. The end-point is not retirement, but the ongoing contributions and successes that are achieved through dedication, intellectual thought, learning, and hard work.

The SMS level focuses on making substantial improvements to organizational capabilities, including enhancing the ability to change. Moreover, it is where the capabilities of the organization, the needs of the business environment, and the strategic direction of the corporation converge. At this level, systems integration provides the means and mechanisms to formulate business strategies and implement action programs. Without taking the full view of the integrated system, most of the opportunities for improvements or the challenges of defects, burdens, and impacts are difficult to discover and manage. SBD, LCT, and management require system-wide assessment, development, and deployment. While improving some elements can provide some benefits, the problems and their causes often lie outside the traditional domain of the corporation, or even its suppliers and customers. Effective, enduring solutions require a holistic view of all of the inputs, outputs, and outcomes to understand all the impacts and to select the proper option for the future.

Systematic change, however, is an ongoing process of building improvements upon improvements. Its power is based on the compounding effects of learning, knowledge enhancements, reductions in wastes, and acceleration of change and improvement. On a product and process basis, Steven Wheelwright and Kim Clark's research showed that fast-cycle competitors significantly outperformed slow-cycle competitors.[8] More importantly, in a fast-paced business environment, the slow-cycle competitor became hopelessly outdated in a relatively short time and had difficulties in surviving. The compounded effects of steady, superior gains provide a basis for achieving competitive advantages and superior positions and capabilities.

The organizational capabilities have to be adaptive as well. As changes require new ways of doing things, people in the organization have to continuously reinvent themselves to become capable of providing high performance in the new realities. Organizations have to undergo substantial and ongoing transitions. This includes becoming more socially responsible and cognizant of social, economic, and environmental considerations. Substantial transitions focus on continuously adapting to the realities of the world and staying ahead of the changing business environment.

At the product delivery level, marrying products and processes to value networks is critical for the complete integration and execution of the initiatives required to move into the future. Synthesis involves connecting the product delivery system with the supply networks and customers in order to maximize linkages and minimize the disruptions and negative consequences. Synchronization means linking new product development with the strategic aims of the operating system and linking capabilities, resources, outcomes, and strategic direction with the needs and expectations of the constituencies over the life cycle of the products and processes. The goal is superior satisfaction at every level and by all constituents.

The ultimate grand strategy focuses on creating value in the present and the future. It enhances power and contributes to sustainable success. There are two main categories of primary considerations and effects: investments and transformations through valued-added processes. The former involve investing in the future of the organization and fulfilling the implicit and explicit intent of the corporation's vision and strategic direction. For example, developing new products creates powerful opportunities to enhance value creation for customers and stakeholders and to sustain the success of the organization. Transforming the value proposition revolves around the mission and the action plans and activities for achieving market and financial success.

Systems and subsystems/processes

Systems

The construct of a management system is one of the most profound developments in management theory in recent years, and provides the mechanisms for translating strategies into realities. The management system typically provides for the following standard functions: (1) policy and management commitment; (2) setting objectives and targets; (3) planning; (4) implementation; (5) measurement, evaluation and risk assessment; and (6) review and continuous improvement.[9] The management system integrates the external aspects of the business environment and the internal resources, capabilities, and processes of the organization into an effective entity. With most management system constructs, senior management establishes the policies, procedures, and practices that form the direction, guidelines, and standards for the organization and its partners.

The constructs for management systems evolved over several decades. The introduction of ISO 9000 in 1987 marked a pivotal shift toward system thinking and management[10] which is based on the prescribed flow of information, instructions, guidelines, policies, actions, and outcomes according to established **pathways**. Systems consist of processes that produce the desired outcomes in the most efficient and effective means possible, minimizing the resources consumed and maximizing the benefits derived.

Policies determine how the elements of the system are to be carried out and provide direction for decision-making. Policies also establish performance targets and the criteria for evaluation. Procedures and practices prescribe the routines for the normal flow of activities and provide guidelines for handling the basic elements of the process. While the use of formal procedures varies considerably, depending on the management philosophy and the need for flexibility, most organizations have well-defined practices that facilitate the interactions between people and the flow of work. Stringent procedures are often used to mitigate high risks. The development of inherently risky products such as pharmaceutical products, jet engines, or automobile tires usually requires more formality and control than the development of less risky products such as tissues and pencils.

The planning process identifies and delineates the upstream and downstream activities, indicating how and what the organization is going to accomplish. It includes defining the scope of programs and processes, assessing opportunities, establishing targets, and determining criteria for success, and the relevant metrics. It also includes establishing procedures for modifying the basic practices to accommodate changes in the business environment. Implementation means executing planned processes and is discussed in detail in chapters 10 and 11.

Measurement reviews and program evaluations are necessary to keep the system on track and to maintain control. Management reviews are the critical steps in processes such as NPD. Using metrics, they measure progress, facilitate decisions related to the future course of actions, and determine the need for change. In many systems, management reviews tend to be a periodic function rather than a continuous one. In certain cases, they occur at critical decision points or when a significant commitment of resources is required.

Subsystems and processes

The transition from vertical management structures to systems and subsystems in which processes flow horizontally is an imperative for making the corporation more responsive to the needs of the business environment and more adaptable to change. The system and its subsystems and processes define the necessary corporate structure, articulate the mechanisms for policy formulation and implementation, and provide ongoing assessment techniques for staying on course and improving.

Processes are management constructs used to define the flow of the activities and actions, ensure that the essential elements are included, monitor performance, identify defects, take corrective actions, and reflect on the outcomes and results. Processes are powerful constructs for managing repetitive flows where there is sufficient data and information to prescribe a desired pathway for doing the work or managing the development program.

Processes are based on theory and practice. A process construct may begin as theory and, as experience is gained, then shift to becoming more pragmatic. Similarly, process management relies on the successes of past experience and learning to better facilitate the successful implementation of programs. Process management suggests that there is a defined route to be traveled in a systematic manner. The goal is to ensure that all of the key requirements are considered and properly implemented, using effective pathways that are similar from program to program.

The four most significant advantages of process management are the following:

- Arranging the flow of activities in a logical pathway that identifies the resources, information, the responsible individuals, the authority for decision-making, protocols, and control mechanisms
- Minimizing the time and effort spent determining the courses of action and the flow of activities and elements
- Increasing the speed at which activities flow because practitioners are familiar with the work and the requirements
- Facilitating analysis of the process because the elements are arranged in a horizontal flow with well-defined inputs and outputs; this also facilitates corrective action because causality is easier to determine.

Process management forms the basis for most operations within the product delivery system because most operations tend to be repetitive. It also is essential for most NPD programs, especially for corporations that have families of related products or for incremental innovations where the new product is similar to the previous or it is related to a particular technology platform. Process management can be divided into continuous, recurring, and intermittent processes. Continuous processes are typically production, manufacturing, and various types of operations where the flow is both steady and linked. Managing the wastewater effluents from a manufacturing facility tends to be a continuous process since wastewater is usually generated an ongoing basis and it is usually difficult and costly to store large quantities to be treated periodically. Recurring processes include the simple improvement processes, NPD processes, and even waste management processes. For instance, most large automobile companies are typically engaged in developing several new products at any point in time and have ongoing requirements for replacing obsolete or older models. Intermittent processes are typically those processes in which the activities or elements and the flow from one element to the next are not directly linked or processes that require only periodic management. Disposal of solid wastes tends to be a time-dependent process requiring intermittent actions. Each element in such processes provides important ingredients to the total story, but the sequencing can vary considerably from case to case.

The typical process management scheme was depicted in figure 3.4 (p. 165). Inputs are transformed into outputs using established methods, principles, and computations. Policies and governance direct process management. Robust processes provide feedback to enhance learning.

Structure

Structure is the term used to discuss the organizational design of the corporation and the enterprise. It pertains to the capabilities and resources of the organization and how they are deployed in planning and executing strategies and action plans. Chandler stated that:[11]

> Structure can be defined as the design of the organization through which the enterprise is administered. This design, whether formally or informally defined, has two aspects. It includes, first, the lines of authority and communications between different administrative offices and officers and, second, the information and data that flows through the lines of communications and authority. Such lines and such data are essential to assure the effective coordination, appraisal, and planning so necessary in carrying out the basic goals and policies and in knitting together the total resources of the enterprise.

Chandler focused on the notion of the enterprise as the primary management level, which fits well with enterprise management methodologies. However, organization design is distinct from structure. It relates to the architecture of the relationships between the people of the organization. In his studies of General Motors, Mobil Oil, Du Pont, Sears, and others, Chandler described vertical structures where lines of authority and communications between the levels were created essentially for planning and execution. Nevertheless, the concept of aligning (or knitting together) capabilities and resources was also a key element in the structure.

Today, the design of an organization dictates how its people fit into the management system and what processes are being used to achieve the desired outcomes. The organizational designs of today focus on building core capabilities and concentrating knowledge and learning in order to achieve critical intellectual capital for meeting challenges and exceeding objectives and expectations.

The management system determines the structure by integrating people into an organizational setting where individuals, teams, and units can easily comprehend, delineate, and perform their roles and responsibilities. Structure includes how teams and other groups are organized and deployed to effectively manage and implement programs in operations, marketing, or developing new products and technologies. The construct of teams runs the gamut from colocated teams of cross-functional members to virtual teams with members who are not in physical contact with each other. Structure links the management levels and subunits within each level. The organizational structure articulates the reporting relationships and the authority and responsibilities of each management position. It is the means for translating direction into action. The organizational structure is ultimately based on the strategies and systems. Therefore, it also serves to reinforce development and performance and orchestrates changes as the business environment and strategic direction change.

Development programs usually depend on team-based organizational mechanisms that rely heavily on individual contributors from various disciplines within the organization. The team is a temporal arrangement that usually has an agenda with beginning- and end-points. However, there are numerous examples of team-based development programs where the team continues its work program after program.

The longevity of an organization structure depends on sustaining the capabilities of the people and growing new knowledge and capabilities through experience and learning. The structure provides the information flow, communications pathways, and coordination to deploy people in response to the vision and objectives of the corporation. Communication is frequently blamed for difficulties when the organization fails, but it is often the lack of integration or focus that is to blame.

Solutions

The people in the business environment (all of the customers, stakeholders, government entities, and others) want solutions, not technologies, products, or services. Corporations and their enterprise provide solutions! While products and services are often powerful means to attract and satisfy customers and stakeholders, their ability to sustain satisfaction in the longer term usually diminishes over time because what customers and stakeholders really want are solutions to their needs, wants, and expectations.

The concept of a "solution" seems to be straightforward, but in reality it is continually evolving as the requirements of the business world change and new expectations develop. The solution is a multifaceted concept that includes the product, the service, the underlying technology(s), and all of the tangible and intangible elements of the system that accompany it. It is temporal as well as physical and psychological. For example, when a customer purchases an automobile, he or she expects it to function well for more than a single day, week, or year. The individual expects and demands that it will function properly for its entire life cycle, as defined by prevailing views or perceptions (roughly 200,000 miles (320,000 km) and fifteen years, or more). Moreover, customers expect their automobiles to be aesthetically pleasing and provide them enjoyment. The automobile solution is determined by these prevailing expectations.

Paul Weaver and his colleagues provide a more poignant example using the home washer and dryer for cleaning clothes. Hundreds of thousands of such appliances are sold each year, yet most customers do not really want to own such devices. People want clean clothes at a reasonable cost, not the hardware to do the laundry. In their book, *Sustainable Technology Development*, the authors discuss the environmental impacts of a "home-based system" versus commercial options.[12] Their case explores the social, economic, and environmental consequences of the choices that people in the industrialized countries have for performing one of the most basic needs of humankind. Their case provides insights about SBD thinking and the view that people simply seek solutions. If the economics are right, people prefer the cleaning service rather than own the resources for doing the laundry.

The solution is framed in the context of the business environment and developed by the provider. Its ultimate form depends on the conditions and trends of the social, economic, and environmental factors and is a moving target. Corporations often mistakenly define the desired solution by what their product does, not by the needs it addresses, or will have to address in the future.

Intel's "Moore's Law" recognizes that the solution is an important consideration.[13] According to a March 25, 2002 *Newsweek* piece, Intel has increased its R&D spending to over $4 billion per year. It has developed a 10 Ghz microchip that is four times faster than the Pentium 4 technology. Intel seems to understand where the technology can go in the future.[14]

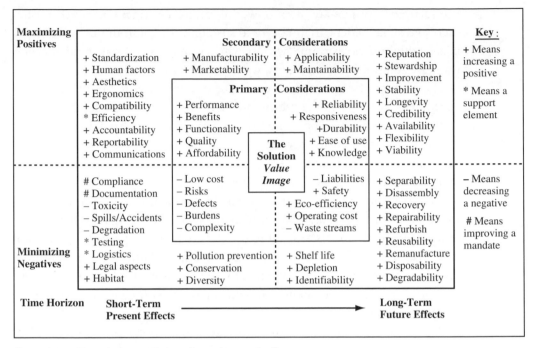

Figure 3.5 The solution matrix based on value creation[a]

Note: [a] The matrix provides a broad perspective on the positive and negative elements and their temporal aspects. Depending on the actual situation or technologies and products, any given element may be positioned differently in the matrix. The critical point is the fact that solutions are multifaceted.

Over the years, IBM has advertised its motto, "It's the Solution," as having linked all of its systems, products, and capabilities together for customer satisfaction. IBM's approach is a great example of a corporation connecting in a meaningful way with its markets, customers, and stakeholders. The solution is the sum of the products, processes, services, capabilities, knowledge, and initiatives that together satisfy specific needs and wants.

Figure 3.5 depicts the elements that make up a solution. From an SBD perspective, it is extremely important for a solution to be based on the value proposition and incorporate improving the positive and reducing the negative, in both the present and in the future. Any given solution has many of the elements, but is not presumed to have all of them. It has primary considerations or benefits that are usually immediately apparent and satisfy near-term needs. It also has secondary considerations and benefits that offer long-term or ongoing satisfaction. Moreover, every solution has short-term and long-term negative effects that can be improved to provide greater satisfaction and enduring results. Good solutions enhance the positives and reduce the negatives.

The solution matrix (the solution) is the convergence of all of the decisions made in an attempt to achieve the corporation's objectives and targets and to meet the needs and requirements of the business environment. It represents the expected outcome of the corporate strategies. People want solutions!

Good solutions are sustainable over a long time horizon and result in beneficial economic, social, and environmental outcomes. The actual time horizon depends on the specific industry and business situation. In electronics, time horizons are measured in months. In the automobile industry, a design is expected to have a life of about five years and the products have typical lives of ten or more years. Most importantly, the solution should bring satisfaction to customers, stakeholders, and other constituents and exceed the mandates of government requirements and industry standards. It should also be adaptable over its life cycle so that it can accommodate variations in the business environment without becoming obsolete. In this way, it must facilitate stability. But, most importantly, in accomplishing all this, solutions must be aligned with the principles of SBD.

Feedback

An important part of formulating and implementing strategies, systems, structures, and solutions is the feedback mechanisms that are needed to ensure that knowledge is deployed beneficially, that learning is captured and understood, and that adjustments are made as necessary. Moreover, the feedback mechanisms should ensure that the solutions and everything that goes into the solutions are internally and externally consistent and beneficial. If the selected solutions make money for the corporation and provide additional internal benefits, but fail to meet the expectations of the business environment, questions about their stability arise. Feedback gives management a sense of the ongoing achievements and sustainability of the management processes.

Feedback makes processes dynamic and provides the mechanisms for instantaneous evaluation and the ability to take corrective action as soon as possible. For instance, the solutions may miss the intended targets; if the difficulty is detected immediately, the implications can be mitigated and the corrected course of action can be executed, avoiding negative impacts. The sooner the information becomes available and determinations are made, the quicker the new or modified solution can become a reality. On the other side of the equation, the original solution may have been appropriate, but the needs of the business environment may have changed. The continuous changes in the business environment require ongoing reflections, assessments, and modifications. In most cases, changes occur over some reasonable period of time. While events such as the attacks on the World Trade Center in New York can have profound and immediate impacts on the macro-environments across the world, most phenomena unfold in a sequence of events that can be analyzed and managed, but it takes time to fully understand and deploy the new solutions. The feedback mechanisms assure that the organization is aware of the changes and is vigilant in keeping pace with these dynamics. In the long term, everything changes as new realities take hold. Feedback mechanisms provide the early warning that strategic responses are necessary.

Determining strategies for SBD

Strategy formulation

The forces affecting business continually evolve and tend to become more intense over time. Expectations rise as new and improved solutions replace old approaches. Management must turn these challenges and concerns into opportunities. For instance, in a conventional setting, competent and ethical business managers would identify the laws and regulations affecting their businesses, study the implications, and develop and implement policies, procedures, processes, and practices to ensure compliance. While compliance is always a positive outcome, eliminating the underlying need for compliance is a more effective means for improving the prospects of the corporation. The goal is to turn challenges into opportunities.

The effective corporation of the future is one that can translate challenges and constraints into strategic advantages. An entrepreneurial corporation leverages its knowledge and understanding of needs and requirements into new ways of meeting expectations. For instance, rather than viewing laws and regulations as barriers, government mandates become pathways to success if the corporation can eliminate whatever causes it to be subject to such mandates. It seeks to discover and meet the needs, demands, mandates, and requirements through a systematic solution.

Formulating effective strategies is a complex subject, especially in the world of SBD. If vision statements provide answers to the "why" question and objectives indicate the "what," then strategies are the "how." While corporate and strategic management represents high-level thinking about the future direction of the corporation, strategies are the means to articulate that direction to the corporation and its constituents. Strategy formulation is an ongoing, evolutionary process that seeks perfection but lives with the imperfections of the prevailing situations. It realizes that the ultimate solutions may never be obtained. Nevertheless, SBD requires corporations to consider the full array of demands and expectations, to provide superior value propositions, and to seek and obtain outstanding performance.

Corporations identify strategic direction by analyzing their position regarding the external forces and comparing their internal capabilities and resources with the needs and opportunities they find. SBD focuses on improving everything; maximizing the positive, minimizing the negative, creating new opportunities, and eliminating old difficulties. Strategies are the plans and the means to achieve that success and to ensure that the future they create satisfies both the external forces and the internal desires. They seek to invent the future through positive actions that are sustainable and mutually beneficial to the communities involved in the business environment. Effective strategies for SBD define a corporation's future direction, and identify objectives and how they can be achieved. The decision process for selecting strategies includes:

- *Assessing the primary external dimensions* The EMM provides a clear construct for assessing the primary forces affecting the corporation and the relationships and networks that exist in the business environment. Effective strategies are based on the implications of a complex array of external dimensions including social, economic, and environmental factors.
- *Examining the value proposition* The value equation provides a powerful construct that includes the essential components for creating and sustaining value. A primary premise of SBD is that each of the elements of the value equation provides opportunities for improving the outcomes and achieving sustainability.
- *Articulating the strategic position and grand strategy* The strategic position maps out the corporation's broad avenue of attack. It defines what SBD means, and how it is to be implemented. The grand strategy is the overarching direction used for formulating and implementing specific strategies, especially for the business units and the product delivery systems. It defines the leadership position of the corporation.

- *Targeting opportunities to make significant improvements*   During the early stages of the SBD paradigm, there are many opportunities for change and improvements; indeed, in most cases there are too many opportunities given the legacies of the past and the deficiencies of existing technologies, products, and processes. The strategic management process must be able to discern the best candidates for effecting improvements and prioritize the opportunities for change. It also defines the process of moving toward sustainable development – i.e. how the existing technologies and products are to be transitioned.

The grand strategy is the most important part of the process from a sustainable development perspective. It sets the tone for changing the paradigms of the corporation. Michael Porter suggests that an organization can achieve a competitive advantage using one of the following generic strategies:[15]

- *Cost leadership*   This strategy requires the organization to focus on cost advantages over competitive or related products
- *Differentiation*   This strategy compels the organization to produce products or processes with features and functions that are unique and not easily duplicated
- *Focus*   This strategy requires the organization to concentrate its efforts on a given market or group of customers where it can achieve an advantage.

While generic business strategies make sense in a well-defined business context, it is difficult to stipulate generalized strategies for SBD. Corporations generally need to provide outstanding value, satisfy customers and stakeholders, produce superior performance, have low cost structures, have high quality standards and results, minimize risks and uncertainty, eliminate defects and burdens, and provide exceptional service and information. While corporations historically dealt with each of these needs individually within the context of separate management systems, such a perspective does not fit into the principles of SBD. Multiple and distinct management systems would result: a SMS for direction, an operating system for production, and an EMS for compliance, etc. In the context of sustainable enterprise management, all these subsystems are integrated into a single embedded management system that involves corporate, business, and operating levels. This is essential for strategy formulation and execution.

The grand strategy of SBD focuses on moving toward the ideal. It is achieving every objective in parallel without compromise. Trade-offs are eliminated as management thinking evolves toward maximizing the positives and minimizing the negatives. The construct is similar to the achievements of the TQM and Six-Sigma thinking of the 1980s and 1990s. During most of the twentieth century the question was "do you want high quality or low price?" TQM and the related management approaches, as developed and practiced by corporations such as Toyota, Honeywell, Siemens, and General Electric, proved that quality and price were not mutually exclusive and that products can have high quality and low price.

The grand strategy of the twenty-first century is even more aggressive and demanding. It is simply being the best at every level and in every element of the value proposition. Former General Electric CEO Jack Welch's requirement to be number one or two conceptually fits into SBD thinking, but from the perspective of value creation and not just winning. Seeking to be the best is a critical factor for sustainable success. Corporations have to reach toward perfection as they achieve business success, social responsibility, economic stability, and environmental excellence. It is that simple.

The framework for developing strategies and their lineage

SBD strategies are based on preemptive, innovative, and creative approaches for achieving short-term and long-term outcomes that represent significant improvements over the prevailing situation. Such strategies also seek to create exciting new opportunities for changing the basis for competitive advantage. The framework for such strategies follows the EMM using space, time, mass, and energy conceptual thinking.

At the corporate management level, the most important considerations are the global reach of the corporation. The key issues are enhancing the social and economic well-being of humankind and lessening the impacts of operations and products, including resource depletion, environmental degradation, and negative impacts on human health and safety. Each of these main categories can have profound effects on all businesses and represent significant opportunities and challenges for sustainability.

Global impacts are the most critical and the most difficult to manage and mitigate. If waste streams and pollution are industry-wide impacts, for instance, then industry-wide or enterprise-wide initiatives are necessary. Examples of strategies for such situations include:

- *Forming an industry coalition* to reduce the effects of the waste stream. The Industry Coalition of the Reduction of Ozone Depleting Materials (ICLOP) is an example of how industry participants formed an effective team to focus attention, reach common ground, and resolve or mitigate problems and concerns. The objective is to neutralize a negative that has very little potential for positive tangible or intangible gains. Table 3.3 shows a few of the advantages and disadvantages of this approach.

- *Creating an alliance with strategic partners* to develop and deploy broad-based solutions to specific areas of concerns so that competitive advantages are achieved, resulting in long-term benefits for the corporation. The strategies include developing new-to-the-world technologies and building infrastructure to support the technologies and their applications. Strategic alliances aimed at developing fuel-cell technologies within the automobile industry fit this strategic approach, as does creating the necessary infra-structure to support such vehicles with hydrogen fuel. Table 3.4 shows a few of the advantages and disadvantages of this approach.

Table 3.3. Sharing responsibilities and solutions: industry coalition

Advantages	Disadvantages
Providing a neutral solution to an entrenched problem for which there are only negative implications	Sharing the responsibilities may include sharing the blame; this is especially a concern for corporations that have had only minor roles in creating the problems
Sharing with others the investment (costs) required to effect a solution	Achieving consensus on the solution may cost more time and money than developing a corporate solution
Reducing the risks of attempting a solution that is not endorsed by the broader communities and participants	Acknowledging responsibilities may carry a risk: a damaged reputation, liabilities, prohibitions, etc.

Table 3.4. Sharing responsibilities and solutions: strategic partners

Advantages	Disadvantages
Gaining a first-mover advantage in capturing a strategic position in a future market that has high potential for growth	Selecting the wrong solution can lead to dead ends and missed opportunities
The use of alliances fits the enterprise management concept	Taking a selected and narrower approach may limit the ability to change in the future
Using alliances allows each member of the team of companies to provide strong capabilities to develop the solution	Choosing the wrong partners may create weaknesses in the alliance and result in the inability to completely execute the strategies and implement the action plans
Having partners allows the corporation to focus its financial and other resources on areas that have the potential for long-term success and outcomes	Coordinating the efforts becomes a strategic necessity and may increase the time and money required to formulate and implement the strategies

Table 3.5. Sharing responsibilities and solutions: SBUs

Advantages	Disadvantages
Creating a business opportunity where the corporation has leadership position superiority allows a corporation to enjoy a period of time where others are trying to catch up	Leading in the development of new approaches is often expensive
	Leaders can have difficulty keeping others from gaining access to the know-how at a significantly lower cost
Leading change has tangible and intangible benefits	Taking a leading role may be premature from a technological perspective
Often the leader gains a lasting reputation for the improvements or for resolving the issues	Future technologies may be more effective in providing the solution, making the investments in existing approaches more expensive than necessary
Gaining proprietary positions allows the corporation to gain from the solution over time, through royalty payments on patents and other intellectual capital	Developing and exploiting new approaches based on the corporation's capabilities requires great strengths and the willingness to expand those capabilities to meet the needs

- *Creating a self-contained SBU* or other constructs to formulate and implement strategies. The strategy is to develop independent responses to opportunities and challenges. For example, Reynolds Metals created a self-contained business for recycling aluminum cans. While the development process was expensive, the company was able to capitalize on the investment for several decades with great success and significant profits. Table 3.5 shows a few of the advantages and disadvantages of this approach.

The actual strategic options often include more alternatives than the selected strategic approaches discussed here. The most crucial aspect is, however, to establish the enterprise framework for achieving success and positioning the corporation for competitive advantage and sustainable outcomes. The focus must be on more than just making profits. It must be on ensuring viable positions in the future that have the potential to sustain and enrich the corporation. SBD translates the vision through selected strategies and strategic positioning to do just that.

While the external forces vary considerably from industry to industry and from setting to setting, there are general strategic approaches that fit many situations. The most important aspect of formulating and implementing strategies at the strategic management level is to think about the integrated systems: the supply networks, distribution channels, customers and markets, secondary markets and retirement options, related industries, infrastructure, and competition. The best overarching strategies depend on the integration of all of these elemental systems and the systematic management of change. This involves linking participants, constituents, and partners over time into strategic relationships that focus on improving the underlying conditions and trends and creating better solutions for the future. Such approaches can transform the capabilities of the entire enterprise into a more effective entity.

From a SBD point of view, strategies should focus on systems thinking, LCT, and holistic solutions. They should seek to eliminate wastes, conserve resources and energy, avoid using or generating toxic and hazardous materials, improve performance, increase reliability and longevity, facilitate reuse and recycling through design and infrastructure, minimize defects and failures, eliminate spills and accidents, enhance safety, make products that are easier to manufacture, remanufacture, disassemble, and market, and provide customer and stakeholders with the information they need to effectively select, use, maintain and retire the products. Table 3.6 provides an overview of selected SBD strategies for improving the SMS.

The general strategies listed in Table 3.6 are discussed in more detail throughout the subsequent chapters. The specific approaches depend on the effectiveness of the management system and the implications of products, processes, and markets.

Design and development strategies

An important construct of SBD is the use of technological innovation and product development (innovation) as the means to affect solutions. Design and development strategies depend on the requirements and specifications of customers and stakeholders and the broader context of the social, political, economic, technological, and environmental concerns and conditions. The most appropriate strategies are ones that satisfy a broad array of needs. Table 3.7 provides an overview of some of these design and development strategies across the product/market continuum.

The NPD process includes two levels of efforts, the conceptual and the operational. The conceptual level includes idea generation, the analysis of each potential opportunity, the development and selection of concepts, and the definition and planning of the improvement program. The conceptual level is typically a low-cost, low-risk, and modest investment. This level does consume time and effort, but the work can be easily redirected, or even halted and later restarted if a significant problem or barrier arises that makes the

Table 3.6. Selected strategies for improving the SMS

	Human health and safety	Resource conservation	Reducing resource depletion	Natural environment protection	Mitigating degradation	Risk mitigation
Supply						
Networks	Eliminate or reduce the use of toxic substances	Use less resource-intensive materials, less mass and energy	Obtain renewable or restorable materials and energy sources	Select suppliers who minimize their environmental impacts	Select suppliers with who have effective management systems	Select high-quality and reliable partners
– Material						
– Energy						
– Information	Select safe and efficient processes that have low impact	Minimize material and energy use and select low-impact materials	Incorporate recovery, reuse, and recycling methods	Partner with suppliers who use life cycle methods	Use sustainable development to minimize present and future impacts	Disclose data about upstream implications and impacts
– Knowledge						
– Life cycle						
– Logistics						
Operation						
– Material	Eliminate or reduce the use of toxic substances	Practice waste minimization and mass conservation	Incorporate renewable energy sources and recyclable materials	Minimize impacts on environment	Use healthy and safe methods; use precautionary measures	Reduce risk, accidents, and spills
– Energy						
– Information	Select safe and efficient processes that have low impact	Minimize material and energy utilization and select low-impact materials	Incorporate recovery, reuse, and recycling methods	Use LCT and life cycle methods to mitigate impacts	Use sustainable development to minimize present and future impacts	Disclose data about upstream implications and impacts
– Knowledge						
– Life cycle						
Distribution						
– Logistics	Select safe processes that minimize handling and exposures	Avoid material losses and energy drains through natural processes	Select efficient transportation and handling processes	Improve protocols for prevention and emergency response	Eliminate unsafe or high-risk processes and practices and those with poor track records	Use risk assessment and risk reduction methods

Table 3.6. (cont.)

	Human health and safety	Resource conservation	Reducing resource depletion	Natural environment protection	Mitigating degradation	Risk mitigation
Markets and Customers – Material – Energy	Conserve materials and energy; avoid hazardous materials/waste	Reduce material and energy use; reduce unnecessary consumption	Create secondary markets for products and materials; reduce unnecessary consumption	Reduce environmental footprint of products during applications and disposal	Withdraw risky products or those that tend to be misapplied; provide means to mitigate such issues	Test all products for potential defects and unexpected problems
– Information – Knowledge – Life cycle	Improve information and disclosures about negative effects	Create more effective methods for the use of products; reduce waste	Provide options for the safe use and disposal of products and materials	Provide information about the footprints and consequences	Disclose information about how to deal with unexpected problems	Disclose information on potential problems
Retirement Disposal	Enhance flow of information to secondary markets	Improve recovery, reuse, refurbishment, and recycling	Create materials flow infrastructure over life cycle	Provide a safety net for the use and disposal of products	Build in disposal solutions during the development of products	Mitigate difficulties in disposing of products

Table 3.7. Selected design and development strategies

Dimension (space)	Design	Life cycle
Product	**Improved product performance and value**	**Improved product performance and value**
	– Improve output/performance	– Improve longevity
	– Increase efficiency	– Increase effectiveness
	– Reduce materials and mass	– Improve reliability
	– Reduce energy requirements	– Improve maintainability
	– Eliminate toxic substances	– Reduce energy consumption
	– Reduce negative impacts	– Enhance stability – social and economic
	– Reduce defects and burdens	– Improve cost structure
Production	**Improved operating system and process performance**	**Improved operating system and process performance**
	– Improve resource utilization	– Recover scrap materials and reuse
	– Improve process safety	– Increase process efficiency
	– Reduce waste streams	– Educate work force
	– Reduce energy requirements	– Improve dialog with constituents
	– Improve process flow	– Improve prevention methods
	– Reduce compliance/permitting issues	– Enhance emergency response
	– Improve emergency preparedness	– Reduce spills and accidents
Market	**Improved Product/Market Stewardship and applications**	**Improved Product/Market Stewardship and applications**
	– Increase information and labeling	– Reduce energy consumption
	– Increase segmentation (focus)	– Build strong relationships
	– Improve awareness and applications	– Improve safe-use and reduce risks
	– Increase customer knowledge	– Decrease potential liabilities
	– Disclose positive and negative effects	– Improve market feedback
	– Improve stakeholder participation	– Eliminate poor products
	– Mitigate risks	– Disclose all pertinent information
EoL	**Improved infrastructure and materials flow**	**Improved infrastructure and materials flow**
	– Reduce materials, mass, and energy	– Improve output
	– Refurbish products	– Increase efficiency
	– Use recovered material	– Reduce energy requirements
	– Reuse and recycle materials	– Refurbish products
	– Create safe dispose/treatment option	– Establish reuse and recycling

viability of the program uncertain. The basic approach is to find viable opportunities and define their potential, or to identify quickly the unsuitable prospects and eliminate them.

The operational level includes the design and development of the product (box 3.1), the verification of the decisions, and launching the new product

Box 3.1 The evolution of BMW's environmental strategies for product design

A global snapshot of the automobile industry

After more than a century of growth and prominence, the automobile industry continues to play a significant role in shaping the economic and social structures of developed industrial countries. During the first half of the twentieth century, the automobile was regarded as one of the most important products, offering mobility, convenience, and flexibility to the motorist and economic power and importance to the industry. Demand was so prodigious that many of the leading business corporations in the world were directly or indirectly linked to the manufacture, distribution, maintenance, or use of the automobile. The automobile industry offered the individual freedom to choose destination, route, and time, and mobility has been a fundamental requirement for highly productive societies.

World-class automotive companies spend heavily to redesign their products, retool assembly lines, and make the technological changes necessary to meet competitive challenges. The automobile is a large, expensive and complex, durable product requiring enormous engineering and manufacturing resources and sophisticated marketing capabilities. Cost, quality, technological innovation, and environmental mandates drive the current market. The most innovative companies, those that have successfully combined high-quality and innovative designs with cost effective production capabilities, set the competitive standards. Capital expenditures and R&D expenses are about 10 percent of automotive revenues for the major players. R&D efforts include increasing engine efficiency, improving safety, reducing emissions, developing better materials and components, enhancing vehicle longevity, expanding manufacturing technologies, and improving reliability. From feature improvements to cost reductions, innovation plays a vital role in shaping vehicle design, parts selection, and manufacturing and assembly.

Environmental regulations also affect design requirements and selections, driving enhancements in safety, reductions in emissions, and recycling. In particular, German legislation and regulations pertaining to solid waste have become the models for many EU countries and across the world. Automobile manufacturers are particularly vulnerable to mandatory legislation pertaining to solid waste because their products are complex assemblies of thousands of parts consisting of numerous materials.

BMW's recycling strategies: precursors to "sustainable value"

BMW was one of the first car-makers in Germany to respond to the pressures of regulation by adopting the goal of producing a completely recyclable car.[1] During the 1990s BMW's executive management viewed the solid waste issues in Germany as a way to attain a stronger position *vis-à-vis* global competitors by enhancing the company's reputation with customers and becoming an industry leader in automobile recycling. By positively responding to environmental issues, BMW not only defended itself against potential threats, but turned them into attractive opportunities.

In 2000, the EU issued the Europe-Wide Directive on End-of-Life Vehicles, mandating that, beginning in 2006, at least 85 percent of the weight of the retiring vehicle must be reused or recycled and, after 2015, allowing only 5 percent of the residual weight to be land-filled.[2] Far from a newcomer to recycling, BMW was able to leverage its existing capabilities and technical know-how into a recycling strategy that catered to the EU political and social mandates. It even claimed that the program was driven by "self-responsibility instead of legislative pressure."

BMW had begun recycling high-value components and systems such as engines, alternators, and starters in 1965.[3] Starting in April 1987, BMW was the first automobile manufacturer in Europe to take back used catalytic converters via a dealer network. Moreover, when the recycling mandate was handed down, its products were already 75 percent recyclable due to a high content of metallic materials.

BMW also has a long history of supporting environmental management initiatives. It has programs to monitor impending government regulations, assess the situation, and initiate voluntary actions to preclude being pressured by government mandates. By taking proactive steps, BMW can help frame the debate and have a better chance of its own protocols becoming the standard solutions. Rather than simply waiting for legislative and regulatory changes to unfold, BMW attempts to drive the solutions to problems. This kind of approach is important because governments often have only limited options such as banning products or materials, imposing taxes, mandating structures, or instituting penalties and fees. Such actions usually deal with the problems after the situation has already developed and may interfere with market dynamics or process efficiencies. BMW is sensitive to the cascading effects of regulations on product economics and market conditions and attempts to proactively manage environmental issues to gain an edge on its competitors.

BMW's recycling strategy evolved from studying how cars could be disassembled and how recyclability could be incorporated into the development stages, so that cars are "designed for disassembly." Technologically, BMW concentrates much of its research efforts on the recycling of plastics, especially polypropylene, which constitutes about 10 percent of a car's weight and is a significant portion of the nonrecyclable content. It also focuses on how to reuse various parts and materials. A significant part of the strategy is the determination of what parts of vehicles can be made from recycled or reused plastic. One example of a success is the use of polyurethane foam from dismantled cars to make soundproof insulation for the next generation of cars. The extent that recycled materials and parts can be utilized in new cars depends upon public acceptance.

As BMW increased its ability to completely recycle cars, recycling infrastructures have become essential for providing closed-loop solutions in its major markets, and BMW's strategic alliances with automobile scrap dealers are essential in creating that infrastructure. BMW works with suppliers to find ways to recycle all of its materials. The establishment of networks of authorized dismantlers, which are fully qualified and monitored for quality, is an important part of the process. The success of such networks depends upon the ability of BMW, along with its authorized dismantlers, to generate sufficient cash flow to sustain their operations.

BMW has explored both a centralized concept customized specifically for handling only old BMW automobiles and a decentralized approach using the existing car recycling infrastructure on an industry-wide basis. BMW believes that both concepts are valid if an "all-around vehicle utilization strategy" is employed where authorized and licensed operators who deal with all of the recycling problems assume full responsibility. With all of these companies working together on a common goal (100 percent recyclable cars), the opportunity for success is greatly improved.

Integrating SBD into corporate strategy

BMW executives view long-term sustainable development as a key element in the company's corporate strategy. The BMW Executive Board adapted the following resolution pertaining to sustainability on February 21, 2000.[4]

> Sustainability is evolving to become a primary approach to [economic] and social prosperity. It also facilitates the interaction between the market and democracy. The BMW group will continue to pursue sustainable development as a principle of corporate strategy.

Most importantly, BMW integrated sustainable development into the mainstream of its corporate life. Dr. Helmut Panke, Chairman of the Board of Management, has stated:[5]

> In our company, we pursue a corporate culture that combines the determination to achieve economic success with cosmopolitanism, trust, transparency and responsibility for our environment. This attitude is reflected in all areas of the company and is absolutely essential if we are to put BMW Group's current product and market offensive successfully into practice and thus safeguard the future of BMW Group on a sustainable basis.

With EoL management as a core competence, management has not only gained a competitive advantage but also redefined the company's strategic direction using sustainable development as the mantra. Executive management appears to be committed to the development and implementation of SBD programs beyond recycling. Indeed, the threat of legislative initiatives is only part of the equation. The most serious challenges involve concerns about the sustainability of the automobile itself. With highly industrialized and densely populated countries, Europe has seen a rise in social and political movements that view the automobile as a significant contributor to the world's environmental problems. Proposed solutions extend beyond legislation affecting disposal costs and recycling mandates. BMW's most critical concern is the impact of social and political pressures on its customers and the possibility of a decline in the social and economic acceptability of the luxury sport sedan. BMW believes that mobility and ecological responsibility are more than ever interlinked with one another. BMW's sustainable mobility model includes the following:[6]

- Intelligent networking of various means of transportation
  - Obtain maximum benefit from each carrier
  - Reduce transportation costs and the space required for vehicles
- Continuous improvement of average fuel consumption
  - Conserve natural resources
  - Reduce vehicle emissions

- Develop alternate drive concepts
  - Long-term preservation of quality of life and economical use of personal transporatation
  - Promote global implementation of hydrogen and the vision of using hydrogen as a renewable energy source
- Recyclable products and return/recycling of used vehicles
  - Conserve natural resources
  - Eliminate/reduce waste.

Environmentally conscious product design and development

In 1973, BMW hired its first environmental protection officer. At that time, there were no counterparts at other companies in Bavaria.[7] At first, the role of the environmental manager was to stay abreast of laws and regulations and keep the company out of trouble. Then, the role changed to pollution prevention, focusing on solving or reducing environmental problems in manufacturing operations. With increased awareness of environmental issues from a market perspective, BMW used pollution prevention methods to stay ahead of customer and stakeholder expectations during the 1990s. Currently, BMW is in a third stage, where environmental management plays a significant role in setting the company's objectives, formulating strategies, and making decisions. The focus is on NPD strategies that incorporate solutions to environmental concerns during the design phase. Dr. N. Hans-Michael Kurz, production general manager at the BMW Munich plant, stated in an interview on June 24, 1999, that "BMW's responsibility for the environment begins prior to the design phase and continues for the entire life-cycle of the car, including assistance with recycling." BMW's approach encompasses the analysis of its products' life cycle and the development and implementation of environmentally responsible strategies. Environmental protection is now an integral part of BMW's overall business strategy.

BMW's product development process, called the product evolution process (PEP), focuses on environmentally compatible designs using computer-aided design (CAD) technologies. The initiatives stretch far beyond the actual life cycle of its product. BMW's main objective is to create a harmonious balance between the utility, mobility, and environmental compatibility offered by its automobiles and operations. BMW has a set of environmentally oriented directives, called integrated product policies (IPP), to guide the design efforts. The overall objectives are to minimize the negative effects on humanity and the environment.[8] A key program relating to the selection of materials involved reducing the number of different materials used in the design of a part or component. For example, the previous instrument panel design consisted of a metal support, polyurethane foam, and PVC film; in the redesigned versions, it is made from a single material which forms the support, foam, and film. By avoiding the construction of a composite, BMW facilitates the recyclability of the component. Another major initiative was the recycling of plastics. Because of their light weight and corrosion resistance, plastics offer the advantages of fuel savings and long life. As designers sought to reduce the number of different plastics in cars, they needed a universal and cost effective plastic that was recyclable. They were able to reduce the types of plastics used from more than twenty to four.

BMW understands that superior innovations are the only way for a car-maker to be successful in the highly competitive future. It believes that the car of tomorrow will not only need to fulfill more complex requirements to meet customer needs, but will have to incorporate advanced technologies to address environmental problems. BMW's R&D efforts systematically convert good ideas into genuine innovations. To ensure efficient integration of its research capabilities in the quest for new solutions, BMW established a centralized think-tank at the FIZ Research and Innovation Center during the late 1980s. This think-tank is near the company's original Munich factory and brings together all parties involved with the development process. Its members work cooperatively on BMW's future vehicles from the design phases through prototyping and production. BMW is using advances in technology to shorten development periods, reduce development costs, and respond more quickly to the needs of its customers.[9] It is striving to ensure that customers will continue to receive what they expect from BMW: the ultimate driving machine, offering sheer driving pleasure in the real world.

One area of innovation on which BMW is focused is the improvement of the fuel economy of its cars. BMW is improving the performance and environmental compatibility of its conventional technologies. Its variable camshaft control and digital engine electronics technologies reduce fuel consumption and emissions for six-cylinder engines.[10] Its fuel saving potential is estimated to be 15–20 percent. Other initiatives include using lightweight materials, new catalyst technology to reduce emissions, enhanced diesel technology, and improved manufacturing processes.

BMW believes it must start now to develop alternatives to the conventional car for 25–50 years into the future. It has engaged in the development of electric cars since the early 1970s and hydrogen-powered cars since the late 1970s. Working to bridge the transition to alternative vehicles, however, BMW has successfully linked the present and the future in a most convincing manner with its hybrid drive.[11] BMW's hybrid vehicle is powered by energy from both conventional fuel and alternative energy. The company's long-term energy strategy, by contrast, seeks to avoid emissions by focusing exclusively on nonfossil forms.[12] To satisfy BMW, alternative energy sources must provide the same range and equivalent performance of today's automobile, but in an environmentally friendly manner.

The electric car was one of BMW's first steps toward providing a cleaner vehicle. An advantage of electric cars is that they produce no exhaust; however, as long as the power station that generates the energy uses fossil fuels, there is no appreciable overall environmental gain. Even with current technology, electric vehicles are still expensive, have short lives, and are too heavy for the amount of energy they store.

In 1995, BMW introduced its natural gas car and became the first car-maker in Europe to launch a standard-production natural gas car. Burning natural gas reduces the emission of pollutants to a minimum. The major drawback associated with natural gas is the complicated storage technology required in the car.

BMW considers hydrogen to be the fuel of the future. In a completely closed cycle, hydrogen is extracted from water, and returns to water again once burned.[13] Produced with the assistance of solar power, hydrogen is the cleanest fuel available. BMW's hydrogen-powered vehicle program is in its sixth generation of vehicles and is presently based on the latest BMW 7-Series models.[14] In addition, the electrical functions on board these cars are powered by a fuel cell. The BMW hydrogen vehicles run with virtually zero emissions, even without additional treatment of the exhaust. The most significant drawback of these vehicles is a lowered power output. This problem can be overcome by increasing engine capacity. Unfortunately, liquid hydrogen currently costs much more than conventional fuel, and there is no infrastructure in place for filling stations. Though providing a complete infrastructure would be costly, BMW has collaborated with others to develop a fully automated system which can fill its car with liquid hydrogen rapidly, safely, and without emissions.[15] A state-of-the-art robotic filling station is now in service at the Munich airport. The vehicles that transport airline passangers from the plane to the terminal operate with hydrogen as their energy source, and utilize the filling station.

All of BMW's production sites are validated according to the European Union Eco-Management and Audit Scheme (EMAS) or certified under ISO 14001.[16] BMW is an active participant in UN initiatives pertaining to climate change and clean energy. The company has made significant investments in training its employees and building sustainable capabilities and is a respected performer in the DJSGI. It is also listed on the Ethics Index FTSE4GOOD-Europe of the *Financial Times*. It has not achieved perfection, but is it working on becoming more capable, sustainable and successful.

Notes:

1. Kim Clark, "Car plastics becoming a colossal waste problem," *Baltimore Sun*, January 5, 1992, p. E12.
2. *Sustainable Value Report 2003/2004: Innovation. Efficiency. Responsibility*, BMW Group, p. 11.
3. *BMW Current Factbook, Recycling*, AK-3, 1991, p. 2.
4. *Sustainable Value Report 2001/2002: Environment. Economy. Social Responsibility: Meeting the Future*, BMW Group, p. 6.
5. *Sustainable Value Report 2003/2004: Innovation. Efficiency. Responsibility*, BMW Group, p. 4.
6. *Sustainable Value Report 2001/2002: Environment. Economy. Social Responsibility: Meeting the Future*, BMW Group, p. 7.
7. *Environmentally Friendly Automobile Production*, Current Factbook BMW AG, AK – 1, 1993.
8. *Sustainable Value Report 2001/2002: Environment. Economy. Social Responsibility: Meeting the Future*, BMW Group, p. 24.
9. *BMW Research and Development*, Current Factbook, AK-2, 1997, p. 2.
10. *Development of Internal Combustion Engine Petrol Engine*, BMW Group Brochure, p. 2.
11. *Hybrid Drive – Taking Two Roads into the Future*, Current Factbook BMW AG, AK – 2, 1997.
12. *Ibid.*
13. *Hydrogen Drive*, Current Factbook BMW AG, AK – 2, May 1999.
14. *Clean Energy – Hydrogen – drive*, BMW Group Publication, January 2001.
15. *Ibid.*
16. *Sustainable Value Report 2003/2004: Innovation. Efficiency. Responsibility*, BMW Group, p. 56.

on the market. This level includes the engineering work for designing the product, the production processes, the development and execution of the market-related program for sustaining the launch, the building or leveraging of the production capabilities, and the financial means and analysis to support the program. The operational level consumes the most time and effort and usually includes an in-depth analysis of every facet of the process. It represents a majority of the investment required to launch a new product. It also represents a significant portion of the risk associated with design and development.

Chapter 8 details specific strategies and approaches for the design and development process.

Performance evaluation system

Overview

Performance measurement and the metrics used to assess outcomes are usually relegated to the operations of the product delivery system. However, corporations engaged in SBD require direct feedback about achievements and required adjustments. Metrics provide the means to determine the effectiveness of SBD and make ongoing improvements and refinements.

The performance evaluation system validates decision-making and provides confidence that the strategic analysis and direction are on track. It also offers insights about the actions required for meeting targets and objectives, or for taking corrective actions. The performance evaluation system measures the corporation's actual performance against the expectations of customers, stakeholders, the community, the regulatory agencies, and other constituencies. It focuses on how well the SMS is meeting objectives and targets, implementing strategies, obtaining desired outcomes, mitigating risks, and achieving competitive advantage and business success.

At the strategic management level, the performance evaluation system examines information and data relating to the metrics to ascertain the probability of attaining the desired outcomes, improving performance, and mitigating potential adverse impacts and risk. The most important contribution of metrics at the strategic level is to provide an early warning of positive or negative trends. They can help companies navigate unprecedented social, political, economic, technological, and environmental contexts.

Objectives and targets communicate what is expected. For instance, laws and regulations often stipulate precisely what companies must do to comply – i.e. they establish the targets. In the twenty-first century, however, the expectations are more complex. Industries and their constituents often set the standards, making the targets more open-ended. Corporations following the tenets of SBD may enjoy setting high standards because it makes keeping up more difficult and costly for its competitors, thereby creating an opportunity for competitive advantages. The drive for higher achievements – higher standards and targets – provides opportunities to excel and make it exceedingly more difficult for competitors to keep up.

Risk mitigation involves assessing and eliminating potential adverse impacts upon the corporation, its constituencies, and the natural environment. Metrics helps signal the impacts that need mitigating. Uncertainty and long time horizons complicate the practice of using metrics at the strategic level.

Table 3.8 lists some of the metrics that may be used to evaluate the SBD performance of the management system at each level.

The strategic metrics vary, depending on the industry setting and the focus of the corporation and its constituencies. The listed metrics are a subset of those that may be used to examine the dynamics of the corporate position and change mechanisms. The actual metrics used depends on the maturity and sophistication of the management systems. It is expected that during the formative years of SBD, a corporation would select several from each category as a means to track performance. As the corporation's capabilities, knowledge, and performance mature, the number of metrics can expand, especially as specific elements become more significant. For instance, there is little point to tracking the number of business units without impacts if every business unit has a large number of impacts and it will take many years to change that.

An overarching metric relates to the corporation's ability to convert external mandates, demands, and requirements for minimizing negative impacts into opportunities. This kind of focus on solutions is pivotal in the pursuit of better positions in the future. The ultimate solution is zero defects and burdens on the environment, and human health and safety, and negligible negative consequences for constituencies. While the ideal solution may never materialize, the corporation must move toward significant improvements.

Performance evaluation from a global perspective

The most critical metrics measure the reduction of the global footprint of the corporation. They assess the impacts and consequences of the corporation's technologies, products, and processes, and their improvement over time. They provide a sense of the sustainability of the corporation and its progress toward a less vulnerable future.

Generally, such an approach is viewed as a prescriptive, "top-down" methodology. It can be argued that such an approach is required if a

Table 3.8. Selected metrics for performance evaluation of management systems

Level	Corporate management	Strategic management	Product delivery
Strategy	% of partners using SBD	% of units using systems integration	% of products based on SBD
	No. of SBD businesses	% of SBD technology platforms	No. of key customers linked
	% of constituents satisfied	% of stakeholders satisfied	% of customers satisfied
	% of cash flow based on SBD	% of units with SBD technologies	% of operations based on SBD
	No. of areas rated as world class	No. of units rated as world class	No. of products rated as world class
	Degree of holistic action	Degree of solving waste issues	No. of waste problems resolved
Innovation	% of programs that involve SBD	% of new technologies with SBD	% of new products based on SBD
	No. of SBD business developments	No. of SBD technology developments	No. of SBD product developments
	% of unique intellectual capital	% of technologies with patents	% of products that are proprietary
	No. of unique SBD solutions	No. of proprietary SBD methods	No. of unique SBD processes
	Rate of acquiring new knowledge	Rate of learning new capabilities	Rate of deploying capabilities
Leadership	Rate of transformation to SBD	Rate of transition of capabilities	Rate of learning and knowledge
	% of information disclosed	% of units beyond compliance	% of products in full compliance
	% of corporation without burdens	% of units with no impacts	% of products at Six-Sigma
	No. of catastrophic events	No. of significant events	No. of incidents
	Amount of SBD investment	No. of programs for improvements	No. of impacts and consequences
	Ranking of corporate reputation	Ranking of global positions	Ranking of product brands/ image

corporation wishes to replace the prescriptive mandates of government regulations with a system that ensures full compliance and/or eliminates the underlying need for the laws and regulations. For global corporations, solutions have to be systematic and enterprise-wide if the corporation is to leverage its resources and capabilities and gain competitive advantages.

Executive management, senior environmental professionals, and their business units conduct the performance evaluations. These executives obtain a comprehensive view of the business units and operations in order to understand the current and future expectations of external stakeholders.

They examine the impacts of current and proposed legislation and regulations and determine what courses of action could reduce impacts and potential liabilities and improve strategic position.

Repsol YPF (formerly Repsol), the Spanish petroleum company, provides an exciting case study on how to integrate EMSs with corporate strategies, business practices, and the precursors to SBD (box 3.2). The case highlights many of the prevailing environmental management approaches, like ISO 14001, an EMS and a performance evaluation system. The Repsol YPF case is used to describe and discuss these environmental management constructs in the context of a corporation rather than just describing the key elements of ISO 14000. Repsol YPF's integration of environmental management into the mainstream strategic thinking of the corporation indicates that executive leadership is bridging the gap between the old constructs and new philosophies of engaging SBD.

Box 3.2 Repsol YPF: integrating an EMS with corporate strategies and business practices

In March 1999, the Spanish oil conglomerate, Repsol, completed its acquisition of Yacimientos Petroliferos Fiscales (YPF), a leading producer of petroleum products in Argentina, in which Repsol had had an investment since the mid-1990s. The new corporation became Repsol YPF, with operations in twenty-seven countries and a majority of its businesses in Spain and Argentina. Repsol YPF is now the seventh largest oil company in the world, with more than 4,500 million barrels of oil equivalents in reserves and producing over a million barrels per day.

Prior to the full merger, Repsol and YPF faced pressing environmental issues in Spain and Argentina, respectively. They started crafting solutions to environmental issues and began formulating and implementing innovative strategies to obtain a sustainable strategic position in the long term. They committed their companies to establishing comprehensive environmental programs to meet society's expectations for a clean environment and a safe work place. Management developed a sophisticated communications plan in 1995 to build awareness for the need to change and to articulate the strategies for integrating environmental issues into the mainstream of corporate affairs. In 1997, management introduced an EMS. After the merger, Repsol YPF continued to manage change proactively through its integrated EMS.[1]

- Establishing an EMS that is in line with the guidelines of the ISO 14001 Standard
- Introducing innovative approaches for improving its operations and gaining the acceptance by customers, employees, stakeholders, and the public at large of its products, services, and processes
- Improving its infrastructure for managing environmental issues to ensure the broadest participation by all stakeholders
- Providing assurance to government officials, financial agents, and customers that it meets their expectations for performance.

Repsol YPF's search for environmental excellence is driven by a proactive environmental policy that supports the overall objectives of the corporation: create value; ensure survivability; achieve growth; foster social responsibility; and improve everything. Repsol YPF views environmental challenges as business opportunities. The overall corporate philosophy was articulated by Alfonso Cortina, Repsol YPF's CEO:[2]

> Our core objective is the creation of value for our shareholders and for the community as a whole, in such a way that short-term benefits should not create untenable imbalances for either sector in the long term. Our aim is to create value while maintaining our values.

When Repsol YPF's executive management recognized that environmental issues presented profound challenges and potential dangers, it decided to develop a strategic context linking environmental management with corporate strategy. The resulting Strategic Plan for the Environment (SPE), and its core elements, is a five-year plan that is updated yearly and is part of the company's overall strategic plan. SPE fits into the corporate strategic policy and includes the necessary measures to ensure compliance with regulations and the strategic initiatives for corrective actions mandated by environmental audits.[3]

Repsol YPF's overarching goal was to integrate environmental management with the overall strategic business plan of the corporation. Integrating environmental, safety, and quality initiatives into the core business areas would at once allow the company to focus on the major environmental concerns, maintain regulatory compliance, achieve operating efficiencies and cost savings, and improve the company's competitive position and reputation. Repsol YPF's SPE provides the company with opportunities to enhance the positive aspects of growing the businesses and satisfying customers with superior products and services, reduce the negative aspects of environmental hazards and liabilities, ensure compliance with laws and regulations, and increase compatibility with the principles of sustainable growth.

Repsol YPF's Top Management Environmental and Safety Committee (TMESC) oversees the company's environmental strategies and programs. TMESC consists of senior management of the various business areas who establish the policies and actions of the company.[4] TMESC defines the objectives and goals, determines the guiding principles for the environmental programs, and monitors the environmental performance. It reviews the performance of the EMS quarterly to determine its suitability, adequacy, and effectiveness and addresses the need for changes to policy, objectives, and the content of the ESM.

An Environmental and Safety Technical Committee (ESTC), consisting of environmental management professionals from the individual business areas, also monitors actions and programs, develops environmental metrics, and coordinates environmental management efforts using common criteria. ESTC leads the company's efforts to achieve environmental excellence. It establishes the required environmental programs based on input from customers and stakeholders, the mandates of regulatory authorities, and the realities of the business units. ESTC ensures that business units conform to the guiding principles and best environmental management practices. It develops efficient and effective programs to address environmental issues and concerns outlined in the guiding principles.

Finally, the business units are essential to the proper functioning of the system. The business line managers are responsible for executing the goals and making sure that performance is achieved based on established policies. They have the responsibility and authority to establish practices and control mechanisms as necessary. They inform the entire organization of the importance of achieving excellent environmental performance.

The EMS adopts ISO Standards to get the job done

While Repsol YPF's SPE links the overall corporate strategy, policies, and organizational structure to the environmental objectives, the EMS is the mechanism by which the company seeks to meet those objectives. It embodies a systematic, interdisciplinary approach for ensuring that the company meets all of its commitments and manages the dynamics of the business environment. The goal is to achieve "world-class" environmental performance in concert with corporate objectives and policies. In the 1999 *Environmental Report*, CEO Cortina articulated the linkage between environmental management and business processes and the iteration of the single company:[5]

> The Repsol YPF Environmental Management System will simultaneously fulfill two aims: to document and systematically improve the Company's performance in its environmental obligations, thus minimizing environmental risks linked to our activities, and to act as a powerful *integration* agent for human resources and management practices formerly pertaining to Repsol and YPF. (Emphasis added)

The main priority was the development of a common management system that would transform the management culture and organizational structure of the two separate operations into a unified corporation and integrate environmental policy with the main management constructs. The goal is a management system that assures quality and environmental responsibility through planning and policies, monitoring, audits, information and communications, and documentation.

Repsol YPF's executive management has moved beyond the typical "profit and loss" mentality by investing heavily in creating an outstanding EMS for its operations. Adopting the ISO 14001 Standard has allowed Respol YPF to measure corporate environmental performance across the entire company. The ISO framework is designed to provide a consistent format for an authoritative overview of environmental performance. The output is designed to be useful for internal environmental and general management purposes and for corporate environmental reporting. Implementing it, however, has required a holistic shift in thinking toward progressive environmental management at all levels of the organization. It has required measurement, evaluation, review, and improvement of all goals. It has also required money. Repsol YPF has spent significant sums of money to obtain ISO 9000 and ISO 14000 certification for its facilities and operations. Today, the company has eight refineries, twelve petrochemical plants, sixteen terminals, three derivatives plants, 96 service stations, two lubricant plants and their marketing systems, six LPG factories, geophysical activities, and nineteen exploration and production operations that are ISO certified.[6]

Repsol YPF senior management has articulated thirteen primary environmental and safety principles that integrate its environmental policies with the business objectives and operations. Table 3B.1 highlights the company's environmental principles and links them to environmental leadership and business integration:[7]

Table 3B.1. Repsol YPF: integrated environmental policies

Repsol's environmental principles	Environmental leadership/Business integration
Integrated environmental and safety management – Leadership and Responsibility – Planning and Life Cycle Thinking	**Environmental leadership/business integration** The leadership holds the ultimate responsibility for implementing the Environmental and Safety Management System. Business line management is responsible for EMS
Impact minimization – Objectives and Targets – Product Life Cycle Assessment – Energy Conservation	**LCT** The company is thinking about how to minimize its environmental impacts and how to use LCA for making improvements
Ongoing adjustments to regulations – Compliance and Beyond – Environmental Responsibility	**Legal and regulatory/operational requirements** The company must comply with environmental regulations at facilities and operations and take legal and international standards into consideration globally Compliance is a necessary and important part of the operating system
Prevention of pollution and evaluation of potential risks – Waste Minimization and Pollution Prevention – Conservation	**Pollution prevention/risk management** The company's basic principle is preventing pollution in all phases of business, including early stages of planning and weighing decisions on all projects
Applying efficiency criteria in solving environmental problems – Eco-effectiveness C/B Analysis	**Eco-efficiency/operational efficiency** Efficiency and effectiveness are measured in terms of C/B analysis when selecting technologies and measures for environmental solutions
Cooperation with society – Community Involvement – Community Relations – Emergency planning/Preparedness – Risk Prevention	**Community awareness/stakeholder management** The company cooperates with the public, communities, governments, associations, and NGOs in the quest for solutions to environmental dilemmas, and regarding the development of new legislation; operations are integrated with the EMS

Table 3B.1. (cont.)

Repsol's environmental principles	Environmental leadership/Business integration
Inclusion of environmental criteria in general business management – Balanced Metrics	**Performance evaluation/business metrics** Environmental criteria associated with processes are on a par with safety and quality requirements Business performance is measured using balanced criteria for ascertaining achievements
Commitment of suppliers and contractors to environmental and safety policy – Selection of Criteria – Development	**Value networks/supply networks** Environmental criteria will be a prime factor in the selection and evaluation of subcontractors who will be required to perform in accordance with in-house standards and regulations
In-house and external communications, the release of information, and relationships with the community – Environmental Reporting – Transparency	**Communications/marketing/customer satisfaction** Provide open communications Encourage in-house and outside disclosures about risks Consumers and users shall receive adequate information to ensure that the use, handling, and disposal will have no undue effects
Planning and provision of technical, human, and financial resources – Planning – Evaluation	**Resource planning/resource allocation** Environmental and safety planning will be based on strategies and programs subject to evaluation, defining the adequate actions to achieve the objectives There will be adequate resources to ensure that programs are implemented properly
Training – Education – Training	**Training and awareness** Customers, suppliers, and contractors will be provided with training Resources will be provided for environmental training to those involved in operations
Customers continuous improvement – Corrective and Preventive Action – Environmental Audits	**Environmental auditing/quality management** Constant efforts will be made in attitudes, practices, and processes to improve the system via regular, systematic evaluation Integrate TQM and environmental quality and seek continuous improvement
Product Stewardship, customer health and safety, and environmental care – Product Stewardship	**Management review** Contribute to preserve the environment and health and safety of customers, making known impacts to employees and collaborators Ensure that there are no ill effects over the life cycle

The items listed in table 3B.1 under environmental leadership and business integration exemplify how Repsol YPF has translated its principles into elements of the ISO 14001 Standard. Environmental communications and Product Stewardship are perhaps the most critical elements tying the entire construct into an effective system, linking the internal operations and practices with the external environmental realities.

The EMS ensures that environmental policies and programs are integrated into an overall business framework that is focused on achieving sustainable environmental performance and outstanding business results. It oversees prevention, detection, and correction of environmental problems, emphasizing improvement through the establishment of suitable goals and the review of operating units to verify accomplishment of the intended results. The EMS also communicates the importance of corporate environmental performance to both the organization and its stakeholders. It provides a link to external stakeholders and ensures environmental communication. The environmental goals clarify the priorities of the corporate-wide ESM programs, and the ESM drives the ownership and responsibility of those priorities throughout the company. The basic elements of Repsol YPF EMS are listed in table 3B.2.[8]

The basic philosophy of ISO 14001 is that all processes require ongoing checking and corrective action. A nonconformance is a deviation from the standard and often involves defects, burdens, and impacts. When these are detected, it is essential to initiate corrective action processes to ensure that problems are resolved as quickly as possible. Repsol YPF's ESTC examines the results of all audits, and compliance reviews, and the root causes of environmental problems, and evaluates the corrective action plans submitted and implemented by business unit management. It continually evaluates the company's environmental performance against its environmental policies and objectives, seeking opportunities for further improvement. The details of Repsol YPF's performance and operations are provided in its *Environmental Report*, which are based guidelines of the European Commission Recommendation (2001/453/EC).

Table 3B.3 provides a map of the EMS framework as it relates to the ISO 14001 elements.

Audit and evaluation

Repsol YPF's Environmental Audit Program is a fundamental management tool for ensuring compliance and continuous improvement. The audit program includes internal audits by trained professionals from unrelated business units, external audits, and ISO 14001 certification audits of the operating centers by third parties. The environmental audit program includes a three-year cycle for operating centers. The audits are basically an examination of the EMS, compliance with regulations, and other technical aspects.[9] "In 2002, 194 environmental audits were carried out at Repsol YPF alone, 125 were internal, 6 were external, and 63 related to ISO 14001 and EMAS certification processes."[10]

ISO 14001 requires audits of the EMS on a periodic basis to provide assurance of its effective implementation, to provide information for management review, and to determine the capability of the EMS in achieving the environmental objectives. The audit program prescribes the audit scope, frequency, and methodology, as well as the requirements for conducting the audits and the reporting of the results.

Table 3B.2. The main elements of Repsol YPF's EMS (SIGMA)

Main Sections of EMS

- *Policies*   Policy statements clearly articulate management's view and are intended to promote outstanding environmental and business performance.
- *Organization*   Provides guidelines on the flow of responsibilities and information to and from the business units. Leadership committees include TMESC and ESTC. Focuses on organizational performance related to the ability, knowledge, responsiveness, motivation, development, and achievement of management and staff.
- *Planning (strategic plan)*   Provides written goals, measures, resources, and action plans that form the basis for direction and performance. The integrated planning methodology results in uniform achievements corporate-wide (five-year plan).
- *Audits*   Establishes the means to assess, understand, prevent, and control outcomes and performance, and provide surveillance of the business units. Audits are generally conducted periodically (every three years) to assure that Operating Centers are conforming to regulations and standards.
- *ISO 14001 certification*   Provide external certification of assessments, audits, and performance. Enables a standard comparison of corporate-wide measurements on a comprehensive/consistent basis.
- *Information: communications and product quality*   Provide ongoing means of communicating information and knowledge of issues and results. Serve as a means to map out the road to environmental excellence.
- *Environmental training*   Includes specific education and training needs to address risks and liabilities and to provide basis for making improvements. Promotes environmental training for those in management and operations.

Table 3B.3. Primary elements of ISO 14001 and Repsol YPF's management responsibilities

ISO 14001 element	TMESC	ESTC	Business units
4.1 General Requirements	R	R	R
4.2 Environmental Policy	Primary	Primary	
4.3 Planning	R	R	
• 4.3.1 Environmental Aspects		R	R
• 4.3.2 Legal and Other Requirements		R	R
• 4.3.3 Objectives and Targets	Primary	Primary	R
• 4.3.4 Environmental Management Programs	Primary		R
4.4 Implementation and Operation			
• 4.4.1 Structure and Responsibility		R	R
• 4.4.2 Training and Awareness		R	R
• 4.4.3 Communication		Primary	R
• 4.4.4 EMS Documentation		R	R
• 4.4.5 Document Control			R

Table 3B.3. (cont.)

ISO 14001 element	TMESC	ESTC	Business units
• 4.4.6 Operational Control			R
• 4.4.7 Emergency Preparedness			R
4.5 Checking and Corrective Action			
• 4.5.1 Monitoring and Measurement		Primary	
• 4.5.2 Nonconformance and Action			R
• 4.5.3 Records			R
• 4.5.4 EMS Audit		Primary	R
4.6 Management Review	Primary	Primary	R

Note: R = Responsible.

Management review also continually evaluates the system's operations and provides opportunity to make changes. Changes to policies, objectives, and procedures may be required because of changes in stakeholder expectations or business conditions, advances in technology, the results of audits, or to pursue continuous improvement. The review process includes the full scope of the environmental dimensions as defined by the EMS, including their impact on business and financial performance.

Repsol YPF's Environmental Reporting System is a conduit to the external media for corporate environmental information and results. It involves the collection, consolidation, analysis, validation, and presentation of available information in a format that is suitable for external use. The system is controlled through standard procedures and guidelines and validated by United Research Services (URS), Repsol YPF's environmental consultant and auditor.[11] The reporting system is intended to reduce the variability between the business units and to serve as an integrating mechanism for comparing environmental results across the corporation. It also supports Product Stewardship, environmental communications, and risk management, and it is linked to competitive advantage and profitability.

The evaluation system offers a balanced, multidimensional approach for evaluating environmental performance so that improvements and progress toward achieving an environmental objective in one area are not made at the expense of performance in another. The evaluation system is divided into six environmental categories or performance measures. Each performance measure is further subdivided into subcategories or environmental indicators (EI). They provide senior management and the business line managers with a process for internally tracking and evaluating the organization's performance and ensuring continuous improvement. Each business unit can evaluate its own processes using EIs that are compatible with the data and information available to them. The environmental indicators are evaluated on a quarterly basis.

The evaluation system includes the selection of the performance measures, the EIs, and procedures for the collection, analysis, and reporting of performance-related data and information. The system and the associated EIs are developed in concert with the elements included in the environmental audit system. However, EIs focus on environmental performance results obtained by the EMS, while auditing is used to verify implementation of the management system. Much of the data and information to support the process such as emissions rates, risk assessments, financial data, and inventory data exist as part of the routine operations of the organization. Information and data of known and verifiable quality is used to provide a reasonable basis for evaluating the performance of the EMS. Appropriate quality assurance and/or quality control functions ensure the validity of the data collection methodologies and modeling techniques.

Assessing performance in each of the areas presents challenges to the company, since not all business units are identical. A technique for evaluating one aspect of the company may not be suitable for all of the business units or operations. Table 3B.4 shows some of Repsol YPF's main categories, subcategories, and select environmental indicators:

Table 3B.4. Repsol YPF's environmental evaluation system

Category	Subcategory	EI	Logic
Product environmental quality	Fuel quality in Spain	– Parts per million of sulfur in gas	Based on pending EU Directives
	Fuel quality in Argentina	– Fuel specifications – Use of Bio-fuels	Meet new requirements for fuels
	Replacement of MTBE		Enhance renewable energy sources
Climate changes	Carbon dioxide (CO_2)	– Tons of CO_2 per ton of production	Efficiently meet emissions
	Greenhouse gases	– Total tons of emission per country	Meet expectation of Kyoto
	Recovery of flare gases	– Tons of gas recovered	Reduce energy consumption
Emissions to air	Sulfur dioxide (SO_2)	– Tons of SO_2 per ton of production	Reduce acid rain precursors
	Volatile organics (VOCs)	– Total tons of SO_2 per country	Improve compliance issues
Water and marine environment	Water management	– Total wastewater discharges (tons)	Reduce impacts and save money
	Water quality	– % of main pollutants in wastewater	Reduce impacts and save money
Waste and soil management	Solid waste generated	– Waste generated per business unit	Improve economics Improve equity and reduce costs
	Quality of liquid waste	– Geographical distribution of waste	
Environmental investments	Improve products	– Total investment, by business area	Improve value and benefits
	Improve facilities	– Environmental expenses, by sector	Improve eco-effectiveness

EIs may be characterized in a number of ways: (1) absolute values; (2) relative ratings; (3) aggregate factors; (4) indexes; and (5) qualitative. The more complicated the indicator, the more difficult it is to interpret. The EI system must:

- Be compatible with the EMS and assist with the attainment of objectives and standards
- Concentrate on measuring the principal causes and effects of environmental concerns
- Be useful as a management tool for taking corrective actions that are related to critical objectives; management must focus on developing a consensus for establishing a common set of metrics that will be used to monitor the business lines
- Be verified externally and be meaningful; they should be cost effective, and emphasize the benefits associated with environmental improvements and provide encouragement for further progress
- Allow self-assessment by the business unit management
- Facilitate comparison with other business units and other companies; this is very important when considering operations in different countries.

Together, the performance evaluation must embody a broad understanding of the environmental liabilities that the company faces. They must indicate a comprehensive view of the operations and activities in order to allow management to determine what courses of action can reduce liabilities and improve the company's strategic position.

The Repsol YPF case study provides many insights about how to deploy a sophisticated EMS and how to begin moving to a richer reality based on SBD principles. The company has established many of the precursors and is working on further improvements. The quest is never-ending.

Notes:
1. http://www.repsol-ypf.com, *Repsol YPF 2000 Environmental Report*, p. 2–7.
2. *Ibid.*, p. 2.
3. http://www.repsol-ypf.com, *Repsol YPF 2002 Environmental Report*, pp. 7–8.
4. *Ibid.*, p. 8.
5. http://www.repsol-ypf.com, *Repsol YPF 1999 Environmental Report*, p. 2.
6. http://www.repsol-ypf.com, *Repsol YPF 2002 Environmental Report*, p. 10. LPG is the acronym for liquefied petroleum gas.
7. N. 3 above.
8. *Ibid.*, pp. 8–10.
9. *Ibid.*, p. 9.
10. *Ibid.*
11. United Research Services (URS) has offices in Spain.

Summary

The strategic management elements related to SBD form a process for strategic thinking and decision-making. The activities, information flow, and analysis within each of the elements are typically ongoing, and the actual inputs and outputs vary enormously from case to case. Chapter 3 has mapped

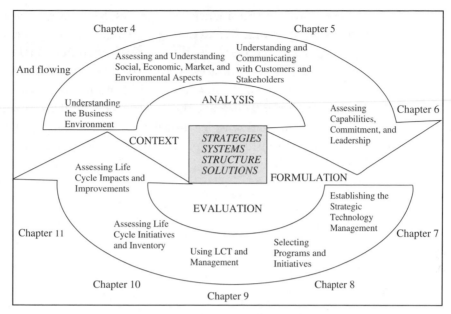

Figure 3.6   Strategic management process for analyzing/selecting SBD programs

out the strategic considerations in understanding the business environment and assessing corporate capabilities for crafting sustainable business strategies and solutions. Figure 3.6 provides the flow of a generic process and how the elements relate to the chapters in the book. The process elements depicted are subdivided into formulation steps at the top of the graphic and execution steps at the bottom.

The process is shown as a circle originating with an assessment of the business environment with its opportunities and challenges, and flowing through an understanding of the market potential (the needs and wants of the external dimensions), analyzing capabilities and resources, and selecting SBD programs. While these elements are the most crucial, there are subelements within each.

Planning and execution are the essence of strategic management. They bridge the initial elements of gathering information for analysis to the understanding of opportunities and their implications. This step leads next to the selection of the types of programs to be explored, from technological innovation and product and process development to simple incremental improvement initiatives. The crux of the process is finally selecting the most viable programs, developing solutions, gaining acceptance, and implementing the solutions in the business world. The process is ongoing, and the next cycle may begin even before the previous one has ended.

The power of the strategic management process for SBD is in the embedded evaluation techniques of LCA and the ongoing performance evaluation of the whole process. Evaluation explores the potential outcomes and determines if the process and the solution are meeting the objectives and targets, or if adjustments have to be made. In addition, evaluation provides a sense of the likelihood of success or failure, and the consequences of such outcomes. Risks are always present, and must be understood and managed. Even doing nothing, a common historical approach, may be highly risky in a world of rapid change and dramatic new technological innovations.

Supplementary material

Learning objectives

Chapter 3 has the following learning objectives that are intended to guide and support students and practitioners:
- Understanding the use of analytical models and business models for strategic analysis and systems integration.
- Appreciating how the business environment (context) drives the formulating and implementation of corporate and business strategies.
- Exploring how global corporations formulate and implement SBD strategies and initiatives.
- Understanding how performance evaluation plays a significant role in ensuring that SBD strategies, initiatives, and programs achieve sustainable success.

Research questions

The following are questions related to SBD in order to facilitate learning and ongoing discussion and analysis of the main topics covered in the chapter:
- What are the linkages between analytical models and business models?
- How do global corporations create a conceptual framework for strategic analysis and systems integration?
- What are the most critical elements of the solution matrix that are important to global corporations and their customers and stakeholders?
- How do global corporations select their grand strategies for SBD?
- How do strategic leaders and managers determine SBD strategies?
- What are the most important elements of a performance evaluation system?

NOTES

1. **Integrated product development (IPD)** is a powerful management construct that systematically links the external business environment and its needs, wants, opportunities, and challenges with the internal dimensions of the organization and its capabilities and resources to create innovative solutions based on improved products and services. It is the concurrent development of new products using cross-functional teams that are aligned strategically and tactically. It is the prevailing form of product innovation.

2. Kenneth R. Andrews, *The Concept of Corporate Strategy*, rev. edn. (New York: Irwin, 1980), pp. 18–19. Andrews was a leading scholar in strategic management and the concept of business strategy at Harvard Business School.

3. Bernard Taylor and Keith MacMillan, *Business Policy: Teaching and Research* (New York: John Wiley, 1973), p. 138.

4. Alfred Chandler, Jr., *Strategy and Structure: Chapters in the History of the American Industrial Enterprise* (Cambridge, MA: MIT Press, 1962), p. 14.

5. Gary Hamel, *Leading the Revolution* (Boston, MA: Harvard Business School Press, 2000), p. 78.

6. C. Roland Christensen, Norman Berg, and Malcolm Salter, *Business Policy: Text and Cases* (New York: Irwin, 1978), p. 125. Their actual definition of corporate strategy included "the patterns of decision in a company that (1) shapes and reveals its objectives, purposes or goals, (2) produces the principal policies and plans for achieving these goals, and (3) defines the business the company intends to be in and the kind of economic and human organization it intends to be."

7. Most scholars agree that organizational learning proceeds at a given rate within an organization and that knowledge and the transformation of capabilities require time to effect. The rate of change or improvement varies from corporation to corporation. Indeed, some corporations such as IBM and Siemens emphasize knowledge and learning as primary objectives.

8. Steven Wheelwright and Kim Clark, *Revolutionizing Product Development, Quantum Leap in Speed, Efficiency, and Quality* (New York: Free Press, 1992), p. 23.

9. This framework is essentially the flow suggested by ISO 9000 and ISO 14000.

10. The inception of the International Organization for Standardization (ISO) in 1979 was critical in the development of management systems. While ISO focused on standards of quality systems, the philosophy was based on the precepts that it is the management system that assures quality and that an effective management system provides the means and mechanisms to positively effect performance and the achievements of targets and objectives.

11. Chandler, *Strategy and Structure*, p. 14.

12. Paul Weaver, Leo Jansen, Geert van Grootveld, Egbert van Spiegel, and Philip Vergragt, *Sustainable Technology Development* (Sheffield: Greenleaf Publishing, 2000), pp. 171–203.

13. Moore's Law suggests that computer processing power doubles every eighteen months.

14. "Upholding Moore's Law," *Newsweek*, March 25, 2002.

15. Michael Porter, *Competitive Advantage: Creating and Sustaining Superior Performance* (New York: Free Press, 1985), pp. 11–16.

REFERENCES

Andrews, Kenneth R. (1980) *The Concept of Corporate Strategy*, rev. edn. New York: Irwin

Chandler, Jr., Alfred (1962) *Strategy and Structure: Chapters in the History of the American Industrial Enterprise*. Cambridge, MA: MIT Press

Christensen, C. Roland, Norman Berg, and Malcolm Salter (1978) *Business Policy: Text and Cases*. New York: Irwin

Hamel, Gary (2000) *Leading the Revolution*. Boston, MA: Harvard Business School Press

Porter, Michael (1985) *Competitive Advantage: Creating and Sustaining Superior Performance*. New York: Free Press

Taylor, Bernard and Keith MacMillan (1973) *Business Policy: Teaching and Research*. New York: John Wiley

Weaver, Paul, Leo Jansen, Geert van Grootveld, Egbert van Spiegel, and Philip Vergragt (2000) *Sustainable Technology Development*. Sheffield: Greenleaf Publishing

Wheelwright, Steven and Kim Clark (1992) *Revolutionizing Product Development, Quantum Leap in Speed, Efficiency, and Quality*. New York: Free Press

4   The driving forces of social-, economic-, and environmental-related change

Introduction

SBD takes place within the context of the business environment. That context consists of social, economic, environmental, and business-related considerations and circumstances, and the ways in which those circumstances are changing. This chapter discusses how this dynamic environment can provide opportunities for corporations to develop, build, and enhance external relationships and create value – and, ultimately, enhance corporate wealth, reputation, and image. The primary focus is on how the corporation affects people and the natural environment as it conducts its affairs, designs, produces and sells products, operates its facilities, and acquires and uses the resources necessary to satisfy customers, stakeholders, and other constituents.

By building key stakeholder relationships among government agencies, NGOs, consumer entities, environmental groups, and other constituents, corporations can anticipate and manage issues and concerns that might otherwise have gone undetected until they had grown into major problems. Being in sync with constituencies and building trust among customers and stakeholders is essential to building strategies for SBD.

The social considerations are the most crucial, yet the most difficult, to define and understand. The concept of corporate social responsibility goes back to pre-strategic planning days (the 1960s and 1970s). Generally, social considerations focus on specific issues that relate to the corporation's involvement in its direct affairs, such as activities and transactions with employees, customers, shareholders, suppliers, etc. Some of the most common concerns are those covered by laws and regulations, including sexual harassment, smoking in the work place, drug abuse, employee layoffs, diversity, and "right to know" mandates. However, social considerations involve more than the "must do" categories of legally prescribed requirements, and include protecting the health and safety of the general population, avoiding harm to the natural environment, developing and deploying ethical standards and practices, meeting cultural and social norms, balancing the interests of the corporation with the interests of society, and being a proactive corporate citizen.

Political considerations are powerful, as well, and generally have direct impacts on the functioning and success of the corporation. Political and regulatory changes are usually a manifestation of the social and economic conditions and issues. For example, public pressure for "Right-to-Know" legislation in the United States was an outgrowth of the chemical disaster at Bhopal in 1984.

Economic considerations are also primary concerns for corporations, their customers, and stakeholders. The focus of economics is often on the direct effects of the exchange of goods and services, the flow of money, and the relationships between the participants. SBD examines those direct effects and their consequences, and also considers the indirect implications of economic activities such as the hidden costs of transactions and the externalities borne by the local community, the public in general, or even the global human population. For example, the health effects of toxic chemicals can become company liabilities and stakeholder concerns that companies must spend time and money tracking, and sometimes eventually remediating them. For instance, global warming is expected to have greater impacts in the "out years" (50–100 years in the future) than in the present. If the trends continue, people will have to make adjustments and create new solutions to deal with these effects.

The most crucial economic questions often pertain to environmental-related impacts: What effects do increasing uncertainty about environmental concerns have on the economic conditions and trends over time? What is the carrying capacity of the Earth? What is its ability to provide resources, digest waste streams, and/or handle disruptions? If resources are depleted, or become scarcer, what are the economic implications? More specifically, what are the long-term impacts of various waste streams?

These and other environmental considerations are some of the multi-faceted negative and unintended outcomes of products, processes, and operations. They lead to *degradation* of the environment, *destruction* of the natural world, *disruption* of the quality of life, and *depletion* of resources. They diminish society's ability to sustain the world of the future.

The basic premises of this book and SBD assume that corporations bear a very serious responsibility to manage their impacts on the social, economic, political, environmental, and market realities of the world. Social responsiveness, economic security, and environmental protection are the key factors for sustainable success. SBD targets the intersection of all of these and integrates them into a holistic perspective so that sustainable solutions may be realized. This chapter examines the following topics:

- The implications of the business environment and the underlying forces affecting social, political, economic, and environmental conditions
- The analytical process for understanding the business environment, including scanning, monitoring, forecasting, and assessment
- The social and political aspects of SBD
- The description and assessment of the main economic implications of sustainable success
- The identification and description of the essential environmental considerations.

Understanding the implications of the business environment

The underlying forces: social, political, economic, and environmental conditions

As a corporation pursues SBD, the choices it makes depend on its understanding of the underlying forces that impinge upon it. These forces are the independent variables that shape the formulation and implementation of the strategies and initiatives of the corporation. They provide the basis for assessing whether the strategic position is viable and acceptable, or if it requires reflection, further assessment, and modification.

The forces at work in the business environment are interrelated and often affect each other in complex ways. Corporations are social organizations conceived to benefit the social and economic aspects of humankind. More specifically, corporations exist to satisfy the needs of their customers, markets, stakeholders, shareholders, and society. The solutions they provide should be based on a broad social perspective – the needs of society at large – and thereafter seek to satisfy the particular, which includes markets, employees, and shareholders. Great solutions combine both the broad and the particular. For example, the PC has greatly influenced many sectors of society and business by increasing capabilities and providing the means to increase effectiveness in the work place and at home. It has done this by dramatically improving the productivity of individuals and the global economy.

While some might argue that examining political forces apart from social forces is an arbitrary distinction, and that a sociopolitical perspective is a more accurate measure, the separation of the political forces from the social is a useful construct for focusing attention on specific issues and concerns. The political milieu definitely affects corporations. Politics converges opinions, shapes mandates, and prescribes the realm of acceptable solutions. From a business perspective, public policy and political decisions represent opportunities for the business community to determine acceptable solutions to problems that were previously left to others such as government to solve. There are many examples of the business community's failure to reach consensus on an issue, and thereby forcing the social and political arenas to mandate the solution. The use of leaded gasoline for automobiles is a striking case in point. Lead in gasoline was recognized as a major source of heavy metal (lead) contamination as early as 1950. It took the governments in the United States, Europe and elsewhere to force a phase-out before the petroleum and automobile industries responded with unleaded fuels and new engine technologies that provided the same performance as the old solution minus the negative effects and impacts.

Historically, political forces have been particularly important in establishing environmental rules and regulations. Political and regulatory changes are major concerns for senior management, business professionals, and technical experts. Often, failure to address the demands of interest groups or the implications of social issues results in political results that could have been avoided. The political environment is a critical factor affecting corporations' means to achieve effective, long-term solutions.

Economics is another powerful driver that is also tied to social and political agendas. The global economic environment is extremely dynamic as financial and trade transactions impact economies, businesses, consumers, and social forces. The economic conditions and trends are significant change mechanisms that often preempt a corporation's desired progress. With the cyclical aspects of the macro-environment in mind, however, it is critical that the analyses of the economic forces take a long-term perspective. In exploring problems and difficulties, the best solutions are found where there is a convergence between all three of these interrelated forces: needs (social), means (economic), and desires (political).

Technological forces also have a significant influence on a corporation's pursuit of SBD. New technologies offer opportunities to create new solutions to current difficulties and past problems. New technologies, such as bioremediation, have created innovative ways to mitigate spills and cleanup landfills and other contaminated areas. Future technologies will provide the means to eliminate the negative implications of many existing products and processes. This topic is discussed in greater detail in chapter 7.

Environmental forces vary from the obvious requirements specified through laws and regulations to the demands and needs of environmental interest groups, local and regional communities, markets and customers, and the general public. Such forces impinge on the product delivery system on a daily basis. Operational management and professionals must comply with legal requirements and manage the products, by-products, residuals, and waste streams that are generated. At higher levels, senior management has to consider the global consequences of the corporation's actions. The environmental aspects of this consideration are covered in more detail in part II.

As the public becomes better informed about the consequences of corporate decisions and actions, it is more difficult for corporations to avoid the implications of residuals, waste streams, and other environmental impacts. Moreover, as government regulations become more stringent, the costs of compliance increase dramatically. The simplification and cost avoidance approaches of the past are now insufficient in the light of the higher costs of managing pollution and the increased taxes, fees, and fines for environmental problems. As hidden costs become apparent, the economics associated with high-volume production and mass marketing are no longer adequate to carry the corporation. A more comprehensive view of the business environment is now required. Figure 4.1 depicts the fundamental interrelationships of the underlying driving forces shaping that environment.

The complex forces affecting the business environment are ever-changing and demanding better solutions. These forces are interrelated, and ultimately tied to social conditions and trends. Indeed, the wants, needs, and expectations of people in the short and long term provide the context for all business decisions.

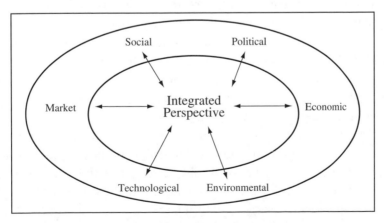

Figure 4.1   The interrelationships between the underlying driving forces

The direct forces: markets, customers, and stakeholders

Markets and customers, along with stakeholders, are the most critical components of the business environment for the corporation. While the underlying social, political, economic, and environmental forces provide a sense of the general requirements, a focus on markets, customers, and stakeholders examines the particular. The market forces are crucial to the viability of a strategic direction. They include customers (buyers and users) and secondary users of the existing technologies and products, and the expected changes in future markets and customers. The former are *relatively* easy to understand since data already exist concerning present-day demand and expectations. Anticipating and understanding the needs and wants of the future is a more difficult feat. Chapter 5 examines market- and stakeholder-related considerations.

The analytical process for understanding the business environment

Perspectives on the business environment and strategic thinking

In exploring the business environment, corporations have to identify, understand, and respond to the legitimate issues and concerns of their external constituents. Assessing the implications of these external factors is one of the main functions of traditional strategic management frameworks. As discussed in chapter 3, the business environment provides the context for determining appropriate strategies and initiatives for SBD. In the normative approach for strategic planning, the situation analysis (assessment of the business environment) usually precedes the determination of strategic direction and the selection of specific strategies. By contrast, in the "preemptive world" of SBD, strategic analysis is continuous and embedded in the whole strategy formulation process. It examines the whole business environment and its critical forces as they relate to every facet of the corporation, including the systems, technologies, products, and processes. It is an ongoing process, with neither a beginning nor an end.

How a corporation responds to its situation analysis of external factors is governed by its desire to compete and succeed but also, increasingly, by its sense of corporate social responsibility, economic stability, and environmental stewardship. The principles of SBD suggest that corporations adopt a stakeholder approach to social responsibility – one that considers the effects of corporate actions on any and all parties involved, no matter how far removed their involvement or where they occur in the life cycle of the product. Again, enterprise thinking plays a role in determining what social responsibility is, and means.

Corporate Social Responsibility (CSR), though widely understood, is difficult to define and prescribe. In simple terms, CSR implies that corporations have a fiduciary duty to both meet the needs and wants of customers and stakeholders and protect the health and safety of humankind and the natural environment. More specifically, it means taking corporate responsibility for the decisions and actions of the whole enterprise, not just those of the corporation and its direct actions. To be socially responsible, a corporation's responsibilities cannot end at the boundaries of its facilities, but rather, must extend beyond the corporation's effects and impacts to include both the direct and indirect impacts of its supply networks, customer applications, and linkages with other entities, as well.

Moreover, in a socially responsible scenario, corporations deliberately choose such linkages and do not limit them to the physical flow of goods and services and commercial transactions. For example, outsourcing certain activities may eliminate direct corporate responsibilities for the wastes and environmental impacts generated by the operations of the suppliers or suppliers of suppliers. However, such approaches (outsourcing) do not lessen the social responsibilities of the corporation. The impacts and consequences are still directly related to the corporation's decisions. The corporation chose the design of the product and the selection of suppliers, and it manages the flow of activities that led to the impacts and consequences. Outsourcing does not reduce social responsibility. In certain cases, it makes the scope of the system more complex and more difficult to manage because the corporation must be ever-cognizant of the operations and activities of its suppliers, agents, partners, etc., and take appropriate actions if the outcomes are not sustainable or in line with the corporation's principles, strategies, objectives, and social responsibilities. It also has an implied responsibility to ensure that the actions of its suppliers, agents, and others are in compliance with laws and regulations. Failure to track such compliance may leave the corporation vulnerable to political and economic problems, including disruption of the flow of materials.

CSR is not a matter of debate. Corporations are inherently and legally responsible for the effects of their operations, products, and processes. The legal aspects are perhaps the easiest to discuss. Corporations have legal and social obligations to understand and comply with all of the laws and regulations that affect their operations, activities and products. Most global corporations have extensive capabilities to manage their legal responsibilities; such capabilities and responses have matured since the 1970s to the point where compliance issues are well understood and executed in a systematic manner. This is not to imply that there is full compliance, or that the mandates are easily met.

The more difficult responsibilities relate to the obligations of corporations to supervise the activities of their suppliers, partners, distributors, and even their customers. This is more open-ended. In most countries, corporations are not directly responsible for the actions of legally independent agents. However, the principles of SBD suggest that corporations have a social responsibility to ensure that such agents, and their agents, in turn, are not only in full compliance with regulations, but have best practices throughout their operations.

SBD also demands social responsiveness and an ethical obligation to eliminate defects and burdens rather than manage them after the problems have been created. It holds corporations to a high standard, expecting them also to mitigate the effects of any defect or burden for which they are directly or indirectly responsible. If the corporation is linked to the issues through its relationships, transactions, and decisions, then it has an implicit, if not explicit, responsibility to ensure that the social, economic, environmental, and market implications of its choices are appropriate and sustainable. While the scope of direct corporate responsibilities may be specific, the implied responsibilities are less definitive and often vary according to the corporation's involvement and the degree of influence that it has on the situation.

A corporation determines the scope of its responsibilities according to its context for decision-making. (LCT, life cycle management, and LCA, as described and discussed in chapters 9–11, provide guidance and direction in determining the scope of such responsibility.) The corporation chooses whether to engage or not engage in technologies, products, processes, operations, and activities. It selects the supply networks and implicitly selects the entities within the supply chain and distribution channels. The greater the ability of the corporation to make choices that would avoid or rectify negative outcomes, the more responsible it may be for any negative impacts. For example, if a manufacturer selects a supplier which generates hazardous wastes in a country with minimal environmental regulations and standards when there are other suppliers of the same materials, parts, or components who do not create any hazardous waste at all, then the corporation causes a situation to exist that could have been avoided or eliminated. In such cases, the manufacturer is directly responsible for the implications of its supplier's actions. Conversely, if a company purchases materials from suppliers, the implications and impacts of whose actions it cannot affect, the purchaser bears less responsibility for the upstream decision-making. For example, electricity is a basic commodity that is broadly used across the world. It is difficult to find acceptable alternatives for power generation that do not have negative impacts. Given that it is usually impossible for the user to specify the source of electricity, it seems unreasonable to hold the user responsible for the upstream activities that generated that electricity. However, as new sources become available and new mechanisms for the delivery of electricity are developed, users may have options.

Fundamental to SBD constructs is the corporation's determination of the standards (both internal and external) that govern its own actions. Ultimately, each corporation has to articulate its social responsibilities based on its own social, political, economic, environmental, and market considerations.

A normative process for analyzing the business environment

The analysis of the business environment is extremely complex, and many elements can be included. The process is limited in this discussion to scanning, monitoring, forecasting, and assessing existing conditions and trends. It is not the intention here to describe a situation analysis in which all external factors are examined, including industry analysis, competition analysis, and market and customer analyses. These analytical techniques belong more to the methodologies of strategic planning.[1] Rather, this section examines the broader aspects of the business environment targeting, instead, general conditions and trends. The focus is on those conditions and trends that the corporation should be aware of and have mechanisms for dealing with. Changes in population growth, demographics, mobility, life styles, technological innovation, social expectations, and laws and regulations are only a few of the change mechanisms that corporations have to scan, monitor, forecast, and assess.

Figure 4.2 maps out the normative process, which includes the following four primary areas of analysis.

- Scanning the business environment to identify the conditions, trends, and the forces of change that exist and to detect the most important issues, concerns, impacts, and implications for the corporation.
- Monitoring those specific conditions and trends that have direct and indirect consequences on the strategies and selected development

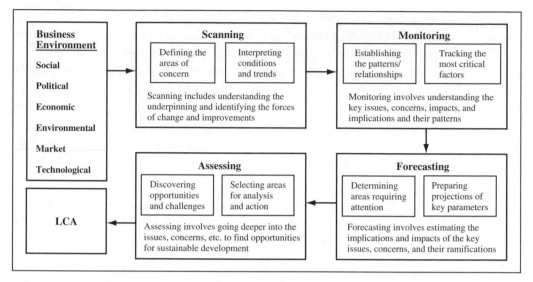

Figure 4.2   A simplified framework for analysis of the business environment

programs of the corporation. Monitoring focuses on the conditions and trends that have been deemed to be the most important in the context of the business.

- Forecasting change and the impacts of the resulting direct and indirect consequences over time.
- Assessing the implications of trends and changes to determine the proper courses of actions.

Scanning

Scanning is the broadest approach used to obtain an understanding of the business environment. It is a sweeping surveillance of the critical social, political, economic, environmental, and market conditions undertaken to find important concerns and issues that may be related to the activities and actions of the corporation and to discover early signals of changes that may have direct and indirect implications for the corporation. These include issues or phenomena that are often viewed as tangential, such as the growing demands for **transparency** and reporting, the pressures to deal with the prospects of climate change, and the expectations of stakeholders for corporations to eliminate toxic substances. Pending changes usually involve new interpretations and views of society, stakeholders, and customers about the prevailing issues and problems. For example, although smoking had negative connotations for decades, it was still largely accepted. During the 1990s pressure groups, through litigation and public awareness campaigns, were able to change public perceptions and reverse public acceptance.

Scanning allows management to stay on top of many issues without having to invest in the full capabilities necessary to monitor them on a full-time basis. It tends to be open-ended without specific or predetermined notions about what to explore, examine, and report and therefore somewhat difficult to define and execute. It requires exceptional skill on the part of practitioners and is most effective when conducted by people who possess an outstanding sense of the business environment and its underlying forces.

The first step is to enumerate the relevant factors and forces pertinent to the corporation and to determine the potential influence they may have on strategies, positions, programs, and actions. The second step is to prioritize those factors and forces. While it may be premature at this point to characterize the forces and factors as opportunities, threats, challenges, or constraints, it is often useful to rank their importance so that appropriate attention can be provided. This step is most useful when there are hundreds or thousands of factors that have to be tracked and it would be impossible to adequately follow everything: prioritizing makes an impossible assignment possible. While prioritization runs the risk of skewing the process toward preordained conclusions, prioritization in the scanning process can be justified when there are limited resources, an overwhelming number of factors to consider, and when management and the professionals involved are aware of the explicit and implicit aspects of the business environment. Such an approach follows scientific logic, wherein observations and theories about the business environment allow the corporation to use informed judgment about what to consider. Experienced professionals generally know what is important and what they have to follow.

Indeed, the normative approach is to combine data, information, analysis, and experience when making decisions about methods and approaches. This is perhaps most appropriate in those cases where unexpected developments are more likely to occur. The more dynamic the business environment, the more useful it is to have an open-ended process. Based on known conditions, corporations can scan for select factors that they know are critical while still retaining an open view for the unexpected. For instance, a corporation might use subject matter experts to track concerns that are well established, such as global concerns about climate change. It might also wish to track the broader topics of the quality and availability of drinking water, for which it would employ specialists in the task of watching other industries or other countries, and the development of new issues, concerns, consequences, and the like.

The third step is to determine the strategic significance of each of the factors and forces. This step includes outlining the conditions and trends and creating a means to select the most crucial ones for ongoing monitoring. For most corporations having a continuous process, this step involves ongoing adjustments rather than definitive and comprehensive actions.

The last step is to ensure that the information and knowledge is available to those conducting the next stage in analyzing the business environment: the monitoring. This is an easy step in those cases where the same people are doing both the scanning and monitoring. This arrangement may be more efficient, require less training, and make it easier to link with the other downstream elements of the analysis process. Still, scanning requires a broad perspective while monitoring necessitates a narrower one. Scanning is intended to discover issues, concerns, threats, and/or problems during their early stages so that additional information can be obtained and ongoing tracking can be affected. The great concern is that there may be a bias towards overemphasizing the most obvious issues impinging on the corporation and not paying enough attention to the newly developing issues.

Monitoring

Monitoring is easier because it involves tracking specific conditions and trends that have been identified as important to the corporation. While there may be hundreds of such items to follow, the process is usually more systematic, with known sources of data and information and established means for discerning patterns and implications.

Monitoring depends on gathering accurate information about the targeted topics and understanding the implications of the patterns and relationships that develop over time. For example, the effects of a single accident may not have significant long-term implications. But a pattern of many similar situations may indicate that there is a defective product or process that requires a solution. As more information became available, it became more apparent that there might be a causal relationship between the tires and accidents.

Monitoring also includes determining the significance of events and understanding the needs and demands of constituencies. Events typically fall into two main categories: the overwhelming and the commonplace. Overwhelming events, such as the terrorist attacks of September 11, 2001, are so catastrophic that it is difficult to ascertain all of their short-term and long-term effects. Such events tend to change many of the basic assumptions about conditions and trends in the business environment. It is impossible to generalize about managing the impacts and consequences of such events other than to recognize that changes will occur and that they may challenge the corporation's basic assumptions of its management practices.

The commonplace category is somewhat easier to track and understand. The demands of constituencies tend to evolve over time rather than change rapidly and dramatically. If the corporation identifies the precursors to unmet constituent demands and acts expeditiously in trying to resolve the situation, the implications can often be mitigated. The commonplace category does not imply that the concerns are unimportant: on the contrary, they may be critical for the long-term success of the industry, its customers, and the corporation itself. The depletion of petroleum resources is an obvious and well-known issue that is easily tracked, but it is difficult to truly ascertain the implications and impacts.

The information gleaned from monitoring can be used to direct the development of solutions and create mechanisms for creating positive outcomes. To gather the best information, monitoring draws from archival records, the available literature, and a careful observation of ongoing events. Like scanning, the steps include identifying the specific factors and forces to be tracked on an ongoing basis, determining the significance of these events, patterns, and relationships, and understanding the key issues, impacts, and implications. Both scanning and monitoring are part of the discovery process that enriches the knowledge and understanding of the business environment. They characterize what is occurring or has occurred and, in this way, provide the information and data necessary to further analyze the business environment for strategic purposes.

Forecasting the implications

Forecasting involves making projections about what is expected to happen in the future. The intent is to make realistic predictions of the expected conditions and trends – but, as one might guess, forecasting is imprecise. Still, it is a critical step, as it sets the stage for assessing likely situations and determining the options available to the corporation. Forecasting is also complex: rarely does any situation depend on a single variable. In most cases, the situation is confounded with many variables that can cause incredible impacts on the expected or potential outcomes.

In the context of the business environment, forecasting not only helps to present the corporation with information on which to base future actions, it also provides a way to understand the opportunities and potential impacts of those decisions in quantitative terms. The fundamental goal is to make projections about the implications of decisions and to determine whether those decisions are desirable choices or if they will likely lead to unacceptable outcomes. During the preliminary stage of developing sustainable solutions, forecasting is used primarily to understand the feasibility of a selected action based on its projected effects and implications on the downstream situation. The projections typically provide insights about resource utilization, waste generation, the effects of production disruptions, and other significant factors. It is about understanding *relationships* more than predictions.

The classic use of forecasting is to determine the expected market conditions and the potential share of market that the company is expected to enjoy. There are numerous techniques used for forecasting, most of which are useful only for short-term, commonly encountered situations. It is relatively easy to determine the social, economic, environmental, and market considerations for the short term for established or mature businesses and their products. It is more difficult to determine the salient factors for new-to-the-world situations where the critical external factors are not readily apparent nor fully developed. In these situations, one of the simplest ways to differentiate the forecasting techniques is to think in terms of the product life cycle. During the early stage of a new product or business launch, the rate of change is usually small, but the potential for change is large. During the growth stage, the rate of change is often larger and more predictable, and there is sufficient data and information available to make reasonable estimates of the situation. At maturity, the rate of change is usually negligible, and the business situation is well established.

Forecasting techniques pertaining to the effects of a new product or activity on the business environment are complicated and difficult to validate. Such techniques must provide accurate results in the long term. The typical situations usually involve five, ten, or even more years ahead, and information from that duration may simply not exist. Forecasting in these situations can be based on the experience of previous technologies or products that have related factors. For example, if the new product or process uses toxic substances, it may have the same stakeholders as previous products. If the product uses large quantities of water during production, it may be competing with the local community or the other local products and processes for the water resources. This qualitative technique examines previous and related situations and estimates the conditions that may arise based on past experience. While this approach is straightforward, great care has to be used to ensure that the new situation is similar to the previous one. However, the validity of this assumption tends to fade over time, and the further the previous experience is from the current time frame, the more likely it is that fundamental changes have occurred in the context that will affect the outcome. While these statements are broad generalizations, they do help characterize the different applications of forecasting. Forecasting related to technologies and products is further defined and discussed in chapter 8.

Assessing

Assessing the business environment translates the results of scanning, monitoring, and forecasting into a definitive understanding of the opportunities, challenges, and constraints facing the corporation. It builds on the work of scanning, monitoring, and forecasting to provide the corporation with a clear understanding of the key issues and concerns and the expected implications and impacts of possible corporate actions to exploit or improve them. While conditions and trends are spelled out during monitoring and forecasting, assessing provides an understanding of their importance. For example, a positive development could be that waste streams are diminishing to the point where they will no longer be a serious concern to stakeholders and may even be eliminated from regulatory oversight. Conversely, there could be a realization that the prevailing means for handling hazardous wastes may be inadequate to meet the requirements of the future. A third possibility is that while the laws and regulations have remained constant, stakeholders are expecting still greater reductions in the quantities produced. Assessing gives meaning to the implications and potential impacts of the expected outcomes over time.

The most effective assessment technique for determining the impacts from new technologies and new products is input-output analysis using LCA. Such techniques can be complicated to use and may take many equations to provide the actual forecast. However, the following simple example indicates the power of the approach. If a manufacturer plans to produce 100,000 units per year of a product that uses lead connectors, that company can forecast the amount of lead discards produced each year. It simply needs to know the waste generated per unit and the reuse or recycling rate. While this is a simple example, it also illustrates a point that is often overlooked. As the wastes increase, the expenditures to treat or dispose of the waste also increase. Additionally, as the level of waste increases, society's willingness to tolerate the waste decreases; the compliance requirements may change dramatically as the manufacturer moves from a low-quantity generator to a large-quantity generator. The social, economic, regulatory, and environmental considerations are not always linear, and as greater quantities are produced the effects may become more serious and the requirements of the business environment more significant. From a business perspective, then, it is critical to estimate and assess not only the sellable products, but also all of the negative implications of their production and sale.

Assessing again selects the most important forces and factors for scrutiny and identifies the constituents that are most influential, so that proper courses of action can be laid out. It does so with the benefit of all the information already obtained by scanning, monitoring, and forecasting, and it does so while focusing on the corporation's required responsiveness to the patterns of change in the business environment. It synthesizes the knowledge gained from the previous steps into a comprehensive understanding of the business environment.

Social, political, and regulatory milieus

The social dimensions

Corporations are social entities. They create outcomes through people and for people. There are numerous views on the purposes of corporations. While the prevailing view is that the most important objectives are to generate profits and cash flow for shareholders and maximize corporate value, satisfying the needs and wants of customers, stakeholders, employees, and selected constituents are also critical objectives of corporations. Indeed, the broader social objectives are often critical for achieving profit objectives.

Customers and markets buy and use the products, services, and intellectual outputs of corporations. Stakeholders are the external entities (individuals, groups, and organizations) that have relationships with the corporation. They influence the corporation directly or indirectly through their actions, opinions, decisions, and/or control mechanisms. Some stakeholders, like government agencies, have formal relationships with the corporation and may even control the activities through regulations, standards, and/or agreements. In the context of the social dimension, stakeholders are defined broadly and may include contractors and partners who provide labor and intellectual inputs into the systems, operations, and processes. They impose the direct social responsibilities of the corporation to be fair and to provide appropriate compensation and reward to its primary contributors. The boards of directors and the shareholders have the overall responsibility to ensure that their corporations behave properly and act according to social

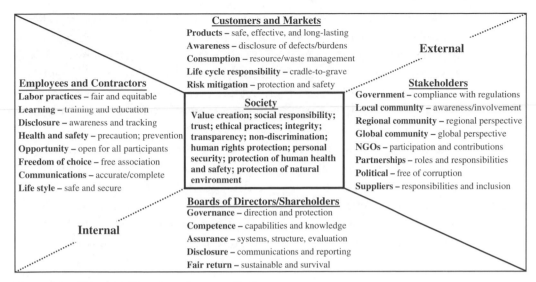

Figure 4.3   The social dimensions of a corporation[a]

Note: [a] Several of the elements are similar or identical to the indicators suggested by GRI, *Sustainability Reporting Guidelines*, 2002, p. 36.

mandates, standards, and norms. It is a complex challenge for most global corporations given the diversity of ownership, external relationships, and partnerships.

Figure 4.3 depicts the social dimensions and several selected elements for each of the principal areas. Several of the key areas are discussed in this section, and many of the areas are discussed in more detail throughout the book.

The core of the social dimension is society in general. Each of the essential subareas embodies a part of corporate life and its relation with external social contacts. The pivotal objective of SBD, from a social perspective, is to achieve success in the present and invent an even better future through value creation. The overall goals are to increase customer value and benefits, improve stakeholder relationships and positions, enhance employee and contractor opportunities, outcomes, and rewards, and to increase shareholder wealth and value, all on a concurrent basis. It may be easy to maximize any one of these elements, and often the focus is on shareholder value, but the true challenge is to improve all of the subareas of the social dimension. SBD implies holistic value maximization, not local system optimization. It also implies fulfilling the inherent social contract of the corporation to ensure that it is socially responsible for its decisions and actions.

Society expects solid corporate performance that provides significant improvements over the past. People generally want more for less. They expect better quality at low prices. They want to have better life styles with fewer difficulties and negative effects. They expect and demand exceptional value from every transaction, product, service, and activity. Value creation is the pivotal perspective that integrates the other facets of the social dimension.

Social responsibility is an essential integrating theme that ties the four subareas of figure 4.3 into the perspectives of society in general. For instance, customers are crucial, but their needs and wants have to be balanced with the needs and wants of stakeholders and other external constituents. Social responsibility is linked to the idea of universal responsibility, which is based on a realization that "the whole Earth community ... is linked and that everyone shares responsibility for the present and future well being of the human family and the larger living world."[2] Universal responsibility also suggests that social issues and their solutions are mutual responsibilities and not assigned to single entities or distributed among entities.

Trust is essential for achieving sustainable success in commercial business. Trust binds people together across the enterprise in the knowledge that the proper actions are being taken and that all precautions have been considered. It implies that corporations provide pertinent facts and information to customers and report all of the salient details about products, operations, and activities to the public on an ongoing basis.

Ethical practices are directly related to trust. It is expected that corporations and their associations will police themselves to ensure that best practices are employed and that individuals, groups, departments, business units, and the entire organization act and behave in a responsible, prudent, and safe manner. Ethical practices involve complying with laws and regulations, mitigating impacts, and informing constituencies about the full implications of products and operations. Ethical corporations do not eliminate questionable practices by outsourcing the processes and activities to "outsiders." They find positive and permanent solutions. They assume responsibility for the impacts of supply networks, value networks, and partners and have them take actions to mitigate impacts to the greatest extent possible.

Great corporations are built on a solid foundation of integrity that protects and enhances their image and reputation. Integrity results from high standards, ethical practices, impeachable outcomes, and proper disclosures. Integrity is achieved through actions and outcomes that consider and protect everyone and everything without any compromises.

Transparency is an integrating principle in a sustainable enterprise.[3] It means open disclosure and reporting of social, economic, and environmental performance, including information about products, processes, practices, and the underlying premises and scientific principles. While such reporting is critical for the multiple constituencies of the business environment, transparency also facilitates good decision-making from an internal perspective. When decision-makers realize that stakeholders may scrutinize the results of their decisions and that outsiders will have the background information necessary to understand the reasoning involved, they will more likely take a balanced perspective. The premise is that good solutions will be made when the whole world is party to the information and data pertaining to them.

Nondiscrimination, human rights protection, and personal security are also central themes of SBD. The exploitation of disadvantaged workers in developing countries is one of the most significant concerns surrounding globalization. Corporations must ensure that their operations, or those of their supply networks, do not treat people unfairly because of their poor social standing, lack of political power, or other weaknesses.[4] Protection of human health and safety and the natural environment are discussed in detail later in this chapter. They are central to sustainable success.

The success of a corporation depends on its responsiveness to **customers** and **markets**. Customers have needs and wants that are based on their social status and condition. They expect solutions with economically viable benefits and a minimum of defects, burdens, and negative impacts. They desire solutions that are safe, effective, and long-lasting. If the solutions are in the forms of products, customers demand full disclosures of all pertinent information to ensure appropriate and safe use of the products. Customers wish to minimize or eliminate any personal risks associated with buying and using the products, they do not want to involuntarily accept risks or other concerns. Most importantly, they expect the producers of products and providers of services to take due precautions to prevent adverse difficulties and problems. They don't like to discover the negative aspects after they own the product and then be faced with limited options.

From the customers' perspective, resource utilization and waste management during consumption are usually viewed as tangential issues. However, as waste disposal becomes more difficult and costly, customers are seeking assurance that such problems are being addressed. They want the producers, the distributors, or governments to prescribe the required actions, and to take them. As discussed earlier, support services and information on appropriate product use and EoL considerations can provide the mechanisms to assist customers with safe and environmentally sound applications of products.

Stakeholders can have specific social and economic interests or take broad responsibilities and actions for the health, safety, and well-being of the public and the natural environment. Governments generally enact laws and promulgate regulations and directives to control the effects of business decisions on society. Often the laws are enacted in response to the pressure exerted by public interest groups. In this way, governments play a significant role in balancing the needs, wants, and objectives of society and business.

Industrialization, population growth, and affluence in the developed countries have had dramatic impacts on communities all around the world. In regions of high population density such as the northeastern United States, Western Europe, and Japan, production and consumption create tremendous residuals and waste management problems. Local communities are becoming more concerned about the ability of the local governments, NGOs, and citizens to handle the impacts. Awareness and concern for managing the impacts of production, consumption, and growth are increasing. Many of these economic and environmental issues have expanded to become regional and global concerns that require broad participation by governments, concerned citizens, businesses, and other constituencies if they are to be resolved. Some of the most pervasive issues are the depletion of water resources and water quality, the negative effects of discharging extensive quantities of nutrients into ponds, lakes, and rivers, and the degradation of air quality due to industrial air emissions and pollution from automobiles. Air quality is a local, regional, and global concern that affects populations near production plants where emissions are concentrated, and more widely through the effects of acid rain, ozone depletion, and global warming.

Stakeholders view most of these concerns as social problems. Society, governments, and businesses have to cooperatively frame solutions respectful of diverse interests and objectives. Stakeholders want improved conditions for people and the environment, and the reduction of impacts and negative consequences. Governments want to serve their citizens and constituents with improved conditions. Businesses need to be cost effective, efficient, and profitable as they eliminate problems, difficulties, liabilities, and risks.

Employees and contractors and subcontract labor have social and personal agendas that include being treated fairly and equitably, having a safe and hazard-free work environment, having opportunities for personal achievements and advancements, and receiving open communications about the conditions and implications of their work. Employees and subcontract labor must be given the necessary and appropriate education and training; they should have opportunities to improve their working conditions and personal life styles as they contribute to the success of the corporation. They seek opportunities to choose their life style, obtain information about the choices that they have, and to become more educated and knowledgeable about their world.

Boards of directors and shareholders have the ultimate responsibilities to ensure that the corporation is fulfilling its obligations. They have a fiduciary responsibility to institutionalize a management framework within the corporation that provides for the proper governance of the enterprise that protects share value and the assets of the corporation, that provides the intrinsic capabilities of the organization, and that fulfills explicit and implicit social, economic, and environmental imperatives. It is their responsibility to provide appropriate disclosures to shareholders and stakeholders, so that a fair and accurate picture of the viability of the corporation is portrayed. Such disclosures help keep the focus on discovering solutions to problems as soon as possible. The overarching objectives of the board of directors and shareholders are to achieve sustainable success and ensure that there is an adequate reward for the capital investments and equity of the corporation. Each of theses duties and objectives is an important part of creating a social structure within the corporation that is supported by and supports the principles of SBD.

The political milieu

During early industrialization of the developed countries, public policy promoted the rapid development, exploration and utilization of natural resources and the expansion of industry. Economic incentives and the lack of regulatory constraints motivated businesses to exploit natural resources without any significant concerns about depletion or the effects and impacts of the waste streams that were generated. Industrialization often took precedence over social concerns, broader economic factors, and environmental problems. There appeared to be unlimited resources, and the impacts of wastes were believed to be inconsequential. Industrial growth took top priority because it was for the "social good," providing employment opportunities for workers and more products and services for consumers.

The industrialists and producers who owned and operated the corporations wielded the political power. Labor and consumers, in contrast, held little influence. Public pressure to affect political solutions for the broad array of social, economic, and environmental concerns that developed were generally ineffective. Labor groups focused their efforts on obtaining fair compensation, better work conditions, adequate health care, quality housing, and the like. Many of the laws and regulations pertaining to social, economic, and environmental considerations addressed needs that industries, corporations, and their leadership had usually neglected. Eventually changes did take hold as social–political dimensions gained power.

Public policy views changed dramatically between the 1960s and 1990s. The failure of private sector entities to anticipate and understand the ramifications of the social, economic, and environmental problems they had created led to public outcry for solutions through government action. As the quantities of wastes being generated and discarded escalated beyond the capabilities of the established waste management infrastructure and industries failed to assume responsibilities for their direct and indirect actions, governments became more involved. Events such as Union Carbide's hazardous chemical release at Bhopal in India that killed several thousand people, Exxon's crude oil spill from the supertanker *Exxon Valdez*, Shell Oil's problems at Brent Spar, and numerous others, along with ongoing pollution and waste generation, spurred a huge increase in the number and scope of environmental laws and regulations.[5] Today, these pressures affect virtually every fiber of every corporation.

Various interest groups typically led the charge. Such groups included environmentalists, trade unions, women's groups, and many others. Some groups advocated for certain issues such as gun control while others, such as the National Rifle Association (NRA), argued against controls. Most groups used whatever political clout they had to force political entities and politicians to become aware of their issues and enact legislation or take other action favorable to their causes.

Social and political changes have transformed the way people think about social, economic, and environmental problems, and what they expect the political structure to do. The four most important factors affecting political change as it relates to SBD are:

- *Social value* People's expectations change as the conditions and trends in the social and political environment change. For most of the twentieth century, people placed a high value on economic growth, job creation, and economic stability. Environmental concerns were present, but were considered to be secondary because the focus was on more pressing issues such as human rights, economic security, and political freedom. Moreover, the public was unaware of some of the critical environmental issues such as the treatment and disposal of hazardous wastes – and, in many cases, the quantities and effects were relatively minor. Environmental issues gained prominence and became social and political issues as people recognized the seriousness of the problems and as other pressing issues, like their economic security, improved.

- *Demographics*   As populations in the developed countries become more equally distributed, citizens identify with the needs and requirements of their demographic group and influence decision-makers to provide solutions that are skewed toward their own agendas. Health care issues exemplify the pressures exerted by certain groups to obtain broader benefits for select classes of people. In the United States, senior citizens have advocated for special government programs to pay for prescription drugs, younger groups want safer work environments and information about the technical aspects of their work place.
- *Life styles*   Life style changes have had perhaps the most profound influence on social and political structures. Affluence, more leisure time, and higher levels of consumption have changed the views of citizens. As many of the basic requirements (food, clothing, housing, etc.) for surviving and succeeding in complex societies are satisfied, health considerations, safety and security, and protection of the natural environment become equally critical for the long-term viability of the social and political structures.
- *Technology*   Technologies are often unregulated during the early phases of commercialization. Their effects are typically minuscule and the impacts are relatively low. However, as the impacts of technologies become widely felt, interest groups, communities, and individuals seek controls or to mitigate the adverse consequences.

The interrelationships between these factors determine their effects on the political entities.

The regulatory milieu

The regulatory milieu consists of the laws and regulations that mandate specific protocols to be followed during the conduct of business operations. The requirements of laws and regulations represent the positive steps initiated by social–political forces to balance the needs and objectives of society with those of businesses. They can specify certain attributes for products, the requirements for waste avoidance and management, the mechanisms for reporting and communicating information and disclosures, and many other activities.

There are four broad categories of regulation: (1) mandated policies and practices within an industry; (2) standards for performance and outcomes; (3) reporting and information disclosure requirements; and (4) incentives and disincentives. The regulation of the nuclear power industry by nation states and the international community is an example of category (1). The requirements are industry-specific and detail a broad array of specifications from design to operations and ownership. Category (2) is more sweeping, cutting across industries with mandates that protect workers, outline wage structures, describe work conditions, etc. Category (3) is relatively new and includes disclosures of health and safety issues related to work conditions, product limitations and unacceptable applications, and information about pollutant emissions and waste streams from manufacturing plants. Category (4) includes subsidizing the production and use of desirable new products or cleaner technologies such as hybrid cars or solar energy and levying taxes and penalties to discourage certain others such as large, inefficient automobiles or to limit undesirable behaviors and activities. Taxing the producers of carbon dioxide on each ton of the pollutant they produce is an economic disincentive that might encourage industries to change their technologies and operations to reduce negative impacts on climate change.

Regulations and regulatory changes typically force corporations to take actions that significantly reduce flexibility. In many cases, regulations specifically define and prescribe acceptable solutions or processes. The following are some examples of how regulations can effect product and process specifications:

- Specific product features and functions can be required to ensure safety, effective use, and longevity. Automatic shutoff devices on consumer household products such as steam irons and coffee-makers provide fail-safe provisions to mitigate the potential for human error.
- Product instructions and information can provide customers and users with the knowledge necessary for the safe and wise use of products and processes. Right-to-know mandates are intended to support and enhance the effective use and longevity of products.
- Process specifications are mandated in many industries to ensure that development cycles have included the necessary and appropriate testing and validation steps. The documented clinical testing that is required to prove the efficacy and safety of pharmaceutical products comes into this category.
- Restrictions and prohibitions can affect the strategies of corporations with respect to technologies, products, and processes. Regulations often set the

"rules of the game," establishing the structure and/or boundaries of the competitive arena of the industry. In the United States, the Fair Trade Commission (FTC) and other agencies define the requirements and limitations for advertising, warrantees, and other claims, as well as the meanings of the terms "recyclable," "reuse," and "biodegradable."

While certain regulations are necessary to provide oversight or maintain a "level playing field" between the rich and the poor, the large and the small, or the old and the new, corporations might view most regulations as their failure to anticipate, understand, and mitigate impacts and consequences of their products and operations. Regulatory changes are typically the result of the needs and requirements of customers, stakeholders, employees, and other constituencies that have not been met. Most laws and regulations are a response to events, situations and/or long-standing problems that were ignored or deemed to be unimportant by businesses. For instance, the disaster at Bhopal which led to "community-right-to-know" legislation in many developed countries was not the first such accident; nor was the *Exxon Valdez* the first supertanker oil spill.

There has been a trend over the last several decades, however, to deregulate industries, deemphasize government rule-making, and address public policy concerns through internal or industry-based standards. In a fast-paced world of technological innovations and globalization, it is becoming increasingly difficult for the government of a single country to promulgate regulations that cannot be circumvented by simply moving production to another country. Such actions can significantly undermine the intent of the regulatory processes, making them ineffective and actually detrimental to maintaining an effective industrial base in the regulated country.

Nonetheless, the regulatory arena remains more regimented than the political milieu. Regulations are usually codified, documented, and readily accessible to practitioners. They are usually written in the language of regulators, enforcement officers, and lawyers, however, making it difficult for the untrained practitioner to understand and follow. Uncertainty about the precise meaning of provisions is a major concern for many corporations. The degree of uncertainty varies, depending on the laws and the regulatory agencies, but for many global corporations the implications of noncompliance are great, and the precise interpretation of what is required is therefore very important. It may be as simple as looking at the quantity of products that are produced. If a small manufacturer produces ten products that are defective from a regulatory perspective, the fix may take only a few days to correct at a relatively low cost. But if millions of products have been produced over several decades, it may take years and millions of dollars, euros, pounds, etc. to rectify, if it can be done at all. For example, lead is used in the production of PCs. When PCs were first introduced, it would have been relatively easy to rectify the problem. Today, after manufacturers around the world have produced hundreds of millions of PCs, it will be extremely costly to handle the lead problem. Moreover, there are special concerns about the proper disposal of obsolete computers – there are new EU directives that mandate the proper disposal of used electrical and electronic equipment and on the prohibition of the use of certain heavy metals such as lead.

Regulations are typically viewed as having negative effects on corporations. While it is easy to understand such thinking, regulations also provide opportunities. One of the main premises of SBD is that superior products and processes provide a means to differentiate the corporation from its competitors. By rising to and even exceeding the challenges of the regulatory mandates, leading global corporations can eliminate the need for and/or effects of certain regulations. The quest to avoid regulatory restrictions and costs can actually provide opportunities for new, cleaner technologies, products, and processes. Since the 1980s, whole industries have emerged that take advantage of the need to prevent pollution, to handle and dispose of waste streams, to abate air emissions, and to treat wastewater effluent.

Primary economic considerations

The economic environment for SBD

Economic considerations are critical in developing strategic management constructs, market assessments and LCAs. They are central to understanding the prevailing business conditions and trends, and are pivotal in decision-making. The primary economic considerations include the prospects for growth and progress in the present business environment, an assessment of options through C/B analysis, and life cycle cost implications. Economics is clearly a huge field of study, and involves many elements. The primary considerations of economics involving SBD are examined here as a foundation for further discussions on environmental concerns and LCT.

SBD maintains that economic growth can, and should, occur in step with the needs of society and the ability of the business environment and the natural world to provide the necessary capabilities and resources. More specifically, it implies that the business environment and the management systems can continually provide and advance the means to manage and mitigate the residuals associated with the production and use of products. The economic challenges include sustaining growth and progress without depleting resources and degrading the natural environment.

Economics and economies of scale typically play a critical role in decisions about new corporate initiatives pertaining to technology and product developments. Most decisions pertaining to investments and NPD programs require intensive study to determine the merits and feasibility of the opportunities. In the short term, economics often favor the entrenched positions – i.e. leveraging existing resources and capabilities. The automobile is a good example. The economic power of the automobile industry cuts across the social, political, and economic spectrums. Investing in new models is relatively easy to justify based on the existing demand structure and price levels. Radical changes that would incorporate new technologies such as fuel cells are more difficult to understand and justify. New resources and capabilities have to be developed that are initially very expensive and have relatively high risks. These decisions require a more thorough understanding of the prevailing and future trends.

Market performance is thus always a significant factor when examining economics. It can be measured in terms of short-term gains and long-term benefits, or according to process efficiency and the effectiveness of the outcomes. Successful solutions have a positive B/C ratio, making the resulting conditions worth the investment of time, effort, and money. Cost effectiveness and B/C analysis are primary considerations for determining public policy and corporate decision-making.

Long-term economic growth is essential for keeping pace with the increasing global population and for improving conditions for humankind (a fundamental requirement for sustainable development). In the broadest sense of macroeconomics, then, it is in the public interest to promote economic growth, improve the state of the environment, and protect the long-term stability of market and social forces. Public policies pertaining to economics and environmental concerns across the world have to focus on converging effective and holistic solutions to the myriad of problems, issues, and negative impacts rather than trading off one difficulty for another.

To make this happen, corporate strategists must move from "supply and demand" thinking to a more holistic view of the economic equation. Traditional supply and demand theory is based on the relationships between producers and customers. The assessment of efficiencies and effectiveness in this approach focuses on the direct inputs and outputs. SBD, in contrast, requires a more comprehensive model for analyzing the flow of materials, information, costs, and benefits between all of the parties involved in all possible transactions.

Fundamentals of the economics of SBD

Economics in simple terms is the study of value creation, distribution, and use, as measured by the flow of goods and information and the exchange of money. The global economy is a vast array of physical and informational transactions and relationships through which goods and services, money, and information flow in order to increase social, economic, and environmental value. The main constituents of traditional economics are production and consumption. They embody the primary processes and activities for determining the designs, quantities, and price levels of the goods and services that are produced and consumed and the technological and physical means to produce and consume them. Economics also involves the actual distribution of goods and services and how individuals, groups, and societies obtain their appropriate and "equitable" share.

Historically, economics concentrated on the primary inputs and outputs of the socioeconomic system. These inputs and outputs included raw materials, parts, components, products, logistics, distribution, and applications. However, every process used during production and consumption involves not only the intended outcomes, but also unintended waste streams and mass flows with potential negative effects. The early view was devoid of these secondary considerations, or "residuals" and their consequences in determining the value created and the feasibility and sustainability of the processes.

To be comprehensive, the socioeconomic system must include the ecosystems and all inputs and outputs, ingredients and outcomes, and effects and impacts of production and consumption from cradle-to-grave. It must consider causes and effects, especially those actions that have long-term impacts and consequences. For instance, concerns about climate change and questions about global warming pertain more to the future than to the present. Such concerns recognize that certain problems must be identified and addressed in the present if the future implications and impacts are to be handled properly. By including this kind of issue in their view of the socioeconomic system, corporations can begin to develop broader solutions and a more positive future. They can become more efficient and successful, producing greater output per unit of input with fewer residuals – more value for society, the corporation, and its shareholders.

Modifying the concepts of supply and demand

Traditional economics is based on the relationships between buyers and sellers (customers and producers). Customers want to satisfy their needs; producers desire to design, produce, and market their products and services for revenues and profits. Market demand for existing products and services drives decision-making toward the cost effective, short-term, or marketing-related solutions. Supply and demand determine price levels and volume. The quantity demanded is a function of the benefits obtained by customers and the prices paid. Supply and demand models usually focus on the primary considerations of resources, products, channels, and markets. Figure 4.4 depicts an expanded (socioeconomic system) view of the conventional model. Here, suppliers provide inputs to the producer who creates and produces products that flow through distributors to customers. Customers buy and use the products during their useful life and are responsible for maintenance and ultimate disposal. The producer's responsibilities are viewed as limited to the actual transactions and product liabilities.

Today, the flow of residuals (pollution, discards, and other waste streams) is critical to the economic viability of products, services, and processes. The simple economic models that examined supply, production, demand, and applications are transformed into more comprehensive frameworks including the design and development processes, cradle-to-grave implications, supply and delivery considerations, consumption and applications, and the effective flow and reuse or disposal of residuals. Figure 4.5 provides a simplified view of the supply and demand structures based on the principles of SBD. The added complexity of the more holistic model is obvious.

The model includes the primary transactions between the suppliers of goods and services and the customers who enjoy the derived benefits and

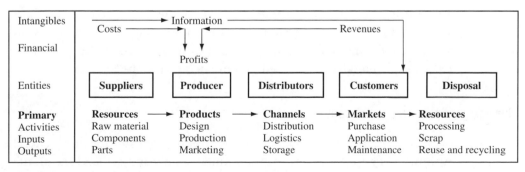

Figure 4.4   Traditional model of supply and demand structures

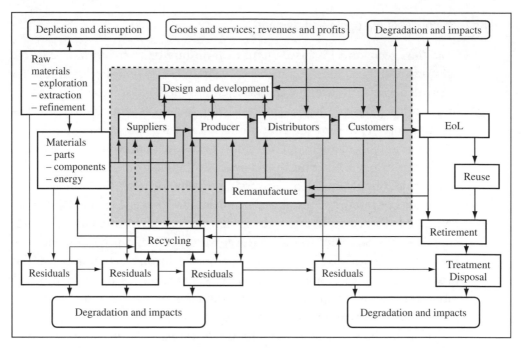

Figure 4.5   SBD model of supply and demand structures

the secondary processes and activities of those providing the raw materials, offering the means and mechanisms for reuse and recycling of products, parts, and materials, and the handling of the residuals. Secondary processes also involve the use of materials and energy (not shown in figure 4.5) which create additional complexities.

The new model has powerful implications. The addition of the residuals and their impacts on the social, economic, and environmental aspects of the business environment more accurately portray the total system and its benefits and consequences over time. Traditionally, residuals were either discharged or discarded to the natural environment as external costs and impacts imposed on society. In the SBD model, suppliers and users are responsible for the implications of their products, processes, and activities. The expanded model is discussed in more detail in chapter 9 as part of LCT.

Managing private and social costs

Historically, corporations assumed responsibilities only for the direct effects, as shown in figure 4.4. Using the traditional "supply and demand" economic structure, they attempted to minimize the direct and indirect costs associated with product creation, production, and delivery activities. These "private" costs included the costs of acquiring the materials, production, distribution, and selling. They usually did not include the costs associated with the residuals and their effects, as shown in figure 4.5. The transition to a broader view of reality, spurred initially by laws and regulations, has forced corporations to recognize and manage many of the external costs as well. Today, the total cost of any operation is the sum of the private costs and the external costs associated with the downstream impacts and costs on society.

The producer and the suppliers and distributors usually pay the private costs that are typically reflected on the income statements and managed using the standard accounting systems. Corporations can reduce these costs through LCT and holistic approaches for mitigating uncertainty and risks. Initiatives to reduce or eliminate impacts reduce both private and external costs. Such approaches usually include expanding pollution prevention strategies and working through external relationships and transactions to mitigate impacts. Educating and training employees, partners, customers, and other related parties about the positive and negative impacts are effective means for minimizing problems. Technologies development and product innovation also offer opportunities to eliminate concerns and impacts, and reduce costs.

The reduction of waste streams at their sources and the reuse and recycling of products and materials became a leading edge phenomenon. Most importantly, producers have expanded their responsibilities to include mitigating external costs, publicly imposed costs, hidden costs, and application-related costs. Corporations are now challenged to be mindful of the potential for defects and burdens that can result in both private and external costs. Corporations have expanded their view of the costs of doing business from the simple "supply and demand" model to a broader, more accurate reflection, as in figure 4.6. This provides an overview of cost categories and some of their implications. The total cost of any business activity is the sum of private (conventional) costs, external costs, publicly imposed costs, hidden costs, and application costs.

External costs, known as *externalities*, are real costs paid by the downstream stakeholders impacted by the products, processes, and operations. For example, a community may be affected by poor air or water quality due to the operation of a local manufacturing plant. Such costs are indirect and manifest themselves over time through increased health problems, degraded water supplies, and other conditions. They are typically the costs of handling the effects and impacts of the problems – i.e. medical treatment for cancer

Focus	Producers	Society	Stakeholders	Enterprise	Customers
Cost elements	Private costs (conventional)	External costs	Publicly imposed costs	Hidden costs	Application costs
Scope	Suppliers Distributors Production Marketing Finance	Degradation Depletion Disruption Destruction	Laws/regulations Communities NGOs Agencies Standards	Employees Society Natural world Markets Corporate image	Customers Users Service providers Maintenance Waste handlers
Time frame	Immediate	Short- and long-term	Intermediate	Longer-term	Short- and long-term
Key elements of cost structure	Plant and equipment Materials/supplies Labor Utilities Tracking	Opportunity loss Health and safety Extinction Tracking Disposal	Notifying Reporting Auditing Record keeping Remediation	Liabilities Penalties and fines Accidents/spills Defects and burdens Disposal	Repairs Energy usage Learning Upgrading Disposal
Mitigation techniques	LCT Risk mitigation Pollution prevention Education/training R&D/innovation	Transparency Involvement Preemption Elimination Treatment	Preparedness Precaution Eliminate waste Reuse by-products	Cradle-to-grave LCA Hazard avoidance Six-Sigma quality Communications	Reliability Longevity Eco-efficiency User friendly Salvage/take-back

Figure 4.6   Elements and perspectives of cost structures

patients, the costs of cleaning up the waterways, and the costs of depletion of resources and disruptions to the natural environment, as well as countless others.

External costs are related to the effects and impacts of pollution and residuals from operations, products, and processes, and are borne by stakeholders, communities, and society. In many cases they are unchecked environmental impacts that are directly related to operations, or that result from the release of residuals from pollution abatement. External costs run the gamut from local pollution caused by such problems as petroleum spills to the global impacts of climate change, ocean habitat destruction, and unhealthy air quality. Identifying external costs has helped change public perception regarding the responsibilities of corporations for managing their residuals. The pollution prevention and waste minimization strategies of the 1980s and 1990s focused on mitigating the external costs and their negative implications for the profitability of products and businesses.

Primary and secondary production processes cause air emissions and water pollution and create solid and hazardous wastes that must be handled, treated, and disposed of. Such residuals depend upon the efficiencies of the processes used. They are also a function of the pollution abatement technologies in use. Nevertheless, there are always some portions of the waste streams that are released to the environment. The external costs of such burdens are normally manifested as degradation of the quality of air, water, and land, destruction of the natural habitat, depletion of resources and diversity, and disruption of life styles. The financial costs of these environmental impacts are difficult to measure, but can include medical expenses related to impacts on human health and safety, the expenses of damage due to pollution such as damage caused by acid rain, economic loss caused by poor air quality, the potential consequences of climate change, and many other environmental expenses. Historically, governments and society pay the cost for disposing of solid wastes from households, operating wastewater treatment plants, and monitoring air quality.

These kinds of external costs result from the impacts of technologies, products, and processes on natural resources and society. The most prevalent forms are medical expenses incurred by workers, customers, stakeholders, and society in general as a result of negative impacts (disease, illness, etc.). Determining exactly what they are in any given situation, however, depends on the prevalent assumptions about the business environment. For example, the automobile requires an extensive infrastructure of roads, traffic control, accident prevention and response, logistics for fuel, and many other elements to provide the opportunity for people to use their vehicles. The extra costs associated with such expenditures that are usually not covered by fees and taxes are borne by society. Car manufacturers assume that society will pay the additional external and hidden costs of this necessary infrastructure and the costs of having poor air quality and related respiratory diseases.

Governments, through laws and regulations, attempt to transfer the costs of such externalities back to the responsible parties if causality can be determined. Additionally, they can assign such costs to corporations through taxes, fees, and fines. Since the 1970s, governments have tended to reduce their role in paying for the indirect burdens that businesses impose on society and to link the sources of pollution more directly to the costs of managing and abating pollution. This **polluter pays principle (PPP)** makes the "cause and effect" cycle a very important reality for the corporation.[6] In the days of subsidized growth (when society shouldered the pollution burdens), the cycle was open-ended. Those who polluted did not have to pay the price of the negative consequences if the costs could be shifted to external entities (society). While there remain some external costs, more of the burdens today are being absorbed by corporations. Moreover, the contemporary **user pays principle (UPP)** invokes the responsibilities of consumers, users, and owners to pay a more accurate share of the costs of using products that create environmental impacts. The objective has become motivating decision-makers to recognize, understand, and pay for the true costs involved in activities and applications.

Publicly imposed costs include the cost implications of laws and regulations and the costs associated with meeting the needs of other stakeholders such as communities, NGOs, public agencies, and industry standard groups. This category has grown significantly since the 1970s as governments in the developed countries through laws and regulations shifted the burden for such costs, usually external costs, from the public to the responsible corporations. The costs imposed include mitigating the effects of pollution and waste streams, providing the tracking mechanisms on the wastes generated, and requiring public reporting and other types of disclosures. Publicly imposed costs are a function of technologies, products, and business activities, as well as the mandates imposed upon a particular industry sector. For example, nuclear power plant operators have to follow industry standards and the specifications of national and international monitoring agencies. Such requirements include notifying the appropriate agencies and stakeholders about emergencies, problems, and other difficulties. They outline the reporting protocols, specify when auditing must occur, and detail record keeping. Stakeholders must also be satisfied when they are involved in determining how to remediate past problems. The best strategy for satisfying them in this kind of situation is to avoid it in the first place. If using a particular substance is going to create cleanup challenges, or if laws and regulations will be triggered by the use of a toxic substance, the solution is to simply avoid using such a material. Reducing the probabilities of spills and accidents and having the mechanisms to mitigate the consequences of potential problems are also effective ways to minimize negative effects.

Hidden costs are among the most difficult to manage and mitigate. Such costs can derive from anywhere within the enterprise and affect individuals or entities. They are unexpected outcomes, with severe social, economic, and environmental consequences that are often not apparent in the short term. Hidden costs include the effects of spills and accidents and the fines and penalties that may be imposed. Such costs are usually not evident until after significant damage has occurred, requiring corrective action and even remediation. In addition, the data and information available about certain impacts are affected by so many other variables that it takes a significant amount of time and analysis to make an accurate determination. For instance, the debate about climate change and global warming is split into entrenched positions that have arguments at the extremes. Scientists are still gathering evidence to indicate the scope and potential severity of such phenomena; doing so may take decades. Nevertheless, there may be consequences that will affect the cost of doing business in the future. Another concern is water. Clean water is a key ingredient in many products, and its availability at low cost is essential for many corporations, from Coca-Cola to Intel. There is always the potential for a problem to arise. For instance, asbestos was widely used during most of the twentieth century, with the negative effects on workers becoming apparent only after decades of exposure and the occurrences of declining health.[7] From the workers' perspective, the impacts and costs were hidden.

Hidden costs affect everyone and everything, from individual employees to society as a whole, from markets and customers to nature, and even corporate reputations. Often lying undiscovered, they are social and economic liabilities that can grow into huge potential costs. For instance, in the late 1990s customers sued General Motors for the failure of the gas tanks on certain light trucks. The design for the gas tanks had been used for more than thirty years, and discovering the problem at such a late stage made it much worse than if it had been discovered during the early stages of its use. Assuming that the company had produced hundreds of thousands of such designs over the decades, the costs of recalling all of the vehicles now would be astronomical. Usually such costs increase dramatically when hidden defects such as this one are discovered later in the process.

Hidden costs include those stemming from unexpected events or situations such as the discovery of defects and burdens associated with, or caused by, the action of the corporation and its relationships. Merck's Vioxx, as discussed earlier, is an example. Hidden costs may also include the costs of complying with unexpected new laws and regulations or correcting defects and burdens from previous activities or responsibilities. In general, hidden costs affect the corporation regardless of whether it is directly responsible for the actions or whether it could foresee the negative implications. For instance, the banning of chlorofluorocarbons (CFCs) due to ozone depletion concerns required producers of air conditioners and refrigeration equipment to design new systems and replace older ones before they normally would have done. It also affected the design and production of electronic devices that depended on the effectiveness of low-cost solvents.

Hidden costs can also stem from customer and stakeholder dissatisfaction. Customers often feel guilty about using products that cause environmental impacts, and they may avoid such feelings by buying alternate products. For example, McDonald's replaced its polystyrene "clamshell" boxes because environmental groups such as the Environmental Defense Fund (EDF) expressed concerns that the boxes were not biodegradable or recyclable and were negatively contributing to the solid waste problem.[8] McDonald's conducted a study with EDF to find a way to collect and recycle the polystyrene boxes, but were unsuccessful in creating a scheme for collecting the containers. McDonald's agreed to eliminate the containers because it wanted to maintain customer and stakeholder satisfaction. As with customer acceptance, the long-term effects of low worker morale and injuries can also reduce productivity and effectiveness, causing a decline in the value proposition of the business. These costs are difficult to determine and are often not even recognized as costs until it is impossible to correct the situation.

Application costs are usually well known, but often overlooked by producers. These are the costs that the customers have to bear after they purchase the product(s). The buyer and/or the user are typically responsible for maintaining the product during its useful life. Such costs may include the training and education necessary for using the product, expenses of owning and repairing the product, the usage expenditures for energy and supplies, and the annual taxes, insurance, etc. The cost of ownership also involves the necessity to dispose of the product at the end of life. Corporations can reduce these costs by enhancing product reliability, performance, and longevity. Superior products are efficient and effective, and have built-in solutions. Salvage or take-back programs can eliminate the customers' problems with disposing of the products at retirement and may allow the producer to exploit the residual value in the discarded products or materials. Take-back may also provide producers with insights about the use of their products.

Economic analysis, B/C analysis, and the value proposition

Economic analysis has been central to effective management and good decision-making for decades. With the proper framework, economic analysis facilitates effectively diagnosing what solutions are needed and how to affect those solutions. Traditional methods use a static view of the situation and limit the scope of considerations to the direct inputs and outputs. Such models often fail to include externalities (external costs and their implications and impacts) and other seemingly tangential or future-oriented effects and consequences. While keeping things simple provides options that are easier to understand and implement, failing to consider secondary or long-term effects and impacts often misleads decision-makers into choosing the wrong solution. This is especially the case if the focus is on the short term and direct costs.

Economic analysis from a SBD perspective focuses on the full context of the business environment with life cycle considerations from cradle-to-grave. Solutions should have low impacts, low costs, and multifaceted outcomes that reduce negative ecological, social, and economic consequences and improve the long-term quality of life and the natural world. Solutions should provide maximum value for the time, effort, and money spent, for it is the quality of an outcome that creates value. For instance, pure water has many life sustaining attributes when it is used for drinking, cooking, cleaning, and bathing. Water contaminated with pathogens, heavy metals, and toxins, however, is useless for such activities and actually imposes costs on society for water treatment and/or disposal. High-quality resources and materials provide economic opportunities and the means to achieve positive social outcomes. Reducing wastes and residuals improves the qualities of the system and makes the total system more sustainable. To move in this direction, corporations must expand their economic perspectives to include the essential temporal and spatial aspects.

B/C analyses are often the essential ingredients in determining products, processes, and practices (see box 4.1). Through them, corporations can systematically examine the benefits to be derived from a project relative to the costs. They are a simple approach for determining the viability, suitability, and sustainability of business initiatives, new programs, new technologies, new products and other investment-oriented innovations. Conventional cost/benefit analysis uses discounted cash flow (DCF) thinking to examine the flow of cash over time relative to the cash invested. The major deficiency of such thinking is that there are many other positive and negative impacts and implications to consider. Moreover, discounting cash flow implicitly favors present outcomes and makes future benefits seemingly less attractive.

This more sophisticated analysis provides a more thorough understanding of the decision-making context, and a better sense of how to make the decisions. The analysis should be based on both short-term and long-term implications and the full costs to all participants, including customers, stakeholders, and society. Good decisions will lead to better investments and a more sustainable strategic position for the corporation.

Life cycle costing

Life cycle costing is the natural extension of the expanded view of B/C analysis. It encompasses the full scope of activities over the full life cycle of a product, and their cost implications across the enterprise. In simple terms, life cycle costing is a culmination of all costs from the cradle-to-grave, direct and indirect, private and external, and short-term and long-term. It therefore includes all of the costs to acquire the means of production, to produce, store,

Box 4.1 B/C analysis

The conventional B/C equation depicts the sum of the benefits divided by the sum of the costs. In simple terms, it is a ratio of expected outcomes to expected costs (investments). Its simplicity is both its strength and weakness. The equation can be expressed as:

$$B/C = \Sigma \text{ benefits } (B) \div \Sigma \text{ costs } (C)$$

While this form is simple, it does not consider the *time value of money*. DCF theory can therefore be added to overcome this shortcoming. The equation becomes

$$B/C = \Sigma \text{ benefits}_t\,(B)/(1+i)^{t-1} \div \Sigma \text{ costs}_t\,(C)/(1+i)^{t-1}$$

where i, the discounting factor, is greater than zero, and is either the cost of money, or the required rate of return for an investment. This equation can be easily converted to the standard form using net present value (NPV) of the investment

$$NPV = \Sigma \text{ benefits}_t\,(B)/(1+i)^{t-1} - \Sigma \text{ costs}_t\,(C)/(1+i)^{t-1}$$

The main concerns in doing this are the difficulty of determining the future benefits and the additional costs associated with defects, burdens, and hidden costs. These difficulties can be overcome by the value equation which depicts the value of an investment or initiative as a VC ratio (value creation ratio)

$$VC = [\Sigma \text{ direct benefits}_t\,(B_d)/(1+i)^{t-1} + \Sigma \text{ lagging benefits}_t\,(B_l)/(1+i)^{t-1} + \Sigma \text{ knowledge benefits}_t\,(B_k)/(1+i)^{t-1}] \div [\Sigma \text{direct costs}_t\,(C)/1+i)^{t-1} + \Sigma \text{ indirect costs}_t\,(Cd)/(1+i)^{t-1} + \Sigma \text{ hidden costs}_t\,(Ch)/(1+i)^{t-1} + \Sigma \text{ external costs}_t\,(\text{defects and burdens}_t\,Ce)/(1+i)^{t-1}]$$

The equation can also be converted into a NPV similar to the conventional form, except that great care must be used to ensure that all elements are accurately expressed. NPV has the connotation of an expected flow of cash over time, which becomes more difficult to measure precisely as intangible aspects such as learning and knowledge are included. The most difficult elements to define are the hidden costs related to social and environmental factors that are future-oriented. It is often impossible to include all such considerations.

transport, and manage the product, process, or service, and to use, maintain, improve, and dispose of it, and account for recycling, disposal, and residuals. While this is a complex array of costs affecting producers, suppliers, distributors, customers, stakeholders, and waste management entities, life cycle costing equations can be simplified to equal the sum of the full cost of development and production, use, disposal, and managing the afterlife. The equation is as follows:

Life-cycle cost = cost of design, acquisition, and production + Cost of use
+ Cost of EoL considerations + Cost of afterlife[9]

Life cycle costing is complicated, requiring an examination of all of the effects and cost implications of design, production, use, disposal, and beyond. Each of the elements has direct costs, indirect costs, hidden costs, external costs, and publicly imposed costs. The direct and indirect costs are traditionally included in the established accounting system or as standard cost elements when doing economic analysis. However, hidden costs and external costs are typically potential liabilities that are not recognized until circumstances turn the liabilities into cost elements for the corporation, or costs paid by someone else. For example, when the *Exxon Valdez* accident occurred, the implications of the oil spill were handled as an extraordinary expense – i.e. a nonrecurring, one-time event. But such potential liabilities are always a factor in transporting crude, and there should be a mechanism in place to account for them. Nonetheless, few oil companies do more than identify the risk and purchase insurance. Life cycle costing can help identify such hidden costs, and corporations can develop social cost accounting systems to track them.

Figure 4.7 provides a general overview of the relationship of life cycle costs and their elements. It provides a sampling of selected direct, indirect, hidden, external, and publicly imposed cost elements and their implications via a life cycle view.

Time Frame	Immediate	Immediate	Long-Term	Long-Term
	Design, supply, and production costs	**Applications, use, and ownership costs**	**Retirement and disposal costs**	**Afterlife costs/ liabilities**
Direct *management accounting system*	Material purchases Direct labor Logistics Overhead allocations Utilities	Ownership Labor Maintenance Energy consumption Supplies	Recycling Treatment Disposal Waste management	Obsolescence Corrective actions Keeping useless assets Maintaining contacts Inspections
Indirect *management accounting system*	Insurance Repairs and refurbishment Community awareness	Training and education Insurance Normal repairs	Testing materials Tracking flows Managing providers	Risks and uncertainty Monitoring (audits) Reporting
Hidden costs *LCA*	Accidents and spills Injuries and damage Penalties and fines Economic loss – cleanups Problems by suppliers	Accidents and spills Penalties and fines Warrantee costs – failures Problems by users Issues with stakeholders	New mandates Contingencies Recycling issues Disposal issue Reputation issues	Litigation Liabilities Reputation loss Remediation expenses Long-term surveillance
External costs *social cost accounting*	Air emissions Water pollution Contaminated land Resource depletion Chemical and fuel spills Health and safety	Health and safety Acid rain Unhealthy air quality Global warming Diseases and deaths Habitat destruction	Residual disposal Hazardous wastes Contaminated sites Leaching of toxins Site closures	Toxins in environment Quality of life impacts Chronic illness risks Bio-diversity risk Eco-systems disruption
Publicly imposed costs	Regulatory compliance Taxes	Regulatory compliance Taxes	Take-back mandates Decommissioning	Record keeping Liabilities

Figure 4.7   Selected direct, indirect, hidden, external, and publicly imposed costs from cradle-to-grave

Cost of design, supply, and production: these typically involve the direct and indirect costs that are paid by the producer. Direct production costs depend primarily on the specifications of the product and the manufacturing processes. They include the costs of materials, labor, supplies, logistics, energy, capital, and overhead allocations (including the costs of regulatory mandates). While certain costs depend on the qualities and quantities of items produced, there is usually a high level of certainty about direct production costs.

Indirect production costs are usually related to the intangible aspects of producing and using products and processes. They involve the myriad activities necessary to keep the operating system functioning properly, including the handling and storage of goods and inventories, the training and managing of employees, the planning, managing, and accounting for activities and processes, the obtaining of permits, and the managing of residuals. For instance, record keeping, reporting, auditing, testing, and mandated training are not hidden, but are direct or indirect costs.

Hidden product and production costs are the most complex. They have a high degree of uncertainty and depend on the probabilities of accidents or spills, or the potential for defects and burdens to be unknowingly designed and built into products and processes. They are generally unknown during design, production, and distribution. Similarly, the true costs of managing residual waste streams, though often viewed as hidden because they are not recognized until the waste streams reach a certain level are, in truth, determined by design and development choices. They are often simply overlooked in decision-making.

External costs associated with design, supply, and production are typically the costs of pollution and wastes across the value chain. The trend now is to attempt to identify as many of the external costs as possible and have the responsible entity pay. Publicly imposed costs typically include compliance costs and taxes.

Costs of use or application costs involve costs that are usually paid by customers and users. Direct use costs are typically a function of the applications, the time and units of use, and the materials, energy, and labor required for effecting the desired outcomes. Corporations and users can often estimate such costs. For example, if an automobile can travel 10 km per liter of gasoline, and gasoline costs $1.00 per liter, then the costs per km is $0.10. Assuming that the user drives 1,000 km per month, the cost per month is $100 or $1,200 per year.

Indirect use costs include the education and training required to learn how to use and maintain products, the cost of expected repairs and maintenance, and the cost burdens implicit with use and ownership, such as insurance. Indirect use costs are deterministic, but variable. They can be reduced or eliminated by mitigating the effects and impacts of products and processes. For instance, avoiding the trigger mechanisms can often eliminate the indirect use costs stemming from regulatory compliance. For example, in the United States a low-quantity hazardous waste generator, whether producer or user of products, can avoid very stringent requirements by keeping the quantities produced per month to less than 1,000 kg. While there may be many hidden problems associated with a product's use, it is difficult to make a comprehensive list. The cost of accidents is a major category. Often accidents are caused by defects in the product or lack of training on the part of users. There may be indirect taxes and compliance costs.

Cost of EoL considerations: this is becoming a significant concern. Governments in developed countries are forcing producers to manage the retirement of products and handle the residuals and wastes. Some requirements even specify the appropriate disposal of the product at the end of its useful life. For example in the European Union, the costs associated with mandatory takeback requirements for PCs and other electrical and electronics products are transferred to producers who have a reverse logistics system available after August 13, 2005 to take back used products. The direct costs for such services are to be borne by the producer. Indirect, EoL costs depend on product characteristics, material composition and the specific requirements for collecting, handling, processing, and disposing of the products. Such costs might involve testing, tracking, handling, record keeping, and managing. For example, materials may have to be tested to determine if they contain hazardous substances. Such testing is costly. Older PCs were manufactured using heavy metals and other toxic substances, yet such information was not generally made available to purchasers, who were left to determine safe disposal strategies.

Hidden costs involving disposal and post-disposal issues are more complicated and difficult to determine. Changing scientific understandings, social norms, and government regulations can make it difficult to anticipate what might be necessary when a product or process reaches the end of its life. Such changes might have cost implications, especially as the understanding of materials can change classifications from benign to hazardous. Even the costs of monitoring the changing attitudes and preparing contingencies constitute hidden costs. Chapter 5 covers additional comments and examples pertaining to EoL considerations.

Cost of afterlife: this involves long-term costs that are often reflected as liabilities. They are the most difficult direct cost category to define. While they are real, they are often assigned to other categories, or not accounted for at all. If such costs are known, predictable, and directly related to production and use factors, they should be assigned as long-term, direct costs. Indeed, many governments recognize a depletion allowance as a real cost in the petroleum business. While the oil depletion allowance is arguably a political and economic incentive in the risky business of petroleum exploration, it does introduce the notion of future or long-term costs that should be recognized as natural resources are consumed and the potential for future economic and social benefits is diminished. This category could be used to handle the problems and impacts of depletion, disruption, and destruction of the business and natural environment that have long-term consequences.

Indirect afterlife costs include record keeping and monitoring, among many others. For example, spent fuel storage facilities from nuclear power plants require ongoing tracking and monitoring. These activities represent future costs that are often not fully recognized during the life of the system or product. In some cases, corporations charge customers for facility closure costs during the sale of their products; this is common with electricity from nuclear power plants, for example.

In the long term, many obsolete, consumed, broken, or useless products and residuals will fill treatment plants, landfills, and other receptacle sites and may become a time bomb waiting to damage human health and the environment far into the future. The costs of such long-term implications are paid through medical expenses, lost opportunities due to restrictions on land use, destruction of water resources, and numerous other impacts. Moreover, the disposal of toxins may create a legacy of concerns and damages that pan out over many generations. In some cases, the effects never go away. The quality of life may decline on the local, if not the regional, level. Such consequences are difficult to quantify and usually take decades to fully appreciate. The cleanup of hazardous waste sites going on today provides a poignant example of the billions of dollars that can be spent to contain and correct the damage caused by the poor practices of the past.

The financial accounting systems of the future must change in order to reflect the total costs of the whole system. To do so will take professionals from many arenas (accountants, lawyers, strategists, technologists, environmentalists, etc.) years to determine the new standards and obtain the required approvals from governments, accounting firms, standards organizations, and stock exchanges. Making such changes is an enormous challenge because it will require consensus of many participants and disciplines to develop "generally accepted practices." In the interim, corporations can minimize environmental and societal impacts, and improve their eco-efficiency, productivity, efficiency, and effectiveness by implementing life cycle costing.

Environmental considerations and implications

The historical trajectory

Until environmental laws and regulations came into existence, most of the residuals of production processes were viewed simply as by-products or losses of the production system that escaped into the air, flowed into the waterways, or had to be buried or burned. They were tangential, rather than primary, concerns. Corporations and society did not understand that pollution actually represents lost resources, resources that could be saved and used if inefficiencies in the systems could be corrected.

During the latter part of the twentieth century, governments in the developed countries began enacting new laws to force solutions to such environmental problems. In turn, corporations managed only those environmental impacts the laws required them to manage. They changed products, processes, and operations in order to comply. While regulations often limited the flexibility of corporations, there were perceived advantages of having governments dictate the protocols. Regulations leveled the playing field and specified what had to be done. Management knew the requirements and assigned people to ensure compliance. Still, it usually handled waste management as tangential to the mainstream business processes. While the requirements, such as those for handling hazardous wastes, were often complex the corporate processes to comply with the regulations were straightforward: do what you are told to do and minimize the effects and costs on the rest of the corporation. The goal was generally to do only what was mandated. Corporations did not like the rules and regulations, but accepted them as a baseline for environmental performance. Such compliance thinking focused on releases, waste streams, pollution, and accidents, and the unwanted effects of production processes and products. The typical questions pertaining to compliance thinking were:

- How much pollution or wastes is allowed under the regulations or permits?
- What are the acceptable levels of releases that will not trigger concerns, cause adverse reactions, or involve failure to comply with the regulations?
- What amounts of toxic substances can be used and still be acceptable to the regulatory agencies, customers, stakeholders, workers, or the public?

- Are there locations where the laws and regulations are less stringent and easier to deal with?
- What is necessary to achieve compliance?

Corporations wanted to reduce the impacts of pollution to be sure, especially those impacts on the company. They also wanted to limit their responsibilities to only what was mandated. This approach left them dealing only with the effects and impacts of the pollution that they generated. The approach was to manage the compliance requirements, instead of mitigating the pollution and waste generation. The approach proved to be expensive; moreover, the investments in capital equipment to manage the waste problems had poor rates of return, and the processes were expensive to operate. Solving problems after the waste streams were generated was not very efficient, nor was it effective. Many of the solutions created new problems that also had to be managed. For instance, stripping volatile organic compounds (VOCs) or other hazardous materials from the land or water and transforming them, through filter media, into solid waste to be landfilled or incinerated created the potential for groundwater pollution from leaching landfills or air emissions from smokestacks, respectively.

During the late 1980s corporations realized the high costs of controlling and managing waste streams and focused on reducing waste generation at source. Concerns about risks and liability containment hit center stage. Pollution prevention and waste minimization became the new buzz words as corporations realized that it was more cost effective to prevent problems than to solve them after the fact. Corporations realized that they had to take the initiative to improve their environmental management. Pollution prevention was an initial, logical step toward SBD. People came to believe that simply following the rules and regulations was not sufficient to mitigate risks and liabilities. The concept of *eliminating* problems instead of managing them was born.

In truth, thinking about pollution must *begin* with the potential impacts. From there, it must backtrack to the causes and effects in order to find ways to prevent the pollution from occurring in the first place. During the 1990s, this redirection began to occur. Corporations began exploring the benefits of proactive EMSs that could provide a systematic solution for managing environmental mandates and issues. The focus shifted from regulatory compliance to the broader perspectives of systems thinking, pollution prevention, waste minimization, and risk mitigation. Minimizing the effects of production through system solutions became the objective.

In 1996, the International Standards Organization introduced its ISO 14000 initiative, providing a standardized format for developing and implementing an acceptable environmental management system. The goals were to facilitate regulatory compliance through systematic processes and procedures, to encourage continual improvements in environmental performance, to prevent and eliminate pollution, and to initiate LCT.[10] ISO 14000 represents a bridge from the old ways of thinking about waste management and compliance to holistic management and LCT as embedded in enterprise thinking and SBD.

Environmental factors: causes, effects, and related impacts

The general theme of environmental regulations has been to provide the rules of engagement and mandate reporting and control mechanisms. By examining the effects of production, government can attempt to reduce or control the causes of those effects. For instance, the production of sulfur dioxide (SO_2) is the unwanted effect of burning sulfur-containing coal or oil at a power plant. The cause of this effect is the sulfur contained in the coal and the process technology used to generate steam for the turbines that produce electricity. Some possible solutions are to use low-sulfur coal, to install flue gas desulfurization equipment, or even simply to obtain permits to release more SO_2. A combination of these actions may also be a solution. However, these are partial solutions at best. While each could have a positive impact on the corporation's problem, they may not address the true problems associated with the emissions. If the downstream impacts and consequences are also examined, it may become clear that the natural or social environment often cannot tolerate any further degradation and destruction, and the specifications of an acceptable solution become more obvious.

The direct environmental effects of most enterprises are fairly easy to identify. They include air emissions, wastewater discharges, production of solid and hazardous wastes, the use and disposal of synthetic chemicals, accidents and spills, and the health and safety of workers and contractors. Most corporations have systems for managing these environmental considerations that result in reasonable accomplishments; however, their EMSs rarely include the effects of their supply networks and customers. Suppliers may have similar production-related environmental issues and, in some cases, even more severe and serious problems. Energy consumption, low efficiencies of processes and products, poor yields, wastes, and discards are only a few of the concerns both upstream and downstream of the primary producer.

Most importantly, once all of these effects have been identified along the production chain, they must then be examined on the basis of their impacts on the local communities, regional economies, and global business environment. For instance, sulfur dioxide releases generally produce acid rain, causing damage over a wide geographical area and resulting in acidification of land and waterways. Corporations must assess the impacts of their sulfur dioxide emissions and determine how best to mitigate the problems. They should focus on the consequences of the environmental factors, not just on what the costs are and how the pollution affects the corporation. The production of carbon dioxide (CO_2) from combustion processes provides a good example of this need for broader thinking. CO_2 is a relatively benign gas that results from burning carbon-based fuels. While CO_2 does not usually cause damage or injury to workers or neighbors,[11] and has minimal effects on the local or regional environments, an increasing level of CO_2 in the atmosphere has contributed to the increasing concerns about global warming and its consequences.[12] Stakeholders' concerns about climate change have to be understood and addressed.

SBD is driven by the impacts and consequences of residuals and pollution. It explores the needs and expectations of all customers and stakeholders and focuses on solutions that provide total satisfaction. It goes beyond the mandates of laws and regulations to look for ways to *protect* health, safety, and the environment. Enhanced performance and positive development, rather than economic growth alone, are at the center of the new business mantra. SBD contends that improving operations, products, and processes are winning strategies regardless of the specific driving forces. Eliminating defects and burdens are in the best interest of customers, stakeholders, suppliers, and the enterprise. Doing so leads to enhanced satisfaction across the broad array of customers and stakeholders, and reduces risks and liabilities. Most importantly, eliminating impacts improves the value provided and fulfills the fundamental social responsibilities of the corporation. It is a win–win strategy.

In implementing SBD, then, corporations begin to create business environments where transparency and eco-efficiency give customers and stakeholders the information and outcomes that they expect. They stop looking only at front-end processes and begin to look at the downstream expectations. They link the system from cradle-to-grave. When they make this transformation, corporations begin to find that contamination of land, air, and water, and the destruction of other natural resources, is leading to economic losses and limitations in the future. Moreover, they find that curing past pollution and contamination diverts investment funding from creating future opportunities. Corporations are left with less to invest in sustaining the future.

The possible destruction of the natural world is perhaps the most severe of the impacts because the consequences are significant and potentially irreversible. The potential consequences of environmental impacts such as climate change, eutrophication, acidification, ozone layer depletion, toxic contamination, habitat loss, and catastrophic illness require corporations to develop sustainable solutions. Such solutions, in all likelihood, will include a more comprehensive understanding of the science driving the causes and effects of these impacts.

Disruption and depletion of the natural environment are usually local or regional in nature, but are profoundly capable of affecting the eco-systems. "Disruption" is a broad category that includes the relatively simple impacts of noise and odors, concerns about the balance of nature, and the compounding effects of such issues as deforestation and ocean contamination. The latter are examples of both effects and impacts: deforestation is itself an impact, but it also leads to other impacts, such as loss of watershed, degradation of land resources, and the loss of flora to absorb carbon dioxide which can potentially exacerbate climate change. Clearly, while disruption seems to be short term, it can have consequences that impact long-term sustainability.

Depletion is often directly linked to corporations, especially the depletion of those resources that are used to produce products and services. The depletion of resources has far-reaching consequences, including the loss of economic viability of industry and the social impacts involved in transforming social and economic requirements to new technologies and products that use alternative resources or ones that are more available. For instance, most industrialized societies depend on the petroleum industry and the production of gasoline and related products from crude oil. Imagine the consequences of the depletion of the world's crude oil in just five–ten years. Valuable assets such as oil refineries, automobiles, supertankers, and numerous others would become worthless, and the world would be seeking alternatives to fill the void. SBD invites corporations to start contemplating such distant possibilities, and the solutions to them, now. The sooner the solution mechanisms are sought, the more time there is to find the sustainable solutions. Change with stability is relatively easy if there is sufficient time to effect the solutions.

Depletion of natural resources is usually not an immediate concern for most corporations, yet in the long term it has profound effects. When natural resources are depleted, new technologies must replace the dependence on the depleted resource. Almost all natural resources, from metals to fuels, have finite limits that are well understood based on current consumption levels. While the usage patterns may change and future technologies may improve efficiencies and effectiveness, the sooner the transition to a new resource or process starts, the less disruptive will be the consequences.

The story of the phase-out of CFCs provides insights about the future economic implications of resource depletion. As CFCs became scarcer, the costs and prices increased dramatically, changing the value proposition of using CFCs from very advantageous (during the 1970s and 1980s) to very disadvantageous (in the 1990s). This was especially the case for their applications as a solvent. CFCs were used extensively as cleaning solvents for electronics because they were inexpensive, nontoxic, and easy to use. At the end of their life story, however, they became very expensive and difficult to obtain. The economic attributes of CFCs shifted from positive to negative. Eventually, CFCs were replaced with new compounds that were less damaging to the environment.

While discussions about depletion usually focus on production materials, the most compelling subject concerns depletion of water resources and air quality. Water is not only critical to carbon-based life; it is an essential ingredient in most industrial processes. It is obviously a central ingredient in the production of food products, an important solvent and cleaning agent for electronics and microprocessor production, and critical to a wide range of other manufacturing requirements. Clean water may be our most precious resource. Air quality ranks in the top category as well: both clean air and water are fundamental requirements for most human activities, and they are easily damaged, requiring extensive investment to remediate.

The depletion of flora and fauna, in turn, threatens the building blocks of human existence. Like other resources, they are difficult to repair or replace. With all of our scientific knowledge, it is still impossible to map out all of the interrelationships between the species and ultimately determine the impacts and consequences when losses occur. In many cases, it takes decades or centuries to understand the implications.

The circle of causes and effects as they relate to impacts and their consequences is possibly the most complex part of managing an enterprise. Management must understand how its operations, processes, products, and activities impinge on both the business environment and the natural world. The effects are usually apparent, and the causes are typically understood. The complicated part is to link the upstream production and use with the downstream impacts and consequences. Figure 4.8 depicts selected elements of cause and effect, and the implications for impacts downstream.[13]

SBD embodies enterprise thinking and management and the full integration of social, economic, and environmental considerations within the value system. Markets and customers are but parts, albeit important parts, of a total system that includes all of the upstream and downstream operations, processes, and activities (see box 4.2). The social and economic factors listed in figure 4.8 are some of the necessary considerations in the complex system of interrelated activities. It is impossible to depict a single graphic the complex story and interactions that occur in the business environment and the natural world.

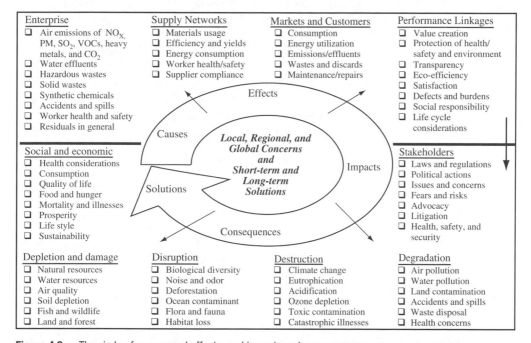

Enterprise
- ❑ Air emissions of NO_X, PM, SO_2, VOCs, heavy metals, and CO_2
- ❑ Water effluents
- ❑ Hazardous wastes
- ❑ Solid wastes
- ❑ Synthetic chemicals
- ❑ Accidents and spills
- ❑ Worker health and safety
- ❑ Residuals in general

Supply Networks
- ❑ Materials usage
- ❑ Efficiency and yields
- ❑ Energy consumption
- ❑ Worker health/safety
- ❑ Supplier compliance

Markets and Customers
- ❑ Consumption
- ❑ Energy utilization
- ❑ Emissions/effluents
- ❑ Wastes and discards
- ❑ Maintenance/repairs

Performance Linkages
- ❑ Value creation
- ❑ Protection of health/ safety and environment
- ❑ Transparency
- ❑ Eco-efficiency
- ❑ Satisfaction
- ❑ Defects and burdens
- ❑ Social responsibility
- ❑ Life cycle considerations

Effects
Causes
Local, Regional, and Global Concerns and Short-term and Long-term Solutions
Impacts
Solutions
Consequences

Social and economic
- ❑ Health considerations
- ❑ Consumption
- ❑ Quality of life
- ❑ Food and hunger
- ❑ Mortality and illnesses
- ❑ Prosperity
- ❑ Life style
- ❑ Sustainability

Stakeholders
- ❑ Laws and regulations
- ❑ Political actions
- ❑ Issues and concerns
- ❑ Fears and risks
- ❑ Advocacy
- ❑ Litigation
- ❑ Health, safety, and security

Depletion and damage
- ❑ Natural resources
- ❑ Water resources
- ❑ Air quality
- ❑ Soil depletion
- ❑ Fish and wildlife
- ❑ Land and forest

Disruption
- ❑ Biological diversity
- ❑ Noise and odor
- ❑ Deforestation
- ❑ Ocean contaminant
- ❑ Flora and fauna
- ❑ Habitat loss

Destruction
- ❑ Climate change
- ❑ Eutrophication
- ❑ Acidification
- ❑ Ozone depletion
- ❑ Toxic contamination
- ❑ Catastrophic illnesses

Degradation
- ❑ Air pollution
- ❑ Water pollution
- ❑ Land contamination
- ❑ Accidents and spills
- ❑ Waste disposal
- ❑ Health concerns

Figure 4.8   The circle of causes and effects, and impacts and consequences

Box 4.2 Royal/Dutch Shell Group and its transformation to SBD

Royal/Dutch Shell Group (hereafter, Shell) is a global oil company that is positioning itself as a diversified energy company that uses its management acumen and technological innovation to meet global energy needs. Shell has developed what it calls "Scenarios to 2050" to reflect on the energy needs over the first half of the twenty-first century. In the company's *Energy Needs, Choices and Possibilities* report published in 2002, Philip Watts, Chairman of the Committee of Managing Directors, made the following comments:[1]

> The ways in which we produce and use the energy the world depends on are bound to change greatly over the next fifty years, in response to three fundamental challenges:
> - giving all people access to the benefits of efficient, commercial energy from which nearly a fifth of us are still excluded,
> - meeting the expanding and shifting energy needs of an urbanizing world as economic development raises the living standards of billions of people, and

- preventing the pollution that damages health, blights environments and threatens vital natural systems.

Shell articulates the fundamental aspects of SBD through a framework that integrates the economic underpinnings of the corporation with social and environmental dimensions. Shell has embraced a stakeholder-based perspective on leading change. However, this was not always the situation. Shell has had a number of significant miscues in the past. Two of the most damaging were its poor track record of exploration and production in Nigeria and the "Brent Spar" oil platform débâcles in 1994. Nigeria is an oil-rich country. Shell acquired development rights and partnerships to exploit the oil reserves. Nigeria did not have sophisticated political, regulatory, or social mandates pertaining to oil exploration and production. Although there were a few regulations, oil companies were allowed to use their own standards and practices. Without governmental constraints, Shell experienced oil spills, oil leaks, pipeline problems, and other operating difficulties affecting the indigenous population. The impacts included polluted water and contaminated land that affected drinking water, food resources, and natural habitant, resulting in social and political unrest.

While the experience in Nigeria was an ongoing situation, Brent Spar was more of a miscalculation that grew into a monumental problem. Shell submitted a plan to decommission an obsolete North Sea oil platform using deepwater disposal. While the British government approved the plan, Greenpeace and other environmental organizations protested it,[2] concerned that the actions would set precedence for future disposal actions. The protest turned into a boycott of Shell's products in Europe. Ultimately, Shell realized that it had to dismantle and properly dispose of the platform. Based on these incidents and growing concerns about Shell's image and reputation, management reflected on the company's vision and strategic direction.

In 1997, Shell took action to move toward SBD in order to preempt difficulties and ensure that management emphasized economic, social, and environmental performance throughout the corporation. In the 2002 *Annual Report and Accounts*, Jeron van der Veer, President, stated the following:[3]

> Showing that we live up to our values – honesty, integrity, and respect for people – is even more important in such troubled times. We believe this requires:
> - engaging people's concerns;
> - articulating clear principles and high standards; having strong corporate governance to ensure that we live up to them throughout our operations; committing to transparency; and
> - communicating effectively.
>
> We believe that contributing to sustainable development is both about how we do business and how business does in the long term.

Shell and the other oil companies now face the challenge of moving their businesses from meeting customers' demand in the short term with petroleum-based products to providing energy services in the long term using more sustainable sources and resources. The scope of the challenge is overwhelming. Each day Shell produces approximately 2.3 million barrels of crude oil and 9 million standard ft^3 of natural gas.[4] The amount of mass that is processed, shipped, and used is staggering. The transformation of a system based on physical assets such as oil platforms and rigs, refineries, and supertankers to a system based on renewable resources will involve enormous investments in technology, plants and equipment, and people. Shell's strategy is to concurrently meet the growing needs for fossil fuels, reduce the associated environmental and social impacts, and build new capabilities for the future. In its booklet, *Meeting the Energy Challenge* that provides statistics on its operations, Shell recognizes the magnitude of the efforts required to meet the needs of the future. The following is its summary statement:[5]

> By 2050, we expect the world to double its energy demand. Developing countries will need five times more. Fossil fuels will remain important, but people are unlikely to tolerate increased pollution, the burden of extra infrastructure and the possible effects on the climate. The world needs to:
> - Deliver the extra energy needed
> - Minimize the environmental and social impacts from extracting and delivering fossil fuels
> - Ensure local communities benefit from energy production
> - Increase energy efficiency
> - Market more natural gas and develop cleaner transport fuels.

The shift requires producing more low-carbon and low-emission energy in the short term and switching to alternatives such as solar power and hydrogen-based applications in the long term. Economics plays a significant role. There are many alternatives to fossil fuels but most are several factors more expensive than the current cost of crude oil and natural gas. Shell is investing in technologies for reducing the costs of solar energy, developing hydrogen fuel cells and the required fuel infrastructure, and using bio-fuels. Specifically, Shell Hydrogen is developing hydrogen stations in Europe and Japan and formed a venture with General Motors to demonstrate hydrogen fuel-cell vehicles and fueling infrastructure in the Washington, DC area.[6]

Shell Hydrogen and Shell Renewables, which focus on alternate energy sources, are commitments to the future. While Shell has made significant investments in future technologies already, there is still the rational tension between providing customers with the products and services of the present (oil, gas, and petroleum products) and shaping a future business landscape that ultimately reduces the value of those products and the related assets. It is a delicate balancing act that benefits from insights and contributions from customers, stakeholders, and other constituents. Fortunately, Shell views openness and transparency as an essential part of the long-term energy solution for the global business environment. It articulated its open perspective in the following statement:[7]

> There are many issues and dilemmas facing the energy industry and it is clear that Shell will only survive this challenging journey if we are open to comments from a wide range of individuals and groups. If we are to close the gap between our perceptions of our business and those of the wider society we need to hear from you. Shell has a commitment to listen and respond.

Inclusion of customers and stakeholders in the equation enriches the discussions and provides a broader sense of reality. The dynamics of the market and competitive forces makes formulating and implementing new solutions for the future extremely challenging. Shell is expected to meet short-term profitability and market share expectations of investors as it moves to a more sustainable future.

The energy sector of the global economy is one of the largest and most complex. Long-term solutions have to be framed in the context of current fuel availability and needs, the environmental and social impacts, the economic impacts of rising fuel prices and the associated influences on inflation and economic instability, and the development of improved and radically new technologies. Shell has embraced the concept of value creation and not just economic gain in the short term. It is value creation that ties the driving forces together.

Shell is recognized as one of the best-performing energy companies from a sustainable development perspective. Innovest, an internationally recognized investment research firm, ranked Shell No. 2 in 2004. Shell is also ranked No. 2 by the DJSI. The corporation has made a remarkable transformation from a laggard to a leader by demonstrating a new commitment to a sustainable future.

Notes:
1. *Exploring the Future: Energy Needs, Choices and Possibilities – Scenarios to 2050*, Global Business Environment, Shell International, 2001, p. 2.
2. http://deanza.edu/faculty/lilly/brentspar.htm.
3. Royal Dutch Petroleum Company, *Annual Report and Accounts*, 2002, Summary, p. 1.
4. *Ibid.*, p. 23. The numbers are rounded off to provide a representation of the magnitude of the operations and not a precise reflection of daily operations. The numbers are based on 2002 production and give a sense of the ongoing needs that Shell provides for its customers.
5. *Meeting the Energy Challenge, The Shell Report*, 2002, p. 15.
6. Shell Brochure, *New Energy*.
7. *Listening* and *Responding* (Houston, Texas: Shell Oil Company), p. 11.

Summary

Social, economic, and environmental considerations are crucial elements within the enterprise management system. Based on the knowledge and experience of the corporation, management can direct the organization and its people toward a positive vision for the future. It takes executive leadership to instill the thinking, encourage the learning, and improve the capabilities to reduce the impacts of operations and their consequences. It takes strategic thinking about the future to transform the social, economic, and environmental status quo into new realities based on trust and value creation. Corporations tend to focus on markets and customers to generate cash flow through reliable and high-quality products and services, but it is equally important to ensure that additional stakeholders are satisfied. Great solutions are built on value creation and balanced benefits across the socioeconomic and environmental spectrum. They provide reduced risks and longevity, effectiveness, and efficiency to all constituents.

Great, sustainable corporations therefore focus on development and improvements, not just on growth and profitability. John Elkington describes his notion of the "Triple Bottom Line"[14] as a more balanced view of corporate objectives that includes social, economic, and environmental considerations. While making money and achieving an adequate return on capital are important, SBD envisions balanced performance and outcomes and long-term improvements. Indeed, one of the main premises of twenty-first-century strategic thinking is that success depends on the rate of improvements in all dimensions, not just the rate of growth of revenues, net income or market capitalization. But improving the management systems at rates that exceed competitors is essential for achieving long-term success. The dot.com failures of the late 1990s and early 2000s made a few people richer, but ultimately thousands lost their investments and became poorer. Sustainable success is not about short-term gains for a few, but rather about long-term gains for everyone.

Corporate social responsibility is the glue that links growth with improvements. Corporations are expected to be responsible and ethical; they are also expected to handle any difficulty and mitigate any risks to the public and society. Doing so is fundamental to the basic *trust* component of public acceptance. Corporations can maintain that trust through effectiveness, openness (**transparency**), inclusiveness, and innovativeness. By deliberately letting the public know of its performance and quest for improvements, they commit to a course of improvements that can only further its growth, development, and success.

Environmental considerations are always at the forefront of public concerns. Compliance with laws and regulation is expected without question or excuse. Preventing pollution and environmental problems and going beyond pollution prevention and waste minimization have become the norm and are absolutely necessary for a business to be considered world class. While the paradigm of the late twentieth century was to reduce the causes of pollution and waste generation, SBD requires much more. It invites corporations to examine the impacts of their decisions across the enterprise and to reduce, if not eliminate, the very causes of the impacts and their consequences. Moreover, it is the responsibility of the producers and the users to mitigate the degradation, disruption, destruction, and depletion caused by the entire enterprise. Figure 4.9 depicts the flow of these fundamental responsibilities across time.

Corporations gain insights into new solutions with increasing experience and knowledge. A sustainable world must derive from the realities of the past, the promises of the future, and the achievements of people over time.

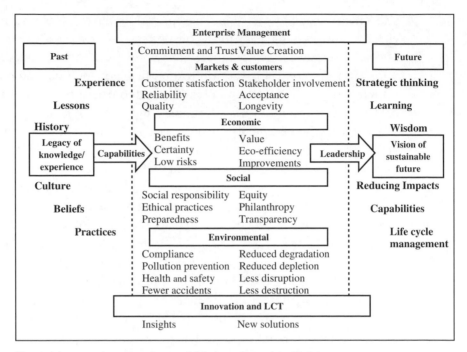

Figure 4.9   The social, economic, and environmental factors of a sustainable future

Corporations who embrace SBD recognize that, in a highly competitive business world, defects, burdens, impacts, and unintended consequences reduce the viability and potential success of the enterprise. Based on the principles of SBD and the vision for the future, leading corporations are beginning to plan, organize, manage, and operate accordingly to invent a new more sustainable future.

Supplementary material

Learning objectives

Chapter 4 has the following learning objectives that are intended to guide and support students and practitioners:

- Understanding the implications of the business environment, especially the driving forces of change: social, economic, and environmental.
- Examining the analytical models used for scanning, monitoring, forecasting, and assessing the business environment related to social, economic, and environmental forces.

- Describing and assessing the social and political aspects of SBD.
- Describing and assessing the main economic considerations of SBD.
- Describing and assessing the main environmental considerations of SBD.
- Appreciating how executives and senior management lead and manage change.

Research questions

The following are questions related to SBD in order to facilitate learning and ongoing discussion and analysis of the main topics covered in the chapter:

- How do global corporations manage the huge array of social, economic, and environment forces that impinge on the strategic and operational systems of the corporation and its enterprise?
- What are the most critical elements of social, economic, and environmental considerations for global corporations, their customers and stakeholders?
- How do global corporations select the most critical issues and concerns?
- How do they prioritize their analytical and strategic efforts?
- How do strategic leaders and managers manage the critical issues?

NOTES

1. Please note that the scope of this book simply does not allow for an expanded description and discussion of all of the topics related to the social concerns. It would take an entire book to discuss topics such as hunger, poverty, and disease. Moreover, the typical areas of concern such as suppliers, distributors, customers, markets, competition, related industries, and stakeholders are embedded within the EMM.
2. National Council for Science and the Environment, *Recommendations for Achieving Sustainable Communities*, 2001, p. 56.
3. GRI, *Sustainability Reporting Guidelines*, 2002, p. 24. GRI suggests that the principles of transparency and inclusiveness represent the starting point for the reporting and are woven into the other principles.
4. This topic is so extensive that it could fill an entire book. The discussion in this book is limited because the focus is on the strategic implications.
5. Union Carbide Corporation's (UCC) plant in India was a joint venture between UCC and the government. Nevertheless UCC has been held primarily responsible. The *Exxon Valdez* was a complicated situation in which the tanker captain, Joseph Hazelwood, was allowed to operate the vessel even though there were issues about his alcohol problems. Moreover, Exxon was slow to respond to the spill, which occurred on March 23, 1989. The company

spent $3.2 billion on the cleanup and is still litigating the $6.75 billion fine and punitive damages ordered by US District Judge Russel Holland. If the 9th US Circuit Court of Appeals upholds the lower court's decision the event (spill) will have cost Exxon over $10 billion. Royal Dutch Shell is the tenth largest corporation in the world. In 1995, it attempted to demolish one of its off-shore oil rigs at sea and sink the remains in the ocean depths. Severe consumer and stakeholder reaction convinced management to dismantle the equipment on land. The Brent Spar incident provides insights about the power of consumers and stakeholders to affect corporate decision-making. Moreover, Shell gained significant insights about the value of sustainable development. It is now recognized by Innovest as a leading oil company in Innovest's EcoValue21 Rating. Moreover, Shell is listed as second in the DJSI.

6. World Commission on Environment and Development (WCED) for the General Assembly of the United Nations, *Our Common Future: The Brundtland Report* (Oxford: Oxford University Press, 1987), p. 221. In 1972, the members of the Organization for Economic Cooperation and Development (OECD) agreed to base their environmental policies on the PPP. The intent was to improve the economic efficiency of decision-making and reflect more of the total costs in the prices of products.

7. There was information available during the early part of the century about the negative effects but significant actions were not taken until severe problems became apparent.

8. EDF brochure, *Partnerships* (2003).

9. David Cohan, Kenneth Wapman, and Mary McLearn, "Beyond waste minimization: life-cycle cost management for chemicals and materials," *Pollution Prevention Review* (Summer 1992), p. 261.

10. ISO 14000 is an internal environmental management system created by the International Organization of Standardization (ISO), based in Geneva. ISO is an international agency whose members include national standards organizations, such the American National Standards Institute (ANSI) and the British Standards Institution (BSI). The following are the main subsections of ISO 14000:

- Environmental Management Systems (EMSs)
  - ISO 14001 EMSs – Specifications with guidance for use.
  - ISO 14004 EMSs – General guidelines on principles, systems, and supporting techniques.
- Environmental Auditing
  - ISO 14010 Guidelines for environmental auditing – General principles of environmental auditing.
  - ISO 14011 Guidelines for environmental auditing – Audit procedures – Auditing of EMS.
  - ISO 14012 Guidelines for environmental auditing – Qualification criteria for environmental auditors.
  - ISO 14014 Initial reviews.
  - ISO 14015 Environmental site assessments.
- Environmental Labeling
  - ISO 14020 Goals and principles of all environmental labeling.
  - ISO 14021 Environmental labels and declarations – Self-declaration environmental claims – Terms and definitions.
  - ISO 14022 Environmental labels and declarations – Symbols.
  - ISO 14023 Environmental labels and declarations – Testing and verification.

- ISO 14024 Environmental labels and declarations – Environmental labeling Type I – Guiding principles and procedures.
- ISO 14025 Type III labeling.
- Environmental Performance Evaluation
  - ISO 14031 Evaluation of the environmental performance of the management system.
- Life-Cycle Assessment
  - ISO 14040 Environmental management – life-cycle assessment – General principles and guidelines.
  - ISO 14041 Environmental management – life-cycle assessment – Inventory analysis.
  - ISO 14042 Environmental management – life-cycle assessment – Impact assessment.
  - ISO 14043 Environmental management – life-cycle assessment – Interpretation.
- Terms and Definitions
  - ISO 14050 Terms and definition guide.

11. This statement is based on the fact that carbon dioxide is not a toxic gas. However, it can cause problems for workers if carbon dioxide has purged the oxygen from the air and there is insufficient oxygen for breathing.
12. There are significant debates about the theories pertaining to global warming. It is not the intent of this book to make arguments about the theoretical and practical aspects.
13. It is the author's intent to write a related book that provides more detail on each of the elements. *Sustainable Enterprise Management: Creating Extraordinary Value through Strategic Leadership and Business Integration* examines, assesses, and describes how an "extended enterprise perspective" of the business environment, a strong enterprise-based SMS, exceptional strategic leadership, and business innovation can create extraordinary business value and sustainable success.
14. John Elkington, *Cannibals with Forks: The Triple Bottom Line of Sustainable Development* (Oxford: Chapstone Publishing, 1997), pp. 2, 109–111.

REFERENCES

Cohan, David, Kenneth Wapman, and Mary McLearn (1992) "Beyond waste minimization: life-cycle cost management for chemicals and materials," *Pollution Prevention Review*, Summer

Elkington, John (1997) *Cannibals with Forks: The Triple Bottom line of Sustainable Development*. Oxford: Chapstone Publishing

Global Reporting Initiative (GRI) (2002) *Sustainability Reporting Guidelines*

National Council for Science and the Environment (2001) *Recommendations for Achieving Sustainable Communities*

World Commission on Environment and Development (WCED) for the General Assembly of the United Nations (1987) *Our Common Future: The Brundtland Report*. Oxford: Oxford University Press

5   The driving forces of markets and stakeholders' connectedness

Introduction

Throughout the 1990s, customer satisfaction reigned supreme in the mindset of corporate executives, managers, and marketing professionals as they tried to differentiate their products and improve corporate performance. While customer satisfaction remains critical for realizing positive outcomes today, it is a subset of the more inclusive view of total satisfaction that also includes meeting broader stakeholder expectations and societal needs. Total satisfaction necessitates solutions that include social, economic, and environmental considerations. Great solutions are balanced from every perspective: they exceed needs, create exceptional value, and satisfy expectations.

With the dramatic expansion of information and knowledge provided through the Internet and world-wide media, customers and stakeholders are empowered with facts, figures, and specifications about products and processes that would have been impossible to obtain a decade ago. In many situations, customers know as much about the products they buy as do the individuals selling them. They can scrutinize the competitive landscape to find the right product at the right price. Moreover, customers and stakeholders can share their opinions and perceptions with thousands of others who are interested in the veracity and accuracy of product claims, advertising messages, process outcomes, waste problems, and any negative impacts associated with production and use. It is becoming more difficult to espouse only positive attributes using glossy marketing campaigns or fancy promotions, or to mislead people through false impressions.

People across the globe expect the truth – and they now have numerous mechanisms for discovering it, both positive and negative – about a corporation, its products and processes, and operations. With the data, information and analysis that are available on millions of web sites, it is difficult to keep secrets. Dysfunctional behaviors and attitudes quickly become common knowledge. The stories of Enron, WorldCom and others indicate that the truth prevails, and inappropriate corporate behaviors can lead to catastrophic results. Most importantly, customers and stakeholders want the whole story, not just the glitz and glamor. The growing expectation is that problems and concerns will be promptly disclosed and corrected. There is also a growing societal expectation that corporations will know the pluses and minuses of their supply networks and product applications, and ensure that the decisions made by outside suppliers, partners, and contributors fulfill their own social, economic, regulatory, and environmental responsibilities.

Before establishing sustainable market and stakeholder strategies, businesses must identify, understand, and articulate the demands and expectations of their markets, customers, and stakeholders. This chapter examines the forces that drive these considerations, business and marketing approaches for managing them, and related techniques for improving corporate performance. It moves us from the broad perspective of the business environment to an examination of specific approaches addressing the needs of markets, customers, and stakeholders. It includes the following four key topics:

- Identifying and exploiting the market drivers, including globalization, market and competitive intensity, market expectations, and life style considerations.
- Understanding stakeholder expectations, including the concepts of the "license to operate" and socially responsible decision-making.
- Building integrity and openness into decision-making and providing balanced marketing communications and corporate reporting to enhance market position and corporate reputation.
- Improving the connectedness of supply networks, customers and stakeholders, and capital markets through dialog and performance.

Understanding the implications of market forces

Globalization and connectedness

Globalization is a complex and ill-defined term that engenders both optimism and fear. It is the linking of economies, markets, and customers through the expansion of trade and the liberalization of market restrictions. It includes creating free trade mechanisms that facilitate the movement of goods, services, information, and capital, and providing support structures that reduce the costs of selling and delivering products, components, parts, and services. It is characterized by the pervasiveness of information and the ability to connect with global suppliers and partners through low-cost telecommunications and logistics, especially the Internet and related infrastructures.

Globalization requires new strategies for managing the complex array of forces that impinge on corporate decision-making. Markets and customers expect customized, sophisticated, high-quality products and services with exceptional value. They demand superior performance, reduced costs and impacts, enhanced safety, and improved longevity and reliability. They want positive results, not compromises. Likewise, stakeholders also expect outstanding solutions that meet the requirements of all constituents without imposing burdens and impacts on society in general, on particular individuals, groups or nations, or on the natural world. Improvements are not realized if one segment gains and others lose.

Markets and stakeholder expectations often cross industry lines and country borders, presenting new opportunities and challenges that confound the traditional views of markets, customers, competition, and industry. The concept of a national or regional market is transforming into two seemingly divergent phenomena: the global product and mass customization.

The *global product* is one that meets the needs and expectations of most customers in many different market conditions and situations. It is designed to satisfy a majority of the potential customers and fulfill the mandates and requirements of stakeholders, including government regulation, wherever it is sold. Such products enjoy incredible cost advantages and are often the market share leaders in their categories. While it is difficult to select the perfect example, Coke and Pepsi are typically cited as global products having global recognition and reputation.

Conversely, *mass customization* involves creating product platforms that allow the producer to change product configurations to meet the unique specifications of selected customers or market segments. While this does not mean that each customer obtains a unique product, it does suggest that products can be tailored to the cultural, social, environmental, and/or application requirements of selected customers and markets. Microsoft's Windows operating system is a great example. It can be tailored to meet the needs of different languages, cultures, costs, applications, and numerous other aspects. While software is relatively easy to change, Windows exemplifies the concept of mass customization and the global trend of corporations trying to design and produce products to customer specifications rather than to company standards.

The two concepts are not mutually exclusive, but are interrelated. Globalization depends on linked entities working together to achieve high-quality, low-cost outcomes that provide total satisfaction. Maximizing the resource base through fabricators and suppliers provides the means to achieve high-value results. Standardized products provide a high volume of cost effective and resource efficient production and distribution. They tend to maximize capacity utilization, minimize costs, and achieve efficient and effective outcomes on a macro-basis. On the other hand, customized products provide specific solutions, while minimizing resource use and wastes on a micro-basis. Either way, the connectedness of the networks through information sharing, standardization of methods, exploitation of advanced technologies, and the understanding of latent and manifested needs is what makes globalization possible. Connectedness is necessary for effective outcomes in the new world of globalization.

Reducing tariffs, quotas and other trade barriers, and creating free trade zones have enhanced globalization. Freer trade has made the exchange of goods, services, and capital less complicated and costly. The following are three key examples of changes in political thinking that were intended to improve connectedness:

- 1993   The North American Free Trade Agreement (NAFTA) between the United States, Canada, and Mexico opened the borders between these countries by eliminating tariffs and other barriers.
- 1993   The European Union replaced the European Economic Community (EEC), establishing free trade and eliminating border restrictions among member countries.
- 1995   The World Trade Organization (WTO) replaced the General Agreement on Tariffs and Trade (GATT), expanded global representation to 132 countries, and established rules and standards related to trade and trade disputes.

There are many more examples of these kinds of actions. The trend toward free trade and greater support for relationships between suppliers, producers, and customers characterizes globalization today. But globalization includes both these kinds of tangible changes that link countries and companies and intangible changes that influence customer behaviors and attitudes. The former improves connectedness, while the latter makes that connectedness more acceptable to the people of the world.

Globalization is the culmination of many forces (social, economic, environmental, technological, and market) that have caused global changes over the last several decades. New technologies have made travel and communication faster, simpler, and cheaper which, together with the expansion of trade, has connected people all across the world. It is now cost effective to process raw materials in one country, ship the outputs to parts fabricators in another, produce assembly modules in a third country, and complete final assembly closer to the final markets. As a result, global corporations have extended their reach to most countries. Governmental pressures for local jobs to support the national economy once worked against free trade; positive outcomes now reinforce the relationships and build trust among the participants.

Yet, globalization is neither inherently positive nor negative. It creates both opportunities and responsibilities. During the early years of globalization, many people, especially those in the developed countries, enjoyed the availability of low-cost goods and services from all over the world. It has kept inflation relatively low in most countries. As time goes on, however, negative effects are also being felt. Already, corporations are finding that the lack of total information about their supply chain inhibits their ability to consider fully the social and environmental impacts of upstream operations, especially those of the suppliers of suppliers. Despite new technologies and communications mechanisms, there remains significant uncertainty. For example, Nestlés' discovered the ramifications of this uncertainty when it was criticized for failing to uncover and eliminate the use of forced labor by its suppliers of cocoa in Africa. As Nestlés' and others discovered, many tangible and intangible elements of remote supply chains can become apparent over time. Producers or suppliers might be using child labor to improve cost structures; or they might be operating in violation of environmental laws and regulations, or taking other illegal or inappropriate actions. Unless the global corporation follows a strict adherence to the principles of SBD and assumes its full responsibilities as the enterprise leader, such defects remain hidden until stakeholder groups or government agencies discover the violations or difficulties. While the global corporation may be blameless from a legal perspective, it may be culpable from a social, ethical, and moral one. It may have failed to conduct sufficient analysis and auditing of the situation to ensure that the proper actions were being carried out. Such responsibilities lay at the foundation of cradle-to-grave perspectives, enterprise thinking, and SBD.

The changes wrought by globalization make SBD an essential management construct for creating a viable future. Table 5.1 depicts a matrix of the forces of change related to globalization and the means to achieve sustainable solutions. The main sections of this chapter examine each of the categories in table 5.1: market and competitive intensity; the influence of stakeholders; the proliferation of information; and the significance of networks.

Table 5.1. Linking globalization and connectedness with sustainable solutions

	Market and competitive intensity	Influence of stakeholders	Proliferation of information	Significance of networks
Globalization (broad aspects)	– Enterprise thinking – Value creation – Total satisfaction – Inclusiveness – Balance	– Discovering needs/mandates – Building relationships – Focus on social responsibility	– Transparency – Global reporting – Validating data and information	– Understanding strategic needs – Creating alliances
Connectedness (specific aspects)	– Understanding driving forces – Discovering latent needs – Learning – Leading change	– Discovering defects and burdens – Mitigating impacts and risks – Focusing on complete solution	– Creating open reporting mechanisms – Facilitating support mechanisms	– Integrating with supply networks – Using LCT – Focusing on advantages

Table 5.1 indicates the power of SBD for meeting the needs of the business environment. That power springs from the development of new management constructs for shaping and developing solutions, and not from the actual solutions themselves. For instance, many corporations are seeking ways to manage climate change concerns. While it may be important to have a management approach for dealing with climate change (e.g. planting trees for carbon sequestration), it is imperative to create an EMS for recognizing and responding to all such issues. Addressing one problem does not create a system for ensuring continuous improvement in all areas.

Globalization brings opportunity in the potential discovery and implementation of solutions through extended relationships. It brings responsibility, too, for the actions of those with whom one is connected. This perspective on opportunity and responsibility is the precursor to developing specific programs for achieving sustainable outcomes.

Market and competitive intensity

In a hypercompetitive business environment, where leading edge technologies and new-to-the-world products are quickly copied, corporations are in a constant search for ways to obtain superior competitive advantage. It is not sufficient to have good products; there is a proliferation of good products. In highly competitive markets, customers expect the best and are unwilling to pay more than the prevailing prices, prices that have already been eroded by competitive pressures. The longevity of powerful product positions is increasingly transient as new solutions become available at a rapid rate. Customers expect improved value with each new product generation.

The primary considerations in this type of business environment are identifying markets and customer needs that do not exceed the capabilities and resources of the corporation, and providing solutions that are balanced and sustainable. The markets and customers provide the context for business and, therefore, help to determine the stakeholders as well. The selection of industry targets and market segments also determines the competition and potential partnerships.

In today's world, even leading edge products quickly become commodities or obsolete. For example, the Gillette Mach III development program did not materialize into a long-term competitive advantage. Rivals like Schick quickly emulated the three-blade concept and then developed a four-blade razor within months of the initial introduction. Commoditization is an ever-present threat to all producers as competitive advantages erode and dominant products become commonplace. Moreover, improvements to low-cost, commodity products really threaten high-end manufacturers. For example, while a €50,000 BMW is still a highly desirable high-end product, customers can choose to buy a €20,000 (approximately $26,000) Toyota Avalon or Ford 500 (to name only a few of the choices), vehicles of outstanding value and nearly as good quality. The abilities of corporations to produce goods and services have grown faster than the number of people in the world who have the means to buy them. In most industries, there are excess capacities.

The Internet has also intensified competition by allowing customers to obtain accurate information about features, benefits, and costs of products and services as well as ways to calculate accurate B/C analysis. Whereas individuals may use objective and subjective perspectives when making a purchase decision, the Internet-based algorithms may skew the selection process to a specific model because it always uses the same logic.

Finally, competitive intensity is also exhibited in terms of quality and performance. As product quality improves on a global basis, customers demand even higher quality. Producers who fail to meet such expectations generally lose market share and fade into oblivion. The successful corporations must continue to improve their quality; the quest toward perfection is never-ending.

Market expectations

Markets are generalizations of groups of similar customers who are seeking to satisfy their needs and wants in specific ways. The historic basis for market generalizations has been the products that corporations have previously sold to the grouping of customers. As the world moves toward mass customization[1] and beyond, markets are becoming more difficult to define, and demand is fragmented into many specific "product/market" segments. Mass customization suggests that there will be a more uniquely designed and delivered product for each customer. Ultimately, future markets may be defined in terms of the solutions provided rather than the products offered by the industry. While products are broad attempts to satisfy needs, solutions are specific, customer-based and stakeholder-based outcomes that focus on exactly what is expected. The solution might include a product, services, and information that provide total satisfaction. For example, jet engine manufacturers, such as General Electric, are selling new engines with thirty-year maintenance built in so that the airline has to think only about flying its planes and satisfying its customers. In the consumer world, electrical appliance producers that offer EoL information and take-back services to the customer provide a more encompassing solution than those that do not offer such services.

The challenge is to discover the needs and wants before others do, and to determine how to meet the requirements ahead of the competitors. This is especially difficult when there are latent needs and expectations and when potential customers are unable to articulate precisely what they want. Products tend to satisfy customers in the short term if they meet general expectations. However, long-term satisfaction requires the best solution, one that may be based on new technologies still in R&D. Nevertheless, history suggests that the impossible becomes possible: witness wireless telecommunications with video! This requires insights and imagination.

Moreover, stakeholders drive the "solution" as well. The myriad of needs and wants of customers, stakeholders, related industries, and other constituencies ultimately determine specifications of the solution. A needs and wants analysis of all of the constituents can provide the requisite information. As shown in figure 5.1, such an analysis provides a matrix of those things sought by customers as well as those articulated by stakeholders, including government and society. The intent is to show the *process* and not to provide a comprehensive listing of all of the elements.

It is paramount to understand customer and stakeholder needs and wants, and how those determine the specifications of the ultimate solutions.

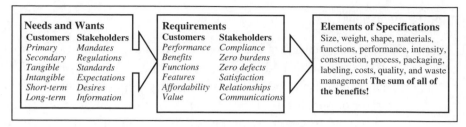

Figure 5.1   Translating needs and wants into requirements and specifications

This understanding, when combined with the demands of the business environment, establishes the basis for selecting product/market strategies and solutions.

Life style considerations

Life style changes during the latter part of the twentieth century have had an enormous influence on our world, creating new social, economic, and environmental concerns. Six of the more profound changes that relate to SBD include:

- *Unprecedented consumption*   The quantities of materials and energy used to produce products and the amount of residual waste generated continue to rise because of increasing populations, growing affluence, and expanding demand *per capita.*
- *The quest for convenience*   The complexities of life and the demands on an individual's time in the industrialized countries translate into pressure to save time and effort through more convenient products. Disposable diapers, throwaway containers, and single-use products contribute to unprecedented material intensity and waste disposal problems.
- *Increased mobility*   Increased mobility has allowed individuals and societies to expand their opportunities for social position, economic power, and enjoying the benefits of life. But it has also brought urban and suburban sprawl, high population densities, greater energy consumption, and vehicular pollution. The desire for more active and exciting leisure time has also contributed to the incredible increase in travel, causing congestion, pollution, infrastructure destruction, and resource depletion.
- *Increased population density*   There are many cities and metropolitan areas around the world that have large population densities of thousands of people per km^2. Such densities put an enormous strain on the infrastructure, causing distortions in the supply and use of resources and the

transportation and disposal of wastes. Such areas, called "megacities,"[2] often have significant problems with pollution, poverty, congestion, crime, and disease.

- *Technological change* The transfer of information, ideas, and technologies around the world can allow developing countries to make huge leaps in their development processes, improving efficiencies and eliminating deleterious effects of growth.

- *Heterogeneity and customization* Demographics in the developed countries continue to shift toward more uniform distribution of the population and away from the traditional normal or skewed distributions. This phenomenon means that there are more subsegments within populations that require specific product forms and solutions to meet their specific needs and expectations. Such diverse requirements translate into demand for fewer quantities of more varied products. More variety means more complexity and greater challenges in establishing standards, achieving economies of scale and compliance, mitigating risk and impacts, and managing EoL considerations.

Consumption is a significant social and economic factor, with both positive and negative implications. It drives the economies of the world and improves the quality of life for producers, workers, and consumers. The level of consumption has increased dramatically over the last fifty years as many innovative technologies and new products have flooded the markets with exciting new opportunities to provide the basic necessities of life along with enhanced leisure and luxury. In the 1950s people had a single telephone, possibly a TV, a radio, and one automobile per household. Today's situation is profoundly different in the developed countries. The typical family might have five radios, four telephones, three TVs, two cars, and numerous computers, video games, DVDs, VCRs, MP3 and iPOD players, and the like. The quantities consumed are staggering. Increased waste generation through production, packaging, transportation, and product retirement accompanies such unprecedented consumption, and concerns mount about the long-term implications of societies that focus on "throw-away" products and over-indulgence. If production and consumption focused on the long-term benefits of the products, the results might be more sustainable. Products having a life cycle and benefits measured in minutes are more problematic than those that can be used and reused over many years. Of course, there are exceptions, such as food and certain health care products, that must be consumed quickly.

The rise and continued success of the single-use package is a prime example of a market driven by society's demand for convenience. As reported in the *Wall Street Journal*, "Shoppers choose convenience over ecological benefits."[3] This was clear when Gerber Products Co., maker of baby foods, switched from a recyclable glass container to a plastic version that was not recyclable and noted that customers never complained.[4] While the recycling rates for plastic soda bottles have declined to a third of the 1995 rate, the quantity of single-serve containers doubled to 18 billion in the United States in 2000.[5] If convenience is a critical life style factor that consumers are not willing to forgo, then the answer may be to incorporate convenience with the principles of SBD. The same *Wall Street Journal* article suggested the following example:[6]

In 1994, Philips Electronics NV billed its eco-friendly, energy saving fluorescent bulbs as "Earthlight." But sales never impressed. In 2000, Philips repackaged the very same bulbs, ditching the environmental angle and emphasizing instead that they were convenient, seven-year life "Marathon" bulbs. Since then, sales have grown 12 percent per year.

Consumers want choices that provide near-term benefits without significant increased costs or negative implications. Very often, they optimize the present and are not connected to the future. The Philips example provides great insights about the power of SBD thinking versus that of the narrower perspectives of "eco-friendly or environmentally-friendly" constructs. The holistic solutions of SBD consider the totality of society's needs and wants. If customers want convenience, then the answer is to find solutions that are both sustainable and convenient – i.e. the Philips "Marathon" light bulb.

Mobility frees society from the limited options available within the local geographical area to the dynamic abundance of globalization. BMW views mobility to be central to its technological and social progress:[7]

Mobility is the economic foundation for the high productivity of the people in the national economy. Since residence and workplace are often separate, we are obligated to be mobile. We also use the car for our leisure time and vacation. Anyone who is not mobile cannot escape from the daily environment, still the thirst for knowledge, search for adventure, get to know new people, or discover new lebensraum.

Mobility, therefore, is not an artificial need created by advertising and in no way is it a short-lived fad. The history of humanity has shown that mobility is a central principle of life and evolution.

Mobility on a grander scale involves changing work environments, moving to different countries, traveling whenever necessary, and interacting with colleagues from every part of the world. The report, *Mobility 2001 – World Mobility at the End of the Twentieth Century and Sustainability*, prepared at MIT (http://esd.mit.edu/tpp/symposium.htm), suggests that mobility has a direct link with social and economic progress. It may contribute significantly to improved life styles, enhanced social interaction, and reduced poverty and social inequalities. Further study is needed to determine whether it is a prerequisite for mitigating the difficulties of poverty in the developing countries. In theory, the lack of mobility limits people's ability to travel, which limits their economic opportunities. The critical questions yet to be answered are: Is mobility a prerequisite to social and economic progress? Is it a cause or an effect of social and economic prosperity? Perhaps it is both.

Studies of nineteenth-century and early twentieth-century life in the developed countries indicate that workers' lack of mobility contributed to their inability to improve their work environment, wages, and life style. The story of the Pullman Company workers is well known in the annals of American management styles and practices. Workers lived within the local community in houses owned by the company. They bought food and commodities at the company store. While Pullman believed that he was providing a quality life style, the system restricted the options employees had regarding work, living, and movement. From a SBD perspective, the objective would be to expand mobility in developing countries while minimizing its impacts.

People also want to travel where they want when they want. Travel for pleasure has increased dramatically since 1975. Air travel to vacation spots and automobile trips to shopping malls have become part of the culture in developed countries; affluence has permitted the luxury of traveling when the individual desires rather than when the transportation system allows.

Population density in the major metropolitan areas around the world is a growing concern. Increasing densities provide job opportunities and achieve economies of scale for creating factories and distributing goods and services. High population densities also allow more economically effective mass transportation systems, the centralized distribution of human necessities (food, water, power, and telecommunications), and safeguard the quality of pristine natural areas. The major concerns, however, are the ones that have plagued humankind for centuries. Larger densities often result in:

- Greater potential for transmitting infectious diseases, especially those spread socially such as HIV and respiratory diseases
- Deterioration of physical health and early mortality due to poor air and water quality
- Poverty enclaves on land masses that are inadequate to support minimal quality of life – i.e. lacking clean water, fresh air, waste disposal, and basic amenities

- Conflict and crime, resulting in deaths, injuries, and ongoing fear and intimidation
- Strained infrastructure and services in the urban and suburban environments; fragile ecological areas may suffer severe effects due to resource depletion and environmental degradation
- Inadequate education and learning of life skills, resulting in ignorance, lack of opportunity, and minimal productivity.

The stress that high population density puts on the environment depends on the quality of the land and its natural resources, as well as the educational level of the residents. The effects appear to be the greatest in fragile lands (those in "arid zones, on slopes and poor soils, or in forest ecosystems"[8]) and in those with undereducated people. Improving such human conditions and the related support mechanisms is critical for enhancing the prospects for the future. Governments, NGOs, citizens, and corporations have to cooperate to create structures that can solve problems in a systematic manner.[9]

Technological changes are primarily a function of social and economic forces. Those forces drive changes in needs, wants, and mandates. In simple terms, people expect better, less expensive, cleaner, safer, more reliable, and higher-quality products having fewer defects, burdens, and negative impacts. People demand and expect superior products. Technological changes and innovations have prompted many of the most profound changes in life styles. The following describes a few of the most important technological and product changes of the twentieth century and how they effected life style changes in industrialized countries:

- *Mobility*   The Ford Model T, introduced in 1908, was originally priced at $850. By 1916, prices were reduced to about $350 and, ultimately, to approximately $300 in 1927 when the Model T was withdrawn from production.[10] A 1933 Presidential Commission surveying contemporary changes in American life stated: "It is probable that no invention of such far reaching importance was ever diffused with such rapidity or so quickly exerted influences that ramified through the national culture, transforming even habits and language."[11] The Model T and its competitors opened the roads of the world to the common person by providing inexpensive vehicles.
- *Flexibility*   Dupont's invention in 1929 of CFCs, trademarked as Freon, radically changed households by providing a safe and effective means to produce refrigerators for every home. The refrigerator allowed people to purchase perishables in greater quantities and, therefore, less frequently. This reduced costs for food providers and purchasers. CFCs and related

inventions basically provided the means to eliminate some of the constraints of daily life.

- *Security*   The development of penicillin in 1929 by Scottish biologist Alexander Fleming and the polio vaccine by Drs. Salk and Sabin improved the health and well-being of millions of people around the world. Such contributions, along with the technological development of the global pharmaceutical industry, have created a more secure and less stressful life.
- *Productivity*   The PC, introduced during the late 1970s and early 1980s, provided individual workers, professionals, and entrepreneurs with the power to control their own work environment. They became independent of "the system," achieving high-quality, self-paced results without the maze of typists, data handlers, and other support specialists who were previously needed.
- *Agility*   The exponential expansion of the Internet during the mid-1990s created a low-cost means to rapidly communicate with others on a global basis and to obtain a plethora of information about corporations, their technologies, products, and processes. The Internet allows people to instantaneously collaborate with others around the globe.

Such significant technological changes share several factors. They dramatically increase the benefits that people enjoy, while reducing the costs and burdens. Most importantly, the improvements are widespread across the business environment and not limited to just products or processes.

Making progress of this magnitude requires creating solutions that provide improved capabilities and outcomes. Falling back on old solutions that are beneficial from only one perspective, such as being "environmentally friendly" is not acceptable. Nor are "negative" choices forced upon people by government mandates, or by fears of future problems. "Green products," for example, do not fulfill customer expectations if they require extreme sacrifices in other "needs and wants" categories. For example, the electric vehicles of the mid-1990s failed to capture a segment of the automobile market because they were more than 50 percent higher in price than the comparable vehicle and were less capable in many essential factors such as speed, range, and size. On the other hand, hybrids such as the Toyota Prius and the Ford Escape promise to meet customer expectations for quality, comfort, and performance while providing excellent fuel efficiency and super-ultra-low emissions. In this way, great technological solutions are not compromises, but rather holistic and sustainable. SBD thinking allows corporations to improve their standing in the social dimension by providing these kinds of solutions.

Sustainable products and process improvements must provide a wide range of life style-changing benefits, including increased product life through reliability and quality initiatives, decreased material usage and power consumption through size reduction and enhanced performance, and improved environmental footprints. Wal-Mart is a global provider of goods and services at "affordable" prices. Its low-price strategy has helped low-income families enjoy the benefits of mass production and mass merchandizing. Wal-Mart's innovations in procurement, distribution, and retailing demonstrate how multifaceted, yet evolutionary, changes can produce incredible outcomes.

Technological changes are fueling humanity's ability to sustain the quality of life and protect the natural environment. While the story line is far from perfect, technology has generally facilitated more production, more productivity, and more sophisticated products at lower costs with fewer defects and burdens. Technological innovations have also produced better processes that result in less waste per unit of production. Most global corporations report decreases in pollution and wastes year after year. While the increased reliance on outside suppliers makes an assessment of pollution reduction across the total enterprise(s) difficult, examining selected, state-of-the-art processes reveals improvements. For example, the average desktop computer today weighs 15 lb (6.8 kg), while the processors of the 1980s weighed more than 30 lb (13.6 kg). The trend continues, as plasma screens and LCDs replace standard computer monitors.

Nonetheless, the debate about the positive and negative effects of technology will proceed for many more decades. Despite improvements in products and their social, economic, and environmental burdens, it is clear that technologies still produce undesirable impacts on the quality of life and the natural environment. The challenge is to continue to strive for perfection. For instance, Wal-Mart has many detractors who are concerned about the company's impact on workers and local communities.

Heterogeneity in life style and demand adds to the proliferation of products and processes and reduces the potential for standardization and high volumes. People want solutions to be tailored to their own specifications. Unlike the early era of mass production in which "one product solved everyone's problem" (e.g. the Model T), today's expanding segments of society and markets translate into more variety and inducements to buy additional goods based on unique features and functionality. It is often difficult to determine whether demand induces the production of many different versions of similar products or if designers create the demand by offering such choices. The result of such product differentiation is certainly greater conspicuous consumption and more difficulty in establishing broad secondary markets.

Demand-side solutions are often better suited to customers' needs than the supply-side solutions that assume that customers are basically alike. Innovations that are tailored to specific needs may avoid the unnecessary "bells and whistles," that use more materials and generate greater waste. In this way, targeted demand translates into more eco-effective designs and better use of resources. Taken one step further, mass customization can produce positive outcomes if the efficiencies gained outweigh the additional costs (social, economic, and environmental) of highly differentiated products. Mass customization, at its best, can mean specifically designing and producing to meet the exact requirements of many customers, while minimizing material and energy consumption and waste and pollution generation.

The demand phenomenon is very complex and is more than a function of utility, functionality, and applicability. The overarching question is that of long-term value. Eco-effective solutions are those that create lasting value and can serve multiple customers over the product life cycle. A high-quality product that has a minimal life and little utility is suspect. For example, "high-fashion" clothing that the owner wears once and is discarded because it is "no longer new" creates instantaneous waste even though the underlying factors are sound. The product could have a long life, but the owner's cultural or social values inhibit such utility.

Understanding stakeholder expectations

The "license to operate"

Corporations are creations of the state and society. They are expected to discharge their obligations to civil society, stakeholders, customers, employees, and shareholders through compliance with laws and regulations, fulfillment of social and economic imperatives, contributions to the well-being of humankind and the natural world, achievements of their mission and strategies, and assurance of proper self-governance. The term "license to operate" refers to the legal standing of corporations as regulated by government in their home country and wherever their operations are located.[12] In most cases, duly organized corporations have to be registered or sanctioned by each of the countries, states, and/or provinces in which they do business in order to be recognized as legal entities. Moreover, corporations and their business units may be required to obtain permits, licenses, and other legal instruments that regulate, control, or monitor operations and sales. This is often the case where there are emissions, effluents, and/or waste streams that impact stakeholders and other constituencies outside of the domain of the corporation.

While trade agreements, treaties, funds clearing processes, and corporate law exist to legitimize business activities corporations, through their boards of directors and corporate officers, have fiduciary duties to protect the assets and well-being of the corporation, to deal fairly with customers, stakeholders, and employees, and to act carefully to ensure that people and the natural environment are not damaged, disrupted, or destroyed. While the particulars vary depending on the laws of the nation states, legal jurisdictions, or corporate structures, the three most significant fiduciary duties for purposes of SBD include:

- *The perpetuation and sustainable success of the corporate entity*   Corporate leadership has an obligation to shareholders, employees, and other related parties to take all reasonable actions to protect the assets, resources, and positions of the corporation and to satisfy the external and internal expectations of society and shareholders.
- *Total satisfaction and value creation*   Executive management has the overarching responsibility to satisfy customers, stakeholders, employees, and shareholders and to create value by maximizing benefits and minimizing negative impacts.
- *Risk mitigation through preemptive strategies and precautionary principles*   Corporations are expected to create positive outcomes for society and to protect people and the natural environment from negative impacts and their consequences.

Governance is the term used to convey the responsibilities of management and the board of directors to ensure that the assets, positions, and people are protected and sustained. It involves fiduciary responsibilities to mitigate challenges to both the well-being of the corporation and to society. The implicit responsibilities include all stakeholders of the corporation and the broader enterprise.

Stakeholders are an essential and often crucial part of a corporation's future. Understanding their views, agendas, and commentaries is critical for managing expectations and leading positive change. While stakeholders are often confrontational, as with Greenpeace, or controlling, as with regulatory agencies, they may also stimulate critical thinking about what the sustainable solutions should involve and how to achieve such ends. Addressing stakeholder issues protects corporate positions, reputations, and invest-ments. It also provides opportunities to outperform the competition. In today's business environment in which powerful differentiated positions and unique competitive advantages can overnight become standard offerings, the ultimate competitive advantage may be a superior business model that includes all constituents and provides total satisfaction.

Stakeholders can crystallize what total satisfaction means, and help man-agement identify the total solution. Using LCA and other management techniques, corporations can acquire and use information from stakeholders to overcome barriers to new products or concerns about existing products and processes, thereby turning adversarial relationships into mutually sup-portive ones. While there are few "magic bullets," and usually no single action can instantly transform entrenched issues or negative relationships, including stakeholders' expectations in the solution matrix can lead to more profound and enduring outcomes.

It is typically impossible to establish exactly why a product or service failed in the business environment, especially if there was initial success. However, one of the most important contributing factors may be the lack of attention to stakeholder concerns and issues over time. This is particularly the case when the impacts of the products and processes were minuscule during the early years of an innovative technology, becoming a serious concern only after millions of products have been sold and used. The PC fits the story almost perfectly. For instance, during the early 1980s few people thought about EoL disposal problems. However, as new technology replaced older versions, the number of units that had to be disposed of grew dramatically. As the numbers increased, the feasibility of "disposal" solutions declined. Moreover, it became widely known that discarded PCs had to be considered hazardous waste, thereby increasing the costs of discarding them. Clearly, the solution was for the producer to consider EoL scenarios during the NPD process.

Working with customers and stakeholders upfront may allow corporations to avoid problems in the first place, or invent more effective solutions than those that would be mandated. Typically, public and stakeholder pressures force government officials to impose mandates. Because mandates tend to encourage a standardized solution, they contribute to commoditization and make it difficult for corporations to differentiate their products and gain a competitive advantage. Mandated solutions also may not fit everyone, and waste streams may, in fact, increase because of the lack of customization. By understanding and responding to stakeholders, corporations may preempt government mandates and avoid these problems.

The story of solid waste management at Proctor & Gamble (P&G) illustrates an example of this kind of proactive corporate thinking. Recognizing the costly effect of negative publicity and stakeholder concerns, P&G began to study the environmental impacts of all of its products in 1985. The importance of solid waste management crystallized in 1987 when national attention was drawn via television to the garbage barge from Islip, NY that had nowhere to go. The situation was characterized by George Greene, P&G Director of Research and Development, Paper Division, who stated:[13]

Here was this barge floating up and down the East Coast with no place to go, no one wanting it. It got us thinking about what we at P&G needed to do about the solid waste we generate, including products and packages we manufacture.

P&G realized the vulnerabilities of its products and packaging and took dramatic action to turn threats into opportunities. Driven by market forces (consumer behavior, stakeholders, and competitors, etc.), P&G formulated and implemented extensive product and process innovations to make its competitive position more environmentally sound. P&G cited its first step with regard to solid waste management as the introduction of the super-absorbent diaper in 1986. This innovative product required only half of the material required in its predecessors. From its experience in Germany, P&G management knew that there was public concern about packaging wastes and that plastic packaging and products could turn into economic penalties so severe that market potential would be negatively affected. Corporate leadership established a task force of middle management to formulate a policy addressing both the real and perceived dangers. The resulting policy statements led to the development of P&G's Environmental Quality Program in September 1988. See box 5.2 (p. 309) about additional information on P&G's programs.

The "License to operate" is grounded in law through the corporate charter, the corporation's shares, and the associated regulatory processes. It is also granted through permits, licenses, and other instruments that allow corporations to function and carry out their activities. Implicit in such requirements and sanctions is the responsibility to exercise due caution and care and perform in a responsible manner that protects humankind and the natural environment. While laws and regulations articulate the "must do" responsibilities, there are many other categories ("should do") that are not explicit and require insight and judgment on the part of management.

SBD legitimizes the "right to operate" by mitigating social, economic, and environmental impacts. The logic of the precautionary principle and preemptive strategies focuses on risk mitigation, which involves understanding problems and potential difficulties, discovering hidden defects and burdens, and taking preemptive actions to resolve them before being forced to do so. Risk mitigation leads to improvements that create rewarding and enduring outcomes.

Integrating stakeholder management into corporate considerations

Global corporations often cite improving corporate reputation and reducing risk as the most important reasons for adopting SBD.[14] While these and other reasons may seem defensive, they are really positive moves to enhance the strategic strengths and market positions of the corporation. Global corporations, in particular, have to turn vulnerabilities into opportunities since they are often in the limelight. They have expansive and growing numbers of stakeholder groups that track operations, processes, products, corporate behavior, and reporting. Moreover, such scrutiny now includes the practices of suppliers and others. Stakeholder groups not only include the neighboring communities, but also NGOs, potential investors, the investment communities in general, and various governments around the world. The scope of the activities of such groups has widened as well. They have access to information and data that profiles a corporation's social, economic, and environmental performance. For example, the US Environmental Protection Agency (EPA) has web sites that provide detailed information about corporate environmental performance including violations, litigation, and fines.

Customers and shareholders are increasingly using disclosures to make informed ethical and social decisions about their relationships with corporate partners and providers. There is a growing realization that social, economic, and environmental performance supports the corporation's financial performance as well. While more study is needed to confirm this link, there is evidence that highly rated corporations using such measures as the DJSI also have good financial performance.[15]

The trend toward more disclosures and the proliferation of data and information about global corporations provides both opportunities and threats. The opportunities include the ability to shape positive perceptions about the corporation through outstanding performance, to differentiate not just the products but the entire corporation, and to reduce the risks of doing business. These accomplishments can lead to extraordinary value creation across the enterprise and sustainable competitive advantage.

Opportunities today lie in a corporation's ability to differentiate itself as fulfilling a balanced and inclusive social agenda and providing a value-based economic framework with environmentally conscious products, processes, and practices. Customers and stakeholders, whether they are consumers, business-to-business (B2B) buyers, or NGOs, expect that corporations will provide superior outcomes at an affordable price with minimal impacts. They expect corporations to do this without sacrificing legal, ethical, and moral imperatives. These expectations are the very "mandate" of sustainable development. Meeting that mandate offers global corporations exciting opportunities to sustain success and become more productive, effective, creative, and competitive.

Failure to broaden management thinking and embrace an integrated perspective about the roles and responsibilities of the global corporation may create threats to long-term survival. Laggards may find that their options decline over time, as well as their strategic positions, reputations, and financial rewards. While it is difficult to prove that such outcomes may occur, the risks associated with a lack of attention to social, economic, and environmental considerations may result in vulnerabilities, such as increased litigation, the imposition of new regulations and directives, restricted market potential, limited community support, damaged reputations, higher costs, lost shareholder value, and constraints on raising capital. Some would argue that these kinds of threat scenarios involve speculation. Nevertheless, there is real evidence that unless corporations improve at rates greater than the change in expectations, the world of the global corporation will become more restrictive and less rewarding. For example, the European Union's Directive Known as Waste Electrical and Electronic Equipment (WEEE) Directive mandates a reverse logistics program that is expected to have far-reaching impact. As we have seen, it required producers to create a product take-back system by August 13, 2005. A related directive restricts the use of heavy metals and hazardous substances and imposes quotas on product recycling rates for various industries.

The strategic choice facing global corporations today is whether to enjoy dramatic improvements though SBD initiatives or worry about the implications of change over the next several decades (box 5.1). The logic of the precautionary principle may resolve the question. Strategies and actions that lead to positive and enduring improvements enhance strategic position and reputation, reduce waste generation, promote efficiency, and advance relationships. Conversely, uncertainties and risks have hidden costs and effects that may not become apparent until it is too late.

Box 5.1 Coca-Cola Company: the convergence of customer and stakeholder considerations

Coca-Cola is the most widely recognized brand of cola soft drink in the world. The Coca-Cola Company is a global corporation with operations in over 200 countries; 72 percent of its revenues derive from outside its home country, the United States. Coca-Cola manages its far-flung business operations and bottling relationships through a form of enterprise management, called "the system." "The system" links company-owned operations, joint ventures (JVs), independent bottlers, and other supplier relationships to achieve sustainable success. According to Douglas Daft, Chairman of the Board of Directors and CEO, sustainable success is "creating economic value while nurturing and protecting the people and natural resources that are essential for our future."[1]

Coca-Cola has formulated four principles of citizenship and published a *Citizenship Report, Living Our Value* (2000). The four principles outlined in the report are articulated as follows:[2]

- *Refresh the Marketplace*   We will adhere to the highest ethical standards, knowing the quality of our products, the integrity of our brands, and the dedication of our people in order to build trust and strengthen relationships. We will serve people who enjoy our brands through innovation, superb customer service, and respect for the unique customs and culture in the communities where we do business.
- *Enrich the Workplace*   We will treat each other with dignity, fairness, and respect. We will foster an inclusive environment that encourages all employees to develop and perform to their fullest potential, consistent with the commitment to human rights in our workplace. The Coca-Cola workplace will be a place where everyone's ideas and contributions are valued, and where responsibility and accountability are encouraged and rewarded.
- *Preserve the Environment*   We will conduct our business in ways that protect and preserve the environment. We will integrate principles of environmental stewardship and sustainable development into our business decisions and processes.
- *Strengthen the Community*   We will contribute our time, expertise, and resources to help develop sustainable communities in partnership with local leaders. We will seek to improve the quality of life through locally relevant initiatives wherever we do business.

Coca-Cola understands that the essence of sustainable success is trust. Customers have to have confidence in the quality, purity, and affordability of the products that they consume. Employees, suppliers, and related entities have to share in the value creation and receive their fair share of the rewards.

Coca-Cola also recognizes the importance of SBD and Product Stewardship, particularly in protecting water resources and ensuring that water effluents are managed responsibly. Preserving the natural environment is directly related to the sufficiency of its most important resource: water. According to its 2003 *Environmental Report*, the company uses 2.90 liters of water per liter of product. Moreover, the total system-wide consumption of water in 2003 was 297 billion liters.

Coca-Cola also attends to community relationships as it conducts its business around the world. The four principles articulate the corporation's responsibilities to customers, stakeholders, the environment, and the community. Together, they integrate the social, economic, and environmental considerations into all the company's operations. The company's sustainable success provides evidence to external parties that the company is worthy of its "right to operate."

The Coca-Cola "system" includes suppliers who have to deliver on the trust relationship. In Coca-Cola's *Supplier Guiding Principles*, the company links its business ethics to its suppliers. The first paragraph of the principles highlights the connections:[3]

> The reputation of Coca-Cola is built on trust. Those who do business with us around the world know that we are committed to managing our business with a consistent set of values that represent the highest standards of quality, integrity, excellence, compliance with the law, and respect for unique customers and cultures in communities where we operate. We seek to develop relationships with suppliers that share similar values and conduct business in an ethical manner.

The company expects its suppliers to become part of the "system" and perform as if they were directly owned or operated by Coca-Cola. Such thinking is precisely what enterprise management requires; suppliers are a connected part of the system even though they are separate legal entities.

Coca-Cola has an environmental management system called eKOsystem, which is a subset of its quality management system. eKOsystem focuses on sustainability and environmental excellence. It combines compliance, risk minimization, impact and cost reduction, and leadership using best practices and technologies. Five guiding principles form the basis of eKOsystem:[4]

- *A Commitment to Lead*   Conduct business in ways that protect, preserve, and enhance the environment. This principle establishes a framework for managing environmental performance worldwide.
- *Compliance and Beyond*   Integrate sound environmental practices into daily business operations. Operations management encourages and rewards innovations that produce meaningful results and practices that exceed laws, regulations, and company policies.
- *Minimizing Impact, Maximizing Opportunity*   Minimize the environmental impact of operations, equipment, products, and packages, taking into account the associated cost or profit for each benefit and minimize the discharge of waste materials into the environment by employing responsible pollution prevention and control practice.
- *Accountability*   Conduct audits of environmental and safety performance and practices, document findings, and take improvement actions.
- *Citizenship*   Cooperate with public, private, and governmental organizations in identifying solutions to environmental challenges.

Coca-Cola's programs reflect a company moving toward SBD. The focus on citizenship, stakeholder performance, and linking suppliers with the system are on the leading edge of enterprise thinking. With a history of superior business performance, Coca-Cola's senior management is now endeavoring to develop a relevant business model that provides a systematic way to achieve sustainable success. This includes ethical management, diversity of thought, appreciation for different cultures, listening and responding to stakeholders, concern for the quality of life, perpetuating best ideas and values, and managing environmental responsibilities.[5]

Coca-Cola and PepsiCo, Inc., its arch rival, are world famous for their "cola wars." While they continue to fight for market share and the minds of the younger generation, the battleground of the future may be their quest for best practices, reduced impacts, and total satisfaction. Coca-Cola is moving in the right direction when it talks about trust, responsiveness, and citizenship. It is clear that it understands that water is the most critical resource in its products and that clean, safe, and bountiful water supports the social, economic, and environmental underpinnings of the world. Coca-Cola's thinking fits the EMM and represents a balanced perspective with respect to social, economic, and environmental objectives. Its outstanding performance and sustainable success may bring an end to "the cola wars."

Notes:
1. The Coca-Cola Company, *Environmental Report*, 2003, Atlanta, GA, p. 1.
2. The Coca-Cola Company, *Citizenship Report*, 2002, Atlanta, GA, pp. 5–7.
3. http://www2.cocacola.com/ourcompany/supplier_principles.html.
4. The Coca-Cola Company, *eKOsystem*, Atlanta, GA, p. ii.
5. The Coca-Cola Company, *Citizenship Report*, 2002, Atlanta, GA, p. 5.

Sustainable marketing and corporate reporting

Building integrity in the marketplace

Building trust, improving brand recognition, and enhancing corporate reputation are at the heart of the transformation to sustainable success. Contemporary management often focuses on marketing as the key for developing demand for the corporation's offering. While conventional marketing may be essential for success in a competitive world, often the products and services do not fully meet customer expectations, and corporations attempt to convince customers that they do. Moreover, the relationships between producers/sellers and the customers are often strained because of the difficulties associated with previous purchases and transactions or the lack of full disclosures about products, processes, and services. Customers are reluctant to repeat mistakes. The traditional corporate response has been to increase marketing expenditures and overwhelm the marketplace with positive messages. Much of modern marketing can be described as "single-sided" marketing that focuses on clever campaigns to promote one side, the positive side, of products or services.

Single-sided marketing may be effective in the short term, but often masks reality. Poor products and services are usually liabilities rather than assets.

They typically lead to problems and dissatisfaction, which cost time and money to fix and require additional marketing expenditures to neutralize, which can become a vicious circle. While it is important to recognize that every product or service has positive and negative effects and impacts, it is also important to realize that problems do not result solely from poor design and development, production, and related internal functions. In fact, many concerns arise from the failure of marketing and sales to clearly identify the most suitable product applications and focus attention on the most suitable customers. For example, small all-terrain vehicles (ATVs) are intended for adults who have the knowledge and experience to drive such devices, yet there are numerous stories of youngsters being injured or worse in ATV accidents. Likewise, household chemical products are often overused or misapplied, creating dangerous conditions for infants, the elderly, or pets.

Building integrity requires a balanced message using straight talk. It means conveying the full story to customers and stakeholders so that they can make appropriate decisions. Customers and stakeholders must be apprised of the negative effects, impacts, and consequences of products, processes, and services as well as their benefits and advantages over the competition. Customers must be encouraged to buy environmentally conscious products and use them safely and effectively. Moreover, they should be given information on how to minimize wastes, energy consumption, and premature failures. Marketing messages have to be simple and effective ways to communicate with customers, yet the information presented has to be factual, balanced, and direct.

Conventional marketing involves building awareness, gaining acceptance, encouraging purchase and use, and sustaining customer preferences. Using a derivative of the solution matrix that was discussed in chapter 3, the attributes and characteristics of a product can be divided into four categories of qualities, which are used to ensure that marketing messages are comprehensive. The approach is to consider elements from each category to provide balance and openness. The objectives of incorporating a more comprehensive view include the traditional approach of promoting the positives, and ensuring that the negatives are conveyed in order to reduce potential problems and liabilities. This is a sensible method for achieving balance and fairness. Table 5.2 provides a simple perspective on these categories.[16]

Category I contains the elements of conventional marketing which focus on the short-term qualities and attributes that excite customers and elicit interest. The elements include the features, functions, and benefits of the products and services that resonate positively with customers. They address

Table 5.2. Categories of effects (generic view)

		Short-term effects (immediate)		Long-term effects (enduring)
Positive attributes (improve/ increase)	I	Features; functionality; benefits; quality; ease of use; affordability; utility; desirability; status; satisfaction; advantages; strengths; economics; awareness; acceptance; use; competitive advantage; bottom line	II	Value; quality; reliability; longevity; responsiveness; stewardship; brand recognition and loyalty; trust; integrity; ethics; transparency; corporate social responsibility; environmental protection; corporate reputation
Negative impacts (reduce/ eliminate)	III	Defects; burdens; safety concerns; spills; accidents; taxes; insurance; waste streams; energy consumption, premature failure; hidden costs	IV	Liabilities; life cycle costs and considerations; EoL considerations; externalities; depletion; degradation; disruption; destruction

the desirability, level of satisfaction, advantages, and applications. The marketing messages usually attempt to create awareness, encourage trial, promote acceptance, and sustain use. When claims are valid and substantiated, such marketing approaches fit generally accepted practices and regulatory mandates. However, if marketers are not always careful, competitors can leverage off from the goodwill that is developed about the products. They can try to imitate the products and messages. Moreover, occasionally marketers overstate the positive and mislead customers into thinking that the products are better or have broader applications.

Category II includes the long-term effects of the product and process elements that are more difficult to imitate. They include intangible elements that are more difficult to emulate because they are dependent on the broader management system and corporate principles and practices. They include the long-term benefits of the products and enduring effects that are critical for sustaining success. The most powerful of these elements are value, quality, reliability, longevity, and responsiveness. The goals are to instill trust and build brand recognition and loyalty. These enhance business and corporate positions for the long term.

Category II also focuses on customer and stakeholder relationships. The approach is to build broader and more enduring relationships based on ethical practices, social responsibility, transparency, and environmental protection. These elements expand the reach of the communications to the larger community and convey more thorough messages. The goals are to connote total satisfaction and build corporate reputation for sustainable success. For instance, astute corporations like P&G recognized the weaknesses in developing marketing campaigns that concentrated on just the product attributes instead of building brand loyalty and enduring satisfaction for the long term. P&G's general approach is to build brand recognition and enhance corporate reputation that can be sustained over time.

Category III focuses on the negative side and includes the short-term negative effects associated with any unintended problems and difficulties. They include defects, burdens, safety concerns, accidents, and others. They also include costs associated with mitigating the negative side, such as insurance, taxes, and penalties. These elements reduce the value of the products and services and cause customers to pay more or enjoy less.

Category IV focuses on the long-term issues including liabilities, life cycle costs, and EoL considerations. It also includes the costs, effects, and impacts of externalities, depletion, degradation, disruption, and destruction. This category provides a more inclusive perspective of social, economic, and environmental concerns and impacts.

Historically, conventional marketing has focused on Categories I and II – the marketing philosophies and methods involved painting the most positive message possible while avoiding any aspect of the negative side. However, there arise legitimate concerns about the "fairness" of just telling one side of the story. Today, there are trends toward a broader, more inclusive perspective. Tylenol's television ads have begun suggesting that if customers are unwilling to read the label and become properly informed about the product, they should not take the medication. Its message is more in line with the concept of inclusiveness. This movement toward a more balanced marketing approaches can be traced to the evolution of "green marketing."

During the 1980s and 1990s leading corporations realized that there was a pressing need to reduce negative impacts and make dramatic improvements to the environmental aspects of their products and processes. They changed their marketing approaches to include the principles and practices of green marketing. Green marketing, also known as environmentally conscious marketing, developed in parallel with pollution prevention and Product Stewardship. It has many definitions, depending on the applications and theoretical framework used. It examines the positives attributes and negative impacts of products and services, and attempts to minimize the negatives or turn them into positives. Green marketing is a response to green consumers who demanded environmentally conscious products and solutions to environmental impacts. It addresses both the business and environmental responsibilities of modern business enterprises. Its strategic objectives to improve product quality, performance, and customer satisfaction are linked to the environmental goals of minimizing air emissions, water effluents, solid and hazardous waste, and other environmental burdens. Green marketing includes all of the elements of our four categories. However, it concentrates on environmental considerations, specifically on Categories II and IV.

Strategic marketing was another marketing paradigm that gained prominence during the 1990s. Global corporations realized the importance of providing more powerful messages that included the concepts of the value proposition, reliability, responsiveness, trust, and many other intangible market and customer considerations. Strategic marketing asks the "why" and "what" questions, looking for opportunities in the business environment and then charting the course for exploiting those opportunities. Strategic marketing focuses on the marketing of product portfolios, the drivers for new technologies and new products, the management of product life cycles, the evolution of product platforms, and the formulation and implementation of high-level marketing programs.

In today's business world of global enterprises, the scope of marketing has to be expanded to include customer, stakeholder, and market considerations. The "four Ps" (product, price, promotion, and place) of conventional marketing become embedded in the more critical perspectives of the total solution, total satisfaction, value creation, and connectedness to the whole system, innovativeness, and openness. Global corporations have to taken on a more enlightened marketing perspective. They must focus on the positive and negative sides of the value equation and incorporate all elements of the four categories. This requires addressing and communicating openly both positive and negative aspects. The theory suggests that it will then achieve more sustainable results.

Marketing for sustainable success is a burgeoning concept that will continue to unfold over the next decade. It combines conventional marketing with the philosophies, principles, and practices of strategic marketing and green marketing. Marketing for sustainable success is "dual-sided," providing messages that include both positives and the negatives. It focuses on satisfying the needs and expectations of people and on building long-term relationships based on trust between the parties, knowledge about the business environment, and confidence in the solutions. Philosophically, marketing for sustainable success takes the high ground in order to build trust, credibility, integrity, and respect. The marketing campaign takes an inclusive approach, providing comprehensive information and connections rather than just creating mechanisms to reach customers and sell products. Customers and stakeholders become part of the process rather than the end of the process.

Table 5.3. Objectives of marketing for sustainable success

	Bottom-line (specific) objectives	Overarching (enduring) objectives
Enterprise/ Corporate management	– Build openness, connectedness, trust, confidence and integrity – Link enterprise partners into the system and promote the system – Promote social responsiveness	– Enhance the reputation of the corporation – Build lasting-value networks with customers, stakeholders, and partners – Promote the "triple bottom line" – Enhance social responsibility
Strategic management	– Create lasting-value networks – Enhance ethical principles and practices and compliance outcomes – Create new solutions through innovation	– Build sustainable brand loyalty – Mitigate risks through information, knowledge, and practices – Enhance life cycle considerations
Product delivery management	– Promote value and trust – Build in credibility through accurate and comprehensive messages and information – Disclose the positives and the negatives – Reduce defects, burdens, and impacts	– Build enduring relationships – Promote Product Stewardship – Build awareness and acceptance – Link product success over time – Eliminate externalities

Marketing for sustainable success (dual-sided marketing) depends more on strategic thinking and leadership, rather than on extensive marketing campaigns, exciting promotions, or clever advertisements. Remember, the EMM is an embedded system that requires management at every level to enhance the reputation of the corporation and ensure that nothing impinges negatively on the drive toward sustainable success. Table 5.3 provides a sense of the integration of marketing for sustainable success within a corporate structure. The objectives depicted in table 5.3 are related to broad initiatives that require ongoing effort and commitment. In each case, there is no endpoint. Corporations can never say they have achieved the ultimate sense of openness, connectedness, trust, confidence, and integrity. Rather, perfection is an ever-present goal.

The objectives are subdivided into two categories: *bottom-line* objectives that focus on specific outcomes and *overarching* objectives that focus on the broader tangible and intangible relationships and long-term desires. The bottom-line objectives are so named because the intent is to obtain results for the overall system, its technologies, products and services, and processes and operations. The marketing efforts associated with bottom-line objectives focus on pragmatic approaches that provide social, economic, environmental, market, and financial rewards. They are shaped by the realities of the world and the needs and expectations of internal and external constituencies.

From an enterprise perspective, however, building trust, customer confidence and integrity are critical elements of marketing success. These are the overarching objectives, and they are more important than simply trying to get people to buy products or services. The former leads to sustainable outcomes, the latter may lead to a sale.

Creating lasting value networks and relationships can provide the support system for creating the required solutions. Ethical practices and outstanding compliance performance reinforce trust and integrity. Conventional marketing techniques focus on selling customers on product attributes, but effective marketing has to improve the value proposition by creating better solutions with fewer defects, burdens, and impacts. Marketing messages must be believable, and supported by defendable marketing data.

These kinds of marketing efforts involve broader, less definitive initiatives that are critical for the short-term and long-term success of the corporation. They may be embedded within marketing programs that have more specific outcomes. For example, Shell produced a series of ads in the *National Geographic Magazine* that promoted its SBD initiatives. The ads sought to improve corporate reputation, enhance brand recognition for its connectedness to social responsibility, and build trust.

The long-term relationships fostered by marketing for sustainable success allow corporations to capture and exploit the value of their marketing investment. Long-term marketing solutions involve supporting relationships, promoting stewardship, building awareness and acceptance, eliminating externalities, and linking product success over time. Though the effectiveness of these investments is difficult to measure, successful outcomes can be translated over the entire enterprise and from product to product. Intel has been successful in translating the value of the "Pentium" name and the slogan, "Intel inside" from one product generation to the next.

The triple bottom line and social responsibility, in particular, connect a corporation to many groups of customers and stakeholders, and over the longer term represent mechanisms to differentiate the corporation from its peers and competitors. Mitigating customer, stakeholder, and business risks is central to marketing for sustainable success.

Dual-sided marketing

Dual-sided marketing provides yet another opportunity to outperform competitors and to differentiate the whole corporation and not just certain products. While the marketing message is important, the process for developing the message is equally important, especially when corporations desire to openly portray all aspects of their products, processes, and operations. Strategically creating the desired solution and articulating its benefits in an open and honest manner can build shareholder confidence, customer knowledge, external trust, and product acceptance and purchase.

Dual-sided marketing integrates marketing communications with the development of overall corporate strategies for SBD. Creating dual-sided marketing communications starts with an examination of the prevailing situation and a determination of the desired outcomes. It includes an analysis of the business environment to find opportunities and challenges and assessment of the internal capabilities, strategies, and objectives. These analyses provide an understanding of reality and a forum for discussions and debates. Through them, the corporation can discover an overarching theme and message for itself. For example, BP plc (formerly British Petroleum) is in the process of becoming a sustainable energy company. Becoming an energy company is both the vision and the grand strategy: it is the dream. In reality, BP is still a petroleum company, but it is investing into renewable energy assets to make the transition to sustainable success. However, it must carefully craft powerful and accurate messages regarding its transformation so as not to be perceived as misleading stakeholders or as conveying false messages. A corporation's theme and messages must be true to its reality in order to build trust and acceptance of the solutions.

Discovering the right theme and articulating it with the right messages must parallel the research and development programs, NPD initiatives, and process improvement approaches. Most importantly, the theme and messages must be "dual-sided," disclosing both the positives and the negatives. Transparency also plays a critical role, as internal and external participants (management, employees, customers, and stakeholders) must be able to contribute based on factual information rather than perceptions or assumptions. It is critical for corporations to avoid being charged with "green wash," viewed as painting positive stories about expected outcomes that are not grounded in reality. Corporations are often accused of green wash when they overstate their vision or intentions through corporate communications to be something that they are not and where the foundation for the intended improvements has not been properly laid. Stakeholders are usually wary of stated intentions from corporations that do not have good track records of achieving positive results.

Figure 5.2 depicts a generalized process for creating overarching themes and messages. The process moves from the examination of opportunities to

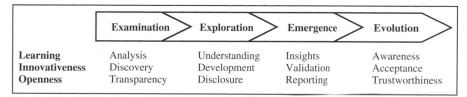

Figure 5.2   A simplified process for developing overarching themes and messages

the exploration and emergence of solutions to the ongoing evolution of leading change and making profound improvements. The objective is to link the vision and grand strategy of the corporation with the reality of its business. Though *dual-sided* marketing communication is a relatively new concept, it will undoubtedly evolve and become more standardized over time.

Examination leads to a better understanding of opportunities. Exploring those opportunities can reveal new ways of doing things, new solutions for creating value and successful outcomes. These new solutions could take the form of new technologies, new products, new processes, or new marketing approaches. Discovery leads to development, including the articulation of new marketing communications methods and techniques.

Ultimately, marketing communications depend on insights gleaned from analysis. These insights facilitate crafting messages that resonate with customers and stakeholders. The development of these messages, and ultimately of solutions that provide satisfaction, requires parallel networking with customers and stakeholders. Creating inclusive value networks means that customers and stakeholders become a part of the solution, understanding the advantages and accepting the benefits. For example, Sony and Philips developed market acceptance of CD-ROM technology concurrent with technological innovation programs. Concurrent development employs two-way communication, providing nonconfidential information about potential solutions to external parties and soliciting their feedback. Such information leads to a better understanding of the potential fit of a technology or product with the business environment.

Marketing communications methods must be validated using market and stakeholder testing techniques. It is critical that there is validation before any theme or message is released to the public. The best-sounding message might easily be misinterpreted. Petroleum companies, for example, are often accused of "green wash" when they advertise their environmentally friendly initiatives. It is imperative that corporations are able to substantiate every claim they make. Validation is complex and involves many mechanisms to prove to the outside world that claims are accurate. The following are five of the most effective ways to provide objective evidence that claims are credible:

- Follow the truth-in-advertising regulations and directives of the country or region (e.g. the European Union) having the most stringent mandates or requirements. The Internet and globalization make it easy for messages intended for one location to be applied or misinterpreted in another location.

- Obtain government certification for the claim being made, if possible. While this approach is usually employed for complex products, there are many opportunities to obtain endorsements for products and processes from government agencies. For example, the EPA's ENERGY STAR program provides standardized and specific ways for corporations to show the energy efficiency of their products and to substantiate claims of improvements.

- Secure private or independent certification for products and processes. ISO 9000 and ISO 14000 certify certain processes used by corporations, indicating that they meet the generally accepted practices of the certifying organization.

- Substantiate all claims through rigorous internal processes and techniques that provide concrete information, data, and analysis. LCA involves systematic and scientific analysis that should lead to valid and provable statements about the benefits of products and processes.

- Educate the business environment about the claims and their meaning. Many of the difficulties pertaining to inaccurate or misleading claims involve definitional problems where the corporation did not understand or follow legal definitions. This is a particular problem, since many terms have various definitions, depending on location. For example, the terms "recyclable," "biodegradable," "compostable," "toxic-free," "energy efficient," and "reduced waste" are often difficult to define and differ in meaning considerably from market to market. New York State challenged P&G on its claims of compostability; the relevant products were not compostable by New York's definition because there were not any composting facilities within the prescribed distance. If there is the potential for questions about the terms being used, it is important to define them and clarify the concerns.

The precautionary principle is useful when thinking about marketing communication themes and messages: it is better to be safe than sorry. It is too easy to have the intended approach backfire on the corporation. The counter-claims and charges of misleading or making false statements are damaging, often far beyond the marginal gains made on a product basis.

One of the most effective ways to offset many of the challenges associated with marketing communications is to provide an annual social, economic, and environmental report. Reporting instruments allow the corporation to preempt criticism by fully disclosing all pertinent information about the systems, products, and processes and the associated benefits, impacts, and challenges. Good disclosures include telling the whole story, defining terms, approaches, and methods of analysis, substantiating the claims, and providing all of the data and information about waste streams, defects, and burdens.

Annual reporting allows the corporation to stay ahead of negative public opinion, skepticism, and competitive pressures. Balanced, honest, and factual communications often disarm skeptics who are looking for targets to attack. Public interest or environmental groups often target global corporations, and hidden problems or the lack of disclosure leave them vulnerable. Preemption in reporting is often the best defense against criticism.

Sustainability reporting, using guidelines from such entities as the GRI, provides a standardized reporting framework that prescribes the reporting elements and disclosure protocols. Such frameworks improve the quality of the reporting documents, provide the rigor necessary to reduce the problem of deception by omission, and facilitate comparative analysis between corporations.

The search for excellence is an evolutionary process that builds on the legacies of the past, the efforts of the present, and the vision for the future. Great corporations systematically use their capabilities and resources to lay solid foundations that can respond to the ever-increasing mandates, requirements, and expectations of the total business environment. As corporations grow and expand, the challenge of informing and disclosing information to customers, stakeholders, and other constituents increases dramatically. Building awareness about the corporation, its technologies, products, processes, and operations is a primary mechanism in an ongoing process to gain acceptance and mitigate risks. Awareness and acceptance do not happen instantaneously; they require a multiplicity of communications methods to get the information out and to reinforce it with positive actions and outcomes.

Corporations depend on customer acceptance of their products and services and the goodwill that it creates for them with society, stakeholders, employees, shareholders, and especially the investment community. But acceptance is a nebulous quality. It is difficult to determine exactly when it occurs or when it is lost. To obtain it requires hard-fought and enduring marketing efforts and management leadership. To lose it may only take a single event. Shell's Brent Spar incident caused significant loss of customer acceptance in the European market.

The problems of suppliers, partners, and other related parties may have negative consequences on the acceptance of the corporation. Acceptance also depends on the prevailing conditions, trends, and standards. As standards change and become more stringent, acceptable outcomes become marginal and then unacceptable. For instance, Four-Sigma quality was viewed as more than acceptable during the 1980s, but now, in the early twenty-first century, is totally unacceptable as many corporations have achieved Six-Sigma quality. It is essential for management to continuously update performance and corporate goals.

Acceptance leads to trust, and trust is what turns marketing communications into successful market positions. Customers buy products and services from corporations that they trust. The implications go beyond the product to characterize the relationship between customers and the corporation over time. Customers want to know: Will this corporation be in business next year? Are there significant defects or burdens in its products?

Likewise, stakeholder relationships depend on the trustworthiness of the corporation. Corporations that have great track records are less likely targets for scrutiny. Government agencies responsible for regulatory compliance are more likely to spend their time and efforts "policing" those companies that have poor performance. Employees, too, gain confidence when they believe that the corporation is trustworthy.

Corporate reporting

Corporate reporting originated in the financial arena where laws, regulations, and directives, as well as the protocols of the responsible government agencies, mandated annual financial reports. In the United States, the Securities and Exchange Commission (SEC) requires detailed reports that follow explicit specifications. In Europe, several countries require corporations to prepare annual reports on their social and economic status, and disclose the impacts associated with their operations. While such reports may not be directly linked to environmental or sustainability reporting, they have been part of the trend toward more reporting, disclosure, and openness.

Environmental reporting was born out of the necessity for corporations to inform the public about their programs, impacts and, outcomes. Specific problems often became newspaper headlines gaining national media attention: the stories of the *Exxon Valdez* and Brent Spar are just two examples.

More importantly, corporations with proactive environmental strategies and good records wanted to improve their corporate reputations and build trust with customers and stakeholders. Companies such as DuPont, P&G and Ciba–Geigy (Ciba) have led the way in publishing comprehensive environmental reports. For example, Ciba's 1992 *Corporate Environmental Report* was twenty-eight pages long and included comments by corporate executives, a discussion of the company's progress toward sustainability, and sections on resources, wastes, products, and safety. In 1992, Ciba executives were on track toward SBD. CEO Alex Krauer and President Heini Lippuner introduced the environmental report with the following statement:[17]

We are convinced that only a strategy of sustainable development can guarantee sustainable success: in the interest of our customers, by providing them with environmentally superior products and services, in the interest of investors and our shareholders, by ensuring qualitative growth and securing shareholder value, in the interest of our employees by taking a long-term approach to business, in the interest of society as a whole, by satisfying present needs in a way that is compatible with future generations. We firmly believe that we will gain competitive advantage with our concept of eco-efficiency. We consider the environmental impact of all aspects of our operations . . . Working toward sustainable development is both a leadership challenge and management task . . . Now for the first time we are providing an overview of our environmental performance of the entire group.

Ciba's proactive management recognized the importance of leading change and establishing a track record for everyone to examine and evaluate. Openness led the way to sustainable improvements and success. Other major corporations also recognized the importance of environmental reporting after they had had significant compliance or public relations difficulties. For instance, Dow Chemical Corporation (DOW) and United Technologies Corporation (UTC) became advocates for environmental leadership and corporate reporting, turning their environmental problems into opportunities to excel. During the late 1980s, Frank Popoff, Dow's CEO, turned a laggard corporation into a leader by moving the corporation from denial to dialog using initiatives such as Responsible Care and Product Stewardship. In 1993 Dow's Environment, Health and Safety Policy included statements that were precursors to its current initiatives for SBD:[18]

At Dow, protecting the environment will become part of everything we do and every decision we make. Each employee has the responsibility in ensuring that our products and operations meet applicable government or Dow standards, whichever is more stringent.

Our goal is to eliminate all injuries, prevent adverse environmental and health impacts, reduce wastes and emissions and promote resource conservation at every stage of the life cycle of our products. *We will report our progress and be responsive to the public* (emphasis in the original).

While Dow was not unique in its advocacy of public reporting and broader corporate disclosures, it was a leader in establishing guidelines for more uniform environmental reporting. It was a key contributor to reporting guidelines developed by the Public Environmental Reporting Initiative (PERI) during 1992 and 1993.[19]

PERI guidelines were intended to be a voluntary, international reporting framework that would facilitate comparative analysis.[20] The PERI guidelines specified that reports must include the following sections:[21]

 (1) Organization Profile
 (2) Environmental Policy
 (3) Environmental Management
 (4) Environmental Releases
 (5) Resource Conservation
 (6) Environmental Risk Management
 (7) Environmental Compliance
 (8) Product Stewardship
 (9) Employee Recognition
(10) Stakeholder Involvement

The context was narrowly focused on environmental performance with links to the operating systems. PERI was relatively simple, yet it formed the basis for today's more sophisticated corporate reporting that has evolved to include social, economic, and environmental considerations.

In 1997, the Coalition for Environmentally Responsible Economies (CERES), with the participation of the United Nations and a number of NGOs, global corporations, consultancies, and universities, established the Global Reporting Initiative (GRI) to formulate and implement a "common framework for enterprise-level reporting on the linked aspects of sustainability: the environment, the economic, and the social."[22] The enterprise-level scope and the inclusiveness of the social, economic, and environmental considerations were a critical change in the thinking about what corporate reporting should include. GRI expanded environmental reporting to encompass the whole of the corporation, not just the operations, and to include external factors indirectly linked to the corporation. Traditionally, reports had included only information directly related to the operations, processes, and products of the corporation – i.e. the direct responsibilities, most of which were related to compliance and operations.

GRI moved environmental reporting from simple management reporting to a balanced accounting of the social, economic, and environmental performance of the enterprise and the corporation's contributions and progress

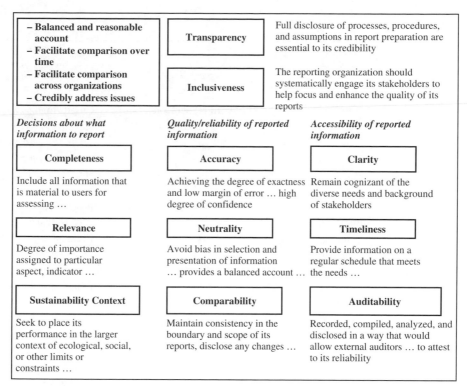

Figure 5.3   GRI reporting principles

toward sustainable development. Figure 5.3 depicts the eleven GRI reporting principles and provides a short description of each. For a more comprehensive understanding of the principles and recommended report content, see GRI's *Sustainability Reporting Guidelines* 2002.[23]

The overarching principles are transparency, inclusiveness, and auditability. Transparency is directly related to openness. Corporations are expected to fully disclosure their positive contributions and negative effects and impacts, and to openly provide customers and stakeholders with the information needed for making informed decisions and for building a trustful relationship with the corporation. In the complex business world of the twenty-first century, with broader responsibilities and more intense requirements, customers and stakeholders want to understand the capabilities and integrity of corporations. Their "need to know" involves much more than just buying products and services.

The principle of inclusiveness helps corporations meet that need. It involves engaging diverse groups of stakeholders in understanding the full

Table 5.4. Indicators in the GRI framework

Category	Aspect	Category	Aspect
Economic		*Social*	
Direct economic impacts	Customers	Labour	Employment
	Suppliers	Practices and decent work	Labour/management relations
	Employees		Health and safety
	Providers of capital		Training and education
	Public sector		Diversity and opportunity
Environmental	Materials	Human rights	Strategy and management
	Energy		Nondiscrimination
	Water		Freedom of association and collective bargaining
	Biodiversity		
	Emissions, effluents, and waste		Child labour
			Disciplinary practices
	Suppliers		Security practices
	Products and services		Indigenous rights
	Compliance	Society	Community
	Transport		Bribery and corruption
	Overall		Political contributions
			Competition and pricing
		Product responsibility	Consumer health and safety
			Products and services
			Advertising
			Respect for privacy

scope of operations, products, and services, as well as the social, economic, and environmental considerations. It also means reporting with performance indicators that cover the spectrum of social, economic, and environmental operations and their impacts across geography and time.

"Auditability" refers to the ease with which external organizations can scrutinize reported information in order to discern the credibility and accuracy of the report – the ability of customer and stakeholder groups to independently validate the report. Inclusiveness and auditability are complementary. Reporting has to be as comprehensive as possible and have information that can be verified by third parties. For example, the less sophisticated reporting guidelines used by individual companies were often selective in what they reported. Corporations reported on indicators that they wished to track, instead of on a broad set of criteria that stakeholders and customers might want to know. Moreover, only the corporation had direct access to the data and information.

GRI represents a major leap forward in reporting guidelines, because the performance indicators are very broad and require a more balanced approach for achieving outcomes. Table 5.4 lists the key indicators.[24]

GRI sustainability reporting is a bold step forward from the selected reporting of environmental initiatives to enterprise-level disclosures about internal and external impacts. While there are many reporting guidelines that include similar frameworks, GRI is indicative of the trend toward more comprehensive reporting. Leading edge corporations are embracing the notion of openness for all of its benefits. They understand that sustainable success is built on trust and confidence in the relationships, transactions, and reputations of the people involved. It may well become increasingly difficult for companies to avoid sustainability reporting.

Box 5.2   Procter & Gamble and the evolution from environmental management quality to SBD

With annual sales of $51.4 billion and profits exceeding $6.4 billion in fiscal year 2004,[1] Procter & Gamble (hereafter, P&G) is ranked as one of the best-performing and most socially responsive consumer goods manufacturers in the world. P&G is a global corporation with operations in eighty countries, selling approximately 300 brands of consumer products to nearly 5 billion customers in more than 160 countries.[2] Global revenues accounted for approximately 50 percent of the total. The company's operations are segmented into global business units (GBU) that include the following product groups:[3]

- *Global Fabric & Home Care*   Bleach and prewash additives; care for special fabrics; dish care; hard surface cleaners; household cleaners; laundry; and, chemicals.
- *Global Beauty Care*   Cosmetics; deodorants, fragrances; hair care; skin and beauty care.
- *Global Health Care*   Water filtration; oral care; pet health and nutrition; prescription drugs.
- *Global Food & Beverage*   Beverages; fat substitute; peanut butter; shortening & oils; snacks.
- *Global Baby, Feminine, & Family Care*   Baby bibs, diapers, and wipes; feminine protection pads and tampons; incontinence products; power towels, toilet tissue, and facial tissue.

P&G's product mix width and depth are considerable, offering customers a full range of products. Sustaining and managing the extensive product groups, brands, and diversified products require ongoing management commitment and investment to product innovation. Product planning is largely the responsibility of the company's strategic planners and brand managers. Longevity is a primary characteristic that typifies many of P&G's products. Some of P&G's best-known brands with the product launch dates are depicted in table 5B.1. The sustainability of the products is a testament to P&G's capabilities to rejuvenate products over time.

Table 5B.1. P&G: best-known brands, 1879–1963

Soaps		Detergents		Cleaners		Paper		Diapers		Shampoos		Toothpaste	
Ivory	1879	Snow	1930	Comet	1956	Charmin	1957	Pampers	1960	Head &	1961	Crest	1955
Camay	1926	Tide	1946	Mr. Clean	1958	Puffs	1960	Luvs	1976	Shoulders			
Zest	1952	Joy	1949	Top Job	1963								
Safeguard	1963	Cascade	1955										

The launch dates are great indications of the enduring life of many of P&G's products. A key to P&G's success has been top management's commitment to product innovation. In 1991, Ed Artzt, P&G's then CEO, stated that:[4]

One of P&G's historic strengths is its ability to develop truly innovative products to meet consumer needs. That commitment to product innovation has never been more critical to P&G than it is today. Product innovation, more than anything else, has been responsible for the company's growth and international success in recent years.

Indeed, innovation provides the critical ingredients to maintain and expand the sustainability of P&G's time-tested products. Artzt also articulated P&G's leadership principles and environmental position of the early 1990s.[5]

Almost everything we do flows from our long-term strategy [globalization and long-term development] for the company. These two principles and others all relate to our total quality effort. One founding principle for the company is that of competitive advantage, which underlies everything we do. And total quality is a means to sustain competitive advantage . . .

In any measurement of consumer satisfaction today, environmental compatibility ranks high. It is very much on people's minds. So to the extent that total quality is a system by which you can continuously improve consumer satisfaction, you can apply total quality principles very directly to environmental issues. The environmental pressures that we are under as an industry are another reason for embracing total quality. Environmental compatibility is a key element of quality in the public's mind.

P&G has effectively used its R&D capabilities to stay ahead of the competition and to exploit opportunities in the marketplace caused by changing social, economic, and environmental conditions and preferences. Moreover, with new consumer and stakeholder challenges continually developing, P&G has accelerated its process of developing new products to draw upon its global experience. Being a global company provides leverage in R&D advantages and offers early warning signals about emerging trends.

During the 1990s, P&G's environmental management system evolved from focusing on total quality environmental management (TQEM) to sustainable development. In the company's 2001 *Sustainability Report*, George Carpenter, Director of Corporate Sustainable Development, stated that:[6]

From the beginning, P&G's embrace of sustainable development has been based on our vision that we can grow the business, shareholder, and stakeholder value of P&G by bringing to the marketplace innovations and technologies that address the frustrations and aspirations of consumers at all levels of the economic pyramid.

P&G viewed environmental quality as a critical construct for maintaining its leadership positions in every product category. As P&G grew as an international company, globalization became a critical element in the company's overall strategy. The company's long-term objectives included being the market leader in each of P&G's product categories and having the international area contribute more than 50 percent of sales and profits.[7]

TQEM is a systematic approach to improve products, processes, and customer stakeholder satisfaction on a continuous basis. The principal premise of TQEM was that environmental problems must be identified and eliminated before they occur, the focus was on the causes of environmental problems and their prevention. The TQEM included product development, product stewardship, process management, and effective communications.[8] P&G believed that the environmental quality provided customers with value in an environmentally sound manner.[9] It was part of the never-ending story of continuous improvement. TQEM design philosophies and concepts were based on sound science and safety principles. From a strategic perspective, P&G uses the "OGSM" concept, which was defined as follows:[10]

- *Objectives*   What outcomes are needed to link environmental considerations to business needs?
- *Goals*   What are the specific outcomes required for tracking and meeting objectives?
- *Strategies*   How can goals be achieved by means of action plans?
- *Measures*   Can numerical assessments of strategy performance and continuous improvement be made?

TQEM action programs for product development consisted of state-of-the-art safety assessments and LCAs, which included holistic accounting of the effects and impacts that a product has on the environment. It focused on consumer research, product performance, and product initiatives, and these programs targeted future improvement. Communications was viewed as a critical means to inform external and internal stakeholders about results and future plans: P&G believed that rapid learning promoted outstanding results.

Continuous improvement became an essential part of P&G's TQM. TQM, along with LCA, allowed P&G to track the potential waste of a product from product concept through commercialization and disposal, using stages in the value chain to control waste. The goal was to avoid generating the waste in the first place and to ensure that releases did not damage the environment. Geoff Place, P&G Vice President of R&D, said that "environmental quality is P&G's top priority for the 1990s."[11] In the company's policy statement, P&G said that: "P&G is committed to providing products of superior quality and value that best fill the needs of the world's consumers." The key element of P&G's policy was to have sufficient information and knowledge about its positions on important issues so that it had responses to vital questions. Decisive resolution of issues in a systematic manner was paramount in mitigating the impact of problems or in gaining the advantage from opportunities.

P&G believed that environmental quality was critical to maintaining leadership positions in its product categories. Yet it recognized that it could not resolve social and environmental issues alone. In many cases, the problems required many more resources than any single corporation had, even one as large and financially strong as P&G. P&G supported solutions through cooperative efforts. Its philosophy was summarized succinctly in the following statement:[12]

> No individual company, institution, or group can effectively do much about the environment alone. Similarly, no single answer will resolve the environmental issues our world faces today. But, by working together, we can meet many challenges successfully.

During the 1990s, P&G developed support associations, joined industry groups, worked with suppliers, assisted in the financing of composting projects, and helped develop industry standards. Using a broad-based and loosely organized array of partnerships, P&G attempted to build an effective infrastructure supporting its recycling and composting strategies. On a global basis, P&G helped form the Global Environmental Management Initiative (GEMI), through which some twenty-three multinational corporations now support environmental excellence. GEMI applies TQM techniques as a means to promote pollution prevention and environmental performance.

In the mid-1990s, P&G established its first set of world-wide goals for improving environmental performance.[13] Pollution prevention, one of the mainstays of P&G's environmental strategy of the early 1990s, became fully embedded in TQEM. By 1995, P&G's priority had become the designing of new products that eliminated manufacturing waste and product and packaging problems early in the design process. Waste reduction was now a key element of the strategic planning process: the approach had evolved from simply analyzing and managing social, economic, and environmental issues and difficulties to a global management system based on policy, performance standards, annual audits, and a philosophy of continuous improvement. P&G began testing a new construct, called "Designing Manufacturing Waste Out" (DMWO). It linked R&D and engineering and manufacturing people together from the beginning of the development process.[14] DMWO marked the transition from concentrating on waste streams after they were created to creating new products with wastes designed out.

In 1996, as part of its continuous improvement strategy, P&G reviewed how the EMS could be restructured to integrate the global aspects of its business. It developed global standards for all of its manufacturing facilities, yet maintained flexibility to accommodate local conditions and necessities. P&G's pollution prevention and DMWO programs saved more than $500 million during 1995–2001, while reducing waste by one-third.[15]

By the turn of the twenty-first century, P&G had changed its overarching approach from TQEM to the concept of sustainability. George Carpenter defined sustainability "as a way to ensure better quality of life for everyone, now and generations to come."[16] Sustainability was an opportunity, not an issue. This profound statement indicated that P&G's environmental management had evolved from focusing on threats and problems to focusing on opportunities and solutions. Sustainable development became a central focus for P&G's global business units. The company created a Corporate Sustainable Development Organization. Its statement of purpose asserts:[17]

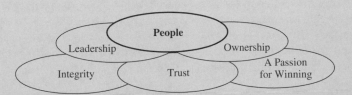

Figure 5B.1 P&G: key perspectives

We will provide products and services of superior quality and value that improve the lives of the world's consumers. As a result, consumers will reward us with leadership sales, profit, and value creation, allowing people, our shareholders, and the communities in which we live and work to prosper.

Sustainable development is about creating value for customers, employees, stakeholders, shareholders, and communities on a regional, national, and global basis. Embedded in P&G's sustainable development program are the TQEM and DMWO constructs. LCA is one of the tools that P&G uses to assess the impacts and improvements of its products and services. The company uses a team approach, often linking with external organizations to acquire new methods or validate its assessments. P&G has elected to use GRI to standardize its disclosures to the public and provide transparency to its corporate information. The 2003 *Sustainability Report* contains many examples of improvement programs.

P&G's business model has evolved from a simple construct focusing on compliance with laws and regulations and cleaning up wastes to TQEM and sustainable development based on environmental, social, and economic objectives. The integration of sustainable development with the global business strategy is the key for obtaining superior outcomes. Innovations create improvements that reduce environmental impacts and consequences. Leadership provides direction and commitment. Figure 5B.1 provides a sense of the key perspectives.

P&G believes that intellectual capital is its most important asset. *People* make the difference, and having the best people provides the means to achieve outstanding performance. *Leadership* is based on vision and commitment, creates opportunities, and eliminates barriers. *Ownership* engenders personal accountability. *Integrity* means being honest and straightforward – operating within the law and upholding values and principles. *Trust* suggests respect of everyone, and it fosters confidence. *Passion for winning* relates to the desire to make significant improvements.[18]

Notes:
1. P&G, *Sustainability Report*, 2002, p. 10.
2. *Ibid.*, p. 5.
3. *Facts About P&G 2001–2002 Worldwide*, p. 3.
4. P&G, *Annual Report*, 1991, p. 4.
5. Karen Bemowski, "Carrying on the P&G tradition," *Quality Progress*, May 1992, pp. 21, 25.
6. P&G, *Sustainability Report*, 2001, p. 4.

7. Brian Dumaine, "P&G rewrites the marketing rules," *Fortune*, November 6, 1989, p. 36. In 1989, P&G was the market share leader in twenty-two of the thirty-nine product categories, see *Annual Report*, 1991.
8. Comments by Michael Fisher, P&G Associate Director, Environments Control Department, March 24, 1993, Alexandra, VA.
9. *Ibid.*
10. *Ibid.*
11. Stephanie Overman, "Environmental interest heats up in oil industry," *HR Magazine*, March 1991, p. 40.
12. P&G, *In Partnership with the Environment*, c. 1991, p. 12.
13. P&G, *Environmental Progress Report*, 1995, p. 16.
14. *Ibid.*, p. 14.
15. P&G, *Sustainability Report*, 2001, p. 34.
16. *Ibid.*, p. 4.
17. *Ibid.*, p. 12.
18. *Ibid.*, p. 13.

Connecting to supporting entities

Overview

Sustainable success depends on relationships between customers, stakeholders, supply networks, and the logistical support systems that ensure that goods, energy, materials, wastes, and EoL residuals flow properly from suppliers and producers to users, recyclers, and disposal providers. Connectedness involves linking all of the entities with each other through trust relationships. This requires disclosure of information across the enterprise and the full participation of all of the players from cradle-to-grave in the process of LCA and improvements. Connecting with supply networks, waste management entities, and EoL logistics is particularly important for obtaining the necessary data and information to understand the full impacts of products, processes, and services. Entities must remain linked and furnish such information on an ongoing basis. Most importantly, each company must assess its impacts and provide such information and analyses to its users, customers, stakeholders, etc.

Networking with suppliers, distributors, partners, allies, customers, and stakeholders requires sharing information, knowledge, and experiences about products, materials, and waste streams. The intent is to facilitate cooperation and collaboration among parties who have common interests and requirements. Information networks can be simple, even informal structures that use the Internet or other electronic media to interact regularly. While some corporations, such as Toyota and Coca-Cola, are adept at developing mutually beneficial relationships with external entities, most corporations have limited experience with building such in-depth relationships and connectedness. Historically, most corporations have dealt with outsiders on a transactional basis, buying and selling materials, goods, services, and energy using formal and legal structures to complete the transaction. The primary effects were handled very properly; however, the long-term relational and informational aspects were not always adequately fulfilled. For instance, buyers usually lacked a full understanding of their suppliers' operations and standards. They focused on the immediate purchase requirements, including quality, delivery, price, and other related topics. The more complex questions were often not addressed. Issues such as the principles, practices, and experience of those who supplied the supplier were usually viewed as outside the scope of interest or responsibility. Moreover, details about the supplier's compliance record and environmental impacts were not always primary concerns.

But, in today's world, these concerns are important to customers and stakeholders – and, therefore, to corporations. Information and data are necessary for making decisions about suppliers and purchases, making connectedness a critical part of the economic equation. Producers need information and support services from all of their contributors (suppliers, distributors, etc.) so that full disclosures and best decisions can be made. Without connectedness there is a huge gap in the information flow, making the necessary analyses difficult. For instance, an automobile manufacturer requires information and analysis from its steel suppliers in order to determine the life cycle impacts of the materials going into the finished product. The automobile manufacturer could estimate the impacts of the steel producers, but the steel companies should actually have the data and information to produce accurate assessments of their impacts.

Connecting with supply networks

Building integrity into products and processes requires close relationships and communications with suppliers, distributors and associated entities. These relationships are becoming even more crucial as global corporations outsource more of the parts, components, assemblies, modules and even products. Sustainable procurement calls for minimizing adverse impacts across the **supply networks** through interactive discussions, actions, education, and information flow. Connecting with supply networks allows the producer of the end product to acquire a more complete understanding of the flow of materials and energy into the product and the implications and impacts of choices and decisions. Despite the sophistication of modern management, most global corporations have only limited information about the processes and activities of their supply networks: historically, the focus has been on quality, delivery, and costs.

Developing richer, more vibrant relationships and information flows with suppliers is essential for LCA. Cradle-to-grave thinking and action depends upon information from the entire enterprise. Table 5.5 lays out the key elements of linking supply networks with the corporation's SBD initiatives. While the process appears to be linear, it is in fact clearly nonlinear, requiring many iterations to reach the point where the process can sustain itself. Indeed, the process is similar to a large spiral where the stages are revisited at more sophisticated levels as time progresses. The rate at which the parties become connected depends upon the resources, capabilities, and willingness of the participants; building such networks requires considerable time and resources. The requirements for connectedness usually expand geometrically, as additional tiers of suppliers and distributors enter the system.

The system includes the trading partners as well as all of the stakeholders and constituents in the various tiers. While it seems impossible to keep track of all these parties, the system can function if it is properly linked and there is a common ground of understanding among the participants. Most importantly, there should be a shared philosophical belief in the value of such integration and a spirit of cooperation, collaboration, and commitment toward making dramatic improvements: participants throughout the enterprise have to behave as partners with common goals. While this goal may seem idealistic, it is supported by TQM achievements over the last several decades. Important and sustainable outcomes involve high-quality outputs across the supply chain and the various production processes. A global corporation simply cannot produce Six-Sigma products unless its suppliers are similarly capable of, and committed to, Six-Sigma quality.

The first step involves identifying and defining the world of the suppliers and distributors and the forces driving change for them, including the regulatory mandates that they must themselves satisfy. The goal is to develop a broad understanding of the business environment of the supply networks

Table 5.5. Selected elements for building connectedness with supply networks

Steps	Elements
Identifying and defining Identifying reality and determining the driving forces in the business environment	– Identifying the driving forces in the business environment – Identifying the regulatory mandates that pertain – Defining environment, health, and safety concerns in each process – Determining key stakeholders throughout the flow of goods and information and determining their objectives, needs, and expectations – Identifying key issues and concerns – Benchmarking important peers and competitors – Identifying trade associations and industry groups that can provide support and information – Obtaining related research from academic communities – Understanding the needs of customers related to supply networks – Determining the uncertainties and risks
Goal setting Defining the short-term and long-term goals, including the actions required for improving the processes	– Reviewing media reports and the literature to determine the most critical needs and expectations – Identifying the information requirements for LCT – Listing specific targets for analysis and improvements – Identifying the most relevant social, economic, and environmental objectives – Determining and prioritizing the opportunities for improvements – Identifying goals for improving compliance and eliminating the need for it – Defining objectives for reducing uncertainties and risks
Action planning Establishing the initiatives to improve outcomes, reduce impacts, and obtain success	– Establishing protocols and information sharing systems to link the participants – Linking supply networks to the enterprise – Creating short-term success outcomes to build momentum – Educating supply networks about sustainable development and their expectations – Changing attitudes about expectations – Building a spirit of cooperation, collaboration, and commitment across the enterprise – Preparing action plans and long-term initiatives
Sustaining Implementing initiatives and programs to achieve balanced solutions Educating people about future opportunities and building awareness, acceptance, and confidence in progress	– Changing mindsets about the value of sustainable development – Establishing new criteria for materials, parts, components, and goods including requirements for minimizing resources utilization, degradation, disruptions, and impacts and improving EoL considerations by facilitating recycling – Communicating the program to suppliers, distributors, customers, stakeholders, and other communities – Auditing progress over time and taking corrective actions – Evaluating ongoing results and making improvements – Reporting on the progress and ongoing challenges – Celebrating and rewarding outstanding achievements – Continuing the process

and to provide assistance in ensuring satisfactory solutions. Understanding the supply chain's key stakeholders and their needs and expectations is crucial to determining actions for sustainable success. This includes mapping out the critical issues and concerns of stakeholders, and the vulnerabilities they may present.

Exploring the systems, products, and processes of important peers and competitors and their supply networks can also enrich understanding. Benchmarking may furnish insights about alternative approaches for satisfying needs and expectations across the enterprise. Trade associations and industry groups related to suppliers and distributors may also provide data and information in a readily available, concise, and accurate form that reduces the need for extensive research; academic organizations may also provide assistance through existing or tailored research studies. While exploring all of these resources can be complicated and costly, it facilitates decision-making about the supply networks, allowing a corporation to improve effectiveness and reduce uncertainties and risks, in both the short and long term.

The overarching goal of connecting the supply network is to create a seamless whole where information flows across company boundaries to those who need it for decision-making. In a connected world, enterprise goals focus on achieving positive outcomes for everyone over time. The relationships of the enterprise support the common goals of all the participants and ensure that total satisfaction is achieved.

The second step involves identifying goals for analysis and improvement. This process starts by examining the needs, wants, and expectations of the participants and stakeholders and determining the information required. Goal setting should include social, economic, and environmental considerations as well the transactional requirements for the exchange of goods, monies, and information. Corporations should approach goal setting from multiple levels, and employ Balanced Scorecard thinking. Table 5.6 lists some suggested target areas for goals.

The suggested areas are very broad. The leadership of the enterprise has to decide exactly what goals make the most sense at any given point in time. The process of choosing goals for enhancing connectedness is selective rather than prescriptive. However, in the European Union, The European Community Program of Policy and Action pertaining to the environment and sustainable development has created structured programs and criteria for improvements in selected sectors and industries, such as energy and airframe manufacturers over both the short and long term. The programs are part of the EU's

Table 5.6. Suggested target areas for setting goals related to supply networks

Level	Suggested target areas for setting goals related to supply networks

Enterprise/Corporate
Improving the connectedness
  of the enterprise from the
  origins of the supply networks
  through production and
  support of EoL considerations
	– Establishing a connected materials flow and information system that
	  is inclusive
	– Establishing the overarching principles and philosophies to guide
	  the relationships
	– Determining the requirements across the enterprise for SBD
	– Convincing executives within the supply networks to embrace
	  sustainable development and its principles, processes, and practices
	– Linking supply networks with the enterprise

Strategic
Enhancing the capabilities of
  the supply networks and
  improving the value of
  products and processes
	– Linking EoL considerations and mandates with the entities of the
	  supply networks
	– Exploring technologies and product families that require significant
	  improvements or replacements
	– Establishing interconnected innovation programs to make requisite
	  changes
	– Improving information flow to support LCAs
	– Creating infrastructures and linking with related industries to
	  enhance product take-back capabilities
	– Creating a spirit of connectedness, trust, and commitment

Product delivery
Improving short-term and
  long-term outcomes and
  making the product delivery
  system more responsive to the
  needs of customers and
  stakeholders
	– Incorporating LCT to discover opportunities for improvements
	– Identifying short-term opportunities to reduce degradation,
	  depletion, disruption, and destruction
	– Identifying long-term opportunities to eliminate degradation,
	  depletion, disruption, and destruction
	– Ensuring compliance within the supply network
	– Educating supply network partners about sustainable development
	  and its explicit and implicit requirements
	– Improving performance on an ongoing basis

research agenda to promote sustainable development and structured improvements. The current program, the *6th Framework Program* (FP6), specifies goals to be accomplished between 2002 and 2006. The previous program, FP5, covered the years 1998–2002. The research agenda intends to achieve ongoing improvements through 2020. Vision 2020 provides a prescriptive view of the technologies, products, and processes of 2020 and outlines the necessary short-term R&D goals (four years ahead) by which it can achieve the desired long-term results. An example of a project is ARTE21, on aeronautical research and technology.[25] (See box 5.3.)

Goals for connectedness should be articulated for each level of the enterprise and flow from the top to the bottom and from the bottom up. At the

Box 5.3 *Aeronautical Research and Technology for Europe in the Twenty-First Century (ARTE21) and the goals for Framework Program 6 (FP6)*

European initiatives Vision 2020 and ARTE21 provide an overarching framework for aircraft manufacturers to use in making improvements in the aeronautical industry through 2020. Industry participants include airframe manufacturers, Airbus and Boeing, helicopter makers Boeing, Agusta Westland and Sikorsky Aircraft, and engine suppliers, General Electric, Pratt & Whitney, and Rolls Royce. The European Commissioner for Research, Philippe Busquin, selected aeronautics as one of the key industries for implementing the European Community Programme of Policy and Action's FP5 and FP6 goals for SBD.

ARTE21 is a bottom-up response by the European Aeronautics Industry to the top-down Vision 2020. The following is an overview of the background for aircraft-related research and technology development (R&TD) as it relates to FP6:[1]

> Acting on the recommendation of the Group of Personalities (GoP), the commission established the Advisory Council for Aeronautical Research in Europe (ACARE). The effort involving all stakeholders in the European Air Transport System is tasked to develop a Strategic Research Agenda (SRA) for the next twenty years (2000–2020), to ensure that the proper research road map is defined and, at regular intervals, critically reviewed (see figure 5B.2).

The framework identifies five areas of challenges to the industry and specifies targets for improvements. The targets are goals for the R&D agendas of the industry participants and the subsequent programs in the future. Validation and integration projects spell out the description, objectives, deliverables, justification, benefits, and partnerships associated with the twenty-three specific projects for FP6. The GoP challenges and the target areas with specific goals are depicted in table 5B.2, listing the GoP challenge as of March 2002:[2]

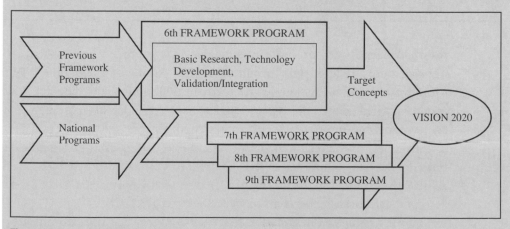

Figure 5B.2 The ARTE21 roadmap

Table 5B.2. GoP challenges and target areas, March 2002

GoP challenge	Target concept	Target concept goals
– Environment	– The Green Aircraft	Per passenger kilometre: 50% cut in CO_2 and 80% in NOX
		Noise nuisance = large city environment
		Reduce impact on global environment
– Safety	– The Safe Aircraft Operation	Five-fold reduction in accident rate
– Capacity and Delay	– On Time Aircraft Operation	99% of all flights <15 minutes delay in all weather
	– ATM of the Future	
	– Airport of the Future	
– Passenger Comfort	– The Passenger Friendly Aircraft Operation	Wait at gate <15 minutes for short haul
		Wait at gate <30 minutes for long haul
		Stress-free travel with home/work services
		Increase choices of flights/locations
– Affordability/ Industry Competitiveness	– The Competitive Aircraft	Steady and continuous fall in travel change
	– The Competitive Enterprise	Capture 50% of market

While understanding the required objectives and the vision for the future can benefit members of the industry, any corporation following such guidelines must also continue to meet, and even preempt, the expectations of its business environment.

Notes:
1. ARTE21 – The Aeronautical Research and Technology for Europe in the Twenty-First Century, March 2002 edition, Aircraft Related R&TD for Framework Program 6, *Towards the GoP 2020 Vision*, p. 3.
2. *Ibid.*, p. 4.

enterprise level, the primary goals are to build connections and relationships. This includes establishing common ground with partners and allies. Moreover, corporate executives need to think about the whole enterprise and how it creates value for both customers and stakeholders. At the strategic management level, management must aim to find innovative ways for improving the benefits and reducing the impacts of the supply networks. Working with suppliers and distributors facilitates making improvements. At the product delivery level, corporations must target short-term improvements and long-term performance gains.

The third step involves establishing action plans for achieving the goals. Again, the critical task is to link the participants in the supply networks in order to enhance communications and information flow. It is crucial that the action plans include short-term programs that lead to immediate gains. Such initiatives tend to build momentum for further progress. Educating participants in the supply networks is a daunting task that can take years to unfold and produce measurable results. It may start with building awareness about the principles, processes, and practices associated with SBD. Educational programs aim to induce acceptance of the initiatives and to promote cooperation and collaboration.

The fourth step involves implementing the action plans and sustaining the improvements. Implementation is not a simple, one-time event but rather an enormous undertaking, multifaceted and ongoing. Nonetheless, the most important element of all of it is changing the mindset of suppliers about the value and importance of sustainable development. Leaders in such organizations have to realize and understand how they contribute to the success of the enterprise, and that their perspectives and efforts are critical for achieving sustainable success. Like TQM, that expanded thinking throughout the business world during the 1980s and 1990s, supply networks have to embrace the principles and criteria associated with SBD and mesh them into their operating systems. Establishing enterprise-wide criteria for decision-making that include targets for sustainable success is critical for creating uniformity of philosophy and purpose across the supply networks. Requiring that all suppliers and distributors obtain ISO 14001 certification is a positive step toward that end. While ISO 14001 outlines specifications for auditing progress, evaluating results, and reporting outcomes, corporations may want to have a broader context by incorporating all of the ISO standards, including the requirements to perform LCA.

Two of the most critical elements for enduring success are communicating goals, actions, and initiatives, and celebrating and rewarding outstanding achievements. Communication is a vital piece of connectedness: all parties must work together under a common banner. The end-product producer has to lead the way through principles, policies, practices, and communications that reinforce goals and requirements. Leaders must articulate a message that will resonate across the enterprise. Given the relative newness of enterprise connectedness, there are many theories and approaches yet to be discovered and structured. Corporations and scholars have to study how individual companies contribute to the whole, how to determine the best mechanisms for linking individual entities in the supply networks, and how best to integrate the networks of relationships and activities into an eco-effective means for providing great solutions, total satisfaction, and sustainable results.

It is a daunting challenge, but it also represents the opportunity to obtain a more lasting competitive advantage. While it may be hard to determine exactly when sustainable success occurs, real world achievements toward a more sustainable position are usually ongoing. Technological innovation, product development, TQM, and the quest for customer satisfaction have resulted in improved product features, functions, and benefits, decreasing the materials used to produce products, and preventing pollution. It is important to celebrate significant accomplishments so that momentum is increased and people are encouraged to achieve more in the future, to continue the relentless pursuit of excellence.

Connecting with EoL considerations

One of the most far-reaching changes affecting business entities since the 1990s is the explicit and implicit requirement to manage EoL issues. This trend is probably most pronounced in the European Union, however, it is a phenomenon that is sweeping across the world. Large corporations, in particular, are affected because they are generally the producers of the end products.

Producers bear an implicit responsibility to ensure that there are solutions for the whole product cycle. Only by doing so can they hope to provide total satisfaction. The creator of a given product, who is directly responsible for the design, development, and commercialization of the product, has the most knowledge and the most freedom to make decisions about it. The decisions made during design, development, and commercialization have consequences across the product delivery system and during the purchase, use, and retirement of the product. The designer/producer is obligated to create the best solution possible, a total solution that maximizes benefits and minimizes impacts over the life cycle. While there are sophisticated upstream capabilities via supply networks with extensive support systems, the downstream considerations, including product retirement and disposal methods, generally lack such sophistication and depth. Managing the EoL considerations is an evolving business endeavor that is becoming a growing area of concern. At the same time, it presents new opportunities for creating value.

EoL management constructs tend to be fragmented. Historically, there were many businesses engaged in the processing of scrap metal, paper, and other commodities to be used as raw materials in manufacturing. The collection, processing, and remanufacturing of steel and aluminum are among the best established. Nucor, a recycler of scrap steel, is now the largest producer of steel products in the United States During the 1990s, BMW and other automobile companies invested in methods and practices for disassembling their products at retirement in order to recover valuable parts and materials and to recycle residuals. They formed strategic alliances with automobile dismantling companies to create a total solution. While such methods and practices have improved the opportunities to affect EoL solutions, the current methods often result in fragmented approaches that lack the sophistication of an operating system.

The formal approach for managing the logistical requirements for reusing, refurbishing, recycling, and processing retired products is often called "**reverse logistics**" or "reverse supply chain management." The Council of Logistics Management (CLM) defines the term as:[26]

The process of planning, implementing, and controlling the efficient, cost effective flow of raw materials, in-process inventory, finished goods, and related information from the point of consumption to the point of origin for the purpose of recapturing or creating value or proper disposal.

The critical part of the definition is the return flow of materials back toward distributors, producers, and suppliers, toward the points of origin. Recapturing and creating value and proper disposal are central to the concept of reverse logistics. Materials flow from the initial point of consumption to secondary points of consumption and finally travel back along a pathway to the original entities in the supply chain. Simply sending materials back to producers or demanding take-back programs may lead to problems if the process is open-ended and little value is created or captured. Reverse logistics involves the flow of materials back to the distribution, production, or supply stages where valuable outcomes can result from their return. Reverse logistics or reverse supply chain management may not be the appropriate term if the materials are simply collected and sent to landfills or incinerators. Product or materials recovery and the value creation associated with capturing residual use or recycling are essential criteria for establishing a successful system. The following are six key definitions of the product or materials recovery options:

- **Reuse**   This is generally the simplest and easiest means to create additional value through secondary use of the products without significant processing.
- **Repair**   Product repair involves fixing or replacing broken or nonfunctioning parts or components. The intent is to return the product to its original use or for reuse by another party.
- **Refurbishment**   Refurbishment involves restoring the product back to the original specifications. The intent is to provide additional useful life for

the primary or secondary users. Refurbished products often have reduced capabilities and limited additional service life.

- **Remanufacturing**   The purpose of remanufacturing is to upgrade the product and improve its quality and performance. Often, the remanufactured products have additional functions and features that were not available at the time of original manufacture. This may include technological upgrades.
- **Recycling**   The purpose of recycling is to salvage as much value as possible from retired products and the inherent materials. This includes reusing parts and components, recovering materials, and capturing some beneficial value.
- **Retirement**   Retirement is a broad term used to characterize the activities involving afterlife treatment of the residuals and/or disposal.

From an enterprise perspective, cost, quality, and availability of the EoL products/materials and the price and demand for such products/materials are essential considerations in establishing stable reverse logistics. An integrated system requires stability and consistency in the pricing, specifications, and quality of the materials. Stability offers suppliers and producers the confidence to invest in the product and process developments necessary to make use of refurbished products and recycled materials. To completely close the loop also requires market development for the sale and use of the resulting products and materials. Figure 5.4 depicts the EMS with integrated reverse logistics.

The EMS and its embedded subsystems facilitate the flow of products and materials throughout the entire product life cycle and incorporate all of the logistical processes needed to get products to customers and deal with EoL considerations. On the primary side of production and delivery, all residual materials (scrap) flow into a system or multiple systems for reprocessing, refurbishment, or recycling, depending on disposition and value of the items. For instance, defective products can be reworked for sale as refurbished products, and scrap from manufacturing can be recycled and used in the enterprise or other enterprises. The objective is to process residuals into more valuable materials and to expand the market potential for such materials. Being connected with the ultimate markets is essential for success.

Traditional solid waste management schemes focus on disposing of wastes. The goal is to eliminate the waste problem rather than finding opportunities to create value. It is a "push system." The flow of waste depends on having a downstream processor who is willing to accept the material. The successful collection of wastes subsequently needs various downstream processors to acquire and use the materials and make the output available to the next

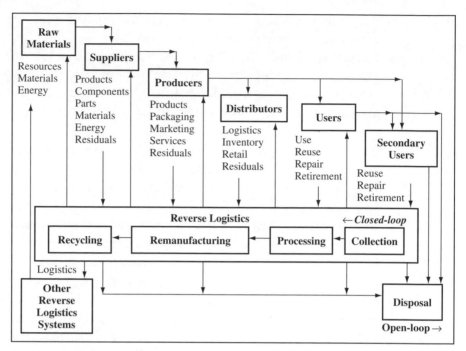

Figure 5.4   The EMS with integrated reverse logistics

processor. Success depends on all of the upstream and downstream businesses carrying out their functions. If the downstream processor is unable to deal with the waste stream, the flow becomes choked at that point, limiting the capacity of the system. The capacity of each operator is easy to calculate, but it may be irrelevant since the system is constrained by the choke point.

Reverse logistics is one of the most important concepts for managing waste problems. It offers many far-reaching opportunities for solving the social, political, economic, and management concerns related to solid waste and discarded products. Reverse logistics usually involves collecting discarded products, transporting the waste streams to processing facilities, remanufacturing those products that can be refurbished, and processing the residual materials into their elemental roots, thus paving the way for the recovered materials to reenter the value chain as raw materials.

Reverse logistics depends on the triad of society's interest and participation, government actions, and private sector product and manufacturing decisions. Since private industry designs products, selects materials, and chooses the manufacturing processes, it has the ability to formulate and implement innovative solutions to the EoL problem. It can lead the way by making products more environmentally acceptable, creating markets for recovered materials, and changing the infrastructure related to the flow of such materials. Moreover, the private sector plays a key role in developing a comprehensive solution by developing technologies, building processing plants, creating remanufacturing methodologies, and incorporating recycled materials in their products and processes.

Building an infrastructure that integrates EoL operations is the central aspect of making reverse logistics work. All of the processes must be part of an overall system. The challenge is to collect, separate, reprocess, remanufacture, and recycle products and/or materials that create value and generate positive results (cash flow) and to do so in compliance with all laws, regulations, and Directives.

A closed-loop recycling system generally involves a complete solution for managing EoL requirements through a comprehensive system of collection, processing, remanufacturing, and recycling of products and materials. The resulting positive outputs flow back to the enterprise participants at various points or to other reverse logistics systems for beneficial alternative applications. The objective is to maximize the reuse, recovery, and recycling of products and materials. Residuals that cannot be used beneficially then flow to environmentally responsible treatment and disposal. An open-loop system would have retired products and materials sent directly to disposal without any attempt to recover value.

Reverse logistics is a broad concept that includes voluntary, self-directed approaches for managing EoL considerations and programs that are based on government mandates and directives. In the United States, reverse logistics is often called product recovery management (PRM).[27] The first step is to determine if there are any risks associated with the process. This is accomplished by analyzing the products, components, or materials. Compiling the information for the analysis involves determining the constituents, their quantities, their potentially hazardous nature, the way they are constructed, and the disposal alternatives. The second step is to identify the waste management options. This includes examining the opportunities for positive outcomes, obstacles to ideal retirement, costs associated with the activities, and the environmental impacts of the processes. The lack of accurate information on the original products, components, and materials is often a problem. The requisite data is generally not available since it was not obtained in the original purchase process, and original equipment manufacturers (OEM) and raw material suppliers are often reluctant to provide such information after the fact. This is especially true if there are environmental concerns. The data may not exist.

In the European Union, the trend is toward prescriptive systems based on government Directives. Directive 2002/96/EC of the European Parliament and of the Council dated January 27, 2002, for example, specifies take-back and systems requirements on WEEE and directives that national governments in the Union shall impose on producers and distributors. The WEEE Directive is a legal framework that requires member states (national governments) to require producers to create a system alone or in partnership with others to collect, process, recycle, recover, and/or dispose of the products (goods) they market after August 13, 2005.[28] It also requires them to require companies to manage a *pro rata* share of recycling these products based on market share. Every company, whether based in the Union or not, must comply. Failure to comply may result in penalties and/or restrictions on selling products in the Union. In addition, as of August 13, 2005, EU countries must have a WEEE collection system in place. Producers must begin paying for the cost of collecting, processing, reusing, recycling, recovering, and/or disposing of all WEEE in EU markets. While there are many provisions identified in the WEEE Directive, some of the most important considerations regarding front-end and reverse processes are:

- Product Design   Producers must incorporate design guidelines that include design for environment, disassembly, recovery, reuse, recycling, and environmentally responsible disposal.
- Channels   Producers and distributors must verify that marketed products are managed at the end of their life.
- Communications   Producers will be expected to provide pertinent information about products through labeling, instructions, and other disclosures, and to inform customers about EoL provisions.

The Directive demonstrates the need for connection with suppliers and distributors and the importance of information and materials flow. It has profound implications, making business in the Union more involved, costly, and difficult for producers and distributors, especially those using virtual methods of doing business. Corporations without a real presence in the Union may find it difficult to adhere to the Directive's provisions.

But, most importantly, the WEEE Directive is part of a trend in which governments and society are holding producers more responsible for the decisions they make in developing, producing, and selling their products. This includes eliminating the negative impacts of the products, providing all relevant information for proper use and retirement, and ensuring that a total solution is available for the products' EoL and residuals. Without a doubt, this presents economic opportunities for completing the loop and capturing value in EoL products. However, the inability of some to handle such considerations may become a barrier to marketing their primary products (box 5.4).

Box 5.4 Xerox equipment recovery and parts reuse/recycling

Xerox is a pioneer in refurbishing retired copying equipment into new products for sale to customers. As part of the company's "Waste-Free Initiative," Xerox established a customer–product take-back process during the early 1990s. The initiative included designing new products with remanufacturing in mind and creating a remanufacture and parts reuse production capability and marketing effort.

Xerox understood that retired copying equipment presented opportunities for creating value and improving the total solution for both customers and stakeholders. Taking back EoL equipment relieved the customer of the cost and effort of disposal. Xerox received equipment that had been in use and could study the implications and impacts of earlier design and production decisions – "forensic evidence" that could help current designers create improved products and better solutions. Xerox designers also received the insights they needed to make their products easier to dismantle, refurbish, and recycle.

Solutions to EoL considerations have to be built in during front-end design and production. Xerox has become a master at thinking about the total solution, incorporating product recovery thinking into design, production, marketing, and return. Customer relationships are the most critical factor in the process. The willingness of customers to return used equipment to Xerox and to purchase refurbished equipment makes the process work; existing or new customers are willing to buy remanufactured equipment because the devices have been upgraded with new technology and have the same quality and reliability characteristics as new products. Customers obtain a great solution and Xerox enjoys higher profits on remanufactured equipment than on other product lines.

While examples of product recovery often focus on the technical and operational elements of the process, the most critical factors are often the changes in marketing, sales, and finance. Executives and professionals in those areas have to recognize product recovery as an opportunity to satisfy customers and generate revenue and profits, and not as cannibalizing

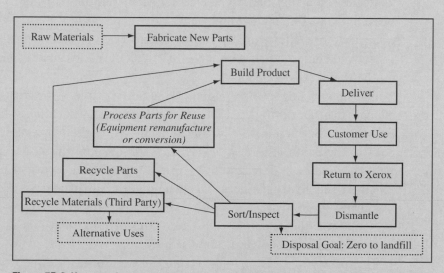

Figure 5B.3 Xerox equipment recovery and parts reuse/recycle process

the potential sales of new products. Philosophically, Xerox does not care whether customers are buying new or refurbished equipment, as long as they are buying from Xerox. Having excellent relationships with customers supersedes all other considerations. Figure 5B.3 depicts the critical elements of the Xerox process. The main business opportunity is in processing parts for reuse (equipment remanufacture), followed by parts and materials recycling.

Xerox's process and program preempt government regulations and Directives for recycled content, recycling, and product take-back. While many corporations view such mandates as a threat to the economic viability of their businesses, Xerox is creating opportunities to provide total satisfaction for customers and stakeholders and to enhance its product portfolio and profitability.

Source: Xerox, *Environment, Health, and Safety Progress Report*, 2003.

Summary

Globalization is a growing phenomenon resulting in the rapid spread of information and knowledge, high expectations from customers and stakeholders, hyper-competition, dramatically increased dependence on supply networks, and a breathtaking rate of change. These changes are forcing corporations to become more connected with their customers, stakeholders, suppliers, distributors, and other partners. Connectedness in thought and action is now, more than ever, crucial for staying in touch with reality. Business leaders once had the time to watch events unfold, contemplate strategies and actions, and then take deliberate responses. Today, they must proactively analyze market and stakeholder expectations and provide solutions for future requirements. Only by being well connected to the breadth of the business environment over a product's full life cycle can a corporation be on the leading edge of change.

The growing importance of total satisfaction was one of the most powerful changes to occur during the 1990s. While customer satisfaction is still critical for sustainable success, total satisfaction means that the expectations of all constituencies are exceeded. Today, expectations continuously increase as new capabilities and technologies provide improved solutions. It is the relentless pursuit of excellence and the ongoing dream of achieving perfection that drives strategic decision-making and action plans. Social responsibility is not tangential, but rather a mainstream consideration that is at the heart of enterprise management and connectedness.

The focus of marketing in the twenty-first century is shifting from selling products to building relationships and trust. The most radical changes involve the move to a more balanced, more open relationship with the public. Dual-sided marketing is beginning to take hold. No longer are companies just inclined to overstate the positive attributes of products and services and understate the negative implications and impacts. The "product" is expanded to a broader concept of a "solution." "Price" is replaced by the "value proposition." "Promotion" is refined to include the full story associated with the solution – the positives and the negatives. "Place" is expanded to include the whole market space in which the solution is framed and provided. Most importantly, "people" move to center stage in the evolving concept of sustainable marketing. The central theme is building awareness of the complete perspective, gaining acceptance and participation in decision-making, and creating trust across the enterprise. The theoretical and practical sides of marketing merge as corporations build corporate and brand integrity and provide customer and stakeholder value and total satisfaction.

Sustainable success depends on having powerful messages that are based on real world capabilities and outcomes and the ability to build awareness, acceptance, and trust. Trust creates loyalty and enduring success. Green marketing concepts are leading the way toward richer, more vibrant marketing methods that create sustainable success.

Leading corporations such as Siemens AG and IBM now view their marketing efforts in terms of "customer relationship management." This perspective applies to stakeholder satisfaction as well. Openness and transparency in disclosures and reporting are essential for building and maintaining relationships and trust. The GRI provides comprehensive reporting guidelines for ensuring that a balanced view of corporate achievements is presented to the communities of customers, stakeholders, and other constituents.

Connectedness is a pivotal factor in achieving sustainable success: it is insufficient to simply link with suppliers and distributors without knowing who they really are, and how they operate. An ongoing connection to all partners ensures full compliance with the legal, regulatory, ethical, and business expectations of customers, stakeholders, and society. Corporations cannot successfully meet the objectives of the triple bottom line without knowing that every entity in the enterprise is performing to the same standards and achieving outstanding results. To outsource without that confidence opens the door to potential vulnerabilities and risks. In today's world, the global corporation is expected to know and manage its supply networks.

Similarly, customers expect producers to take responsibility for EoL solutions. While there is still an evolving view of what those responsibilities should be, there is also a trend, especially in the European Union, to prescribe the requirements through Directives and take-back provisions. Solving all of the customer's problems, including EoL considerations, is the source of opportunities for sustainable success. Building relationships and trust – i.e. building connectedness – is the way to capitalize on those opportunities.

Supplementary material

Learning objectives

Chapter 5 has the following learning objectives that are intended to guide and support students and practitioners:

- Understanding the market drivers for SBD, including the effects of globalization, market expectations, competitive pressures, and life style considerations.
- Appreciating stakeholder expectations and requirements, including how corporate social responsibility can play a significant role in SBD.
- Examining the importance of values such as integrity, honesty, and openness in making decisions.
- Describing and assessing the importance of sustainable marketing and the concept of dual-sided marketing.
- Understanding the linkages and connectedness with supply networks, customers, and stakeholders.
- Appreciating how executives and senior management contribute to sustainable marketing and managing supply networks.

Research questions

The following are questions related to SBD in order to facilitate learning and ongoing discussion and analysis of the main topics covered in the chapter:

- What are the most significant market forces impinging on global corporations?
- Who are the most critical global stakeholders that most corporations have to consider?
- Is sustainable marketing (dual-sided) realistic, and what are the advantages and disadvantages of deploying it?
- What are the most important benefits of increased connectedness with supply networks, customers, and stakeholders?

NOTES

1. J. B. Pine, II, *Mass Customization* (Boston, MA: Harvard Business School Press, 1993). Pine describes the construct of mass customization which suggests that customers can have the economic benefits of mass production and the selectivity of a customized producer. The title recalls the topic introduced by S. Davis in 1987 in his book, *Future Perfect*.

2. *Sustainable Development in a Dynamic World: Transforming Institutions, Growth, and Quality of Life. World Development Report 2003* (Washington, DC: World Bank, 2003), p. xiii.

3. Gregory Fowler, "Green sales pitch isn't moving many products," *Wall Street Journal*, March 6, 2002, p. B1.

4. *Ibid.*

5. *Ibid.*, p. B4.

6. *Ibid.*, p. B1.

7. "Economic Significance of the Car Industry," *Current Factbook*, AK-1, 1994, p. 2.

8. *Sustainable Development in a Dynamic World*, p. 59. It is estimated that 1.3 billion people inhabit such lands, and most of those people live in extreme poverty.

9. While this is critical, the discussions about human conditions and the social implications are so extensive that they cannot be covered in detail in this text. Read Bjørn Lomborg, *Global Crises, Global Solutions* (Cambridge: Cambridge University Press, 2004), for outstanding insights and information about these social implications.

10. Carroll Pursell Jr., *Technology in America: A History of Individuals and Ideas*, 2nd edn. (Cambridge, MA: MIT Press, 1990), pp. 177–210. The story of "Henry Ford and the Triumph of the Automobile" was written by James Flink, and appears as a chapter in the book.

11. *Ibid.*, p. 177.

12. Global Environmental Management Institute (GEMI), *Environment: Value to Business*, (Washington, DC, 1998), p. 13. The concept of the "License to Operate" involves the public trust that the company will operate in a safe and responsible manner. It involves the responsibility to act in a safe and prudent manner that does not jeopardize society, customers, employees, and related entities. It is based on the legal responsibility to comply with laws, regulations, and Directives and the ethical responsibilities to ensure that outcomes are positive and do not involve unreasonable risks.

13. Laurie Freeman, "The green revolution: Proctor & Gamble," *Advertising Age*, January 29, 1991, p. 16.

14. Ans Kolk and Mark van der Veen, *KPMG International Survey of Corporate Sustainability Reporting, 2002* (Maasland: KPMG, 2002), p. 26.

15. The DJSI was explained in chapter 2. It rates the best-performing corporations on social, economic, and environmental considerations.

16. The list of elements in each of the categories is not comprehensive. The elements are intended to illustrate the essential concepts used to develop the marketing campaign.

17. Ciba-Geigy Limited, *Corporate Environmental Report 1992* (Basle: Ciba-Geigy, 1992), p. 2.

18. Dow Chemical Company, *Environment, Health and Safety Policy*, April 8, 1993.

19. PERI included a number of major corporations and several stakeholder organizations. They included the Business Council for Sustainable Development (BCSD), International

Institute for Sustainable Development (IISD), Deloitte & Touche, the Coalition for Environmentally Responsible Economics (CERES), the Council on Economic Priorities, the Investor Responsibility Research Center, and the GEMI.

20. PERI guidelines were written to accommodate the reporting requirements of the following: Chemical Manufacturers Association's Responsible Care; the US EPA's Toxic Release Inventory; the European Union's Environmental Management and Audit Scheme; the UK's BS7750; the National Pollution Release Inventory and Accelerated Reduction Elimination of Toxics in Canada; the Ministry of International Trade and Industry(MITI) guidelines in Japan; and the emissions inventory in Mexico.

21. PERI Guidelines, May 1994.

22. GRI, March 1999, *Sustainability Reporting Guidelines: Exposure Draft for Public Comment and Pilot Testing*, p. 1.

23. GRI, 2002, *Sustainability Reporting Guidelines 2002*, pp. 22–30.

24. *Ibid.*, p. 36.

25. *Aeronautical Research and Technology for Europe in the Twenty-First Century* (ARTE21), March 2002 edition, Aircraft Related R&TD for Framework Programme 6, *Towards the GoP 2020 Vision*, p. 21. The section includes I/V 12 – The environmentally friendly helicopter:

1. *Description*   The acceptance of the helicopter as a transport mode is of growing importance, especially in the civil sector. However, passengers expect from helicopters the same level of comfort that they are accustomed to from fixed-wing aircraft, which comply with the operator's interest of high-quality customer service at low cost. People living near heliports, on the other hand, demand low noise emissions. International regulations (International Civil Aviation Organization, ICAO, limits) that are in force greatly reduce the mission possibilities of helicopters and in view of increasing environmental sensitivity, even tougher limits can be expected. Although considerable progress has been made in recent years in terms of noise and vibration reduction, further efforts are required in order to be able to offer true passenger and environmental friendly helicopters at an acceptable cost.

2. *Overall objective*
   - Reduction of fuel consumption by 20%
   - Significantly reduced noise levels to be 10 decibels (db) below the current ICAO limits
   - A marked reduction of airframe vibrations to reach values below 0.05g and of internal noise levels to below 70 decibels absolute (dba) in order to provide a comfort level equivalent to that of today's fixed-wing aircraft ("jet smooth")

3. *Deliverables*
   - Reduction of emission through drag reduction (novel shapes and propulsion concepts)
   - External noise reduction (aerodynamic and propulsion)
   - Enhanced passenger comfort

4. *Justification*   The project addresses the research challenges "Environment" and "Passenger Comfort" drafted in the "Report of the Group of Personalities" for the *Vision 2020*. It is related to the target concepts "Green aircraft" and Passenger friendly aircraft operation of the ARTE21 document.

5. *Industrial benefits*   The activities planned aim at improving the characteristics of the conventional helicopter to provide an attractive product for the operator, passenger, and public. The general idea is to minimize the negative influence of main and tail rotor

in forward flight by utilizing a main rotor with "low drag" hub concept (allowing for a level fuselage attitude) and to optimize the general shape of the helicopter by minimizing the control surfaces and utilizing advanced concepts of tail rotors or alternative anti-torque devices.

Noise reduction should be achieved by utilizing an advanced design of the main rotor (multibladed rotor with low tip speed and highly efficient airfoils with advanced blade platforms) and quiet engine installation. In addition, "low-noise" flight procedures will be investigated. To achieve these challenging goals, an intense collaboration between research establishments, industry, and universities will be required.

6. *Partnership* Helicopter manufacturers, component manufactures, aeronautical research centers, universities, and laboratories

26. Dale Rogers and Ronal Tibben-Lembke, "An examination of reverse logistics practices," *Journal of Business Logistics*, 22 (2), 2001, p. 130.

27. The purpose of product recovery management is to salvage economic value by determining appropriate options for the disposition of items to be discarded and to ensure that dispositions are carried out in compliance with all laws and regulations.

28. *Official Journal of the European Union*, February 13, 2003, Directive 2002/96/EC of the European Parliament and of the Council dated January 27, 2002 on waste electrical and electronic equipment, p. L 37/24–38.

REFERENCES

Global Environment Management Institute (GEMI) (1988) *Environment: Value to Business.* Washington, DC: GEMI

Global Reporting Initiative (GRI) (1999) *Sustainability Reporting Guidelines: Exposure Draft for Public Comment and Pilot Testing*, March

Global Reporting Initiative (GRI) (2002) *Sustainability Reporting Guidelines*

Kolk, Ans and Mark van der Veen (2002) *KPMG International Survey of Corporate Sustainability Reporting 2002.* Maasland: KPMG

Lomborg, Bjørn, (2004) *Global Crises, Global Solutions.* Cambridge: Cambridge University Press

Pine, J. B. II (1993) *Mass Customization.* Boston, MA: Harvard Business School Press

Pursell, Jr., Carroll (1990) *Technology in America: A History of Individuals and Ideas*, 2nd edn. Cambridge, MA: MIT Press

Rogers, Dale and Ronal Tibben-Lembke (2001) "An examination of reverse logistics practices," Journal of Business Logistics, 22(2)

Sustainable Development in a Dynamic World: Transforming Institutions, Growth, and Quality of Life. World Development Report 2003. Washington, DC: World Bank

6 Crafting a sustainable enterprise through leadership and capabilities

Introduction

Executive leadership and management commitment are two critical requirements for leading change, achieving exceptional performance, and sustaining success. Management must lead at all levels; executives and senior management must create a vision for the future, position the enterprise to realize that vision, and inspire people to transform the corporation's existing capabilities into world-class competencies. Leadership must engage people across the enterprise, imbue an awareness of and commitment to the principles and objectives of SBD, and build the knowledge, capabilities, and actions necessary to support the transition or transformation to a richer reality. Leadership accomplishes all of this by discovering opportunities for growth, development, and improvements, and by mitigating defects, burdens, and impacts.

Leadership of a corporation includes the executives, corporate management, senior management of groups, business units, and subsidiaries, and operational management at the product delivery level. Executives are usually officers of the corporation. Executives and other senior corporate management are responsible for setting the strategic direction, policies, principles, and values and for assuring governance, reporting, and ethical behaviors. Moreover, they have the overall responsibility for ensuring that the corporation meets its objectives, performance criteria, and social responsibility goals.

A corporation's vision determines the direction, strategies, systems, programs, and processes of the organization and, therefore, the potential for achieving sustainable success. For this reason, executive leadership is at the pinnacle of leadership responsibility for SBD. Executives fulfill a dual role, articulating this all-important vision as corporate officers, while also ensuring that the enterprise meets its social, economic, environmental, and business obligations to customers, stakeholders, and society. Corporate leadership, in turn, creates an atmosphere in which people are empowered to translate the vision into a reality, to learn, and to excel. It provides the overarching principles for creating innovative programs and achieving competitive advantages and sustainable positions across the enterprise. Without executive and corporate management's commitment to the principles and percepts of SBD, the organization and its constituents may not fully appreciate what is required to create a sustainable future. The organization may be confused about corporate priorities, strategic objectives, and desired outcomes. It may focus just on short-term objectives because immediate or near-term goals are easier to understand and obtain than long-term ones.

Corporate and strategic leadership of the enterprise integrates the value chains and supply networks so that there is consistent thinking regarding the enterprise's vision, policies, direction, and goals. It ties internal organizational groups and external entities into an integrated system that reaches beyond the immediate to create a new, more sustainable world. These responsibilities comprise a dynamic model for inventing the future rather than merely fighting for prevailing competitive positions, exploiting current resources and capabilities, and producing revenues and profits. While the latter are important, creating extraordinary value and sustainable success are critical for inventing the future, which is what corporate leaders should spend most of their time doing.

The strategic leadership of the enterprise, SBUs, and related subsidiaries identifies the strategic logic for innovation, cultivates innovative solutions for the future, and provides the necessary resources and organizational capabilities. Strategic management concentrates on formulating and implementing business strategies, integrating the business units, processes, and practices into effective forces, managing the people of the organization, and leading change. It thinks about what the organization must become in order to move beyond the prevailing situation to enjoy a sustainable future. It encourages and promotes learning. It governs the people, the assets, and the resources and determines how they are developed and deployed to create value and wealth for all of the constituents of the enterprise, including customers, employees, shareholders, and society. Strategic management works to transform old approaches and methods into new constructs and strategies for achieving dramatic improvements and sustainable success. Strategic leaders should balance their time between making investments for the future and achieving success in the short term.

Operational management concentrates on sustaining the product delivery systems that link the corporation with its customers, stakeholders, and support relationships. It involves engaging, inspiring, supporting, and directing

Figure 6.1   The interrelated nature of leadership constructs

the people of the enterprise to achieve the desired outcomes and to sustain successful results over time. Operational leadership also integrates activities and processes to improve performance and achieve business objectives. It must communicate and coordinate with the other levels of the organization in order to be part of a cohesive organizational force moving in the same direction. Operational and functional leaders should focus mostly on ensuring the proper operations and performance of the product delivery systems to achieve near-term goals and should contribute a reasonable portion of their time and efforts to creating and building a more sustainable future. The latter often involves participating and leading new product and process development programs and continuous improvement initiatives.

Leadership and management are dynamic constructs that can energize and enable the enterprise to achieve its desired future. Leadership creates the core capabilities and competencies of the organization – i.e. the fundamental skills and knowledge required for executing the vision and mission and obtaining the specific distinctive strengths that can translate into competitive advantages. SBD requires effective leaders who recognize the need to think across the full scope of the enterprise in order to create new landscapes for meeting the needs and dreams of all constituencies. Figure 6.1 provides a simple representation of the interrelated nature of leadership constructs within the corporation and the whole enterprise.

In a 1990 *Harvard Business Review* article titled, "The core competence of the corporation," C. K. Prahalad and Gary Hamel declared the importance of **core competencies**, and articulated their meaning:[1]

Core competencies are the collective learning in the organization, especially how to coordinate diverse production skills and integrate multiple streams of technologies . . . If core competence is about harmonizing streams of technology, it is also about the organization of work and the delivery of value . . . Core competence is communication, involvement, and a deep commitment to working across organizational boundaries. It involves many levels of people and all functions . . . Competencies are the glue that binds existing businesses.

Core competencies remain critical to the success of a corporation today. However, SBD involves going beyond the existing core competencies as the approach is to create new and even more compelling and powerful capabilities. Moreover, it requires that a corporation determine what, and where within the enterprise, the core competencies need to be. SBD realizes that core competencies and capabilities may exist outside the corporation, but within the enterprise – i.e. the corporation plus its supply and value networks. Competencies may be viewed as *strategic* and capabilities may be viewed as *operational*.

Core capabilities are also important in the context of the global corporation. They are the critical knowledge and skill sets required for carrying out the processes and practices of the enterprise. While they may not represent unique or even high-level competencies, they are nevertheless critical to the proper execution of the operating system. Competencies and capabilities are part of, and help to determine, an organization's culture, its values, beliefs, methods, and practices. That culture provides stability and harmony and often defines how decisions are made. It is imperative that an organization's culture embraces SBD and recognizes the importance of embedding SBD principles deep within the fabric of the corporation.

This chapter examines the essential elements of leadership and decision-making, core capabilities and learning, the cultural aspects of organizations, and the constructs for managing change. It describes and evaluates enterprise leadership and core capabilities, including the following four key topics:

- Identifying leadership constructs for creating a sustainable enterprise
- Examining the development of core competencies and core capabilities
- Managing change across the enterprise
- Changing the organizational culture and mindset.

Leadership constructs for creating a sustainable enterprise

Executive leadership in the twenty-first century

Staying ahead of changes in the business environment is a monumental challenge in the twenty-first century. Executives normally formulate the vision of the corporation and communicate it throughout the organization using every means possible to reinforce the message. SBD depends on executive leadership's acceptance of its principles and commitment to integrating those beliefs into organizational culture and beyond into the whole enterprise.

Executive leadership has to devote its time and effort to the whole and not just to the parts. Often executive attention is focused on optimizing the present, while the implications of innovations and change are considered secondarily. While it is difficult to generalize on what executives should be doing, it is clear that they must articulate the vision for the future, select the strategies that will be used to pursue success, and ensure that the organization has the resources and capabilities it needs to do so. It is, to say the least, a demanding challenge.

Executives should have broad exposure and knowledge about every facet of the enterprise, they should be generalists with multiple skills and talents in many fields. They have to make decisions that improve the prospects of the enterprise at a rate greater than that of its peers or industry competitors. To be world class, a corporation must be in the top 10 percent of the competition, exceeding 90 percent of comparable corporations.

Executives and corporate management are the prime drivers of corporate strategies and the architects of the enterprise's future positions. While many executives are concerned about the financial status of their corporations, the paradigm of "inventing the future" demands a more dynamic approach toward discovering opportunities and exploiting them to create sustainable competitive advantage. It demands exceptional management skills to realize the objectives of the short term without sacrificing the prospects for the future. Indeed, SBD is actually about achieving outstanding results in both the short and the long term.

In order to achieve success in a global business environment, executives and corporate management have to create management systems that include the cradle-to-grave aspects of the multidimensional enterprise (supply networks, customers, users, competitors, related industries, and afterlife entities). This includes integrating the value networks of customers, partners, allies, stakeholders, and government agencies and the internal structures and relationships for performing activities and meeting expectations. Executives' work is about integration, innovation, and leadership.

Executives have to go beyond creating the strategic intent of the corporation and structuring organizational capability. They must promote change, for dramatic improvements in performance require substantial change and a commitment to ongoing change. While executives can *motivate* people to improve performance in the prevailing situation, they have to go further and *inspire* people to embrace change and to become part of the change process. They must establish change as the norm, and work to keep people from just accepting the status quo, encouraging them to move toward a sustainable future. This requires an interactive management style that allows people to participate in strategic and tactical decisions. People at each level must be party to discussions and be able to contribute to solutions. Moreover, executives must participate in the processes with people to move and transform the enterprise. Active participation of the executive ranks provides the evidence of leadership and commitment and encourages managers and employees to reach beyond normal expectations and seek the extraordinary. Only then will they want to become part of the vision.

Leading this kind of continual change involves seeking new opportunities from every vantage point. Success comes through cooperation and collaboration, and builds the foundation and structure for sustainable competitive advantages. Success involves achieving that delicate balance between short-term results and positioning the corporation for even greater accomplishments and outcomes in the future.

For instance, the theory of profit maximization is fundamentally a narrow, and possibly a limiting, perspective because it addresses only a single perspective – profits: it values profits above all else. While profits are important to the long-term success of a corporation, they do not guarantee success. Often maximizing short-term profitability affects long-term positioning and future success. Philip Fisher, financial consultant and entrepreneur, believed that successful corporations had to balance both short-term and the long-term prospects. His philosophy on what contributed to above-average performance formed the basis for Warren Buffett's management and financial tenets. Fisher believed in sustained growth and profitability. He noted that:[2]

Many companies have adequate growth prospects from existing lines of products and services that will sustain these companies for several years, but few have policies in place to ensure consistent gains for ten to twenty years. Management must have a viable policy for attaining these ends with all of the willingness to subordinate immediate profits for the long-range gains that this concept requires. Subordinating immediate profits should not be confused with sacrificing immediate profits. The above-average manager simultaneously has the ability to implement the company's long-range plans while focusing on the daily operations of the company.

Fisher's philosophy leads to one of the most important principles of strategic management. Management is not about maximizing profits or shareholder value in the short term, because that may be relatively easy to do if the corporation is willing to sacrifice its future; nor is management about investing everything into long-term prospects: it may be impossible to survive the cash flow constraints or the risks and uncertainties of making investments without seeming rewards. Rather, management is the art and science of achieving appropriate results, including financial rewards, in the short term and investing and being prepared to take advantage of opportunities in the long term, and in achieving sustainable success. Using Fisher's language, "above-average" companies, with their management focus on both, and are able to achieve both. It is not an "either/or" proposition. Great management has the capacity to obtain extraordinary rewards during the immediate term and sustain such rewards over the long term.[3]

Finally, leadership must provide mechanisms for information to flow throughout the enterprise and facilitate broad understanding. SBD requires that professionals and practitioners operate with full information. Leadership must promote both internal and external relationships that will increase knowledge and perspective. Most importantly, leadership must ensure that problems and solutions are discussed openly without fear of retribution.

Leading change in the world of SBD

From a business perspective, ongoing change may be the greatest opportunity of the twenty-first century. While the most significant management constructs of the twentieth century, including strategic management, technological innovation, IPD, TQM, mass customization, lean production, and transformational leadership, are still prevalent and gaining significance, many corporations have found that the best way to keep up is to actually outpace changes in the business environment and become an agent of change.[4] Setting the pace of change and influencing the standards and expectations of the future are prime ways to achieve sustainable positions and outcomes. The old notions of reacting to change or anticipating changes are defensive, and lead to vulnerabilities as conditions and trends rapidly change.

But confronting rapid change requires agility and flexibility, along with the ability to implement strategies quickly and at the same time eliminate the negative aspects of past decisions as quickly as possible. Many global corporations have legacy issues that require significant resources to mitigate, but provide no benefits for future opportunities. The best examples are the numerous remediation projects that corporations have undertaken to cleanup wastes from past operations. Investments in remedying the effects of the *Exxon Valdez* tanker accident or the Love Canal incident consumed capital without tangible benefits to the corporation.[5] Such problems reduce the resources available to meet the needs of the future.

Agility and flexibility enable corporations to embrace change. Agility is the ability to move quickly in new directions, and flexibility means being able to transform existing core capabilities into new ones that are in sync with new realities: agile corporations are more likely to encourage change and discover new opportunities than to think about threats. Agility depends upon the skills, knowledge, and processes of the organization. It is also a function of the organization's ability and willingness to learn. Rapid change necessitates rapid learning and there must be willingness to move from the old to the new.

Most agile corporations have flexible management systems that can quickly accommodate global change and exploit opportunities. These are the corporations that can aggressively position themselves to preempt the business environment and meet new needs. Eight of the key processes that facilitate rapid response are:

- *Global surveillance of the business environment*   Training people to think globally, to recognize opportunities, and to embrace the changing business environment enables corporations to discover opportunities wherever they may be.
- *Reinventing strategic direction and leadership*   Change necessitates a continuous reassessment of strategic direction and the development of new strategies to meet rapidly changing conditions. Such strategic changes require organizational constructs that are fluid enough to be reconfigured on an ongoing basis. Rapid strategic development is essential for keeping pace with reality, as is the ongoing development of competent leaders and capable people. Adept leadership is often the scarce resource.
- *Cultural perspectives on change*   Expertise, knowledge, and capabilities are subject to change. Organizations have to invest in resources and capabilities to acquire new knowledge, methods, and practices in order to lead rather than follow. The organization must be willing to replace the old with the new even when the old has world-class core competencies. Leadership, trust, and inspiration win consensus and buy-in.
- *Change management prototypes*   Having a flexible means to assess the advantages and disadvantages of change and to determine the most appropriate courses of action accelerates decision-making. Prototype processes allow management to understand the implications of change. This is most critical for organizational design and new structures that involve uncertainties: prototypes can provide feedback on a small scale before changes are instituted more broadly.
- *Organizational learning process*   The strengths of core competencies and capabilities automatically decline over time as others emulate them,

reducing powerful advantages to commonplace abilities. Corporations must begin building new organizational competencies and capabilities before they are needed. They must work diligently to educate and train people to keep ahead of the pack.

- *Innovation management*   Innovation provides the means to create a new reality. It involves converting knowledge, learning, capabilities, and insights into valuable and creative new perspectives, products, and productive outcomes. Innovation is more than change: it is making incremental and/or radical improvements to systems, technologies, products, processes, and practices.
- *Building strategic partnerships*   Enhancing strategic partnerships and relationships across the enterprise is one of the most important actions of global corporations. Global reach requires multifaceted, diverse resources that are often best provided by outside entities. Partnerships facilitate rapid change by eliminating the need to invest in new strategic assets.
- *Supply network development*   Supply networks are crucial to meeting customer and stakeholder needs for new products and processes without providing all the necessary resources from within. Developing suppliers and distribution channels that have quality capabilities and values and the necessary sense of urgency is vital to creating the physical and virtual reality needed.

The most important processes of a corporation are those that prepare it for the future. Historically, companies have focused on the capabilities of the product delivery system. The ability to change in response to the changing business environment, however, requires processes that facilitate strategic thinking, business analysis, and sound decision-making. Like a rapid deployment of military forces that are specially trained to be able to move toward many different targets depending upon the situation, these processes must be flexible and able to function in diverse situations.

The use of management systems, rather than organizational structure, to execute strategies is central to a corporation's agility and flexibility. It is easier and quicker to change the management system than it is to reorganize the corporate structure. Teams and other flexible organizational constructs allow the corporation to meet the challenges of change without losing time to determine "superior–subordinate" relationships, job titles and descriptions, and other structural aspects that can hinder change. Moreover, the management system can often be changed to accommodate the new requirements without threatening the stability of the organization.[6]

Agile corporations are dedicated to change, creativity, and innovation. They partner with external entities that share the same values and seek

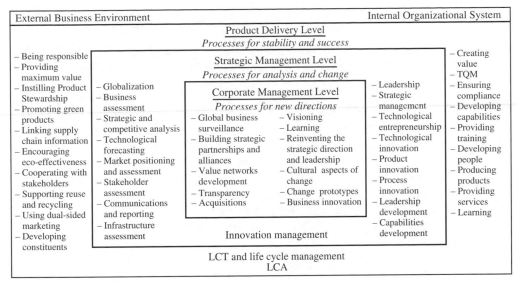

Figure 6.2   Selected key processes for advancing SBD, leadership, and capabilities

improvements at every level of the enterprise. They have a collective mindset that welcomes opportunities and challenges.

Figure 6.2 provides a graphic representation of the key elements or processes for managing change. At the corporate management level, the key elements are discovering opportunities and creating insights about the future. At the strategic management level, they are analysis and leading change, at the product delivery level, they are creating stability and achieving success.

The processes within the corporate management level are the most critical because they focus on the future. By concentrating on positioning and reinventing the potential and promise of the corporation, they develop a new vision for the future. They identify opportunities and lead to initiatives that implement innovations and renew corporate strategies. For instance, based on surveillance of the global business environment, corporate management may redirect the corporation toward more sustainable activities or processes. BP plc is doing just that by building more renewable energy assets (see box 6.1, p. 346). The most important requirements for this kind of change are generating acceptance within the corporate culture and building relationships with the value and supply networks that support sustainable development.

The outer portions of figure 6.2 list processes that are the short-term outcomes of building this new future. The global business processes at the strategic management level seek to maintain agility while providing a balance between managing change and ensuring stability. Senior management must

Box 6.1 Executive leadership bringing change at BP plc

BP plc (hereafter, BP) is the third largest oil company and the fifth largest global corporation in the world. It is headquartered in the UK and has operations in seventy countries. Petroleum exploration, production, refining, and marketing sustain the company's financial viability in the present, but gas, power, and "renewables" are the wave of its future. BP is also a leading global photovoltaic supplier.

BP began its life as the Anglo-Persian Oil Company in 1909 with most of its resources in Iran. When Iranian assets were formally nationalized in 1954, the company changed its name to British Petroleum and expanded the scope of its operations to Kuwait, Iraq, and Qatar. Being acutely aware of the vulnerabilities of a company with most of its reserves in the Middle East, BP continued during the 1960s and 1970s to lessen its dependence on that region through exploration and development programs in the North Sea and Alaska. Today, BP is also acutely concerned about the long-term viability of petroleum and the dependence on dwindling reserves. Industry estimates suggest that there is approximately forty years' petroleum reserves remaining based on current production and consumption.[1]

Concerned about the public's negative perception of oil companies and based on the need to integrate acquisitions, BP in 2000 again moved to reinvent itself and its vision, changing its name from British Petroleum to simply BP plc. While BP enjoyed a good track record, especially relative to some of its competitors, executive leadership understood that even companies with good records are vulnerable to misperceptions and stereotyping. Executive leadership believed that building "trust" relationships with all of its stakeholders would be essential for long-term success.

BP's vision today is to become an energy company rather than a petroleum company. It is moving its production and distribution resources from nonrenewable assets to a mix of renewables and nonrenewables and plans to continue the conversion over the twenty-first century by adding more of the former and reducing reliance on the latter. BP realizes that existing customers depend on the petroleum products of today, but expect better energy solutions as new technologies are developed. While the transformation of the physical assets may take decades to implement, executive leadership is actively engaged in transforming the management philosophies and systems of the corporation to lead to more sustainable positions. Lord John Browne, BP Group CEO, highlighted the situation in a speech at Stanford University in 2002. The following is an extract from his comments:[2]

> There is no single solution . . . but there are many ways forward. What we and others have done shows that there are rich and wide-ranging possibilities . . . Our aspiration then is to sustain the reduction in emissions we've made. And by doing that contribute to the world's long-term goal of stabilization. Not by abandoning oil and gas – but by improving the ways in which it is used and produced so that our business is aligned with the long-term needs of the world.

The automobile and petroleum industries are linked through social and market needs for mobility and energy. The support of such needs requires large infrastructures of roads, the logistics of fuel storage, transport and sales, and communications. BP and the other oil companies support their customers with products that are essential for keeping the economies of the world moving in reasonably good order. Yet, there are finite petroleum resources, and the future of energy is expected to change significantly over the twenty-first century.

BP is changing its mindset about the petroleum business. While BP still identifies shareholder value as the most important criterion, its policies incorporate the commitments, roles, and responsibilities of the entire enterprise. The following statement articulates BP's commitment to external relationships:[3]

> We [BP] believe that long-term relationships founded on trust and mutual advantage are vital to BP's business success. Our commitment is to create mutual advantage in all our relationships so that others will always prefer to do business with BP. We will do this by:
> - Understanding the needs and aspirations of individuals, customers, contractors, suppliers, partners, communities, governments, and nongovernmental organizations.
> - Conducting our activities in ways that bring benefits to all those with whom we have relationships.
> - Fulfilling obligations as a responsible member of the societies in which we operate.
> - Demonstrating respect for human dignity and the rights of individuals.

In its 2003 *Sustainability Report*, BP states that "sustainability means the capacity to endure as a group by renewing assets, creating and delivering products and services that meet the evolving needs of society, attracting successive generations of employees, contributing to a flourishing environment, and retaining the trust and support of customers, shareholders and communities."[4] While BP sees itself as a "first mover" toward SBD, its primary focus remains shareholder value and its petroleum assets. It believes that these are critical to maintaining corporate value as it moves to being an "energy company."

BP leadership in corporate governance is a critical factor in its transition to SBD. It is among the leaders in its industry, as noted by the DJSI. The DJSI identifies BP's management capabilities as its strength. BP's enterprise-level management system provides strategic direction and integrates the entire corporation with its external relationships. The overall focus is on proper governance of all aspects of strategies, operations, and performance. At the corporate (enterprise) level, BP's corporate management system specifies the architecture of corporate policies, strategies, objectives, and values. Group leadership defines the "destination" and the path toward the desired competitive advantages that create value for shareholders. This decentralized approach is intended to empower people at the operational level to be responsive, accountable and entrepreneurial. The business units are: (1) Exploration and Production; (2) Gas, Power, and Renewables; (3) Refining and Marketing; (4) Petrochemicals. Exploration and Production focuses on supporting the needs of the prevailing market conditions of the traditional businesses based on crude oil. Gas, Power, and Renewables focuses on the future direction of providing low-emission and low-carbon fuels, renewable energy, and innovative technologies. Refining produces the products, and Marketing sells products to customers around the world. The marketing efforts are supported through regional organizations: (1) Europe; (2) the Americas; (3) Africa, Middle East, Russia, and the Caspian; (4) Asia, the Indian sub-continent, and Australasia. They provide regional context and linkages with the stakeholders, establish regional strategies, and form supportive and sharing relationships across the organization within the region. Petrochemicals provide specialty products such as lubricants.

Management used the 2002 *GRI Guidelines* in preparing the 2003 *Sustainability Report*. The goal is to provide transparency and dialog within external individuals and entities. However, it is clear that, at BP, economic performance and the creation of value for shareholders enjoy more emphasis than they would in a more balanced approach.

Notes:
1. BP, *Statistical Review of World Energy*, June 2002, BP plc, p. 4. The report indicates the world-wide reserves at the end of 2001 were 1,050,000 million barrels. At current consumption, reserves are expected to be depleted between 2040 and 2050.
2. BP, *Environmental and Social Review*, 2002, BP plc, p. 15.
3. *Ibid.*, p. 8.
4. BP, *Sustainability Report*, 2003, BP plc, p. i.

initiate development programs that both support near-term improvements and radically change the prospects for the future. Both pathways must exist and lead to superior results that are balanced and sustainable.

At the corporate management system level, the focus is on change, while at the product delivery system level, the focus is on stability. The sustainable approach is the combination of these.

Strategic leadership for energizing performance

SBD is based on the premise that corporations can create superior performance and create extraordinary value. Strategic leadership sets the stage for success. It determines the plans and programs, provides the resources and capabilities, and ensures that the courses of action are appropriate and executed properly. Leading change of this kind means energizing the organization to operate at the highest level of performance. This includes educating people and facilitating their contribution to the corporation; linking people together through an interactive system of relationships is what results in the positive transformation of inputs to outputs.

Leadership also involves translating objectives, information, analysis, communication, interactions, and feedback into a comprehensive understanding of reality for achieving exceptional outcomes. This kind of leadership exemplifies its commitment to positive transformation by putting its principles into action through its decisions, by "Walking the Talk."[7] Executives must demonstrate this kind of commitment to SBD if they hope to energize their employees and management teams and build credibility in the external business environment. And they must demonstrate this commitment continuously.

This kind of committed leadership affects six key characteristics in an organization:

- *Productivity*   The organization and its people are able to carry out the mission and achieve their objectives effectively using resources and capabilities that are adequate to the task.
- *Effectiveness*   Strategic thinking and logic is predicated on the concept of selecting the right way to achieve results. Effectiveness improves when the best processes, practices, and methods are used.
- *Efficiency*   The use of resources and the consumption of time and money generate long-term value and represent the precise ratio of inputs to outputs that minimizes economic and environmental waste. Lean business practices focus on waste minimization and effective utilization of resources.
- *Ability to satisfy*   Outcomes result in more than satisfactory benefits and rewards for every participant, including employees, partners, customers, stakeholders, and shareholders. Such benefits are both tangible (money, promotion, value, products, etc.) and intangible (status, prestige, reduction in risks, etc.).
- *Innovativeness*   People within the organization think about new solutions and how to create and execute new technologies, products, processes, and practices to enrich the future and achieve more with less.
- *Agility*   The organization is ready to meet the needs and requirements of the future and change accordingly. There is no such thing as the status quo: either the organization is moving ahead or it is falling behind. The former is exciting, but takes hard work; the latter is the pathway to oblivion.

People perform because they are excited about the activities, the process, and the results. For long-term programs, the work itself has to be satisfying so that people can enjoy what they are doing on a daily, monthly, and yearly basis. If it takes years or decades to accomplish the end-results, the process for getting there has to be fulfilling. Good leaders know this and are able to draw the best out of people on both short- and long-term efforts.

A dynamic view of core competencies and core capabilities

The changing landscape of the underlying capital of the corporation

Capital assets were the prevailing source of strategic advantage during most of the twentieth century. Corporations with overwhelming production capacity were generally the leaders in their industries. US Steel, General Motors, and Exxon are examples of the titans who ruled their industries, and even their customers, by their sheer hold on so much capacity and power. Their incredible economic and financial positions allowed them to convert production and marketing capabilities into dominant and long-term positions. As long as the rate of change was modest, the resources of such giants proved to be overpowering.

However, the paradigm shifted after the 1970s, and the power of capital assets and corporate resources fell second to that of the intellectual capacity, competencies, and capabilities of the people within the organization. This transformation has been a function of the rate of change and the dynamics of the business environment. High rates of change make existing resources and capabilities less valuable, and innovation and creating the future more important for long-term success. Intellectual capital and learning are the key ingredients for responding to change by reinventing the technological, product, and process capabilities of the corporation. As the rate of technological obsolescence continues to increase, and the need for replacements and new solutions accelerates, the capability of an organization to invent new technologies, products, and processes becomes the predominant source of strategic competitive advantage. As past inventions and existing positions decline in value, innovation and intellectual capital become the source of preemptive power.

The **intellectual capital** of a corporation includes its knowledge and experience, its intellectual property (patents, trade secrets, protocols, databases), and the creative talents of the people within the organization. Executives, managers, and professionals often hold in high regard the experience and know-how of the organization. However, experience and know-how are the products of the past; they are valuable as long as the past or present situation remains fairly static. However, if the business environment is changing dramatically, the relevance of the experiential base declines, and the usefulness of some of the knowledge base is affected as well.

Transforming an experiential-based business model to one based on learning

The challenge in a fast-paced world is keeping up with the need to expand core capabilities and competencies. Corporations depend on the knowledge, experience, and know-how of their organizations to perform the required operations, processes and tasks. In concert with information, data, and knowledge, experience and know-how provide the foundation needed for

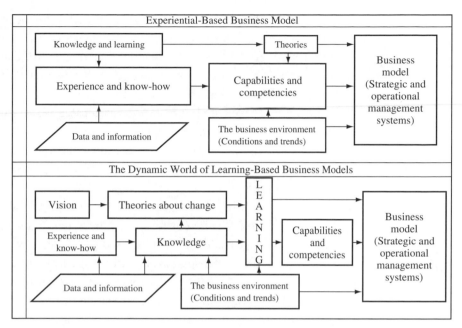

Figure 6.3   The transformation to the dynamic world of learning and new capabilities

the proper functioning of the management systems. However, as the rate of change increases, the value of the experiential factor decreases. Indeed, if there are radical changes in the business environment, past experience may even become a liability or constraint. For example, as corporations created digital systems for designing new products using advanced computer-aided design and computer-aided manufacturing (CAD/CAM), the knowledge and experience of the draftsman using two-dimensional drawings became irrelevant. While there is always some residual value in past knowledge and experience, the change to CAD/CAM was so dramatic that new capabilities had to be learned and the old ways had little usefulness.

Corporations today find that knowledge is best enhanced through multiple means of learning, rather than just experiential learning. Figure 6.3 provides a graphical representation of the transformation from an experiential-based business model to a learning-based dynamic business model.

Perhaps the most profound change that is involved in this transformation is the realization that the experiential base has become less meaningful than it once was and that learning from external and internal sources is now a more effective mechanism for building new capabilities and competencies. Moreover, corporate vision and the theories about leading change are critical for determining the levels of knowledge and learning that are necessary.

Learning has to occur ahead of the needs, since it provides the means to meet them. Corporations must rely on the theoretical frameworks for understanding how the business model(s) should be constructed. Clayton Christensen, Scott Anthony, and Erik A. Roth suggest that good management theory links cause and effects.[8] They say that good theory has:[9]

(1) An underpinning of robust circumstance-based categorization that provides a guide to the situations managers encounter.

(2) A causal statement that explains why certain actions lead to certain results and that describes how the result of actions will vary from one circumstance to the next.

The intellectual capabilities of the organization are the principal means for creating the "right" future for the corporation. They are enhanced through the dynamics of knowledge building, learning, and acquiring new experience. SBD involves not only outperforming peers and competitors, but also learning and acquiring new knowledge and capabilities at significantly greater rates than others. Knowledge and learning are parallel constructs. Learning begets new knowledge that facilitates understanding and decision-making to create a future based on what reality has to be, as opposed to what it is. While truly understanding reality is an extremely difficult task, formulating a definitive vision of what it should be is even more challenging. This ongoing and iterative process focuses on inventing a business model that provides an effective framework for guiding the corporation to the future. For example, BP is becoming an "energy company" that involves building new capabilities in photovoltaic and other solar energy technologies among many other new competencies and capabilities (see box 6.1).

The implicit and explicit aspects of future needs

Most corporations use a *strategic planning model* that examines the prevailing organizational capabilities and projects out into the future, typically five–ten years, to create a scenario of the expected situation. This is simply forecasting what is expected based on the prevailing business context. In contrast, one of the innovative approaches from a SBD perspective is to use **backcasting** to invent the future. "Backcasting" is a method used by Swedish oncologist Dr. Karl-Henrick Robert, founder of the Natural Step, with others, to connect the needs of the long-term future to the present by identifying the actions required for creating the desired future state. "Backcasting" involves a fundamental change in the mindset of strategic thinking. It starts with the *desired future* business conditions, organizational capabilities, and strategic positions and then explores the strategic options available to achieve those targeted outcomes. Backcasting examines future needs and expectations and determines what has to be accomplished over a predetermined time horizon (say, thirty years) to get there. The premise is based on "what must be accomplished" instead of on "what can be achieved."[10]

The implicit factors affecting this process are those less tangible elements: understanding, knowledge, and learning. They form the basis for creating the business models and the desired solutions. Understanding and knowledge help in developing the framework for analyzing the business environment and the enterprise. Learning transforms existing core capabilities into enhanced and/or new organizational strengths. New knowledge, acquired through learning and experience, may reveal new opportunities, new theories, for changing reality. While certain pragmatic practitioners argue that theories are unreliable and not grounded in reality, a theoretical foundation for examining options and potential solutions is essential for charting a course to the future that appreciates historical experience while imagining what is both possible and desirable. Moreover, it establishes a means to avoid guessing or trial and error and allows practitioners to understand the basis for their potential solutions. In reality, SBD is less theoretical than previous business models because it is based on enterprise thinking and LCA which dig into the realities of the whole business environment, both in the short and long term, to *understand* the key variables rather than making assumptions about them. There are usually many potential initiatives for realizing any given solution, and that's where vision comes in. The vision of the corporation ultimately guides the selection of the best specific initiatives to move toward a sustainable future. The vision imbues the theoretical with practical direction. It directs the implicit – the understanding, knowledge, and learning – as the means and mechanisms to create the explicit – the strategies, actions, and methods to be followed.

Strategists then formulate actions based on analysis of the business environment and the prevailing realities of the enterprise. Strategists may undertake an in-depth life cycle analysis of the whole enterprise or study only selected critical portions of it. The choices depend on the time and resources available and the strategic needs of the corporation. The preferred approach is a comprehensive analysis of the whole so that informed and balanced strategies can be formulated. Corporate leaders differentiate the strategy options for pursuing SBD and guide the corporation toward the most effective. The selected strategies focus on "the why" and "the what," while the actions they prescribe focus on "the how" and "the who." They specify programs needed for development and

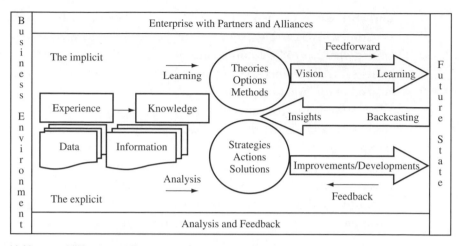

Figure 6.4   Linking capabilities across time

improvement. Figure 6.4 provides a simplified view of the key elements of the process of linking capabilities across time.

Ultimately, learning supports the development and growth of the enterprise. Solutions come from insights that derive from new knowledge. These solutions represent a leap from the theory, based on the implicit elements of experience, knowledge, and learning, to the explicit elements of information, data, strategic analysis, and action-based initiatives.

The most challenging requirement imposed by the rapidity of change is the continuous transformation of the organization to new and higher levels of knowledge and learning. Corporations that are pleased with their existing core competencies and which base decisions on their strengths and capabilities rather than building new ones may be embedding themselves in the present instead of shaping themselves for the future.

Developing and improving core capabilities

The notion of core competencies was the rage of the 1990s. While it is clear that core competencies are desirable, they can also be a double-edged sword unless they are dynamic enough to be relevant over time. Core competencies and capabilities provide the corporation with a favorable position based on the strengths that are currently enjoyed. Corporations with broad core competencies usually have more significant and enduring positions than ones having a narrower focus. For example, P&G has incredible skills and capabilities in brand management, product development, marketing, and distribution. Its ability to generate new products, reinvigorate existing ones, and serve customers is legendary. Such core capabilities are more sustainable and meaningful than simply being the best in soap-making. The former is easily transferred to the next technological innovations and business opportunities, while the latter may be useless if soap becomes obsolete because of new inventions or solutions. Similarly, being the best in developing new products may not be effective if the rest of the organization is incapable of translating the new products into market successes or sustaining them over the long term. However, if such strengths are augmented with many related competencies, it is more difficult for the strengths to be neutralized. It is also easier to translate such strengths into productive and enduring outcomes. The best core competencies are multifaceted, covering a broad range of strengths across the organization. 3M has recognized this and encourages everyone in the organization to become expert in its innovations and join in the development processes.

Capability building is an overarching strategic initiative. While technological and product innovations are the means to build a sustainable future, nothing is possible without talented, knowledgeable, and creative people who are inspired and committed to realizing enhanced positions and producing superior performance. Capabilities are acquired through experience, knowledge, and learning. They are the means to create value and wealth.

Frederick Betz, in *Managing Technological Innovation*,[11] suggests that five kinds of wealth creation for humanity are provided through technology and innovation:

- *Functional capabilities*   New functionality provides the means and mechanisms for humankind to explore, acquire, and exploit new solutions.
- *Availability of resources*   Inventions and innovation provide ways to create solutions from natural resources.
- *Productivity*   Knowledge and skills allow practitioners to produce more for less input, making products more affordable.
- *Increase in knowledge*   Technology provides the means to disseminate learning and to distribute the gains across many fields.
- *Improve the environment*   Innovations require improvements, not just change. Moreover, improvements involve positive contributions without negative impacts.

According to Betz's explanation, wealth creation has much in common with SBD. Improvements are derived from innovations and the capabilities of people to translate knowledge into functional realities. Knowledge and capability are precursors to innovation, but without strategic direction and action plans, they may not be exploited to their full potential. With an understanding of the prevailing conditions and the corporate vision for creating the future, the corporation's intellectual capital can be invested in transforming existing capabilities into more powerful positions for the future. The conversion process is open-ended and complex.

The first step is to examine the implications of creating new capabilities for the future. This includes a thorough analysis of the implicit and explicit requirements for realizing the corporate vision and strategic direction. Most corporations view their vision statement as a wonderful and inspiring message about what it would like to be in the future. These statements run the gamut from well-thought-out premises about the future and the commitment to realize that future to a shallow proposition without substance or meaning. The former can create excitement within the enterprise and all of its relationships for building the future that the corporation has set forth. The latter is often simply a marketing effort intended to convince customers to buy products and services. For corporations that are serious about inventing the future, the vision statement is the precursor to understanding the implications of the strategic direction that has been set and the need to create the organizational capabilities to pursue that direction.

The second step is to identify and assess the strategic and operational capabilities that are necessary to realize the vision and future direction. The process is more dynamic than conventional capability assessment, which traditionally focuses on what is, instead of what has to be. The more inclusive approach is to examine capabilities and requirements within the organization and within the enterprise (suppliers, distributors, partners, allies, etc.). While it may be cost effective to have selected activities, functions, and/or operations "outsourced," there are strategic implications that have to be explored before such decisions can be made. It is executive management's ultimate responsibility to continuously probe the importance of existing capabilities and the need for new ones and to ascertain the means to acquire or build such capabilities. The most difficult part of the identification process is to determine the essential competencies and capabilities that may be required by future positions. For instance, in high-tech businesses such as electronics and computers, there may be several overarching functional or strategic areas that are embedded in most technologies, products, and/or processes that necessitate internal competencies. Some examples are the need to exploit digital technologies, use wireless devices, make devices smaller, develop high-quality outputs, reduce wastes, and improve value. Such areas may not be core capabilities by definition, but they are increasingly being demanded.

While it is impossible to generalize and develop a list of essential require-ments, Table 6.1 offers some suggestions, categorized according to the levels of management and their time frame.

The list of suggested processes that require core competencies and cap-abilities could be endless. The critical point is that management at each level has to be thinking about improving capabilities in the short and long term as they achieve the desired level of performance on an ongoing basis. They have to think in terms of balanced solutions; they have to realize the objectives of the current period as well as invest in future capabilities in order to realize their vision. Building and creating capabilities and competencies represents a dynamic process of understanding the present and optimizing results at the same time as one is reconfiguring the capabilities of the enterprise to seam-lessly invent more sophisticated positions for a sustainable future.

Corporations usually focus extensively on the core capabilities – the funda-mental existing strengths – of the existing product delivery systems and the specific capabilities and resources that provide the means to obtain or exploit competitive advantages. The strategic problem with such a limited perspective is that it may lead to vulnerabilities in the future. Overly optimizing the present often improves short-term financial performance and promotes attainment of near-term objectives. However, core capabilities have to be viewed from a more dynamic perspective that determines whether there are effective capabilities and resources, in both quality and quantity, and in strategic and operational areas for creating a sustainable future. The seven important questions are:

- Does the organization have the knowledge, skills, and leadership talent necessary to formulate and implement strategies and programs?
- What are the strengths and weaknesses of its current core capabilities?
- What are the requirements for the future for sustaining the corporation?
- What are the combined capabilities of the enterprise?
- What are the essential capabilities that have to be secured within the corporation or through acquisition to ensure its survival and growth?
- What are the capability shortfalls and resource limitations?
- Does the corporation have the means and mechanisms to create the requisite capabilities for the future?

The capability assessment should be an in-depth analysis of the capabilities of the corporation at the product delivery level, the strategic management level, and the corporate management level. The analysis must identify the essential requirements and the strengths and weaknesses of the prevailing case in the light of future needs. It must examine the organization's existing technology and product portfolio, its technical and engineering capabilities,

Table 6.1. Selected examples of broad-based core competencies and capabilities

Level of management	Short and intermediate terms (Directing and executing)	Long term (Transforming and sustaining)
Executive level – corporate management	Instituting SBD Developing competent leaders of the corporation Acquiring sustainable capabilities and resources Ensuring ethical and legal behaviors Encouraging social responsibility Identifying opportunities for improvements Benchmarking for the most effective methods	Creating a vision that transforms the enterprise Transforming the enterprise in terms of the vision Leading change through preemptive strategies Developing sustainable partners and networks Creating transparency across the enterprise Energizing people to embrace a sustainable future Eliminating unsustainable assets and resources
Strategic Level – SMS	Developing strategic partners and networks Validating decisions for initiatives Developing R&D programs for new technologies Encouraging social responsiveness Instituting LCT Improving enhanced production means Creating full disclosure marketing	Building sustainable businesses Creating and developing clean technologies Managing change through innovation Growing the capabilities of the organization Educating and protecting people Using LCA for decision-making Eliminating impacts and burdens
Operational level – product delivery system	Assessing the life cycle of products and processes Managing with high quality and reliability Eliminating wastes, pollution, and residuals Managing in full compliance Mitigating uncertainty and risks Creating reuse and recycling initiatives Developing improved products and processes Developing high-quality supply networks Developing people at all levels	Becoming eco-efficient Creating balanced solutions for all constituencies Moving toward zero defects and burdens Developing sustainable new products and processes Avoiding hazardous materials and processes Creating open dialog via Product Stewardship Creating an infrastructure for closed-loop recycling Assuring effective retirement of products/materials Training people to create needed capabilities

market-related skills and knowledge, and its financial resources and management capabilities. The assessment asks:

- Does the corporation have the capabilities, resources, skills, knowledge, and people to identify, analyze, and manage opportunities and then create, design, development, test, finance, produce, market, distribute, and deliver the best solutions (product delivery level)?
- Does the organization have the qualities and capabilities to successfully define, innovate, and execute the requisite development programs (strategic management level)?
- Can management lead change, integrate the enterprise, and instill a commitment to the new strategic initiatives (corporate management level)?

The third step is to determine the capabilities that are essential for the future. Incremental innovations and improvements usually evolve through small changes to the core capabilities of the organization over time. These ongoing learning and development initiatives are often adequate for keeping pace with needed evolutionary changes. Radical innovations and dramatic changes typically require more substantial, even revolutionary, changes in the capabilities of the corporation. In most cases, global corporations have to think about both categories. Table 6.2 provides a simple list of skill-based core capabilities.

The fourth step is to create mechanisms that focus on developing future capabilities and positions. While most corporations have education and training programs for improving the knowledge, skills, and competencies of their employees, most such efforts relate to the existing situation. However, in a fast paced world, the question of future capabilities is always a pivotal concern. Understanding the capabilities needed for the future is complicated, and there are no predetermined methods for determining them. The approach has to be highly stylized for each level of the management system and the business context, and the process involves continuous changes and improvements.

While it is impossible to stipulate the exact percentage of time that management at each level spends on inventing the future, the following rule of thumb may be instructive:

- *Enterprise (corporate) level*   A majority of management's time is invested in inventing the future of the enterprise, and a minority of management's time is spent ensuring the effective flow of strategic initiatives and realizing outstanding short- and intermediate-term business performance.
- *Strategic level*   Management's time and efforts are more or less balanced between creating new opportunities and repositioning core capabilities to meet future requirements, and managing innovation, integrating business units and activities, and achieving exceptional short-term performance.

Table 6.2. Selected examples of skill-based core competencies and capabilities

Level of management systems	Incremental innovation (Evolutionary changes)	Radical innovation (Revolutionary changes)
Executive level – corporate management system	Improving the management systems Investing in the most effective opportunities Improving technological foundation Enhancing the value propositions Developing the people of the organization	Establishing a new business model Building new relationships across value networks Establishing new means of governance Determining metrics for the organization Acquiring new resources/assets to support businesses
Strategic level – SMS	Improving technology platforms Satisfying customers with effective solutions Selecting improvement programs Integrating supply networks Developing new products	Forecasting the needs for radical technologies Finding the initial users (customers) and their needs Building the supply networks for the system Developing the people and their skills and capabilities Leading change through positive rewards
Operational level – product delivery system	Improving quality and reliability Satisfying customers better Managing assets more effectively Improving resource utilization	Creating producible and marketable products Reaching new customers with the "message" Creating value networks Integrating the management system

- *Product delivery level*   A majority of management's time and efforts is focused on assuring effective utilization of capabilities, achieving desired performance, and mitigating the barriers to success, and a minority is invested into improving the prospects for the future, including eliminating defects and burdens.

The exact time allotments have many variations, depending upon the industry structure, business conditions, and the prevailing rate of change. In the aircraft industry, the time horizon for new products is approximately ten years. On the other hand, the electronics industry measures its time horizon in terms of months. The more dynamic the business environment, the more senior management has to devote its time and efforts toward investing in the future and empowering subordinates to manage the present. Implicit in such efforts is building the requisite capabilities ahead of the specific needs. These capabilities are the limiting factor for inventing the future. For example, as BP plc converts from a petroleum company into a fully integrated energy provider it has to transform its existing resources into multifaceted capabilities incorporating a broader spectrum of technologies and business systems. Fortunately, change in the petroleum industry is relatively slow, giving management time to effectively make the transformation.

The fifth step is to integrate the exploitation of intellectual capital and core capabilities into the management system and the action programs of the corporation. The latter are covered in detail in chapters 7 and 8. While the process outlined above suggests that identifying, determining, developing, and exploiting core capabilities is a sequential approach, the process is more of a continuum with many steps being implemented on a concurrent basis. It is based on management's realization that capabilities are developed concurrently with the formulation and implementation of strategies, technology and product development programs, and normal business operations. Developing new capabilities is pivotal in sustaining competitive advantages. Even in a business environment of slow change, the leading entities are often at work developing higher-level capabilities. Indeed, corporations such as Siemens, IBM, and Toyota, are developing new capabilities that will set themselves apart from their competitors. As the compounding effects of such improvements are realized, weak competitors will become hard pressed to produce acceptable financial results.

Enhancing core capabilities has become an essential requirement for doing business. Corporations have to develop and improve their capabilities in many cases just to keep up with peers and competitors. Simply meeting expectations does not create exceptional value, nor does it provide a comfort zone. The corporation must exceed expectations by some large margin (say 10 percent) if it is to outperform its competitors on a consistent basis.

Managing change across the enterprise using cross-functional and cross-company integration

Converting organizational structure into enterprise-wide capabilities

Intellectual capital provides the means for creating opportunities. Having a broad scope of talent and knowledge available during the formulation of new ideas, concepts, and approaches provides rich potential for innovation and change. Historically, large corporations relied on vertical structures for managing organization, affecting the flow of information and linking decision-makers with those responsible for the execution of strategies and actions. This can be viewed as Stage 1 in the evolution of corporate structure and integration.

During the latter part of the twentieth century, the hierarchical nature of the vertical organization was transformed, placing a strategic management group at the top and a more horizontal organizational structure at the operating levels. While there were many variations, and it is difficult to generalize, this matrix-type organization epitomized the new management thinking. Theoretically, it provided the advantages of more linear flow of activities through the process while retaining the strengths of a functional organization (knowledge pertaining to the subject matter). It resulted in a streamlined flow of activities and decision-making. Where the once vertical organization was characterized by numerous transactions between decision-makers at various levels, the horizontal organization allowed participants to determine the flow of activities and to solve many problems themselves. This was Stage 2 in the development sequence.

This streamlined approach worked sufficiently well for routine processes such as manufacturing and distribution. However, the linear nature of the structure caused difficulties when people were engaged in innovative activities, projects, or programs. The slow pace and the lack of interaction between different groups within the structure were a problem. The sequential nature of the flow of process steps consumed a lot of time and meant that participants were not linked across time. Fortunately, since the 1980s, management frameworks began to focus more on people and less on activities. People became the architects for creating the future, and the principal organizational construct for managing innovation became the cross-functional team. Cross-functional team constructs can be viewed as Stage 3.

Cross-functional integration affects collaborative behavior among participants from different backgrounds and functions within and outside of the organization. Cross-functional teams link downstream activities with upstream decision-making. Knowledge of downstream capabilities and limitations allows the upstream team to select solutions that are appropriate for the needs and requirements of the whole program. Cross-functional teams can apply a broad array of talent, skills, experience, and knowledge to discover and develop a wide range of new opportunities.

The concept of cross-functional teams is an embellishment of the horizontal structure, an evolutionary change to the notion of using horizontal processes to affect the proper flow of activities. It is often viewed as a distinct model because it includes the time dimension as a critical factor in managing

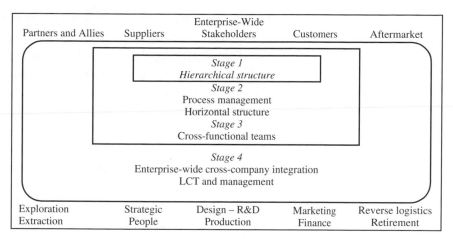

Figure 6.5   Enterprise-wide model of cross-functional integration

processes, especially technology and product development processes. In addition, cross-functional team concepts, such as IPD, view suppliers and customers as important sources of new product ideas and innovations and participants in the development processes. Indeed, this use of external participants was a revolutionary change that greatly broadened development processes.

The next stage in the development of a more interactive system is cross-functional integration across the enterprise using cross-company integration. It can be called Stage 4. This approach is a logical extension of cross-functional teams with selected suppliers, customers, and others in the value networks. Figure 6.5 depicts enterprise cross-functional integration.

Enterprise-wide, cross-company integration includes every level of the corporation and all of the constituents across the enterprise. Executive leadership may still be a vertical structure, but senior management must play a broader role to ensure that the whole enterprise, not just the internal organization, is functioning and performing properly. The horizontal structure and process management provide the means to execute the operational requirements of the corporation. While the horizontal structure includes implementing strategies, developing programs, and executing action plans, the principal focus is on product creation, development, and delivery. This is the center stage of the production/consumption system. The prime metrics are creativity, productivity, effectiveness, and satisfaction. Economic and social responsibilities are critical external factors.

Enterprise-wide, cross-company integration uses all of a corporation's resources and capabilities to obtain the best solutions possible. It is an open-ended approach that can easily incorporate LCT to ensure that every possible option has been explored and that the ultimate solution is among the best. Moreover, it can facilitate mitigating defects and burdens by providing a thorough assessment of the business environment. It expands capabilities by effectively including the whole value system as part of any solution.

Linking people across the enterprise

The journey to SBD depends on the involvement of people across the enterprise. LCA, for instance, requires the contributions of suppliers, distributors, customers, stakeholders, and related industries. They provide details about inputs and outputs, energy and materials consumption, processes, applications, residuals, and other wastes streams. Even with detailed information about the external side of the LCAs, it is difficult to understand the implications and impacts without the direct involvement and experiences of the external constituents. Without linking with them, it is impossible to handle the increased complexities of the world. Indeed, the most effective corporations are those with a solid knowledge about their entire sphere of influence from cradle-to-grave.

While most corporations understand the need to use cross-functional teams for developing new technologies and products, the extension of cross-functional integration throughout the entire enterprise is a growing construct. Several factors are driving this trend: the outsourcing of more of the production of components, parts, and products to global suppliers, the diversity of the product applications across many markets and geographical areas, and the explicit and implicit requirements for managing waste streams and EoL considerations. As the number of entities increases, managing relationships becomes a critical aspect of managing performance. The benefits of integration become more obvious.

For example, multiple parties and fragmented linkages characterize the traditional supply network. Each step in the process fulfills its responsibilities without much input from the other participants in the system. The upstream activities normally include processing numerous types of materials and operations to support downstream processors. Each processor depends on all of the upstream and downstream businesses to carry out their functions, but is often unconnected to them and lacks the information it needs to make good decisions.

Outsourcing is an ongoing phenomenon that makes enterprise-wide integration more critical. Theoretically, outsourcing allows the corporation to invest its resources and capabilities in the areas which will bring it competitive advantages. James Brian Quinn, in *Intelligent Enterprise*, has suggested that, "if one is not the 'best in the world' at a critical activity, the company is sacrificing competitive advantage by performing that activity internally or with existing technique."[12] Quinn's maxims for dealing with core competencies indicate that most other activities, those that are not core competencies, should be out-sourced if they are not strategic.[13] The concern with this theoretical thinking, however, is that the lack of integration of the outsourced activities may intro-duce problems and constraints. Outsourcing does not eliminate the need for oversight or for ensuring that suppliers or partners perform in accordance with accepted practice and fulfill their social, ethical, economic, and environmental responsibilities. In fact, the corporation may have to invest its intellectual capital and financial resources to ensure that this is the case. The effort and cost to do so may be higher than the costs to engage in the activities directly.

In addition, outsourcing may introduce complexities and vulnerabilities that would not exist if the activities were managed internally. For instance, the lack of information and knowledge about the ingredients used in external processes may create long-term liabilities for the corporation that could be avoided if it had not outsourced the operation. For example, large financial service corporations have often contracted with "value-added resellers" to purchase, configure, and manage their PC assets. PCs are complex devices that require a sophisticated management system, and managing a broad array of PCs in a corporate setting has become an expensive proposition. Outsourcing such activities seems to save time, effort and involvement in nonstrategic areas; however, some corporations have experienced difficulties because they did not have sufficient information and knowledge to handle the long-term implications. Many simply purchased computers to fit the pre-vailing needs of their businesses. Decisions were generally based on the price and performance of the products and services and paid little heed to EoL considerations for refurbishment, reuse, and retirement. When the time came to retire machines, problems arose. Often it was difficult to determine what the components were made of – and, accordingly, how to dispose of them. Many of the older generations of PCs contained hazardous materials such as lead and phosphorus. If these machines went to a landfill and ultimately polluted the groundwater, the corporation could be held responsible.

Clearly, the short-term gains of outsourcing must be weighed in terms of the total requirements, including the need for investing in an expanded knowledge base. That knowledge should include information about the ingredients that go into the products, the processes that are used to produce the components, and the other vulnerabilities that are inherent to the flow of goods, information, and outcomes. Moreover, the corporation has to keep track of the activities and operations of the external entities to ensure that appropriate decisions are made, acceptable practices are used, and impacts and their consequences are anticipated.

Outsourcing often means that corporations must invest in internal resources as well. As the business activities of the corporation move from highly centralized locations, with wholly-owned production facilities, to diverse supply networks, communications processes for information and management control become more complicated. While establishing the communication system may be simple, using the Internet and other means of mass communications, determining the required information flow and handling the details are much more involved. The former is based on technology and systems, while the latter involves people. Breakdowns in ensuring that information is processed correctly and put to good use are often caused by the original objective of outsourcing the work: saving money and eliminating people from the payroll. People are still needed to keep track of the activities of the enterprise partners and ensure that corporate responsibilities are fulfilled. The payroll may not be reduced as much as was hoped.

Outsourcing aside, the effective linking of people across the enterprise is essential for sustaining an effective management system. The "enterprise-wide team" is a simple, but effective, means to achieve this. It is similar to the cross-functional team within the corporation, except that it links external entities with each other and with the responsible corporate functional areas. The network that is created fulfills many functions, including processing information, tracking transactions, completing contractual responsibilities, mitigating risks, defects, and burdens, solving problems, and providing oversight and control for social, ethical, economic, and environmental impacts and consequences. This integrated flow of information will allow the communication process to become proactive in anticipating and solving difficulties.

James Brian Quinn discussed managing the intelligent enterprise and articulated several key requirements for partnerships to work effectively. The enterprise-wide team is based on a quasi-partnership so Quinn's comments are relevant:[14]

For partnering relationships to be as "seamless" as possible – i.e. to minimize transaction costs – requires much proactive management . . . participants in alliances agree on three things that will reduce these costs most: (1) an overriding goal-congruence, (2) strong mutual trust, (3) an integrated information system that allows continuous real-time monitoring of all of the key variables. Without these partnerships prove disastrous.

Quinn's points provide insights for developing effective partnerships in enterprise-wide teams. They have to have common goals that encompass the product or service life cycle from cradle-to-grave. It is difficult for the global corporation to strive for SBD unless its supply networks and other partnerships are in league with it. Each party owes support to the others and provides the requisite information and assessments to ensure that responsibilities are understood and fulfilled and that improvements can occur continuously across every facet of the enterprise. The integration of the entire enterprise links everyone and everything. Trust is the key to a successful enterprise-wide team.

Enterprise-wide teams are necessary for formulating and implementing LCAs. Indeed, the structure for such teams follows the flow of inputs and outputs through the life cycle of products and services. Enterprise-wide thinking and actions also embody a collaborative approach for managing the life cycles of operations and processes, and for encouraging participants at each stage to contribute to successes and mitigate defects and burdens.

The enterprise-wide team approach uses a horizontal structure to help participants learn more about the implications of their activities. Team members (companies and their people) and their leaders establish the basis for performing the work, set the priorities, specify assessment activities, and evaluate the results. The teams operate on a concurrent and ongoing basis, minimizing transactional mandates because participants are interacting with and inspiring each other.

The enterprise-wide team is not a silver bullet, just an innovative method that links activities across the enterprise without increasing costs and complexities. It is a time-based mechanism that shortens the process because participants automatically provide the information and support necessary for effective assessments. These topics are further described in chapter 9.

Cultural aspects of organizational dynamics and the agile enterprise

Resistance to change and its implications

Organizational culture encompasses the intangible philosophies, principles, values, and beliefs that define the personality of the corporation. It includes the intellectual underpinnings that create a constructive atmosphere for the organization and the ethics that guide decision-making. It is often grounded in the legacy of past experiences, the core competencies of the present organization, and its prevailing practices and methods.

Culture is usually the stabilizing force that helps corporations deal with turbulence, conflicts, and disruptions. Corporate culture can also cause difficulties for corporations trying to make dramatic changes, however. Dorothy Leonard-Barton discussed core capabilities and core rigidities in her book, *The Wellsprings of Knowledge*. According to Leonard-Barton, core rigidities are the factors that inhibit the flow of knowledge and change. They might include things such as insularity, overshooting the target, limited problem solving, the inability to innovate, limited experimentation, and screening out new knowledge.[15] Core rigidities are often the reasons why corporations fail to make improvements or reject new paradigms. The corporate culture attempts to stabilize and protect the corporate personality, its capabilities, and way of conducting business. Moreover, the individuals within an organization reinforce core rigidity because the uncertainties and risks of change often threaten them. For instance, radical change may eliminate the value of certain core capabilities, making the individuals possessing those capabilities and related knowledge less valuable. These people typically respond by resisting this kind of change. Highly competent automobile engine mechanics, for example, have little interest in promoting fuel-cell technology. Such a radical change would make their contributions less valuable in the long term; eventually, their expertise may not be needed at all.

Leonard-Barton also discussed the hierarchy of the difficulty of change. Figure 6.6 depicts the susceptibility of core rigidity to change.

The research indicates that changing physical and managerial systems require considerable time, effort, and money. However, given that they are usually based on assets and resources, people often embrace such changes as improvements to their work environment. On the other hand, changing skills sets and knowledge within the organization often meets resistance because it directly involves people: people become concerned about their jobs,

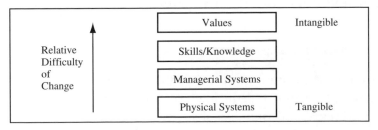

Figure 6.6   Leonard-Barton's susceptibility of core rigidity dimensions to change

positions, and futures. Likewise, trying the change the culture and value system is also very difficult because people have become entrenched in the prevailing thinking and have a specific mindset about the way things should be done.

The more dependent the culture is on the well-defined core competencies and the legacies of the past, the more likely it is to resist change and promote the status quo. Powerful strategic positions reinforce the desire of the organization to maintain its dominance in the business environment. It is often difficult to get leaders to embrace new concepts, new approaches, or new technologies because they threaten the power base. However, corporations with strong cultures that are based on innovation and strategic leadership like change. Toyota is one of the leading automobile companies in the world. It has effective technologies (especially its lean-burn internal combustion engine), strong market positions, and many leading products. It has an enviable position that might be difficult to maintain if it had to convert to new technologies like fuel cells. However, Toyota is developing new technologies in conjunction with its existing ones to smooth the way to a new reality if necessary. Toyota has linked its present strengths with its future direction to encourage a seamless transformation to the future, whatever the technological underpinnings may be. Toyota's strong culture of embracing change and technological development is helpful in promoting acceptance of the new technologies.

Weak cultures are those that are static. They are narrow and self-centered. They focus on perpetuating the existing strengths of the organization rather than improving the capabilities of the entire enterprise. They attempt to perpetuate the prevailing situations as long as possible. They want to maximize or optimize the existing systems.

Resistance to change has been a key concern of executives and strategic management for many decades. It may start at the highest levels of the organization, where leaders of highly successful businesses may view any change as resulting in less desirable outcomes. Even innovative leaders such as Henry Ford resisted changing his product, the Model T, because it meant suboptimizing what he perceived to be an optimized system. Most importantly, Ford believed that his cost effectiveness would be compromised if he introduced new models. The old axiom, "if it isn't broken, don't fix it," is often the prevailing thought.

Resistance to change is more likely in highly authoritative (centralized) organizations with top-down management styles, because of the rigidity of the reporting relationships. Employees' and mid-level management's lack of empowerment and involvement in decisions can lead people to "wait and see" how new initiatives and programs will work. Such resistance, though often indirect, may negate the objective of making dramatic changes in a short time frame. Without direct contributions from within the organization, new programs are generally introduced more slowly and require more time and effort to achieve the desired results. Senior management must provide incentives to ensure the success of the changes. If the change mechanisms are successful and prove their value to the organization, people may accept the changes and integrate the new mechanisms into the organizational modalities. Though resistance may have cost time and money, the final outcomes may be fruitful.

If the changes prove to be undesirable from an organizational perspective, however, there may be a divergence between upper management's desires and the operational levels' view of the proper approaches. Such divergence may lead to chaos and hinder progress. Recovery requires an incredible amount of dialog.

Even in cases where the organization plays a significant role in determining the change mechanisms, resistance to change is a significant concern. Broad participation in the process does not automatically overcome negative attitudes. People may not accept the need for change, or may not like the speed of change. They may not comprehend the logic associated with the changes, and may not understand their roles and responsibilities in the new approaches, or they may not like the actual change mechanisms. Regardless of the management approaches, people most often resist change if it threatens their value and contribution to the system, making them irrelevant. This is especially the case if new technologies and new methods are introduced.

Mitigating resistance to change and shaping a SBD culture

Rosabeth Moss Kanter, Barry A. Stein and Todd Jick, in *The Challenge of Organizational Change*, discussed change actions that they called "bold strokes" or "long marches."[16] "Bold strokes" are revolutionary actions that translate into new realities from the top down in a short time frame. They involve the rapid conversion from the old to the new. For example, BMW converted to digital auto design using CAD/CAM in 1998, revolutionizing the way it developed new automobile models. "Long marches," on the other hand, are intended to be enterprise-wide initiatives that require everyone's participation and are executed over a long time frame, generally decades. Long marches are usually evolutionary actions that create improved capabilities and enhanced stability in the long term.

Managing change in the context of SBD requires both bold strokes and long marches. Preemption means initiating significant changes that result in revolutionary outcomes that are superior to what competitors and peers are accomplishing. These bold strokes can result in extraordinary improvements across the enterprise. However, even with dramatic improvements in the near term, SBD also requires ongoing long marches over the decades to achieve continuous improvement, dramatic shifts in identity, and minimized impacts.

Management can lead change within their organization by promoting learning and enhanced knowledge. People are more willing to change if they recognize the benefits of the new reality and understand the strategic logic for creating it. A sustainable enterprise embraces both evolutionary changes that improve its foundation and systems and revolutionary changes that provide new opportunities and create enhanced strategic positions for the future. This is possible when practitioners participate in the change processes and have the means to become even more successful under the new conditions and requirements.

Managing change involves experimenting with many alternatives to find the solutions for the future. It means allowing people to fail when taking on a new initiative, but to gain from the experience and learn how to handle the next opportunity. Managing change requires encouraging innovative solutions and prudent risk-taking. It involves influencing positive behaviors and rewarding significant achievements.

Change is an ongoing necessity, and managing it is one of the most important responsibilities of senior management. Leadership must emphasize the benefits of proposed changes and allow people the autonomy to assess the implications and make their own judgments about the opportunities and challenges those changes bring. Leadership must be committed to energizing the organization to continuously make both incremental improvements and radical changes.

Corporations that adopt SBD as their guiding business model must be adaptive and embrace change. Their cultures must view change as the norm. The challenge is to embrace change while also promoting stability and a smooth transformation to the future. The ultimate strategic competitive advantage in a fast-paced world is often found in the ability and flexibility to change quickly to meet the needs of the prevailing conditions. Theoretically, a SBD corporation functions on the basis of relationships, both internal and external, which can be reconfigured quickly and easily without conflict, resistance, or turmoil. This is not to be interpreted as everyone simply accepting the new direction without discussion or debate. On the contrary, effective change includes broad participation of people with divergent views that are addressed and resolved through openness and empowerment. New solutions become possible because the corporation shares its values and beliefs across the enterprise with both internal employees and external entities in a nonthreatening way. The notion of "winning" is replaced with the concept of "succeeding."

Reshaping the culture of the corporation around the needs of the entire enterprise requires executive leadership to focus on the benefits of change and the strategic advantages of inventing the future. If the capabilities of the corporation are based on skills and knowledge related to technologies and products, then the challenges for the future rely on building new knowledge and skill sets through education and training. As the corporation moves from the old technologies, products, and processes, the adaptive organization has to learn how to function in the new realm by acquiring the knowledge necessary to perform to expectations. The resistance to change that has plagued management for decades is often a result of management's failure to transform its organizational capabilities and mindset for inventing the future. People resist change if they believe that it will make them less valuable. Such resistance is mitigated through interactive participation in the change processes and by providing the necessary education and learning for people to bring new value to the corporation.

It is imperative to ensure that the people of the enterprise are included in the strategic thinking about SBD programs. While it is impossible to simplify the many ways people affect program developments, leaders can improve the integration of the development professionals and practitioners in the process by keeping in mind three key perspectives: *respect*, *recognition*, and *reward*. These three "Rs" can encourage people to enthusiastically and energetically embrace opportunities for creating a more sustainable future and become an essential part of the ultimate solutions. Leaders must *respect* the capabilities and contributions of the people involved in the programs. Regardless of the individual's position within the corporation, everyone has a significant role to play and deserves respect for his or her commitment and contributions to achieving sustainable success. Leaders often take people for granted and fail to inspire great efforts and accomplishments. They typically blame others for their lack of success when, in reality, they should examine their own leadership style and ability.

While respect is an intangible that bonds people together, recognition and reward are more tangible ways to encourage people to seek the impossible and achieve the extraordinary. *Recognition* is the link between respect and reward. It is a manifestation of respect through the regular acknowledgment of significant achievements. It provides opportunities to bolster people's feelings about their efforts, allowing everyone to realize that they are making progress. This is especially critical for long-term programs. Recognition can take many forms, from trophies, plaques, and certificates of achievement to award ceremonies. *Rewards* are much broader and can include financial payments, promotions, and other tangible benefits. They may be bestowed on individuals and whole groups. Indeed, providing rewards to an entire group instead of to individuals can be an effective way to encourage positive group dynamics.

One of the best examples of a corporate commitment to respect, recognition and rewards is the development of Nucor Steel under the dynamic leadership of Ken Iverson. Jim Collins cited Nucor as one of the eleven "Good to Great" companies.[17] Iverson, now the former CEO, had tremendous respect for the company's managers, professionals, and work force. He focused his attention on creating a corporate culture of achieving superior performance and leading change through technological superiority. Nucor used electric arc melting technology and mini-mill operations to create innovative systems for producing high-quality, low-cost steel. With only nineteen people on the corporate staff, Iverson deployed his resources in lean and efficient operations. He recognized that people, not machines, produced results, and he recognized achievements biweekly as the various production teams outperformed expectations and standard requirements. One of the most brilliant decisions that Nucor made under Iverson was to pay bonuses to workers on a per-pay period basis. The leadership realized that although the executives could be rewarded for achieving objectives on an annual basis, workers had to receive recognition over a shorter time frame. Iverson's leadership propelled Nucor into becoming the leading US steel producer. He clearly understood that it takes motivated people to achieve great results. Moreover, he knew that the right programs and leaders could inspire ordinary people to do extraordinary things.

The agile enterprise

Agile enterprises can change quickly in response to the dynamics of the business environment and are prepared to change whenever necessary. There is no universal prescription that will make an enterprise agile, however, it is clear that agility derives from skills, knowledge, expertise, and capabilities. The agile enterprise enjoys the following nine key attributes:

- Full understanding of the total business environment, including relationships, linkages and networks with customers, stakeholders, supply networks, related industries, and others.
- A corporate culture that supports the open exchange of ideas and views, empowers people to participate in decision-making, and creates an atmosphere of collaboration within the organization and with its external partners and allies.
- Principles and practices that enhance internal and external linkages for building rapid exchange of information, know-how, experiences, and processes, and promoting ethical and responsible behaviors.
- Win–win relationships within the organization and with external entities that enhance the value created across the enterprise.
- Shared information across the enterprise, so that LCAs can be easily prepared to make improvements in every facet of the business enterprise.
- Learning quickly from acquired knowledge and experiences, including successes and failures from innovations, feedback from customers, stakeholders, supply networks, related industries, and other constituents, and new methods and practices in other industries and business in general.
- Competent leadership and multiskilled management and professionals who have the knowledge and capabilities to lead, manage, and function in different business environments.
- Explicit and implicit criteria for measuring performance throughout the enterprise.
- Continuous inspiration for improvement beyond the expected and elimination of defects, burdens, and impacts, wherever they may be.

These attributes characterize the agile enterprise as one that thrives on positive changes, learning new skills and knowledge, acquiring new means and mechanisms, transferring methods and techniques across the enterprise, and dealing with uncertainties and risks. While it is easy to articulate these qualities, it is difficult to specify how to build and maintain them. The agile enterprise is innovative, flexible, and knowledgeable. The linchpins for these characteristics are learning and knowledge, and a full understanding of the enterprise and its interactions and relationships. Agility relies on information, knowledge, and experiences, and functions through distributed authority and responsibility.

Enterprise management provides the means and mechanisms for agility. For instance, enterprise thinking links the entire enterprise and provides the information and knowledge for management and professionals to understand the implications of decisions, actions, relationships, and flows across the enterprise. This kind of complete knowledge reveals the full scope of the prevailing situation, facilitates LCA, and reveals opportunities for improvements and change. The corporation and its partners are better prepared to embrace the future because they understand the current situation, the benefits of change, and how to change.

But, to become agile, corporations must also alter the power and control mindset of executive management, which is often adversarial in nature, into a shared sense of accountability and responsibility, as each participant across the enterprise understands the why, what, how, and who of the relationships and networks and assumes leadership for improvements and change. Creating widespread awareness of the *dependencies* and *capabilities* of the entire system facilitates agility. The broader knowledge and expertise of the enterprise allow for more effective decision-making on a distributed basis. As the saying goes, management and professionals have to think globally (the entire system) and act locally. These changes will provide the corporation with the cultural foundation necessary for change, and those seeking SBD will have this culture in place before its competitors and peers are even thinking about the need for change.

Agility has become the precursor to sustainable success, making it possible for organizations to respond rapidly to the fast-changing business world. Agility and SBD are complementary constructs that are equally necessary for achieving the desired outcomes. People and knowledge are the essential ingredients for both. Continuous learning and acquiring new skills are pivotal for sustaining achievements and maintaining the capabilities to change.

Summary

Leadership is the most critical core competency of twenty-first-century corporations. Human capital is the strategic resource for leading change and improving performance as the complexities of globalization, shortening product life cycles, and the proliferation of information, among many other driving forces, make decision-making more challenging. The capabilities and qualities of executive leadership are among the most important variables in creating future value and sustaining long-term performance. While capital assets can be purchased or acquired, the growth of intellectual capital requires well-thought-out strategies. Creativity and strategic thinking are the hallmarks of corporate leaders who have the capacity and willingness to exceed customer and stakeholder expectations and shareholder and employee objectives.

Given the dramatic increase in the complexities of managing modern enterprises, large and small organizations are scrambling to discover, develop, and deploy the leadership talent needed for improving and sustaining corporate performance. In a world full of uncertainties and risks, astute, knowledgeable, and competent leaders are the essential ingredients for achieving sustainable success.

Leadership provides real world, outcome-driven strategies and innovative methods for leading change. It involves theories, concepts, strategies, and practices for turning opportunities and challenges into extraordinary outcomes. Leadership is pivotal for all corporations, but especially for those embracing SBD. Executive management must commit to developing an enterprise-wide perspective that includes relationships, linkages, and networks with external entities. SBD and enterprise thinking are fundamental constructs for the formulation and implementation of preemptive strategies that seek dramatic developments and improvements in every facet of the business environment and the corporation itself. SBD requires long-term commitment to change the basic structure of the corporation and to create a culture dedicated to the relentless pursuit of excellence. Management at every level has to engage change and energize the organization to become the best. Moreover, SBD necessitates having external entities that are just as involved in improving the enterprise as is the corporation.

SBD involves developing new core capabilities that allow the corporation to outperform its peers and competitors. It means having competencies that are ever-growing and adapting to the new realities of the future. It requires agility and flexibility for changing and improving the skills, knowledge, and capabilities of the organization. The focus is on opportunities and challenges as the corporation seeks to eliminate barriers to success.

Supplementary material

Learning objectives

Chapter 6 has the following learning objectives that are intended to guide and support students and practitioners:
- Identifying and understanding the leadership constructs for creating a sustainable enterprise.

- Examining the constructs of core competencies and core capabilities and how they play roles in developing a sustainable enterprise.
- Understanding the processes for leading and managing change.
- Understanding the development and applications of cross-functional and cross-company teams.
- Understanding the cultural aspects of organizational dynamics and managing resistance to change.
- Appreciating how executives and senior management can lead the corporation to adapt new methods and approaches.

Research questions

The following are questions related to SBD in order to facilitate learning and ongoing discussion and analysis of the main topics covered in the chapter:

- Why should corporate executives and senior management lead change?
- Who are the most important leaders in developing SBD within the corporation and outside it?
- What are the most important leadership constructs for leading change and adapting SBD?
- What are the differences between core competencies and core capabilities?
- How does corporate culture play a role in leading change?
- How do corporate, business, operational, and functional leaders overcome resistance to change?

NOTES

1. C. K. Prahalad and Gary Hamel, "The core competence of the corporation," *Harvard Business Review*, 90(3), 1990.
2. Robert G. Hagstrom, Jr., *The Warren Buffett Way* (New York: John Wiley, 1995), p. 42. Part of the quote was taken from Philip Fisher, *Common Stocks and Uncommon Profits* (New York: Harper & Bros, 1958) and a monograph, *Developing an Investment Philosophy*, The Financial Analysis Research Foundation.
3. This principle or tenet is derived from the philosophies and approaches of Fisher and Buffett. There are other authors who have articulated similar principles.
4. This approach is similar to the "proactive leader" suggested by Derek Abell, "Competing today while preparing for tomorrow," *Sloan Management Review*, Spring 1999, p. 75.
5. These comments are not intended to imply that the investments into cleaning up the sites were not necessary, or that the communities and people involved did not benefit from the expenditures. If the companies had taken an SBD approach, they might have avoided the

difficulties altogether. Most importantly, the point is that such legacy problems reduce a company's viability in the future, causing it to spend money on past problems that could have been used to sustain the future.

6. The topics of organizational structure and organizational development are not covered in this book. There are many suitable texts covering these topics from Alfred Chandler's work, *Strategy and Structure*, to Gary Hamel's book, *Leading the Revolution*.

7. Charles O. Holliday, Jr., Stephan Schmidheiny, and Philip Watts, *Walking the Talk* (Sheffield: Greenleaf Publishing, 2002). The book is an official publication of the WBCSD. It provides case examples of corporations that have walked the road to sustainable development.

8. Clayton Christensen, Scott D. Anthony, and Erik A. Roth, *Seeing What's Next: Using the Theories on Innovation to Predict Industry Change* (Boston, MA: Harvard Business School Press, 2004), p. xv.

9. *Ibid.*

10. Paul Weaver, Leo Jansen, Geert van Grootveld, Egbert van Spiegel, and Philip Vergragt, *Sustainable Technology Development* (Sheffield: Greenleaf Publishing, 2000), pp. 171–203. Chapter 8 provides an example of backcasting.

11. Frederick Betz, *Managing Technological Innovation: Competitive Advantage from Change* (New York: John Wiley, 2003), pp. 196–197.

12. James Brian Quinn, *Intelligent Enterprise* (New York: Free Press, 1992), p. 32.

13. *Ibid.*, pp. 34–35. Quinn identified four maxims.
    - Maxim One: For maximum long-term strategic advantage, companies focus their own internal resources on a relatively few basic sources of intellectual or service strength – or classes of service activities – which create and maintain a real and meaningful long-term distinctiveness in the customers' minds.
    - Maxim Two: The key to competitive analysis and competitive advantage is to approach the company's remaining capabilities as a group of service activities that could be either "made" internally or "bought" externally from a wide variety of suppliers specializing or functionally competing in that activity.
    - Maxim Three: For continued success companies actively command, dominate, and build barriers to entry around those selected activities critical to their particular strategic concept. Concentrating more power than anyone else in the world on these core competencies as they affect customers is crucial to strategic success.
    - Maxim Four: Strategists plan and control their outsourcing so that their company never becomes overly dependent on – or later dominated by – their partners.

14. *Ibid.*, p. 385.

15. Dorothy Leonard-Barton, *The Wellsprings of Knowledge: Building and Sustaining the Sources of Innovation* (Boston, MA: Harvard Business School Press, 1995), pp. 29–56.

16. Rosabeth Moss Kanter, Barry A. Stein, and Todd Jick, *The Challenge of Organizational Change: How Companies Experience It and Leaders Guide It* (New York: Free Press, 1992), p. 492. The authors identify two types of change actions that leaders can initiate: bold strokes and long marches. Bold strokes are top-down decisions intended to achieve fast results. Long marches are operational initiatives that are driven by the organization and require a long time frame. Deploying the two types are situational-determined: the former is more appropriate for introducing radical changes such as phasing out product lines.

The latter is more appropriate for long-term change such as improving quality across the enterprise.

17. James C. Collins, *Good to Great: Why Some Companies Make the Leap . . . and Others Don't* (New York: HarperBusiness, 2001), p. 201.

REFERENCES

Abell, Derek (1999) "Competing today while preparing for tomorrow," *Sloan Management Review*, Spring

Betz, Frederick (2003) *Managing Technological Innovation: Competitive Advantage from Change.* New York: John Wiley

Christensen, Clayton, Scott D. Anthony, and Erik A. Roth (2004) *Seeing What's Next: Using the Theories on Innovation to Predict Industry Change.* Boston, MA: Harvard Business School Press

Collins, Jim (2001) *Good to Great: Why Some Companies Make the Leap . . . and Others Don't.* New York: Harper Business

Hagstrom, Jr., Robert G. (1995) *The Warren Buffett Way.* New York: John Wiley

Holliday, Jr., Charles O., Stephan Schmidheiny, and Philip Watts (2002) *Walking the Talk.* Sheffield: Greenleaf Publishing

Kanter, Rosabeth Moss, Barry A. Stein, and Todd Jick (1992) *The Challenge of Organizational Change: How Companies Experience It and Leaders Guide It.* New York: Free Press

Leonard-Barton, Dorothy (1995) *The Wellsprings of Knowledge: Building and Sustaining the Sources of Innovation.* Boston, MA: Harvard Business School Press

Prahalad, C. K. and Gary Hamel (1990) "The core competence of the corporation," *Harvard Business Review*, 90(3)

Quinn, James Brian (1992) *Intelligent Enterprise.* New York: Free Press

Weaver, Paul, Leo Jansen, Geert van Grootveld, Egbert van Spiegel, and Philip Vergragt (2000) *Sustainable Technology Development.* Sheffield: Greenleaf Publishing

Part II

Innovation management, life cycle considerations, and insights

Part II discusses the relationships between SBD and innovation management, and how LCT, life cycle management, and LCA can provide the understanding of opportunities and challenges that is necessary for making significant improvements. SBD and innovation are inexorably linked. Moving toward SBD also requires a broad strategic perspective that LCT and LCA can provide. The first two chapters of Part II (chapters 7 and 8) examine the significant roles of technological innovation and product development in achieving sustainable success. Technological innovation focuses on inventing new or dramatically improved technologies that accentuate positive implications and mitigate negative consequences. Product innovation deals with improving products and applications through incremental change.

Part II includes an overview of LCT and life cycle management, LCA, and the associated methods and techniques. Chapters 9–11 cover the basic methods and techniques and quantitative and qualitative approaches for LCT, life cycle management, and LCA. Discussions include customer and stakeholder needs mapping, benchmarking, gap analysis, and other analytical tools. Part II includes:

- Chapter 7   Sustainable technology management and development
- Chapter 8   Crafting and implementing sustainable business development programs
- Chapter 9   Life cycle thinking and framework
- Chapter 10   Life cycle assessment formulation: initiation and inventory assessment
- Chapter 11   Life cycle assessment implementation: impact and improvement assessments
- Chapter 12   Inventing the future through enterprise thinking and sustainable business development

Chapter 7 provides an integrated perspective of how technological innovation and product innovation can play key roles in achieving sustainable success. It examines how innovation can provide a complex and delicate balance in meeting the needs of the SMS and the organization. Innovation requires creativity, inventiveness, knowledge, experience, learning, and effective decision-making. Topics include examining core technologies, managing technological innovation, understanding technological forecasting and assessment, managing technological change, managing radical technological innovation, and creating customer value through product innovation.

Chapter 8 examines development programs for managing environmentally conscious technological and product innovation. Environmentally conscious innovation uses a systems approach to create an alignment between the external requirements and the internal capabilities of the organization. The objectives are to create value, improve product performance, minimize the negative impacts on the external environment, and produce sustainable and cost effective designs. The chapter focuses on how corporations can establish guidelines for selecting, developing, and implementing sustainable development programs. The guidelines define the scope of the analysis, establish the boundaries, methods, costs, and schedule of the programs, and set the baseline for the comparative analysis of impacts and improvements. The specifications of the requirements cover the design considerations, including pollution prevention, liability containment, compliance issues, health and safety concerns, and waste management.

Chapter 9 discusses LCT and life cycle management for developing new technologies and designing new products. It includes life cycle considerations and inventory mapping of the upstream supply networks and manufacturing and the downstream aspects of product use and retirement. Life cycle management examines existing situations and explores the possibilities for systematic improvements through product and process developments and improvements. It includes determining whether specific materials are required or not, evaluating potential new materials and suppliers, analyzing options, and selecting the most economic and environmentally conscious option.

Chapter 10 focuses on the LCA of products and processes. LCA is a systematic method used to analyze and evaluate the resources and outcomes and the environmental burdens associated with a product, the related processes, distribution requirements, and applications. The assessment is undertaken to identify, quantify, and evaluate the materials and energy used to produce and use the product over its entire life cycle. The approach is a multistage input-output model that examines all of the inputs and outputs and their impacts, including materials, products, wastes, and emissions. LCA includes an inventory analysis of the resources and energy inputs for products and processes, and the outputs from each stage of the product life cycle.

Chapter 11 focuses on the applications of life cycle management techniques and methods for evaluating impacts and determining improvement strategies. LCA includes an impact assessment that examines the potential consequences of the inputs and outputs on the eco-systems and human health. Techniques also include improvement assessment, risk mitigation, and performance evaluation techniques. Effective performance evaluation provides management with a process for tracking the stated goals and expectations of the improvement process.

Chapter 12 examines the implications and future directions of enterprise thinking and SBD. The overarching goal of building a sustainable enterprise involves creating value streams and environmentally sound processes and practices that are based on the strategic needs of the business and society. Positive linkages with constituents ensure that management approaches are balanced for all involved. The purpose of a business is not just to increase shareholder value; it is to maximize the value derived by every entity. Such approaches provide total satisfaction and sustainable success.

Sustainable technology management and development

Introduction

Strategic technology management, technological innovation, and product development play vital roles in developing solutions to social, economic, environmental and market-related problems and in creating new opportunities. They provide the means and mechanisms to fundamentally change the enterprise in its quest for achieving excellence.

"Technology" is a complex term that includes art, science, engineering, devices, methods, and know-how that are applied in a beneficial manner. It usually takes the form of products and processes (hardware and software) that can be used to create solutions. At the beginning of the twentieth century, technology was typically viewed as the application of science, engineering, and art for developing useful apparatuses with complementary and supporting devices. The automobile is a good example. Automobile technology provided the means to create a self-propelled vehicle based on the internal combustion engine technology that converted chemical fuels into mechanical propulsion. However, the automobile is actually the fusion of many technologies into a useful end-product. The related technical devices used in the automobile met functional requirements: for instance, mechanical brakes, though unrelated to the primary function of vehicular motion, were critical for stopping the automobile.

In the twenty-first century, our view of technology has expanded beyond what is embodied within the products and processes to include the theories, knowledge, concepts, and constructs for creating beneficial outcomes. The Internet is the prime example. The Internet is a multifaceted linking of computers, servers, telecommunications, and software to create networks, information storage and retrieval systems, and protocols that require the cooperation, support, and management of far-flung organizations.

Because people discover, create, produce and improve technology using their knowledge, skills and talents, technology is dynamic. It has to be constructive and positive in order to be useful. As new needs and problems are recognized, new solutions are sought and discovered. Corporations make strategic decisions to invest capital, effort, and time into technology and product developments. Technologies are also occasionally discovered through serendipity when new solutions happen unexpectedly.

Strategic technology management is the management of technological solutions. It involves planning and analysis, formulating and implementing technology strategies, selecting and executing development programs, and evaluating performance and results. It also includes taking advantage of opportunities that become apparent and turning them into competitive advantages and sustainable positions. Due to the rapidity of change and innovation, strategic technology management has shifted from problem solving and managing existing technologies to proactive decision-making focused on improving outcomes, creating clean technologies, and moving toward more ideal solutions.

Technological innovation is a subset of strategic technology management. It is the systematic creation of new-to-the-world technologies that are superior to their predecessors and the improvements of existing technology platforms and portfolios. Technological innovation also occurs when improvements are made to the use and effectiveness of knowledge, or when technological sophistication and organizational learning are advanced. These new developments depend upon understanding the forces of change, managing creativity, developing new technologies and new-to-the-world products, mitigating risks, reducing liabilities, satisfying customers and stakeholders, and earning profits (rewards).

Product innovation involves managing and improving the development processes for creating new products and processes. It involves making evolutionary changes to the products and products lines employing the prevailing technologies and organizational capabilities. It generally includes the initiatives, methods, techniques, and processes for making incremental changes and improvements to existing products and services. Product innovation and related development processes, methods, and techniques are covered in chapter 8.

This chapter examines strategic technology management and its connection to SBD, enterprise thinking, the logic of technological innovation, and the technology development process. The discussion follows a hierarchical flow as strategic management drives first technological innovation and then technology development. It examines following topics:

- *Strategic technology management* Connecting technology management and technological innovation to the SMS.

- *Managing technological change* Managing change and determining technological direction based on social, economic, and environmental considerations.
- *Technological forecasting and assessment* Understanding the opportunities and challenges for technological integration and innovation.
- *Strategies for innovation* Assessing the options and choosing the right approaches for developing new technologies, improving existing ones, and creating new products and processes.
- *Technological innovation* Managing technologies, knowledge, and capabilities and determining the best processes, methods, and practices for effective development programs.

Technological innovation often changes the entire nature of the practices, processes, and relationships in the organization. Such changes are key to creating value and sustainable success. Corporations can and must enhance conventional technology management constructs with new ways of thinking so that they can create a better future around the concept of SBD.

Strategic technology management

Overview

Strategic technology management is an essential part of enterprise thinking and the strategic management of the corporation. It includes managing all of the knowledge, technological capabilities, technologies, technological innovation, and development processes for managing change and creating new technologies, products, and processes. It provides the architecture for integrating and managing knowledge and technologies and for being creative and leading change through technological innovation, product innovation, and the related development processes. Strategic technology management focuses on future needs and capabilities as well as on existing core competencies and capabilities. It embraces change that facilitates stability, growth, and exceptional performance.

Strategic technology management is built on the principles and practices of enterprise thinking and SBD. The leadership and management of the SMS are the critical ingredients of effective strategic technology management. Figure 7.1 depicts a generalized overview that includes the fundamental considerations.

The precepts of SBD can provide the overarching logic for technological and product innovation. While the SBD construct is not prescriptive, it is

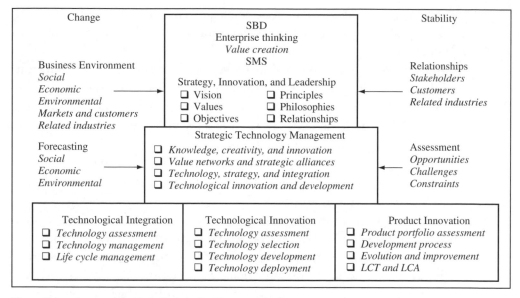

Figure 7.1   An overview of strategic technology management

directive. SBD seeks dramatic improvements to the existing technologies, products, and processes and explores the potential for more radical solutions through new cleaner and more effective technologies and products that eliminate the defects, burdens, and impacts of previous technologies and products. It attempts to move the positive and negative aspects toward the ideal. While the ideal represents perfection, the objective of the quest is the pursuit of perfection.

Strategy technology management involves the ongoing applications and improvements of technologies and products in the commercial world. It seeks to focus the corporation's resources and capabilities on the common goal of enhancing the effectiveness of the enterprise and its relationships. It also focuses on adapting technologies and enhancing their acceptance in the business environment. The primary means of gaining acceptance is through improving the underpinnings of technologies and products and providing improved solutions through the product delivery system and the value networks.

Technology: the cause or the solution?

Technology is the lifeblood of industries and corporations. It is intertwined with the social–economic–environmental structures of nearly all of our human endeavors. While it is possible to discuss specific areas of technological applications such as manufacturing or computer technologies, technology must also be viewed in the broader context of devices, know-how, resources, people, relationships, capabilities, knowledge, learning, and processes and the associated implications, impacts, and their consequences. Technology is a human construct and is highly dependent on imagination, creativity, risk-taking and risk mitigation, and rewards. It is a social construct because it provides the theoretical and practical solutions to maintain the human condition and enhance the quality of life. It is also an economic construct because technology provides the means and mechanisms to create, develop, produce, transport, distribute, use, and dispose of the products and services that generate benefits for users and competitive advantages and wealth for producers. Moreover, technology is an environmental construct with significant positive and negative impacts.

That has been the paradox of technology: it is both the cause of, and the solution to, many of society's ills. Barry Commoner argued in his book, *The Closing Circle*, published in 1972, that technology was the significant contributor to environmental and other social problems.[1] On the other hand, Paul Ehrlich in his 1968 book, *The Population Bomb*, argued that population growth was the main culprit in our destruction of the natural environment.[2] Both authors used the simple formula $I = PAT$ to provide evidence pertaining to their arguments. In the formula, I represents impacts, P is population, A is activities, and T is technology. The equation suggests that relationships are linear and that each contributes directly to impacts. Commoner argued that "the predominant factor in industrial society's increased environmental degradation is neither population [people] nor affluence [more activities], but increasing environmental impact per unit of production due to technological change."[3] Whereas antagonists can provide compelling evidence about technology's contributions to environmental impacts, technology and innovation are also clearly precursors to improvements and a cleaner environment. The $I = PAT$ formula itself demonstrates how technology can enhance solutions.

The automobile provides a simple example. The impacts are the sum of all of the negative outcomes related to the waste streams (T), multiplied by the number of automobiles in use (P) and the total level of activities in terms of miles (km) driven and hours used (A)

$$\Sigma I = T \times PA$$

Improvements can certainly be achieved by reducing the population or the activities. But, from a technology perspective, reduced impacts could also result from new technologies, improvements to existing technologies, and/or improvements for handling the impacts of technologies. Indeed, technology and technological innovation represent potential solutions to existing problems and, for this reason, are central to SBD.

SBD as it relates to technologies and technological innovation provides a strategic, analytical, and rational framework for decision-making. Solutions are derived through comprehensive and reflective thinking, overarching principles, good policies, processes, and practices instead of dogmatic views of what should or should not be. Great care has to be taken to ensure that new solutions are improvements in the long term and do not create more problems than they solve. Jesse H. Ausubel, in his chapter, "Regularities in technological development: an environmental view" in Ausubel and Sladovich's book on *Technology and Environment*, discusses how the railroads of the nineteenth century were consuming wood, especially for cross-ties which decayed within a few years of use, at such an alarming rate that many feared that the destruction of the forests could not be prevented.[4] Chemically treating the wood with creosote became one of the saving technologies for the railways during the late nineteenth and early twentieth centuries. However, the solution itself became a significant environmental problem during the latter half of the twentieth century. The solution (creosote) begot a new problem. Creosote is a toxic substance containing phenols and creosols; the former is classified as human poison although there is a lack of solid carcinogenic evidence, and the latter is suspected of causing damage to kidneys and the liver. Moreover, it is also important to recognize that the simple solution of using wood for the cross-ties involved renewable resources – wood products and forests. The presumption that the solution of employing renewable resources is also better than using nonrenewable ones has to be tested in the real world as well. It may be a good short-term solution but it may not be sustainable if resource depletion is excessive and the destruction of natural resources are threatened. A great technological solution today, even one grounded in renewable resources, may become an environmental crisis in the future.

Ausubel also makes a comparison between horses and automobiles in terms of the solid and liquid wastes from the horses versus the gaseous emissions from automobiles. The mass of waste streams from a horse per mile is approximately 175 times greater than that from automobiles.[5] While the example is hypothetical, and it would be impossible to use horses in the way and manner that cars are used, Ausubel's calculations provide excellent insights about the implications of technology in the SBD and LCT context. The question is not which solution is better from a philosophical perspective but what information and evidence is required to properly determine the implications and impacts of alternatives and make the best choice possible for both the short and the long term. Sustainable solutions, though they seek to address future needs, must also be developed in the context of the current business environment. Technologies must accommodate the situation.

Stability, change, and the technology portfolio

Technologies are intellectual assets. They are important building blocks for the strategic positioning of corporations and the foundation upon which products and processes are built. Strategic technology management encompasses the management constructs and practices for integrating technologies with enterprise management and strategic direction. Strategic technology management focuses on both stability and change.

Stability relates to obtaining results in the present and the near term and sustaining performance over the long term. The corporation must satisfy customers, stakeholders, and other constituents on an ongoing basis to ensure that success is not transient: it is pointless to make huge gains if they are followed by big losses. Stability involves balancing short-term and long-term outcomes to achieve sustainable success. If the rate of change is so aggressive that technologies change very quickly, then the investments required to create the technologies are not rewarded with sufficient return; the processes become unsustainable. Still, stability does not mean maintaining the status quo. It means that new technologies or technological improvements have life cycles that are sufficient to warrant the investment of time, effort, and money needed. While learning and knowledge are often the long-term reward, the situation has to have balanced social, economic, and environmental outcomes.

Change is the other important part of strategic technology management. Change focuses on improving the near term and inventing new solutions for a dramatically improved future. Change is inherent in every system. It is the rate of change and the benefits derived in the present and the future that provide the ability to exceed expectations, avoid obsolescence, and become sustainable. New technologies are created to solve existing difficulties, meet new needs, overcome limitations, and explore and exploit opportunities. They must produce positive results in the aggregate.

The technology portfolio embodies the knowledge of the organization, the capabilities of its people, and its technological assets. Many corporations focus on the technologies themselves to capitalize on market opportunities.

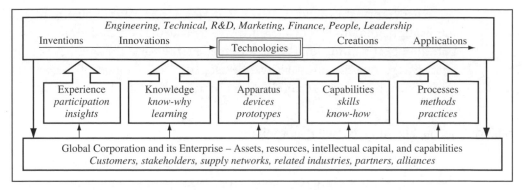

Figure 7.2   The technology portfolio of intellectual capital and property

While this view is pragmatic, it is narrow. The technology portfolio actually also encompasses the knowledge, experience, capabilities, and processes of the whole enterprise as well as that of the corporation. It also includes the contributions of supply networks, customers, stakeholders, related industries, and technology partners who contribute intellectual capacity and technology resources. Such enterprise thinking is complicated because it comprises the embedded knowledge, the evolutionary learning processes, the achievements, and the technological resources of the entire enterprise. The technology portfolio also expands over time, as new knowledge and experiences add to capabilities and technologies.

The technology portfolio may have a starting point for entrepreneurial organizations, but for well-established global corporations, the process of developing the technology portfolio is simply a spiraling effect of constant improvements that hopefully continues forever. Figure 7.2 is a simplified representation of the linkages and implications in the technology portfolio. While the model appears to be static, it is one of the most dynamic flows in the enterprise. New knowledge is always being discovered, experiences expanded, and capabilities enhanced, all of which advance the business' apparatuses and devices (the prototypes or initial product forms using a new technology that indicate its viability/commercial benefits/reliability). Knowledge may be the essential ingredient for sustainable success. The acquisition and application of knowledge reveal the opportunities for change.

However, as technologies change, the value of experience changes as well (see chapter 6). In some situations, the experience factor diminishes as new technologies become dominant and previous experience becomes irrelevant. Capabilities are determined by experience, knowledge, and learning, and they are always in flux as new knowledge is gained through experience, external sources, and participation in development programs. Technologies are often manifested in the form of hardware and software. In those cases where patents are sought, an apparatus has to be developed and validated through prototyping to prove the commercial viability of the innovation.

Technological capabilities are the means for integrating the requirements of productive outcomes. The technology portfolio is similar in structure to the product portfolio. It represents the core capabilities of the corporation and defines what will be the basis for its strategic focus. The processes used to develop new technologies are as essential to success as are the invention and innovations themselves. Sustainable success is achieved through the integration of the internal functions and resources of the organization with the assets, resources, intellectual capital, and capabilities of all of the enterprise's participants. The alignment of technological capabilities and strategic direction is essential for sustainable success.

Categories of technologies

Technologies are not all equal. They can be ranked in a hierarchical structure starting with base technologies that are essential commodities with well-known advantages and disadvantages to new-to-the-world technologies that are not completely proven and that possess potential positive benefits and negative impacts that are not fully known. Arthur D. Little, Inc., a technology-based consulting firm in Cambridge, MA, categorized technologies according to their competitive implications.[6] Table 7.1 provides an overview of the standard construct. While there are other, similar and newer approaches, the "A. D. Little, Inc." construct still provides a good relative distinction between the categories.

Most technologies are relatively old and exist in the public domain. Anyone who wants to use such technologies can do so without charge or difficulty because the information and know-how is readily available. This bottom tier in the hierarchy is the *base or basic* technologies. They have few consequences on the competitive situation and, if they have significant negative impacts, can be replaced with new solutions. Assessing base technologies and improving their weaknesses offers opportunities to turn disadvantages into competitive strengths. Improving the negative aspects of base technologies is often an unrecognized opportunity that may provide competitive advantages even in commodity-type situations. For example, Reynolds Metals created an enormous business opportunity through its aluminum recycling technology and infrastructure. It found new opportunity from the disposal problems associated with used beverage containers (see box 1.1).

Table 7.1. Categories of technologies[a]

Descriptor technology	Impact or relative sense of importance	Comments about the category and its broader impacts
Emerging *Highest tier*	Technologies that have not demonstrated the potential to change the basis for competition They often have outstanding attributes	Emerging technologies are the future technologies that can potentially change the nature of competition and the business environment
Pacing (leading edge) *Strategic tier*	Technologies that have the potential to change the entire basis of competition, but have not yet been embodied in a product or process These technologies often develop into key technologies of the future	Pacing technologies have generally demonstrated the ability to change the basis for competition and provide the developer a competitive advantage They have superior attributes that facilitate change
Key (core) *Operating tier*	Technologies that are the most critical to competitive success because they offer the opportunity for meaningful process or product differentiation These technologies yield competitive advantage	Key technologies are the proprietary technologies that form the basis for differentiation and core capabilities Often the crux of the technologies is patented and provides strengths that are difficult to duplicate
Base (basic) *Bottom tier*	Technologies that although necessary and essential to practice offer little potential for competitive advantage These technologies are typically widespread and shared	Base technologies are the *commodities* that are embedded in products and processes They are widely available, offer little distinction, and are not the source of value and wealth

Note: [a] Russel *et al.* (1991), p. 64.

The second tier of *key or core* technologies is more difficult to discern because they typically provide the foundations for the prevailing products and processes. While the argument for changing these technologies is more complicated, assessments of social, economic, and environmental impacts can provide an understanding of their "fit" in the value proposition and the need for change. Eliminating the negative impacts of core technologies can improve existing products and make them more sustainable in the marketplace.

Pacing or leading edge technologies are those that require significant investments of time and money before generating a competitive advantage. They are often difficult to change if they have already been commercialized. Defects and burdens should therefore be discovered and cured before commercialization. Using LCA may facilitate this kind of enhancement during development, when it is usually more cost effective.

Emerging technologies are the hope of the future. They represent the future direction of the corporation. For instance, renewable energy from photovoltaic technologies may provide solutions to the high costs and carbon dioxide emissions of petroleum-based generation of electricity (see box 2.4). While the new technology is still in its infancy, the promise for the future looks bright. Siemens AG is now producing photovoltaic energy systems in the 7–10 MW range. The higher-tier technologies have the potential to provide sustainable competitive advantages when they are fully developed and proven. It is important to realize that not all emerging and pacing technologies become successful, because a hidden defect may cause their premature decline or elimination. The story of Vioxx in chapter 3 highlights such concerns.

The importance of existing technologies decreases as the higher-tier technologies with great potential for generating value move the old technologies toward the bottom tier, the base technologies. Most existing technologies are destined to become commodities, just as the higher-value technologies embedded in PCs and microprocessors quickly become basic commodities and eventually become obsolete. It is just a matter of time. This is true for most technologies. The business environment evolves, and new technologies replace the old. In many industries, the emergence of completely different ways of fulfilling customer needs and wants has actually caused the collapse of the previous technologies. For example, the PC played a significant role in the demise of the typewriter. The CD-ROM replaced the vinyl discs for recorded music and floppy discs for data storage. Moreover, the corporation itself may become obsolete because of new technologies: think about what digital cameras have done to the fortunes of Polaroid and Kodak.

Toyota's technology development provides an excellent example of these categories of technologies. Using fuel cells for power instead of the internal combustion engine technology is Toyota's emerging technology. The hybrid engine, which combines the internal combustion engine with an electric motor, is the pacing technology in its Prius automobile. Its lean-burn internal combustion engine is its key technology, currently providing Toyota with a competitive advantage in the marketplace and an environmental improvement over previous designs.

Technology life cycle

The technology life cycle is a time-based theory of technological change that uses the "S" curve to depict the development and growth of a technology. The

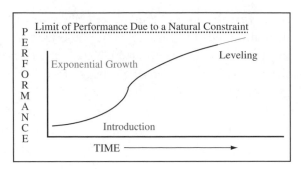

Figure 7.3   A generalized life cycle of technological change

concept is based on biological life cycles, which include early development, rapid growth, maturity, and decline over the life of an organism. The "S" curve generalization describes the growth of a technology with slow growth during the early stage due to a number of mitigating factors (lack of awareness or acceptance) followed by exponential growth during mid-life, reaching an asymptote during maturity, and declining as newer technologies become available in the future. The logistic is given by the equation

$$y = e^{ax}/(1 + e^{ax}/b)$$

with a and $b > 0$ and has the value of b as $x \to \infty$. The "S" curve life cycle of technological change is depicted in figure 7.3.

The introduction of a new technology usually requires a significant investment to overcome the natural concerns about change and the uncertainties inherent in new technologies. People need time to become aware of the innovative technology, to understand the implications and benefits, and accept it as a possible solution for the future. Moreover, they need time to learn how to use the technology and to acquire the support structures to obtain its full benefits. Weaknesses often limit the advantages of the technology and, in certain cases, the first generation of a new technology may actually be inferior to existing technologies. The corporation (innovator) may then improve the new technology to overcome its disadvantages or weaknesses. Likewise, competitors may improve the existing technologies to emulate the advantages of the new technology. In the long term, the technology with superior attributes and characteristics often prevails. Ultimately, if the new technology has extraordinary advantages it may replace the prevailing technologies.

The history of the steel-belted radial tire is a good example. When Michelin introduced its radically designed tire in the United States in the early 1970s, its progress was slow because it did not have adequate promotion mechanisms and distribution channels. Customer acceptance was hindered by a poor infrastructure and lack of awareness. Fortunately, Michelin had large resources and was able to form a supply alliance with Sears, America's largest retailer at the time, and overcame its structural weaknesses to gain market share. Goodyear and Firestone, the largest US tire manufacturers during the 1970s produced conventional bias tires, which were relatively poor in "wearability." While US competitors researched steel-belted radial tire technology, their immediate response was to improve their conventional tire technology. They did achieve some success, but ultimately they could not match the superior performance of the steel-belted radial tire technology. They were forced to convert to the new technology.

Technology reaches a rapid growth phase after critical mass has been obtained, markets, customers, and stakeholders have accepted the advantages, and the producers and providers have mitigated many of the disadvantages, such as high costs and the typical startup problems. The causes and effects of the growth phenomenon are complex, and vary considerably from case to case. Improving cost structure and reducing prices of products and services are among the primary reasons for rapid growth. The availability of related products and services and the expansion of infrastructure are also significant contributors to growth and success. The early years of video cassette recorder (VCR) technology, for instance, were fraught with high prices, for both VCRs and the blank tapes. Moreover, the lack of video rental establishments and the limited choices of movies on the format made owning such technology expensive and marginal in terms of benefits. Digital cameras suffered the same problems during the early 1990s. They were expensive and had poor resolution in comparison to film-based photography. However, they did exhibit many positive attributes, including instantaneous results, connectivity with PCs, and superior environmental performance. As digital cameras improved with each new generation, the price differences dissipated and the quality of the pictures improved dramatically. Digital cameras now significantly outsell conventional cameras.

Eventually, all technologies reach maturity as growth slows, markets become saturated, and demand reaches a plateau. There are many reasons why potential starts leveling out. The most important explanation is that it has reached a natural limit: the technology becomes constrained due to physical laws or structural barriers that cannot be exceeded beyond a certain point. For instance, the speed of a microprocessor cannot exceed the speed of light. In other cases, the limitation may be the inability to manage waste streams or the availability of resources. Fossil fuel power plant technology is limited not only by the availability of low-sulfur bituminous coal but also by the emissions produced – specifically, the regulations imposed and the diminishing capacity of the environment to tolerate the impacts.

The "S" curve is a tool for understanding the relationship of time and space with respect to technological phenomena. It is imperfect and provides only a relative sense of position and potential. It provides a pattern that most technologies follow, but it does not foretell what will happen to any given technology. It does not predict premature failures, the length of time required for reaching the growth stage, or how long any stage will last.

While a single technology may follow the "S" curve, a family of technologies evolves over time as the older generation becomes obsolete and is replaced by a new generation. The more frequently generations change, the more critical technological innovation becomes. *Technological innovation* is the primary means for sustaining growth when the technology life cycle is short. Conventional thinking implies that "short" means less than five years. Intel and its microprocessor technologies change generations in less than two years. Intel focuses on creating the next generation of its Pentium and related technologies; each generation represents a significant commitment of time and money to achieve at least a 200 percent improvement in the technology.

Product innovation is the primary means for making improvements if the underlying technologies change less frequently, say every ten or more years. The automobile is the historic example. Most innovations in the automobile industry are incremental changes to prevailing technologies. The internal combustion engine technology has ruled supreme for more than a century.

Figure 7.4 provides a simple graphic depiction of technoloical evolution. The automobile industry is characterized by slow change; consumer electronics exhibit rapid change.

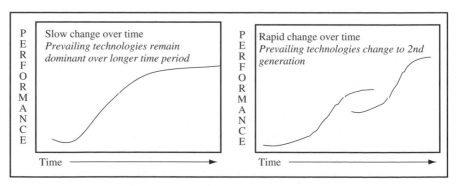

Figure 7.4   Technological evolution: slow change versus rapid change

The evolution of technologies presents enormous implications for SBD. For long-life-cycle technologies, SBD considerations are more complex since the opportunities for change are less frequent and the implications of design decisions are long-lived. In cases of slow technological change, SBD can be embedded in the change process with continuous improvements being built into the sequence so that it continues moving on the quest for perfection. Conversely, the more rapid the change process the less likely it is worth investing in the structural fabric of the existing technology to make it long-lasting. In such cases, technological innovation is often the answer. If the underlying technologies are on the decline, then it pays to develop new technologies as replacements.

Types of development programs

A look at the types of development programs provides a critical understanding of how technologies change through corporate investments over time. Generally, new-to-the-world technologies that are developed within the corporate structure are a result of R&D or related programs. The outcomes of such programs are often radical breakthroughs that establish viable new technologies, usually the first of their type and having significant weaknesses. However, these new technologies typically have one or more attributes that outperform the existing technologies and offer great promise for the future.

Figure 7.5 depicts a framework for the types of development projects articulated by Steven Wheelwright and Kim Clark during the early 1990s.[7] It remains one of the most important constructs for examining technological development and related product and process changes. The concept of a *platform* is pivotal in understanding how technologies are shared across technology portfolios and product lines.

The *research and advanced development project* (type 1) involves new-to-the-world technologies that are based on inventions that may lead to radical technological innovations. This type includes stand-alone projects that produce complex technologies such as the space shuttle and the F117 stealth fighter. *Radical breakthroughs* (type 2) create new technologies that provide the basis for new core products and processes. Breakthrough technologies are relatively rare and may form the basis of a new "S" curve. The new technology may create a new business venture, or even a new industry sector. It may rival the existing technologies and force them to change and, in some cases, it replaces the prevailing technologies completely. The cellular telephone technology is a good example of this kind of breakthrough. Originally, the technology was

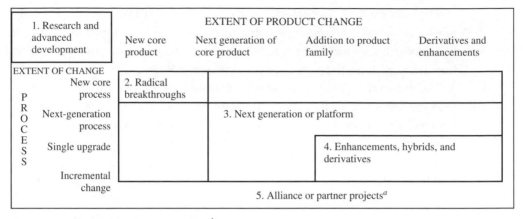

Figure 7.5   Types of development projects[b]

Notes:
[a] The four primary types of projects (programs 1–4) differ in the degree of change they require in product and process technology. Type 5. alliance or partnered, involves joint work with another organization. While any of the four types could be partnered, partnering occurs most often with those projects involving substantial change, not with incremental or enhancement projects.
[b] Wheelwright and Clark (1993), p. 93.

expensive and limited in scope and capacity. It offered mobility and flexibility that wire-based telephone systems could not provide. However, as later generations of the technology were improved and the technology became more cost effective, it started to compete head-on with the conventional systems. As new technology improves, old technology often loses its ability to compete in the marketplace. The new becomes the dominant technology, and the old withers away. In Finland, 80 percent of all telephone devices use wireless technologies. Their users are moving toward 3rd-generation technology.

The *next generation or platform* (type 3) project seeks to improve the prevailing technology by eliminating weaknesses and enhancing advantages. It produces the new platform that provides the technological underpinnings for a family of products. The automobile industry typically produces multiple models from one platform. The Toyota Camry and Lexus ES have the same platform, for example. The next generation type is best typified by the Intel's Pentium line. Each new Pentium is a new generation in terms of technology.

Most changes and new products and processes, however, are *enhancements, hybrids, and derivatives* (type 4) of existing products. These changes are incremental improvements rather than radical innovations. Most new products and processes fit into this category. They are related to the existing products except for incremental improvements and share the same underlying technologies.

Wheelwright and Clark's framework is an important construct for SBD programs. Radical new technologies are not only rare, but are usually difficult to develop due to the complexities involved in revamping the business environment, the supply networks, related industries, and infrastructure. For instance, the radical innovations associated with the conversion of automobiles to fuel-cell technology are incredibly complex. Assuming that the new technologies will use hydrogen-based fuel, the technology developments include the power cells, the interfaces, and the hydrogen infrastructure, among many other complementary and supporting technologies. Incremental improvement programs are less complex and present a wider range of opportunities for change and improvement while maintaining stability within the system. However, in order to achieve dramatic improvements and outperform competitors, a corporation has to consider radical changes as well. The right approach is generally a combined one.

A generalized construct for managing technological change

Determining strategic actions based on driving forces

One of the most profound questions pertaining to SBD is how to select the strategic actions for managing technological change. Given that technological change is an *a priori* requirement for proactively meeting the expectations of the business environment, corporations have to identify the best strategies for advancing technological changes to achieve superior performance. Their choices are critical for long-term success. If significant technological change is needed and the corporation responds with incremental improvements, it will likely meet with suboptimal results. Even if the corporation achieves its own targets for improvements, it may nonetheless fail in the context of the global business environment because such minor improvements were insufficient to meet the changing environment. For example, if society is demanding the elimination of hazardous substances such as heavy metals and bromine flame retardants in response to new EU Directives, and the corporation's response is a planned reduction in using such materials by 10 percent per year, or whatever, the organization's objective may not be sufficient to meet the mandates or the expectation of stakeholders and other constituencies.

Conversely, radical change may not be sustainable if the business environment is not prepared for the change processes and the innovations are disruptive to social, economic, and environmental conditions. For example, the complete elimination of petroleum products (nonrenewable resources) would create chaos since most automobiles, trucks, airplanes, diesel locomotives, ships, and other types of vehicles using petroleum-based fuels would become useless. Moreover, it would be impossible to convert the applications of those vehicles to some other approach in a short time-frame. This action would lead to instability and a deteriorated business environment.

The theories, principles, processes, and practices of SBD suggest that the general flow of inventions, innovations, creations, and applications is toward more sustainable outcomes with cleaner technologies, products, and processes that are more efficient, effective, productive, and economically and environmentally viable. While this statement has not been proven, the evolution of businesses, technologies, products, and processes clearly indicates a pattern of improvements and increasingly sustainable outcomes.

SBD is based on the precepts of exceeding the expectations of the business environment and creating superior value and outcomes for everyone. It is driven by future requirements and needs as well as by the existing opportunities, challenges, and constraints. SBD is a natural fit for world-class corporations that wish to lead change and be proactive in creating a better world for all humankind. The central challenge of SBD leaders is to determine how aggressive the corporation should be in moving to its envisioned future. Both change and stability have to be integrated into the solution matrix, however.

In his chapter on the aggressiveness of a firm's innovation strategy, in his book on *Implementing Strategic Management*, H. Igor Ansoff discusses five levels of change in the business environment.[8] Ansoff characterized these levels as stable, reactive, anticipatory, exploring, and creative. The construct used in this book is similar to Ansoff's, with the exceptions that his definition of "stable" implies maintaining the status quo, which is not feasible in a dynamic business environment, and his "reactive" level is outside the realm of SBD since it involves taking proactive actions to preclude problems or to solve difficulties as rapidly as possible.

Rather, the approaches for managing change within the context of a global corporation using SBD can be viewed as preemptive, innovative, or creative. This construct takes a relative, rather than absolute, view of conditions, trends, and needs. The meaning of each category varies according to the particular industry and the forces driving change within that industry. Global corporations often have only a relative sense of the dynamics of their industry and of the social, economic, and environmental implications for it. It is difficult to achieve an absolute sense of the change mechanisms.

The following are three generic SBD technology-related response strategies:

- *Preemptive* Being responsive to the needs and wants of customers and stakeholders before the external forces mandate changes. "Preemptive" means improving at rates that exceed the prevailing expectations by a factor of two or more. For example, if peers and competitors are improving at 5 percent per year, then preemptive means improving at 10 percent or more per year. Preemptive strategies and programs are based on improving existing technologies and products. They work best when the social, economic, political, and environmental underpinnings are well understood and relatively stable, and when the industry structure and constituencies are known (Toyota's lean-burn internal combustion engine technology is an example).

- *Innovative* Discovering the wants and needs and the underlying causes of change before they become apparent to mainstream communities and taking aggressive actions to eliminate the causes of difficulties; eliminating impacts and the negative consequences of the technologies and products. Innovative solutions make quantum improvements with respect to impacts and implications. The social, economic, political, and environmental underpinnings of these changes are more difficult to predict and understand because they create major changes in the business environment. Innovative solutions are those that attack the root causes of problems and initiate actions that resolve them (Toyota's hybrid technology is an example).

- *Creative* Inventing radical new solutions that require expanding the reach of the enterprise. Creative solutions require inventing new systems for meeting the expectations of customers and stakeholders. They eliminate impacts and create a new reality. The social, economic, political, and environmental underpinnings of the business environment are changed profoundly, and old concerns evaporate as new, unpredictable patterns of behaviors develop (fuel-cell powered automobiles are an example).

The preemptive strategies are similar to Ansoff's anticipatory level, except that they imply a more comprehensive awareness of the business environment. They require taking actions to make significant improvements before others do. Innovative strategies are those that put a corporation on the leading edge of technological innovation through the development of new products and processes that significantly change the underlying issues. Creative strategies involve creating a whole new solution for meeting the needs of the business environment. They eliminate concerns and impacts by

Table 7.2. Strategic actions and the most appropriate management constructs for leading change

Level strategic action	Product delivery system	SMS	Corporate management	Change
Preemptive	**Product/process innovation**	Derivatives of existing technologies	Business integration and leading change	*Evolutionary*
Innovative	New technology generation	**Technological innovation**	Radical innovation	*Quantum*
Creative	Breakthrough technologies	New-to-the-world technology development	**New reality**	*Radical*

developing new-to-the-world technologies and overcoming the constraints that formerly limited the solutions.

These types of changes are relative constructs. They provide a sense of how significant the change mechanisms should be. Solutions vary from incremental improvements of existing products and processes to radical changes that create a new reality. SBD implies that even for incremental changes the level of improvement has to be at least better than the prevailing rate of improvements in the industry. Simply reacting to changes or defending the status quo are both inconsistent with SBD and are not considered acceptable options. The business environment demands improvement. The variable is how much improvement, and how quickly.

Table 7.2 suggests appropriate strategic actions based on the change mechanisms required by the business environment, or those that strategic management deems appropriate for the conditions and trends. Preemptive moves are basically evolutionary innovations to improve the technology portfolio and product lines of the enterprise. Innovative strategies are more aggressive approaches for leading change that focus on eliminating the underlying causes of impacts. Creative strategies replace existing technologies, products, and processes with a new reality.

The strategic actions identified within the matrix are suggested initiatives that generally fit the required levels of technological change. The actual constructs should be determined based on a full analysis of the business environment and the capabilities of the organization. While the basic construct suggests a potential solution pathway, the actual journey depends on the long-term implications of the forces driving the change.

Figure 7.6 provides a graphic view of the strategies, and the distinctions between them. While there is not always a direct link between strategic actions and the resultant changes, it is generally accepted that strategic

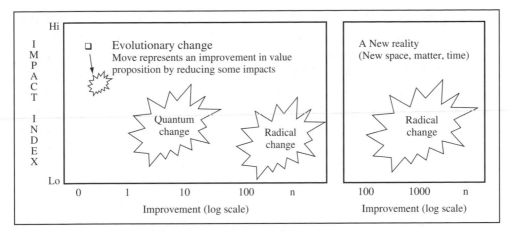

Figure 7.6   A graphic view of evolutionary, quantum, and radical change

actions result in changes. Preemptive actions typically lead to evolutionary changes to outperform peers and competitors, but are still within the prevailing strategic context of the enterprise and its business environment. Innovative actions lead to quantum leaps that often stagger the imagination. Such actions often have significant effects on the industry and its supporting structures. They are profoundly affected and are unable to maintain a viable position in the industry unless they follow suit. Creative actions induce radical change and initiate new enterprise perspectives for the corporation. The new construct may coexist with the old until the transformation process is complete.

Preemptive strategic actions

Since preemptive actions are intended to gain a competitive advantage by significantly improving products and processes, such actions are generally an extension of the corporate programs for technology improvement, product innovation, pollution prevention, stewardship, compliance, and beyond. The focus is primarily on the product delivery system and its portfolio of products and services. Preemptive actions cause corporations to examine their technology platforms and explore opportunities for improvements and strategic advantage. The intent is to create derivatives and enhancements that are superior to the existing portfolios of technologies and products but which still use the underlying technologies, resources, capabilities, and assets of the corporation. From a corporate management perspective, the focus is on business integration and leading change.

Preemptive strategic actions provide an orderly transition from the pre-sustainable world of the twentieth century to the expectations and dreams of twenty-first-century life. The main advantage of preemptive strategic actions is that they provide stability in terms of strategic position and resource utilization since the corporation has time to convert its strategic advantages and assets to more powerful opportunities without risking near-term object-ives. The pathway to the future can take more of an "emergent" pattern, allowing for appropriate adjustments along the way.[9] Other advantages include facilitating implementation and acceptance from the business envir-onment, and the full integration of the business model. Preemptive strategic actions concentrate on improving existing positions in a systematic way that provides continuity over time. While the intent is to make dramatic improve-ments affecting the underlying opportunities, difficulties, and challenges, the desire is to avoid disruptive (unstable) changes to the enterprise. Preemptive strategies appreciate that long-term objectives can be achieved through progressive improvements that stretch goals and accomplishments.

The main disadvantage of preemptive strategies is that they continue the pattern of investing in existing technologies and products that may become obsolete or lack the potential for significant improvements. Allocating resources and building assets that have a marginal remaining life cycle to such areas may be a waste of time, money, and effort. Preemptive strategies also have limited potential for gaining a significant competitive advantage. It can also be difficult to determine the required level of improvements and to control all of the implications of the changes. The direction for achieving the objectives is never precise. Table 7.3 depicts the salient points when using the preemptive approach.

Preemptive strategic actions are often difficult for others to emulate because they are tangible and based on real improvements to technologies, products, and processes. It often takes considerable time to develop improved technologies, products, and processes, although the benefits are enduring. The effects can be even more beneficial if the actions are sustained over long periods. When compounded over many years, preemptive actions have the potential to create insurmountable leads and superior positions.

In a simplified sense, the focus of preemptive action is on the value proposition. Improving the benefits of products, reducing the defects and burdens, and other enhancements to the value proposition are the basis for achieving success. The intent is to improve as many of the elements of the value equation as possible, focusing on the most achievable elements first. However, while preemptive moves appear to be a variation of incremental

Table 7.3. Preemptive strategic actions at three management systems levels

Level *Preemptive*	Product delivery system	SBU	Enterprise management	Essential factors
Focus	**Product/process innovation**	**Derivatives of existing technologies**	**Business integration and leading change**	Evolutionary change
Strategic actions	Enhanced portfolio of products and processes	Improved core technologies and improved image	Increases corporate wealth and reputation	*Enterprise thinking*
Space (prime real estate)	Superior product positions with better competitive advantages	Global technological leadership	Synthesis of relationships	*Holistic thinking*
Time frame to obtain results	Near term ($\geq$3 years)	Immediate term (3–5 years)	Long term (+5 years)	*Strategic thinking*
Organizational	Enhanced capabilities Rapid learning	Strategic leadership Integrated systems	New knowledge Linkages with networks	*Systems thinking*
Market perspective	Improved value proposition Quality/reliability	Improved life cycles Continuous improvements	Value networks Better resources utilization	*Solutions thinking*
Social	Reduced defects and burdens Enhanced Benefits	Social and economic links and reduced consequences	Equity and value Transparency	*Triple bottom line thinking*
Economic	Reduced defects Improved cost structure	Longevity Competitive advantages	Eco-effectiveness Stability	*Value creation thinking*
Environmental	Less degradation Less depletion	Less destruction Less disruption	Reduced impacts Improved footprint	*LCT*

innovation, there is a profound difference in intent. Preemptive strategic actions solve problems, eliminate defects, and reduce burdens by using a comprehensive set of social, economic, environmental, and business metrics that foster development programs and initiatives to create competitive advantages. Preemptive actions also expand the scope of product development from the domain of product designers, R&D personnel, and marketing professionals to environmental professionals and all of the relationships of the enterprise.

From the product delivery perspective, preemptive strategic actions examine the strengths and weaknesses of product lines and concentrate on making dramatic improvements to the product portfolios and the positions they occupy. The potential initiatives include enhancing quality and reliability, improving the cost structures and overall benefits, and reducing environmental degradation and resource depletion. The time horizon is relatively short, typically less than three years for most initiatives. The task is to identify challenges and turn them into opportunities.

From an SBU perspective, the focus is on discovering technology derivatives that have improved characteristics with respect to market, social, economic, and environmental expectations. The goal is to create value for customers and stakeholders above that of the competition, thereby enhancing strategic position and reputation. Technologically, the goal is to obtain leadership and preeminence. Most initiatives are intermediate-term (three–five years) and focus on leadership and systems integration. The potential initiatives include improving life cycles, enhancing social and economic linkages, reducing negative impacts, and eliminating destruction and disruptions.

Corporate actions focus on business integration and leading change, linking strategic partners and internal resources into a holistic system that outperforms all other choices. The enterprise perspective links all business units and strategic alliances technologically. It builds relationships that create knowledge and capabilities for the future. Most initiatives are long-term (+five years). The potential initiatives include creating new knowledge and capabilities, enhancing equity and transparency, improving eco-effectiveness and stability, and improving the overall footprint of the enterprise.

The discussions on design for the environment (sustainability) in chapter 8 provide details and examples that are based on preemptive change. Preemptive strategic actions employ advanced new product development processes that are balanced and exceed the expectations of society, markets, and stakeholder groups.

Innovative strategic actions

Innovative strategic actions are based on technological innovation and creating new technologies that eliminate the deficiencies of the previous versions. The intent is to discover the means and mechanisms to improve the positive side of the value equation and minimize the negative side. Innovative effects are achieved through a combination of improving the performance of the existing products and processes and introducing new technologies. Improvements to the PC during the 1990s are a good example. Improved

Table 7.4. Innovative strategic actions at three management systems levels

Level *Innovative*	Product delivery system	SMS	Corporate management	Essential factors
Focus	New technology generations	**Technological innovation**	Radical innovation	**Quantum change**
Strategic actions	New technological solutions	Building the support structure	Leading change across the enterprise	*Technological thinking*
Space (prime real estate)	Superior technological positions	Global technological leadership	Synthesis of enterprise	*Network thinking*
Time frame to achieve results	Near term (≥ 7 years)	Immediate term (7–15 Years)	Long term (+15 years)	*Long-term thinking*
Organizational	New capabilities New knowledge	New learning New structure	New leadership New systems	*Paradigm thinking*
Market perspective	New value proposition	New networks	New business model	*Full value thinking*
	New customers/ markets	New partners/ allies	Enhanced integration	
Social	Eliminate defects/ burdens	Eliminate consequences	New value creation	*Beyond bottom line thinking*
	New reality	Full balance	Full transparency	
Economic	Eliminate negatives	Longevity	Stability and change	*Ideal solution thinking*
	Lower cost structure	Competitive advantage	Full effectiveness	
Environmental	Eliminate degradation	Eliminate destruction	Eliminate impacts	*Cradle-to-grave thinking*
	Eliminate depletion	Eliminate disruption	Eliminate footprint	

technologies have made PCs much more powerful and significantly less expensive.

Innovative strategic actions do not simply rely on improving the products and processes, however. They are driven by technological innovations across the enterprise and across time. They involve developing improved or new technologies that have superior attributes, including ones that reduce or eliminate negative impacts. Corporate leadership plays a significant role in determining what direction the selection process takes. It may even dictate the solution set and outline the process for achieving the desired end. Table 7.4 depicts the salient aspects of innovative strategic actions.

Technology development is crucial for discovering breakthrough technologies leading to new-to-the-world products and applications. In terms of product delivery, the key is to achieve superior technological positions. Given a high degree of uncertainty, there are often vulnerabilities to both existing positions and new ones. With significant changes in the business environment, products may become obsolete, rendering resources, assets, and capabilities worthless. Discovering the right opportunities for investment is essential to future success.

The key product delivery level task is to select the right technologies and positions for the future. This depends upon the ability to analyze current and future business conditions and trends and identify the most appropriate selections. Most initiatives are near-term, requiring less than seven years. They typically seek to create new capabilities, new knowledge, new value propositions, and new markets that are superior to the old ones. From a market perspective, the objective is to enhance the value proposition and reach out to new customers and markets. Moreover, the intent is to advance technology in ways that will eliminate social, economic, and environmental weaknesses.

From the strategic business perspective, it is essential to lead change through technological innovation and build complementary support structures for the new technologies. The objective is to establish global technological leadership through innovative technologies. Most initiatives to this end are seven–fifteen years in duration. They launch new learning and new ways to eliminate negatives. The primary market drivers are the desire to build improved value networks through partnerships. The social and environmental imperatives include eliminating any negative consequences of the technologies.

The enterprise perspective focuses on managing technology innovation across the entire enterprise with the aim of creating new business models and practices. To some extent, this level is the most difficult because the solution is less tangible. The most significant challenge is to both encourage change and instill stability. To succeed requires full transparency, new value creation, and the elimination of impacts and their consequences. Corporate leadership has to guide and inspire the organization and its networks to dedicate themselves to change that may take more than a generation to complete.

Creative strategic actions

Creative strategic actions are the most radical and difficult to articulate. They involve starting or creating whole new business approaches, reinventing the whole business model or a significant part of it, or creating new

Table 7.5. Creative strategic actions at three management systems levels

Level *Creative*	Product delivery system	SMS	Corporate management	Essential factors
Focus	Breakthrough technologies	New-to-the-world technology development	**New reality**	**Radical change**
Strategic actions	Radical technologies	New dimensions	New business venture	*Innovative thinking*
Space (prime real estate)	Superior positions Sustainable advantages	New value networks	Global business leadership	*Global thinking*
Time frame to obtain results	Long term ($\geq$10 years)	Long term (10–20 years)	Long term (+20 years)	*Long-term thinking*
Organizational	Exceptional capabilities Rapid learning	New knowledge Linkages with networks	Total leadership Integrated systems	*Paradigm thinking*
Market perspective	Best value proposition Total customer satisfaction	Improved life cycles Total networked Sustainable marketing	New business model Total solution	*Solutions thinking*
Social	Best value Total stakeholder satisfaction	Zero difficulties	Equity and value Full transparency	*Beyond bottom line thinking*
Economic	Zero defects Exceptional value	Superior life cycles	Stability with change Sustainable solutions	*Ideality thinking*
Environmental	Zero burdens	Zero problems	Zero impacts Zero consequences	*Sustainability thinking*

opportunities. Table 7.5 depicts the salient aspects of creative strategic actions. The most important perspective is their intent to create a new reality without the problems of the past. They demand strategic thinking about how to invent a future that is balanced and moving toward ideal solutions. Radical innovations are the precursors to establishing business models and constructs that eliminate most of the negative impacts across the social, economic, and environmental landscapes. The time horizon for such changes is expected to be greater than twenty years.

The product delivery systems, business units, and corporate management will be fully integrated with the business environment and ensure that solutions provide the greatest value possible with the least degradation, depletion, disruption, and destruction. While it is difficult to map out the expected development over twenty years, the objectives can be specified and the pathways to the future can be determined using SBD principles.

Creative strategic action is impossible to fully define because there are limited examples of corporations who have been able to create new businesses or operations with zero defects and burdens. The quest to develop zero-emission vehicles is an example of creative strategies. Fuel-cell powered automobiles may provide new solutions for achieving that quest. While corporations may be able to imagine the ideal state, it may take decades to actually develop the full construct. For product delivery, it would mean that customers and stakeholders would be fully satisfied, and there would be no negative aspects.

Chapter 8 examines creative strategies further as it describes initiatives to start new businesses based on the principles and strategic actions of SBD.

Technological forecasting and assessment

Overview

Technological forecasting and assessment are essential for analyzing and understanding the business environment, and for determining the needs for technological innovation and the related development programs. The construct is similar to the assessment of the business environment discussed in chapter 4, except that the focus is on technologies. Technological forecasting and assessment are among the most difficult challenges facing senior management. The available constructs are limited and generally provide qualitative rather than quantitative results.

Figure 7.7 shows a simplified version of the normative framework for analyzing technologies to discover and understand both opportunities and threats. The framework is depicted as a process rather than a flow chart because it represents ongoing efforts that are critical to determining the conditions, trends, and patterns of change.

The framework in figure 7.7 shows the parallel processes of assessing the factors affecting technology and those affecting markets and stakeholders. These assessments are crucial for SBD because technological solutions must work in reality. Technological assessment is a close look at the technological aspects of the broad context of the entire business environment.

Scanning is the simple, open-ended approach of watching and evaluating change in the broadest context and looking particularly for technological changes that may benefit the enterprise even if they may not directly relate to the corporation. It is nonspecific and cuts across industries and business

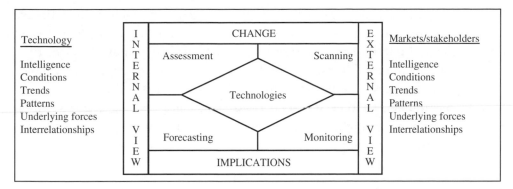

Figure 7.7   A simplified normative framework for technological assessment

sectors. For example, a peer corporation may develop best practices for improving environmental impacts. Such practices might be adaptable even if the originator's lines of business substantially differ from those of the entity scanning the situation. The electronics industry has created many solutions to difficult environmental problems that corporations in other industries could "adopt and adapt." For instance, Intel is a world leader in the recycling of water for industrial processes. Through technological scanning corporations can detect early signs of technological change and determine the implications and potential applications.[10] This is a form of benchmarking, **brainstorming**, and competitive intelligence.

Scanning is extremely difficult given the rate of technological change in the business environment and the incredible quantity of data and information available. Moreover, looking for changes far afield is an undertaking potentially huge in scope. It may involve tracking patent applications across the world to determine innovative technologies that might be useful. Scanning may include going to trade shows in different industries in order to research their innovations. It may involve reading numerous publications and academic papers to determine who and what are on the leading edge of technological change. The challenge is enormous.

For these reasons, monitoring is a more achievable endeavor. It is more focused and generally addresses well-established target areas. It involves determining the trends of selected social, economic, environmental, and market conditions pertaining to technology. Monitoring involves the real time study of the implications of the technological changes that are occurring, and their technological relevance.

Through monitoring, corporations can seek to understand the future implications of these changes. Technological forecasting is the art of determining those expected implications. It generally results in quantitative projections that provide a sense of the scope and timing of the expected impacts of technological changes in the business environment. It describes not only the conditions, but also the rate of change, the expected technological outcomes, and the key factors in the business environment.

Technological forecasting and assessments engage each of these activities, interpreting the findings, and fitting the new understanding into the strategic context of the enterprise.

Technological forecasting

Traditional technological forecasting techniques typically provide answers to quantitative questions regarding the scope and timing of opportunities and challenges. However, the most critical question pertains to the corporation's ability to accommodate and sustain the technological change and the technologies involved. Standard forecasting techniques focus heavily on market demands and requirements of existing customers. But market demand is just one of many indicators of the viability of technology, or the need for new ones. Indeed, the latent needs of current and future customers and stakeholders can determine the viability of existing technologies and pressure corporations to develop new ones.

Technological forecasting is the wide-ranging surveillance of the potential of a technology and its "fit" into the business environment over time. It is an analytical technique dealing with one or more characteristics of the technology, such as the performance or the functional parameters that satisfy potential needs. Technological forecasting is essential for determining the sustainability of a technology. The most important reason for preparing forecasts is to ensure that decisions are as sound as possible and investments are made on the basis of the future potential of the technology, and not its current level of performance and output. There are numerous examples that highlight the importance of forecasting and the need to predict future implications.

A look at the US steel industry during the 1960s and 1970s illustrates the difficulty of forecasting. While the demand for various steel products continued to increase during most of the 1960s, the performance of the US steel industry declined because its technologies were obsolete. Newer processes using basic oxygen technologies were being deployed across the world, and Japanese companies had taken the technological lead.

From a SBD perspective, the forecasting technique has to examine the need for the technology, the impacts and implications over time, and the limits of its applications, and produce both quantitative and qualitative information about each element. The potential of the technology is expressed in terms of its application in various market segments in a given period of time. The standard quantitative result estimates the number of products or the amount of material produced and consumed during a specific time frame. This is often viewed as the demand for the applications of the technology.

While such approaches are inappropriate for emerging technologies that may not have a demand structure or fit into the normal economic picture, there is nevertheless a need to forecast the potential applications of emerging technologies.

Technological forecasting is extremely complex because the actual development of a technology and its long-term potential depends on many factors:

- The corporation's commitment to developing the technology and providing ongoing support to improve and sustain it over time.
- The acceptance of the technology by society, markets, customers, stakeholders, and other constituencies during the life cycle of the technology.
- The industry's contribution to the development and support of the technology, and related factors that affect its applications and implications. The Competition may offer alternative forms of the technology to enhance the choices users have, thus making the technology more mainstream and more viable. Related industries may provide the supplementary products and services that increase the value of the technology. For example, DVD movie rental companies make owning a DVD player more valuable; they enhance the value proposition of the DVD manufacturers.
- Technology is often commercialized based on its benefits and performance – i.e. the positive effects. In the longer term, the negative consequences often impact the prospects, usually reducing its potential.

Forecasting is highly dependent on external factors causing change in the business environment. Technological implications vary, depending upon the stage of the development process. During the introduction stages, the effects of the technology are not well understood, making it difficult to predict weaknesses and outcomes. During the growth stage, many of the positive and negative attributes unfold. At maturity, the key factor becomes the new technologies lurking on the horizon that may replace the existing ones.

Technology assessment

Technology assessment is the act of interpreting the results of the scanning, monitoring, and forecasting in order to understand how the business environment and selected technologies converge toward a solution. Technology assessment basically translates the implications of strategic issues and technology development into a decision-making context. It takes the broad forecasts and provides a constructive view of the implications and impacts.

Technology assessment includes: (1) understanding the forces driving a changing technology; (2) determining the key issues; (3) reviewing the scientific underpinnings of the technology; (4) determining its potential effects; (5) determining its principal applications; (6) understanding the benefits and limitations of those applications; (7) determining the potential products and processes; and (8) making an overall evaluation of the social, economic, and environmental viability of the technology. The assessment outlines the advantages and disadvantages of the technologies with respect to the business environment. It also identifies any barriers to or critical factors for success and determines the levels of risk and uncertainty. These are expanded upon below, under each of the types of innovations.

Strategies for radical technological innovation, technological innovation, and product and process innovation

Overview

The basic premise of SBD from a technology perspective is that *leading change* involves proactively developing new technologies, improving existing ones, creating new products and processes, and improving existing ones. It also includes integrating these technologies, products, and processes into a fully articulated management system using principles of enterprise thinking and LCA. The primary objective is to exceed every expectation in order to gain competitive advantage and upstage the competition. Leading change – the premise of SBD – becomes the norm. The question then becomes how dramatic the changes should be. The following categories of innovations help to define the options:

- *Radical (technological) innovation* (creating new-to-the-world technology) brings about revolutionary changes that may create a brand new industry or market structures or involve dramatic changes to existing ones. It may involve starting a whole new business unit or subset of it, or making substantial changes to existing SMS, including developing new customers, new markets, new supply networks, and other related entities.

- *Technological innovation* (developing new generations of existing technologies) changes the existing industry(ies) or market structure(s) by making dramatic improvements through new generations or platforms of technologies and the related products and processes. It brings significant, if not revolutionary, changes to customers, markets, and stakeholders.
- *Product innovation* (making incremental improvements and changes) enhances existing technologies, creating new derivatives and hybrids that add significant benefits to, or eliminate major defects from, products and processes. It represents modest changes to the prevailing system.
- *Process innovation* (aligning resources and capabilities) improves the management system by improving technologies, products, and processes and by reducing or eliminating redundancies and problems.

Radical (technological) innovation involves creating, developing, and managing new-to-the-world solutions that are significantly enhanced using new technologies. It means blazing new trails by building new capabilities and approaches. This kind of innovation may be most advantageous in situations where the prevailing technologies are significantly deficient, and improving them is not possible or is not warranted from a time or financial perspective. It may also be the best solution for corporations that have a weak industry position. Managing this kind of innovation, however, is highly complex. The standard management constructs, methods, and techniques that work under well-established business conditions may not be useful in the setting of radical technological innovation. Senior management, professionals, and practitioners must be able to manage in open-ended situations and think "out-of-the-box." The radical technological innovation may have disruptive effects on the corporation and its business environment. Still, if the approach is mapped out properly and implemented over a long time-frame such potential implications for the enterprise can be mitigated, and the positive effects can provide sufficient benefits to overcome the challenges.

Technological innovation typically involves improving technologies, especially eliminating the negative effects associated with customer applications and waste disposal issues. It is a broad approach for developing new solutions because it often involves R&D, followed by product and process developments, and then developing the means to commercialize the technology. The general construct includes creating the new technologies that fit into the existing management systems, developing the next generation of the prevailing technology, or combining two or more of the existing technologies into an enhanced solution – the latter is called "technology fusion." Technological

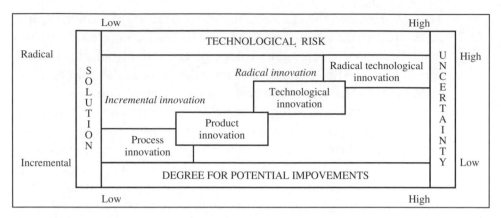

Figure 7.8   Relationship matrix of technology and development strategies

innovation focuses on both the development of the technology and its fit within the enterprise.

Product innovation involves designing and developing new products or making incremental, but dramatic, improvements to existing ones. Product innovation methods are based on the prevailing business environment and generally assume that the development programs can be completed in five years or less. Process innovation involves improving the technologies associated with production processes and the ways in which activities are executed.

Innovation involves improving the technological and product underpinnings of the corporation. It includes assessing the advantages and disadvantages of the technologies, products, and processes, and those of the supply networks, and making improvements where significant difficulties are found. The intent is to examine the technological fabric of the whole enterprise and then improve the positives and eliminate the defects, burdens, and impacts.

The strategic decision regarding which way or combinations of ways to proceed depends on an analysis of the situation, the vision and strategic direction of the corporation, and its capabilities and resources. While there are significant overlaps between the types of innovation described above, the general scheme involves a hierarchical relationship. Figure 7.8 provides an overview of the linkages between technology and development strategies.

The matrix figure 7.8 depicts the relationship between the new solution, technological risks, the level of uncertainty, and the potential for improvements. It does not indicate that one approach is superior to the others, but merely that outcomes vary depending upon these variables. However, the potential for dramatic improvements in eliminating defects and burdens increases as the solution set moves toward more radical innovation. New-to-the-world technologies have the potential to be designed and developed in a manner that avoids many of the difficulties and problems of the past. Still, radical technological innovations come with a higher degree of uncertainty regarding risks and required investment. The uncertainties cut across the full domain of the business environment, including the capabilities of suppliers and customers. Moreover, great promise is not always realized, and the new-to-the-world technology may have defects and burdens as well. There are no guarantees.

When determining the appropriate technology and development choice:

- Selections should be based on the strategic analysis of the business environment and the capabilities and resources of the corporation.
- The choice of innovation and development mechanisms significantly influences the techniques, methods, and practices used to achieve the end-game.
- Leading change is not simply an option for SBD; it is essential. The choice is not to change or maintain the status quo, but rather to select the specific means and mechanisms by which to change, and the degree of change to pursue.
- Selecting a technology-related strategy is not an all-or-nothing proposition. Depending on the business environment, a corporation may have some of its units selecting new technologies while others seek to create next product generations or product improvements.

Change and improvement mean different things to each corporation, industry, or market sector. Some industries, such as consumer electronics, change their technologies in a matter of months or a year or two. Other industries or corporations, such as airframe manufacturers and automobile companies, require five or more years to change their technologies and products.

Table 7.6 highlights some of the advantages and disadvantages for each type of innovation management.

There is no simple or risk-free approach. SBD calls on corporations to be as aggressive as possible in creating better solutions and a better world. However, solutions that are more aggressive often have greater complexities and higher probabilities of not achieving their objectives. While executives have to provide the means and mechanisms to achieve success, they also have to be tolerant of failures in order to secure their successes. Ultimately, their success lies in identifying the best opportunities, the best means to exploit them, and responding with appropriate development programs.

Table 7.6. Advantages and disadvantages of innovation management approaches

Construct	Radical innovation	Technological innovation	Product innovation
Fit and benefits	• Provides a significant competitive advantage, distinction and an improved position, if successful • Creates new value proposition, establishing a win–win situation for customers, suppliers and the entire enterprise • Restructures the business environment in a more favorable light • Reduces the negative side of the equation and reaps long-term savings	• Brings potential to transition technologies and products to more sustainable position • Builds resources and capabilities for more sustainable competitive advantage • Brings potential for new opportunities to make improvements and enhancements • Brings potential to make dramatic gains within a known context	• Provides ongoing improvements for long-term, sustained effort • Improvements are made across the spectrum of the management system • Reduces the risks of not achieving substantial results • Based on the prevailing conditions and information flow • Short time frame allows for faster feedback on successes and failures
Concerns	• Have to build awareness, acceptance and new learning • High level of uncertainty/risk • Potential lack of acceptance • High probability of failure • Long development cycle • Change may be disruptive, destroying valuable assets (plant, products, processes, etc.)	• Investments are generally high and still at risk of being replaced by new technologies • People may be unwilling to adapt new behaviors, gain new skills and knowledge • Lack of awareness requires considerable effort to communicate benefits	• Incremental change may not be sufficient to meet expectations • Investments in improving old assets, technologies, and products may be a waste of money and effort

Selecting the right technology strategy

Technology strategy links the strategic management of the corporation with the management and development of technologies. The strategic direction of the enterprise largely determines how the corporation is going to lead change and select, develop, modify, manage, and/or retire its technological resources and capabilities. The strategic decisions associated with technologies and innovations are central to achieving results in the near term and creating an environment for sustainable advantage and success in the long term. The fundamental logic of what the enterprise is, and wants to become,

Table 7.7. Technology strategies matrix: key elements

Strategic actions	Strategies	Technologies	Products services	Processes resources	Knowledge capabilities
Acquire (buy)	**Diversification** Expansion	**Multifaceted** Hardware/ software	**Multifaceted** Hardware/ software	**Multifaceted** Hardware/ software	**External sources** Industry-based
Invent (create)	**Radical innovation** Basic research	**New-to-the-world** Invention	**New-to-the-world** Development	**New-to-the-world** Development	**New-to-the-world** New learning
Develop (Innovate)	**Innovation** Applied research	**New generation** platforms	**Derivatives** Enhancements Hybrids	**Derivatives** Enhancements Hybrids	**Internal sources** People
Deploy (integrate)	**Integration** Applications	**Adaptation** Acceptance	**Diffusion** Commercialization	**Product delivery** Value networks	**Core capabilities** Knowledge
Improve (maintain)	**Modification** Problem solving	**Customization** Differentiation	**Improvements** Quality/ reliability	**Improvements** Effectiveness	**Educational** Learning
Divest (dispose)	**Divestment** Recapturing	**Substitution** Shifting	**Phasing out** Retiring	**Closing down** Shifting	**Transferring** Transitioning
Alliances (partner)	**Joint development** Venturing	**Technology fusion** Sharing and linking	**Relationships** Networking	**Alignments** Linkages	**Collaborative** Connecting

provides an overarching sense of how to make the proper choices for long-term success.

Technology strategy determines what technologies to acquire, invent, develop, deploy, improve, and divest. It integrates the existing positions with the future needs and requirements to sustain the success of the corporation over time. Technology strategy occurs in a multidimensional matrix that articulates multiple action plans across the entire enterprise. Table 7.7 lists the key elements of such a technology strategy matrix.

The technology strategy matrix serves to align multiple technology strategies into a seamless strategic perspective. It is a dynamic construct, with strategic business sectors within the corporation selecting their own set of strategies to meet the challenges of their own business environment. Choices can be broad, encompassing all of the matrix, or narrow focusing on select strategies.

The standard approach is to innovate through progressive improvements and to maintain the prevailing capabilities as defined by the portfolio of technologies and products. Life cycle constructs suggest that eventually the technologies and products become mature and obsolete, requiring replacements. Solutions to such situations include acquiring technologies and products from others or creating new ones using the R&D capabilities of the corporation. Such strategies necessitate ongoing development through technological and product innovations. They also require building new capabilities and acquiring new resources.

To pursue the more aggressive entrepreneurial strategies of radical technological innovation and diversification, however, requires new or enhanced knowledge and rapid learning. Diversification takes many forms, from simply acquiring or merging with another corporation to purchasing assets, technologies, and other intellectual property. The discussions here focus on the development of technologies and knowledge and not on the corporate financial aspects or acquisition methodologies. The entrepreneurial strategy, with its focus on creating new-to-the-world technologies, products, and processes, is often driven by the vision of the corporation to become a more powerful entity having an enhanced value proposition. It requires radical technological innovations that can result only from significant changes to the knowledge, resources, assets, and structure of the enterprise. Entrepreneurial approaches mandate new ways of thinking and new mechanisms for managing.

Technological and product innovation strategies are the most familiar to corporations, and have a broad array of subsets. They focus on applied research and typically involve improving existing technologies and products through development programs. The possibilities range from creating new generations of technologies to producing derivatives of current products. Corporations generally initiate these strategies using internal capabilities and prevailing knowledge.

Technological integration is a corporation's ongoing initiative to apply and improve technologies and products in the commercial world. It seeks to align the corporation's resources and capabilities to enhance the effectiveness of the enterprise and its relationships. The primary means of gaining acceptance is improving the product delivery system and the value networks. Integration is a subtle, but effective, way to enhance the potential of technologies and products.

Modifications are the incremental improvements that are made every day. Most modifications are based on problem solving, aimed at eliminating defects, reducing burdens, and/or enhancing quality and reliability. From a technology perspective, modifications customize the salient aspects of the technology to improve its fit into specific segments of the business environment. They often provide a means for differentiation. These approaches are particularly critical during the later stages of the life cycle.

At the end of the life cycle, or when the technology becomes a detriment rather than an asset, the question of divestment arises. The strategic approach is to make such determinations as soon as possible and to recover assets and resources to the greatest extent feasible. The more time there is for initiating such actions, the greater the probabilities of transforming the remaining value of the old into new.

Joint developments with other corporations can be viewed as a strategy, but it is often used in combination with one of the other strategies discussed above. Usually, it means venturing with other corporations to develop new technologies or significant refinements to existing ones. It is used when neither entity has the resources or capabilities to proceed alone. It is often used when the risks of failure are high and the potential gains in the business environment are uncertain.

Selecting a technology strategy involves one or more of these strategic options. There are many combinations and alternate forms of strategies, and figure 7.9 depicts the "nesting" effect within the strategic choices.

Selecting the right type of technology strategy depends on the situation and the requirements for change. The appropriate selection lies in the

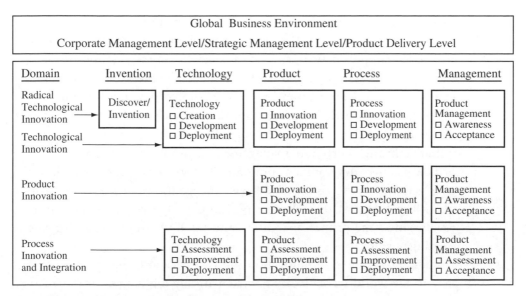

Figure 7.9   The "nested" hierarchy of innovation and integration

expectations of customers and other constituents, and the willingness and ability of management to lead change.

Radical innovation is the most difficult to orchestrate. The pathway of this kind of development is uncharted; often only a skeleton outline of the project elements can be identified and mapped using project management techniques. Much of the detail has to be determined as the program unfolds. The same is true for other forms of technological innovations that focus on new-to-the-world technologies.

Technological and product innovations that improve existing technologies and products generally employ well-established process management approaches. This is an enormous advantage because the process can be articulated in advance, and every participant can become familiar with the process elements. The same is true for process innovation programs. However, process innovation may include examining the technologies used to create and produce the products for opportunities for improvements. Process innovation also includes developing the means and mechanisms for deploying the improvements.

Radical technological innovation

Overview

In the context of a global corporation, radical technological innovation involves creating new-to-the-world technologies along with the market structure, supply networks, and associated infrastructure needed to support its development and deployment. In the hierarchy of technology strategies, radical innovation involves creating a new market, intellectual property, and knowledge using "out-of-the-box" thinking and methods. Generally, it emanates from the highest level of the corporation and is initiated through corporate management resources such as an R&D center or new business development program. The strategic logic for such initiatives is based on the vision to radically change the enterprise, or a portion of it. The intent is to seek new positions in the commercial world, to revolutionize the prime capabilities, and to eliminate the negative side of existing positions.

Radical technological innovation can take several forms, from inventing new-to-the-world technologies to systematically building an infrastructure, and growing all of the salient value networks required for achieving a sustainable business. It often means creating an entire business entity with a new foundation and superstructure. This requires substantial investment for selecting the appropriate opportunities, creating the necessary internal dimensions, structuring a viable business reality, developing the related products and processes, validating the outcomes, and gaining acceptance in the business environment. It also involves substantial efforts to create an appropriate structure for the external dimensions such as establishing the market space, supply networks, and support products and services, and building the necessary infrastructure. The principles, approaches, methods, and techniques are based on starting a new venture on a large scale. While small-scale entrepreneurship is a well-established subject, the theories and constructs for creating large-scale radical technological innovation are based on the case histories of such corporate initiatives. The main limitation to developing a generalized methodology is that most of the previous initiatives represent unique situations. Moreover, most of the existing case studies are not based on sustainable development.

Radical technological innovation is highly dependent on the business environment and the changes that may occur over an extended time frame. Creating new-to-the-world technologies and the related management systems is a long-term venture fraught with many curves and possible dead-ends that require the retracing of strategies, action plans, and activities. Thus, while the primary elements are easy to identify, the details of planning, formulating, implementing, and evaluating such developments are not. They depend upon specific and complicated networks of relationships and strategic actions.

Radical technological innovation requires imagination, creativity, and agility. Both management and the participants have to be able to make decisions and take actions as development occurs on a real time basis. They have to have the fortitude to persist in a long-term initiative requiring new internal and external dimensions.

The hallmarks of radical innovations are the uncertainties and risks involved and the difficulties in determining the correct methods to use. There are uncertainties and risks in every step – in the development of the technology, the selection of the best applications, the economic feasibility of the investments, the possibilities of hidden defects, and in banking on the acceptance of the technology by society, markets, stakeholders, and global communities. Yet, for this reason, and because of its potential for realizing tremendous corporate and personal growth, radical innovation remains both exciting and desirable.

Principles of radical technological innovation

Radical technological innovation involves creating new realities that are not related to the existing business situation. For this reason, it is even more important to rely on principles and policies, rather than rules and procedures. Senior management establishes the principles and policies for managing and controlling the development and provides direction based on enterprise thinking and SBD precepts. A corporation opts to pursue radical innovation when it desires to change the status quo, make dramatic improvements, succeed through recognition, financial rewards, and social and economic accomplishments, and achieve valuable outcomes. The principles for managing strategic actions and achieving this kind of success are open-ended constructs that vary from corporation to corporation and situation to situation. They are broad statements pertaining to the inherent objectives of the enterprise and the end-results that it aspires to. They articulate hopes and dreams and provide the underlying basis for making good decisions about the future and achieving SBD. As such, they provide a steadying sense of guidance and comfort in the difficult and risky situations that characterize radical technological innovation. Table 7.8 lists several of the most profound principles, that can overcome barriers to initiating and sustaining complex strategic actions.

While the list could be expanded, it is important to have long-term initiatives that are embedded within the organizational culture as well as to develop a tolerance for failures during the short term. Management has to balance the seemingly contradictory desires for maintaining tight control and promoting a high degree of creativity and flexibility. Guiding principles provide the direction required by management and help determine that balance.

Managing radical technological innovation

Managing radical innovation requires an entrepreneurial mindset and spirit with close coordination and cooperation among all participants. The development programs are typically based on the leadership of the corporation and the capabilities of the entire enterprise: the corporation's internal capabilities, assets, and external partnerships. Even in those cases where the corporation is able to develop the technology on its own, it still needs the cooperation and contributions of its strategic alliances and others in the value networks to fulfill the requirements of external dimensions, especially

Table 7.8. Selected principles of radical technological innovation

Principle	Underpinnings	Implications
Create value and improve the value proposition	Value is the overarching construct This is particularly important when there is a high level of uncertainty Value is easier to determine than profits or customer satisfaction	The value equation provides answers to the sustainable aspects of the new technology If defects and burdens are reduced and performance is enhanced, the technology exhibits the potential for success
Acquire and enhance knowledge	Discovery, understanding and invention are based on intellectual capital Knowledge and experience are crucial for developing state-of-the-art technology Knowledge is based on observations and engagement	Technology is the complex arrangement of science and art based on scientific principles and experience Program failures can be considered a success if they improve knowledge
Use insights and lessons learned	Insights provide the empirical foundation for creative thought Innovations are often based on combinations of technologies that lead to a new capability or understanding	Analogous situations or solutions may provide inspiration and creativity Using lessons learned from others facilitates the process and reduces trial and error
Enhance the learning process, build capabilities	Capabilities and learning are the centerpieces of discovery Learning decreases uncertainty and enhances knowledge Learning builds intellectual capital and the ability to understand the variables and construct a solution	When uncertainty is high, learning is paramount for success Answers are time- and activity-dependent Learning allows the process to converge toward a solution
Create enthusiasm for the program	People are the essential ingredient in creativity People have to be inspired and rewarded	People are emotional and logical Motivation is both self-induced and generated by short-terms gains
Maintain objectivity	Professionals should follow scientific thinking It is important to be skeptical about observations until there is sufficient evidence to draw conclusions All technologies have positive and negative aspects	Maintaining objectivity is critical People often accept too many unproven theories Solutions should be based on objective evidence and sound methods Discover the leading and lagging effects
Understand the driving forces	Markets, stakeholders, and corporations do not want technologies They want solutions and applications to fulfill their needs Understand all of the driving forces, not just the market forces	The forces driving change make or break a technological solution All driving forces, including government regulations, change over time

Table 7.8. (cont.)

Principle	Underpinnings	Implications
Consider social, economic, and environmental implications	Technology is a social and economic construct It has to benefit people in ways that are overwhelmingly positive and cost effective Environmental burdens detract from the positive aspects	Technology has to fit the social and economic realities of the business environment People require benefits that are worthwhile They have to be able to afford the solution
Maintain integrity and honesty and build trust	Provide credible evidence about the technology and its benefits, and communicate the negative aspects as well Be honest about the technology; do not oversell its potential Corporate reputation is often the most valuable asset	Lack of integrity and honesty tends to mislead stakeholders about the viability of the technology Effective corporations communicate problems early and resolve them before huge investments have been made
Build long-term commitment	Persistence is necessary for complex programs Answers and solutions are sporadic Management and participants feed each other	Success is a long and uneven road Difficulties and frustrations are part of the equation Giving up too early is a common difficulty

infrastructure. The technology and its value networks are only part of the total value equation required to achieve success.

Still, radical technological innovation is more than just developing a technology package. It requires dynamic interfaces with the business environment to obtain the information needed for decisions and within the corporation to obtain the maximum benefits of its knowledge, experience, and capabilities. But radical technological innovation has to be based on future expectations and not on the prevailing situation. Insights and forecasts are necessary to determine what the business environment is likely to be, rather than what it is. For example, existing customers may not have the capability to assess how a new technology meets their needs and expectations if they are not familiar with the attributes of the technology – or, more importantly, if the technology requires more than ten years to develop. The Iridium telecommunication program that cost billions of dollars to develop is an example of basing technology development on the existing conditions and not understanding the implications of change during the ten years of

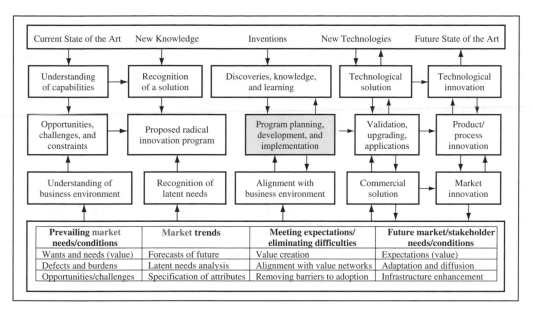

Figure 7.10 The dynamics of radical technological innovation

execution. The model mapped out in figure 7.10 provides an overview of this very complex dynamic.

Corporations undertake radical technological innovation to create significantly enhanced value and new solutions for customers and stakeholders. The intent is to expand opportunities for competitive advantages, to meet social, economic, and environmental challenges, and to eliminate constraints to success. Solutions are combinations of outcomes that are based on the technological capabilities and means of the corporation and meet the expectations of the business environment.[11] They are the convergence of concepts, new knowledge, inventions, and technologies with the needs and expectations of the business environment. The alignment of strategic actions with the capabilities of the infrastructure is essential for the integration of the total solution – i.e. the technological solution married with the commercial (market) solution. Solutions must be validated in the real world and any deficiencies must be improved.

The development of strategic logic is the initial stage of a multistage process. The second stage is the development of technological innovation, which focuses on finding applications and modifying the technology to suit those applications. The third stage is product/process innovation, which leads to product development and commercialization. In certain situations, however, products are not developed from the initial generation of a new technology because too many weaknesses have made the technology unviable in the marketplace. The process continues, with developers continuing to improve the technology through technological innovation.

Technological innovation

Overview

Technological innovation involves developing new technologies that fit into the prevailing market space, improving existing technology through the development of next generations, or enhancing the existing technology platform. The development of new technology is similar to radical technological innovation, although the change mechanisms are not necessarily so disruptive. Technological innovation involves technology developments that are relatively straightforward improvements or replacements of prevailing technologies. While the technology exploration and exploitation processes may be complicated and require significant changes, the underlying management systems and the linkages with the business environment remain basically the same. The change mechanisms involve the replacement of an old technology with a new one. The transition process is relatively smooth, using much of the existing management approaches and infrastructure. Similarly, the next generation or new technology platform generally represents significant improvements to the underlying knowledge base and technological capabilities. The degree of improvements can range from changing one or more facets of the technological foundation to making dramatic improvements in the very structure of the technology itself.

Technological innovation is more predictable than radical technological innovation. It usually focuses on the existing business environment and the core capabilities and resources of the corporation. It is not particularly concerned with the stability of the business environment or the effectiveness of the management system, as the underlying market structures and stakeholder considerations remain fairly constant. There may even be evolutionary effects, but not revolutionary ones. While there are always risks and uncertainties associated with innovations, technological innovation attempts to use well-defined approaches, processes, and capabilities to affect a more sustainable future without the threat of destabilizing the business environment or absorbing the costs of an enormous investment in radical changes to the industry structure or the enterprise management system.

The principles of technological innovation

Technology innovation involves basic and applied research. It is often commingled with the construct of product innovation. But technological innovation is technology-based. It involves creating and building technical capabilities and the technological means to exploit them. Technological innovation actually creates devices that then facilitate new and beneficial solutions. The development of new products and processes is possibly the most common and most important outcome, but there are other ways to exploit the technology, including licensing or selling the innovations to others.

The strategic logic of most technological innovations is to make dramatic improvements to the core capabilities and technological underpinnings of the corporation. While these improvements spring from creativity and new knowledge, they are also often based on the existing capabilities and external networks of the organization. The change mechanisms, though often revolutionary in terms of outcomes (new-to-the-world products), are not radical themselves. They do not substantially change the business environment or how technologies are deployed. For example, wireless telecommunications have restructured the telephone industry, the value networks, and the applications and usage of telecommunications. The outcomes represent revolutionary changes and have created whole new enterprises and value networks. On the other hand, while each new generation of Intel's and AMD's new microprocessor technology is a quantum improvement over the previous generation, the fundamental structure of the industry and the value networks remain relatively stable and unaffected.

The management of technological innovation includes technology scanning and monitoring, technology forecasting and assessment, technology planning, development programs, and the control and evaluation mechanisms. The goal is to form and implement effective business–technological–commercial interfaces that link the creation of technologies, or the improvement of them, to the business environment.

Technological innovation usually involves more of the formal mechanisms and organizational constructs within the corporation. R&D centers, whether centralized or decentralized, are typically responsible for developing new technologies and new generations. Their work is driven by the need to replace existing technologies because they are ineffective, obsolete, or have overwhelming defects and burdens. This also stems from the recognition that significant improvements are needed to satisfy customers and stakeholders, or from the desire to exploit new opportunities.

Table 7.9. Selected principles of technological innovation

Principles	Underpinnings	Implications
Identify the strategic fit	Developing new or improved technologies represents significant investment and commitment Therefore, great care has to be taken to ensure that the resulting programs are aligned	Poor fit results in lost opportunities and wasted efforts Given the long time frame for most related programs, making the right choices is critical to achieving the desired outcomes
Build in adaptability and flexibility	Technological innovation is a mix between well-defined pathways used to develop new products and processes and the open-ended project-type approaches used for technological entrepreneurship	Technological innovation often requires a combination of methods that can be difficult to predict and articulate The organization has to be adaptive to changing requirements
Involve senior management early and throughout the process	Many of the most important strategic decisions are made during the early stages of technological innovation programs Senior management has to provide leadership, commitment, and decisions	Senior management often gets involved at the point when decisions to commit funds are made, often after the preliminary decisions have already been taken
Use collaborative methods	A holistic management approach requires input and cooperation from every internal and external part of the enterprise	Good decisions require inputs from all parties involved in the development and deployment of new or improved technologies
Establish screening up-front	Objective screening criteria are essential for making good choices about the opportunities to pursue Selecting criteria up-front eliminates some of the bias that may occur later on	Screening criteria are often based on the strategic objective of the corporation It is relatively easy to obtain agreement on such criteria before the actual programs are at stake

The principles of technological innovation are similar to those listed in table 7.8. The time frame for technological innovation tends to be shorter (seven–plus ten years), and the scope is narrower and easier to define. Table 7.9 summarizes some selected principles.

It is an essential part of the management process to identify and articulate the specific principles guiding each program. Technological innovation may involve both project management techniques and process management methods. If the technological innovation involves new-to-the-world technologies, the methodologies are more likely to focus on project management. Conversely, if the technological improvements are related to previous

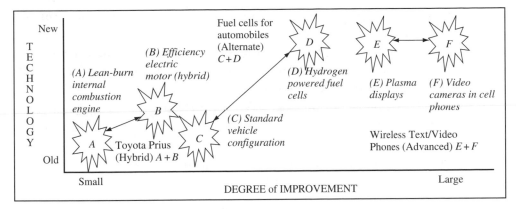

Figure 7.11   Select examples of technological fusion

generations and the development pathways are well established, process management approaches are more appropriate.

Fusion of technologies

Technology innovation often involves the **fusion** of two or more technologies, providing enhancements and new capabilities. Technology fusion can combine two old technologies to create a hybrid technology, develop a new technology to go with an old technology, or integrate two or more new technologies. Figure 7.11 depicts selected examples.

The expected results are capabilities that are greater than the sum of the parts, or a new technology that improves upon the weaknesses of the earlier one. The exact benefits of technological fusion usually depend on the circumstances. For example, the Toyota Prius (a hybrid) combines the lean-burn gasoline engine technology with an improved version of a standard electric motor that uses regenerative braking energy recovery. The result is a super, ultra-low-emission vehicle with fuel efficiency that doubles that of conventional automobiles. The system is actually more efficient in traffic because the electric motor is able to conserve energy during braking that would normally be lost as heat. As fuel prices increase, the product will become even more valuable.

Automobiles that use hydrogen powered fuel cells combine old technology with the new technology of the hydrogen-fueled power plant. They achieve dramatic improvements in fuel efficiency and zero emissions at the point of usage. Such technology requires radical changes to the infrastructure, however. This kind of technological innovation may well require two separate programs, one to develop the radical innovation (fuel cells) and a simpler technological innovation program to marry the two technologies together.

Fusion of two or more new-to-the-world technologies can be considered technological **entrepreneurship**. Often such technologies require the discovery and codevelopment of many solutions simultaneously. TV is a good example. Cathode ray tubes (CRTs), TV network cameras, transmission capabilities, and many other devices were necessary to invent the world of TV. Today, LCDs, plasma screens, digital networking, and many other technologies are combining to change TV from a commodity business to a great opportunity for creating value.

Box 7.1 Toyota Motor Corporation: environmental leadership, technological innovation, and the "realization of a sustainable society"

Toyota views environmental protection as a vital issue. Former president of Toyota Motor Corporation (hereafter, TMC), Hiroshi Okuda, believed that "Toyota must strike a balance between business and corporate citizenship."[1] Okuda used unequivocal language when he described the challenge facing TMC and the automobile industry. He suggested that without decisive industry action, the automobile might cease to be a viable option. He characterized the situation as follows:[2]

> I do not believe environmental protection and economic growth are mutually exclusive. Economic growth that ignores environmental consequences is in my view reckless, but on the other hand, attempting to resolve global environmental issues without recognizing the need for economic growth is unrealistic. I believe our objective should be sustainable growth.

These statements reveal TMC's perspective on its global business situation and strategies for the future. In its *Global Vision 2010*, announced in 2002, Toyota mapped out the company's strategy for sustainable growth in the twenty-first century. It included balancing the needs of people, society, the economy, and the global environment. TMC's CEO, Fujio Cho, articulated TMC's desire to be a global leader in the regeneration of technologies and products to support customers world-wide and to scrutinize environmental actions over the entire product life cycle. TMC would, wrote Cho, provide new directions for achieving the dual goals of protecting the environment and offering consumers a wide range of environmentally friendly vehicles. Appropriately, the theme of *Global Vision 2010* is "Innovation into the Future – A Passion to Create a Better Society."[3] "The fundamental thinking for *Global Vision 2010* has three elements: (1) to step beyond "harmonious growth" and demonstrate our responsibilities as a global leader; (2) to benefit society through the manufacture of value-added products; and (3) to share prosperity with our employees."[4] Most importantly, *Global Vision 2010* represents a paradigm change that is based on technology and product development.

Why does TMC want to be the No. 1 environmental car-maker in the world? Is it the result of altruistic leadership? Or is it due to competitive pressures from others pursuing similar initiatives, namely Honda, GM, Ford Motor Company, and Daimler-Chrysler? Many internal and external forces are driving TMC to change the way it does business and influencing its strategies, policies, and structure. The major external change agents are:

- Societal concerns and attitudes about environmental protection and pollution.
- More stringent regulations world-wide pertaining to automobile emissions in order to protect the environment and the health and safety of the general population.
- Wide fluctuation in the economics of automobile manufacturing, principally driven by uncertain fuel prices and costs associated with waste streams.
- Rapidly evolving technologies, both within the industry and in other sectors.
- Expansion in the number of market segments based on the needs and wants of customer groups.
- Globalization of the industry.

These changes are increasing business risk and uncertainty. Public policy debates are resulting in a more conservative view of the potential dangers and long-term impacts of automobiles, and perceptions are changing. New regulatory mandates that will further restrict the allowable levels of emissions loom on the horizon. In the United States, the California Air Resources Board (CARB) is charged with improving the state's smoggy air. It has mandated that auto-makers' sales by 2005 must consist of 10 percent zero-emission vehicles.[5] Around the world, other governments are also mandating greener vehicles. The European Union has agreements with the European Automobile Manufacturers Association (ACEA) to reduce carbon dioxide emissions by 25 percent over ten years. In Japan, ambitious targets under regulatory consideration would slash vehicle emissions of nitrous oxides, carbon monoxide, and hydrocarbons by 80 percent, and those of carbon dioxide by 20 percent. Additionally, the 1997 Kyoto Protocol is pushing significant cuts in greenhouse gas emissions in many nations.

While the threat of these regulations is prompting many improvements, new market opportunities – particularly in the developing world – are providing exciting potential. It is expected that most of the real growth in auto sales exists in the developing world; sales in Europe and Japan appear to be flat, and growth is slow in the United States. For markets in the developing world, a more environmentally benign product makes sense. The price of gasoline is very high, which is a significant factor given the relatively low wage rates. Moreover, the severely polluted air in many of the mega-cities will only deteriorate further as more vehicles are used.

In 1991, TMC's management created the *Toyota Earth Charter* to foster the development of safe, clean automobiles and a green earth. The *Charter* was designed to direct important environmental programs and to promote environmental protection company-wide.[6] In January 1992, the company formed an environment committee and three subcommittees to study critical environmental issues and develop appropriate corporate policies for making significant progress toward environmental goals. The commitment of senior management established the importance of the program, but the entire organization had to actively participate in achieving its objectives. The three subcommittees operate as follows to make this happen:[7]

- Environmental product design assessment committee – studies critical environmental protection issues related to TMC vehicle development, sales, and post-use disposal.

- Plant environment committee – determines environmental protection polices related to TMC manufacturing activities.
- Recycling committee – studies the design of easy-to-recycle vehicles and develops recycling and collection systems.

The *Charter* is a systematic approach for addressing environmental impacts across all product lines, all related technologies, and the production system. The *Charter* was revised in April 2000. It now incorporates four profound points that clearly go beyond pollution prevention and regulatory compliance:[8]

- *Contribution toward a prosperous twenty-first-century society*   Aim for growth that is in harmony with the environment and promote achievement of zero emissions throughout all areas of business activities.
- *Pursuit of environmental technologies*   Pursue all possible environmental technologies, developing and establishing new technologies to enable the environment and the economy to coexist harmoniously.
- *Voluntary actions*   Develop a voluntary improvement plan based on improving preventive measures and surpassing compliance, one that addresses environmental issues on the global, national, and regional scale and promotes continuous implementation.
- *Working in cooperation with society*   Build close and cooperative relationships with a wide spectrum of individuals and organizations involved in environmental preservation, including governments and local municipalities, as well as with related companies and industries.

TMC's strategies are still evolving as it moves toward developing and implementing the individual new product programs to fulfill the directives of the *Charter* and *Global Vision 2010*. The initiatives are complex and involve investments of billions of dollars. The multifaceted array of product development initiatives and technological innovations are implemented through R&D programs operating in separate units located in Japan, Europe, and the United States. TMC allocates approximately 5 percent of its revenues for such spending. The essential challenge is to link these activities with customer and stakeholder needs and integrate the development programs throughout the entire enterprise.

TMC has been working on environmental solutions for vehicle technology for decades. It has continuously improved the performance of its conventional engine technologies through product improvement. Such improvements to existing technologies offer cost effective means to meet environmental mandates, while at the same time preserving its investments in the existing product lines and capital structures. For example, TMC can meet the CARB requirements for low-emission vehicles (LEVs), but as the challenge escalates over time, its entire fleet will one day have to achieve LEV status and better. TMC's technological solutions to environmental issues have been a combination of traditional business practices for managing technology and NPD and advanced technological innovation methodologies for reducing environmental burdens through the design and development process.

TMC's technology development strategy is a three-pronged approach:

- *Incremental innovations of existing product technologies*   improving conventional engine technology using lean-burn methods that increase fuel efficiency while reducing emissions. This includes gasoline and diesel powered LEVs and ultra-low-emission vehicles (ULEVs).

- *Hybrid technological innovation*   developing vehicle technology that exploits the benefits of electric power with the support of lean-burn conventional technology, bridging the gap between the dominant technology of the internal combustion engine and future technologies.
- *Radical technological innovation*   exploiting electric vehicle technology and developing fuel-cell technology for automobile applications. This includes other new technologies based on new methods and means to deliver power to the vehicle.

The investment in the existing technology, the internal combustion engine, has two principal objectives: keep the current products and models viable in the marketplace as long as economically possible and establish the true benchmark for what the new technologies have to accomplish. The design parameters for improving this technology are based on what customers and stakeholders need and want and the options available. TMC designs its vehicles to reduce environmental impacts and burdens throughout their life-cycles. The concern for the environment starts during the design and development process. TMC seeks to conserve resources and energy, minimize waste, and recycle whenever possible. This approach extends across the entire system, from development, manufacturing, and use to waste management. The process also focuses on identifying customer needs and expectations and developing new products that satisfy those needs. TMC updates its technologies and product lines to incorporate sustainable methods and practices. Each new product is an opportunity to enhance the corporation's position by improving the environmental impacts of the management system.

NPD provides intermediate-term solutions to the environmental issues. TMC's hybrid technologies integrate solutions from the old and the new as the company converts its capabilities and assets into effective future solutions. Investing in hybrid technologies represents a transformational step. The uncertainties are somewhat tempered by the knowledge of the existing technologies and their platforms. The changes are substantial, but the underlying product structure has many common features and functions with the conventional designs. The commonality of parts and components and customers' familiarity with vehicle characteristics make investment in transitional technologies a little easier to justify.

Alternative technology vehicles are a more significant challenge. Radical innovations that are significantly different from the prevailing conditions of the industry are the most demanding to embrace: the technology and the market are both unknown. Stepping away from the time-tested dominant technology is highly risky, even when it is on the right track. Customer needs and wants are ill defined. There is uncertainty about the urgency to develop such technology; it is clear that existing legislation and regulations provide mandates for advanced technologies, but the strategic value of being a leader is unclear, and the benefits of the new technologies are open-ended.

In theory, the transformation of the automobile has to continue to meet customer needs and expectations, society's concerns, and government mandates. There is no magic bullet to the solution. In fact, the solution is apparent in the model: unless all of the internal and external dimensions are considered concurrently, the solution will be flawed. Only using total integration can the proper result be derived.

Notes:
1. Toyota brochure, *Car of the Future: Toyota Automotive Eco-Technologies*, 1998.
2. *Ibid.*
3. Toyota, *Environmental & Social Report*, 2003, p. 4.
4. *Ibid.*
5. *Ibid.*
6. Toyota brochure, p. 92.
7. *Ibid.*, p. 91.
8. Toyota, *Environmental and Social Report*, 2003, p. 12.

Product and process innovation[12]

Product innovation is the primary innovation management construct for making incremental changes and improvements to products, services, and processes.[13] It includes the conceptualization, design, development, validation, and commercialization of new products for customers and markets.[14] Product innovation accommodates the needs and expectations of customers and market(s), the driving forces in the business environment, and the strategic requirements of the organization. Product innovation runs the gamut from improving existing products to discovering entirely new ways for satisfying customers and stakeholders. It also includes process innovation for enhancing the means and mechanisms for producing and delivering products and services.

Product innovation is challenging because of the dynamics of the business environment, the changing needs of customers and stakeholders, the intensity of competition, and the difficulties associated with understanding the present and forecasting the future. However, there are common pathways to define, describe, assess, and manage the processes used for developing new products. Moreover, most organizations have information systems to support the required analysis and decision-making. Product innovation requires contributions from strategic management, engineering, marketing, finance, production and operations, supply networks, distribution channels, and customers. A diversity of knowledge, skills, creativity, and insights is essential for success.

IPD is the most widely adapted product innovation methodology. It systematically links the external business environment and its opportunities, challenges, and concerns with the internal dimensions[15] of the organization to create innovative solutions based on improved products and services. IPD uses cross-functional teams that are strategically and tactically aligned, such that those involved from inception to commercialization are involved in the product development process. IPD is the NPD construct used by most global corporations.[16] There are many case studies, as well as much empirical data, to suggest that it is the most effective product innovation methodology.[17] It employs process management techniques that integrate capabilities and requirements into seamless flows of activities which ensure creativity, quality, thoroughness, and speed.[18]

The prime objective of product innovation is to produce cost effective product designs that meet or exceed customer and stakeholder needs and expectations and provide exceptional value for all constituencies. The organizational goal is to maximize performance of both the people and the management system and to minimize the negative impacts of new products on the external business environment. Product innovation includes the NPD programs that develop improvements to existing products and the product development process of R&D programs that create new-to-the-world products based on next-generation technologies. The greater the departure from the prevailing technologies and market conditions, the more likely the type of innovation changes from product to technological, and from incremental to radical. The development processes used for product innovation and technological innovation are discussed in chapter 8.

Summary

Leading change through radical technological innovation, technological innovation, and product innovation allows corporations to translate opportunities into meaningful and sustainable outcomes. Inventing technological solutions to the complex realities of the business environment requires strategic direction, creative thinking, and a firm understanding of the business environment. It requires SBD, the powerful construct that guides the entire enterprise to develop solutions that exceed the social, economic, environmental, market, and technological needs of the day. SBD is the all-important connection to ongoing success.

Conventional improvements occur through small modifications to underlying technology and product forms, features, and functions. Designing and developing new products based on existing technologies is relatively easy from a technical standpoint, but often involves significant challenges from a market perspective. For incremental innovations, the required attributes are

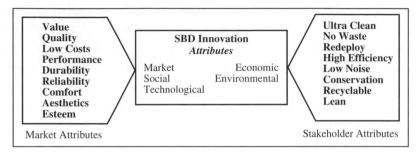

Figure 7.12 The convergence of balanced technological and product attributes

usually mapped out and well understood in the context of designing and producing the product. However, stakeholder requirements are not always as well known, and the forces of change may be felt sooner than expected. For existing products, the technology and market aspects are in alignment, but the requirements for meeting environmental mandates and expectations are often difficult to precisely determine. The answer to these challenges lies in the convergence of product development and environmental improvements. Indeed, global corporations have integrated the social, economic, and environmental conditions and trends into the decision-making processes for creating new products, leading to fundamental changes that provide balanced solutions.

SBD thinking focuses on creating clean technologies and designing the best products possible. The underlying premise is to achieve outstanding product performance and excellent social, economic, and environmental attributes as well. Figure 7.12 provides on overview of this convergence.

In today's business environment, innovation management is an essential means for gaining a competitive advantage. The most important players are the customers and the stakeholders. Ultimately, they define value, performance, benefits, and even the price of the product.

Supplementary material

Learning objectives

Chapter 7 has the following learning objectives that are intended to guide and support students and practitioners:

● Understanding the connections between strategies and technological and product innovation.

- Exploring how to lead change through radical and incremental innovations.
- Examining how to assess technological opportunities and challenges.
- Understanding the processes for selecting the right programs for technological change.
- Determining the best processes, methods, and practices for effective development programs.
- Appreciating how executives and senior management contribute to technological innovation.

Research questions

The following are questions related to SBD in order to facilitate learning and ongoing discussion and analysis of the main topics covered in the chapter:

- What are the main categories of strategic technology management used by most global corporations?
- How do strategic technology management leaders manage technological change and select innovation programs?
- What is the strategic management of technological innovation in the context of SBD?
- What are the differences between radical technical innovation, technological innovation, product innovation, and process innovation?
- How do technology leaders manage change?

NOTES

1. Barry Commoner, *The Closing Circle: Nature, Man, and Technology* (New York: Alfred A. Knopf, 1972), pp. 140–177.
2. Paul R. Ehrlich, *The Population Bomb* (New York: Ballantine Books, 1968), pp. 17–35.
3. Barry Commoner *et al.*, *Population, Environment and the Quality of Life* (New York, Halsted Press, 1975), p. 67.
4. Jesse H. Ausubel and Hedy Sladovich, *Technology and Environment* (Washington, DC: National Academy Press, 1989), pp. 71–72.
5. *Ibid.*, p. 76.
6. Philip Russel, Kamal Saad, and Tamara Erickson, *Third Generation R&D: Making the Link to Corporate Strategy* (Boston, MA: Harvard Business School Press, 1991), p. 64.

7. Steven Wheelwright and Kim Clark, *Revolutionizing Product Development: Quantum Leaps in Speed, Efficiency, and Quality* (New York: Free Press, 1993), p. 93.

8. H. Igor Ansoff, *Implanting Strategic Management* (Englewood Cliffs, NJ: Prentice Hall International, 1984), p. 225.

9. Henry Mintzberg and James Brian Quinn, *The Strategic Process: Concepts, Context, Cases,* 3rd edn. (Englewood Cliffs, NJ: Prentice Hall, 1996), p. 12. James Quinn's article, "Strategies for Change," suggests that strategy is a pattern, especially if the pattern is consistently moving toward the intended results. It is emergent when the pattern does flow along a precise path but achieves the end-result in a more circuitous way.

10. Ansoff, *Implanting Strategic Management*, p. 22. Ansoff developed the notion of "weak signals" as a means for early detection of environmental change. Such weak signals can be precursors to significant trends and change mechanisms.

11. Donald Marquis, *Managing Advanced Technology, volume I* (New York: American Management Association, 1972), pp. 35–48. The model is based on the notion that a solution requires a need to fulfill and the technical means to accomplish the required outcomes.

12. This section is derived from the author's book, David L. Rainey, *Product Innovation: Leading Change through Integrated Product Development* (Cambridge: Cambridge University Press, 2005), pp. 21–27.

13. The book uses the term product(s) to include products or services. For the sake of simplifying the text, products stand for products and services. The notions of incremental and evolutionary changes and improvements are similar in context.

14. Product innovation focuses on the outcomes (products or services), the mechanism (the new product development process), and the means (the people within an organizational context, their capabilities, and the available resources). A new product is any change, improvement, repositioning or new-to-the world product or service. The NPD process includes identifying new product ideas and opportunities, understanding their implications, formulating new product concepts, designing and developing the actual product(s), evaluating the potential and fit, and launching the commercial results.

15. The internal dimensions include strategic management, engineering, marketing, finance, production, and operations.

16. IPD is a widely used term for developing new product using cross-functional teams and parallel processing of activities rather than the older sequential approaches in which functional departments would complete their assignments before their colleagues in the other disciplines became involved. Extensive amount of time and energy were required to manage the sequential processes. Whereas there are many variations, most IPD models have a similar construct.

17. R. G. Cooper, "Developing products on time, in time," *Research Technology Management*, 38 (5), 1995, pp. 40–50. It is difficult to prove that one process is more effective than another is, unless it is in the context of the development opportunity. Time to market is a good indication of effectiveness. The sooner the product gets to the market the better are the chances of achieving the desired cash flow. IPD, with its parallel processing, supports time to market objectives.

18. The discussions in later chapters (especially chapter 8) pertain to the NPD process, which is based on IPD principles. The terms are interrelated.

REFERENCES

Ansoff, H. Igor (1984) *Implanting Strategic Management*. Englewood Cliffs, NJ: Prentice Hall International

Ausubel, Jesse H. and Hedy Sladovich (1989) *Technology and Environment*. Washington, DC: National Academy Press

Commoner, Barry (1972) *The Closing Circle: Nature, Man, and Technology*. New York: Alfred A. Knopf

Commoner, Barry *et al.* (1975) *Population, Environment, and the Quality of Life*. New York: Halsted Press

Cooper, R. G. (1995) "Developing products on time, in time," *Technology Management*, 38(5)

Ehrlich, Paul R. (1968) *The Population Bomb*. New York: Ballantine Books

Marquis, Donald (1972) *Managing Advanced Technology, Volume I*. New York: American Management Association

Mintzberg, Henry and James Brian Quinn (1996) *The Strategic Process: Concepts, Context, Cases*, 3rd edn. Englewood Cliffs, NJ: Prentice Hall

Rainey, David L. (2005) *Product Innovation: Leading Change through Integrated Product Development*. Cambridge: Cambridge University Press

Russel, Philip, Kamal Saad, and Tamara Erickson (1991) *Third Generation R&D: Making the Link to Corporate Strategy*. Boston, MA: Harvard Business School Press

Wheelwright, Steven and Kim Clark (1993) *Revolutionizing Product Development: Quantum Leaps in Speed, Efficiency, and Quality*. New York: Free Press

8 Crafting and implementing sustainable business development programs

Introduction

This chapter explores product and technology development and related programs and processes, as they may be used to support SBD. It examines program types, planning models, and selected development processes, including the identification, selection, planning, implementation, and integration of development programs for sustaining the vision and strategic direction of the enterprise. The constructs discussed are based on enterprise thinking and SBD. Their aim is to create innovative solutions that involve significant improvements to the strategic position of the enterprise and the value propositions for its constituents.

The selection of effective development programs depends on the capabilities, skills, knowledge, desires, and resources of the corporation. The selection may be determined by the requirements, mandates, and standards of the business environment and by the strengths and weaknesses of the existing technologies, products, and processes. The underlying social, economic, and environmental considerations and the identifiable needs and wants of customers and stakeholders also play significant roles. Selecting programs uses methods, processes, and analytical techniques that link technological innovation, product development, and process improvement to the objectives and strategies of the enterprise.

The basic philosophy for building a sustainable enterprise is to invest in development programs that create value streams that exceed social, economic, environmental, technological, and financial requirements and expectations. Value streams and outcomes must focus on delighting customers and stakeholders and building a foundation that provides great solutions for all constituents. The intent is to do so while decreasing resource requirements, defects, and burdens, and negative impacts on the business environment. SBD programs are the key to this kind of success.

SBD programs necessitate sophisticated management constructs, methods, and techniques for selecting the best design and development configurations. The selection process depends on many variables, including the strategic fit of the programs, the value derived by the enterprise and its constituents, financial (investment) considerations, available capabilities and resources, the level of improvements sought, the time required to achieve the intended outcomes, and the longevity of the expected competitive advantages.

SBD programs can be categorized as those having an immediate impact on the prevailing business environment, those that require a short-term investment of time, money, and effort before there is a payback, and those that require more than five years of investment before generating significant gains. Strategic initiatives for improving the future may require facing significant uncertainties, risks, and other challenges. Dramatic change is always fraught with both excitement and anxiety.

This chapter also explores the related quantitative and qualitative constructs that facilitate analysis and decision-making. The most important of these are enterprise thinking, technological innovation, product development, and process improvement. The discussion explores:

- *Program types*   The methods and criteria for choosing appropriate development programs and determining the most attractive opportunities for sustainable successes. The discussion examines the range of development programs, from those resulting in incremental improvements to those promoting technological innovation and radical innovation.
- *Managing improvement programs*   The planning regimes for executing process improvement and development programs.
- *Managing development programs*   The planning regimes for executing product and technology development programs.

Figure 8.1 shows the general relationship of the innovation program types in terms of their level within the corporate systems and the expected life of the technology and related products. The **bold** font categories indicate technological and product innovation programs, while the regular font categories represent improvement programs. While the matrix depicts the typical case, there is variability in actual selections. The strategic logic is based on the implications of the investment and its expected duration in the business environment.

The logic is relatively simple. The longer the time frame for the development program, the more money and time must be invested before the rewards are felt. There may be exceptions – such as in the world of electronics, computers, and telecommunications where product life cycles are very short and the intensity of

	Process Focused	Product Focused	Technology Focused	Business Focused
Corporate Management System	Special cases	Technological innovation – Developments	Radical technological innovation – New technology	Sustainable-enterprise Business model innovation
SMS		Product innovation – Developments	Technological innovation – New technology	Technological innovation – New technology
Product Delivery System	Process improvements Product stewardship Pollution prevention	Product innovation – Improvements	Product innovation – New-to-the-world	Product innovation – New-to-the-world
Operating System/ Processes	Waste minimization Compliance	Process innovation – Changes	Process innovation – Dramatic changes	Process innovation – Radical changes
Duration of Expected Cycle	Ultra short-term cycles ≥2 Year	Short-term cycles ≥5 years	Intermediate-term cycles 5–15 years	Long-term cycles +10 years

Figure 8.1   Strategic fit of innovation program types

the activities is significantly high. In figure 8.1, such cases are shown as "special cases." However, the simpler types of development programs are usually relatively easy to orchestrate, and the funding is modest. The more complex development programs require significant levels of funding and are driven by senior management's commitment to, and its participation in, the program.

This chapter examines the roles of program selection, development, and implementation in creating a sustainable enterprise.[1] While the list of program types is extensive, the chapter covers three main categories: process improvements, product development, and technology development. Specifically, it examines the following topics:

- Selecting innovation SBD programs.
- Understanding innovation program management regimes.
- Managing process improvement programs.
- Managing product development programs.
- Managing technology development programs.

Selecting SBD innovation programs

SBD innovation program types

There are many ways to characterize SBD innovation programs. They may be described according to size, the rate of change relative to the business environment, the degree of intended change, the area of focus (process, product, technology, business, enterprise), scope or management level (component, process, system), the investment required, the time to completion, and the degree of risk. Regardless of their defining traits, all such programs focus on change, improvements, and creating value. Given the fundamentals of enterprise thinking and maximizing value, the most appropriate way to view the options for SBD programs is in a matrix depicting their degree of change or inventiveness in relation to different program scopes.

The types of SBD programs are primarily defined in terms of the intended outcomes – i.e. what specific needs are addressed and the value that is expected from the program. The program types or categories can also be defined according to organizational structure, top-down being directed by senior management, or bottom-up using a team of employees responsible for the program. Table 8.1 provides a general sense of the types of development programs and the most salient aspects of planning and selection. The insights provided in the matrix are a generalization of the typical applications.

In simpler terms, SBD programs can be divided into two broad areas: (1) those focusing on major *improvements* to the existing technologies, products, and processes; and (2) those representing new *developments* in business systems, technologies, products, and processes. The former have shorter time horizons and typically use resources and capabilities of the existing management systems and organizational structure for supporting the initiatives. It can be argued that they are crafted around the core capabilities and existing resources of the corporation. The latter types have much longer time horizons and depend on a combination of existing and new resources and capabilities. The corporation must assess its ability to execute programs that represent significant changes in the prevailing business situation. It also must understand the willingness of the organization to change in order to enhance the organizational capabilities to meet the needs of the programs. This model was depicted in figure 3.1, showing continuous improvements for improving the near term on the left and major development for achieving sustainable solutions for inventing the future on the right.

Selection approaches

Selecting improvement and development programs is one of the most difficult and important strategic actions for corporations. Choices have to be made in the context of the business environment. "Doing nothing" or "wait and see" are not viable options if the corporation wants to lead instead of follow.

Table 8.1. Salient aspects of generic SBD innovation program types

Program Focus	Specified need	Scope	Size	Investment	Duration	Risk
Process improvement	Correcting specific defects and/or burdens in the product delivery system	Usually internal processes but can include supply chain elements	Small to moderate; focus on internal aspects	Typically modest funding requirements; programs can be subdivided	Short term; most programs are completed in one–two years	Low risk during execution; lost opportunity to improve
Process	Improving process capabilities to reduce cost and waste; may be driven by stakeholders	Requires input from the value networks; may involve customers and stakeholders	Moderate; requires resources adjustments and contributions of supply network	Modest funding requirements but could mean duplication of capabilities and resources	Short term; most programs are completed in one–two years	Low risk during execution; may have impacts during transition
Product/process improvement	Improving product attributes that require improved processes; add benefits and reduce negatives	Requires input from the value networks; may involve customers and stakeholders	Moderate; requires new resources and contributions of supply network; some learning	Modest funding requirements; have to convert resources into productive inputs	Short term; most programs are completed in less than three years	Low risk during execution; may have impacts during execution
Product	Replacing existing product or add new one; enhance attributes and reduce defects and burdens	Requires input from the value networks; involves customers and stakeholders	Moderate; requires new resources and contributions of supply network; new learning	Medium-scale funding; have to convert resources into productive inputs	Short term; most programs are completed in less than five years	Moderate risk; can be mitigated by NPD process

New-to-the-world product creation	Expanding product capabilities; improve attributes and reduce defects and burdens	Requires input from the entire value network; involves customers and stakeholders	High; requires new resources and capabilities, contributions of supply network; focuses on new learning	Large-scale funding; have to create new capabilities resources	Intermediate term; most programs are completed in five–ten years	Moderate risk; can be mitigated by NPD process
Technology improvement	Improving the technology; adding new functionality and benefits; faster, cleaner, better	Requires input from the entire value network; involves customers and stakeholders	Moderate; requires new resources and contributions of supply network; new learning	Moderate-scale funding; involves converting technology into products	Intermediate term; most programs are completed in five years	Moderate risk; usually making dramatic improvements within scope
Next-generation technology development	Enhancements through new platform; less expensive, less waste, cleaner, and safer	Requires input from the entire value network; involves finding latent needs and expectations	Broad scope involving value networks from cradle-to-grave discovering hidden impacts	Large-scale funding; have to create new capabilities resources	Intermediate term; most programs are completed in five–fifteen years	High risk; many changes can occur during the program
New-to-the-world radical technological innovation	Dramatic increase or new value proposition; reduced impacts and consequences	Requires input from the entire value network; involves finding latent needs	High; requires new resources and capabilities; contributions of supply network	Large-scale funding; have to create new capabilities resources	Long term; programs may require more than fifteen years	High risk; many changes can occur during the program

In most industries, competitors are making improvements at about 5–10 percent per year.[2] If a corporation does not keep up, it will fall behind. Simply making small improvements will not suffice in many situations since global corporations are expected to exceed the norm and outperform expectations. Moreover, expectations are changing at rates that make keeping up difficult.

The choices are many. The focus is often on the short term, using modest programs to rectify problems in existing products and technologies or to improve them in very specific areas to enhance their attractiveness to customers and stakeholders. The strategic benefit of such modest programs is that they are easier to plan and execute. It is also easier to understand the customer- and stakeholder-related benefits and outcomes. Moreover, because the implications to the corporations are usually straightforward, they are simpler to assess and approve or reject. The time horizon for such programs is generally less than five years, and the investments are in the low–moderate range. However, long-term programs are usually more complicated and require significant investments of time and money. As the time horizon expands, the resource commitments become more crucial, and the impact on the future business situation becomes more difficult to forecast and assess.

Steven Wheelwright and Kim Clark in their book, *Revolutionizing Product Development*, identify three development models; Model I – R&D Driven, Survival of the Fittest; Model II – A Few Big Bets; and Model III – Focused.[3] Model I represents cases in which there are many opportunities for development programs, generally with near-term implications and relatively easy to analyze, prioritize, select, and develop. The basic construct is to have an intensive screening process that can quickly discern the best candidates based on predetermined criteria. Wheelwright and Clark suggest that Model I is suitable for large corporations.

Model II is similar, except that the goal is to select candidates from a relatively small number of larger opportunities and concentrate on developing big wins. The general intent is that such a program would represent a significant, strategic opportunity and typically involves changing the technology platform or developing new-to-the-world technologies and/or products. Model III is a combination of the two, having the ability to handle numerous opportunities in a short period of time through a well-established screening process and develop as many successful candidates as money, resources, capabilities, and time allows.

While Wheelwright and Clark's models were developed in the context of product innovation, the models can be used for technological innovations as well. Generally, corporations establish funding levels for development programs through a financial resource allocation system. The programs range from process improvements and product enhancements to new-to-the-world technologies. Given that there is usually a fixed level of funding, the choices for development programs not only depend on the business environment but on how the corporation chooses to balance the short and long term and the nature of its current and future businesses.

The allocation and selection models can also be characterized using conventional funding perspectives:

- A "*Balanced*" approach involves selecting several initiatives with both large and small development programs that balance the risks of failure and time horizons. Toyota's triad of development programs is a good example of this approach (box 7.1, p. 434). Its lean-burn engine technology focuses on the near term; the hybrid focuses on the intermediate, while the development of fuel-cell technology is dedicated to the long term. While there is a balance of types, "balanced" does not mean that the funding or investments are exactly equal.

- A "*Focused*" or concentrated approach usually attempts to develop breakthrough or radically new technology that has the potential to change the essence of the business environment and provide a significant competitive advantage. Motorola's investment in the Iridium System is an example of the focused "big bet." With many big bets, however, success is often fleeting. Big wins typically involve a high risk of failure.

- A "*Multifaceted*" approach of many small programs attempts to solve difficulties with existing technologies, products, and processes, enhancing current offerings, and providing greater variety. While this may be viewed as a "scatter gun" approach, the intent is to fund candidates that are worthy of investment. One variation is to fund all such programs that meet the development criteria to the extent of available resources. A good example is 3M's pollution prevention programs in which candidates that make economic, environmental, and technological sense are funded.

- A "*Portfolio*" approach involves selecting a combination of product developments and technological innovations as well as programs to improve knowledge through learning and experience. GM, the Ford Motor Company, and other automobile manufacturers typically divide their investments, with 80 percent of their development funding going to product innovation and 20 percent toward technological innovations. The portfolio approach is a modification of the "balanced" approach and may involve investing in different technologies, products, processes

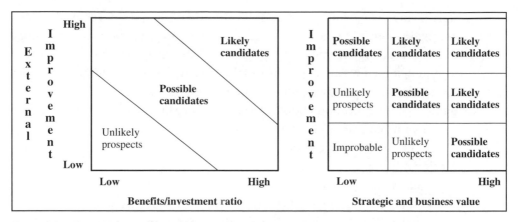

Figure 8.2   Simplified perspective for examining viable candidates

or even licensing arrangements to obtain more diversity in the corporate arsenal. The portfolio approach also involves spreading improvement and development programs across business units and product delivery systems.

These approaches represent options for allocating development funding and selecting programs. There are many alternatives. Figure 8.2 shows a general scheme that facilitates strategic thinking about viable candidates. Obviously candidates that exhibit more value and strategic importance or higher benefits/investment ratios are better candidates and are more likely to be selected.

Figure 8.2 provides two perspectives on the selection of development programs that derive from the basic premises of SBD. External improvements such as reduced environmental degradation, resource depletion, and eco-systems disruption are more likely to be deemed feasible when the strategic and business benefits are commensurate with the external gains. The programs that have a higher probability of being selected are those that offer many benefits, both internal and external. Programs that bring only marginal improvements from an external perspective yet require substantial invest-ment are unlikely candidates. On the other hand, programs providing excep-tional external improvements and internal benefits in relation to the investment are better candidates. Likewise, from a strategic perspective, the most likely candidates are those offering high strategic and business benefits in concert with significant external improvements.

Identifying potential candidates is the initial step in selecting programs. For most global corporations, there are numerous opportunities for improvements and developments. The difficulty is in choosing the best options. While it is impossible to prescribe a "best game plan" methodology, the corporation's vision for the future and strategic direction, in combination with SBD principles and management fundamentals, can facilitate decision-making. Corporate values, beliefs, and philosophies are also helpful in making the right choices. The strength of organizational capabilities and the availability of financial resources are critical criteria, but occasionally are the limiting factors.

Options in selecting programs

Most global corporations allocate or budget a prescribed amount of capital for improvement and development programs. Assuming that the funding is fixed in a given time frame, the critical decision is then how to allocate the money among candidates for development. In their book, *Managing Product Families*, Susan Sanderson and Mustafa Uzumeri developed a framework for examining the development choices based on a variety of products and the rate of technological change.[4] The basic choices they outline form a matrix between variety and rate of change. The four categories that result are: simple (slow change and few types); change-intensive (few types and fast-paced change); variety-intensive (many types and slow change); dynamic (rapid change and many types).[5] In a stable business environment, variety-intensive programs seem to improve the short-term competitive posture of the corporation. However, great care has to be exhibited to ensure that each variation makes sense to the markets, customers, and stakeholders. Many global corporations have a proliferation of product forms that are so similar that additional variations detract from value creation and market success. The fact that change is slow allows corporations to invest in increased variety within the existing technology platform(s) seemingly without significant risks. However, in a turbulent business environment, change-intensive programs are often necessary for keeping pace with the dynamics of the external forces. They represent opportunities for leading change and achieving significant outcomes. While there is no single answer to the complexities of the selection process, Sanderson and Uzumeri's model provides insights about how to structure the selection process based on the rate of change and the needs of the business environment. Figure 8.3 shows the relationships they describe between variety and rate of change in development program choices.

The "simple" category is attractive because of the ease of development, implementation, and management. However, the category usually involves commodity-type offerings that are easily copied and may not have any competitive advantages other than low costs. Unless the corporation is the

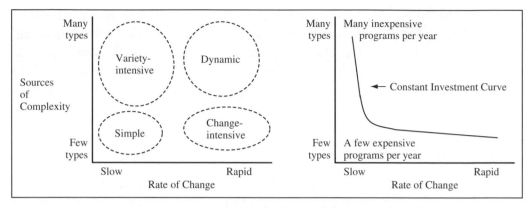

Figure 8.3   The Sanderson and Uzumeri model of development program choices

low-cost leader, there are significant risks from competitive actions and the results may have questionable long-term viability. The model suggests a trade-off between variety-intensive and change-intensive programs. There may be a tendency to invest in variety-intensive programs because they have a shorter time horizon and are often linked to the existing organizational capabilities and prevailing market needs of the corporation. They offer the possibility to differentiate the products and overcome the problems associated with commodity-type products. The difficulty with the variety-intensive approach is that if there are significant flaws in the underlying technologies or systems, then the corporation is creating more products with the same related problems. Change-intensive approaches are more focused on the solution and represent a logical approach, especially if the business environment is in flux. However, they call for strategic choices. They usually focus on improving the underpinnings of technology and the related processes. While the dynamic arena seems to be a good compromise between investing in the present and the future, if it is based on simply hedging bets, it may result in a dilution of resources and outcomes instead of a well-thought-out strategic approach.

Wheelwright and Clark's models agree with Sanderson and Uzumeri's constructs in figure 8.3. The "multifaceted" approach is similar to a variety-intensive one. The "focused" approach is similar to a change-intensive approach. "Balanced" and "portfolio" approaches are variations of a strategy to ensure that candidates for innovation programs are selected from a broader array of options. The types of programs that will be selected depend on the short-term needs and the long-term vision of senior management. The more money that is available, the more aggressive the corporation can be in achieving its SBD objectives.

The curve of constant investment in figure 8.3 (right-hand side) provides a sense of the relationship between extremely large and costly development programs (usually involving new-to-the-world technology) and more modest investments in improving and expanding existing technologies and products. It suggests that choices typically involve a few larger programs or many smaller ones.

Principles of program selection

The principles of SBD provide the underpinnings to ensure that program selection is made on the basis of inventing a better future. They provide the logic for determining the screening criteria. Table 8.2 provides a list and examples of the most important general principles that can be used as program selection criteria.

Framework for selecting development programs

Choosing development programs means eliminating candidates that might be viable and even desirable. Funding is often limited, however, and only so many programs can be initiated and executed during a specific time frame. Great care has therefore to be taken to ensure that the right programs are selected. Selecting the wrong programs dilutes resources and translates into wasted actions. While there are never any guarantees, and the selection process tends to be complicated, the situation can be improved by having a well-articulated selection process.

Selecting development programs involves defining the scope and boundaries of the program, establishing the objectives, targets, and selection criteria, determining the basis of comparison for computational assessments, setting priorities, and developing the required organizational structure. The SMS manages the program selection process in most global corporations. The framework for selecting development programs depends on the type of development programs and what is needed to execute the programs. It provides ways for mapping out the actual selection process, determining the screening criteria, and linking the selected programs to the program management process.

Program selection requires insights about the future, understanding the prevailing situation, and sophisticated techniques for making difficult decisions. It is affected by upstream strategic management through the corporation's vision, grand strategies and objectives, and by downstream

Table 8.2. SBD principles and their use as program selection criteria

Principles	Applications	Examples
Philosophy	The guiding philosophy focuses on the corporation's values, culture, character and vision The philosophy provides direction, guidance, and focus Building quality and value into products and processes is a critical principle	GE views innovation programs as opportunities to create distinctive competencies that will provide competitive advantages in the future Motorola's philosophy focuses on Six-Sigma quality and exceptional customer value
Value creation/ proposition	Value creation is the underlying reason for engaging in development programs Growth and success are achieved by creating superior value for all constituencies Improving the value proposition enhances the capabilities of the corporation to compete in diverse settings	Southwestern Airlines is able to successfully compete and maintain profitability during poor economic conditions because it provides outstanding value
Market and customer satisfaction	Customer satisfaction is critical for the viability of products and services If the products fail to meet the needs of potential customers, the materials and energy consumed have a high probability of being wasted Failed products cost money and consume valuable resources that could have been used more productively	Nucor Steel is the largest steel producer in the United States It recycles scrap steel into valuable metal products for the automobile industry Customers are pleased with low-cost, high-quality steel Nucor has made significant investments in continuous strip technology to minimize energy losses
Stakeholder satisfaction	Stakeholder satisfaction is often just as critical as customer satisfaction Stakeholders can be strong proponents or opponents of technologies and products and related development programs An understanding of stakeholder requirements helps define requirements and product specifications	Weyerhaeuser has many stakeholders that have to be satisfied if it wishes to harmoniously harvest trees and produce lumber and paper products Minimizing the footprint of its logging operations contributes to economic, social, and environmental solutions
Fairness	Fairness relates to equity Solutions have to be balanced in terms of current and future generations and across economic and social groups They should also be balanced across the geographic and demographic dimensions	Johnson and Johnson's credo is inclusive and protective of various groups and all constituents

Table 8.2. (cont.)

Principles	Applications	Examples
Eco-efficiency effectiveness	Sustainable development provides solutions that make wise and effective use of resources and energy Eco-efficiency and effectiveness involve using only what is necessary to achieve the outcomes and then insuring that the outcome is long-lasting	FedEx was one of the first corporations to realize that system effectiveness was just as important as the efficiency of the processes Its system simplified the logistics of rapidly shipping packages
Stability and change	The dilemma is to lead change for positive outcomes while maintaining sufficient stability to allow the benefits of the change mechanisms to be enjoyed Development programs focus on change, while improvement programs focus on stability	Toyota is attempting to create significant change in the automobile industry through technological innovation, yet it is pursuing strategic actions that allow the market to keep pace with the changes

methods for identifying opportunities and action plans for SBD. Program selection also considers the broader opportunities that may exist with strategic partners. While this discussion concentrates on internally developed programs, working with partners is a significant part of the complete development picture.

The program selection process can be divided into three main parts: (1) defining and screening opportunities for SBD programs; (2) establishing the program management constructs; and (3) managing and reviewing progress of the selected programs to ensure that the desired outcomes are achieved. The first element tends to be a periodic function of analysis and decision-making. The second element translates decisions into actions, and the third element is the dynamic process of implementing programs into reality. Figure 8.4 provides a simplified flow chart of the essential elements of the selection process.

Opportunities for SBD programs

Opportunities are the lifeblood of SBD. Given the diversity of the global competitive situation and the expectations of society, stakeholders, and markets, there are incredible numbers of potential programs. Corporate management focuses on high-level opportunities that match the organization's vision for the future and its ability to achieve sustainable success. They

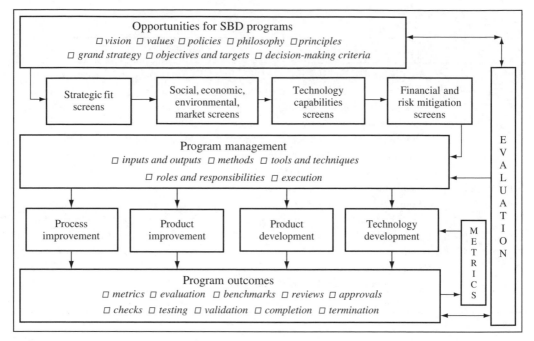

Figure 8.4   Selection process for SBD programs

also focus on change means and mechanisms that have potential to improve the corporation's prospects for the future. Such opportunities often involve radical change and establishing a new paradigm.

Strategic management, in contrast, focuses on opportunities with the potential to improve the SBU. SBU management chooses opportunities depending upon how they relate to the intellectual capital of the organization and its ability to lead and manage technology and product developments. Strategies and objectives determine the logic of the selection: there should be a strategic fit. These initiatives are also intended to fulfill technology and product requirements for the future.

Product delivery system management typically focuses on opportunities to improve the prevailing products and processes. There are often enormous opportunities at this level to correct problems, remove defects, and eliminate burdens and impacts. While product or operations management does not often appreciate the value of discovering hidden defects and potential problems, such discoveries are in reality opportunities for gaining new competitive advantages. Moreover, every issue, concern, and difficulty, if addressed properly, can become a source of insight for creating or improving technologies and products.

Screening process

Screening mechanisms are crucial for selecting SBD programs that balance the needs of the corporation and those of its constituents. The screening criteria are usually based on four critical areas: (1) strategic fit; (2) social, economic, environmental, and market-related requirements; (3) the intellectual and technological capabilities of the organization; and (4) financial implications and risks. Corporate management establishes screening criteria according to the principles of SBD, corporate values, strategies, and objectives. Screening involves a multistep process for determining the suitability and desirability of the candidate programs that have been identified as viable. The first screening examines the candidates in light of the corporation's strategic management constructs. It determines if the candidates fit the vision and grand strategy of the corporation. It asks:

- Why invest in this program? What value will be created?
- If successful, will the proposed SBD program meet the future needs of the corporation and its constituents?
- Will the corporation become more sustainable upon the implementation of the program?
- How will the proposed program contribute to the short-term and long-term success of the corporation?
- Will the program improve the future prospects, reduce the negative side of the value proposition, and add to the positive side?

The screening for strategic fit provides the first cut and is critical in saving time and money on further analysis of strategically inappropriate programs. If a candidate fails to meet the criteria of this screening, it can be discarded, shelved, or possibly sold to others. Those candidates that survive are next funneled into the most difficult and complex screening criteria, those pertaining to external forces. Such externally oriented screenings consider candidate programs in the light of the primary external factors and ensure that selected programs can meet the multiple expectations of stakeholders and constituents. While it is difficult to generalize about such screenings, there are several key areas they must examine:

- Does the proposed program create sufficient value to justify the investment and satisfy the constituencies?
- Is the life cycle of the outcomes of the program (technologies, products, processes, etc.) long enough to provide a sustainable solution?
- Are the social benefits in line with the expectations of external constituencies and strategic direction?

- Are the economic implications balanced and sufficient to meet short-term and long-term needs?
- Are there any stakeholder issues that have the potential to reduce the expected outcomes?
- Are there any laws and regulations that can affect potential outcomes?
- Are there any special interests and NGOs that must be considered during the development process?
- Are there any unreasonable risks or environmental, health, and safety issues that have to be explored?
- Is the market/customer potential sufficient to provide a sustainable need for the proposed program's solution?
- Are there any competitors who have the ability to thwart long-term success?

Strategic management prepares a comprehensive list of screening criteria. The screenings focus on the proposed program's potential to satisfy all of the constituencies. Many of the elements of the solution matrix in figure 3.5 (p. 178) could be used as screenings for determining the value created for customers and stakeholders. With the screening of external considerations, management pares down the pool of potential candidates to a set of potential programs that fit the strategic direction of the corporation and have the potential to fulfill the expectations of the business environment.

Figure 8.5 portrays the theoretical flow of a standard program screening process. In reality, the screenings may be applied in any order. It generally makes sense to flow from high-level, strategic, and external requirements to internal considerations, for there is little point in determining the corporation's capabilities for a potential program if the demands of the business environment are moving in a different direction.

The resultant list will then be assessed further to ensure that the corporation has the right focus for developing and executing the program. Success often depends on the corporation's leadership, core capabilities, and resources. Knowledge, skills, and technical capabilities are the essence of creating, developing, and implementing SBD programs. Management must assess the corporation's capabilities, and its current and expected strengths and weaknesses. The assessment is dynamic because it relates to what is and what has to be. The results may suggest that new capabilities have to be developed during the implementation of the program. If the corporation has the means to develop the required capabilities, then the screening process may simply identify the necessary capabilities and provide a mechanism for developing them.

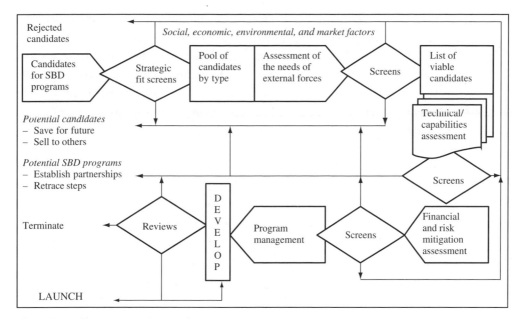

Figure 8.5   Program screening process

The following are five of the questions that might be included in this assessment:

- Does the organization have the intellectual capital and capabilities and resources to execute the proposed program?
- If not, what are the missing ingredients?
- Can strategic partnerships or alliances be formed to supplement the organization's resources and capabilities?
- Are there specific gaps in the skills set and knowledge base that must be filled before the proposed program can be implemented?
- Can strengths and capabilities in other areas be leveraged to support the initiatives?

Capabilities are both the precursor and end-result of program execution. If a program makes the organization more capable of achieving solid performance in the future, it may have been effective, even though other objectives may have been less than successful.

Typically, management focuses on making money, and the financial screenings are the primary determinants for selecting potential programs. However, in addition to cash flow and profitability, the financial picture also involves the long-term viability of the corporation. In certain cases, corporations must invest in developing new capabilities, long-term positions, and new opportunities. Financial considerations have to be balanced across time.

The difficulty in establishing financial screening criteria is that DCF thinking using internal rates of return (IRR) based on a cost of capital approach is useful for short-cycle programs (less than five years), but not for long-term programs (greater than ten years). It is not as simple as stating a required IRR for a given investment. For programs with a short time horizon, an IRR or NPV requirement may be fine. For longer time frames, more sophisticated screenings are necessary. A more detailed discussion is presented at the end of this chapter.

Finally, risk mitigation screenings ensure that candidate programs adhere to the important SBD principle of reducing risk. Typically, managers view development programs as a greater risk than "doing nothing" or maintaining the status quo. But, the "do nothing" approach is not risk-free. Leaders may inadvertently let obsolescence become the mode of operation. Development programs generally have five main areas of corporate risks:

(1) *Strategic risks*   Will the development program lead to the expected outcomes? Will it meet the strategic objectives? Will it contribute to the vision and grand strategy of the corporation? Is there a more suitable program? Is management betting the corporation or one of its business units?

(2) *Reputation risks*   Will the development program enhance or threaten the reputation and image of the corporation? Will the program meet the needs of the corporation's constituencies? Could a catastrophe result that would damage reputation or financial viability of the corporation? Is management risking the corporation's reputation?

(3) *Market or stakeholder risks*   Will the development program enhance or threaten the corporation's market position or harm customers or market entities? Will the program meet the needs of the corporation's customers and market entities? Could a catastrophe result that would damage the economic or market positions of other products?

(4) *Compliance risks*   Will the development program meet the mandates of laws and regulations? Can the development program meet the standards of the broader business environment?

(5) *Financial risks*   Can the development program return a cash flow sufficient to cover the investment and make a reasonable contribution to the future? Are the estimated expenditures affordable? Is there sufficient confidence in the estimation process? Is the expected return adequate to justify the commitment of time, money, and effort?

The actual screenings used depend on the situation. The financial screenings, in particular, are highly dependent on the type of development program and its expected time horizon. The screenings are used to shed light on the positive and negative implications of a proposed program. They filter out the programs that do not fit and would not provide the benefits needed for sustaining the corporation. As figure 8.5 suggests, candidates can be accepted and implemented, rejected and discarded, shelved for the future, sold, or implemented in partnership with others. Management monitors and manages the selected development programs over the development period. The program management construct includes periodic review for ensuring the ongoing suitability of the program. If problems are detected, they are either cured or the program is assessed or terminated.

Improvement and development program management

Improvement and development program management constructs must accommodate the needs of the business environment and the capabilities of the corporation. There are four main configurations for technological and product innovations: process improvement, product improvement, product development, and technology development.

Process improvement simply explores the processes associated with the production of products, looking for opportunities for improvements. Such programs are enhancements to the prevailing situations and attempt to rectify discrepancies, defects, and burdens. Product improvements explore the existing products to discover opportunities to make improvements by correcting difficulties, problems, defects, and burdens. Such programs can also include process improvements. They create derivatives of the existing products that are superior to the previous versions. Product development programs include the design and development of dramatically changed or new-to-the-world products. These programs are typically based on the existing technologies or technology platforms.

Technology development programs run the gamut from providing new generations or platforms to new-to-the-world technologies. They involve creating the technology or new platform and developing new products and processes. Program elements include shaping the infrastructure, forming partnerships with other industries, supporting stakeholders, discovering needs and wants, and linking supply networks. While there are many other possible program constructs including ones that involve new-to-the-world business models, their one common focus is on the ways the corporation can enhance its future. Figure 8.6 depicts the key elements of the selected improvement and development program configurations. Radical technological innovation and technical innovation were both discussed in chapter 7.

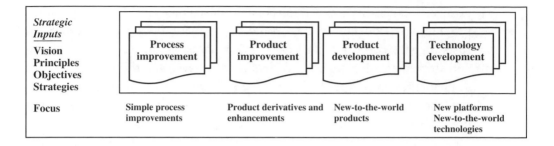

	Process improvement	Product improvement	Product development	Technology development
Strategic Inputs Vision Principles Objectives Strategies				
Focus	Simple process improvements	Product derivatives and enhancements	New-to-the-world products	New platforms New-to-the-world technologies

Scope	Narrow	Broad	Broad	Broad/Deep
Integration	Value system Value chain	Supply networks Value networks	Value networks Enterprise	Enterprise Business environment

External Dimension				
Market	Known market conditions	Known market trends Known needs and wants	Uncertain market conditions and trends	Unknown future markets
Stakeholders	Laws and regulations Key issues, defects	Known expectations Prevailing requirements	Unexpected needs Uncertain issues	Unknown stakeholder issues
Supply Networks	Established relationships	Known information Supporting relationship	Enhancing relationships	Forming new relationships
Competition	Well-known Benchmarks	Well-known Benchmarks	Unsure responses Uncertainties	Unknown competition
Infrastructure	Well-established Limited needs	Well-established Incremental changes	Existing Modifications	Lacking structures Major developments
Related Industries	Well-established Few changes	Well-established relationships	Supporting alliances and partners	Linking with other industries

Internal Dimension				
Product/Market	Product/technology assessment	Product/market attributes	Product architecture	Product development plan
Marketing	Market research (wants/needs)	Customer needs and requirements	Target product specifications	Marketing development plan
Production	Resource assessment	Production resources Leveraging suppliers	Production planning Supplier planning	Production/logistics development plan
Financial	Objectives restated Value analysis	Unit cost estimate Investment	Financial targets	Financial development plan
Organization	Core team selection Leadership	Organizational design	Program management	Management development plan

Evaluation Methods and Metrics				
Market	Market assessment	Market analysis	Concept testing	Market screens
Technical	Feasibility	Performance	Success factors	Technical screens
Economic	Viability	Unit cost	Economic analysis	Economic screens
Risk	Overall risk analysis	Investment risk	Risk/reward	Risk screens
Timing	Do-ability	Time to market	Program duration	Strategic screens

Figure 8.6   Main configurations of improvement and development programs

The purpose of establishing an innovation management construct is to identify the essential elements of the improvement and development program(s) and arrange them into an explicit framework. The generic flow can be modified to suit the specific needs of any program or organization. Process and product improvement programs focus on incremental improvement to existing products and processes using the core technologies and capabilities of the corporation. Chapter 9 examines the ways they can integrate LCT and management constructs. Product and technology development programs, in turn, are much more complicated and require more definitive constructs for mapping out their processes and elements.

Managing improvement programs

Process improvement programs and design for Six-Sigma

Process improvement programs for SBD have to be integrated into the mainstream methodologies of the corporation at each level. **Six-Sigma thinking** has gained significant acceptance since the 1990s and is becoming a mainstream methodology for process and product development. It seems a logical next step to enhance six-sigma constructs to include enterprise thinking and SBD constructs.

Six-sigma thinking has its roots in the TQM methodologies articulated by W. Edwards Deming, Joseph Juran, Armand Feigenbaum, Kaoru Ishikawa, Philip Crosby, and Genichi Taguchi. These quality management leaders laid the foundation for TQM and its related practices that have evolved over the last thirty years into six-sigma quality methodologies.

Six-sigma thinking is more than a quality methodology; it is a business philosophy and a way of managing processes for production, operations, or product development. It focuses on achieving "world-class" performance and distinction by eliminating defects and problems, making it perfectly aligned with SBD thinking. Design for Six-Sigma (DFSS) represents the integration of TQM and product development processes. It seeks to maximize value by providing customers with the exact products they want and eliminating the defects and burdens that can reduce benefits. DFSS is a process-oriented methodology that targets the elements associated with improving a product or developing a new one. It provides a systematic means to achieve higher quality and world-class performance with a high degree of customer and stakeholder satisfaction.

Incremental "process improvement": the five-phase DMAIC Six-Sigma methodology

The most basic DFSS construct is intended for managing simple improvements to existing processes or products. The phases include define, measure,

Box 8.1 Overview of Six-Sigma thinking

Six-sigma is actually a statistical measurement representing the area of a normal distribution that includes approximately 99.99966 percent of the total. Achieving six-sigma performance means that there are only 3.4 defects per million opportunities. The level of quality depends on the complexity of the product or process and the number of independent transactions that occur in the life of that product or that process. The more complicated the product or process, the greater the opportunities for defects.

At Four-Sigma, the number of defects is about 6,210 per million opportunities. Defects are significant costs that are difficult to measure. How does one calculate on a per-product or per-process basis the problems associated with failed products such as the Ford Explorer/ Firestone tire problems? The cost of achieving a Four-Sigma level of quality is estimated to be 10 percent of revenues. Reducing defects increases the value propositions and provides additional cash flow for investments and profits.

Motorola was a leader in six-sigma thinking during the 1980s. In 1981, its CEO initiated a five-year program to improve quality ten-fold.[1] The company successfully completed the first, second, and third phases to achieve six-sigma quality within fifteen years. Its ultimate goal is zero defects and best-in-class in everything.[2] Motorola, IBM, Texas Instruments, Xerox, and later, Allied Signal (who merged with Honeywell), General Electric and several other *Fortune 500* companies adapted a NPD methodology that focuses on Six-Sigma.[3]

Six-Sigma thinking complements LCT. Both approaches focus on improving products and processes and reducing defects and impacts. Defect prevention in quality circles is similar to pollution prevention. If problems and wastes are avoided through effective quality and design processes, social, economic and environmental considerations are enhanced and the corporation's strategic position is improved as well.

During 1996, GE's Jack Welch, Jr. established six-sigma goals across every process. Since then, DFSS has become GE's product development process for ensuring that GE meets customer expectations for quality. It called for "critical-to-quality" (CTQ) deliverables based on statistically derived, quantifiable metrics. CTQs include variable cost, inventory levels, productivity, and service levels. Jeffrey R. Immelt (Welch's successor) has continued to move GE into a Six-Sigma corporation.

Notes:
1. Gregory Bounds, *Cases in Quality* (New York: Irwin, 1996), p. 229. Information derived from an article, by Richard Buetow, "The Motorola quality process: Six Sigma."
2. *Ibid.*, p. 243.
3. Matt Barney, "Motorola's second generation," *Six-Sigma Forum Magazine*, 1(3), 2002. The article is located at www.asq.org/pub/sixsigma/past/vol1_issue3. Six-Sigma is a statistical construct that results in approximately three defects per million opportunities. A Six-Sigma level means that products and processes satisfy the customer 99.99966 percent of the time. A Four-Sigma company has approximately 6,210 defects per million opportunities.

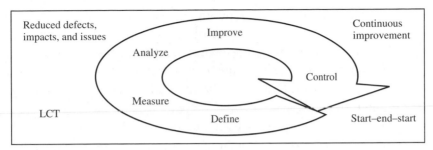

Figure 8.7   The DMAIC process: define, measure, analyze, improve, and control

analyze, improve, and control (DMAIC) with emphasis on analyzing and improving. This is an information- and data-intensive methodology for achieving ongoing improvements. DMAIC is a great fit for simple SBD programs. Objectives and outcomes that fulfill the CTQ parameters drive the process. Each phase is interconnected and can be implemented quickly. The process flow is easily understood and action-oriented, with well-defined objectives, typically a short (one or two years or less) timeframe, and modest investment. Program justification is simple and takes days rather than the weeks or months that may be needed for more sophisticated programs. Figure 8.7 depicts the DMAIC process.

The beauty of the DMAIC construct is its simplicity, that begets speed, effectiveness, and efficiency. It is a targeted approach that implies continuous improvement. *Kazien* is a Japanese term denoting continuous improvement through concentrated, short-duration initiatives aimed at specific improvement opportunities or selected problems. The typical *kazien* consists of four or five days of intense effort. Often, like the *kazien*, DMAIC is used to cure specific problems or difficulties without a large investment of time and money.

DMAIC is the construct of choice when the underlying base is solid and a company desires to keep the current processes and products viable. It fits well when technologies, products, and processes are reasonably well positioned in the business environment and have overwhelming strengths and only minor weaknesses. Minor changes can augment strengths or mitigate weaknesses.

During the *Define phase*, managers identify opportunities for improvements and expected outcomes. This requires an understanding of the business environment and the management system, establishing goals related to customers and stakeholders, determining what is CTQ, identifying analytical processes, and forming the organizational structure for implementation. Essentially, definition involves selecting targets of opportunity and determining how the improvement process will be executed.

DMAIC programs are typically small and may target parts of products or processes. For example, in June 1999, Sikorsky Aircraft conducted a four-day *kazien* event to improve the environmental impacts of the landing gear on its UH-60 helicopter. The improvement methodology followed UTC's Design for Environment, Health, and Safety (DEHS) methodology, using constructs similar to DFSS.

DMAIC depends on determining the right initiatives to pursue. There are numerous opportunities for improvements in the product delivery systems of large corporations; management must select the most advantageous ones for DMAIC initiatives. From an environmental management perspective, Dr. Thomas Graedel's streamlined assessment matrix provides a straightforward means to obtain a first cut at determining needs and opportunities for improvements (Graedel is Professor at Yale University's School of Forestry and Environmental Studies). Graedel's model is a two-dimensional matrix of life cycle elements (pre-manufacturing, logistic, operations, distribution, use, and retirement) and environmental consequences (natural environment, depletion, degradation, disruption, and destruction).[6] It is used to discover any grave concerns about impacts and implications, which represent potential opportunities for improvements. Graedel's model is explained further in chapter 10.

During the *Measure phase*, managers identify defects, obtain baseline information pertaining to the products or processes, and establish specific criteria for evaluating results. At this point, the focus is on measuring existing product and process performance and the opportunities to improve them. Carefully examining and documenting weaknesses ensures that future development programs are based on established needs. Managers and subject matter professionals characterize processes, review applicable laws and regulations, determine the compliance status, describe and assess the operating system, map out the driving forces, and identify needs and goals. They further articulate the desired outcomes and the process variables that, when improved, will support the achievement of the desired results.

In the *Analyze Phase*, managers explore improvement opportunities using functional and statistical analysis (discussed in detail in chapter 10). They focus on the root causes of the difficulties and what can be done to cure the defects and burdens. They look for variables that have the most significant impacts and determine the CTQs that are important to customers and stakeholders. They then assess the ability of the organization to meet these expectations.

The *Analyze phase* requires using qualitative and quantitative methods to understand functional performance and to identify and quantify the gaps between "what is" and "what is desired." Statistical methods provide the objectivity that is needed when communicating results to internal participants and external constituencies. They help focus attention on the real issues. The analysis examines the product and process design in light of customer and stakeholder wants and needs. Concerns may pertain to safety and/or human health implications, and the analysis results in statements or conclusions about these issues. If it appears unlikely that an issue can be resolved or mitigated, an alternative course of action may be required, including addressing product and technology development options.

During the *Improve phase*, managers refine the proposed solutions based on the knowledge gained during the *Analyze* phase. The ultimate solution balances all the needs and requirements; it incorporates the most important customer and stakeholder wants and needs with the most critical product and process characteristics. In many cases, there may be an overwhelming requirement that takes priority over the others, and certain product attributes may have to be suboptimized in order to fulfill the specific requirement. For example, concern about the use of lead in a manufacturing process might force management to eliminate the material in the design of the product, even if the product performs better when lead is used.

The Improve phase also includes testing and validating the decisions to ensure that they are accurate and appropriate. The key questions to ask are: Will constituents accept the solution? Is the solution an improvement? Does the solution mitigate the key concerns and reduce the gap between what is and what is desired?

The *Control phase* represents the implementation stage. At this point, managers seek to ensure that the company can effect the improvements as planned, and sustain the solution over time.

Incremental "product improvement": the five-phase DMADV Six-Sigma methodology

A similar incremental product improvement process is the five-phase define, measure, analyze, design, and verify (DMADV) process for developing new products. The main difference between DMAIC and DMADV is the final "design and verify" phases that depend on creativity and new approaches for satisfying needs and objectives. DMADV is structured to predict and prevent defects, and is in perfect alignment with SBD. The scope is broader and the objectives and expected outcomes are more intense. DMADV is new product development methodology that is intended to be implemented on an integrated basis. The process flow appears to be linear.

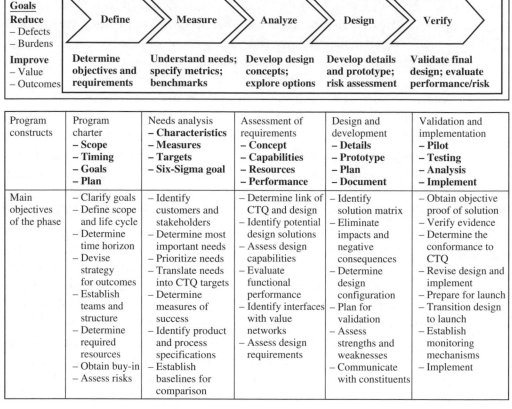

Goals	Define	Measure	Analyze	Design	Verify
Reduce – Defects – Burdens					
Improve – Value – Outcomes	Determine objectives and requirements	Understand needs; specify metrics; benchmarks	Develop design concepts; explore options	Develop details and prototype; risk assessment	Validate final design; evaluate performance/risk

| Program constructs | Program charter
– **Scope**
– **Timing**
– **Goals**
– **Plan** | Needs analysis
– **Characteristics**
– **Measures**
– **Targets**
– **Six-Sigma goal** | Assessment of requirements
– **Concept**
– **Capabilities**
– **Resources**
– **Performance** | Design and development
– **Details**
– **Prototype**
– **Plan**
– **Document** | Validation and implementation
– **Pilot**
– **Testing**
– **Analysis**
– **Implement** |
| Main objectives of the phase | – Clarify goals
– Define scope and life cycle
– Determine time horizon
– Devise strategy for outcomes
– Establish teams and structure
– Determine required resources
– Obtain buy-in
– Assess risks | – Identify customers and stakeholders
– Determine most important needs
– Prioritize needs
– Translate needs into CTQ targets
– Determine measures of success
– Identify product and process specifications
– Establish baselines for comparison | – Determine link of CTQ and design
– Identify potential design solutions
– Assess design capabilities
– Evaluate functional performance
– Identify interfaces with value networks
– Assess design requirements | – Identify solution matrix
– Eliminate impacts and negative consequences
– Determine design configuration
– Plan for validation
– Assess strengths and weaknesses
– Communicate with constituents | – Obtain objective proof of solution
– Verify evidence
– Determine the conformance to CTQ
– Revise design and implement
– Prepare for launch
– Transition design to launch
– Establish monitoring mechanisms
– Implement |

Figure 8.8   The five-phase DMADV Six-Sigma methodology[a]

Note: [a] David L. Rainey, *Product Innovation: Leading Change through Integrated Product Development* (Cambridge: Cambridge University Press, 2005), p. 123.

Figure 8.8 provides an overview of the essential elements of the DMADV process. Like most product improvement or development processes, there are many variations to the standard form.

The *Define phase* is similar to the conceptual level of any new product development process. It involves identifying the scope of the program including the life cycle considerations. The most critical step is determining the boundaries of the management system that is to be measured and analyzed, the elements of the system, and the goals and priorities.

The Define phase also establishes the timing and time horizon for the program. It defines the program life cycle and translates objectives into plans for execution. It usually involves establishing an organizational framework for implementing the actions, typically a team-based construct with a definitive charter for linking the participants and the external business environment. The charter defines roles and responsibilities and the time line. It identifies resources and specifies their allocation.

During the *Measure phase*, managers establish targets and metrics that are critical to customers and stakeholders. From a preliminary assessment of the business environment, the professionals or the team members review the opportunities for improvements in the products, prioritize the needs and expectations, and prepare preliminary product specifications for the analysis phase. This phase focuses on the external forces to ensure that the program addresses the needs and wants of constituencies. It also involves benchmarking other corporations in order to ensure that another corporation will not surpass the proposed goals and targets.

This phase can involve examining qualitative and quantitative data to determine how the corporation is meeting the expectations of customers, stakeholders, the community, employees, and regulatory agencies. Managers determine what metrics can be used to interpret the effects of management constructs such as environmental stewardship, risk management, competitive advantage, cash flow management, and the effectiveness of decision-making. Much of the information needed to support the Measure phase (emissions rates, risk assessments, financial and inventory data) may already exist, gathered as part of routine operations. It can be used for evaluating performance. Appropriate quality assurance functions must be in place to ensure the validity of the data collection methodologies, modeling techniques, etc. This is particularly important if the information is to be used in external reporting requirements.

The *Analyze phase* involves identifying and selecting the most appropriate opportunities for product improvements. Management analyzes product performance in terms of CTQs, the principles of SBD, and the constructs of continuous improvement. They also review performance relative to industry peers, benchmarks and best-in-class corporations, and other products, operations, and sites. This includes checking for compliance with government mandates and for success in meeting customer expectations, finding unresolved difficulties, and determining elements with high negative impacts. There are numerous techniques for determining the strengths and weaknesses of the existing products and candidate improvements, including LCA, product functional analysis, quality functional deployment, failure modes and effects analysis, and others.[7]

In the Analyze phase, managers also generate potential solutions to meet the objectives and goals by formulating preliminary design concepts.

They articulate a plan for implementing the program and gaining acceptance and commitment across the organization. In addition, they may conduct a capability assessment to ensure that the organization has the capacity to execute the program. If not, they must identify the means to eliminate the gap.

The *Design phase* includes translating the preliminary design concept into product specifications and detailed engineering instructions and drawings that define the physical aspects of the product. The product specifications break down the entire product into subsets and then provide a building-up process for assembling pieces into parts and components, modules, and the final product. It includes calculations for determining the material requirements, the strength of the materials, the arrangement of the components and parts, and the life cycle considerations. It also specifies techniques for mitigating risks and liabilities.

The Design phase also includes the development of a verification plan to ensure that potential failures are identified and mitigated. This plan ensures that the design incorporates as much of the requirements of the external dimensions as possible. The focus is on items that are CTQ.

Customer and stakeholder satisfaction are some of the most important metrics of any design program. The primary elements of the solution matrix identify what customers are seeking. Generally, the secondary elements focus on stakeholder expectations. Government stakeholders are particularly important because the new product has to comply with public policy concerns and applicable laws and regulations. Legal requirements often determine what can and cannot be done. Compliance issues may also have an impact on the time required to complete the development program.

The *Verify phase* includes building prototypes and pilot plants to test the validity of the design and the suitability of the new product in the business environment. The intent is to ensure that the product will perform properly in the intended applications and that the potential for defects and burdens has been significantly reduced and the risks have been mitigated. This phase validates quality and performance before the product is launched on a large scale. If difficulties are discovered, they can be rectified before production more easily and at a lower cost. Resolving difficulties early improves the value proposition and enhances the financial picture.

The DMADV process is used for simple, new product development programs that make incremental improvements to existing products. It emphasizes defect and burden reduction and impact prevention.

Development program management

Design for sustainability and IPD

NPD programs that represent major changes to the product attributes, specifications, and characteristics, or involve new-to-the-world product innovations are more complicated to formulate and implement than standard DFSS types. They generally are based on the principles of IPD, which involves the concurrent development of a new product using integrated teams of development professionals from engineering, production, marketing, finance, and environmental functions along with participants from external organizations. The more sophisticated IPD constructs are based on the principles of SBD and DFSS and the strategic thinking and management of the executive leadership of the enterprise.

IPD is a management process that enables senior management, strategic leaders, product managers, program leaders, and designers to make quick determinations about the feasibility and acceptability of a new product, to review the expected requirements and outcomes, and to plan for the NPD program. IPD provides a descriptive, analytical, and structural framework that enables management and practitioners to integrate all of the required resources on a real time basis. Management can make informed decisions because the upstream and downstream participants are involved concurrently. It starts with a strategic assessment of the vision, objectives, and strategies of the corporation, and the forces at work in the business environment. It ends with new and improved products.

The IPD model discussed in this chapter is a derivative of the standard IPD used by global corporations. It incorporates the basic constructs of IPD and Design for Sustainability (DFS),[8] also referred to as Design for the Environment (DFE). However, the former implies a broader context that includes social and economic considerations as well as environmental ones. The convergence of the IPD and DFS methodologies bring LCT and SBD considerations to bear on a concurrent basis. DFS is built on the philosophy that LCT and assessment have to be fully integrated into new product concepts and designs during the NPD process, and not after the new product has been commercialized. This leads to an efficient and effective construct for creating new products that provides better solutions with superior value and fewer defects and burdens. DFS may not be the ultimate NPD process, but it

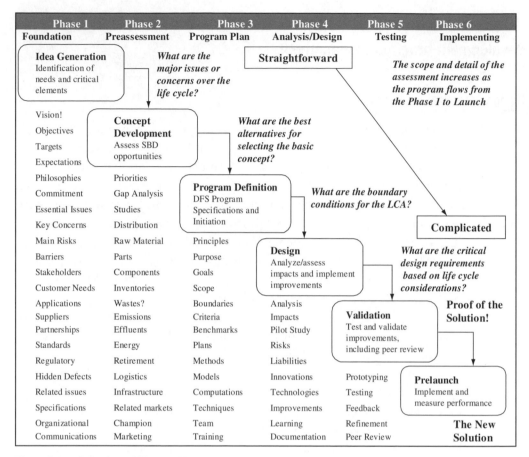

Figure 8.9   Embedding DFS with IPD

is moving in the right direction. The essential philosophical and practical changes are the inclusion of LCT and LCA as an integrated part of the process and the linkages with DFSS and the other constructs. Ultimately, there will be a unified development methodology that includes all of the management perspectives, such as quality, value, social, economic, and environmental considerations, etc. Figure 8.9 indicates how some of the DFS elements embed within the generic IPD process.[9]

The DFS construct contains many of the elements embedded in IPD and DFSS. DMADV is more intensive than DMAIC; likewise, DFS is still more sophisticated than DMADV. More elaborate constructs are needed as the requirements for the program increase. New-to-the-world NPD programs have more uncertainty and greater risks than the simpler improvement programs.

The theoretical proposition of DFS is that it is easier to assess life cycle considerations during the design and development of the new product than after commercialization. It is more effective and less costly to discover defects and burdens systematically before the business environment becomes dissatisfied and seeks remedies through litigation, political action, recalls, or other market/stakeholder actions. For example, it is more cost effective to design out toxic substances than it is to manage their effective use.

DFS represents the full integration of enterprise thinking, TQM, LCT, clean technologies, inspirational leadership, and many of the other constructs within the design and development process for new products.

Idea generation

New products are born from insights and inspiration. In the life cycle management setting, new products are created to take advantage of opportunities to replace existing products with improved ones, or to correct significant embedded deficiencies that cannot be resolved using more incremental approaches because of expense or technical limitations. Most importantly, new products may be necessary to eliminate unintended impacts that can no longer be tolerated. There are many reasons for seeking new products, some of which are suggested in table 8.3.

One of the main motivations behind DFS is the desire to understand the requirements for the future and preemptively provide solutions before being forced to do so. The crux of generating new product ideas is improving the value of the solution(s). Customers and constituents want solutions. Customers buy products because they provide solutions, benefits, and positive outcomes.

The other main inspiration and aspiration for new product ideas are the desires and objectives to mitigate the negative aspects of a product. The platform construct is built on the premise that each new generation improves in both performance and in reduction in negative impacts. The notion of reducing negatives is well established in management theories and practical approaches. For instance, lowering the cost structure of the existing product is one of the most often used means for improving the value proposition and the prospects for the products involved. A lower cost structure makes the products more affordable and profitable. Likewise, mitigating impacts is central to improving the value proposition and DFS. Heightened public pressures, increased regulatory requirements, expanded competitive actions, and the explosion in liability claims provide incentives for reducing and/or eliminating negative impacts. LCT and LCA offer sophisticated tools for creating future

Table 8.3. Compelling reasons for the search for new products

Management level	Capture opportunities *Focus on needs*		Improve positives *Focus on value*		Mitigate negatives *Focus on impacts*
Enterprise (corporate)	– Realize vision – Create alliances – Encourage communications		– Enhance image – Create stability – Improve longevity		– Reduce depletion – Reduce degradation – Improve health and safety
Strategic	– Improve stewardship – Improve infrastructure – Enhance related products		– Increase value – Improve performance – Achieve equity		– Eliminate gaps in portfolio – Eliminate liabilities – Protect environment
Product delivery	– Partner with supplier – Improve distribution – Find new applications		– Meet new customer needs – Support stakeholders – Facilitate applications	–	– Improve affordability – Eliminate hidden defects – Reduce retirement problems
Operating	– Improve capabilities – Increase efficiencies – Improve effectiveness		– Improve quality – Use clean technologies – Improve economics		– Reduce operating risks – Mitigate burdens – Meet government mandates
Functional	– Improve social aspects – Enhance prevention – Improve services		– Improve marketability – Improve financial aspects – Increase knowledge	–	– Reduce waste streams – Improve reuse and recycling – Enhance treatments

products that are easier to market and sustain because the typical issues, problems, defects, and burdens have been designed out of the solution.

Concept development and selection

The Concept Development and Selection phase is a continuation of the Idea Generation phase. This is when managers and professionals further expand those ideas that, based on assessment thus far, show promise. They turn ideas into concepts by further defining the potential properties of the new product, its marketing, production and financial implications, and its expected outcomes. Concepts represent a more complete picture of the new product opportunity. Figure 8.10 provides a view of the essential elements of concept assessment, including a preliminary LCA. If a robust LCA is required because of the complexities of the product specifications or due to high risks, then a thorough assessment can be made at this time. If the social, economic, and environmental concerns and risks appear modest, and the potential for hidden defects is low, then a cursory LCA may be carried out and a more

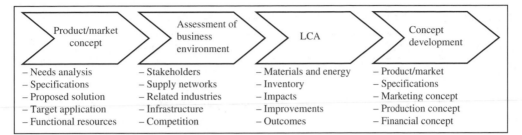

Figure 8.10 Concept assessment with life cycle considerations

comprehensive assessment made during later phases. The goal at this phase is to minimize effort and investment until there is a full commitment to the development program.

The most important consideration when developing a new product concept is how well the candidate meets the wants and needs of the business environment. The more a concept meets the needs of customers and stakeholders, the more likely the new product is to meet the vision, mission, and objectives of the corporation. These external forces determine product specifications that, in turn, determine the expected benefits, functionality, and features. The solution matrix, as depicted in figure 3.5 (p. 178), forms the essential elements of the technical specifications for the proposed new product.

The concept is typically defined by the expected applications of the new product. A product/market concept focuses on generating and developing new products for specific market segments, applications, and outcomes. The product/market notation combines the essence of the product in a market segment and defines the product attributes based on market position. Knowing the intended applications helps preclude decision-makers from selecting attributes that are not appropriate for certain applications. For example, industrial cleaning agents must be restricted from consumer uses if the applications require positive ventilation, which may not be possible in a closed building such as the typical house.

The initial assessment in the Concept Development and Selection phase examines how the proposed concepts fit within the business environment. Practitioners must understand how a product concept will affect each dimension of the business environment; some of the key elements to consider are listed in table 8.4.

Life cycle considerations are central to SBD methodologies. But, at what point in the NPD process should managers conduct the LCA? The advantage for doing LCA during the Concept Development and Selection phase is that, if strong negative implications are discovered and cannot be cured, the

Table 8.4. Requirements through the dimensions of the business environment

Dimensions	Explicit requirements	Implicit requirements
Markets	– Good value proposition	– Zero defects and burdens
	– Exceed needs and expectations	– Embedded health and safety solutions
	– Excellent solutions	– EoL management
Stakeholders	– Applicable laws and regulations	– Information and communications flow
	– Identification of stakeholders	– Cultural requirements
	– Understanding of key issues	– Defined industry standards
Supply	– Availability of raw materials	– Suitability of information and data
Networks	– Quality level of parts/components	– Waste management constructs
	– Material handling safety	– Potential for hidden defects and difficulties
Related	– Identification of critical	– Required information flow
Industries	relationships	– Potential impacts
	– Linkages at critical points	– Economic and social consequences
	– Dependencies and implications	
Infrastructure	– Critical requirements	– Information and data flow
	– Support levels and potential gaps	– Reverse logistics
Competition	– Identification of critical competitors	– Aggressiveness of competition
	– Capabilities of strongest competitor	– Influence of competitors
	– Level of turbulence	– Political impact of industry structure

investment in the program is still relatively low and the loss is minimal. The major disadvantage is that the field of candidates is often not yet fully defined, and there are many uncertainties. Not all concepts will be selected for full development, and conducting a LCA for all candidates could mean huge expenditures of time and money that may not be necessary. The pragmatic approach is to conduct a LCA as soon as there is assurance that the probability of proceeding with a program is reasonably high (say, greater than 80 percent). Often the decision depends on the type of program or the risks that are involved. For example, Boeing may only have one or two new product candidates in a given period of time, and it makes sense to ensure that detailed analysis is available before proceeding to the more complicated and expensive phases. Boeing is currently considering the viability of the "787" program, a long-range, mid-size wide-body jet that is expected to be very fuel efficient. Chapters 9–11 provide greater detail about LCT, life cycle management, and LCA.

The final two steps in the Concept Development and Selection phase are to screen the candidates and select the right DFS programs for further development. The screening process may include testing concepts using experts or potential customers and stakeholders to provide feedback about the proposed new product. LCA may also be used to screen new product candidates.

If the candidate fails to offer significant positive benefits, or has overwhelming negative impacts, it fails the screening. Some find combining screening with an effective LCA protocol saves effort and increases their confidence that the right proposal has been advanced. Table 8.5 lists selected screening criteria that can be used to discern the most appropriate DFS program candidates.

The selection process is both qualitative and quantitative. Corporations may select DFS programs on the basis of their overall position with respect to the screening criteria. However, management may also use more subjective approaches, such as its past experience, in making the determinations. The selection methods have nonetheless to be flexible because DFS programs are generally one-of-a-kind and may not fit precisely into the rating system. There is always the possibility of selecting the wrong candidate or eliminating the right one.

Program definition

The Program Definition phase involves fleshing out the proposed program in sufficient detail to anticipate the scope of the program and the boundaries of the system. The intensity of the Program Definition phase depends on the management system and the NPD process. If process management constructs are fully articulated and the new program is related to previous initiatives, the Program Definition phase may be short and include only an overview of the core requirements for going forward. Management usually follows a well-specified process management script that is used on a repetitive basis. They specify overall objectives, the time duration for the program, the resources needed, and the metrics that will be used to measure performance. They estimate the total investment and the capabilities the proposal will require.

If the NPD program is a one-of-a-kind effort or it is a new-to-the-world product development, however, the Program Definition phase is often more elaborate. Project management constructs may have to be used to detail the key requirements if there is not a history of similar programs to follow. They require a precise mapping of the program elements over the program life cycle. The Project Management Body of Knowledge by the Project Management Institute (PMI) presents an effective model for mapping out and managing such NPD projects.[10] The initial decision involves defining the scope of the program and identifying the essential elements. Scope definition includes establishing the system boundaries (internal and external), determining the critical issues, setting the program goals and priorities, assigning the resources, identifying the barriers to success, and establishing

Table 8.5. Selected screening criteria

	Strategic direction	Capabilities and resources	Risks mitigation
Enterprise	– Fits with vision – Fits with relationships – Aligned with goals	– Have knowledge and learning – Have sustainable resources – Can lead change	– Limits damage to reputation – Eliminates constraints/ issues – Improve negatives
Market	– Fits needs and wants – Is attractive – Creates lasting value	– Enhances life cycle/ longevity – Links to markets/ relationships – Can gain acceptance	– Provides customer protection – Eliminates defects and burdens – Can be adequately tested
Stakeholder	– Meets mandates – Exceeds standards – Improves quality of life	– Promotes awareness – Ensures involvement – Facilitates responsibilities	– Limits liabilities – Promotes problem solving – Enhances health and safety
Social	– Meets equity expectation – Is fair and efficient – Provides broad opportunities	– Fits employee expectations – Is compatible with social norms – Fits within knowledge and learning	– No adverse disclosure problems – Protects human rights – Promotes education and training
Economic	– Meets value proposition – Is feasible for customers – Provides lasting results/stable	– Provides for an adequate return – Is efficient and has high yield – Has reliable sources of materials	– Does not transfer risk to others – Can be sustained over time – Has modest level of uncertainty
Environmental	– Builds reputation – Reduces defects/ burdens – Is eco-effective	– Has knowledge of impacts – Can mitigate negative effects – Difficulties can be solved	– Reduces degradation/ depletion – Reduces potential for accidents – Does not effect biosphere
Competition	– Is not easily copied – Creates better choices – Exceeds competitive positions	– Monitors competitive responses – Creates defendable space – Has a sustainable advantage	– Limited unexpected responses – Avoids anti-competitive behavior – Can sustain competition

standards. Defining the scope also includes determining the computational models and the metrics to be used to measure success.

Establishing the system boundaries is a critical point in the Program Definition phase. The broader the definition and scope of the management system, the more complex the assessments become. However, the more thorough the analysis and development regime, the more likely defects, burdens, and impacts are to be discovered and addressed during development. Moreover, a more comprehensive system provides more accurate and precise final results. This is especially critical if many of the key concerns are with the supply networks, and the scope must include suppliers of suppliers. However, there are real world considerations too. The greater scope and depth of analyses usually require more time and money. The longer it takes to get the new product to the market, the less time there is to reap the rewards and the greater the probability that competitors will find a similar or better solution.

Focusing on the critical issues helps to define the scope. If the major concerns are within the expected operating system of the new product, the boundaries of the system can be narrowed. Generally, the greater the understanding of the total system, the easier it is to make such decisions. If the critical questions extend beyond the normal operating view, the scope has to be expanded to include those elements that might provide the necessary input. Moreover, if there is a high level of uncertainty about the main areas of concerns and potential impacts, the scope should be expanded.

The subsequent step is to determine the goals and priorities of the program. The goals often derive from the vision, grand strategy, and strategic direction of the corporation. Prioritizing is more difficult, however. In many cases, the strategic direction and prevailing conditions are not in sync. It may be impossible to make strategic investments when there are perilous survival questions at hand. When the situation is not so extreme, corporate decision-makers often balance priorities between short-term and long-term benefits. Short-term achievements make the process doable and provide confidence that the gains are meaningful. Long-term outcomes allow the corporation to enjoy future successes and mitigate difficulties over time. LCT can help provide this sense of balance. It examines opportunities on the basis of both current and future implications.

Establishing program metrics is another important step in moving a concept through to commercialization. Metrics provides management and participants with an understanding of the progress being made and builds confidence in the ability to succeed. This topic is discussed in more detail at the end of the chapter.

When an NPD represents significant product change, more detailed mapping of the NPD program is needed. The five key elements for this kind of project mapping are:[11]

- *Activity definition*   identifying the specific activities that must be performed to produce the various project deliverables
- *Activity sequencing*   identifying and documenting activity dependencies
- *Activity duration estimating*   estimating the number of work periods required to complete individual activities
- *Resource planning*   determining what resources (people, money, equipment, and materials) are required and what quantities of each should be used to perform activities
- *Schedule development*   analyzing the activity sequencing, activity duration, and resources needed to create the schedule.

Activity definition depends on the scope of the program. The depth of the supply network analysis is crucial. The common approach is to examine the implications of first-tier suppliers. In a more comprehensive scheme, the assessment may cover many tiers of the supply chain. Similarly, corporations often focus on customers and users on the applications side. Using LCT, the entire chain of use, reuse, recycling, and disposal may be covered. Activity definition also includes all manufacturing and distribution processes.

Activity sequencing is pivotal. Certain activities have to follow others because they depend on the results of the previous activity. However, there are many activities that do not directly depend on certain predecessors. There are alternative approaches for including these activities. For instance, if LCA has not been explored during the Concept Development and Selection phase, it can be completed in a series of activities over several phases or during the Program Definition or Design and Development phases.

Estimating the amount of time required for completing an activity might be relatively easy if similar programs have been executed in the past. However, for new-to-the-world products that are not related to previous experiences estimating the time duration is difficult. Examining other types of activities may be necessary in order to estimate how much time it may take to complete the assessment. For example, LCA may have many similar activities to pollution prevention programs: management can use the experiences with the latter to obtain estimates for the former.

Resource planning is always a challenge. It clearly depends on what the proposal is and how intensely it is implemented. The biggest challenges pertain to people. Management has to select the right number of people who have the capabilities to implement the program requirements. It is especially important to have people with the right training and background for doing LCAs and a systems perspective on developing new products.

Developing the actual schedule integrates sequencing and resource planning into a comprehensive game plan. Allowing sufficient time to perform in an exceptional manner and achieve the desired results is important. The goal is to accomplish the mission in the most comprehensive way possible on a timely basis without sacrificing anything.

Design and development

The Design and Development phase is typically the most crucial phase of the NPD program. At this stage, the conceptual foundation from the previous phases is transformed into an executable form. Managers and practitioners create the technical design and examine the marketing, production, and financial implications. The technical design often determines the other functional requirements. The design elements are the solution matrix. They are the basis for the improved value proposition. The design process is integrative and iterative. Figure 8.11 depicts the interrelationships between the primary elements of the design process.

The centerpiece of the design process is goal setting. While program goals are set during earlier phases, and the solution matrix is often articulated prior to the start of the program, it is often useful to reexamine the specific goals of the design to ensure that the direction is still on track.

Product mapping focuses on what the new product has to be and how the designers are going to achieve the end results. Product designers use input from the business environment to configure new products to provide the

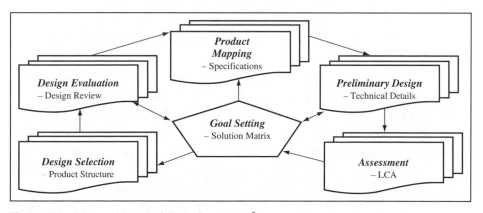

Figure 8.11   Primary elements of the design process[a]

Note: [a] Rainey, *Product Innovation*, pp. 471–513.

most effective solution, given the realities of the past and the expectations of the future.

The preliminary design translates product specifications into technical details via specification sheets and drawings. Engineers break the entire product down into subsets and depict the process of building the pieces into parts and components, modules and, ultimately, the final product. This kind of work breakdown structure is effective for complex products or new-to-the-world technologies that have components or modules requiring significant development.

Design assessment examines the solution from the eyes of the constituencies and the support dimensions of the enterprise. It focuses on the benefits, implications, impacts, and potential improvements provided by the new design. The assessment covers the key dimensions of enterprise thinking and incorporates LCT and LCA. As discussed earlier, the actual timing of LCA depends on the type of program and the importance of knowing results of the assessment. The details for conducting LCA are discussed in chapters 10 and 11.

Design selection involves many technical considerations and assessments. While the prevailing view is to optimize the design from every perspective, there are always choices that have to be made. Design selection should incorporate the most important customer and stakeholder wants and needs with the most critical product characteristics. However, in special cases, there may be overwhelming requirements that take priority over the others, and certain product attributes may have to be suboptimized to fulfill the specific requirements. For example, environmental considerations may require designers to eliminate certain materials that might make the product last longer, but that also make it more difficult to dispose of. Such is the case with paint containing cadmium; the cadmium improves the weathering characteristics of the product for marine applications, but is a toxic heavy metal that creates a hazardous waste.

Design evaluation is the final step. While it is possible to incorporate the elements of this step during the previous activities, a final check of the rigidity of the design is often beneficial. This is especially powerful when independent parties having no vested interest in the design or the program perform the evaluation. Such an approach provides management with the confidence that all reasonable actions have been performed during the Design and Development phase, making the new product one that meets SBD criteria. The Design and Development phase includes similar process elements for determining the marketing and production requirements for the product.

Validation

The Validation phase is actually a continuation of the Design and Development phase. It is directly linked to the design elements, but is often described as a separate phase in order to reinforce the importance of verifying the decisions and the rigor of the entire NPD process. Validation includes testing the design for defects or burdens using internal and external means.

Validation involves examining risks and uncertainties. Risks are identified and analyzed to ascertain their potential impact on the success of the new product. One of the major goals of validation and the related testing protocols is to assure management, and indirectly all constituencies, that the NPD program can achieve all of its objectives, including time to market, development cost (investment), product performance, unit cost, risk mitigation, and reduction of burdens and impacts. It is not easy to achieve such difficult and often opposing objectives. High-risk situations require intense testing. When safety is concerned, extensive testing ensures that every reasonable precaution has been taken. There are no simple answers. Each situation has to be analyzed and carefully thought through before arriving at an appropriate conclusion. The protocols and methods used to effect sustainable solutions invoke the precautionary principle and the philosophy of minimizing environmental impacts and negative implications. The health and safety of users and bystanders makes the validation phase critical. It is pointless to launch a new product that threatens the well-being of society or the natural environment in any way.

Validation may also include scrutiny by outsiders who have no vested interest in the new product. They can provide a peer review of the design and its implications, and offer valuable insights about its suitability in the business environment. Such feedback helps produce the best new product possible and also offers suggestions for improving the NPD process.

Pre-launch

The Pre-launch phase (also called the Pre-commercialization phase) involves preparing for the market. This includes producing products and creating inventory levels suitable for meeting initial demand, initiating the marketing communications plan and program, and coordinating all of the participants in the supply networks.

The NPD process using DFS constructs is intended to be rigorous in its ability to discover and eliminate defects and burdens, yet have sufficient flexibility to allow the corporation to create new products that meet customer expectations and market needs on a timely basis and at a reasonable cost. The process has to be flexible in order to meet the wide array of new product situations. There are always many more areas to explore than time and money will allow. The overall objective is to achieve sustainable competitive advantages that are difficult for others to copy. With the principles of SBD embedded in the designs, new products are less vulnerable.

Still, it is important to remember that the answers lie in the solutions and not in the products. People seek solutions! They are more interested how a solution meets their needs or wants than in the nuances of the technologies or the products. In the long term, business success depends on the sustainability of the solution.

Technology development programs

Overview

Sustainable technology development creates and manages emerging technologies for future markets and business environments. The level of uncertainty is high, and the ability to understand the forces driving change is paramount. While there are numerous well-established approaches for developing new products, such as IPD and DFSS, generic versions of technology development processes are difficult to find and even more difficult to adapt to a specific corporate situation. Technology development usually involves unique inventions and new-to-the-world discoveries. In addition, the related programs are based on strategic management directives that are project-oriented, with senior management playing a vital role during the early stages.

Because technology development defies generalization, it is difficult to identify the essential elements of a system for developing sustainable new technologies. However, three critical areas must be explored and developed simultaneously: (1) the invention or technology itself, (2) the business environment, and (3) the implications of the vision and strategic direction of the corporation.

There are many pathways for creating new technologies, and they are largely unique and uncharted. For instance, the discovery phase for one invention may last for many years before the idea and underpinnings for that invention actually moves into the NPD phases. Still, in very broad terms, an invention or discovery based on corporate vision and understanding of the business environment typically leads to a research program that explores opportunities for, and obstacles to, creating a new technology or a new generation of existing technologies. Breakthrough or new-to-the-world technologies usually require a significant amount of research, typically in a R&D lab, research center, or similar facility, before the efforts are transferred to the

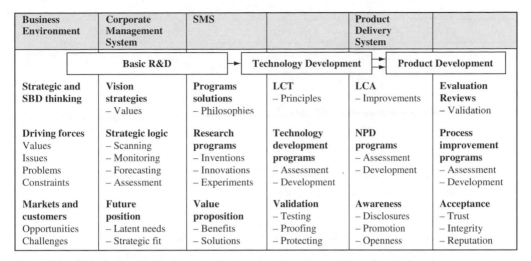

Business Environment	Corporate Management System	SMS		Product Delivery System	
	Basic R&D		Technology Development	Product Development	
Strategic and SBD thinking	**Vision strategies** – Values	**Programs solutions** – Philosophies	**LCT** – Principles	**LCA** – Improvements	**Evaluation Reviews** – Validation
Driving forces Values Issues Problems Constraints	**Strategic logic** – Scanning – Monitoring – Forecasting – Assessment	**Research programs** – Inventions – Innovations – Experiments	**Technology development programs** – Assessment – Development	**NPD programs** – Assessment – Development	**Process improvement programs** – Assessment – Development
Markets and customers Opportunities Challenges	**Future position** – Latent needs – Strategic fit	**Value proposition** – Benefits – Solutions	**Validation** – Testing – Proofing – Protecting	**Awareness** – Disclosures – Promotion – Openness	**Acceptance** – Trust – Integrity – Reputation

Figure 8.12   Relationships between new technology development elements and the business environment

development stage where a prototype or similar device can be created to demonstrate and test the technology. Creating these kinds of technologies is complex and often requires building complicated relationships, structures, and infrastructures.

Figure 8.12 depicts, in simplified form, the relationships between some of the elements necessary for initiating technology development programs. Here the relationships between the business environment, the analytical techniques for understanding market opportunities and needs, the internal assessments, and the strategic management considerations become clear. Technology development flows from its origin via discovery or invention through research and development-related programs to product development and beyond. Figure 8.12 also shows the relative flow of life cycle considerations, portraying the complexities involved, if not all the elements and their precise relationships.

Many elements overlap – and, often, subsequent elements begin before the predecessor has been completed. There are so many variations that generalized forms are difficult to specify. But, most importantly, technology development occurs like a cascading flow from one arena to another, with many elements developing separately and then being integrated at the appropriate time. Orchestrating such activities is extremely difficult and demands significant effort and leadership by senior management.

The critical attribute of technology development is the inherent uncertainty that is present through the formulation and early implementation stages. Program management and leadership have to ensure that the program elements are linked together and that progress is made at the proper rate.

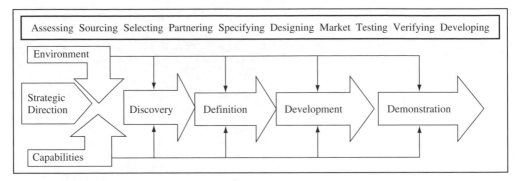

Assessing Sourcing Selecting Partnering Specifying Designing Market Testing Verifying Developing

Environment

Strategic Direction

Discovery

Definition

Development

Demonstration

Capabilities

Figure 8.13 Simplified technology development process

While it is always challenging to pioneer new discoveries, the prospects of the rewards and the excitement of discovery and creation buoy up the program and its participants to find direction and achieve significant outcomes. Such programs often need special people who love challenges and are not afraid of failure. Typically, the R&D or entrepreneurial individual is a pioneer who enjoys the flexibility and freedom to create new technologies, new processes, and new ways of doing things. Figure 8.13 depicts the essential elements of a simplified technology development process.

Regardless of the circumstances, there is always strategic direction. It may be the vision of the corporation, an elaborate strategic plan, or the leadership of executive management. It is often based on the opportunities and challenges of the business environment and the intellectual capabilities and resources of the organization – elements that together provide the ability to discover new technologies and related inventions and innovations. But a great discovery has to be followed by a plan for exploiting the opportunities. The Definition stage provides the mechanisms to articulate that plan, to create a framework, and organize the management constructs for implementing a development program. The subsequent Development stage is the broadest and most difficult to define, because there are numerous ways to carry out the work. And, finally, demonstration is the ongoing effort to validate the devices created during development.

Discovery

The Discovery stage is full of excitement and fraught with challenges. Thomas Edison's system for electric lights is one of the greatest examples of the trials and tribulations of the inventor and his team. The team created an integrated system that included generators, switches, incandescent lamps, and complex circuitry. Edison understood that invention, business, finance, and engineering were interrelated and that each contributed to the overall success.[12] The electric light bulb was not the only successful outcome; it was the entire system of producing electricity, distributing it to the applications, and the excitement of using such products to improve people's lives. Many people contributed to its success including Edison's compatriots who worked with him in his laboratory in New Jersey, and his rivals like George Westinghouse and Nikola Tesla.

The story of the Comstock Lode is another excellent example of discovery. The story is about exploration and mining for gold and other precious metals, but provides interesting insights about discovery and innovation. During the late 1850s, the "easy digging" in California had played out, and the gold miners began seeking new opportunities to find gold. In 1857, miners had discovered mineral deposits in West Nevada, but claims were never filed. In 1859, Pat McLaughlin and Peter O'Reilly claimed gold deposits there in an area known as Six-Mile Canyon. Henry Comstock also made claims to the same land. The three miners settled the dispute by forming a partnership. Comstock eventually sold his share for only several thousand dollars. The mine was not very profitable because the gold was difficult to mine, the gold miners were handicapped by a sticky blue-gray mud that made digging difficult. One astute miner became interested in the mud. He took a sample back to California to get it assayed. It was not gold, but silver ore worth over $2,000 a ton in 1859 dollars![13] The discovery represented a great opportunity, but it was not what the miners were expecting. They were looking for gold, and instead found silver ore, over $300 million worth. Moreover, their unexpected discovery required additional curiosity and patience. The value contained in the mud could be reaped only after technologies were created for extracting the ore. The Comstock Lode demonstrates the importance of having an open mind, not cashing in too early, and looking at the whole system and not just the product (gold).

Discovery is an open-ended process that includes a broad array of programs and projects at R&D lab and research centers, and both formal and informal dedicated methods. Informal, autonomous methods vary from Lockheed's famous "Skunk Works" that concentrated on dedicated projects with specific objectives and targets in mind to the small teams of scientists working independently on new biotechnology, nanotechnology, or other new-to-the-world technologies. Autonomous methods typically involve dedicated teams configured to effect a specific solution. The "Skunk Works" at Lockheed was made famous by the U-2 and SR-71 Blackbird projects.[14] The Department of Defense (DoD) and Central Intelligence

Agency (CIA) had a clear understanding of the specification for the recon-naissance airplane. "Kelly" Johnson and the Lockheed teams created a sim-plified system for developing unique technologies for the aircraft they designed. The team concentrated its full efforts on the project and, in the process, developed new technologies that had large-scale impacts on aircraft performance and manufacturing.[15] The Lockheed team worked with many contractors to develop the materials and components necessary to make their designs into realities.

More formal efforts include the great R&D efforts of the past and present from Bell Laboratories and DuPont R&D centers to the systems integration approaches of IBM, NEC, Siemens, Hitachi and others.[16] Large and generally centralized approaches are most appropriate for complex situations where the solution matrix is ill defined and the discovery process is broad, such as in the discovery of a new pharmaceutical compound. Marco Iansiti, a leading authority on R&D methodologies, promotes the construct of system-focused R&D organizations using integrated teams early in the development process to create knowledge and learning and manage complexity.[17]

An alternate approach is to form alliances or partnerships with smaller companies to broaden the intellectual basis for discovering new opportu-nities. Expanding the network of alliances makes it possible to reach areas that are outside the corporation's core capabilities. For example, Pfizer benefits from its alliances with organizations supporting drug discovery and development.[18] ArQule, Inc. provides know-how on how to rapidly synthesize compounds. Evotec BioSystems and Aurora BioScience offer test-ing protocols for screening compounds. Other companies are also integrated into the system and serve to accelerate the discovery and development of new technologies and new products.

Inventions and discoveries are events that require incredible up-front efforts and collaboration but are impossible to precisely predict. They may be the result of the efforts of a single individual or a large team of diverse participants who collectively create the new technologies. Even Edison depended on the talents of glass-makers, electrical technicians, and mechanics. Today, global corporations depend on a wide array of suppliers, distributors, customers, and others to find technological solutions for the world of tomorrow.

SBD may provide the impetus for discovering new technologies and new ways of achieving the desired outcomes. For instance, the need to improve efficiency and reduce emissions is driving efforts to create a fuel-cell powered automobile. This need offers corporations like UTC, with its International Fuel Cells unit, an opportunity to participate more directly in the automobile industry.

New technologies are also being created to cure the harmful effects of previous technologies and their various generations. Early in the life cycle of a technology the negative effects are often tolerated and even viewed as progress. However, as the harmful effects accumulate, tolerance decreases, and improved technologies are mandated. Leaded gasoline is a good example of a new product being seen as a great solution, yet the new product was inherently flawed because it contains an extremely toxic substance (lead). In August 1924, GM and Standard Oil of New Jersey created the Ethyl Gasoline Corporation and gave the new corporation their patent rights in the anti-knock technologies.[19] The anti-knock technology had solved the limitations of the internal combustion engine by using tetraethyl lead (known as ethyl). However, the federal government (principally the Surgeon General, Hugh Cumming), various universities including Columbia and Harvard, and industry leaders recognized the toxicity of the chemical. Alfred Sloan, president of GM responded by saying that if they could not control the toxic qualities of tetraethyl lead he would close the business.[20] Yet, after several studies and improvements, the product was put on the market. The positive effects of the products seemed to outweigh the negatives that were tolerated because the public, government, and industry believed that the effects could be managed. However, during the 1970s, with the proliferation of automobiles in Europe, Japan, and the United States, there were renewed pressures to solve the leaded gasoline problem. Slowly companies converted their internal combustion engine technologies to run on unleaded gasoline, and tetraethyl leaded gasoline was phased out.

The "ethyl" story is relevant to many technologies of the present era. Technologies have advantages and disadvantages, and the general scheme over time has been to focus on improving the advantages with new generations of the prevailing technologies and occasionally even creating new technologies. But global corporations are wise to examine the disadvantages of their technologies and products as well. The disadvantages might be tremendous sources of inspiration and insights for new discoveries and great new solutions for satisfying customers and stakeholders and making money.

Corporations can also facilitate discovery by continuously screening potential technologies as opportunities are identified and defined. Many corporations use a periodic review to determine the merits of continuing with the program. The review allows time for reflection and decision-making. Programs that are selected for further investment often include a Definition phase for mapping out the program details.

Definition

The Definition stage for technology development has similar constructs to the Program Definition phase for developing new products. The intent is to identify the key elements of the project and define the time, money, work elements, resource requirements, and organizational capabilities that will be required. Technological innovation programs generally do not have predecessors. The program elements have to be determined based on the goals of the programs. The high level of uncertainty demands flexibility and adjustments along the way.

In many cases, the stages of the technological innovation program are transformed into phases and reviews of NPD during the later stages. This is especially likely when the technology has been developed and verified and the activities shift to developing new products using the technology. Some corporations have two distinct programs, one for technology development and a related one for NPD. The other prevailing option is to combine the two development programs into a single program that is linked from the inception of the technology to the commercialization of a new product.

Planning, budgeting, and resource allocation are critical activities that occur during the Definition stage. Planning relates to the same elements here as in product innovation: activity definition, sequencing, estimating duration, resource planning, and schedule development. The most important element is determining the essential activities. The Definition phase activities should seek to answer the following seven questions.

- What is the purpose of this development?
- What has to be done, in what sequence, and when?
- Where is the work to be performed, and by whom?
- When does a work activity start, and when is it finished? What are the criteria for knowing that it has been completed?
- What are the targets and measures for success?
- What are the quality requirements and standards for performance?
- What is the cost estimate for the work?

Identifying *targets and metrics* is especially crucial for SBD programs that use LCT, since performance expectations cut across social, economic, business, and environmental considerations. The description of the program with the established boundary conditions provides an overview of the strategies, objectives, and approaches to be used. The *boundary conditions* set the parameters to be explored, and the breadth and depth of the analysis.

The planning step also includes a detailed work breakdown and schedule that is tied to the organizational design. It specifies resource requirements and allocations with a cost budget for the critical elements. The budget provides an estimate of the total investment for the program, including subcontracted and outsourced elements.

Development

The Development stage for technology development is more complicated and less specific than for product innovations. During the Development stage of a new technology, the focus is on translating the invention (the concept or discovery) into a practical solution. This stage generally involves designing a technological solution. The invention or discovery is often an integration of knowledge, imagination, and ingenuity that has to be transformed into a device. Yet, the device is a generic form of the technology that requires further development and validation. It can ultimately be transformed into products either internally or licensed to others for development and application.

During the Development stage, eco-efficiency design considerations should be explored from a broad perspective, allowing SBD principles to shape the proposed solution. From inception, the effects of social impacts, environmental degradation, resource depletion, and waste generation are important considerations in creating future outcomes. Cradle-to-grave thinking should be incorporated into the system.

In addition, design selections should not be based on trade-offs or "either/ or" thinking. Rather, they must reflect the *total solution* required by the entire constituencies. Older design philosophies were founded on the principles of mass production and consumption. Designs tended to reflect the "average" position based on the most desirable attributes from the customer's perspective. Other considerations were viewed as secondary, given primacy only when mandated by laws and regulations. Today's design philosophies focus on inclusiveness, innovativeness, connectedness, and effectiveness. The objectives are to create the total solution that provides total satisfaction for customers, stakeholders, and others.

During technology development, design focuses on the device and its ability to demonstrate the technology and validate its viability and suitability. It tends to be a technical function rather than a commercial approach. While it is imperative to think about customers and applications, particularly lead users during the early stage of technology development, it is even more important to select the right technological parameters and understand their social, economic, and environmental consequences.

The principles of eco-efficiency can offer profound guidance during technology development. Thinking about the long-term implications of the design selections is critical for ensuring sustainable positions over time. Designers should ensure that the "carrying capacity" of the eco-systems is adequate to provide a sustainable solution.[21] If a certain material is critical for the functionality of the technology, the pivotal question becomes: is that material sustainable in the future? For example, if there is a preference to use renewable energy sources, and ethanol is selected as the fuel of choice for the next-generation automobile, designers must consider the long-term implications of using ethanol-fueled vehicles in large quantities. They must determine the ability of the agricultural sector to "carry" the new technology when launched on a large scale. Many authenticated sources indicate that the production of fuel derived from agricultural sources may have a negative impact on the global problems of food and hunger.

The "ecological footprint" – i.e. the impacts and consequences – of the technology is similarly a critical factor. During the development of a new technology, the negative implications may not be apparent. The history of technologies and products is replete with stories of great products turning into monumental disasters. Such products include DDT, PCBs, CFCs, asbestos, and tetraethyl lead in gasoline, to name only a few. As discussed earlier, the railroads of the nineteenth century consumed incredible quantities of timber for rail ties to provide a solid foundation for the tracks. The impact was devastating for the forests.

Technology development focuses on improving solutions in terms of both positive and negative impacts. New technologies must target wasteful practices, polluting processes, nonessential features, and materials and energy consumption. Technological innovation offers enormous opportunities to rectify the problems of the past and to create new, more sustainable paradigms for the future. The less developed the design, the more latitude there is in making selections that reflect the full scope of considerations, and not just the conventional economic and profit-making objectives. Table 8.6 provides some general insights about conventional and ecological design principles.

Whereas principles offer guidance, design parameters define what the technology is intended to be, and how it fits into the strategic positions of the corporation. Design parameters for products are relatively simple and are typically the specifications developed from the input of customers, stakeholders, other constituencies, and internal participants. In technology development, however, design parameters are more complex and broader in scope. Most importantly, customers and stakeholders are usually unable to definitively

Table 8.6. Conventional and ecological design principles[a]

Issue	Conventional	Ecological design	Added commentary[b]
Material and energy selection	Usually nonrenewable and destructive; relying on fossil fuel or nuclear power; design consumes natural capital	Renewable where feasible: solar, wind, small-scale hydro, or biomass	"Where feasible" is a critical distinction; every proposed solution requires analysis to ensure that it is a good solution
Material use	High-quality materials are used wastefully and result in toxic and low-quality materials that are discarded in soil, air, and water[c]	Restorative materials cycles in which waste for one process becomes input for the next; designed-in reuse, recycling, flexibility, ease of repair, and durability	The solution matrix discussed in chapter 3 provides designers with the essentials for improved technologies and products. Efficiency and effectiveness of resource utilization should be prime considerations
Pollution	Copious and endemic creation of residuals and waste streams; little regard to the problems of waste given the primary considerations of economic viability	Wastes are minimized; the amount and composition of wastes conform to the ability of the ecosystems to absorb them. Lean production techniques should be used to conserve resources and minimize wastes	Minimizing wastes is a primary consideration; the expected wastes must be calculated before committing to technology/product design. Balanced solutions are the most important
Toxic substances	Common and destructive, ranging from pesticides for apicultural production and carcinogenic chemicals for industrial applications to toxic chemicals for household use	Used extremely sparingly in very special circumstances; replacing toxic chemicals with benign substitutes. Creates natural means to produce products and food	The negative effects often outweigh the positive, especially in the long term; analysis of materials and energy is imperative to determine the most efficacious selection; in the long term, all toxic material must be eliminated
Ecological accounting	Limited to compliance with mandatory requirements such as environmental impact reports; minimal disclosures pertaining to social, economic, and environmental impacts and risks	Sophisticated and built-in transparency of operations, products, and processes; covers full analysis of wide range of impacts over entire life cycle of the project, from extraction of materials to final recycling of components	Requires extensive effort to incorporate ecological accounting into the mainstream of business thinking and management; requires input and approval of standards setting organizations. Necessitates full reporting and disclosures

Table 8.6. (cont.)

Issue	Conventional	Ecological design	Added commentary[b]
Ecology and economics	Perceived as mutually opposing perspectives; short-run view that favors economic considerations above all others	Perceived as compatible; long-term view that indicates that they are not only compatible but they reinforce each other Good economic choices must be ecologically sound	Designs of the future have to build-in solutions that are balanced and inclusive; SBD requires positive outcomes that are socially, economically, and environmentally harmonious
Design criteria	Economics, customer needs, and convenience, and other performance-related criteria are given precedence	Human and eco-systems health and safety considerations, ecological impacts, and economic realities are coequal in the design considerations	Design criteria are based on input from all constituencies and a long-term perspective
Sensitivity to ecological context	Standard templates are replicated all over the planet with little regard to ecological considerations of the place	Responds to bio-region; the design appreciates local soils, vegetation, culture, climate, and topography; solutions are based on the local context as well as the global	Customized solutions provide improved efficiencies and greater effectiveness; designs are fine-tuned to regional conditions, avoiding unnecessary material or functionality
Sensitivity to cultural context	Tends to build homogeneous global culture – for instance, skyscrapers look the same from New York to Cairo	Respects and nurtures traditional knowledge of place and local materials and technologies; fosters a rich diversity of life styles	Sustainable development fosters social considerations; good solutions respect the cultural and social diversity of humankind and maintain bio-diversity
Knowledge base	Narrow disciplinary focus based on core competencies that are specific to the prevailing situation	Integrates multiple design disciplines and a wide range of sciences; comprehensive knowledge – and, most importantly, accelerated learning	Technological innovation and technology development are about learning and knowledge; greater knowledge begets better solutions; the learning rate dictates progress

Whole system	Tends to work at one scale at a time; divides system along boundaries that do not reflect underlying natural processes	Works with whole system; produces designs that provide the greatest degree of internal integrity and coherence	Holistic thinking is paramount for creating great solutions; management must understand all of the implications and impacts
Role of nature	Design must be imposed on nature to provide control and predictability, and meet narrowly defined human needs	Includes nature as a partner; whenever possible, substitutes natural solutions instead of relying on materials and energy	Spatial aspects include multiple dimensions; each must receive due consideration; spatial aspects include cradle-to-grave perspective
Underlying metaphors	Machine, technology, product, and part	The eco-systems, the enterprise, and LCT	It is the solution, not the product! People want solutions, better solutions with fewer impacts

Notes:

[a] Adapted from Sim der Ryn and Stuart Cowan, *Ecological Design* (Washington, DC: Island Press, 1996).

[b] These comments are intended to add insights and reflections.

[c] These comments are broad generalizations that have to be proven. There is no doubt that such conditions do exist.

provide input because they are unfamiliar with the proposed technologies. The following are seven of the key questions they must address:

- *Strategic intent*   How does the technology fit into the enterprise and its spatial and temporal dimensions? How would it affect the value system and the value propositions? What are the critical factors for success? What are the constraints?
- *Market context*   What is the market potential for future applications of the technology? Generally, this question focuses on future customers and markets and the overarching needs of society, economical underpinnings, and environmental imperatives.
- *Strategic relationships*   Who are the advocates for the technology and the solutions derived from it? Who are the potential users, and what are their needs? Who are potential partners and allies, and what do they think is needed for success?
- *Leading effects*   What are the "must haves" or "should provides" for this technology? Such effects may be concepts such as mobility, enjoyment, convenience, risk mitigation, savings, longevity, etc. They generally pertain to the value propositions and the solutions.
- *Standards*   What are the most critical government and/or industry standards that pertain to the new technology? If the standards do not exist, how can they be developed?
- *Risk mitigation*   What are the most significant risk factors? How can they be reduced or eliminated? What are the means to avoid the negatives and accentuate the positive aspects?
- *Change management*   What are the best ways to encourage change and adoption of the technology both externally and internally? Who are the potential change agents, and how can they play a role in supporting the new technology? It is important to emphasis the importance of building critical mass for the acceptance of the solutions.

It is difficult to articulate all of the design considerations necessary to invoke a new-to-the-world solution. Strategic intent recognizes the centrality of technological innovation for achieving SBD. Ecological designs with new architectures face the social, political, economic, and environmental realities of the business world and attempt to eliminate, mitigate, or solve the negative impacts of existing technologies, products, and processes.

The market context for technology development is based on the broader view of balanced solutions and enhanced value propositions. Leading change requires understanding the latent needs of potential customers, developing the market conditions to prepare the way for suitable applications, and building awareness and acceptance. Technology development often takes ten or more years to create the new technology. Communications with potential markets and customers are typically not viewed as priorities during the early stages because the means to reach potential customers have not been developed. However, selling the advantages of the technology and building acceptance can start once there is definition about the technology. Building market awareness in this way is an integral part of the Design and Development stage.

Creating technology designs for a complex invention necessitates building many relationships across the value networks. Moreover, LCT and life cycle management mandates the inclusion of all of the essential partners and allies to analyze the advantages and disadvantages of the technology and to structure the most appropriate value chain for developing and implementing the technology. The best solution is not always apparent, and the flow of value-added actions and activities depends on the relationships between the producer, all of the other contributors in the enterprise, and the customers. For example, certain suppliers may be better able to provide the solution than the primary producer. Sikorsky Aircraft has certain key suppliers who handle some plating and coating requirements, because they concentrate on those lines of business and have state-of-the-art equipment for managing the regulatory mandates.

The justification for developing a new technology is typically based on leading effects, the advantages that create excitement in the markets and with other constituencies. Corporations typically explore the positive effects to seek opportunity and competitive advantage. Occasionally, the negative effects of existing technologies and their related products and processes drive change. Nevertheless, leading effects are central to the design of new technologies.

When considering the feasibility of a new technology, a prime factor may be its ability to reduce the myriad risks associated with the prevailing conditions. Risk mitigation facilitates better outcomes.

The creation of standards is a somewhat isolated parameter, but it is crucial for achieving success and mitigating problems. Standards facilitate applications and make it easier for the broader communities to understand and use the technology. With a uniform approach that is articulated to all constituencies, customers and the value networks can invest in the solution without any concern that there may be other forms that have to be accommodated as well. The story of the development of CD-ROM technology provides insights. Sony and Philips collaborated on the design so that they could establish a common format. Each recognized that it needed the power of a partner to standardize the technology. Once their standard was established, it was difficult, if not impossible, for a competitive form to gain acceptance.

Standardization has played a pivotal role in the development of many industries. The railroads became more successful when standard-gauge track was employed. Similarly, by creating standard grades of metal with precise formulas, the steel industry provided customers with accurate information about the products they were buying. Standards support sustainable development. They reduce the number of variants and improve the economic feasibility of EoL options. For instance, standards make recycling more attractive because there are only a few alternatives to handle and generally more of a common material to use in other applications.

Change management is inherent and obvious when developing new technology, but it is often not fully contemplated. People must have information and knowledge to move from the old to the new. They must become comfortable with the changes and the implications. When creating new designs, the impacts of the changes have to be considered and built into the solution.

Demonstration

The Demonstration stage focuses on the technology and not on the potential products. It examines the prototype that is created to test the feasibility and viability of the technology, and seeks to build credible evidence that the technology warrants full implementation. It may involve extensive testing and should include the perceptions of potential customers. For example, the pharmaceutical industry clinical trials as required by the US Food and Drug Administration (FDA) may require between five and ten years of studies, beginning with laboratory animals through to clinical patients. The purpose is to determine the efficacy and safety of the potential applications before the end-product is marketed. Discovering potential defects before developing commercial forms of a technology allows corporations to address them early, or to even terminate the program before commercialization. Negative impacts can be managed more easily during development stages, but may require substantial expenses to cure after the technology has been in use for several years.

The demonstration of new technology is similar to the validation of new products, except that the focus is on technical and economic feasibility instead of on proof of design and the verification of factors for production, marketing, and finance. It focuses on obtaining objective evidence that the technology fits the criteria for SBD. This evidence is often obtained by testing prototypes. Prototype testing gives concrete information about the advantages and disadvantages of the technology, including data about the economics. This allows further investments to be based on proven solutions and not on promises or assumptions.

Box 8.2 Canon, Inc.: aiming to be a truly excellent corporation

Canon is transforming itself to be a sustainable company. Its overarching ambition is to become "an excellent global corporation based on the *Kyosei* philosophy, using cutting-edge technology to support the environment and create a sustainable society."[1] Fujio Mitarai, President and CEO of Canon, defines *Kyosei* and puts it into context:[2]

> Kyoei stated concisely is "living and working together for the common good." And a broader definition is "all people, regardless of race, religion or culture, harmoniously living and working together into the future." The ideal behind *Kyosei* is the same as that for a sustainable society.
>
> Corporations, and especially manufacturers like Canon, are in business to provide products and services that enrich people's lives, making them happier and more convenient. I firmly believe that, at the same time, these products must be environmentally conscious, both in terms of manufacturing and marketing, to ensure that the environmental burden is reduced and the products contribute to the goal of establishing an environmentally and economically sustainable society.

Canon's aim to be a truly excellent corporation is support by its technological and product innovations to create products without rival in quality and service. Product innovation is based on three sustainable product strategies, focusing on energy efficiency, resource conservation, and the elimination of hazardous substances. Using LCA methods, Canon maps out the burdens for each product and establishes targets for making improvements. The environmental information on products supports product design and development processes with details about the benefits and burdens associated with the decision making from the planning phases through development, testing, procurement, and production. Canon uses three-dimensional CAD to manage the information, to assess design options, and to create prototypes for testing.

The Product Environmental Information System includes assurance activities to integrate suppliers into the design and development processes so that they are fully qualified to meet environmental, quality, cost, and delivery (EQCD) requirements. Suppliers have to be deemed capable for meeting all requirements. The Green Supplier Management System ensures that suppliers are successful contributors to Canon's vision, mission, and objectives and are capable of meeting standards and performance.[3]

Figure 8B.1 provides an overview of the Product Environmental Information System.

Canon's design and development process provides an interesting perspective on how to embed environmental management considerations into NPD. The assessments are basically reviews to determine whether to proceed or not. Supplier evaluations include green procurement standards to improve efficiencies and eliminate hazardous materials. For instance, Canon is already in compliance with EU Directives to eliminate certain hazardous substances

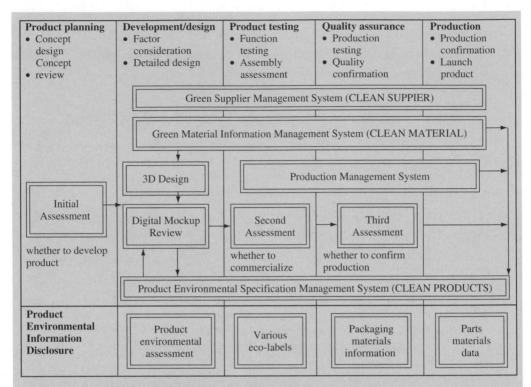

Figure 8B.1 Canon's Product Environmental Information System

such as lead and cadmium. Canon's NPD process incorporates EoL considerations. Resource recycling management is aggressively pursued to support life cycle management and to maximize resource utilization. For example, Canon recycled 110,000 tons of used toner cartridges in 2003.

In 1993, Canon adapted its Environmental Charter, revised in 2001 and based on the corporate *Kyosei* philosophy. The fundamental policies for environmental assurance seek to achieve sustainable business activities and offer green products through innovative improvements. The eight specific targets are:[4]

(1) Optimize the organizations for promoting the Canon Group's global environmental efforts, and promote environmental assurance activities for the Group as a whole.

(2) In product planning and development, explore ways to minimize the environmental burden and conduct EIAs.

(3) Promote the development of technologies and materials essential for environmental assurance, and share the achievements with society.

(4) Promote energy and resource conservation and elimination of hazardous substances in all corporate activities.

(5) When possible, practice green procurement and purchasing – give priority to selecting materials, parts, and products with a lower environmental burden.

(6) Establish EMSs to prevent environmental pollution and damage, and steadily reduce the environmental burden.

(7) Actively disclose to all stakeholders information on environmental burdens and keep them updated on the progress of environmental measures.

(8) Raise the environmental awareness of employees and educate them to take initiatives in environmental protection. Maintain close relationships with governments, communities, and other interested parties, and actively support and participate in environmental protection activities.

Canon portrays many of the attributes of a sustainable company. Its Charter reflects the principles, philosophies, and practices of a company that believes in the triple bottom line. Canon has an inclusive view of its enterprise and maintains openness through reporting mechanisms. It is connected to its customers, stakeholder, and suppliers through its various Green Product initiatives. Most importantly, it is pursuing excellence through innovation and business integration. Leadership is setting the stage for extraordinary performance and achievements for the company and society.

Notes:
1. www.canon.com/environment, *Canon Sustainability Report*, 2004, p. 3.
2. *Ibid.*
3. *Ibid.*, p. 30.
4. *Ibid.*, p. 7.

Summary

Selecting improvement and development programs involves complicated processes that are based on the strategic direction of the corporation and its vision for the future. They also depend on the capabilities and knowledge of the organization and its willingness to change technologies, products, and processes. Corporations may seek simple improvements to products and processes, or radical technological changes. They select improvement and development programs based on the dynamics of the business environment and the overall needs of customers, stakeholders, and other constituents for improving the prevailing situation.

The overarching goal of improvement and development programs is to integrate management systems, technologies, products, and processes into a seamless framework that focuses on innovation and creativity for solving problems, eliminating difficulties, and creating significant competitive advantages. Strategic leaders of global corporations are expected to achieve exceptional results. They have to outperform the competition and satisfy the needs and expectations of all of their constituencies. It is clear that dramatic changes are crucial for success. The challenge is how to proceed.

There are numerous approaches for making changes and improvements: the actual choices depend on the situation. If the corporation is just beginning to pursue SBD, the simpler methods of process improvements might be appropriate. Achieving success in process innovation can provide the knowledge and capability to move on to the more involved product development and technology development programs. Senior management has to decide the path to take, and the urgency for obtaining the desired outcomes. The approaches are not prescriptive, but the outcomes may be. It is expected that significant and meaningful gains will be made on an ongoing basis as the corporation fulfills its obligations and objectives under the SBD paradigm. Moreover, as improvements are realized, additional improvement and development programs should get easier to accomplish. Like the TQM approaches of earlier decades, success will lead to additional programs for further improvements and gains. Also like TQM, the improvements will profoundly change the business environment and the competitive arena. The capable corporations will grow stronger and become more successful; the weak will struggle to survive.

Supplementary material

Learning objectives

Chapter 8 has the following learning objectives that are intended to guide and support students and practitioners:
- Understanding how to select appropriate SBD innovation programs.
- Understanding the means and mechanisms for managing SBD innovation programs.
- Describing the essential elements of SBD process improvement programs.
- Describing the essential elements of SBD product development programs.
- Describing the essential elements of SBD technology development programs.
- Appreciating how executives and senior management contribute to innovation programs.

Research questions

The following are questions related to SBD in order to facilitate learning and ongoing discussion and analysis of the main topics covered in the chapter:

- What are major types of SBD innovation programs of global corporations?
- What are the main screening criteria for selecting SBD innovation programs?
- How can corporations integrate DFSS into SBD?
- What are the main phases of product development programs used by large corporations?
- What are the main stages of technology development programs?

NOTES

1. The concept of an enterprise was discussed in chapter 2. The concepts of a sustainable enterprise and how to develop new business models are so extensive that they would require an entire book to elucidate the salient theories, concepts, strategies, processes, and practices. I am currently writing a book (to be published in 2007), entitled *Sustainable Enterprise Management: Creating Extraordinary Value through Strategic Leadership and Business Innovation*.

2. The actual rates vary considerable year to year and industry to industry. For example, the leading corporations in the chemical industry, DuPont and Dow Chemical, improved many of their waste management metrics by 90 percent during the 1990s. The results represented approximately a 6.5 percent improvement per year.

3. Steven Wheelwright and Kim Clark, *Revolutionizing Product Development: Quantum Leap in Speed, Efficiency and Quality* (New York: Free Press, 1992), pp. 119–127.

4. Susan Sanderson and Mustafa Uzumeri, *Managing Product Families* (Chicago: Irwin, 1997), p. 19.

5. *Ibid.*

6. Thomas E. Graedel, *Streamlined Life-Cycle Assessment* (Englewood Cliffs, NJ: Prentice Hall, 1998), pp. 235–249.

7. This book is intended to provide a high-level perspective of development programs. For details on NPD and techniques such as quality function deployment and failure modes and effects analysis, read Rainey, *Product Innovation*.

8. Rainey, *Product Innovation*. For an in-depth understanding of IPD, read chapter 3 in Rainey, *Product Innovation*. The subsequent chapters provide details about the phases of the NPD process as discussed in this section. The intent of *Sustainable Business Development* is to provide a high-level view of IPD and the NPD process.

9. Rainey, *Product Innovation*, p. 580.

10. Project Management Institute (PMI), *A Guide to the Project Management Body of Knowledge* (Philadelphia: Project Management Institute, 1996). The book provides an effective guide for using project management techniques.

11. *Ibid.*, p. 31.

12. Carroll Pursell, Jr., *Technology in America*, 2nd edn. (Cambridge, MA: MIT Press, 1990), p. 126. Taken from Thomas Parke Hughes, "Thomas Elva Edison and the Rise of Electricity," chapter 11 in Pursell's book.

13. http://www.vcnevasa.com/history.htm. The article is entitled, "History of Virginia City, Nevada and the Comstock Lode," by Don Bush (1992).
14. Ben Rich and Leo Janos, *Skunk Works* (Boston, MA: Back Bay Books, 1994), pp. 193–219.
15. C. Johnson with Meggie Smith, *Kelly – More Than My Share of It All* (Washington, DC: Smithsonian Institution, 1985), pp. x–xii.
16. Marco Iansiti, "Real world R&D: jumping the product generation gap," *Harvard Business Review*, May–June 1993.
17. *Ibid.*
18. A. Barrett, "How big is too big?," *Business Week*, August 28, 2000, pp. 216–222.
19. Joseph Robert, *Ethyl: A History of the Corporation and the People Who Made It* (Charlottesville, VA: University of Virginia Press, 1983), p. 119.
20. *Ibid.*, p. 122.
21. Bleet Scmidt *et al.*, "Statement to government and business leaders," Wuppertal Institute, WBCSD, 1997, p. 6. The carrying capacity of the earth to provide the resources or tolerate the waste streams is the primary concern – i.e. the long-term implications of design selections. Certain selections may be feasible in the short term but may not be sustainable over time.

REFERENCES

Barney, Matt (2002) "Motorola's second generation," *Six Sigma Forum Magazine*, 1(1)
Barrett, A. (2000) "How big is too big?," *Business Week*, August 28
Buetow, Richard (1996) "The Motorola quality process: Six Sigma," in Gregory M. Bounds, *Cases in Quality*. New York: Irwin.
der Ryn, Sim and Stuart Cowan (1996) *Ecological Design*. Washington, DC: Island Press
Graedel, Thomas E. (1998) *Streamlined Life-Cycle Assessment*. Englewood Cliffs, NJ: Prentice Hall
Iansiti, Marco (1993) "Real world R&D: jumping the product generation gap," *Harvard Business Review*, May–June
Johnson, C. with Meggie Smith (1985) *Kelly – More than My Share of It All*. Washington, DC: Smithsonian Institute
Project Management Institute (PMI) (1996) *A Guide to the Project Management Body of Knowledge*. Philadelphia: Project Management Institute
Pursell, Jr. Carroll (1990) *Technology in America*, 2nd edn. Cambridge, MA: MIT Press
Rainey, David L. (2005) *Product Innovation: Leading Change through Integrated Product Development*. Cambridge: Cambridge University Press
Rich, Ben and Leo Janos (1994) *Skunk Works*. Boston, MA: Back Bay Books
Robert, Joseph (1983) *Ethyl: A History of the Corporation and the People Who Made It*. Charlottesville, VA: University of Virginia Press
Sanderson, Susan and Mustafa Uzumeri (1997) *Managing Product Families*. Chicago: Irwin
Scmidt, Bleet *et al.* (1997) "Statement to government and business leaders," Wuppertal Institute, WBCSD
Wheelwright, Steven and Kim Clark (1992) *Revolutionizing Product Development: Quantum Leap in Speed, Efficiency, and Quality*. New York: Free Press

9   Life cycle thinking and framework

Introduction

LCT is an intellectual methodology for examining, assessing, and improving technologies, products, and processes. It includes "cradle-to-grave" evaluation – i.e. evaluation of the upstream supply network management and manufacturing, the downstream aspects of product sale, use, and EoL considerations, and all of the entities related to any of these processes. LCT may be viewed as a subset of enterprise thinking, or a more specific form of it, depending on the management's perspective. LCT generally focuses on operational considerations while enterprise thinking focuses on strategic management considerations. LCT takes an integrative perspective on the linkages and relationships within the entire enterprise, in order to find new and improved ways to select and deploy inputs and processes that will create better outputs. It also looks at the business environment and its opportunities and challenges as a whole. Nothing is considered in isolation.

LCT involves a revolutionary philosophy about how to progress from achieving satisfactory results and continuous improvement to leading change, making significant improvements, and eliminating the causes of social, economic, environmental, and business problems. Rather than just focusing on maximizing growth and profits, LCT is aimed at finding opportunities to improve and achieve sustainable outcomes. The goal is to create value streams and networks that are strategically aligned and functioning effectively over time so that negative consequences are minimized and positive benefits and implications endure, justifying the investments of time, money, and resources.

Progress in the twenty-first century is measured in terms of generating maximum value, benefits, and positive outcomes using a minimum of resources and energy and creating the least amount of wastes and pollution. While this is a challenging goal, technological and product innovations in many fields are providing the means and mechanisms for realizing dramatic improvements. The essence and functionality of most technologies and products are significantly better than they were even in the 1990s. For instance, processes are producing less waste per unit of production and products are generally smaller, more powerful, and more cost effective. Moreover, new technologies are eliminating certain impacts by circumventing the waste generating processes. While digital camera technology is not perfect, it has eliminated the requirements for hazardous chemicals in the processing of photographs.

LCT explores what the situation "will be," "has to be," or "could be," instead of "what it is." It presumes that future outcomes will move product positions closer to the ideal. The PC, for example, has been transformed from a simple device used mostly for word processing to a multifunctional platform of utility and productivity that has become less expensive, less burdensome, and more powerful with each new generation. LCD displays are eliminating the use of cathode ray tube (CRT) monitors that contain toxic substances. The long-term trend is clearly moving toward more effective solutions with fewer difficulties and less wastes.

Most problems that develop with a given product or process over time appear minuscule during the early stages of development. For example, CFCs were not recognized as a problem until their usage expanded dramatically when they became the preferred cleaning solvent for electronics. While it is impossible to reconstruct history, CFCs might have survived if the applications had been restricted to devices where the materials could be controlled. LCT can avoid this type of situation because it focuses attention on future impacts and implications when examining the business environment and proposals for new products and technologies.

The **life cycle framework** broadens management's view of market space and time. Most management constructs are based on reductionism (thinking about the parts) in order to simplify the analyses required to understand the complexities of the real world. They generally explore the parts of the system or the local conditions and not the whole. LCT is a pivotal change, adopting a systems perspective about the enterprise, the corporation, its relationships, networks, interconnections, and subsystems. LCT and the life cycle framework examine the implications of past difficulties, existing concerns, and future needs and desires. The intent is to be as inclusive of the whole business environment as possible and to examine all aspects, not just the desired outcomes.

LCT includes the following six essential elements that are also the topics of this chapter:

- *Improving performance through LCT*   Using management constructs that focus on opportunities, challenges, constraints, and concerns, and on improving performance.

- *Systems integration*   Positioning the enterprise and its technologies and products in the most favorable position for sustaining its future through systems integration.
- *LCT at the product delivery system*   Linking LCT with the product delivery system and requirements.
- *Design and development principles using LCT*   Establishing design and development principles and guidelines for decision-making that provide management and professionals with balanced criteria for achieving sustainable outcomes.
- *Creating a life cycle framework*   Ensuring that the full scope of internal (marketing, engineering, production, finance, environmental, etc.) and external dimensions (customers, stakeholders, supply networks, related industries, the infrastructure, and competitors) is included in determining improvement and development programs.
- *Developing an analytical framework for research*   Developing an analytical model for exploring opportunities using LCT.

This chapter provides an overview of life cycle considerations and how they fit in to the complex business world. It sets the stage for an understanding of qualitative and quantitative techniques pertaining to LCA.

Improving performance through LCT

Fundamentals of LCT

LCT is predicated on the notion that a holistic view of the spatial and temporal implications of a process, product, technology, or system provides the best understanding of the opportunities, challenges, constraints (limitations), and concerns associated with their application over time and the capabilities of the enterprise to deal with them. It springs from the philosophical belief that it is management's responsibility to ensure that designs and operations have been analyzed in sufficient detail to determine the positive and negative implications and impacts. It is a fundamental construct for examining and improving the effects of products, processes, and systems. To apply LCT is to thoroughly examine the product, process, or system to discover ways to make improvements, create opportunities, reduce challenges, and eliminate constraints and concerns. LCT involves examining the social, economic, environmental, and business aspects of the product or system over its entire life cycle. Figure 9.1

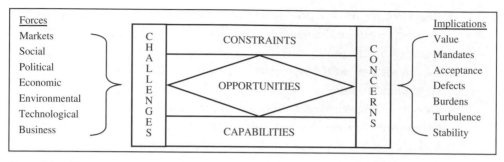

Figure 9.1   The strategic logic of LCT at the senior management level

depicts a simple representation of the strategic logic of LCT at the senior management level.

The model indicates that corporations seek opportunities to improve (develop and expand) their business prospects using their capabilities, resources, and intellectual capital. As tangible and intangible assets are enhanced, the corporation theoretically has the ability to enhance its strategic position and to expand its reach into market space. However, the ability to expand is often limited by the constraints that exist in the system and the business environment, constraints that are multifaceted, difficult to categorize, and often result from the products or systems themselves. For example, the output of certain production plants may be fixed, based on the level of air emissions or water effluents generated in the manufacturing processes. Such plants usually have government permits that restrict the amount of pollution they may generate, thus limiting the capacity and output of the operation. Such constraints are not natural limits, but are a result of inadequate technologies, poor designs, and process inefficiencies. Reducing the pollution generated per unit of production would allow the plant to increase its output while still complying with the discharge limits. The impact of the constraint would be reduced.

While constraints tend to be concrete, concerns are more relative. For example, customer concerns about the value, reliability, and longevity of products are limiting factors. Improving products across their entire life cycle can eliminate these concerns. Acceptance of products by customers and society in general is a critical factor for sustainable success. Corporations depend on the trust that people have in their products and systems. People expect corporations to exhibit the proper ethical, legal, and quality standards in developing and delivering products. If these expectations are not met, people become concerned about the stability of the corporation and its viability as a world-class business. Such situations cause turbulence and limit growth.

Concerns may be based on the perceptions of the people involved – and, in many cases, are just as difficult to remove as more tangible constraints. For example, the perceived dangers of nuclear power plants after the Three Mile Island incident in 1978 were probably much greater than the actual risks in most cases. Nevertheless, once the public's trust was lost, it became very difficult to convince people that the technology was safe and had actually been dramatically improved. Defects and burdens can also increase the power of stakeholder groups and lead to additional government mandates that attempt to rectify the situation.

Challenges are the demands and indirect needs of the external business environment. In conventional business strategies, they provide the counterpoint to opportunities. They are the signals that customers, stakeholders, or other constituencies send to the industry or to individual companies telling them they need to change the standard approaches and offer better solutions. For example, BMW recognized that it had to invent the means to disassemble its automobiles at the end of their useful life and recycle the parts and components if it was going to convince automobile dismantlers to handle the processing. More importantly, BMW wanted to assure its customers that at the end of the useful life of the car there were approved means and mechanisms to retire and dispose of the product. Challenges and opportunities are often intertwined. If government mandates require the safe and environmentally sound processing or disposal of a product, they present an opportunity for those corporations that can provide the solution, and a threat to those that cannot.

SBD engenders a positive strategic position that involves leading change and proactively handling challenges. Threats simply become situations that can be transformed into opportunities for those who can manage change and invent a future that benefits all constituents. Challenges provide opportunities to infuse new blood into the fabric of the corporation.

LCT provides a management construct that explores the full scope of the implications of products, processes, and systems. It examines the flow of impacts over time from the perspective of customers and all of the other constituents involved in the production, use, and retirement of the products. It views challenges as potential ways to obtain competitive advantages. Corporations that embrace the challenges of markets, society, economics, political entities, and environmental issues enrich their business environment and create opportunities to outperform and outpace their peers and competitors.

Challenges, concerns, and constraints are not the opposite of opportunities. While they do have the potential to reduce opportunities, they also can become opportunities for those with the right, sustainable perspective.

Philosophy of LCT

LCT reverses the conventional way of viewing the management of systems and processes. It embraces the idea of corporations taking direct and indirect responsibilities for the impacts and implications of their systems and products. It considers the whole situation, not just selected parts of the business environment, and it considers them from cradle-to-grave, across their life cycle. The philosophical underpinnings are the creation of value for customers and stakeholders by maximizing benefits and minimizing defects and burdens. Moreover, the objective is to discover hidden defects and burdens during the development processes and take every step possible to improve the implications and impacts. If such improvements are impossible, then the intent is to find alternative opportunities for improvements, such as new products and processes. Simply stated, profits and cash flow are the rewards for providing outstanding solutions and positive outcomes for customers and all other constituents. They are the result of providing *total solutions*. The focus for such rewards is on positive outcomes and not on the rewards themselves. Great corporations seek to design, produce, and deliver outstanding solutions which are then rewarded by way of cash flow and profits.

There are many examples of products or materials that could have been improved if the corporation had focused on the problems as soon as they were discovered. Asbestos is one of the most tragic stories. The defects were known, but little action was taken until the government stepped in. If action had been taken sooner, perhaps its use could have been restricted to only those applications where health and safety could be assured.[1] Clearly fewer people would have been damaged and the corporations involved may have had the time, money, and resources to find alternatives.

LCT expands the sphere of responsibility beyond the normal boundaries of the corporation. It suggests that senior and operational management are also responsible for the actions of the supply networks, the applications of the products, and the post-customer retirement requirements. While this notion varies from industry to industry and country to country, there is growing pressure for corporations to take certain responsibilities for the actions of their suppliers, distributors, and even customers. The logic is based on the view that the corporation selected its suppliers and distributors, and in that process has the responsibility to ensure that they are fully capable of meeting all of the expectations of the business environment, not just delivering the contractual outcomes. Moreover, if the boundaries of responsibilities are narrowly defined to just those operations directly owned by the corporation, some fear that senior management would outsource certain operations that generate large quantities of wastes and pollution or those with particularly problematic hazardous substances requiring stringent management. LCT stipulates that the corporation is still responsible for all of the products, processes, and waste streams, regardless of who produced them.

Daimler-Chrysler, at its Mercedes-Benz plant in Stuttgart, Germany, is developing an integrated IT system that will link its logistics operations with all of its more than 1,000 suppliers and their suppliers on a global basis.[2] While the system is still being developed, and the intent is to manage the flow of information and goods, such a system could also include details about life cycle considerations, waste management implications, and improving solutions across the enterprise.

Leading change through life cycle considerations

LCT is about transforming the existing organizational order into an energized organizational structure that focuses on continuous improvements and ongoing change. It depends on assessing products and systems so that decisions pertaining to improvements can be made on the basis of facts. It requires an organizational mentality that is open to discussing any difficulties that may be embedded within product architectures and operating systems. Open communications is essential for discovering opportunities; management also must create an atmosphere of trust in which assessments and changes are welcomed.

But change is difficult because it brings many uncertainties about the future. Transforming a corporation into a more capable organization using LCT and life cycle management can be an overwhelming challenge. It requires management commitment to a broad-based program that could take decades to fully implement and execute. It requires new ways of thinking and management: management must assess the needs for change, defining what has to be improved, and how it is to be improved.

As discussed in chapter 6, leading change is inherently part of the SBD paradigm: that the corporation will change is not in question. Rather, the question is the degree of change that will occur and the mechanisms that will be used. Niccolò Machiavelli made the following comment about change in *The Prince*:[3]

It should be borne in mind that there is nothing more difficult to handle, more doubtful of success, and more dangerous to carry through than initiating change . . . The innovator makes enemies of all of those who prosper under the old order, and only lukewarm support is forthcoming from those who would prosper under the new.

Managing change on a broad scale requires management systems and organizational structure to keep people on course over an extended period of time. The structural aspects provide the "glue" that holds the change management together. People are linked by the vision, aligned by the philosophies of SBD and continuous improvement, and directed through executive leadership that communicates and inspires. The pathway to the future is an infinite road of ever-new expectations, realizations, accomplishments, needs, and requirements. Leading change through LCT travels that road toward zero defects and burdens. The elimination of every negative impact is the ultimate objective.

Systems integration and LCT

Systems integration in the LCT context

LCT is inherently complex, introducing detail by adding analytical depth to the management of systems. Many of the more simplistic approaches of the twentieth century failed to include all of the essential elements of the enterprise. For example, most of the economic and business management constructs did not include waste management as essential parts of the system; waste management was viewed a tangential aspect.

The lack of true integration of environmental considerations is apparent from the number of separate management systems that exist. For instance, ISO 14000 was developed as a stand-alone system rather than integrating the elements into the quality management system, ISO 9000, and other systems. While the evolution of such decisions is understandable, it has resulted in less integration, not more. The problem springs from a focus on specific outcomes and solutions. While solutions must be broadly defined within the context of the whole system, small companies can afford to concentrate on specific opportunities or local markets and define their position accordingly. Global corporations do not have the luxury of taking such a narrow perspective. Their business environment is global, complex, and ever-changing. The interrelationships are mind-boggling, and accordingly, they face the need for and challenge of integration.

System integration facilitates systems thinking which examines the interconnections between the elements of the strategic and operating systems of the corporation and also the interrelationships between the various organizations and people within the corporation. Systems thinking helps to optimize

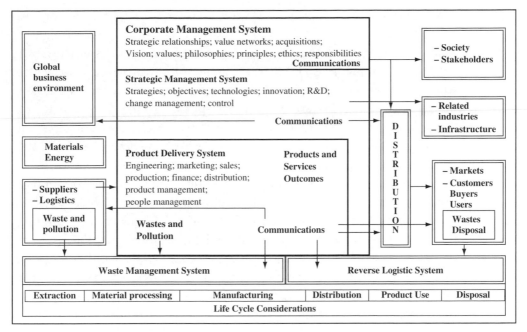

Figure 9.2   Systems integration of the essential constructs of the enterprise

the whole and improve the parts to produce the best solution possible, given the state of technology and the sophistication of the management systems.

The most significant enhancement using life cycle considerations is the addition of time-based thinking to the frameworks and more rigorous analysis of data and information for making decisions. Figure 9.2 depicts a systems integration using life cycle considerations. The actual management model is even more complex than what can be shown on a simple two-dimensional graphic. However, figure 9.2 does portray the essential aspects of the management system for a life cycle perspective. Senior management defines the scope, intent, and direction of SBD initiatives and programs. Initiating and maintaining communication and messages with all constituencies is crucial for ensuring the proper two-way flow of information about intents, achievements, and expectations.

Executives are primarily thinking about the future and leading change in the enterprise to promote the desired strategic positions. Their most critical decisions relate to the future expectations of the constituencies, the sustainability of the strategic positions, and the selection of new resources and capabilities. All of these contribute to the reputation and image of the corporation, one of the most compelling reasons for implementing LCT and SBD.

For global corporations, the SMS leads change for specific lines of businesses that are related through common structures and industry settings. For example, P&G divides its businesses into five global business units (GBUs) with broad product lines. Each GBU has an SMS, with senior management who are responsible for establishing direction and achieving the desired outcomes. These SMSs are ultimately responsible for ensuring that each line of business has the proper subsystems in place to fulfill the requirements of the business environment. They apply LCT to integrate the supply networks, distribution channels, markets, and aftermarket considerations.

Like the corporate management system, the SMS focuses on communications with customers and stakeholders in order to proactively identify and address any difficulties and negative implications. Establishing an information system for the collection and dissemination of information regarding products is essential for staying ahead of expectations and avoiding surprises. The information flow allows the corporation to assess situations and take positive steps to improve any negative aspects. Reporting or disclosing the full range of details about the positive and negative aspects of a system without disclosing confidential information can also reduce the shock to constituents who discover adverse information after investments have been made in new products, processes, and systems. This latter communication requires a feedforward and feedback information management system.

This full disclosure practice is directly in line with public right-to-know legislation that exists in various forms in many developed countries around the world. Even without such legislation, more and more information about products and manufacturing processes is made available to the public by numerous interest groups that track certain industries or selected companies or through the Internet. With advances in technologies for sampling or scanning emissions and effluents, it is becoming more and more difficult to generate waste streams without the public knowing about it. The best logic from a strategic management perspective is to simply disclose the information. Ongoing disclosures avoid the difficulties of explaining why previously known information was not released when it became known. Society cannot expect perfection in products and services, but it can expect that corporations will always act responsibly. Society, customers, and stakeholders can also expect that a corporation will address any negative aspects of its operations directly, leading to improvements and leaving nothing to be discovered and publicized by a third-party group.

LCT calls on strategic management to assume responsibility for all of the waste generated, regardless of where it is produced in the system.

Management analyzes all of the implications of the products and services and determines how to produce the best products with the least amount of waste and the fewest impacts. While strategic management thinks about the broad constructs for formulating SBD initiatives, the implementation of such initiatives and programs is typically carried out by the product delivery system.

The product delivery system includes the operating units that deliver the products and provide the services. The product delivery system is action-oriented and involves the repetitive activities of producing products and managing processes. In most corporations, a majority of the activities occur within the product delivery system. The time-based focus is on the present and near term. Management typically is concerned with outputs and inputs and views everything in terms of how it can help transform inputs (raw materials, parts, components, and energy) into outputs that are more desirable than the other options available to customers in the market place.

While the primary focus is on the effects and impacts of products and processes, LCT suggests that all of the effects of the product delivery system have to be considered and managed to meet the expectations of the business environment. Consideration of secondary effects have evolved over the last thirty years as laws and regulations have forced management into more effectively dealing with waste streams and preventing pollution. The operating systems in most global corporations include waste management systems – or, in the broader context, an EMS that focuses on integrating environmental management issues into mainstream business operations.

While it can be argued that many of the EMSs deployed by global corporations are intended to function strategically at the higher level, such systems usually direct most of their attention toward operational aspects. For instance, even though ISO 14000 EMS includes policy, planning, objectives, and targets, most of its elements deal with implementation and measurement. Even so, EMSs have provided enormous benefits to corporations. They have facilitated significant gains in regulatory compliance and pollution prevention.

But, today, global corporations are moving to a higher level of thinking, toward systems integration and a strategic management perspective for managing the concerns, consequences, and impacts of the corporation's operations. Systems integration and the broader view of LCT are transforming the perspective from simply operational considerations and near-term implications to the strategic examination of the whole life cycle and insuring that product development and technological innovation are improving prospects for the future.

LCT at the product delivery level

The traditional life cycle management model

Traditional life cycle models and techniques are based on the SETAC constructs for examining the life cycle inventory of processes. The basic model is a simple input-output model that includes the flow of materials, energy, and water across the value system for producing products and the related benefits. The value system includes the intended outputs plus all of the waste streams that are created by the individual processes within the system.

Most systems and processes were originally designed to maximize the benefits. The focus was on the commercial outputs and not on the negative defects and burdens produced by the system. The SETAC life cycle inventory analysis model made a significant contribution to improving products and processes. It put attention on the total outputs of the system including the negatives. It caused companies to assess the efficiency and effectiveness of their processes. The basic concept is shown in figure 9.3.

The SETAC model establishes the fundamentals for understanding and assessing both systems and their inputs and outputs. The outputs typically provide both the benefits and concerns. The efficiency and effectiveness of the transformation processes are critical as well. Inefficient processes may require more input than necessary. Processes cause noise, illnesses, injuries, other defects, and environmental burdens.

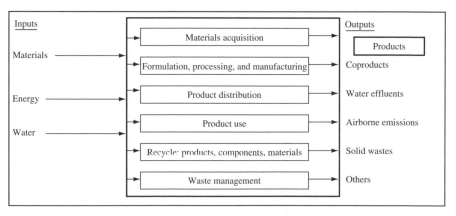

Figure 9.3   SETAC's life cycle inventory analysis

Source: Adapted from the Society of Environmental Toxicology and Chemistry, *A Technical Framework for Life Cycle Assessment*, 1991.

Examining the life cycle stages is critical for understanding where the problems are, and contemplating possible solutions. The basic model provides a construct that is similar to econometric models for industry analysis. It is also related to the engineering construct of energy and materials balances for a system. Such analysis examines the inputs and outputs of the processes to determine what alternatives fit the needs of the corporation and provide the best solution. The methodology is supported by scientific principles and provides a means to increase the rigor of design selection for future products and processes. It also provides a construct for improving existing products and processes.

Integrating life cycle considerations with product delivery

Global corporations made significant progress during the 1990s in reducing the waste they generated and becoming more effective in solving environmental problems. Many of the improvements were made through effective waste management, including using waste minimization and pollution prevention. The most important improvement, however, was the change in philosophy that occurred regarding the responsibilities of manufacturers with respect to the upstream suppliers and downstream distributors and customers. Historically, the scope was narrow, with linkages only to first-tier suppliers and direct customers who purchased the products. Little consideration was given to the whole system and what happens to the products during and after use. Moreover, most processes depended on virgin materials, and there was little concern for recycling and reusing products. While secondary markets did exist for certain products, and there was an infrastructure for recycling valuable materials such as steel and aluminum, most used products were discarded in landfills or incinerators. Figure 9.4 shows the traditional scope of management considerations.

While this perspective has been used as the basis for significant reductions, there are limits to the improvements that can be achieved without looking at

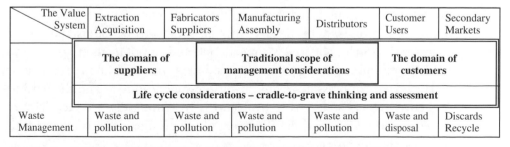

Figure 9.4 Traditional scope of considerations for managing the implications of waste

the full system. The technologies, products, and processes themselves can often be improved dramatically through innovation and integration. For example, BMW initiated a program to improve the recyclability of its automobiles at the end of their useful life. While there was an existing industry structure for dismantling discarded automobiles, the degree of recyclability was limited by the design configuration and the way in which the product was manufactured. BMW, to its credit, studied how to effectively disassemble its automobiles and changed the material selection process to facilitate reuse or recycling of the parts and components. Unless the corporation had been willing to expand its scope or the boundary of its management system, these broad-based solutions would have remained out of reach.

By integrating life cycle considerations with the broader constructs of enterprise management and the expectations of stakeholders and society in general, the scope of corporate responsibilities is beginning to mirror the scope of the enterprise. This expansion of the business model is also grounded in the reality of waste management and pollution prevention. Waste management requires the support and cooperation of many providers who must have high-quality operations in order to comply with laws and regulations and provide a cost effective solution. But, most importantly, pollution prevention is now reaching out to the traditional customer domain to provide solutions to the problems of product retirement and disposal. In addition, many countries now require companies to "take back" their products at the end of their useful lives. In such situations, corporations must invent solutions for handling the discarded products. As discussed in chapter 5, these solutions vary from refurbishing the product for additional use by primary customers to remanufacturing them for secondary applications, reusing the parts for servicing primary and secondary applications, or even recycling the materials in the initial applications for secondary uses.

Pollution prevention also reaches out to the supply chain for information about the materials and processes, so that more detailed information can be provided to customers and users to ensure safe and effective applications. Source reduction is more effective when customers truly understand proper usages, recycling is enhanced when materials and components are coded and labeled with information instructing customers about use and retirement.

These kinds of pressures from the business environment and the need to proactively create solutions to problems is redefining the product delivery system. Figure 9.5 depicts the alignment of the product delivery system with life cycle considerations.

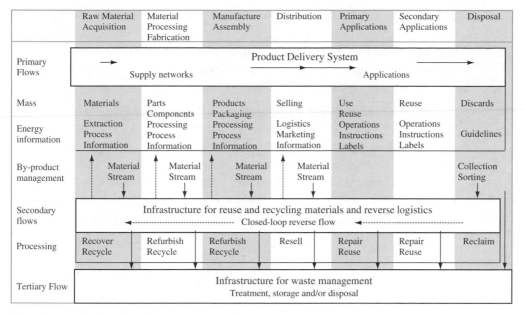

	Raw Material Acquisition	Material Processing Fabrication	Manufacture Assembly	Distribution	Primary Applications	Secondary Applications	Disposal
Primary Flows	Product Delivery System ——→ Supply networks ——→ Applications ——→						
Mass	Materials	Parts Components	Products Packaging	Selling	Use Reuse	Reuse	Discards
Energy information	Extraction Process Information	Processing Process Information	Processing Process Information	Logistics Marketing Information	Operations Instructions Labels	Operations Instructions Labels	Guidelines
By-product management	Material Stream	Material Stream	Material Stream	Material Stream			Collection Sorting
Secondary flows	Infrastructure for reuse and recycling materials and reverse logistics Closed-loop reverse flow						
Processing	Recover Recycle	Refurbish Recycle	Refurbish Recycle	Resell	Repair Reuse	Repair Reuse	Reclaim
Tertiary Flow	Infrastructure for waste management Treatment, storage and/or disposal						

Figure 9.5   Product delivery system based on life cycle considerations

Figure 9.5 depicts a linear flow of mass and energy across the product delivery system as products are constructed from materials and energy is consumed. The model indicates the responsibilities of the product delivery system as the products are converted from the material world of suppliers to the application world of customers and users. The model shows the primary flows of the product and the secondary, reverse, flows that recover discarded products and materials after retirement. The tertiary flows are the processing of the waste streams that flow from suppliers, producers, and users after recycling has captured as much of the recoverable material as possible.

With an integrated systems approach for life cycle considerations, information from suppliers is translated into instructions and guidelines to enable customers and downstream users to make effective decisions about the applications of products. For most corporations, the primary flow is relatively straightforward, and only refinements are necessary to enhance outcomes and move toward full integration. The missing pieces are typically a lack of information about the details of the products and processes. In some cases, the information is not available, or it is not in a reliable form. In other cases, the suppliers do not wish to provide the information. This is particularly true about information pertaining to waste streams.

The diagram in figure 9.5 depicts the flow of materials in the reuse and recycling streams. The providers of these processes and services can be independent of the product delivery system. As in the case of BMW, the primary responsibility in managing the product delivery system is to facilitate the creation of the infrastructure and to provide information and support for ensuring the proper flow of recovered materials.

LCT takes a holistic view of the formal and informal relationships that can be analyzed and improved in terms of performance, cost effectiveness, quality of outputs, and environmental impacts. Again, the intent is to minimize the defects and burdens generated by the system and to provide solutions to all of the needs of the system's constituents. The primary responsibilities for minimizing the impacts of the system rest with the entity that creates the final products. Usually the global corporation facilitates linkages with the supply networks and relationships with customers and users. It has the responsibility to ensure that there is an infrastructure to handle the flow of discarded products and wastes. It must select suppliers who can manage the waste streams according to government mandates and best practices in order to minimize the environmental consequences.

Creating an infrastructure for managing post-customer discards is a complex part of the system that is evolving in many industries. Solutions such as the recycling of aluminum cans and the take-back programs for used computers are piecemeal steps to affect a more global solution. While significant gains have been made since the 1990s, most systems are still far from the goal of having a closed-loop, reverse logistics system. As with many of the constructs of SBD, the full implementation of product recycling and reuse requires new technologies, intellectual and financial capital, and time.

Design and development principles based on LCT

Integrating life cycle management with product development

LCT oversees the flow of information, materials, components, products, services, and waste streams from the acquisition of raw materials through distribution, market application, and retirement. It also examines the nature of design, the design process, functional requirements, and design constraints with emphasis on health and safety issues, the environmental impacts of design decisions, performance indices, and safe material selection strategies. It reviews product design strategies by analyzing product requirements and selecting the most economic, technical, and environmentally conscious product architecture and specifications. An "appropriate" design is one that

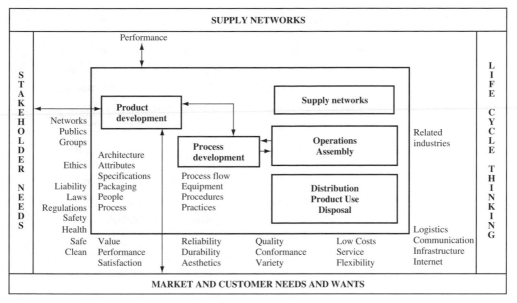

Figure 9.6   NPD and LCT

satisfies the entire set of product requirements, thus creating a sustainable design from every perspective. The product design establishes the material and energy requirements and determines the flows of goods, services, and information. The choices made during the process are directly linked to creating better solutions and eliminating defects, burdens, and potential liabilities.

Figure 9.6 shows the relationship between the critical dimensions of NPD from a life cycle perspective.

The general goals of product development are to create new solutions in the form of advanced products that meet business and environmental criteria and have a competitive advantage over alternatives. Product development from a life cycle perspective includes selecting product specifications based on social, economic, and environmental criteria that lead to improvements across the life cycle. The selected criteria are based on inputs from customers and stakeholders, along with contributions from the supply networks, related industries, and the infrastructure. Product development includes the entire chain of decisions, from determining customer and stakeholder needs to engineering specifications, manufacturing operations, and distribution, use and disposal. It relates the product, parts, processes, and operations with the suppliers, the infrastructure, the related industries, and potential competitors.

Principles of design and development using LCT

SBD requires the convergence of design and development methods and practices and the concepts and constructs of SBD itself. The theory is that traditional design principles and guidelines and LCT are not mutually exclusive. Corporations can achieve environmental and business objectives, as well as providing for the interests of society and stakeholder groups.

The principles of SBD maintain that:

- The focus of a corporation is on creating value and sustaining its cash flow.
- Management should create products and processes that enjoy sustainable competitive advantages in the marketplace.
- Core capabilities, knowledge, and learning are essential factors for achieving successful outcomes.
- Resources should be allocated strategically and deployed effectively and efficiently.
- Products, processes, and practices should meet high quality standards and provide cost effective results.
- Customer loyalty and the image and reputation of the corporation are among the most crucial factors for achieving positive outcomes.
- Customer satisfaction and responsiveness to customer needs are critical factors for success.
- The ability to create new technologies and new products is fundamental for maintaining and sustaining the corporation over time.
- Executive leadership has to inspire and reward the contributors in the corporation. People and intellectual capital are the modern corporation's most important assets.
- Knowledge is the glue that links technologies, products, processes, and practices.
- The preemptive strategies demonstrate and sustain a differential advantage over competitors.
- Management at all levels has to determine the risk factors and mitigate risks to an acceptable level.

Managerial leadership establishes the principles and guidelines for directing actions and effecting decision-making. In the fast paced and ever-changing business environment of the twenty-first century, management faces the difficult challenges of making decisions about technologies, products, and processes. There is always a myriad of choices for the next generation of technologies and new products. Corporations have to determine, analyze, select, and implement new and better solutions faster than ever before. Choosing an incorrect solution costs money, time, and effort as well as lost opportunities, greater liabilities and risk, and lost market position.

Articulating a list of design and development principles using LCT is an even more forbidding task. First, designs must adhere to the mandates of laws and regulations. Second, but equally important, they must respect the evolutionary tracks of pollution prevention, waste minimization, Product Stewardship, and the precepts of enterprise management and LCT. From the perspectives of global corporations, there are ten fundamental principles that relate to life cycle considerations:

- Resources should be deployed in the most effective and efficient means possible given availability, processes, and best practices.
- Resources should be used in a manner that minimizes the potential for environmental degradation, depletion, disruption, and destruction.
- The materials used in products and processes should be nontoxic and safe to use during extraction, processing, manufacturing, transportation, application, and disposal.
- The quantity of waste generated in processes should be close to the theoretical minimum, and plans to further reduce the amount of waste produced should be made.
- Products should be designed and produced in ways that provide the highest level of quality, reliability, safety, longevity, durability, maintainability, serviceability, and disposability.
- Communications with customers and stakeholders should provide the full factual information needed for the safe and effective use, reuse, recycling, retirement and disposal of the products. It is the responsibility of the primary producers to create and articulate solutions for the safe and effective discard of EoL residuals.
- The impacts of the technologies, products, processes, and operations should not adversely affect the quality of life of the local, regional, and global communities, or the natural environment, in a significant manner.
- Products should be designed and produced to maximize the ability to reuse, recycle, remanufacture, and refurbish the products, component, parts, and materials.
- Safety and human health should be primary considerations when designing and operating facilities, plants, and processes and when designing and producing products.
- Increasing performance and benefits and decreasing defects and burdens are the critical factors in improving outcomes.

Some of these principles are close to the prevailing views of the environmental interest groups and the WBCSD. The WBCSD advocates the principles of **eco-efficiency** as effective guidelines for businesses when making decisions that may affect the environment. It maintains that the two overarching economic and environmental considerations should be:[4]

- Increasing resource productivity so that more is obtained from less energy and raw material input.
- Creating new goods and services that increase customer value while maintaining or reducing environmental impacts.

Eco-efficiency essentially means maximizing outputs and minimizing inputs and wastes (doing more with less). The WBCSD suggests that eco-efficiency will enhance the mainstream objectives of corporations, and it has developed seven key guidelines:[5]

- Reduce material intensity
- Minimize energy intensity
- Reduce dispersion of toxic substances
- Undertake recycling
- Capitalize on use of "renewables"
- Extend product durability
- Increase service intensity.

The WBCSD's principles of eco-efficiency are intended to provide assistance and guidance to practitioners and management as they reinvent existing products and processes and create new ones. The guidelines help to save time and money during the assessment and evaluation processes. Judgment has to be used in specific cases to ensure that nuances of the situation do not favor an alternative to the principles. For instance, environmental groups such as EarthWatch advocate the use of renewable energy resources instead of fossil fuels, which have been labeled as nonrenewable. However, it is not proven that a mass-scale use of renewable energy such as photovoltaic, wind energy, hydropower, or biomass would cause less depletion, less pollution, and fewer environmental impacts than the existing forms of petroleum-based resources. It is clear from the historical record and the data collected each year that the environmental impacts for petroleum products are significant. However, there is insufficient evidence to suggest that biomass or hydropower would be better. Both deplete natural resources and have long-term effects on the natural environment. For instance, dams dramatically change the habitats of the rivers and cause silt to back up near the dam structure. Biomass in certain forms may lead to soil depletion and may not be available in sufficient quantities to effect an economically viable solution and sustainable outcome. Great care has to be taken not to be presumptive about the viability of given solutions. Indeed, one of the most important principles of LCT is the realization that the answer can be derived only through thorough analysis of the situation.

Linking LCT and business considerations

Design principles provide guidance and support rather than rigid requirements for the specifications of products and processes. They should provide a convergence of the business and SBD objectives, leading to solid solutions that meet the needs of all constituencies instead of compromises that result in inferior outcomes. Corporate competitiveness and environmental quality are complementary concepts that together can contribute to long-term success.

For example, the reduction of hydrocarbon and carbon monoxide emissions from automobiles has over the last twenty-five years allowed the automobile industry to meet the regulatory requirements of various governments around the world. The industry has improved the overall viability of the internal combustion engine, a technology that might have been forced out of existence if air quality had continued to be significantly degraded.

The interrelationship of the primary design and development considerations with life cycle management principles provides a matrix that combines the requirements of the corporation with the needs of constituencies. The matrix encourages inclusion of all of the primary considerations. Decisions are driven by the concept of mutual gain instead of trade-off. A good design incorporates all of the requirements necessary to provide an acceptable solution for customers and stakeholders. Table 9.1 provides a sense of how the main considerations are interrelated, and their implications.

LCT focuses on enhancements to the prevailing constructs for making determinations about products and technologies. The principles used to make selections must be balanced and broad across time and space. The criteria used for initiating and selecting programs and action plans have to be responsive to the full scope of participants and considerations.

Designs are generally intended to have a reasonable life cycle that allows the developer the time and means to exploit the outcomes sufficiently long so that the capital can be recovered and a reward created to justify the time, money, and effort involved. Moreover, it is critical from the social, economic, and environmental perspectives that the resources are deployed efficiently and effectively and that products and processes provide solutions to meet the needs of customers and stakeholders without damaging the health and safety

Table 9.1. Interrelationship between business and LCT

Primary business-related design and development considerations

	Financial	Market	Organization	Resources	Position	Risk
Primary business considerations	Cash flow Profits Value-added	Satisfaction Competitive advantage	Core capabilities Knowledge Learning	Allocation Utilization Effectiveness	Customer loyalty Reputation Image	Identification Assessment Mitigation
Prevent degradation	Waste streams cost money to dispose of	Applications may be restricted	Professional have to spend effort to manage wastes	Pollution destroys resources	Product defects and failures cost money	Products may be restricted or banned
Reduce depletion	Economics changes as materials are in short supply	Lack of available resources is inconvenient	Lack of resource means finding new substitutes and new methods	Depletion changes the economic equation	Poor product life costs money for repairs	Lack of stability creates uncertainties and risks
Reduce material/ energy intensity	Inefficiency and high-input flow costs money	Low material content provides savings	Heavier products are more difficult to handle	Heavier products consume more	Inefficiency and high-energy use costs money	Energy/material use costs money and cuts into resources
Minimize toxic impacts	Products with toxic substance require special handling	Health and safety risks reduce market size	Employee illness and injury are major health problems/ issues	Toxic and hazardous waste require resources to handle	Toxic substances and the products are affected by laws and regulations	Unsafe products cause liabilities and damages

of humankind and depleting and degrading the natural environment. It is crucial that solutions are free of defects and burdens to the greatest extent possible, given the state of the art in technology and management constructs. The general expectation is not perfection, but the assurance that every reasonable precaution has been taken and every required action implemented. Obviously, in product and technology categories where the inherent risks are high, the requirements may necessitate perfection.

Creating a life cycle framework

Overview

Identifying linkages throughout the life cycle of a product or service is crucial for establishing a life cycle framework. Suppliers generally are the first link in the chain, providing the inputs to manufacturing and assembly processes. Their contributions include a broad array of upstream activities that culminate in a stream of specific materials, components, and parts that are used to produce the products to the specifications of the design requirements and customer needs. The supply chain includes all upstream inputs, from the primary ingredients that are embodied within the final product to the secondary and complementary inputs such as packaging and instructions for the proper applications of the product. Judgments often have to be made about the importance of a given element to the ultimate solution. If the effects are minuscule, then management may decide that they are not material and can be removed from in-depth consideration. However, care has to be taken to ensure that seemingly small or incidental elements that have significant negative effects are not overlooked. For example, Product Stewardship focuses on ensuring that customers use products properly. To that end, operating instructions with safety guidelines and instructions for proper applications can help prevent premature failures or even catastrophes.

Figure 9.7 depicts a simplified life cycle framework. It represents an operational dynamic that links the entire product delivery system over time. Suppliers provide physical materials and products and related information. The process actually starts with suppliers of suppliers and moves up the production chain to include every facet of production, consumption, and disposal. LCT requires all participants at every level to understand the full implications of their actions and to provide the appropriate information and knowledge downstream so that proper decisions can be made during every

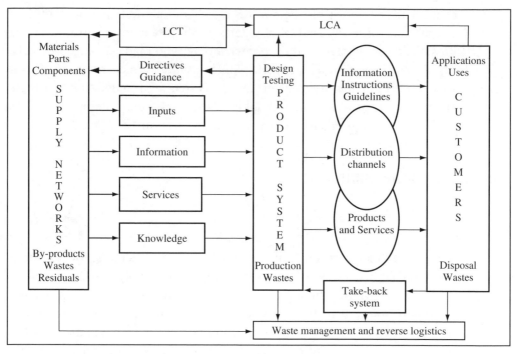

Figure 9.7   Simplified life cycle framework

step of the process. One of the main goals is to uncover hidden defects and burdens as early as possible, and to cure such problems before they become intractable.

LCT extends product responsibilities into the realms of both the users and the suppliers of materials and energy. This includes responsibilities for the safe and effective use of the products, the proper handling and disposal of the waste streams generated during use, and the proper retirement of the product itself. Manufacturers are assuming, or being forced to assume, the responsibilities for their products both during and after the product's life. In Germany, manufacturers are even responsible for taking back the packaging that they send to customers to ensure safe transportation and storage of the products.

A life cycle framework provides a systematic view of all participants and stages in production. It is useful for discovering and understanding opportunities to dramatically improve products and processes, enhancing the linkages and communications between the entities, and improving value creation by the entire system. The most critical aspects of the framework are the linkages of goods and information about the positive and negative implications of products and processes. It is a feedforward and feedback system, and depends on effective IT systems.

Three critical elements of the framework go beyond the conventional view of supply networks:

- The entities involved are responsible for their inputs and outputs beyond the simple contractual responsibilities defined in accordance with the prevailing commercial codes. The responsibilities include the downstream implications of the use of the materials, parts, components, and products over time and the upstream impacts of suppliers' operations (waste streams affecting degradation, depletion, safety, and human health and the environment).
- Producers have the duty to provide full disclosure of information to ensure the best use of the products and processes. This includes providing information about the negative aspects of the products and processes, as well as the positive in order to facilitate a comprehensive assessment of the impacts.
- The process is dynamic, with the participants proactively discovering and curing the negative aspects and mitigating any implications and impacts.

These requirements present important challenges to creating sustainable products and processes. But they lead to more sustainable positions in the long term. While it may be difficult to validate the benefits of the expanded view of corporate responsibilities, history is replete with examples of corporations that made significant investments into products and processes that later had to be changed or withdrawn from the market because of discovered defects. Merck's Vioxx is an example. The intent of LCT is to investigate opportunities and challenges in sufficient detail to ensure that the potential for future problems has been minimized. Therefore, there is not only the environmental, but also the social, economic, political, and business implications of decision-making to be explored. Figure 9.8 shows the critical areas of LCT that cut across the enterprise and require careful consideration during product design and delivery.

While this list is not exhaustive, it does show that many problems are difficult to detect and manifest themselves over time. Category I items are generally well established, and the life cycle perspective is to minimize and eventually eliminate such difficulties. Category II items are linked to the products and processes. These are more complicated, because they are derivatives of many products and processes and are time-dependent on many other factors. Solutions to such problems require extensive changes to the materials, parts, components, products, processes, and technologies and improvements to the management systems. Both Categories I and II are generally known and are the targets of pollution prevention and waste minimization programs.

	Known	*Known*	
Direct	**I Inherent, systemic problems** *(Problems that are well known and based on selection criteria)* ❑ Toxic substances ❑ Air emissions and releases ❑ Water effluents ❑ Solid waste storage and disposal ❑ Hazardous materials ❑ Energy consumption	**II Negative consequences** *(Downstream implications of upstream decisions)* ❑ Impacts and consequences ❑ Accidents, spills, and pollution ❑ Acid rain and acidification ❑ Eutrophication ❑ Remediation requirements ❑ Retirement and disposal issues	**Indirect**
Direct	**III Hidden defects and burdens** *(Difficulties that were not assessed or were not viewed as consequential)* ❑ Cancer-causing residual agents (toxins) ❑ Equipment or product failures ❑ Liabilities and risk exposures ❑ Constraints and new mandates ❑ Safety and hygiene concerns ❑ Human health and habitat impacts	**IV Lagging externalities** *(Problems that manifest themselves over time or result from cumulative usage)* ❑ Global climatic changes ❑ Ozone depletion ❑ Resource depletion ❑ Biosphere or habitat degradation ❑ Growth constraints ❑ Sustainable development concerns	**Indirect**
	Unknown	**Unknown**	

Figure 9.8   Categories of critical LCT concerns

Categories III and IV are the most troubling since their impacts are generally unknown. In the former, new products and processes may be selected, designed, and developed using technologies, materials, and other inputs that are defective, thereby creating problems and burdens in the future. These defects and burdens are often not readily apparent during the early stage of the development, or even after the launch of a new product.

Though no management construct can totally eliminate surprises, life cycle management attempts to minimize them. As the matrix in figure 9.8 depicts, this management construct takes management thinking beyond the obvious problems to deal with the implications of the whole product over its entire life cycle. By identifying the potential for future problems, it encourages management to dig into that potential, and to understand all of the implications. This exercise could be the critical one in finding the optimal product design.

Supply networks and LCT

Linking the framework

Cradle-to-grave thinking makes the supply chain a vital part of the decision-making process when designing products and processes and selecting the inputs for those processes. The operations of suppliers and distributors have to be fundamentally sound from a social, economic, and environmental perspective so that the entire product delivery system maximizes opportunities and value and minimizes negative consequences. Great care has to be taken to ensure that the negative implications of materials selection and processing are not transferred to upstream participants.

Since the mid-1990s, with the applications of lean management principles, suppliers and distributors have streamlined their processes to improve customer service, reduce excess inventories, cut costs, and form new relationships to facilitate interactions and communications. Suppliers and their suppliers have begun to coordinate their efforts so that the best overall solution is provided and an integrated, systems approach is created between all the upstream providers. This includes identifying the details of the processes and activities, collecting information about the implications and impacts, developing a comprehensive view of the current and future state of the supply chain, and effectively managing the flow of goods and information over time.

The continued improvement of the supply chain depends on several factors: (1) an articulated framework for integrating all of the tiers in the supply chain; (2) well-defined processes with well-defined principles and decision-making guidelines for all the participants; (3) action plans that drive supply chain improvements; and (4) early visibility of the impacts and consequences of processes and products along the supply chain to allow an integrated and effective understanding of causality. Most importantly, actions have to be initiated quickly to rectify any problems and eliminate the related issues.

LCT aims at selecting and integrating the best processes, methods, and techniques for the supply chain. The challenge is to initiate throughout the chain the best practices available in all areas: strategic, financial, technical, informational, legal, and regulatory. The principles of life cycle management provide guidance for decision-makers. The management framework should establish the minimum requirements of product or process content and specifications, along with the intent of sustainable development. Thereafter, the suppliers must decide what works best for them. The framework should continue to provide the means to identify, describe, analyze, and manage the entire supply chain. Opportunities for standardization and replication in common areas should not be missed.

Establishing criteria

Expectations drive the management of procurement requirements. It is pointless to develop and implement a life cycle framework that extends into the supply networks unless the suppliers understand the requirements and

Box 9.1 Philips Electronics and its supplier involvement program

Koninklijke Philips Electronics NV (hereafter, Philips) is a leading consumer and medical systems electronics company headquartered in Eindhoven, the Netherlands. It is using sustainability as a key driver to explore to new business opportunities and new markets, and to make dramatic improvements to its general business practices and its relationships with partners, customers, stakeholders, and suppliers.

Philips is a global corporation with manufacturing sites in thirty-two countries. Its products are sold in 150 countries. It is recognized by the DJSI as the best in class for its market sector.

In December 2003 the Board of Management adopted a new version of the General Business Principles (GBP) that govern management decisions and actions throughout the world and form the basis of the Purchasing Code of Ethics. The GBP apply to the internal business system, which includes R&D, product development, supply management, communications, manufacturing, and services. It also applies to the extended business system, consisting of suppliers and various other stakeholders, including the financial community, customers, consumers, governmental organizations and NGOs.[1] Philips recognizes the importance of the whole enterprise. Its embedded business system is an integral part of achieving sustainable success. This view is expressed in the *Philips Sustainability Report 2004*:[2]

> After years of being internally focused, companies must now broaden the scope outside their own organizations. This is critical in today's networked world where there is a growing interdependence on extended parties.
>
> To have a truly sustainable business, we also need sustainable suppliers. We started an extensive supplier involvement program in 2003. Our supplier program includes the Philips Supplier Declaration on Sustainability, which outlines the essential principles in the areas of environment, health and safety, and labor conditions, including child labor.

Philips clearly understands the importance of capable and high-quality supply networks. In 2004, the company spent €20 billion on purchases to support its production and sales efforts. This represented 66% of revenues; 80% of outsourcing is based on long-term partnerships.[3] Philips developed a supplier assessment and certification process to ensure that partners were qualified and were in compliance with the GBP.

Notes:
1. Philips, *Sustainability Report 2004* (February 2005), p. 18.
2. *Ibid.*, p. 19.
3. *Ibid.*, p. 80.

are prepared to provide the information and manage their operations accordingly. The first step is to articulate the criteria and guidelines to be used, which define the intent of the life cycle considerations. In some industries, the process is relatively simple because there is a high level of sophistication within the supply networks. For example, the automobile industry has an integrated supply base with many global corporations providing high-level components and products for the major producers. These suppliers have excellent management systems.

The criteria can take many forms. They can specify the expected results or define the processes required. The former make definitive statements about what is required of the supplier and may be viewed as a "rule-based" approach. The latter specify that well-defined processes or established protocols be used, but leave the actual execution of the process up to the supplier. There are advantages and disadvantages to both approaches. Having specific process requirements may preclude the supplier from adapting better methods as new technologies and processes become available. Detailed rules are generally clear about what the expectations are, and this approach is also easier to implement in conjunction with other mandates, including the regulatory requirements promulgated by governments. Participants understand the system and can manage the process accordingly. The major disadvantage is the loss of flexibility.

Process-based approaches offer more flexibility. One such process approach is found in the provisions of ISO 14040 *Environmental Management – Life Cycle Assessment Principles and Guidelines*. The standard defines the fundamental requirements for life cycle management and the principles and guidelines for developing LCAs. LCAs are discussed in detail in chapters 10 and 11. Other process-oriented criteria include "design for the environment," "design for sustainability,"[6] or "design for eco-efficiency,"[7] and the various quality and reliability management constructs such as DFSS.

Criteria for supply networks generally focus on the upstream processes for extracting, refining, and producing materials and those associated with the fabrication of parts and components. The upstream processes include all of the handling, transportation, and storage activities. While it is impossible to spell out criteria for every conceivable activity, the criteria can be based on the practices of other sources within the industry and others performing similar processes and activities. The idea is to mirror the best practices and have the supply networks emulate the world-class entities. Table 9.2 provides generic guidelines for establishing the criteria for supply networks.

Guidelines are most effective when the requirements are broad and the specifications cover a multiplicity of concerns and impacts that are both apparent in current designs and might be anticipated for future versions. Information about goods and processes are essential for effective upstream life cycle management.

Table 9.2. Generic guidelines for establishing criteria for supply networks

Step	Flow elements	Principles and guidelines
1	**Benchmark suppliers** (gather and analyze data to determine the requirements for making improvements)	Select similar goods or those related to the family of goods and determine the specifications and quality standards for minimizing impacts and implications
2	**Determine the criteria for evaluation** (evaluate the effectiveness of the criteria to be used)	Develop an effectiveness profile for the criteria to be used for evaluating the supply networks: specifications; quality requirements; and management system; ISO 9000 and ISO 14000; ISO 14040
3	**Link criteria with product design, production, marketing, and finance** (integrate solutions)	Determine the most effective and desired parameters; examine the impacts on operations; compare options, and evaluate the financial and other implications
4	**Prioritize criteria in terms of needs and effectiveness** (determine the critical requirements)	Identify the criteria that are essential and determine how they fit into the overall system Determine the absolute requirements Select supporting elements
5	**Develop action plans for implementation** (map out the action plan for each element)	Determine the content of the action plans and the timing for their implementation Articulate the criteria to the supply networks
6	**Communicate the action plans**	Prepare a document and disseminate it to participants

The ultimate criteria depend on the contributions of the suppliers and their position in the supply system. Extraction processes are different from refinement and manufacturing processes. Likewise, transportation and logistics involve significantly different activities and require criteria with a service orientation rather than a product or production focus.

The supply networks have to provide sufficient information and factual data about their operations to facilitate solutions that maximize the positives and minimize the negatives. It is the flow of information from every contributor in the total process that makes life cycle management possible and effective. Great outcomes are possible only if the entire system – from cradle-to-grave – is integrated and the results are used to make continuous improvements.

Incorporating suppliers in the design equation

LCT begins with the creation of a new product and the related manufacturing processes. From the inception of the product concept to commercialization, the strategic suppliers should be involved in the selection of materials, parts,

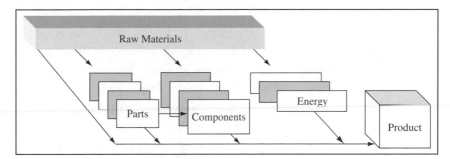

Figure 9.9   Simplified view of material and energy inputs to product design

components, and energy requirements, as well as the product's functionality, quality, and reliability. Integrating suppliers into the design process and understanding their operations and impacts can only enhance decision-making.

The more strategic or more important a particular input, the more crucial it is to have the relevant suppliers participate in the early design decisions. This is especially true when inputs are the subject of regulatory mandates or when they have profound effects on the environment or health and safety. Figure 9.9 depicts a simplified view of material and energy inputs to a product design. The shaded inputs represent special concerns that require the suppliers to become active in mitigating any negative implications and impacts.

This schematic can be expanded to include other critical issues. The actual integration of the selected suppliers into the design process depends on the complexities of the situation. Confidentiality and cost containment must be considered. Usually the biggest determinant is the willingness of suppliers to commit to the design. If such commitments can be made during the concept phase, suppliers may become partners in solving certain problems and environmental impacts. The later the inclusion of suppliers in the process, the more difficult it is to obtain the full benefit of their insights and knowledge. Early supplier integration leads to a more cost effective, environmentally conscious design.

Linking the distribution channels

The distribution channel provides a means to reach potential customers. It consists of intermediaries, wholesalers, retailers, and/or agents who link the organization with the ultimate customer and provide the flow of information and physical products. The channel may include many entities that add value by providing specific functions to enhance the benefits received by customers, or it may be a single connection between the organization and its customers.

Distributors often provide a two-way flow of information to and from the customers and markets. Often the channel is the customer's main means of communications about the product and its implications.

The marketing and distribution methods of the past focused heavily on communicating one side of the value proposition, the positive side. LCT means that the producers of the products and their agents in the delivery system have an inherent responsibility to ensure the proper disclosure of relevant information and full instructions pertaining to applications, safety, and environmentally conscious use. This requirement is more complex than it appears, because it implies that the distribution channel members have to be qualified to provide the full range of product information for potentially hundreds of applications and situations. It can be a daunting requirement, requiring training and education or the services of specialty organizations that understand the customers' needs and know how to convey the appropriate information. For regulated products, formal training programs are mandated to ensure that practitioners are adequately informed and knowledgeable about proper protocols.

The distribution channel may also provide for the flow of used products back to the producers for refurbishment or recycling. In some cases, the channel provides such services for customers, or they resell the refurbished products to other customers. Similarly, the channel may relay information about opportunities for handling the afterlife of the products, providing connections to the support infrastructure of dismantlers, recyclers, and materials handlers who function as intermediaries for effectively processing residuals. Table 9.3 provides examples of how the channel functions in distribution and reverse logistics.

The list in table 9.3 is intended to illustrate the potential contributions that distribution channel participants can make in affecting improved solutions. The opportunities are multifaceted, and the challenges they present are complex. The BMW case offers insights about how solutions require the input and contributions of the OEM, the dealer network, and the support system provided by the scrap handlers and dismantlers.

The market dimension: applications and uses

The customer value proposition

Customers are the pivotal element in the life cycle of products: they can make or break the value creation process. Customers exist in market space and time, comprising the relevant product or market segment during the useful

Table 9.3. Functioning of distribution channels

Dimension	Expected outcome	Considerations and concerns
– Customers	– Safe and effective use of the product during its life cycle – Obtaining the maximum benefits and longevity from products – Understanding how to safely dispose of the product at the end of its useful life – Taking appropriate and responsible actions	– What are the best methods for using the product? – Should a defective component be replaced with a new or used part? Or should the product be retired? – Are its components near the end of their useful life and likely to fail? – Should the product be repaired or retired? – Is there another customer for the used product? – What is the best retirement option?
– Channel participants (outflow)	– Understanding the responsibilities inherent in the handling of the product – Knowing what information has to be conveyed to customers for the effective use of the products	– What are the critical factors that have to be managed to ensure the safe and effective use of the products? – What information is essential for the customers to ensure proper use and applications? – Are restrictions adequately communicated to customers and stakeholders?
– Channel participants (reverse flow)	– Providing information and potential solutions for product retirements – Facilitating the flow of materials through the infrastructure to affect solutions	– What are the needs for the channel to provide services to customers and users for product disposal issues? – How can the channel link the service providers to ensure a complete solution? – What are the necessary communications mechanisms?

life stages of the product. Customers are enthusiastic about enjoying the maximum benefits derived from products with the least amount of discomfort and costs. They want to maximize positive gains and minimize negative aspects. The customer or market dimension reinforces the logic of life cycle management and sustainable development. Social, economic, environmental, and business concerns all converge at the customer. Figure 9.10 presents selected customer expectations in time and space.

Category I includes the direct benefits that improve the functionality, performance, and benefits of the product from the customer's perspective. These improvements mean getting more out of the product for the investments in producing and using it. Improvements mean a single product does

Primary effects (Increases in benefits and knowledge)			
Space	I Improvements to product (Improved value proposition) *Increasing value to customers and society* – Enhanced performance – Improved functionality – Improved quality – Increased marketability – Increased compatibility – Improved packaging and instructions	II Improvements to life cycle (Improved longevity and usefulness) *Many years of value-providing* *applications* – Increased reliability – Improved applicability/ease of use – Enhanced repairability – Enhanced maintainability – Enhanced safety and health – Improved durability	Time
Space	III Enhancements to the bottom line (Improved economics and ecological aspects) *Minimizing negative effects and impacts* – Improved affordability – Improved material/energy conservation – Reduced environmental burdens – Reduced social and economic defects – Lowered health and habitat impacts	IV Enhancements to value over time (Improved time-based applications) *Reducing the loss of value over time* – Reduced cost of ownership – Enhanced reusability – Improved disposability – Increased recyclability – Improved refurbishment	Time
Resultant factors (Reduction in costs, defects, and burdens)			

Figure 9.10 Selected customer expectations in time and space

more, or it can even replace two or more products because of its enhanced capabilities. For example, wireless telephones may eventually replace all of the wire-based telephone lines, provide the functionality of a personal digital assistant, and offer Internet access as well. Improved compatibility with other devices increases capabilities, reduces the needs for specialized products or interconnectivity, and enhances the flexibility of the interrelationships between products. It also may improve the product life cycle by making a product that meets future requirements as well as present ones. Improved packaging and instructions can convey more information to the customer and better protect the product from damage.

Category II includes enhancements to the longevity and usefulness of the product. With proper use and care, robust products with a high level of reliability should achieve their targeted life span. Poor reliability and durability, inadequate maintainability and repairability, and the lack of attention to the safe and appropriate use, as described in the instructions and training manuals, result in failures and problems that reduce the time that the product can be effectively used. Such difficulties mean that products have to be produced and consumed in a shorter time period than is theoretically necessary. Fortunately the trends in many product categories are positive. For example, the average life of automobiles in the United States is approximately ten years. In 1980, the average life span for automobiles was 5.5 years. The significant improvement in the longevity of automobiles is not only an economic benefit, but an environmental benefit as well. It means the entire system is approximately 40 percent less material-intensive than it was during the 1980s. However, there are usually secondary factors that have to be considered to understand the full implications of such changes. Simply extending the life of the automobiles means there is a greater tendency to have older, more polluting technologies still on the highways.

Category III improvements are reflected in the bottom line of the value equation. The investment required for any product or economic activity is a significant factor for the customer when assessing the merits of a product. The value equation can be improved without decreasing the price by improving the defect rates and reducing the economic and ecological burdens associated with the product. Economic defects and burdens are obvious to the customer: they simply make owning and using the product more expensive. The costs of insurance and extended warranty policies are clear examples of how producers transfer the burden of defects and costs to customers. In the short term, customers often pay the price, but they also seek better solutions for the future. Loyalty may be lost.

Environmental defects and burdens are a little more difficult to appreciate. Products that involve toxic substances and hazardous materials, for example, require the customer to take special precautions. Often these precautions include obtaining additional training and knowledge to understand and manage the special handling, regulatory permits, periodic reporting, environmental audits, and special disposal protocols that may be required by law. In some cases, cradle-to-grave waste management is mandated, and the owner has to provide safeguards and solutions for the materials over extended periods of time. Environmental burdens also affect society in general, influencing the quality of life for many generations. For example, the potential impacts pertaining to the concerns about climate change are likely to be more pronounced in the future than today. Future generations may suffer the consequences of the actions, or lack of actions, of today's decision-makers.

Category IV contains those improvements that affect the long-term implications of products and their residuals. The primary concern is often the cost of owning the product. An inexpensive product can ultimately prove to be expensive if the product is unreliable, difficult to maintain or repair, or requires costly materials and energy to affect suitable outcomes. On the other hand, efficient products generally have lower operating costs and are more valuable to owners and buyers in the secondary market. Reusability enhances value: the secondary market may not be willing to pay as much for the product as when it was initially sold to the primary customer, but the secondary customer provides a means to capture some of the residual value and temporarily solve the disposal issue. It allows enhanced utilization of the resources deployed in the product and reduces the need to produce another one, at least for a given period of time.

Disposability is an inherent requirement of every product. Ultimately, unless the product or material becomes part of a building or apparatus with an indefinite life cycle, the product has to be disposed of at the end of its life. Enhancements that make the product easier to dispose of through reuse, refurbishment, remanufacturing, and recycling reduce such costs and burdens. The ability to eliminate the residuals of a product is becoming an important feature. As governments and customers demand take-back programs, the retirement question has to be addressed during product design and development.

Box 9.2 Alcan, Inc.: from enterprise thinking to LCT about water

Alcan is the second largest producer of aluminum, with a mission of turning raw material into more valuable metal resources and products. As a primary and secondary producer of aluminum, Alcan created a corporate sustainability framework for "doing more good" through design and application of innovative products and by enhancing stakeholder engagement. President and CEO Travis Engen discusses sustainable development in the *Alcan Sustainability Report 2004*:[1]

> Integrating sustainability into our business is not an easy path to take – it requires a senior-level commitment, the understanding, resourcefulness, and dedication of our employees, and a consistent and long-term approach to partnering with our stakeholders. Our sustainability framework is firmly entrenched and supported at all levels of the organization through the three components of [the Alcan] Integrated Management System (AIMS): Maximizing Value, Continuous Improvement, and our commitment to environment, health, and safety excellence . . .
>
> We are not simply "talking the talk" – we are on the fast track to "operationalize" sustainability throughout Alcan for the benefit of current and future generations and the company, today and tomorrow.

With its headquarters in Montreal, Canada, Alcan is a global corporation with operations in approximately fifty-five countries and over 70,000 employees world-wide. Its main businesses include bauxite and alumina processing, aluminum smelting and production, engineered products, and recycling. It is creating a corporate culture that embeds sustainability at the center and builds a business model that focuses on internal and external roles, responsibilities, and practices. Its culture embraces the principles of integrity, accountability, trust, transparency and teamwork. It focuses on the well-being of employees, the development of the local communities, protecting the environment, and using resources responsibly. The focus has shifted from "doing less bad" to the more integrated current perspective of "doing more good."

Alcan's thinking has expanded dramatically during the last several years from focusing on its products, processes, and operations to a more holistic perspective of an integrated business system based on an enterprise view of its responsibilities for customers, stakeholders, and employees. Its enterprise thinking forms the foundation for company values, the corporate mindset, and short- and long-term objectives. Alcan is committed to the harmonious development of social, economic, and environmental outcomes that are efficient, effective, and enduring.

AIMS sets the stage for sustainability and moves Alcan from the narrow perspective of environment, health, and safety (EHS) to the more inclusive enterprise view of cradle-to-grave responsibilities and actions. Management created a strong EHS management system, called EHS First, that has been very successful. The philosophical underpinnings have evolved toward the more comprehensive view of facing the full range of impacts across the enterprise, including those on customers and their customers. EHS First is now fully integrated into AIMS.

Alcan's Sustainability Framework provides a great overview of the most important elements of the system. The overarching focus is on value creation and increased growth. These underpin the key success factors of improving corporate image and reputation, protecting value, improving strategic position through cost reduction and preparation, and ensuring its survival. The framework provides insights and guidance for developing strategies and initiatives for achieving sustainable success. It links Alcan's grand strategy of being a value-based company with the context of the business environment and the necessity to maximize value creation and reduce social, economic, and environmental negative impacts. Value protection is especially dependent on conservation and prevention. Figure 9B.1 provides a graphical representation of the Alcan framework.[2]

The framework and Alcan's enterprise thinking both set the stage for understanding its integrated business management system and the life cycle impacts of its products, processes, and operations. While aluminum processing is energy-intensive and the mining

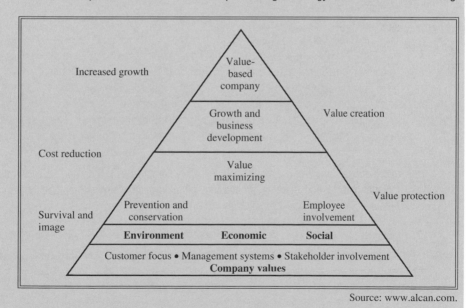

Source: www.alcan.com.

Figure 9B.1 Alcan's Sustainability Framework[a]

Note: [a]Adapted from Alcan's own framework. see www. alcan.com for full details.

operations involve large quantities of raw materials, one of Alcan's primary concerns is water. CEO Engen expressed the importance of water to Alcan:[3]

> While water is not our core business at Alcan, without it, we would have no business. As a critical component of our business cycle, water enables us to generate hydropower for most of our aluminum smelters. It is an indispensable input to our diverse industrial processes. We also recognize that the same water is an inevitable output for us, with downstream impacts such as water level issues and industrial releases to both surfacewater and groundwater environments . . . In the end, water binds us to each other, no matter where we live or work.

Water is a precious resource that requires diligent management. To understand the implications and impacts of its water use, Alcan uses LCT to determine the most important issues and to formulate action plans for managing the problems, difficulties, challenges, and opportunities. LCT builds awareness of the critical inputs and outputs and their effects and impacts, and sheds light on potential concerns as well. While the production of aluminum is generally material (4 kg of bauxite to produce 1 kg of aluminum) and energy-intensive, most of the energy is derived water from hydropower (hydropower provides 83 percent of the electricity).[4] Alcan believes that LCA is fundamental for having an accurate assessment of water resource management issues. LCA focuses on the needs and provides the logic for selecting appropriate R&D initiatives for making improvements. In Alcan's brochure on water, *Committed to the Sustainable Management of Water, One of our Most Precious Resources*, Alcan shows a graphic of the life cycle of aluminum. The graphic, "Our Aluminum Life Cycle: Key Water Issues and Impacts at Alcan," identifies the most critical water-related issues across the enterprise.[5]

The framework is not intended to be comprehensive. It shows the essential processes of the enterprise and indicates some of the principal areas pertaining to water issues and impacts. The life cycle framework provides an overview of the relationships between aluminum production and water. It provides management with the foundation it needs for developing water strategies and action plans for improving the utilization of water resources and to reduce vulnerabilities to degradation and depletion.

In June 2004, Alcan joined the United Nation's Global Compact.[6] It was selected by the Dow Jones Sustainability World Index (DJSWI) as the top performer in the category of basic resources.[7] Alcan is recognized as one of the most admired corporations. It is one of the leaders in SBD and has gained significant advantages through its leadership, business integration, and innovation.

Notes:

1. Alcan, *Sustainability Report, 2004*, p. 3.
2. *Ibid.*, p. 18.
3. "Committed to the Sustainable Management of Water, One of our Most Precision Resources," Montreal, Canada: Alcan Inc., December 2003, p. 3.
4. *Ibid.*, p. 10.
5. *Ibid.*, p. 9; see Alcan's website (www.alcan.com), or obtain the pamphlet from Alcan for details.
6. Alcan, *Sustainability Report, 2004*, p. 16.
7. www.sustainability–indexes.com.

Analytical research frameworks: the precursors to LCA

Foundations for assessment and discovery

Business executives, senior professionals, and practitioners are constantly seeking to discover and understand new information about the business environment. Synthesizing new knowledge and developing theoretical constructs for analyzing the business environment is a crucial part of sustainable development. LCT and LCA depend on knowing and understanding the needs of a broad array of external constituencies. But using LCT is more complex than standard approaches because the research methodologies have to be rigorous and comprehensive, yet flexible.

The challenge for the professionals involved in developing a logical conceptual framework for the discovery and assessment of the business environment is to determine a research model that is based on scientific principles (rigor) and the strategic needs of the corporation (flexibility). Researching the forces of change involves a myriad of disciplines. Examining the whole system requires a fundamental shift in the way researchers think and act. The approach is top down. The framework starts with the whole and then narrows down to the pieces. The methods and techniques of the investigation must prescribe the flow of the research, address the critical questions, use objective evidence to support the theoretical constructs, and lead to sound and unbiased insights and conclusions. The researchers must be proficient in the techniques they use.

Preliminary research

The basic framework for LCA involves a multiphase process for defining, developing, implementing, and evaluating the work. The starting point depends on the information about the subject that exists in the literature, practitioners' knowledge, and the public domain. Preliminary research is the initial phase, a precursor to the actual study. It identifies the critical questions and determines the scope of the ultimate research program. It defines and refines the most important issues, challenges, and opportunities. It is based on scientific reasoning, requiring both a theoretical view and a fundamental understanding of the corporation and its business environment. Preliminary research uses a variety of means to acquire knowledge about the corporation and its business environment that can help to formulate the proper research questions.

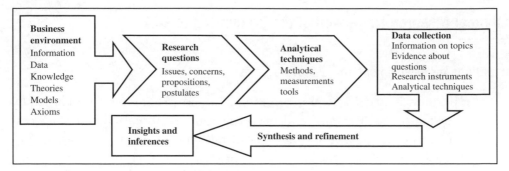

Figure 9.11   Preliminary phase in establishing a research agenda

The context for the research is also the subject of the research – the business environment– and there are general theories about behaviors and interactions in the business environment. It is useful at the outset to identify the prevailing theories, models, and axioms, those well-established truths and scientific principles that are generally accepted by all of the constituents.

Based on this fundamental understanding of the business environment derived from preliminary research and generally accepted knowledge, the next step is to determine appropriate research questions to guide the discovery and assessment process. These questions pertain to the most important issues, concerns, constraints, challenges, and opportunities, always reflecting the dynamics of the external forces and how the corporation relates to them. They are often propositions that can be assessed using analytical methods such as LCA and risk assessment and techniques of scientific inquiry.

Synthesis and refinement involve the preliminary assessment of the information and data so that a view of the dynamics can be formulated and the research methodology can be refined. Figure 9.11 provides a schematic of this preliminary stage in establishing a research agenda.

From a management perspective, the research questions are the key to understanding the prospects for LCT and life cycle management within the corporate setting. Developing the best research questions requires creativity and out-of-the-box thinking, as well as a clear understanding of the prevailing conditions, trends, and scientific knowledge. LCT involves exploring the implications of the entire enterprise and its impacts. Establishing a research agenda is a precursor to LCA. It sets the stage for the transition from thought processes to assessment. Most importantly, executive management and business professionals have to determine their own perspectives for conducting the underlying research and doing the assessments.

Research methodology

The intent of business research is to improve the general understanding of the dynamics of the business environment and the corporate condition, and to increase the certainty and confidence management has about its vision, strategies, and direction. This depends on an intuitive process of developing conceptual approaches into a logical framework for questioning, challenging, and assessing propositions and constructs. The conceptual approaches and propositions define the business setting in terms of generalizations, accepted knowledge, or axioms. The research methodology then establishes and implements a research plan to test these "truths." The research questions are the postulates that, when applied to these axioms, reveal further knowledge about the business environment. The framework that results provides a means for creativity, study, comparative analysis, and insight.

The research methodology typically follows the generalized approach suggested in figure 9.11. It engages practitioners in seven key steps:

- Identify the main *questions and propositions*, as determined by the preliminary study. What are the most compelling issues, problems, concerns, challenges, threats, and opportunities?
- Define the fundamental *truths and axioms* pertaining to the situation. What are the generally accepted theories about the situation? What does the literature provide about the propositions?
- Identify *innovative constructs* for creating alternate solutions. What are the main debates about the research questions and alternate views about the key questions? How can imagination and creativity contribute to new ways of thinking?
- Select *analytical techniques* for investigating and assessing the questions and propositions. What are the most appropriate methods for understanding the situation and exploring the information, data, and evidence?
- Collect *information and data* pertaining to the questions and propositions. What are sources of information? What is the critical evidence for generalizing the implications of the conditions, the trends, the situation, and the future prospects?
- Compare the *observations, conclusions, and insights* with the metrics and expectations of the constituents. What are the profound outcomes? How can the results be used to improve the management system and constructs of the corporation?
- Create *theories or generalizations*. What are the proposed changes that further SBD?

The research plan defines the purpose of the study and the expected outcomes, identifies the design of the study and the scope of the effort, states the boundaries of the system and the key constituents, stipulates the research questions, specifies the analytical constructs, and determines the research methods.

Based on the observed phenomenon and evidence, a coherent explanation can be proposed and tested. The synthesis of the research insights, conclusions, and inferences varies considerably, based on the evidence and the depth of the study. Understanding of causality is a fundamental outcome of the research. In scientific research, causal explanations are often the primary focus. For example, in astrophysics, finding the cause of the "big bang" would provide evidence supporting the related theory about the origin of the universe. Causality provides compelling support about the validity of an argument or theory. Evidence supports the theories and provides answers to the questions. The basic approach in LCT is to make determinations based on facts and information and not on presumptions and preconceived notions. While not everything can be assessed using scientific methods, it is critical in charting the right course for the future to ensure that the foundations are as solid as possible. Great care has to be used to eliminate stereotypical views, whether they support the traditional perspective that business is just about making money, or that there are overwhelming problems, such as global warming, or prescribed solutions, such as renewable energy, that take priority over everything else. SBD involves strategic logic, assessment, and effective and balanced decision-making.

Summary

A corporation has to undergo a substantial change in its vision, philosophies, and principles to focus on SBD. It may actually need to undergo a complete paradigm change in beliefs, attitudes, behaviors, and practices. It may require new competencies, capabilities, rigorous analysis, and understanding of multiple dimensions across the global context of the business environment. Sustainable answers are based on analysis rather than prescription, and that analysis depends on the critical assessment of programs, processes, practices, and people from start to finish. That analysis depends upon LCT and life cycle management.

A paradigm change usually occurs when the older paradigm is inadequate for meeting the requirements of the business environment – i.e. when there

Table 9.4. Key factors related to SBD

	Near-term initiatives	Long-term programs
Environmental	Regulatory compliance and lobbying	Conservation and preservation
	Pollution prevention and waste minimization	Reduced degradation and preparedness
	Stewardship and communications	Reduced depletion and effectiveness
	Ethics and principles	Impact reduction and risk mitigation
Social	Distribution of goods and services	Quality of life and equity
	Needs and fairness	Symbiosis and eco-efficiency
	Rights and expectations	Rationalism and relational views
	Problem solving and customer satisfaction	Risk management and life expectancy
Economic	Growth and development	Wealth creation and sustainability
	Utilitarianism and balance	Learning/knowledge and solutions
	Short term and long term	Value maximization and profitability
	Industry performance and success	Effective change and stability

are too many unresolved problems and difficulties that cannot be solved using the old theories. New solutions must be determined through understanding and knowledge.

During the early stages of SBD, many of the essential elements are still in transition as new learning and experiences provide greater insights about the most effective theories and constructs. Table 9.4 provides a sample of some of the key factors. A few of the topics relate to the older paradigm, a few take on new meanings in light of LCT, and several are still being debated.

LCT is critical for including considerations that cross space and time. The intent is to ensure that the solutions include all key considerations, reflect on the implications over time, and are comprehensive. Moreover, LCT forces management and professionals to be responsibility for the actions of direct and indirect participants, including suppliers and their suppliers and customers and their relationships as well.

LCT establishes a mindset and a framework for understanding the whole, and the need for change. It provides insights about opportunities and challenges. It sets the stage for determining the requirements for further assessment. It is the precursor to LCAs.

Managers and professionals have to understand and manage the whole and not just the parts (functional areas). They have to have broad exposure and knowledge about every facet of business management. They have to have the ability to integrate business operations and to make decisions that improve the prospects of their businesses at a rate greater than the general rate of improvements of their peers or industry competitors. They must focus on

discovering opportunities and exploiting them to create sustainable competitive advantages and future success as well. LCT involves the knowledge,
intellectual capabilities, creativity, and inspiration to think strategically, lead
change, and create breakthrough solutions that meet the business opportunities and challenges of the global environment, both now and in the future.

Supplementary material

Learning objectives

Chapter 9 has the following learning objectives that are intended to guide and
support students and practitioners:
- Understanding the meaning and importance of LCT.
- Understanding systems integration and LCT in the context of global
  corporations.
- Describing the essential elements of LCT and life cycle management for
  designing and developing products and processes.
- Describing the essential elements of an analytical research framework.
- Appreciating how executives and senior management can use LCT.

Research questions

The following are questions related to SBD in order to facilitate learning and
ongoing discussion and analysis of the main topics covered in the chapter:
- What are the most important aspect of LCT for global corporations?
- What are the design and development LCT principles used by global
  corporations.
- How can corporations integrate LCT into their mainstream thinking?
- What are the elements of analytical research programs?

NOTES

1. The point is that known defects were allowed to persist. The companies involved in the
   situation seemingly failed to take corrective action that might have mitigated some of the
   problems. It is not my intent to speculate about what the outcomes could have been, or to
   address old problems.

2. Information was provided during a discussion and presentation of the plan on June 3, 2001, during a visit to the plant.
3. Quote is taken from Niccolò Machiavelli's *The Prince*.
4. WBCSD, "Eco-efficiency: sustainability module," March 2004, p. 20.
5. Ibid., p. 27.
6. Joseph Fiksel, *Design for Environment: Creating Eco-Efficient Products and Processes* (New York: McGraw-Hill, 1996, p. 3).
7. Liivio DeSimone and Frank Popoff, *Eco-Efficiency: The Business Link to Sustainable Development* (Cambridge, MA: MIT Press, 1997), p. 119.

REFERENCES

DeSimone, Liivio and Frank Popoff (1997) *Eco-Efficiency: The Business Link to Sustainable Development.* Cambridge, MA: MIT Press

Fiksel, Joseph (1996) *Design for Environment: Creating Eco-Efficient Products and Processes.* New York: McGraw-Hill

Machiavelli, Niccolò (1916) *The Prince.* London: Macmillan

Society of Environmental Toxicology and Chemistry (1991) *A Technical Framework for Life Cycle Assessment*

World Business Council for Sustainable Development (WBCSD) (2004) "Eco-efficiency sustainability module," March

10 Formulation of life cycle assessment: initiation and inventory assessment

Introduction

This chapter defines and examines LCA, a derivative construct of LCT that looks at products and processes to expose the full scope of their resource and energy utilization from cradle-to-grave and all the implications and impacts. While LCT explores the broad perspectives, LCA examines the particular, studying products and processes using rigorous quantitative and qualitative analyses to determine the inputs and outputs of materials and energy, causes and effects, problems and solutions. While standard LCA techniques are evolving, including ISO 14041, the constructs vary considerably, from streamlined versions focusing on the primary concerns to more elaborate holistic models that attempt to encapsulate the entire system.

LCA usually focuses on finding potential difficulties and curing the defects and burdens during the early phases of product and process development processes or during the early stages of product delivery. LCA is a means to obtain a significant amount of information about the whole system, from external suppliers to end-use customers and beyond. It can also be used to examine existing products and processes if there are significant problems that must be cured. If such efforts reveal the need for significant changes, the requisite improvement initiative may become an NPD program.

LCA is a rather radical break from the traditional business approaches of focusing on primary considerations and internal matters to a richer view of the full spectrum of the impacts and consequences of management decisions. It is action-oriented, identifying positive initiatives that can correct defects and burdens and/or improve products and processes. It can be viewed as an analytical technique for moving to higher levels of quality and capabilities through continuous improvements and profound changes. Actions and outcomes, not just good intentions, lead to gains.

LCA is still in its infancy, and there are relatively few concrete examples of comprehensive LCAs that have examined entire systems. LCAs are time-consuming, costly, and difficult to perform because of a lack of information and structure. Furthermore, they are expansive and tend to increase exponentially as additional levels of examination are added. However, complexity can be handled by selecting definitive boundaries for the analysis. For example, Electric Boat and the US Navy limited their LCA to the top twenty first-tier suppliers and selected EoL considerations during the design of the *USS Virginia*, the US Navy's newest submarine. Alternatively, a streamlined LCA may focus only on the most salient considerations. Minor effects and those known to be benign may be neglected, or rules may be established to decrease the scope. While there is always the risk of neglecting important parameters, the intent is to reduce the time and effort needed to obtain meaningful results. Such logic might follow Pareto thinking: 20 percent of the activities produce 80 percent of the results.

This chapter describes and discusses the methods, applications, and benefits of LCA and includes the following topics:

- An overview of the LCA construct and its prime components.
- The context of LCA, key considerations and applications.
- The fundamental LCA framework and the Initiation phase, including goals, definition, purpose, and scope.
- The Inventory phase, including computational models for analyzing, interpreting, and understanding data and information.
- Decision constructs for deploying the Inventory phase of LCA in a business setting.

The objectives behind LCA are multifaceted. The most critical objectives are to obtain knowledge and insights about possible improvements and changes in order to formulate and implement strategic initiatives for achieving sustainable success. LCA facilitates improved strategic positions and reduced negative impacts. It also helps expand organizational capabilities and economic stability. In a complex world of shared information, extensive litigation, and radical changes, it is incumbent upon management to exercise appropriate precautions and ensure viable solutions. LCA is the manifestation of the "logic-based" precautionary principle. It assures that the best decisions are made and that future considerations are deemed just as important as current ones. It supports good decisions and effective solutions based on the principles of SBD.

The LCA construct

Fundamentals

LCA can have strategic implications for SBD. Corporations can use LCA to find ways to reduce uncertainties, mitigate risks, reduce liabilities, and facilitate positive outcomes. LCA incorporates analytical techniques to determine and cure defects and burdens across the entire life cycle of a product or process. It seeks to recognize and solve social, economic, and environmental difficulties at the earliest possible stage in the technology or product development cycle. It is an evolving methodology that traditionally consists of inventory, impact, and improvement analyses.

Life cycle inventory analysis examines material selection, product evaluation, product design review, and policy determination. Impact analysis explores the effects of defects, burdens, and impacts. Improvement analysis involves discovering ways to improve outcomes. Table 10.1 provides an overview of the three main phases in the traditional LCA process.[1] The steps in the traditional process are intended to identify potential problems, determine their severity, and invent solutions for improving the situation.

LCA is based on scientific principles that frame the analysis in objective terms. It is a realistic view of products and processes and their implications and impacts. It provides a comprehensive, balanced, and unbiased basis for decision-making, a way to compare options, and a mechanism for improving defects and burdens.

Main elements of LCA

Initiation

LCA begins with a clear definition of purpose and scope. Whereas the theoretical scope of an LCA takes a "cradle-to-grave" view, it is imperative that the scope of the actual assessment is defined by clear limits. Practitioners must determine what is to be analyzed, how many processes are to be examined, and the baseline for the assessment. A full LCA may not be necessary to gain a comprehensive view of the social, economic, and environmental aspects of the design, production, and use of a product and the related processes. Moreover, practicality may compel management to divide complex situations into manageable subprograms that can be executed in a reasonable time frame (two–three years).

Table 10.1. Phases in the traditional LCA process[a]

	Inventory assessment	Impact assessment	Improvement assessment
Elements	An objective quantification of environmental burdens and product and process defects	An evaluation of the effects of the burdens and defects and the related impacts and their consequences	A systematic evaluation of the opportunities to reduce the burdens and improve the products and processes
Key Aspects	Identification of the elements and quantification of inputs and outputs	Resource depletion, human health risks, safety concerns, environmental degradation, disruption, and destruction	Changes needed to bring about the desired improvements and improved solutions
Goals	Identification of inputs and outputs; classification and evaluation of levels, loading, and sources	Understanding the potential implications of the difficulties with products and processes and the viability of potential solutions	Opportunities to reduce the environmental burdens and defects, thus improving longevity and sustainable outcomes

Note: [a] Bruce Piasecki, K. Fletcher, and F. Mendelson, *Environmental Management and Business Strategy: Leadership Skills for the Twenty-first Century* (New York: John Wiley, 1999), p. 148. The chapter in the book, "Converging integrated new product development with design for environment" was written by David L. Rainey.

Practitioners may limit the scope of the analysis by ranking the importance of the product elements and the processes in the management system and selecting the essential elements. For instance, a cursory assessment may indicate that the most significant impacts occur within the supply networks, suggesting that the LCA should focus on upstream considerations. Moreover, certain processes within the supply networks may create hazardous wastes. In such a case, the LCA may omit suppliers who contribute less than 1 percent of the materials and those whose materials are benign, unless there are other significant concerns about the impacts and consequences of the materials or products involved. Likewise, scope could be limited to only key suppliers if a preassessment determined that the downstream implications were more important than the upstream aspects. Such an assessment would suggest that the application side (customers and users) may contribute to a majority of the difficulties and should therefore be the focus. EoL considerations may require special attention to ensure that controls are initiated to manage wastes and burdens.

Inventory assessment

The **inventory assessment** is the in-depth identification of the material and energy flows within the product delivery system and the quantification of inputs and outputs at each step of the processes used to design and produce the products. This includes identifying the design, production, and application processes and their elements, ascertaining the availability of information regarding the materials and energy flows, determining the environmental status in positive or negative terms, and providing a means to categorize the data and information. In some cases, the inputs or outputs are shared by a number of products. The information about a specific product's use of a material or production of waste may not be readily available because of aggregation of the data: for example, there are numerous cases where waste streams are combined into a single tank for security or cost reasons. This practice can make it difficult to determine the specific sources of the wastes. Often such waste streams are simply allocated over all of the products in the facility or the process. This makes LCA more difficult or even impossible. But even more importantly, it often requires more sophisticated and costly technologies to cure the problems. Table 10.2 lists the main elements of an LCA inventory.

Inventory assessment is an important phase since it identifies environmental concerns and provides a preliminary sense of the potential opportunities for improvement. The findings of this phase help management determine the courses of actions for curing problems. However, it is implicit that discovered problems be rectified. This obligation can be a particularly serious concern if the problems are several tiers deep within the supply chain. Solutions to such problems can require multiple levels of interaction to cure, and the required solutions may be expensive and unpleasant. For instance, if a serious problem is identified and the supplier is unwilling to resolve the difficulty, a new supplier or a new solution may have to be selected. Still, LCA assists corporations in discovering problems and remedying them sooner than if it were not used at all. Problems that are not found early often surface during applications of the products, or are discovered by stakeholders who monitor the corporation. The consequences then are much more severe and costly.

Impact assessment

Impact assessment evaluates the waste and energy flows to determine the impacts and consequences of resource utilization, waste generation, and disruptive and destructive activities. The inputs and outputs may create environmental defects and burdens that require categorizing, characterizing, assessing, prioritizing, and then decision-making.

The prevailing approach is to evaluate the impacts of a product and its product delivery system according to the following categories: (1) environmental health; (2) human health; (3) social and economic health; and

Table 10.2. Elements of an LCA inventory

Life cycle stage	Selected categories of inputs	Selected categories of outputs
Extraction processes; precursors to materials; acquisition of resources	Overburdens; processed mass; water resources; land resources; energy to extract ore; capital equipment; infrastructure; transportation energy; labor	Ore; overburden; slag; depletion of natural resources; air emissions; dust; water effluents; habitat disruption; degradation of land; solid waste; noise
Material processing; raw materials and energy	Ore; natural resources; energy; water; capital equipment; labor; land; combustion air; parts, components, materials, products	Slag; scrap; wastewater; air emissions; refined material; by-products; solid wastes; other residuals
In-bound logistics	Fuel; capital equipment; vehicles; energy; lubricants; wear parts; tires; labor; land and infrastructure	Movements; air emissions; dust; noise; spills; health and safety considerations; accidents; cleaning water residuals; noise
Production processes	Raw materials: energy; capital equipment; catalysts; supplies; repair parts; filters; media; water, air; land	Products; by-products; spent fluids; solid waste; excess chemicals; ash; scrap; defects; accidents
Distribution and logistics	Fuel; capital equipment; vehicles; energy; lubricants; wear parts; tires; labor; land and infrastructure	Movements; air emissions; dust; noise; spills; health and safety considerations; accidents; cleaning water residuals; noise
Application and use	Products; infrastructure; related industries; energy; complementary products; repair materials; supplies; labor	Solid wastes; wastewater; air emissions; land impacts; spills; accidents; residuals; spent products; discards
Service and maintenance	Maintenance supplies; repair parts; service facility; labor	Used parts; spent materials; cleaning agents; energy
Reuse	Used products and materials; repair materials; labor; logistics; storage facilities; supplies; water, air, land	Secondary applications; solid wastes; wastewater; air emissions; land impacts; spills; accidents; residuals; discards
Remanufacturing	Used products and materials; refurbishing materials and energy; supplies; water, air, land	Refurbished products; solid wastes; wastewater; air emissions; land impacts; spills; accidents; residuals; discards
Recycling	Used products and materials	Secondary materials
Waste management	Products; wastes; logistics; storage	Water effluents; air emissions; wastes

Table 10.3. Selected examples of impacts and their assessment

Categories	Selected impact areas	Assessment
Environmental health	Ozone depletion; hazardous waste; smog; eutrophication; global warming	Intensity of effects, time scale, media; types of impacts; risk mitigation strategies
Human health	Toxicity; carcinogenicity; allergenicity; odors; noise; residuals; living environment	Hazard identification; risk characterization; exposure assessment; risk management
Social and economic health	Economic losses; social stability; quality of life; fear; product safety and integrity; human rights; discrimination	Costs and benefits; value assessment; risk sensitivity; liability containment; disclosures; security assessment
Resource depletion	Soil depletion; water resource and quality losses; air quality degradation; decline in species diversity; degradation; disruptions	Longevity; sustainable outcomes; availability assessments; environmental assessments; risk mitigation

(4) resource depletion. Environmental health is the broadest and most complex category. It covers the use of materials and energy, the residuals of processes, and ongoing and accidental releases that may affect the eco-systems. The human health category includes assessing the impacts on the human physical system. The social and economic health category covers the impacts on the stakeholders in social, economic, and political terms. Finally, the resource depletion category covers the consequences of using renewable and nonrenewable resources. The impact assessment examines the impacts in all these categories, and the linkages between them.

Characterizing the effects of a product or process requires information pertaining to a broad array of social, economic, environmental, and human health issues. It is often difficult to determine the direct impacts on each category. For example, the results of resource utilization (depletion) or releases of waste streams to the environment (degradation) may take decades to manifest themselves. The analysis involves establishing the relationship between the cause and effect, evaluating the routes and the potential affected areas, and determining the severity of the outcomes. It examines the downstream consequences of the critical activities in terms of local, regional, and global impacts. The evaluation includes qualitative and quantitative measures and an objective estimate of the probability of a negative effect occurring. Table 10.3 provides examples of selected impact areas within the broad categories.

Impact assessment examines the impacts, and ranks them in importance. Prioritizing the results of the analysis provides a foundation for selecting opportunities for improvement.

Improvement assessment

During the improvement assessment, practitioners identify opportunities for changing the operating system in ways that will lower the social, economic, and environmental defects and burdens. Improvements must be based on a systems perspective to ensure that the outcomes have positive effects. The improvements can cut across a wide range of elements in the operating system – from waste minimization to fundamental changes in the practices used to produce the product and NPDs. Improvement assessment is the never-ending quest toward perfection. It involves actions for making products and processes more ideal.

LCA from a development perspective

The most obvious application of LCA is in the NPD process. It is relatively easy to implement LCA concurrently with the design and development of a new product. The required analytical work parallels the elements of the NPD plan and provides decision-makers with real time information on the environmental implications of their designs.

LCA can also be used in the redesign of existing products though existing design parameters tend to be more limiting. The redesign situation offers opportunities to improve the product by reducing or eliminating defects that reduce its viability. LCA can be carried out on a limited scale or in its full scope, depending on the time available and the objectives of the program.

A full LCA can uncover issues pertaining to compliance with environmental laws and regulations or provide the means to withstand the scrutiny of customers and stakeholders (environmentalists) who expect improvements and better solutions. From a SBD perspective, LCA provides an in-depth analysis of products and processes, their design, production, applications, and retirement. Such a comprehensive review of the complete value network provides a valuable tool for making decisions: decision-makers are able to make dramatic improvements to the value proposition and to reduce environmental burdens and defects that could cause a product's premature death.

Conscientious management focuses on establishing plans and programs to enhance performance and reduce problems and liabilities. LCA offers an outstanding management tool toward that end. Ongoing efforts to optimize product parameters or process elements may incorporate LCA to find opportunities for improvement.

The contextual implications of LCA

Overview

LCA is intended to shed light on products, processes, and product delivery systems. It is a means to better understand their implications and impacts, to generate the information and data that contribute to knowledge, transparency, and effective communications with stakeholders and customers, and to ultimately make significant improvements.

LCA focuses primarily on products because the product reaches across the enterprise, linking customers with operations and supply networks. The products are the means for corporations to translate technologies, resources, and intellectual capital into value and wealth. Processes, on the other hand, are derived constructs that depend upon the product structures.

Products represent the "mass" in the product delivery system, and are the end-results of the materials, components, and parts that are used to construct solutions for customers and stakeholders. They exist in space and time. While products include mass and energy, the primary considerations often focus on "resources." Energy comes either directly from the sun or is indirectly stored as chemical or potential energy. For example, coal and petroleum products are stored chemical energy. When they are burned, their energy is released. The main implications of this kind of energy center around the mass of coal or oil that is extracted, processed, transported, and combusted, and the resources and materials involved in and produced by these processes.

LCA exists within the context of the business environment. The desires of customers, stakeholders, and society for fewer defects and burdens motivate it. But LCA is not about discovering the obvious weaknesses of the product or process, nor is it about reaffirming the positive attributes or benefits. Although such results are welcome, the purpose of LCA is to examine a product or process in its entirety, from supply networks to final applications and EoL, in an attempt to disclose all of the potential implications, impacts, and consequences of that product or process. The ultimate objectives are to identify, define, and mitigate any negatives and corroborate, and specify and communicate the positives. LCA is preemptive.

As stated in chapter 4, the seven primary product or process impacts are:

- *Destruction* of the bio-system. Waste streams from industrial processes and product applications can destroy the chemical, physical, and biological equilibrium of nature and have significant adverse local, regional, or global effects. It is often difficult to assess and mitigate damage to a bio-system, making these impacts a serious concern. The destruction of the ozone layer is possibly the best-known example.

- *Degradation* of the environment through manmade waste streams. Pollution of the air, water, and land, and deposits of solid and hazardous wastes in the natural environment are an ongoing concern. Pollutant volume, concentration and duration of releases are significant factors in determining the negative impacts. The medium in which a waste stream is released can have a large effect on the handling and treatability of the wastes. For instance, once air emissions are released to the atmosphere, they disperse and become difficult to cleanup. Some effects are immediate, like unhealthy air caused by smog. Others, like acid rain that destroys vegetation, lakes, and ponds, have long-term implications.

- *Damage* to the business environment or natural environment. Most industrial chemical spills fall into this category. While spills have negative effects, in most cases they can be remediated to mitigate the long-term effects.

- *Depletion* of resources. Resource availability plays an important role in the economics of products and production processes. As resources become scarce, they tend to become more costly and more difficult to acquire. As resources are used faster than they are replenished, the viability of the products and processes that depend upon them becomes questionable. For example, the settlers of Easter Island consumed the wood of the native forests faster than it could regrow. The islanders destroyed both the trees and nature's ability to replace them. In modern society, the depletion of petroleum is one of the most critical social, economic, and environmental concerns.

- *Disruption* of the natural environment. Nature is complex, and introducing an industrial activity, a manmade waste stream, or altering the eco-systems in any way can have significant ramifications. For example, hydroelectric power plants were once viewed as renewable sources of energy. However, the current assessment is not quite as positive: dams can restrict the spawning of fish, the flow of nutrients to the river basin, and have a negative impact on the natural habitat.

- *Disturbance of the natural environment*. This is typically a local impact caused by a new activity, such as seismic testing for oil reserves. Often, corrective actions can mitigate disturbances quickly.

- *Defects and burdens* in design, production, and application. These impacts are especially critical to the health, safety, and well-being of both people and the natural environment. Defects lead to uncertainties, risks, and liabilities. They result in compromised solutions that may not be reliable or sustainable. Burdens are the negative impacts caused by products and processes. All materials have the potential to be hazardous or toxic; however, there are certain materials – such as heavy metals and certain man-made organic compounds – that are inherently toxic and may be viewed as inherently defective. These materials impose burdens that have to be mitigated.

The context of LCA is the realm of corporate responsibility for protecting and improving the business environment, the people in it, and the natural world. That responsibility includes ensuring that the product delivery system and the enterprise itself meet the social, economic, and environmental needs of its constituents. LCA attempts to systematically uncover and eliminate potential negative impacts by identifying and avoiding questionable products, processes, or activities, preventing impacts whenever possible, or mitigating them. The primary focus is on eliminating or minimizing the impacts using analyses, knowledge, and preemptive actions. It also involves improving the management system so that it is better able to explore sustainable solutions.

Protecting the business environment and improving the management system

The use of LCA fits perfectly with the global trend toward Six-Sigma quality and defect-free products and operations. Global corporations have a vested interest in ensuring that their business solutions remain viable over time and that the means of production and future operations are not threatened by the negative impacts and consequences of previous decisions. Many of the large corporations that face severe challenges today are those plagued by legacy problems. Those problems often include unfunded pension and health care benefits for retirees, environmental problems caused by improperly discarded wastes and pollution from past operations, and uneconomical operations caused by high structural costs (inefficiencies and poor work flow) resulting from past decision-making.

LCA makes it possible to know the trouble spots and avoid them. For instance, using heavy metals such as lead and cadmium will make products unmarketable in the European Union and create disposal problems for customers. The solution is simple: do not use heavy metals.

LCA generally invokes positive responses from employees and professionals within the enterprise. Reducing uncertainty and expanding knowledge facilitates effective management and improves the management system. LCA has the potential to reduce the number of problems and difficulties. For instance, US chemical companies spent more on remediation during the 1990s than they did on R&D. Curing problems took priority over discovering and creating new technologies and developing new products. LCA can help a corporation to anticipate these kinds of problems and avoid them. Its use improves the business environment and the management system.

The LCA framework

Overview

LCA depends on the temporal and spatial relationships between the essential dimensions of the enterprise and its participants. The LCA framework is directly related to the EMM. Primary considerations are the duration of the life cycle and the longevity of products and processes. Historically, LCA has followed the activities of the producer, but a more innovative perspective examines the implications of the product during its useful life and retirement. This *market-driven approach* focuses on the perceptions of customers and stakeholders, and looks at what should be developed instead of what has been developed. It places more attention on preventing defects and burdens from a customer's viewpoint than on meeting design standards and complying with mandates. It represents the convergence of pollution prevention and design for environment (sustainability) with SBD.

Because LCA depends on so many variables, it is difficult to create a generalized format. While it may be important to be inclusive and innovative, often the demands of the real world preclude a full analysis of the life cycle. Because of time constraints or process issues, other options may have to be examined and structured. For instance, the commercialization of a new product may require early introduction to the market; time constraints limit the amount of detailed analysis that can be performed. Nonetheless, management has a fiduciary responsibility to ensure that products are safe and effective for their intended purposes. A streamlined version of the LCA may be the answer; however, it is only one of many options. Many choices will have to be made, based on the context of the situation.

Determining the LCA framework

Practitioners can tailor the LCA framework to specific situations. However, there must be a defendable logic to the choices made. In theory, the LCA framework should include the full scope of the life cycle and examine every element and every impact. While this is the ideal, practicality may dictate otherwise. The full LCA may cost more money and take more time than the value derived from the analyses, especially in certain areas of the product structure or applications. For example, the typical food product has a life span of hours or a few days: an analysis of its use over time may not be warranted. Conversely, an automobile has a life span of many (ten–fifteen) years, during which it may consume vast quantities of gasoline (approximately 20,000 kg). The consumption of fuel over the life cycle may be much more significant than the other life cycle considerations of the vehicle itself.

The alternative to a full LCA is to conduct a **streamlined life cycle assessment (SLCA)**. Many companies have used SLCA to achieve more immediate results and to simplify the complexities of a full LCA. This can be especially helpful when the data and information required for a full LCA are not readily available.

SLCAs are used to limit the life cycle stages, focus on selected impacts, reduce the number of parameters or processes examined, and overcome the weaknesses related to the availability of data and information. In his book, *Streamlined Life-cycle Assessment*, Dr. Thomas Graedel provides an excellent perspective on how to use SLCA and its implications, suggesting several ways to abridge the LCA framework.[2] His book offers insights on how to select a SLCA and explains many techniques that can be used to improve the analytical constructs for making improvements.

The SLCA approach examines the essential elements of the system using a predetermined logic for choosing what elements to include or exclude. It uses select product characteristics or life cycle implications to concentrate on either the product side or the application side of the value system. The intent is to ascertain the most crucial concerns about the product and its applications and construct a LCA framework that addresses the major issues systematically without becoming overwhelmed with nonessential parts of the equation.

In determining the LCA framework, one of the most important aspects is the complexity of the product and its value networks. Complex products generally use more elaborate technologies and have more complicated structures. Complicated structures, in turn, have a greater probability of incurring problems or difficulties. As the number of tiers in the supply chain increases and the number of interfaces in the production process expands, the opportunities for something unexpected to occur also increase.[3] For example, two materials used separately may have only a minimal impact on the environment; however, when the two are combined, the results can be significant. Aluminum and plastic material used separately are easily recovered and recycled, but when they are made into a composite, the final product is difficult, if not impossible, to recycle. In addition, the manufacturing processes for the latter often have lower yields and produce more solid wastes.

The temporal aspects play a significant role as well. If a preliminary assessment indicates that most of the concerns are exhibited during the use of the product and not during its production, the focus of the LCA may shift to the application side of the equation. Traditional LCA models are intended to be comprehensive, but the constructs are relatively simplistic involving four main phases (initiation, inventory, impact, and improvement). The LCA framework can take any of the following six product perspectives:

- *Product platform* (holistic)   For related products or product families, the product platform provides a holistic perspective of the entire product delivery and NPD systems. The advantage of using a product platform approach is that many products can be included in the LCA, and multiple benefits can be achieved. The challenge is the complexity of the system and all of its implications.
- *Product system* (holistic)   This approach is also holistic, because it focuses on all of a product's implications and support structures. Still, the product system is narrower in scope than a platform approach and less complicated. When using this system, the pressures to get new or improved products to the market may make it difficult to complete the analyses of the entire product.
- *Component or assembly* (selected piece)   Selecting a component or an assembly of a product simplifies the framework and reduces the difficulties involved in trying to examine the entire product. It simplifies the scope of the work. It can be a defendable approach if the impacts associated with a product are well known and are concentrated in one or two areas of the product architecture. For example, the internal combustion engine of an automobile may produce most of the emissions from the product and that fact is well known from the historical record; therefore there is defendable logic in concentrating the LCA on the engine assembly. The disadvantage to this approach is that other interrelated aspects of the product are not analyzed. Still, this less holistic approach can be part of a larger program that includes all of the components or assemblies.
- *Supply network* (selected piece)   Choosing to focus the LCA on the front-end of the value system or on the product delivery system is most appropriate for consumer products that have a useful life of one month or less.

This kind of LCA framework concentrates on the acquisition of materials and energy via the supply chain and the manufacturing processes used to produce the product. While there are short-lived products that have significant concerns on the application side of the equation, most such products have the larger portion of their impacts on the producer's side. Taking this approach can improve product design and architecture. The disadvantages are that one may miss potential defects or burdens on the application side.

- *Market segment* (selected piece)   Focusing on certain markets makes the LCA more doable. This approach provides a complete analysis of one market segment at a time, making the first LCA available sooner than if the entire market is addressed. The advantage is that the LCA can be prioritized to complete the most critical segments first, allowing the most important concerns to be addressed first.
- *Application* (selected piece)   This approach is similar to the market segment approach, except that the focus is on a specific category of users. In industrial markets, the top ten companies using a product such as an aircraft may represent a majority of the usage; focusing on the top ten airlines in the world may cover 80 percent of the applications. This approach allows corporations to focus on the most significant applications of their products. Any corrective actions or improvements that are made immediately benefit a majority of the customers. This approach could overlook the experience of smaller companies that may have difficulties using the products.

The actual LCA framework that is chosen obviously depends on the product and market considerations. While there are numerous ways to articulate the types of product/market situations, the three intrinsic distinguishing dimensions are space, mass, and time. These are independent variables that relate to products, markets and resources. The space dimension refers to the position occupied by the product in the market and the management system. It defines the location in the business environment and the value system that a product enjoys. It includes the full scope of actions that occur in the enterprise to produce and consume the product. Mass represents the resources and energy consumed, transported, and otherwise affected across the product life cycle. Time relates to the life cycle of the product and the duration of satisfaction that the product or solution provide. Space, mass, and time have three LCA implications:

- *Space*   The depth of the supply networks and the number of tiers in the supply chain are related to the complexity of the product. Complex products depend on inputs from many entities in the value network. Likewise, on the application side, the number of users and the implications of owning and using products add to the complexities of the system. Product retirement also plays a profound role in determining viable improvements.

- *Mass* The quantity of products produced and used is directly related to their impacts. For instance, the pollution per unit may be low, but if millions of units are produced and used, the impacts can be significant. Retirement and disposal can then become significant issues. In addition, the more massive the product is, the more resources are required to produce it. Heavy products require more energy to move them and contain more mass to process at retirement.
- *Time* The longevity of a product's applications has major implications for energy and resource consumption. The longer the life span, the more important the application side generally becomes.

The LCA framework for a given situation depends on many factors, including the objectives and goals of the corporation, the need to validate the outcomes, the desire to communicate the results to constituencies, and the ability of participants to perform their roles. The availability of certified and credible information and data also influences the framework. It may be impossible to execute a full LCA because of the lack of objective information and the limited sophistication of participants. While it is difficult to generalize, there is often more relevant information about manufacturing processes than there is about applications and EoL considerations.

Based on the goals and objectives of the analysis and the complexity of the product, practitioners can determine the scope of the LCA. Table 10.4 offers some suggested frameworks for determining the most appropriate approach.

Table 10.4. Suggested frameworks for LCA based on time and complexity

Time horizon	Short term	Short term	Intermediate	Long term
LCA framework	Supply networks	Streamlined LCA	Modified LCA	Full LCA
Focus	Components	Applications	Markets	Product/product platform
Product life cycle	1–10 days	1–10 months	1–10 years	+10–100 years
High value examples	Pharmaceuticals	Clothing	PCs and TVs	Manufacturing facilities
	Food products	Shoes	Appliances	
	Packaging	Video games	Furniture	Houses and aircraft
	Newspaper	Chemicals	Books	Automobiles
				Roofing
Commodities	Gasoline	Plastics	Carpeting	PVC piping

There are other key dimensions, beyond product complexity and life cycle duration, that can contribute to a systematic methodology for selecting the LCA framework. Indeed, four other parameters are critical to the framework:

- *Severity of impacts*   Impacts can be characterized from low or minimal to high or catastrophic. Low indicates local or short-term effects that can be corrected quickly using readily available technologies and methods. High indicates global and long-term effects that require dedicated efforts to correct if possible.
- *Intensity of energy consumption*   Energy consumption can also be characterized as low to high. Low indicates that very little energy is required to produce or to use the product. An automobile is an energy-intensive device, requiring between 500 and 1,000 gallons of fuel per year for the typical operator. The amount of fuel consumed is approximately equal to or greater than the weight of the vehicle. This factor has both environmental impacts (usually degradation caused by the creation and use of the energy source) and economic consequences in usage costs.
- *Intensity of resources deployed in the product*   This parameter is similar to the previous one. Low resource intensity means that the mass of the product is low and the product does not significantly deplete materials during its use. This factor has environmental, technological, and economic impacts. For instance, electronic devices such as wireless telephones have become less resource-intensive with each new generation.
- *Intensity of resources deployed in the production and supply chain processes*   This parameter is similar to the previous one, except that it tends to be more dynamic. There may be numerous processes required to produce a product from its inception. The amount of mass that must be processed depends on the materials used in those processes.

If there are significant amounts of toxic substances used in the production and consumption processes, the LCA should be skewed toward the areas of concern. In this case, the severity of impacts may be the most important consideration to combine with the complexity and longevity aspects. If the impacts are potentially severe, the LCA framework should be more comprehensive than when the impacts are known and less problematic.

Options for establishing a LCA framework discussed in this section are provided for guidance and pertain to the general situation. Practitioners must consider their own situations and act accordingly. Furthermore, determining the LCA framework can be an iterative process, examining component by component in series to achieve a level of understanding sufficient to establish the best framework.

Defining the main elements

The LCA framework follows the conventional approach. It starts with the Initiation phase, which includes the subphases of goal setting and LCA definition. Figure 10.1 portrays the phases and individual steps of the LCA framework. The most important step is setting the overarching goals for the LCA: these set the stage for all of the other elements in the process. Establishing the direction and framework for the execution of the work occurs in concert with goal setting. Mapping out the process elements and the basis for the analysis is equally important and prescribes the flow of the effort. Goal setting, LCA definition, and inventory assessment are discussed in this chapter. Impact assessment, improvement assessment, and program evaluation are covered in chapter 11.

The standard LCA approach is similar to the DFSS model used for improving products and processes. The DMAIC process, as described in chapter 8, also parallels LCA. The essence of both approaches is the analysis of the system, technologies, products, and/or processes to discover opportunities for improvements. The goal setting and LCA definition have similar elements to the "Define" phase of the DMAIC process. The DFSS "Measure" phase parallels the inventory assessment of LCA that focuses on obtaining

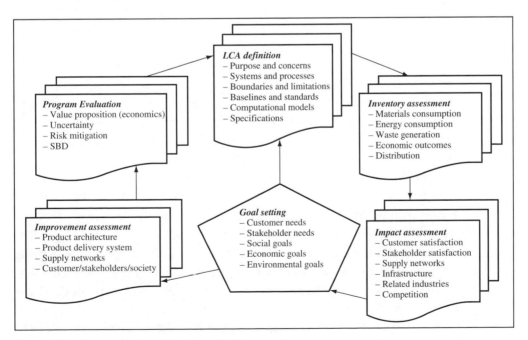

Figure 10.1   Phases and steps of a standard LCA framework

information about products and processes. LCA's impact assessment is a more specialized version of the general approaches used in DFSS. Likewise, LCA's improvement assessment is similar to the "Improve" phase of DFSS. Finally, the Program Evaluation phase of LCA is part of implementation and control. Like the "Control" phase of DFSS, this step in LCA ensures that the method has been implemented properly and that the results can be used for their intended purposes.

The initiation

Goal setting

LCA goals derive from SBD principles; the overarching objective of LCA is to create the best possible products and processes – those that are free of defects and burdens and are of the kind and quality that customers and the public expect. Attaining this objective results in an enhanced value proposition and a more sustainable future.

Goal setting links the LCA to the NPD program, the product or process improvement program or, in the broader sense, to the strategic intent of the LCA initiative. It articulates the most crucial desired outcomes that warrant the investment of time, money, and effort in the LCA. The goals relate to the social, economic, and environmental imperatives that form the triple bottom line. Customer satisfaction goals have to include not only an improved value proposition, but also solutions that have a better overall "fit" within the business environment. Customers have needs that may not be apparent to them when they acquire a product. For example, if a product has toxic substances in its components, it may be difficult to dispose of at the end of its life. Customers may not realize that they have assumed a burden that will cost them time and money in the future. Similarly, stakeholder satisfaction goals have to be framed in the context of both the present and the future.

Articulating the objectives for meeting social expectations is possibly the most difficult task. While most corporations understand the pressing needs of the social dimension, the role that they can or should play in answering those needs is not always clear. Corporations usually recognize their mandates under laws and regulations. However, their goals pertaining to the social dimension tend to be fragmented and dependent on geographical location. SBD imperatives suggest a common set of goals, regardless of location and background.

Economic goals relate to the objectives of the enterprise and its constituents. Successful corporations generally understand that their economic health is linked to the satisfaction of their constituents. Economic goals must promote everyone's success. For example, if a product provides profits for the corporation, but fails to meet the expectations of customers and society over the long term, both the corporation and its constituents will suffer.

Environmental goals are multifaceted and often related to the other categories. While goals relating to laws and regulations are often most critical, the purpose of LCA is not just to specify the obvious. The focus is on selecting goals that result in a more sustainable future. The most radical, but often the most necessary, way to handle certain environmental impacts is to simply prohibit the production and use of the product or its problematic ingredients. The demise of CFCs is a good example. CFCs were among the most effective products ever produced. They served as safe ingredients for refrigeration, effective cleaning solvents, and in many other valuable applications. CFCs are no longer in use because they are linked to ozone depletion, a serious environmental impact.

Definition of LCA

Purpose and concerns

LCA definition explores deep into the product structure and the product delivery system to determine the suitability and long-term viability of decisions made during the NPD process and to understand the impacts and consequences of those decisions. It is a precursor to the actual assessment phases. LCA definition does not seek to find every potential problem or those phenomena that may never happen. It seeks to generate sufficient understanding to allow a high level of confidence that the product and processes meet all expectations. LCA definition focuses on determining the driving forces for conducting an LCA and the specific purpose for the assessments.

The following are the five primary areas of concern when undertaking LCA:

- *Hidden defects and burdens* One of the most significant reasons for conducting a LCA is to discover unknown problems and impacts. LCA adheres to the precautionary principle by offering a reasonable way to verify that the product architecture and the product delivery system provide safe, sound, and appropriate solutions.
- *Implications and insights* LCA is a positive way to ensure that solutions are balanced and based on a full view of the possibilities. Examining the

inputs and outputs across the value system provides a broad understanding of the opportunities for improvement.

- *Comparisons and contrasts*   The LCA provides a means to articulate differences across the value system and between competitive products and processes. Using validated information, the corporation can communicate to its constituencies the advantages of its products or services. LCA is particularly powerful in validating the corporation's advantages based on factual evidence and solid analysis. Such advantages can be used to create powerful, provable marketing messages.
- *Stability and clarity*   SBD depends on stability and longevity. Thoroughly understanding the impacts and consequences of the products, the product delivery system, and the supply networks affords the corporation a clear view of the expected outcomes and their implications. It provides management and practitioners with the knowledge they need to make informed decisions, decisions that can result in more stable solutions.
- *Uncertainties and risks*   From a management perspective, uncertainties and risks are two of the most profound concerns in managing the value systems, developing new products and technologies, and leading change. The selected products and processes may be adequate and potentially free of defects. However, they may not be the best solutions for the situation if they have short life spans. Often uncertainty results from simply not having the proper information.

With the increasing complexities of managing a business system and producing products, decision-making must become increasingly sophisticated. The insights and awareness gained through the LCA effort are part of that necessary sophistication. They facilitate better solutions – and, in turn, competitive advantages. The improvements may even open new strategic positions that can be preemptively exploited.

The business environment today insists that those corporations that wish to be successful and lead the world must find ways to discover opportunities and mitigate threats. As transparency becomes increasingly important, the validated and objective information gained through LCA can be used to communicate with constituencies. Public disclosures of such information is becoming expected, as more and more stakeholders and customers demand to know the implications and consequences of the corporation's products and processes.

Systems and processes

The critical step in LCA is to identify the specific systems and processes to be included in the analysis. The full framework includes all of the stages of the

Suppliers	Producers	Distributors	Applications	
Inputs/Outputs	**Inputs/Outputs**	**Inputs/Outputs**	**Primary users**	**Secondary users**
Resources	Products	Products	Use	Reuse
Materials	Processes	Processes	Reuse	Repair
Energy	Packaging	Packaging	Repair	Recycling
Supplies	Marketing	Distribution	Retirement	Retirement
Parts	Service	Marketing		
Components	Waste management	Service		
Remanufacture	**Remanufacture**	**Remanufacture**	**←Recovery ↓**	**←Recovery**
Recycle ◄—	**Recycle** ◄—	**Recycle** ◄—	**Discards→**	**Disposal ↓**
↑	**Logistics**	**Logistics**	**←Closed-loop**	**Open-loop→**
Reprocess	**Support services**	**Support services**	Reclamation	Treatment
			Processing	Storage
			Logistics	Disposal

Figure 10.2   Selected elements of the simplified product delivery system

product life cycle, from raw material extraction to EoL considerations. However, the actual LCA can be modified to meet the purposes and objectives of the initiatives.

LCAs focus on products and the product delivery system, or on what many practitioners call the "operating system." These constitute how the corporation is currently meeting the market, production, technical, and financial requirements. The product and process innovation capabilities of the corporation support LCA. The operating system can be divided into two parts: the supply networks and the value networks. The former consists of all of the suppliers and their suppliers, along with all those in logistics and the distribution channels and all of their processes. The value networks consist of all of the entities and processes on the application side. Figure 10.2 provides a graphical representation of the product delivery system in its simplest form. It is a modification of the models discussed in chapter 4.

LCA explores the implications of the primary inputs and evaluates the applications of the products and their secondary uses and processes. The secondary aspects include repair, reuse, refurbishment, remanufacturing, recycling, and other afterlife concerns. The most crucial addition to the system is the inclusion of the waste streams and their impacts.

The LCA of the producers and supply networks includes an examining their willingness and ability to provide the best solution for customers and stakeholders. Traditionally, producers were concerned only about the flow of their products to the customer. The LCA framework suggests that producers must be concerned about the primary and secondary flows as well, especially the reverse flow of products and materials after retirement. The supply base not only needs to reduce the use of toxic and hazardous materials, it must move to a closed-loop system for recovering

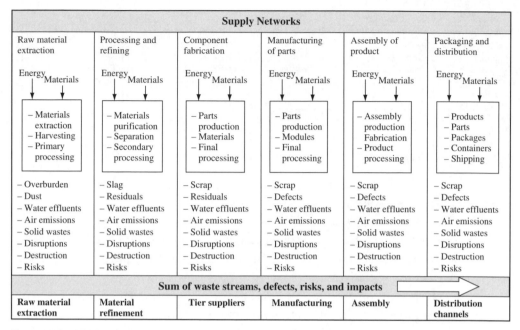

Supply Networks					
Raw material extraction	Processing and refining	Component fabrication	Manufacturing of parts	Assembly of product	Packaging and distribution
Energy Materials	Energy Materials	Energy Materials	Energy Materials	Energy Materials	Energy Materials
– Materials extraction – Harvesting – Primary processing	– Materials purification – Separation – Secondary processing	– Parts production – Materials – Final processing	– Parts production – Modules – Final processing	– Assembly production Fabrication – Product processing	– Products – Parts – Packages – Containers – Shipping
– Overburden – Dust – Water effluents – Air emissions – Solid wastes – Disruptions – Destruction – Risks	– Slag – Residuals – Water effluents – Air emissions – Solid wastes – Disruptions – Destruction – Risks	– Scrap – Residuals – Water effluents – Air emissions – Solid wastes – Disruptions – Destruction – Risks	– Scrap – Defects – Water effluents – Air emissions – Solid wastes – Disruptions – Destruction – Risks	– Scrap – Defects – Water effluents – Air emissions – Solid wastes – Disruptions – Destruction – Risks	– Scrap – Defects – Water effluents – Air emissions – Solid wastes – Disruptions – Destruction – Risks
Sum of waste streams, defects, risks, and impacts					
Raw material extraction	**Material refinement**	**Tier suppliers**	**Manufacturing**	**Assembly**	**Distribution channels**

Figure 10.3 LCA framework for assessing the "front-end" of product delivery

materials, resources, and waste streams. Integrating reuse and recycling into the value network is an important step in achieving environmentally and economically sound practices.

The LCA framework thus goes beyond primary production and use of the product, to examine secondary customers as well. It explores how all of the market participants can promote the economic and environmental strengths of the product. Market aspects include the repair, reuse, and recycling of the product, the goal being to maximize the value available by discovering as many secondary applications as possible for the product or the materials. For instance, the market for used automobiles helps to sustain the primary market by creating outlets for the older vehicles. Customers are pleased to use a product that has this kind of residual value. The framework explores the connections between upstream and downstream elements. The supply networks require detailed assessment. Figure 10.3 provides a general overview of the framework for assessing the "front-end" of product delivery.

The LCA framework links the operating level in all directions through process management. Process management affects the stages of extraction, fabrication, production, assembly, and distribution. Processes convert resources and energy into outcomes (parts, components, products, etc.) using intellectual capital, information, know-how, and equipment. They

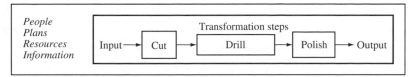

Figure 10.4   Example of a simple flow

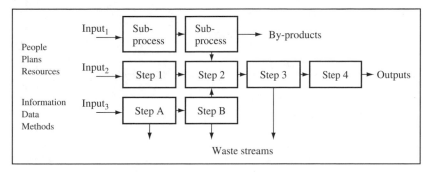

Figure 10.5   Example of a compound process flow

can have many elements in series, in parallel or some combination and have subprocesses within processes. Moreover, processes can extend across the supply network or the value system.

The simplest process includes a single step or only a few steps to accomplish the end-result. For instance, filling the car with gasoline may involve only two or three steps. The number of steps is not as important as the link between them. If the elements are all directly linked, and the flow is sequential, the process may be viewed as simple. Figure 10.4 indicates a simple flow with several linked steps.

Compound processes include several subprocesses within a process, with the subprocesses confined to a single entity or establishment. They are usually confined within self-evident boundaries. In many cases, the process has to be analyzed in totality in order to understand its characteristics and impacts. Figure 10.5 provides a view of a compound process flow.

Compound processes are more complicated and difficult to understand and map. Most involve multiple entities, usually the producer and various tiers of the supply chain. They cut across the value system and often require many interfaces between the participants in the process. The typical compound process has many inputs, and those inputs likewise have numerous inputs. Each input may require its own subprocess to transform its inputs into the output for the next subprocess. In addition, there may be a significant amount of logistics involved in moving the resources/materials from

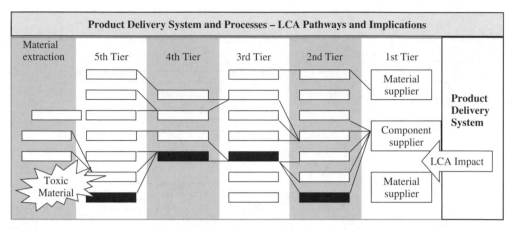

Figure 10.6 Compound process involving multiple tiers of suppliers

their place of origin to the location of the process or subprocess. Complex products such as automobiles and aircraft commonly involve such processes.

Figure 10.6 provides a sense of the complexities of a process involving multiple tiers of suppliers. The suppliers have their own processes and subprocesses at each point. The black boxes show the route one component takes as it contributes to the final assembly process for the end-product. The component supplier has many "tier-two" suppliers providing inputs for the component. Many of the "tier-two" suppliers, in turn, have "tier-three" suppliers who are providing inputs. In fact, some of the requirements run six-deep in the supply chain, all the way back to raw material extraction. An analysis of the flow, depicted in figure 10.6, indicates that there is a serious issue with toxic materials upstream in the fifth tier.

The production of an aluminum engine is an example of a compound process. The engine includes hundreds of parts from tens of suppliers who are linked to each other through many tiers in the supply chain. The aluminum block itself requires casting, milling, boring, and heat treating during fabrication. Upstream, the aluminum stock is produced at a smelting and finishing plant. Further upstream, the aluminum metal is obtained through a reduction process that applies electricity to aluminum oxide which, in turn, was refined from bauxite at a processing plant, usually near the ore extraction locations in the equatorial regions around the world.

Boundaries and limits of LCA

Establishing boundaries and/or limits for the LCA is often a necessary but problematic challenge for management. It is actually part of establishing the

LCA framework and must be based on strategic logic. It further defines the scope of the system, often limiting the processes to be examined and the depth of the analysis. Boundary conditions should be determined as early as possible to avoid the appearance of predetermining the conclusions of the LCA. This is especially critical when outcomes are to be made public or used to make marketing claims about the product.

Often, LCA boundaries are determined not by the practitioners but by factors beyond their control. These unintended limitations include:

- *Lack of integration* across the enterprise, especially within supply networks. The lack of specific information and data about the inputs and outputs of suppliers is often a serious deficiency. LCA is not yet a mainstream phenomenon. Most companies are not set up to handle the necessary information flow.
- *Lack of detailed information* about specific products and processes. Many companies do not collect data and information from certain processes that relate to specific products. Much of the available data is in aggregate form, making it difficult to apportion the inputs to the correct outputs, or to ascertain the cause and effect relationships. This is particularly the case for commingled waste streams that are a result of many processes or the production of many products.
- *Fear of discovering hidden liabilities* that would have to be disclosed. This fear runs counter to the principles of SBD and LCA and is typified by the old adage, "if it's not broken, don't fix it." Some senior managers and professionals would still prefer not to know about the negative aspects of their products and processes. This short-term thinking usually leads to difficulties in the long term.
- *Absence of critical specific information and data* about certain subprocesses or parts of processes. There may be missing information that makes determining all of the facts impossible. In many cases, the information and data were never collected because it was not viewed as important. This is especially critical when the missing pieces are vital to a full understanding of the process or the impacts of products. For example, knowing the toxicity of a certain material in a product or process is often pivotal to the acceptability of subprocesses or downstream applications. If that information is not available, managers may come to the wrong conclusions. For many existing products, such information has never been collected.
- *Inconsistencies in data and information*   Some data may be provided on a per-unit basis while other data exist on a per-period basis. This is similar to communicating messages using two different languages.

- *Lack of knowledge and training* Most organizations are still limited in their knowledge and understanding of how to perform LCA. While there may be a cadre of educated professionals who can map out the LCA framework, a full LCA requires the contributions of many individuals, from shop-floor operators and product designers to environmental professionals with a background in LCA. As with TQM, everyone contributes, rather than just the experts.
- *Lack of well-known and widely accepted methods* The lack of generally accepted practices and methods makes LCA more difficult to complete. While there are defined methods such as ISO 14042, they may not fit every situation.
- *Time and money pressures* Management and professionals alike have a tendency to concentrate on the speed to market and return on investment – in their view, the main objectives of the NPD program. While time and money are critical for success, it is pointless to commercialize a defective product.

These limitations are significant, and in many cases, they mean that only streamlined or abridged LCAs can be performed. Still, they do not preclude LCA entirely, but do represent concerns that have to be managed as part of the process.

Baselines and standards

Baselines identify the existing situation and thereby facilitate determining the amount of improvement a corporation has achieved, or the level of improvement that is required. They are also critical for determining the potential for improvement. Baselines can be constructed for the management system, the products, and/or the processes, depending upon what kinds of information must be compared. In this way, they can link the present and future expectations. For example, UTC formulated a 10X improvement program, which stipulated that it would improve selected environmental targets ten times over a ten-year period.

The baselines for a LCA depend on the context of the business environment. They may be set by regulatory requirements, industry standards, or by the prevailing situation. They are often expressed using the amount of production in the base year. For example, DOW reported its improvements over the 1990s based on its position in the year 1990. As with the pollution prevention programs of the 1990s, however, the *rate* of improvement in a relative sense can be just as important as the *absolute* level of improvement. For instance, if the waste generated per unit of production is improved

Table 10.5. Categories of selected baselines relative to LCA

Category	Company-related baseline	"Best-in-class" baseline	"Ideal case" or "target" baseline
System-wide LCA	Total waste generated during the current period Can be broken down into subsystems or processes	Total waste generated during the current period by the top performer in the industry peer group or a world-class performer	The total waste generated if the ideal system were available Zero waste is the ideal, but may not be possible
Product platform LCA	Amount of recycled content used in products across the product lines	Amount of recycled content in the best application of recycled materials	The maximum amount of recycled content theoretically possible if it is not 100%
Product/process LCA	Resource depletion of the current model The total degradation caused by the process (per unit)	Resource depletion of the best in class The total degradation caused by the process (per unit) in terms of the best	Ideal resource use Zero degradation.

(reduced) by 50 percent, the corporation may claim significant achievement even if the overall waste generated by the corporation increased due to higher volumes of output.

An easy way to establish baselines is to continuously report on the social, economic, and environmental implications of the enterprise and make such information available on an ongoing basis. Such practices are especially beneficial if the corporation is making improvements and achievements that are being documented over time. This approach encourages constituents to focus on improvements, and such openness allows practitioners and others to easily make comparisons.

In certain cases, baselines are based on "best-in-class" or "best-in-world" performers. This approach is particularly important for the underachievers of the past. For instance, if the corporation is in the bottom quartile in selected performance categories, even significant improvements may find them still in the bottom half of the peer group and requiring yet further improvement. Table 10.5 provides a sense of the relationships between the categories of selected baselines and the LCA framework.

Baselines are often difficult to determine because waste stream and material utilization rates are aggregated across many products and processes, making it difficult to ascertain cause and effect. It may cost time and money to obtain the necessary data and information related to each product or process, if it is possible at all. A number of techniques need to be used to approximate

Table 10.6. Generic process for developing baselines (benchmarks)

Step	Guidelines for establishing baselines	Process
1	Benchmark systems, products, and processes (internal and external) (Analyze data to determine the requirements)	Select similar products or ones related to the family of products and determine the most important criterion and the targets to be achieved based on a logical fit to the system, the products, and the processes
2	Determine the most effective criteria for establishing baselines (Evaluate the effectiveness of the elements)	Develop a profile for each of the critical areas of concern, including depletion, degradation, disruption, destruction, and defects and burdens Determine what the criteria should be
3	Link baselines with product design, supply networks, production, and applications (Integrate solution with other functions)	Determine the most effective baseline parameters Examine the impacts on operations and evaluate the social, economic, and environmental implications
4	Prioritize the baselines in terms of their effectiveness in making improvements (List the critical requirements)	Identify the baselines that are essential and determine how they fit into the overall framework Examine the ability to compare and contrast with other options
5	Document the baselines details so that they can be used for comparative analysis	Determine the content of the document If the information is available in the literature, describe how to glean the required details If the information has to be obtained from primary sources, spell out the means to acquire the details Surveys and other instruments may be used

quantitative values, and it is important for peer groups or independent parties to validate baselines in order to establish their objectivity.

Baselines derived from external sources are even more difficult to determine and verify. The best approach is to use publicly available information published by peers or competitors in credible reporting documents such as the GRI. Government documents pertaining to environmental reports are usually good sources of information as well since reporting entities are required to be truthful. Other sources of information include web sites, sustainability reports, environmental reports, research studies prepared by reputable third parties, reports from trade organizations, articles and publications in the general literature, and research by academic organizations. Table 10.6 provides a generic process flow of a methodology for obtaining information for establishing baselines. It is similar to the construct in table 9.2 (p. 536).

The development of the Honda Insight hybrid automobile may serve as an example. The Insight was commercialized in the United States in

December 1999. It is a front-wheel-drive, two-seat coupé that is powered by a conventional gasoline engine working in combination with an electric motor. Honda calls this technology fusion, the Integrated Motor Assist (IMA) system. The vehicle has a fuel efficiency of 70 miles per gallon (30 km/liter). The Insight's engine is the world's lightest, most compact, 1-liter, 3-cylinder gasoline engine. The engine uses advanced lean-burn technology, low-friction design and lightweight materials and has advanced nitrogen oxide catalysts to achieve low emissions. The electric motor component of the IMA consists of a 144-volt nickel–metal–hydride battery pack with advanced electronic power control. The Insight uses regenerative braking. The question is: what is the right baseline for the Insight? Honda can compare it to its conventional cars that get 35 miles per gallon (15 km/liter). It can compare it to other conventional cars manufactured by competitors. It can select a baseline using US government CAFE standards of 27 miles per gallon (11 km/liter).[4] The criterion, in the example, is fuel efficiency, but it could also be emissions. The baseline is then compared with the design choices to determine what the outcomes should be. In this case, the Insight is twice as efficient as Honda's conventional cars and more than two and half times the CAFE standard. The next steps are to select other baselines, to prioritize the baselines, and document the comparisons.

The research methodology is an intensive topic in its own right. Some of the ramifications of research methods as they relate to LCA are discussed in the following section.

Computational models
Mass and energy balance

The fundamental computational models for LCA are simple input-output models based on the conservation of mass and energy. Mass balance is a primary technique based on the conservation of mass in a system or process. Similarly, an energy balance can also be examined. In simple terms for products and production processes, this is:

$$Mass_{in} \text{ and } Energy_{in} = Mass_{out} + Energy_{out} + By\text{-}products + Emissions + Wastes$$

Processes do not create or destroy mass or energy; they transform the materials into different forms. The equation accounts for all of the material and energy used in the processes, as well as all of the environmental releases. While energy is equally important in the analysis, most energy is derived from the use of material resources. The computational models are thus either a

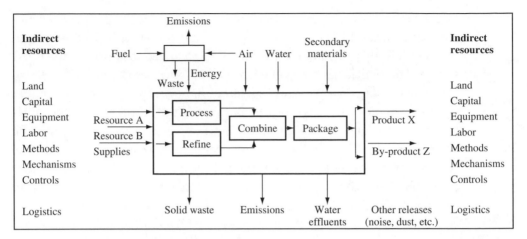

Figure 10.7 Computational model for the conversion of inputs into outputs

combination of mass and energy balances or an inventory balance including the energy implications of the input and output materials. The latter approach has the advantage of putting all of the inputs and outputs on a common basis (mass). Unless energy is obtained directly from the sun, wind, or water (hydroelectric), it derives from the conversion of chemical energy contained in mass (fuel oil, gasoline, coal).

The **mass-balance equation** is the sum of all of the direct inputs of mass plus the air, water, and secondary materials (like packaging) which then must equal the sum of the outputs of product(s), by-products, and waste streams. The model can be enlarged to include the entire system of processes and subprocesses. The form shown in figure 10.7 does not indicate all of the subprocesses required for handling the waste streams. In fact, each of the waste streams has a mass-balance equation that describes the materials flow of the associated treatment processes. Likewise, the energy input has a mass-flow diagram indicating the flow of resources to provide the energy component of the process. Figure 10.7 depicts a simple computational input-output model.

Flow diagram

A flow diagram depicts the process or subprocess within a system using mass flow or mass balance from cradle-to-grave or as modified by the LCA boundary conditions. The flow diagram shows one or more of the pathways to the products and their use, recycling, and retirement. For example, if a product contains a certain chemical, the flow diagram includes all of the inputs required for producing the chemical from whatever point in the process described by the LCA mapping. The flow diagram is a powerful

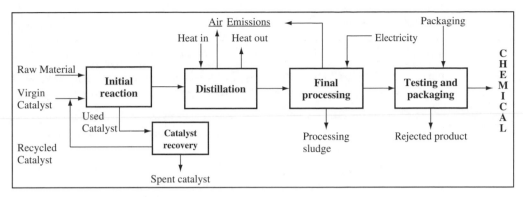

Figure 10.8   Example of a simple flow diagram

computational model because it allows the full analysis of a pathway. It can also be used to expand or limit the scope of the LCA by including certain flows and not others. In some cases, the most problematic pathways are known before the start of the LCA, and selected flow diagrams can be studied in detail to ascertain the defects and burdens. In figure 10.6, the highlighted pathway indicates that there is a serious concern about hazardous materials in the supply chain at the fifth tier. A flow diagram would show the full implications of these materials and the related processes across the supply chain. Figure 10.8 illustrates a simple flow diagram of a chemical process.

The process flow diagram depicts a simple process that includes the catalyst recovery operation as a subprocess. The mass and energy balance includes mass inputs of raw material and catalyst and energy inputs of heat and electricity. The diagram clearly indicates the waste streams generated during the process. Recovering and recycling some of the catalyst reduces the inflow of new catalyst. Moreover, the diagram shows inputs of heat and electricity and a heat output. The actual mass flow depends on how the heat was generated and the electricity produced. If both energy sources were derived from solar panels, the effects on the mass flow of the process would be small.[5] However, if the heat and electricity were produced from coal-fired plants, the effects would be significant. Table 10.7 provides a simple example of the mass flow of the process.

Using the weights indicated in table 10.7, the flow diagram indicates that the efficiency of the process is 80 percent and that 20 percent of the mass is converted to wastes and by-products. The energy balance should be included if it has a significant effect on the mass flow. Again, if the energy inputs are generated from fossil fuels, the mass flow from the energy requirements may be greater than that from the production of the chemical itself.

Table 10.7. Simplified mass flow elements

Elements	Mass inputs				Mass outputs			
	Raw material	Virgin catalyst	Packaging	Air emission	Spent catalyst	Processing sludge	Rejected product	Chemical/ packaging	Recycled catalyst
Mass (kg)	100	2	2	2	2	8	10	82	2
Efficiency (%)								80	50

Recycling the spent catalyst reduces the catalyst requirement by half. It means that the actual need for 4 kg can be met by obtaining 2 kg from virgin sources and 2 kg being recycled. Recycling also decreases disposal requirements and cost. While the recovery subprocess is shown as a simple mechanical step, such activities often consume materials such as filters or require energy inputs.

Yield and efficiency

The efficiency of processes plays a pivotal role in affecting the amount of mass consumed in transforming inputs into outputs. One of the key measures of a process or subprocess is how close the real inputs and outputs are to the theoretical equation. For instance, in theory, material *A* and material *B* combine to produce product *C*. In science and engineering, stoichiometry describes the theoretical requirements when combining two or more chemical materials. The stoichiometric value represents the theoretical outcome. For instance, product *A* and product *B* produce exactly product *C*. The simple example is carbon and oxygen ($C + O_2$) combining to produce carbon dioxide (CO_2). In the real world, carbon and oxygen, when combined, produce carbon dioxide, carbon monoxide, unburned carbon, and excess air (which results in energy loss due to heating additional mass without any benefit). The more accurate formula is material *A* and material *B* combine to produce product *C*, by-product *D* (carbon monoxide), and residuals of material *A* (unburned carbon) and material *B* (excess air). Obviously, more of product *A* and product *B* are required to obtain the desired amount of product *C* than in the ideal case. The real world case is not only less efficient, it produces waste streams that have to be addressed.

For this reason, the concept of yield is critical when calculating the actual or anticipated resources required and produced by a process. In the example above, the theoretical yield is not realized. In addition, some of the finished products may be damaged or have low quality. Or the product may consume more material than expected. For example, if a company has to produce

125 products to obtain 100 products that are free of defects, the yield of the process is equal to the quality units produced divided by the total units produced.

$$Yield = 100 \div 125 = 80\%$$

In this example, the poor yield means that more mass is being used than is theoretically required and more by-products or waste streams result that require treatment and disposal.

As you might guess, yield can affect the economic viability of products. The production process for the product consumes approximately 25 percent more resources than is theoretically necessary, thereby increasing the cost of the products produced.

$$Input = 125; \; Output = 100; \; Resource \; consumption \; percentage = 125 \div 100 = 125\%$$

This lower yield (inefficiency) indicates a likely difficulty in achieving a sustainable position and can be viewed as a competitive disadvantage. It suggests that a competitor with better production capabilities could improve its own cost structure by the difference between the two corporations' production processes.

Specifications for inventory assessment

SBD thinking moves the solution toward the ideal.[6] While twentieth-century product decisions were based on the concept of trade-offs, twenty-first-century approaches focus on achieving the best solution possible. Trade-offs often led to unreasonable compromises, improving product life, and economics at the expense of increasing health and safety risks and liabilities, or some other negative implications. For example, pressure-treated wood using copper, chromate, and arsenic (CCA) for exterior applications dramatically increased the useful life of the wood, but created the risk of arsenic poisoning especially in small children, which may lead to short-term and long-term health consequences. The long-term impacts depended on the individuals involved and the extent of exposures. While CCA wood is being phased out in many countries, the liabilities will remain for decades. CCA wood is an example of solution trade-offs that focused on present economic benefits rather than on the longer-term social, economic, and environmental consequences.

The ideal solution is one that has many positives and no negatives. When looking at the value proposition, the top of the equation is enhanced and the bottom of the equation is minimized. While the ideal may be impossible, moving toward it is a fundamental precept of SBD.

The specifications for LCA definition are guidelines for applying LCA to assess and improve products and processes. They facilitate decision-making in the LCA process, and ultimately in product development. Generally, the specifications come from customer needs, stakeholder expectations, government mandates, industry standards, and company criteria. Moreover, the specifications may be based on the principles of SBD. Table 10.8 offers some selected specifications related to the LCA specifications.

The suggested specifications for LCA mapping are similar to the selected design strategies indicated in table 3.7 (p. 189). The "good news" since the mid-1980s is that product and process trends have generally followed the precepts of table 10.8. As a result of microprocessor technologies, software developments, TQM techniques, Six-Sigma methods, and many other innovations, products and/or processes have become smaller and more streamlined, more powerful and user-friendly, and more efficient and effective. Most of these trends have also demonstrated the value of SBD principles. The specifications for LCA can translate the more open-ended goals of SBD into a more focused directive for practitioners.

Inventory assessment

Material consumption

Material consumption is a primary consideration because upstream inputs have dramatic implications on downstream activities and outcomes. Noting the flow of materials from the inception of a pathway to the final products can help practitioners understand the consumption of materials, both direct and indirect, and provide insights into opportunities for improvement. The flow diagram such as that shown in figure 10.8 provides a detailed listing of the materials consumed in the processes or incorporated into the product. However, the actual quantities of materials used may vary with the volume of the product being produced and the quality of the subprocesses. Generally, processes are less efficient at low process utilization than at full output. Most production processes can measure the consumption of raw materials, parts, and components and relate that to the production output. If a process is stable and operating at a set rate, the calculations are straightforward. However, if there are significant swings in production rates, and if the efficiency of the

Table 10.8. Selected specifications for LCA definition

Specifications/Criteria	Implications	Comments/concerns
● Material resources		
Less is better	Using less mass in the product or the process means less depletion and usually less waste	The product may be less robust and have a tendency to fail prematurely
Seek higher yields that reduce inputs per outputs	The more efficient the process, the less mass and energy must be consumed to obtain the product	More efficient processes may cost more or be more complex; They may have higher failure rates
Avoid toxic substances	Toxic materials create complexity and downstream impacts that take time and money to mitigate; Typically, there may be hidden defects that cause problems in the future.	All materials and energy sources have the potential to have a negative side; The alternative may be more problematic than the original solution
Reuse resources and materials	Reusing scrap and used products reduces the need for virgin materials and the effects of wastes and their disposal requirements	Reused material may require special cleaning and handling methods that are costly and add to waste streams and the complexity of the processes
● Waste streams		
Prevent pollution and degradation	Avoiding pollution at its source is one of the most effective means of reducing impacts and improving products and processes; Source reduction affects inputs and outputs	Pollution prevention is not always cost effective in the short term; It takes an investment of time and money to reap future rewards
Keep waste streams homogeneous	It is easier and typically less expensive to enhance the recovery, reuse, and recycling or treatment of homogeneous waste streams	Managing separate waste streams may increase the amount of equipment necessary to produce the product or treat the waste streams
Minimize or prevent leaks, spills, and accidents	Leaks, spills, and accidents generally mean a loss of resources, turning assets into liabilities and expenses; Preventing such events saves money and avoids burdens and impacts	Avoiding these unintended events is often costly and requires up-front investment and training; It becomes increasingly more difficult to reduce the potential for spills as the processes improve
Avoid the transfer of waste from one media to another	Cleaning one process at the expense of another is not always effective and is generally a waste of resources	There may be government mandates calling for such protocols; Often cleaning one waste stream merely transforms one form of pollution into another; For example, cleaning air pollution creates a solid waste via dirty filters that must be disposed of

Table 10.8. (cont.)

Specifications/Criteria	Implications	Comments/concerns
• Energy		
Improve energy efficiency	The more efficient the process, the less mass and energy consumed in obtaining the product and using it over time	Energy efficient devices are typically more expensive to produce and may create more wastes during production
Reduce energy losses/conserve energy	Saving energy through conservation and insulation eliminates the need to produce energy and transport it	Insulation and conservation may cost money to implement and may not be cost effective unless usage is reasonable
Use renewable sources or those that can be replenished	Renewable energy sources tend to have the fewest impacts, especially solar energy Energy sources that can be replenished quickly also tend to maintain stability and long-term viability	Great care has to be exercised to ensure that energy sources, especially solar, are indeed reducing impacts For capital-intensive processes, the source may have zero impacts during use, but have significant upstream impacts
Increase energy density	Higher power energy sources take less space and often require less mass to achieve the desired outcomes In a moving device, the power unit requires energy to move it along with the device	Devices with high energy density are often more costly and occasionally more dangerous
• Temporal		
Improve product viability	Product viability in the market is a function of customer preferences, perception, quality, technology, and economics Products that are enduring save on design costs and resources	The viability of a product in the market depends on competition, customers, the availability of support products, etc. Technology plays a key role in the life cycle
Increase life span	Expanding the useful life of a product means that its replacement and all of the resources and environmental impacts of that replacement can be reduced/avoided	Products may be obsolete long before their useful life is exhausted If the product designed outlasts its technological life, it may result in wastes
Increase shelf life	Increased shelf life reduces the amount of product that spoils or has to be discarded due to time restrictions	For food products, increased shelf life may require more packaging or more complex technologies such as composites
• Spatial		
Decrease footprint	Lower space or volume requirements often translate into less disruption of the environment	"Footprint" is a nebulous term that could mean the specific spatial impact or more broadly, the entire impact of a product or process

Increase open spaces	Ensure that the product or process does not affect or impact selected areas A safe zone around a manufacturing facility assures neighbors of fewer disruptions and better aesthetics	Such restrictions may be counter to the rights of society or the obligations of the producer There is always an economic cost to providing open spaces Determining who is responsible to do so is a difficult question
• Informational		
Develop easy-to-use products and processes	Because of the diversity of applications and users, products and processes should be relatively easy to use Simplicity is most crucial where there is less control over outcomes	Products are becoming more complex as technologies and economics force better and more cost effective solutions Sometimes it is necessary to increase the complexity of products and processes in order to mitigate other factors
Promote communications and disclosure of data	Encouraging the proper use of products reduces incorrect applications LCA builds in the requirement to provide data back to the manufacturer Disclose the positives and the negatives	Information and data have to be accurate and validated The marketing methods and customer understanding of dual-side marketing (providing both positives and negatives) is a new concept and requires time to fully develop
Educate employees, customers, and stakeholders	Knowledge is powerful and helps mitigate potential risks and impacts Educating people about the products and processes reduces the potential for mistakes and misapplications	Creating effective educational programs and materials requires significant investments Care has to be taken to ensure that the knowledge conveyed is correct and appropriate
Enhance feedback	Communications are a two-way street It is imperative that designers listen to their constituencies and incorporate suggestions when feasible	Customer and stakeholder inputs are complicated and often difficult to interpret. Constituents do not always say what they mean
• Recovery		
Enhance secondary use	Refurbishing and reclaiming products and parts eliminate the need for new ones, avoiding all of the associated impacts	Secondary applications may not be as safe or beneficial as primary ones Users may lack the information necessary for sound use
Recover products, parts, and materials with the highest value	Recovery of those products, parts, and materials with the greatest economic value achieves the greatest benefits Early intervention in the recovery process captures more material and avoids downstream impacts	Certain products and parts may have hidden defects that decrease their value or may have exceeded normal life expectancy thereby increasing risks and potential future impacts
Create a recovery infrastructure	Creating the means to recycle and reuse scrap and other discarded materials is imperative for the effective recovery and reuse of resources	Creating an infrastructure is complicated and requires the input and support of many partners and related entities
Enhance recycling and material recovery	The recovery and reuse of scrap from manufacturing or post-customer use should be designed into products and processes	Creating product take-back systems is complicated and costly The best options are not always clearly identified

process depends on output (more efficient at full capacity), the actual material utilization per unit of production may be higher than ideal.

There are several ways to quantify the flow of materials. Practitioners may measure all of the inputs and outputs during a formal testing and validation of the process. Or they may obtain data from the nominal rating of the plant and/or equipment, or calculate it from the total flow and consumption over some period of time, typically on an annual basis. Finally, they may determine it from government statistics about the industry and its primary processes and outputs. Table 10.9 provides a listing of the most important balance and inventory assessment methods and their advantages and disadvantages.

The best approach is to combine design-based estimates with actual data from production. Of course, if the system or process is in the design phase, actual data will not be available. Design estimates can be verified during actual tests of the operations. The material flow data may have to be supplemented with data and information from suppliers who will be following the same approach. If the relevant information is not available, it may be necessary to use the supplier's aggregate company data until the supplier matures to the point where it can furnish the required details.

Air and water are often the inputs in many processes. Both should be considered in the life cycle inventory. Air is often used in combustion processes in which oxygen is reacted with fuel. The nitrogen component is heated to the exit gas temperature, but does little else. A small quantity may be converted to nitrogen oxides (NO_x). Water is used as a solvent and as a cleaning fluid. It is also used in large quantities for cooling and condensing steam. In most countries around the world, water resources are scarce and the availability of clean water for production processes is limited. In these regions, wasting water reduces the amount available for irrigation and food production. However, even in areas where water is plentiful, treating waste-water effluents is expensive and results in solid waste streams that have to be managed and controlled.

Energy consumption

Energy consumption is much more difficult to generalize. Primary energy sources include electricity (derived from various means), solar energy, nuclear, hydroelectric, wind, and fossil fuels (natural gas, coal, and oil). Secondary sources include geothermal, waves, and waste-to-energy. Electricity is a convenient and efficient mechanism for distributing energy.

Table 10.9. Categories of materials balance and inventory assessment methods

Method	Simple description	Advantages	Disadvantages
Nominal case derived from design estimates	The material flows are determined on the basis of the plant and/or equipment design	The data and information are readily available and expected to be accurate especially if tests were performed during start-up to verify the calculations	Modifications to the operations may have significantly changed the operating characteristics, making once-accurate calculations no longer pertinent
	Mass and energy balances are calculated for nominal capacity and often at the mid-range point	The estimates may have been used to obtain permits and may have the sanction of government agencies.	The assumed efficiencies and flows may be better or worse than expected
	The calculations of the inventories are the expected case for the operation	This provides consistency with other submissions	There may be unexpected inputs or hidden outputs that do not show up in the theoretical calculations
Actual data from production	Actual data from operations at prescribed conditions are used to create a mass balance for the process	If properly validated by experts or an independent third party, the data are deemed reliable and accurate	The data set may contain only data about the operations tested
		It is up to date, reflecting any changes to the plant or equipment that may have been made	Data and information outside of the boundaries would have to be obtained using alternate means
			The acquisition of the data is costly
		The test conditions can be established to provide data that match the needs of the LCA	The tests might be conducted using ideal conditions or employing expert operators that are not normally available
Estimates from company aggregate data	Companies keep records of all of the purchases and dispositions for all their operations over the course of a year	The data and information exist in the databases of the company and can be accessed easily and inexpensively	The results represent a weighted average of all such plants, processes, or equipment within the company
	Such aggregate data can be allocated to specific plants on a weighted basis	The data include materials that are lost during transit and material handling	The results are based on the assumption that all of the plants or processes are similar
		This approach provides results that are typical for the entire company	But each plant may have different suppliers affecting the quality of the outputs
		It is an average or an expected value	Supplier details are not readily available

Table 10.9. (cont.)

Method	Simple description	Advantages	Disadvantages
Estimates from industry aggregate data	Government statistical databases track various industries using self-reported data from the participants The data represent the aggregate materials flows for the industry	Such data are readily available at little cost and are assumed to be accurate The data typically include the operations of upstream suppliers and downstream distributors This approach provides results that are typical for the industry It is an average	The results represent a weighted average of all such plants or equipment within the industry The results are based on assumptions that all of the plants are similar Some plants are more efficient than others The approach may allow the worst producers to appear to be better than they really are

When electricity is the energy source, LCA requires determining how that electricity is produced and the impacts of that process. For example, electric cars were perceived to be zero-emission vehicles. However, such views were correct only on a per-unit basis. The actual vehicle may not produce emissions, but the plant that generates the electricity used to power the vehicles probably creates significant waste streams. Inevitable inefficiencies in the combustion process and in transforming heat to electricity in the generation process result in energy losses. There are also transmission line losses. Moreover, there are possibly many sources of inefficiencies in the manufacturing process of electric vehicles. So, while electric vehicles improve the air quality of locations surrounding the vehicle, the broader implications may not be as positive. Analysis is needed to determine the true impacts.

Nonrenewable energy sources have been criticized and characterized as bad, and renewable energy sources have been touted as good. While there is logic in the desire to use renewable resources for energy supplies, it is not as simple as saying they are inherently preferable. Again, the best source of energy for any given project or process depends upon the sum of the impacts and how they are mitigated. Nonrenewable energy sources that are stable and result in efficient and effective processes may be acceptable when compared to renewable energy sources that have severe impacts. For example, using biomass for energy may lead to increased rates of soil depletion, water consumption, and degradation of the land due to the use of agricultural chemicals. While there are inherent advantages to renewable sources, it cannot be inferred that they are always superior.

Disruption of the bio-system is also a factor. Although hydropower does not have significant effects on inventory assessments, it raises some concerns that are difficult to quantify. Habitat loss and land use interruptions that accompany hydropower development have long-term consequences that affect a broad array of human and environmental considerations.

Energy consumption has multiple implications. If fossil fuels are used to produce the energy, mass and energy consumption and their impacts have to be all factored into an inventory assessment that includes the flow of resources into materials and energy. This approach simplifies the calculations, since there is only mass to balance.

Waste generation

The ideal process would convert inputs into outputs without any **waste generation**. However, most real world processes are less than ideal and generate waste streams. Traditional inventory assessments identify three categories of waste streams: air emissions (gaseous residues), water effluents (liquid residues), and solid waste. In each category, there are often many different wastes that are generated and released. The inventory assessment includes all of the regulated waste streams (wastes that are hazardous or cause serious concerns because of their negative effects) and other waste streams that are significant in terms of volume or impact. Most regulated waste streams are subject to pollution abatement devices and measures. The inventories include the waste materials as well as the materials and energy used to collect the pollution.

Air emissions generated from production processes or the combustion of fuel are quantified on the basis of the actual flow to the emission control devices. Based on the collection efficiency of that device, the inventory of the releases to the atmosphere can be calculated or measured. Typical air emissions include particulate matter, nitrogen oxides (NO_x), volatile organic compounds (VOCs), sulfur dioxide (SO_2), carbon monoxide (CO), ammonia, lead, aldehydes, and carbon dioxide (CO_2). Many others could be listed, including fugitive emissions of chemicals and fuel products. Some of the most pervasive are gasoline emissions (evaporative) from the fueling of trucks and cars. Moreover, the loading and unloading of transportation vessels and vehicles typically involves evaporative emissions as well as the potential for spills and accidents. CO_2 is a naturally occurring, nontoxic gas that supports photosynthesis. However, the tremendous number of combustion sources has increased the levels of CO_2 in the atmosphere to the point of possibly affecting the earth's ability to effectively radiate heat.

Scientists are concerned that global temperatures may be rising as a result. Global climate change concerns have placed special emphasis on reducing gases that potentially contribute to this greenhouse effect. The 1997 Kyoto Conference and 2002 Johannesburg Summit focused heavily on CO_2 emissions and global warming.

Water effluents are particularly problematic, since clean water is vital to life on the planet. Polluted waterways take decades to recover, and the effects on marine life can be devastating. Water effluents include chemical discharges from industrial plants, pollution from nonpoint sources (generally agricultural activities), spills and releases of fuels and chemicals, biological agents that deplete oxygen levels (biological oxygen demand), and other chemical compounds that consume oxygen (chemical oxygen demand). Other waterborne wastes include suspended solids, dissolved solids, metals, cyanides, phosphates, microbes, and petroleum products, to identify just a few. Such effluents cause a myriad of problems, from algae growth because of phosphates to pathogens and other disease-causing microbes. Even if the wastewater is only slightly contaminated with salts or petroleum residues, the effects on the environment can be significant if there are large quantities of discharges. Wastewater from industrial operations is often regulated and thereby subject to treatment technologies to reduce contaminants.

Solid waste is often the most visible waste. Since it does not readily disperse or flow, solid waste requires immediate action for treatment and disposal. Industrial solid wastes are the residues and by-products remaining from processes. They are generally classified as hazardous or nonhazardous, and regulatory burdens depend on the toxicity of the materials. The more toxic and concentrated the wastes, the more significant are the regulatory, social, and economic concerns. Such materials and processes require special consideration, regardless of where they occur in the life cycle. The intent of SBD is to drive such outputs to zero.

Consumer waste streams include the packaging and unusable portion of the product. Post-consumer wastes are a special category that includes such items as left-over aluminum cans, empty containers, discarded computers, or "dead" cars parked in a field.

Transportation is a special subprocess that links the major stages in a life cycle. The materials, parts, and eventually the product itself are transported from the point of inception to the next stage, and ultimately to the customer. As previously discussed, in most cases the energy flow can be translated into mass flow.

Integrated flow

Assessing the material flows across a product life cycle should be based on the full integration of mass flows across the production system. In the conventional perspective of environmental management, it is easy to deal with unacceptable or problematic materials by outsourcing the supply of the goods for the most difficult processes or some similar approach. However, examining the whole enterprise eliminates this seeming cure because, no matter where the difficulties are, they remain the responsibilities of the producer.

The integrated flow diagram includes the full range of materials, energy, and waste streams. Figure 10.9 represents a simple system for the mass-balance of material flow.

The sum of inputs equals the residual product at the end of life plus the sum of the gaseous, liquid, and solid residues, and any by-products. Efficient processes and subprocesses require less total inputs for the final output. Residues are nonproductive inventories that increase resource depletion

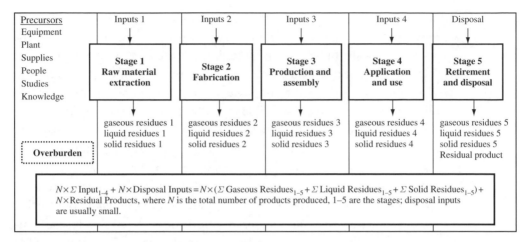

Figure 10.9 Mass-balance of materials flow

and add to environmental degradation. They are double problems since they both consume valuable materials and resources and turn them into negative burdens that require more resources and energy to rectify. Each data field can be summed to obtain a two-dimensional matrix of the inventory across the stages and the sum of the waste streams within each stage.

LCA is about examining every process and finding every opportunity to improve the system. The underlying philosophy is that everything is important and every element of a process can contribute to success. LCA uses an inventory assessment of materials and energy balances to ascertain the implications of the flows and to determine the expected outcomes in the future. The simple example is the aluminum can. The raw material is bauxite; the bauxite is refined to produce alumina which is then reduced in a smelting process to produce aluminum. The aluminum is then alloyed with other metals into can stock which is shipped to users (beer and soda manufacturers) who produce cans and fill them with their products.

The effects of reuse and recycling

The pollution prevention and waste minimization methodologies of the 1990s concentrated heavily on the benefits of product and material reuse and recycling. These methods are still central to environmental management strategies and play a significant role in reducing the need for virgin materials. These strategies provide both economical and environmental benefits to the corporation and to society. However, the extent of the benefits enjoyed

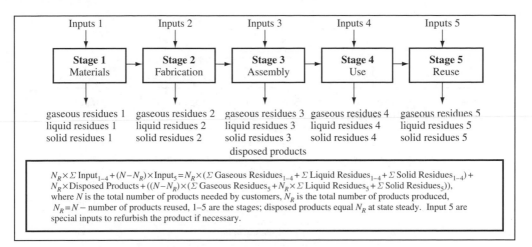

$N_R \times \Sigma\, \text{Input}_{1-4} + (N-N_R) \times \text{Input}_5 = N_R \times (\Sigma\, \text{Gaseous Residues}_{1-4} + \Sigma\, \text{Liquid Residues}_{1-4} + \Sigma\, \text{Solid Residues}_{1-4}) + N_R \times \text{Disposed Products} + ((N-N_R) \times (\Sigma\, \text{Gaseous Residues}_5 + N_R \times \Sigma\, \text{Liquid Residues}_5 + \Sigma\, \text{Solid Residues}_5))$, where N is the total number of products needed by customers, N_R is the total number of products produced, $N_R = N -$ number of products reused, 1–5 are the stages; disposed products equal N_R at state steady. Input 5 are special inputs to refurbish the product if necessary.

Figure 10.10 Mass-balance of materials flow adjusted for reuse

depends on the material and its inherent value. For instance, newsprint, which is inherently low-cost and low-value, is difficult to recycle economically and requires special conditions or economic and noneconomic subsidies. Aluminum, on the other hand, enjoys a high demand and value, making aluminum cans readily recyclable. Despite these differences between materials markets, reuse and recycling remain an important part of SBD.

Successful creative options are based on fully understanding the base case. Recycling and reuse includes the recovery and refurbishment of components, the repair and reuse of parts, and the recycling of commodity materials. These practices reduce the upstream requirements of the processes for which the recycled/reused materials are inputs. Including the benefits of reuse and recycling in the analysis is therefore critical. Figure 10.10 gives a sense of the effect of reuse.

Reuse and recycling are typically downstream processes that attempt to mitigate the effects of products, parts, components, or materials. They are after-the-fact attempts to deal with some of the negative aspects, focusing on what is, instead of what should or could be. This thought is especially important if the ingredients used are inherently undesirable. For instance, recycling chromium may be viewed as a means to maintain chromium as a viable material instead of simply recognizing that it has to be taken out of use based on the principles of SBD. Similar statements can be made about certain manmade compounds, especially certain classes of chlorinated compounds (halogens, vinyl chlorides, etc.), heavy metals, and all of the cancer-causing or suspended carcinogenic materials.

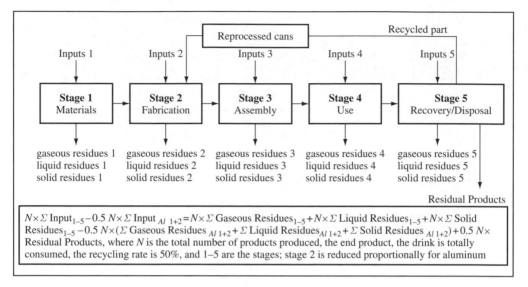

Figure 10.11 Mass-balance of materials flow adjusted for one component (stage) recycling

The most powerful solutions are those that positively influence more of the upstream processes. Reuse has linear effects all the way upstream to the first stage. In figure 10.10, it is easy to determine the benefits of reuse by examining the relationship of N_R to N. The smaller the ratio, the more effective is the reuse approach. Reuse not only reduces the input requirements, however, it also decreases the amount of residues that have to be handled as waste. While the equation in figure 10.10 does not include the economic implications, reuse and recycling can bear economic benefits as well. The ultimate solution is the approach that best satisfies all perspectives.

Reuse can be implemented with recycling to improve the utilization of materials and reduce waste generation. Recycling takes many forms, from the simple recycling of one material or part to the recycling of the entire product in the strategy of BMW (see box 3.1). The trend since the 1980s has been toward increased recycling by primary producers and a growth of secondary producers who recover, refurbish, reuse, recycle, and regenerate products, components, parts, and materials. The infrastructure is often complex, with many participants in the process to recover value and avoid depletion and degradation. Many of the concepts were discussed in the BMW case.

Figure 10.11 shows how recycling a simple component can affect the materials flow of a product.

The example might be aluminum cans that contained Coke or Pepsi. The end-product is carbonated water with special ingredients. The raw material is water, which is obtained and purified during Stage 1. The ingredients are mixed and prepared during Stage 2. The formula is canned in an automated process during Stage 3. The product is shipped to retail outlets and sold to consumers who use the product within the limits of the shelf life. Finally, the empty aluminum can is recycled through the reverse logistics infrastructure that delacquers the can, melts and reforms the aluminum sheet, and produces new cans. The example assumes that 50 percent of the cans are recycled directly back into the production system, closing the loop by capturing recycled materials within the producer's value system. Open-loop systems do not recycle materials or allow them to be recycled and used elsewhere.

The recycling of the material is advantageous if the burdens added by reprocessing the aluminum cans are less than the burdens associated with acquiring the raw materials and producing the aluminum can sheet in Stages 1 and 2. If the economics and social implications of recycling the aluminum are sound as well, the process is a viable option on the road to SBD.

Projections based on inventory assessments

Sales forecasting provides decision-makers with a sense of the expected demand for a given product over time. The goal is to determine the demand structure for the product and estimate the production volume required for meeting the demand. There are numerous techniques for accomplishing this, ranging from simple projections based on past demand to more elaborate methods that examine the causes of demand and the economic implications.

Inventory assessment explores the full scope of inputs and outputs on a per-unit basis under current demand conditions. The fundamentals of inventory assessment provide valuable insights and spotlight areas of potential improvements. However, inventory assessment can be taken to the next level by examining the projections of sales volume over time or by estimating the inputs and outputs of various hypothetical scenarios. While it may be customary to calculate projected volume and the need for selected inputs, such as the projected requirement for titanium and aluminum in the production of aircraft, the practice of calculating the projected waste streams has gained prominence only with pollution prevention techniques. Such practices are still in the early stages of development, but are proving extremely important for mapping out the implications of products and processes and for determining the suitability of selected practices. Certain practices that are feasible for low-quantity operations become impossible to manage at higher quantities.

For example, the common practice during the early part of the twentieth century of storing scrap automobiles in junkyards became a social problem (not in my backyard!) as well as an environmental concern (leaking fluids, rusting metal, rotting fabrics, and leaching heavy metals to name a few) when the numbers grew large. During the 1970s and 1980s, industrial countries such as the United Kingdom and Germany were discarding approximately 10 million automobiles per year. Failing to consider the implications of this waste stream was only one side of the situation, however. The other side was the lost opportunities associated with the scrap products and materials. The inherent value of the discarded cars represented a rich source of wealth for those engaged in recovery and recycling efforts. As Reynolds Metals proved with the aluminum can in the 1970s, recycled materials are viable substitutes for virgin materials and, in many cases, they provide better economic and environmental solutions.

Projections of the waste streams are a critical part of inventory assessment and determining the priorities and strategies for managing residues. The estimates can be rough approximations that provide a sense of the scope of the requirements for handling the waste streams. They may be a simple formula related to the expected production of the products, or complex econometric models that examine the aggregate demand by customers. The former has the advantage of being direct and related to the production capabilities of the corporation. However, waste stream problems are often shared across an industry. As noted in the earlier discussion, Union Carbide recognized that it had to work with other chemical producers along the upper Potomac River if it was going to make significant improvements in the water quality. Simply improving the outflows from its Institute, West Virginia plant would contribute to mitigating the problem, but would not alleviate the concerns of citizens and stakeholder groups worried about the pollution in the river.

Using more complex models examines the problem from the broadest perspective. While one of the industry participants may believe that the waste streams can be handled, an industry-wide assessment may shed light on the true nature of the concerns. For example, a conscientious producer or user of CFCs might believe that it has sufficient control over the materials, and assume that there is no problem. The broader models are often at a disadvantage, however, as they require detailed data and information that may not be available.

Inventory assessment provides the framework for a critical examination of the impacts of the products and processes. The most crucial considerations are the future implications. Unlike most of the traditional environmental management constructs that focused on what happened, inventory assessment focuses on the future, and the impacts that might be expected.

Deploying inventory assessment

The cradle-to-grave flow of LCA data and information brings new concerns about the veracity of data and information, especially those from external entities such as suppliers and customers. Data must be high quality if they are to serve the purposes of most LCAs. Inventory assessments also depend on accurate, timely, and reliable data and information from numerous sources, each with its own system of calculating inputs, outputs, and waste streams.

The data and information should be normalized if possible. For instance, if the flows from unit operations are used, the time of day, week or year that was used to obtain the data should be consistent across the system. This will avoid seasonal variations such as those in rivers, a common repository for wastewater effluent. It is also important to understand the variability of the data and whether averages, when used, do represent an expected case. Some of the extreme values might turn out to be the norm when the process is monitored carefully. The aggregation of data and information over time, especially when based on total output, tends to smooth out the fluctuations due to incidental factors.

On the negative side, some participants or supply network entities may try to provide inappropriate information to skew the results. For example, they may provide information based on the best operating characteristics of their processes, rather than the typical results. Using ranges (e.g. a 95 percent confidence level) to establish conditions rather than a single data point may help provide a better sense of the real situation, and allow for a sensitivity analysis as well. Indeed, it could help establish the expected upper and lower conditions of a process or subprocess.

Furthermore, most inventory equations assume a linear relationship. Generally, processes tend to be linear within a certain range and nonlinear at the extremes. Data collected under selected conditions may be of limited use. There is no guarantee that interpolations or extrapolations can be validated.

Similarly, missing and estimated data and information are always a problem. If estimates are used, especially from industry data, it is important to ensure that equivalence is established. The basis – geographic area or technology, for example – should be the same.

Data and information required by a regulatory agency are accurate and readily available in most cases. Information about unregulated emissions is often more difficult to obtain. For instance, carbon dioxide is a greenhouse gas that has become a primary concern. However, CO_2 emissions have not been tracked historically and are often available only through indirect calculations. Fortunately, the process flow information for most primary processes is readily available.

Summary

The primary purpose of LCA is to validate new products and processes, or to improve the performance of existing ones. It does this by discovering concerns and impacts, especially hidden ones, and by gaining insight about how to mitigate burdens and defects. For this reason, the scope of an LCA should be as open-ended as possible. However, practitioners must consider the cost and effort involved when they establish the objectives and priorities of the LCA. Difficult choices must be made.

Establishing the framework for the analysis and determining the guidelines that the organization and its related entities will use in obtaining, analyzing, and interpreting the information and data is perhaps the most important step. It lays the foundation for the remaining phases of the LCA. The scope may include every product and process, or only selected elements. The notion of a streamlined LCA or an abridged version has gained acceptance as many corporations have discovered that they need to build capabilities and knowledge in order to execute a full LCA. The abridged version allows them to get started and to learn the intricacies.

LCA requires an evolutionary learning process. The organization has to institutionalize the flow of information pertaining to impacts so that it becomes more systematic and participants can provide input as requested. It is analogous to the developments in TQM and the six-sigma techniques that have evolved since the 1980s.

Inventory assessment is the listing of inputs and outputs of processes and subprocesses. It is the second phase of the LCA process and includes the information required to fully understand the mass and energy balances of the system. Together, establishing the LCA framework and inventory assessment constitute the front-end of LCA because they map out the structure of LCA and provide an understanding of what is expected. The two front-end phases can actually be a simple version of an abridged LCA. With knowledge of the

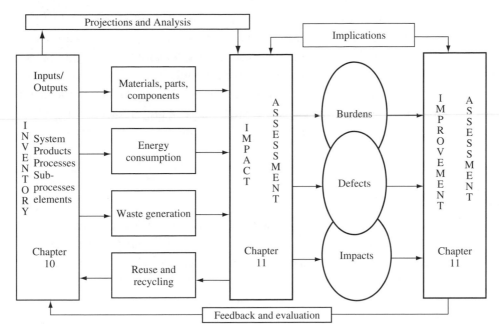

Figure 10.12 Impact and improvement assessment phases of LCA

protocols and a mapping of the processes, participants can execute many of the key elements of the impact assessment and improvement assessment phases without a formal structure or a huge investment. However, formal approaches are still better than informal ones if there are no other options.

The Impact and Improvement assessment phases of LCA are discussed in chapter 11. Figure 10.12 depicts the LCA phases, which are directly connected to NPD and process and product improvement.

Impact Assessment focuses on needs, and Improvement Assessment focuses on desired outcomes. The so-called "triple bottom line" in these final phases of LCA is to reduce, if not eliminate, defects, burdens, and impacts and to create better products and processes from the social, economic, and environmental perspectives.

Supplementary material

Learning objectives

Chapter 10 has the following learning objectives that are intended to guide and support students and practitioners:

- Understanding the LCA construct and its prime components.
- Determining the context of LCA, key considerations, and applications.
- Understanding the fundamental LCA framework and the Initiation phase, including goals, definition, purpose, and scope.
- Understanding the Inventory phase, including computational models for analyzing, interpreting, and understanding data and information.
- Assessing the decision constructs for deploying the Inventory phase of LCA in a business setting.

Research questions

The following are questions related to SBD in order to facilitate learning and ongoing discussion and analysis of the main topics covered in the chapter:

- What is the most important aspect of LCA for global corporations?
- How can LCA be used during the design and development of the new products and processes of global corporations?
- How can corporations integrate LCA into mainstream thinking?
- What are examples of effective LCA approaches?

NOTES

1. B. W. Vigon *et al.*, *Life Cycle Assessment: Inventory Guidelines and Principles*, Office of Research and Development, EPA, 1993, p. 5.
2. Thomas Graedel, *Streamlined Life-Cycle Assessment* (Englewood Cliffs, NJ: Prentice Hall, 1998), pp. 87–93. Graedel credits Keith Weitz of North Carolina's Research Triangle Institute and his coworkers for identifying nine approaches for modifying the LCA. The nine approaches are (1) Screen the product with an inviolate list; (2) Limit or eliminate components or processes deemed to be of minor importance; (3) Limit or eliminate life cycle stages; (4) Include only selected environmental impacts; (5) Include only selected inventory parameters; (6) Limit consideration to constituents above threshold weight or volume values; (7) Limit or eliminate impact analysis; (8) Use qualitative rather than quantitative information; (9) Use surrogate data.
3. TQM and six-sigma quality constructs examine the levels of defects in terms of defects per million opportunities for defects. The more complicated the product and process, the more opportunities there are for defects.
4. CAFE means corporate average fleet efficiency. It is the average fuel efficiency that automobile manufacturers have to achieve for their entire fleet of cars.
5. The production and construction of the solar panels consume materials and energy, and such effects should be included in a full LCA.

6. This concept is reinforced by the "Theory of Inventive Problem Solving" (TRIZ), developed by Genrich S. Altshuller. TRIZ focuses on the Law of Ideality, which states that a system throughout its life tends to be more reliable and effective. See http://www.personal.engin.umich.edu.

REFERENCES

Graedel, Thomas E. (1998) *Streamlined Life-Cycle Assessment*. Englewood Cliffs, NJ: Prentice Hall

Piasecki, Bruce, K. Fletcher, and F. Mendelson (1999) *Environmental Management and Business Strategy: Leadership Skills for the Twenty-first Century*. New York: John Wiley

Vigon, B. W. *et al.* (1993) *Life Cycle Assessment: Inventory Guidelines and Principles*. Office of Research and Development, EPA

11 Implementation of life cycle assessment: impact and improvement assessments

Introduction

The implementation phases of LCA include impact assessment and improvement assessment. These phases transform information and data organized during the inventory phase into meaningful and valuable analyses and actions. These phases of LCA can touch all the life cycle stages of a product or process, putting SBD principles into action on the broadest scale. Implementation involves intensive activities aimed at improving the value proposition (economics), enhancing the viability of products and processes (social), and mitigating the consequences and impacts (environmental).

As discussed previously, impact assessment transforms the inventory assessment into a comprehensive awareness of the strengths and weaknesses of the product architecture and the process structures that can then reveal improvement opportunities. It explores processes and subprocesses to verify that decisions are appropriate and in line with the corporate objectives and the expectations of constituents.

Improvement assessment then translates the identified opportunities into realities. It is the least definitive of the phases since it depends on context. Improvements may include proving that everything meets specifications, enhancing existing positive attributes, reducing defects and burdens, mitigating impacts, and ensuring longevity. It is impossible to spell out all the possible scenarios.

This chapter focuses on major risk-reduction methods involved in implementing LCA. Despite the ever-present potential for hidden defects, management must strive to ensure that products and processes are safe, appropriate, effective, and meet the expectations of all constituencies. The logic-based precautionary principle suggests that LCA is a necessary means to achieve the "triple bottom line," as the corporation moves toward SBD.

The chapter includes the following topics:

- Impact assessment for understanding the opportunities for improvements.
- Improvement assessment to improve the triple bottom line.
- Tools and techniques, including evaluation and metrics, risk mitigation, and quality methods.
- LCA implications for SBD.

The costs of LCA in terms of time and money have to be balanced with the benefits it brings. The major benefit is the additional knowledge obtained. Participants are better equipped to understand the effects of corporate decisions and what the solutions are expected to be. As more LCA programs are performed, the body of knowledge increases, thereby decreasing the cost and time required to obtain the information and to perform the assessments. Systematic approaches such as LCA also improve as the number of initiatives increases. A single program performed during the early years of SBD may not provide the benefits to justify the investment. However, in the long term, the ongoing efforts build a "critical mass" of LCA capabilities, knowledge and actions that result in a more sustainable future.

But LCA is not intended to be a stand-alone process. Ultimately, it should be embedded within technology development programs, NPD programs, and related development and improvement programs. The full integration of LCA within such programs will facilitate all these efforts, reducing time requirements, lowering the necessary investments, and improving overall results. Most importantly, LCA will enhance management confidence that decisions are sound and based on best available analysis and approaches.

Impact assessment

Definitions and categories

An impact is a positive or negative result of an effect of a product, process, and/or activity, including all the social, economic, and environmental consequences and implications. Negative impacts can affect the eco-systems and natural resources, human health, safety and quality of life, and economics and society. They include defects and the burdens. Impact assessment is the process of determining the severity and significance of defects, burdens, and impacts and related implications and consequences. It includes an examination of the stages of the life cycle in order to identify, prioritize, and specify concerns, uncertainties, risks, and hidden defects in each one.

Based on the objectives and scope of the LCA, impact assessment interrogates the inventories to ascertain the real or potential negative effects that have to be prevented, mitigated, eliminated, or managed. The identified impacts determine the actions taken.

Impacts can be characterized according to the following categories and subcategories:

- Relational: *direct, indirect, and tangential impacts*   These categories describe how the impacts are connected to the enterprise, its systems and supply networks, constituents, and the natural environment.
- Temporal: *immediate, intermediate, and long-term impacts*   Impacts vary according to their timing and their effect on the future.
- Spatial (geographic): *local, regional, and global impacts*   Geographic impacts vary according to their origin and their reach.

These categories describe the various ways that impacts are related to the enterprise, and not their importance or severity. Traditional LCA methods used more formal language for the same categories, although they employed fewer distinct categories.

Direct describes those impacts that are linked to the system, process or subprocess that management and practitioners have to deal with on a regular basis. It describes impacts related directly to the enterprise, its supply networks, customers, partners, allies, and others. The LCA participants are usually aware of the material flows and implications, and these impacts are typically evident. However, participants may not fully understand all of the potential impacts and their consequences. There may be hidden defects, unknown risks and impacts, and their consequences that have not been realized or experienced. For example, it is clear that certain incinerators or mass burn plants *can* create dioxins. However, it may not be obvious whether a new mass burn technology *actually does* create dioxins or other toxins. The potential impacts would be in the "direct" category since they are a consequence of the combustion process. Direct impacts also tend to be both immediate and local or regional in nature. They include air emissions causing acid rain, water effluents polluting water quality, solid waste requiring treatment and land-filling, and spills and accidents forcing emergency responses. Obviously, the list is extensive.

Indirect impacts are those that are caused by other parties not directly related to the enterprise. Typically, indirect impacts are related to the infrastructure or other industries that provide resources and services used by the first industry. For example, many industrial processes use electricity that is distributed from the generating plants to the users via transmission lines.

An indirect impact of the transmission lines is the health and safety effects of the electromagnetic force (EMF) and the potential for the lines to disrupt natural wildlife habitat and the aesthetics of nature. The primary producers and suppliers of the electricity often manage these impacts, which are directly related to their operations. Such impacts may still have consequences – i.e. "indirect" impacts – on third parties. As you can see, there is often a fine line between direct and indirect impacts. Even car theft can be seen as an indirect impact of the automobile because the automobile producers do not have any direct means to deal with the impacts of such crimes. However, automobile manufacturers may respond by enhancing the capabilities of the owners to avoid such problems through advanced locking mechanisms, alarms, and other anti-theft devices. While there may be aftermarket providers who make profits from such problems, the OEMs generally have mixed views about such requirements because the anti-theft devices add to the cost of the vehicles but are not always fully recognized by customers as exciting attributes. However, the willingness to provide such solutions indicates that OEMs recognize the impacts of their business and the implicit responsibility they bear to do something about it.

Tangential impacts are those that are relatively small and seemingly inconsequential or those that have only a remote connection to a product or process. Corporations have various rules on how to handle these minor impacts, and it often makes sense to follow the *de minimis* trigger of many regulations.[1] Tangential impacts are often resource streams or by-products that have little or no impact. For example, the loss of vapor from a cooling tower at a power plant may represent a large flow of water vapor, but since the release of water to the atmosphere is a naturally occurring and beneficial part of the hydrocycle such releases should be not be considered as part of the LCA impact assessment. Eliminating "tangential" impacts from the scope of an LCA can facilitate the assessments without arbitrarily defining limiting boundaries. The boundaries can remain broad, yet the impact assessment can be focused on the truly significant impacts.

Immediate impacts are those whose consequences are felt quickly. For example, a petroleum spill into a waterway has immediate impacts on the quality of the water and the organisms living in and around it. Immediate impacts may also set in motion additional consequences that may take days or weeks to fully manifest themselves. For instance, a worker inadvertently exposed to certain radioactive materials is immediately harmed, even though it may take days for the full destructive effects of his exposure to become apparent. "Immediate" includes impacts that are apparent or not. In most cases, immediate impacts elicit an immediate response, as in the case of an accident or a spill. However, a response is not a condition for characterizing an impact as immediate. The release of VOCs into the atmosphere, for example, has an immediate impact but often with little remedial recourse.

Intermediate-term impacts are those impacts whose effects do not occur immediately, but rather take many months or several years to appear. Certain impacts must mature in the environment before they become significant. Often this is related to exceeding a certain concentration or accumulation of the released substance in order for the impacts to be fully felt. Generally, lakes and ponds can absorb a certain amount of acid rain before the acidification causes problems. This is particularly true when the lakebed or adjacent soil has a significant amount of calcium carbonate ($CaCO_3$) to neutralize the acid. However, over time, perhaps even several years, the neutralizing effects diminish, and the quality of the water in the lake or pond declines.[2]

Long-term impacts require a decade or more for the effects to present a significant challenge to the prevailing conditions. Long-term impacts are not necessarily unknown and do not always require many years for the implications to become recognized. Rather, the general effects of these impacts increase very slowly. These effects tend to be difficult to measure and require scientific research in order to document their significance and severity. Often there is a high level of uncertainty surrounding them. For instance, CO_2 is the primary product of most combustion processes, and billions of tons of it are produced each year.[3] CO_2 is a greenhouse gas, which contributes to global warming and climate change. While it is clear that CO_2 production has risen from pre-industrial levels of approximately 280 parts per million (ppm) to 365ppm today, the causes and effects are not as clear, nor is there agreement about what has to be done to rectify the situation.[4] Moreover, there is a significant lag between the releases and the consequences of the climate change, because of the thermal capacity of the oceans and other natural phenomena.

Local impacts are those having a relatively short geographic range. "Local" typically means in and around the plant and its surrounding community, or the areas where products are in use. Local impacts can affect the social and economic conditions of the community in which operations take place or the one where input materials are derived or the products are used. For instance, logging has local, regional, and possibly global impacts. The local impacts involve deforestation and disruptions that affect soil conditions, habitat preservation, the aesthetic values derived by humankind, and the quality of life in the area. The local impacts also include resource depletion, as harvesting trees can render the soil less capable of sustaining new growth.

Regional impacts affect a broader geographic area, including whole countries or even several countries. They can include impacts to the cultural and social conditions of a nation state and surrounding areas. Regional environmental impacts affect natural resources and the eco-systems, the quality of human life and health, and the social and economic well-being of people. For example, air quality is usually a regional concern because the conditions are felt downwind of a given location. If a community or even a small country has a very effective pollution prevention approach, its air quality may still be poor if its upwind neighbors fail to take similar actions.

Global impacts affect everyone and everything, connecting points of cause and effect around the globe because of the interrelatedness of the elements of our biosphere. Global impacts generally affect the biosphere, atmosphere, oceans, and the availability and quality of resources. Such effects can impact weather and climate, the availability of water, and the quality of life across the earth. Population, consumption, and waste generation have global impacts. For example, there is a small island in the Pacific Ocean where the population is worried about the effects of climate change caused by excessive emissions of CO_2 around the world and other phenomena. Since the highest elevation is approximately 4m, it is easy to understand the islanders' concerns and their urgent desire for a solution. Table 11.1 portrays the temporal differences of direct geographic-related impacts using selected concerns and impacts.

Table 11.1 contains some of the more frequently discussed concerns and direct geographic-related impacts that global corporations are facing. Usually they are linked to the management system and its supply networks and to customers and stakeholders.

Impact assessment explores the severity of the impacts and attempts to deduce the probability of occurrence and the potential consequences over time. The impact assessment process section (pp. 615–29) provides an overview of quantitative and qualitative means for making such determinations.

Many of the concerns listed for direct impacts also pertain to indirect ones. The actions causing the indirect impacts, however, are usually further upstream or downstream of the management system. Some of the most important direct or indirect impacts are those that threaten the corporation, but the corporation usually has more control over internal operations than it does over those of external entities.

Table 11.2 depicts the temporal aspects of selected indirect geographic-related impacts. It shows the relationship between the geographic and temporal continuums. The list is not intended to be comprehensive.

Table 11.1. Temporal nature of selected direct geographic-related impacts

	Immediate		Intermediate term		Long-term	
Local						
	Impacts	Concerns	Impacts	Concerns	Impacts	Concerns
	Worker injuries and fatalities	– Safety standards – Work conditions	Decline in process viability	– Cost increases – Loss of acceptance	Increased liabilities	– Litigation – Economic viability – Use of hazardous materials – Disposal of hazardous wastes
	Pollution from chemical spills	– Linking storage tanks – Inadequate procedures – Poor training	Decline in water quality	– Use of fertilizers – Discharge of hazardous materials – Oxygen depletion	Damage to human health	
	Decline in air quality	– Use of VOCs – Vehicular emissions – Increase in diseases	Damage to natural resources	– Destruction of land, water, and air – Decline in food production	Decline in natural (economic) resources	– Depletion of strategic resources – Decline in economic and social stability
Regional						
	Industrial or residential development	– Loss of open spaces – Habitat loss	Disruption in quality of life	– Increased noise, odors, wastes, congestion	Increase in burdens	– Added to costs for remediation – Loss of capital
	Release of industrial pollution and residues	– Effects of treatment processes – Transportation and storage risks	Decline in air quality	– Use of carbon-based fuels – Emissions of particulate matter, SO_2, NO_x	Decline in bio-diversity	– Habitat loss – Use of toxic chemicals – Use of pesticides and herbicides

Catastrophic releases from industrial plants	– Nuclear radiation – Chemical releases	Waste disposal	– Landfills – Incinerators – Storage – Nuclear wastes	Decline in economic base	– Destruction of viable land – Congestion – High costs
Global					
Worker injuries and fatalities	– Safety standards – Work conditions	Decline in process viability	– Cost increases – Loss of acceptance	Increased liabilities	– Litigation – Economic viability – Training
Volcanic eruption	– Increase in particulate matter in atmosphere	Soil depletion; Resource depletion	– Loss of food supplies – Decrease in raw materials	Global climate change	– CO_2 emissions – CH_4 emissions – Land destabilization
Disease	– Increased illness and mortality due to pathogens	Ozone depletion	– Use of CFCs – NO_x emissions – Halons emissions	Population decline	– Chronic diseases – Higher mortality – Decreased fertility – Quality of life

Table 11.2. Temporal nature of selected indirect geographic-related impacts

Local

Immediate		Intermediate term		Long-term	
Impacts	Concerns	Impacts	Concerns	Impacts	Concerns
Increase in negative footprint	– Worker injuries – Fatalities – Loss of habitat	Resource availability	– Decline in the materials/parts – Increase in costs – Depletion	Increase in destructive behaviors	– Human rights issues – Social responsibility
Lack of regulatory compliance	– Government interdiction – Delays in output – Shutdown or bankruptcy	Decline in quality	– Increase in defects – Added liabilities – Added cost and involvement	Damage to corporate reputation	– Illegal or inappropriate practices – Use of hazardous materials – Liabilities
Production of waste residues	– Life cycle implication of large waste streams	Damage to the natural resources	– Destruction of land, water, and air – Decline in food production	Decline in natural (economic) resources	– Depletion of resource – Decline in economic viability – Social stability

Regional

Immediate		Intermediate term		Long-term	
Impacts	Concerns	Impacts	Concerns	Impacts	Concerns
Decline in social and political viability of products	– Reduced acceptance due to defects and burdens	Decrease in economic viability of products	– Users' fees and restrictions – Disposal costs – Prohibitions in certain markets	Increased resistant to product applications	– New laws and regulations – Added penalties – Increased opposition

Global

Immediate		Intermediate term		Long-term	
Impacts	Concerns	Impacts	Concerns	Impacts	Concerns
Unexpected changes or mandates	– Resource availability – Disease (SARS) – Instability (war)	Required changes	– Significant changes – Mandated technologies	Product bans or restrictions	– International protocols and treaties – International agreements

The geographic-related categories are also extremely important from a management system perspective. The ability to manage and solve the impacts often depends on the geographic scope of the impacts. In theory, the local management group is best equipped to handle local impacts, strategic management manages the regional impacts, and corporate management leads the entire organization in finding creative solutions for global impacts. For instance, it is difficult for a plant manager in a given country to find the time and expertise to rationally formulate and implement programs for managing global issues. Understanding and articulating positions on issues such as global climate change at the various international conferences takes a huge commitment of time and effort and requires substantial knowledge, both of which are generally possessed only by senior management and subject matter experts at the corporate level. The impact categories are important for defining the role and responsibilities of the organizational participants and management in addressing impacts. Management at the appropriate level must have the resources and capabilities to affect appropriate solutions.

The impact assessment process

The actual impact assessment process translates inventory assessment elements into an understanding of the actual and/or potential impacts that can be assessed to determine the required action plans. In general, impacts are difficult to characterize because they have components that are absolute, relative, dynamic, and perceptual. For example, leaded gasoline contains tetraethyl lead, which is a known toxin with well-established characteristics. Lead is a heavy metal that creates hazardous waste, but it was not usually considered as dangerous as mercury. However, the enormous use of leaded gasoline led to significant social, environmental, and health concerns that ultimately led to the phasing out of the product. Societal perceptions changed from acceptance to intolerance.

The impact assessment process includes the following:

- *Identifying potential impacts*   Using the life cycle stages and the inventory assessment, practitioners identify all of the potential impacts, characterize them, determine their consequences on the business and natural environments, and put them into appropriate categories.
- *Assigning responsibilities*   Identify and assign the ultimate responsibilities for understanding, managing, and mitigating the impacts and their consequences.

- *Assessing severity/risks*   Assess the impacts to determine the severity of the consequences and the probabilities of occurrence. Determine the quantitative and/or qualitative implications.
- *Assessing needs*   Assess the needs of stakeholders, customers, and other constituents in concert with the needs, goals, and priorities of the corporation. Ensure that regulatory mandates have been included in the analysis and that the implications are understood.
- *Screening*   Select and prioritize the improvement programs for implementation.

There are many versions of this general process, from simple three-step approaches to elaborate constructs that represent the full LCA model. The version used depends upon the context of the LCA situation. For a NPD program, the impact assessment should be integrated into the overall development program and implemented concurrently with the Design and Development phase. However, for large, complex, new-to-the world products such as the Airbus A380, it is wise to accelerate the LCA and execute the impact assessment early in the concept phase. For incremental improvement programs, the impact assessment can parallel the decision-making process, providing valuable evidence in support of the improvement process.

Impact assessment is not simply a detailed analysis of the standard approaches, materials, or products; impact assessment goes further to examine and reveal *alternative choices* that may be available to designers and decision-makers.

Identifying impacts

Based on the inventory assessment, impacts can be characterized and placed into categories. The conventional approach follows the stages of the life cycle, identifying impacts by examining processes and subprocesses. There are numerous techniques for identifying and characterizing the most crucial concerns including Dr. Thomas Graedel's "Environmentally Responsible Product/Process Matrix: Scoring Guidelines and Protocols."[5] The key to the assessment is to examine the flows and document the impacts. Figure 11.1 provides a simplified life cycle impact assessment of an automobile using this method.

Only selected impacts are included to show the flow of the impacts across the stages of the life cycle. The initial stages tend to result in some direct and many indirect impacts while later, downstream, stages create direct impacts. The textured boxes depict direct effects. Clear boxes are some direct and mostly indirect effects. A diagram such as figure 11.1 indicates how the

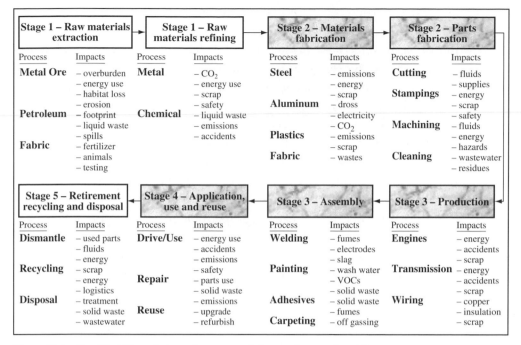

Figure 11.1 depicts stage four of the life cycle of an automobile: product

Figure 11.1 Simplified life cycle impact assessment diagram for an automobile

impacts are identified and listed. Creating a diagram helps practitioners scrutinize each impact so that it may be categorized. This exercise helps them to thoroughly understand all of the impacts. In this way, the assessment examines hundreds, even thousands, of individual elements that have, or potentially have, implications for the social, economic, and environmental fabric of the business environment.

The impact assessment includes delving deeply into product design, process flows, and facility operations. The design is often the most crucial aspect because it establishes the requirements for the parts, processes, and facilities. It represents the decisions that are made to realize the product specifications and applications. It feeds forward in terms of life cycle implications and impacts and backwards in terms of requirements on supply networks. Indeed, direct effects can often be traced back to product design, while indirect effects are often those impacts that occur regardless of design specifications.

Again, using the automobile as an example, an essential consideration in designing and using the product is safety. While there are safety concerns about workers in the fabrication stages and assembly operations, the most critical safety considerations occur during the use of the product. Figure 11.1 depicts stage four of the life cycle of an automobile: product use. A subelement is safety, and one of the safety concerns is the "blind spot." The blind spot is the area behind the vehicle that the driver cannot see. The most crucial concern is the safety of small children who could be injured or killed if a driver moves in reverse without checking the pathway. The typical sedan has a "blind spot" of approximately 20 ft, while the larger, sport utility vehicle (SUV) typically is two–three times worse. The "blind spot" is not only an example of a problem that can result in a potential impact. It might also be viewed as a "hidden defect" of a particular design. Assuming that such a hidden defect represents a direct impact, it then becomes incumbent upon the designers to mitigate the risk to small children and drivers that was created during the design process. The discussion about the solution is part of the impact and improvement assessment phases. Some automobile manufacturers are using cameras and radar devices to eliminate the "blind spot" with a visual image or an audible sound to alert drivers to something in the path. BMW provides optional equipment for sensing objects that are too close to the car and alerting the driver.

For most products and processes, most of the impacts occur during one of the LCA stages. For the automobile, the use of the product generates the greatest waste streams, including emissions of CO_2, hydrocarbon, carbon monoxide, and nitrogen oxides. Moreover, the average automobile consumes approximately 1,000–1,500 kg of fuel per year, or an amount equal to the weight of the vehicle itself. The impacts of operating a car over an average life time of ten years are significant, and generally outweigh the impacts caused during manufacturing.

Determining the significance of the impacts is also an important part of the identification process. Significance is the measure of the consequences of the expected impacts. Impacts are not all equal: some are much more significant than others. For example, in the automobile industry traffic accidents are common problems. If a particular automobile model is in an accident and the passengers are seriously injured, the consequences are serious concerns that arise about causality and the role that the design may have played in the accident. In this case, the impacts of an accident may be severe, but just one accident may not be a significant concern. However, in the case of Firestone's tire problems, in which more than 100 accidents involving fatalities occurred, the impacts were both severe and significant.

It is difficult to establish a precise ranking of impacts and concerns. Generally, the logic for ranking holds that the greater the risks to human health and safety and the natural environment, the more significant the impacts. Given the importance of protecting human life, priority (1) is to eliminate the risks of death and serious injury. It is unacceptable to put people at risk.

The next most important impacts are those that threaten the eco-systems and the natural environment. Such subordination is based on a philosophical view of the primacy of humankind, but also on the commonly held belief that protecting the world from destruction, degradation, disruption, and depletion is critical for the long-term well-being of everyone and everything (priority(2)). In reality, priority (1) and (2) are interrelated, and it may be impossible to achieve the first without the second.

The third most important objective in mitigating impacts (priority(3)) is supporting the economic and social stability of the world. Environmental equity, or ensuring that impacts are not skewed to those who have the least ability to mitigate the consequences, is part of this consideration. But, again, social satisfaction can also be linked to one's health and safety. The distinctions are always difficult to justify in light of the complexities of the real world. Still, economic stability is critical to the proper functioning of the business environment and the success of business activities and operations.

The fourth ranked impacts (priority(4)) are those that threaten the resources of the world and the diversity of species. However, the argument can be made that priorities (3) and (4) are interrelated, and it is difficult to achieve one without the other.

The identified impacts should be prioritized within and between these four levels of significance so that action plans can be initiated and responsibilities for actions assigned. In the ideal situation, every negative impact would be addressed and mitigated to the greatest extent possible. In the real world, such an approach might dilute the resources and capabilities of the corporation to such an extent that little is accomplished. The actual approach taken is a management decision that requires both insight and introspection.

Significance is also determined by how the impacts affect the corporation, its vision, reputation, and successes, and failures. Extreme and unmitigated impacts have the potential to seriously harm the corporation. Some of the most serious impacts are those that damage the corporate name and reputation, threaten the viability of products and processes, produce financial losses or incur liabilities, provoke litigation and actions resulting in criminal and civil penalties, and result in irreversible losses, including deaths, injuries, and property damage. Impacts and risks are prevalent in both society and business; they are an inherent part of nature and life. However, it is the responsibility of corporations and their management to ensure that impacts are mitigated or eliminated to the greatest extent possible.

Corporations assume special responsibilities when selecting the materials and resources to be used in products and processes. Such decisions trigger many upstream and downstream impacts and consequences that have to be considered. For instance, the use or production of heavy metals, VOCs, chlorinated compounds, and other toxic substances is a particular concern because they cause serious impacts across the life cycle. As inputs they impact human health and safety, and as outputs they represent regulated waste streams that create liabilities from cradle-to-grave. Corporations must categorize the impacts of their products and operations and clearly spell out the significance of such impacts. Unfortunately, there is no one absolute way to rank materials and wastes that can guide the design process. Of course, regulations often tell practitioners what must be done, and there are also industry standards, and international and national organizations and protocols that facilitate the ranking of impacts.

Table 11.3 provides some examples of significant impacts and concerns.

Since a primary impact can cause secondary and tertiary ones, it is important to assess each impact in depth and examine the potential for additional impacts, especially lagging ones. For example, clear-cutting of forests destroys habitat for flora and fauna. The destruction of protective vegetation and animal life may, in turn, contribute to accelerated erosion and lead to sediments filling adjacent lakes and ponds. This, in turn, will affect aquatic life and water quality. If the water is used for human activities, the clear-cutting will obviously affect the communities that use it and the quality of life they offer. One thing clearly leads to another.

There are also cases where the primary effects are not significant, but the secondary ones are. It could be argued that ozone-depleting materials fit this classification. The direct effects of CFCs are benign, and CFCs are safe and efficient in application. Indeed, for decades CFCs improved the quality of life by making effective refrigeration possible, enhancing productivity in the electronics industry, and improving the quality of life through air conditioning. Most importantly, they played a significant role in increasing the shelf life of food products, thereby reducing the amount of spoilage and premature discards.

Practitioners can also use statistical analysis and other quantitative methods to determine significance in a given situation. This can be helpful, as significance often depends on the future implications of an impact. For instance, the number of cellular telephones being discarded in 2005 may be relatively small and therefore, insignificant, but the projections for 2010 may indicate a huge increase in the discards, creating a serious issue. On the other

Table 11.3. Selected examples of significant impacts and concerns

External factors	Significant impacts	Internal factors	Significant impacts
Across all factors	Death, injury, accidents, spills	Across all factors	Death, injury, accidents, spills
Customers	Safety concerns, loss of value, premature failures, high maintenance costs, loss of economic value	Management system	Viability of system, risks, uncertainties, liabilities, reputation, image, truth
Stakeholders	Health hazards, noise, odors, toxic pollution, hazardous waste, water quality, air quality, habitat protection	Technology	Validation, uncertainty about future impacts, unexpected effects, hidden defects and burdens, obsolescence
Supply networks	Waste generation, pollution, health, and safety hazards, resources consumption, corruption, availability of resources	Product design	Lack of sustainable resources, hidden defects, satisfaction, longevity, risks, suitability, liabilities
Related industries	Inappropriate claims and actions, lack of support, poor practices, waste generation and disposal problems	Engineering	Limited knowledge, improper testing and verification, faulty design decisions, poor selections, errors
Infrastructure	Support structure, safety, security, longevity, maintenance costs, capabilities to provide means of mitigation	Production	Safety and health, mistakes, defects, errors, waste generation, waste handling and treatment, storage
Competition	Inappropriate claims and actions, improper instructions and information, poor practices, waste generation and disposal problems	Marketing	Inappropriate claims and actions, improper instructions and information, poor practices, lack of focus on negative impacts

hand, if new technology is expected to eliminate the concerns, the impact of used cell phones may not be as significant as it first appears. Similarly, in a NPD situation, Xerox might view the structure of its new office-sized copying machines and the resources required to produce them as insignificant if its strategy is to make the machine an investment that will be refurbished and reused many times in the future.

Determining the significance of impacts once they have been identified and undergone a preliminary analysis is one of the best ways to further define the scope of the LCA. It allows the corporation to make informed decisions about what should be studied in depth. The main limitation to this method of defining a LCA is the lack of well-established norms, standards, criteria, and/or metrics for stipulating what is significant.

Assigning responsibility for mitigating impacts

Assigning responsibility for eliminating or mitigating impacts to an individual, team, or business unit depends, again, on the situation. Management generally assigns responsibility after identifying and determining the importance of the impacts. It simply makes more sense to assign responsibility only after the corporation is fully committed to resolving a particular impact. Most corporations have an extremely large number of impacts to manage, and they cannot afford to spread their capabilities so thinly that very little will be achieved. This is also why it is so important to understand the significance of impacts in order to prioritize them. Decades in the future, it may be possible to take on all impacts because the numbers have reached more manageable levels.

Responsibility for managing an impact takes many forms. Five conventional approaches for assigning such responsibilities are:

- *The preemptive leader* is the CEO or other senior executive that takes responsibility for eliminating impacts without regard to return on investment or profitability. This leader philosophically believes in the need for a solution or in the solution itself if it is apparent. David Reynolds from Reynolds Metals exemplified this kind of leadership in the recycling of aluminum. George David, CEO of Technologies Corporation, is also preemptively leading change through SBD initiatives and his 10X initiatives.
- *The champion* is a senior manager or professional who has assumed, or has been given, the overall corporate responsibility for resolving an impact. This approach is especially useful when the impact cuts across many products, product lines, and even business units. It is also relevant for situations where the solution is multifaceted and requires new technologies, new products, and/or new processes. The champion leads change and drives the invention of the solution.
- *The advocate* gathers information about the impact and the related internal aspects. As a team or an individual, the advocate works to achieve consensus on the issues throughout the enterprise, and focuses on aligning the external views of the solution with the internal capabilities and resources.
- *The manager* is usually the individual manager or designated professional within whose area of responsibility the impact falls. The manager may be the product manager, the facility director, the vice president in charge of

operations, etc. Impact assessment and management is typically considered a duty of managing.

- *The facilitator* simply keeps track of information and data about the impacts. This approach usually employs an individual or small group that compiles the organizational knowledge pertaining to the issues. The individual or team may take initiative to make improvements.

Leadership is critical in tracking, assessing, and understanding impacts. The organizational design for such activities should be built into the management system. Organizational design should allow management, teams, and individuals the freedom to seek to resolve the implications and consequences of impacts. At 3M, for example, employees are given the flexibility to spend some of their time to initiate and manage innovation programs including 3M's famous "Pollution Prevention Pays" initiative that originated in 1975 and led to significant reductions in wastes streams and negative impacts over the following decades.

As stated above, the assignment of direct or indirect responsibility for selected impacts depends on the nature of the impacts and the expected solution. Certain impacts are related to the entire product line and have to be addressed on a macro-basis. Pratt & Whitney (hereafter, P&W) has a "Green Engine" program that examines the impacts of P&W's turbine engines and makes recommendations for improving the environmental impacts of the products. Other impacts may be isolated to a given plant or location. One of the major concerns at Anheuser–Busch's (hereafter, A–B) brewery in Los Angeles, for example, is the availability of clean water. The company has a team of professionals managing every aspect of the procurement, use, recycling, and discharge of water at that location.

In a NPD situation, specific issues, concerns, or impacts can be delegated to design teams who develop options for eliminating or mitigating the problems. For instance, during the design of the *USS Virginia*, Electric Boat established the "Environmental Compliance Team," a departmental-level group that studied numerous environmental impacts (known and suspected) to develop alternative solutions for the overall design to reduce the potential impacts over the product life and to improve EoL considerations, especially environmental problems during dismantling.

The actual approaches are probably less important than the notion of establishing corporate, business unit, product, and/or process responsibilities for mitigating impacts. It is the fiduciary responsibility of senior management to understand and manage impacts in the most prudent and effective ways possible. Clearly, many impacts cannot be cured instantaneously and require long-term commitment and effort. However, for every significant concern there should be a mitigation plan and a party (or parties) assigned to carry it out.

The severity and the likelihood of impacts

The difference between significance and severity is often subtle. Severity can be viewed as one step beyond significance. It relates to the consequences of impacts on the corporation, its supply networks, customers, and other constituencies, and the implications they may have on the business environment and the natural world. For instance, the potential impacts of climate change are debatable. While some impacts appear positive, the prevailing view holds that the majority of the potential impacts are negative. As a result, most corporations have identified climate change as a significant concern. However, the potential consequences are more severe in certain locations than in others. For instance, coastal areas a few meters above sea level are more easily impacted by small increases in ocean levels than are the mountain ranges. Increasing global temperatures may have significant impacts on the interior of the continents, such as disruptions on agriculture and depletion of water resources, but catastrophic (i.e. severe) impacts at the seashore.

As this example indicates, severity involves the criticality or gravity of the impact. This is often measured on a scale of one to ten, with one being negligible and ten being catastrophic. Impacts that have the potential to exhibit severe consequences should be assessed in detail and mitigated to the greatest extent possible. However, the risks to humankind and the environment associated with any impacts depend not only on the severity of the impact, but also on the probability of its occurrence. The severity could be extremely high, but if the probability is very low, the risk is only modest at most. A large meteor hitting the earth is often cited as an example of such an extremely unlikely event that would have major consequences if it did occur. In his book, *Inevitable Surprise*, Peter Schwartz, Chairman of the Global Business Network, discusses just such a "final calamity."[6] While such impacts would be catastrophic the concerns are relatively low because the probability of such an event is deemed to be remote.

Risk is the measure of harm that can be expected from an impact with a particular level of severity and an assumed or calculated probability of occurrence. In simple terms, the risk is the product of the severity and the probability of occurrence. High severity combined with a high probability of occurrence (one in ten) results in high risks

$$Risk = Severity \times Probability$$

Moreover, the risk of a specific harmful impact increases as the number in the population increases. The Poisson distribution of low-probability events deals with rare occurrences. However, often the expected number of opportunities for such events is not small because the population is large. For example, if the probability of being involved an automobile accident is once for every 200,000 km driven, then the expected number of accidents is relatively large if the population drives 10 billion km per year. The expected number of accidents in a year would be 50,000.

While there are numerous traditional quantitative and qualitative techniques used to assess the risks of any given impact, there is a special case that warrants consideration: it is the case where the severity is unknown and the probability of occurrence is unknown as well. This case is more likely to occur when developing new-to-the-world technologies and products. The lack of experience and the inability to think through all of the possible scenarios during technology and product development programs make it impossible to determine all of the potential impacts, their severity and probability of occurrence. For example, hybrid automobiles or fuel-cell powered vehicles are relatively new. Certain phenomena, such as a failure of the battery or hydrogen system, may take several years to manifest. Since this type of vehicle is new, the manufacturers or responsible agencies do not have full knowledge about what could go wrong, the probabilities of occurrences, and how they would handle the problems. The logic-based precautionary principle suggests that they should conduct an extensive amount of product and application testing to validate their claims about the products and unearth any hidden defects or potential problems.

The histories of previous products and processes and the fact that most changes are incremental make it possible to anticipate many impacts. There is usually a general understanding of the expected concerns and how the corporation must respond. However, impact assessment is about finding and mitigating the unknown difficulties as well as the obvious problems.

Reassessing needs and objectives

Reassessing the needs of constituencies and the objectives of the corporation is a pivotal step in the process of selecting the impacts to mitigate. In an ideal world, every impact would be selected. However, recognizing that there are limits to the financial and human resources available to execute improvement programs, it is imperative that the most crucial programs be implemented quickly and the less important ones follow as soon as possible. The process is iterative. During the inventory assessment and impact assessment phases, changes may occur or new knowledge may be acquired that provides insights about the choices to be made.

It is critical that corporations formulate and implement solutions that are aligned with the expectations of customers, stakeholders, and the other constituents of the business environment. Most importantly, solutions have to reflect the needs of the future as well as the expectations or problems of the present. Too often problem solving simply exchanges one problem for another. Through analysis and understanding, LCA attempts to break this pattern of simplistic problem solving (linear thinking, one problem at a time) and move toward holistic solutions that create a more sustainable position.

Reassessing the needs of the corporation and its constituents includes ensuring that government mandates are fully met. While this seems to be an obvious step, inventory and impact assessments may uncover information that triggers a new regulatory requirement. Such discoveries require actions on the part of the corporation to achieve compliance. For example, the corporation may not have been aware of the use of certain heavy metals in the construction of vendor-supplied electronic devices. If the corporation sells its products in the European Union, this discovery means that corrective actions will be immediately required to bring the products into compliance with regulations. Once the discovery is made, the corporation cannot plead ignorance. Additionally, a petroleum company that is shipping huge quantities of crude oil using supertankers cannot contend that it was unprepared for a spill because it had not had any occurrences in the past. It should be prepared for spills because they have happened to others, and could happen to them. Ignorance is a weak excuse: the failure to connect new knowledge with required actions is unacceptable.

Screening and selecting improvement initiatives

Screening potential action plans is an open-ended step that, again, depends on the situation. The needs and wants of customers and constituencies, the objectives of the corporation, and the principles of SBD provide guidance for establishing screening criteria. Practitioners should also use the significance and severity criteria for making choices. Most importantly, the LCA definition can be used to measure the urgency for improvements and the viability of the desired outcomes.

In general, improvement initiatives should lead to meaningful gains that are sustainable over time. They should be balanced, focusing on the triad of social, economic, and environmental concerns in concert with business-related objectives. While producing zero defects and zero burdens is a theoretical dream, in the practical world it is important to have great accomplishments in addition to great dreams. Plans for outstanding results have to be tempered with the realization that actions require time, effort, and money. There has to be a commitment to taking action and following through to completion. In many cases (depending on the urgency of the solution), it is more important to select initiatives that will be implemented properly and on a timely basis than to have large numbers of very aggressive initiatives that linger forever.

A simple approach to selecting potential action plans is to rank all of the target impacts in order of severity or risk and significance. This allows the corporation to retain all the candidate initiatives for eventual implementation. As conditions and trends in the business environment change over time, priorities may change, and the lower-ranking initiatives may move up the list. The disadvantage of this inclusive approach, however, is that the list of inactivated initiatives may imply that the corporation is unable or unwilling to deal with many of its impacts that have been identified as important. This could lead to difficulties in that the corporation had identified problems but that it had then failed to take action.

Ultimately, each corporation has to select the most appropriate criteria for selecting improvement initiatives. Table 11.4 provides a ranking example, but does not indicate a precise method. It shows the rating on one initiative that would be compared with the rating of others to determine the relative ranking between all of the potential initiatives. This suggests that scores that are relatively close are essentially equal and should be treated the same. On the other hand, if there is a large difference between two potential or proposed initiatives, then the one with the larger score would have a higher priority.

This is one of many such constructs that may help decision-makers. Great care has to be used to ensure that the data used are accurate and that the ranking is unbiased.

The ranking may be sufficient to prioritize the candidates, but is truly meaningful only if all appropriate categories and elements are included. Table 11.4 provides an example that is not comprehensive; it therefore provides a relative sense rather than an absolute sense of the rankings. In such a case, the first priority grouping might include candidates with the highest severity numbers regardless of the overall score of the criteria. The second-ranked grouping might be those candidates with the highest potential to cause difficulties for the enterprise – i.e. those with the highest calculated risks (not including severity). The third grouping might be

Table 11.4. Ranking candidate improvement initiatives

	Risk (X) Criteria (10 = high; 1 = low)	Significance (Y) Criteria (5 = high; 1 = low)						
	X	1	2	3	4	5	X × Y	Comments
Resource depletion								
• Total mass required	3		✓				6	
• Efficiency/yield	4			✓			12	
• Toxic substances	8		✓				16	
• Availability/Strategic importance	1		✓				2	
Social implications								
• Meeting expected benefits	9			✓			27	
• Negative consequences	6				✓		24	
• Longevity of life cycle	3			✓			9	
• Performance/price	5			✓			15	
• Reliability	5				✓		20	
Waste generation/Degradation								
• Solid residues	3			✓			9	
• Liquid residues	6			✓			18	
• Gaseous residues	8				✓		32	
• Hazardous wastes	9			✓			27	
• Disposal aspects (incineration)	5		✓				10	
• Accidents/Spills	3			✓			9	
• Packaging aspects	1				✓		4	
Production/Procurement								
• Production cost	7			✓			21	
• Production capabilities	3				✓		12	
• Supply chain impacts	8				✓		32	
Economic considerations								
• Investment requirements	4			✓			12	
• Low unit cost potential	5				✓		20	
• Product risk	9			✓			27	
• Process risk	9		✓				18	
• Residual value	2			✓			6	
Stakeholders								
• Potential impacts	9			✓			27	
• Relationships	3				✓		12	
Infrastructure								
• Supportive	5			✓			15	
Related Industries								
• Supportive	5				✓		20	
Total							**462**	

candidates that can best achieve social, economic, and environmental improvements. It is fundamentally sound to implement initiatives with these broad benefits. The last grouping would include all of the other potential initiatives, listed in order of the ranking number or overall importance.

The advantage of using a ranking approach is that the logic for decision-making is established up-front, making decisions defendable. The disadvantage of using the ranking approach is that criteria are often subjective and the ranking can be skewed to reflect the desires or predetermined views of management or functional groups. It is difficult to create purely objective mechanisms for ranking and selecting candidates. The preferred approach is to establish the selection criteria early on, and use a systematic approach for selecting candidates. A logic-based approach eliminates randomness and leads to consistency and effectiveness. The methods focus on creating a logic-based approach that uses evidence and objective criteria and does not rely on opinions and personal perspectives. While insights and judgment are always important, the ultimate approach should provide the rationale for the selection process and be based on a logic that is defendable to customers, stakeholders, and other constituents.

Improvement assessment

Overview

Before spending any time or money on improving impacts, senior management or the responsible party(ies) or entity(ies) should make a preliminary determination about the viability of the product or process given the status of the impacts. If the impacts are so severe that corrective actions are extremely costly, not feasible, or impossible, the decision may be made to discontinue the product or process. While it is never simple to eliminate or phase out a product or dramatically reinvent a process, the return on such strategies may be much higher in the long term than that of trying to address the severe impacts. This path is particularly powerful for corporations that are aggressively moving toward SBD and quickly want to eliminate as many defects and burdens as possible.

On a corporate basis, continuous improvement of every product and process is the most plausible strategy for making long-term competitive gains, as well as enhancing its social, economic, and environmental positions.

It is imperative to minimize weaknesses across product lines, facilities, operations, and practices. As competition becomes more intense, weaknesses become the Achilles' heel in achieving and sustaining competitive advantages. *Improvement assessment determines the gains that can be realized through strategic and tactical actions.*

Improvement assessment involves responding to the impact assessment and the prioritization of the required initiatives. It focuses on the "how" while the latter focuses on the "what." There are two broad categories for addressing the required solutions. They are strategic actions, generally using innovation and development programs, and tactical actions, involving improving the operating system and its processes.

Strategic actions focus on innovation programs and improvements that are more revolutionary. They include:

- Instituting *new business models* that improve the effectiveness and efficiency of managing the business environment, minimizing defects, and mitigating impacts
- Creating *innovative clean technologies* that eliminate the impacts associated with old technologies
- Developing *sustainable product platforms* and product lines that mitigate the impacts of existing products and processes
- Improving the *links and communications* with supply networks and strategic partners to reduce impacts wherever they exist
- Deploying *sustainable marketing* approaches that openly and honestly promote the benefits and inform about the negatives
- Creating an *infrastructure* for reusing and recycling products, components, and materials, and for sharing information across the stages of the life cycle.

Tactical improvements are the incremental changes that mitigate impacts without fundamentally altering the underlying technologies or products. They focus on products and processes and include:

- Increasing the life of product platforms and products themselves, thus making the inputs and outputs more effective on a per-unit basis
- Improving the quality, reliability, and longevity of products and processes so that fewer premature failures occur
- Improving the efficiency and effectiveness of processes so that less waste is generated and more output is achieved
- Increasing the integration of suppliers, distributors, and customers in order to minimize losses and wastes
- Reducing the amount of materials required to produce the products

- Substituting benign materials for toxic substances, as well as using materials that are easily reused and recycled
- Enhancing the material life cycle through closed-looped recycling, thus getting more value from the inputs and outputs
- Improving the public and market awareness about the life cycle of products and processes through effective communications and disclosure of technical information.

The strategies for instituting strategic improvements were discussed in chapter 3. They generally require a significant commitment and investment, but often lead to more substantial and sustainable improvements and long-term competitive advantages. The tactical improvements listed are but a microcosm of the specific actions used to achieve sustainable development. They are generally simpler and easier to implement, but may fail to eliminate the cause of the impacts.

Strategic and tactical actions are both necessary for effective impact improvements. Often the exact mix depends on the product life cycle. If the technologies and products are relatively new, corporations usually make incremental improvements to enhance positions and correct defects and burdens. Unless there are serious strategic concerns, these kinds of evolutionary changes are preferred since the corporation has to protect its investments and receive an adequate return before it has the financial resources to launch another development program. On the other hand, if the technologies and products are old and close to obsolescence, spending financial resources to improve them is often a waste of time and money. In such cases, incremental improvements may do very little to make a difference in the competitive arenas and, ultimately, may waste resources. Revolutionary changes may be more appropriate and beneficial.

Developing and implementing tactical improvements

Tactical improvements include all of the methods used in implementing pollution prevention initiatives discussed in chapter 8, along with the initiatives for improving the tangible and intangible aspects of products, processes, and practices. Such initiatives are based on creating less pollution, less wastes, and increased efficiency and effectiveness. They realize quick gains that achieve recognition and reward without having to justify profound change. These initiatives lead to positive business and environmental outcomes, and allow the corporation to build momentum toward even greater improvements. The following examples are simple initiatives that can reduce the impacts of existing products and processes:

- Develop improvements that reduce material resource use and energy consumption. Reducing the size and weight of products translates into less input and waste across the life cycle. For example, more efficient and powerful electric motors translate into better small appliances that consume less electricity.

- Phase out toxic substances, especially those that produce hazardous wastes or those that have known or suspected negative health effects. Toxic substances create impacts at every stage of the life cycle. The simple solution is to eliminate their use.

- Increase the longevity and durability of products and packaging. Investing in higher quality and reliability pays off in the long term. This includes making products repairable and reusable. This approach reduces the impacts per unit – for example, if an automobile has a life of twelve years instead of eight or achieves an average usage of 300,000 km instead of 200,000, the 50 percent improvement means that only two automobiles are required to drive 600,000 km instead of three. Moreover, it significantly reduces the quantity of impacts.

- Enhanced product performance, to ensure that the product does more than the competitor's alternative does. Make the product provide more per lb, more per unit energy consumed, etc.

- Use recycled material and post-consumer content in products and packaging. The use of 25–33 percent post-consumer recycled content is widespread. Such initiatives reduce the need for virgin materials upstream and eliminate a proportional amount of inputs and outputs and associated impacts.

- Communicate with consumers about the applications of the product and its restrictions. While most corporations are effective at informing potential customers about the benefits of their product, making the limitations transparent to buyers, users, and stakeholders is an evolving practice that is typically driven by regulations and not by corporate policy.

These suggested initiatives represent only a small number of improvement opportunities that can lead to incremental changes. SBD involves continually making such improvements across the enterprise and requires the efforts of suppliers, distributors, customers, and stakeholders.

Acquiring and providing information are essential to the effective integration of the system and the ability of the system to reduce, mitigate, or eliminate impacts. Suppliers have to be informed and educated about the initiatives and have to understand their roles in the improvement process. For instance, Toyota and Honda both have extensive supplier development programs that allow suppliers to improve quality and environmental performance.

The physical aspects of impacts are only one side of the picture. Societal values represent an important, yet less tangible, piece of the equation. Perceptions about impacts on the quality of life and the environment are critical factors in achieving superior and sustainable product and process positions. People expect to enjoy the beauty and diversity of the natural world. They want the benefits of technology, products, and services without feeling guilty about the negative impacts.

The essence of improvement assessment is to systematically understand impacts and make every effort to improve their consequences. The philosophical underpinnings of SBD do not demand perfection. They do require efforts to improve positions, mitigate impacts, and enhance the future prospects of the enterprise and its constituencies.

The benefits of improvement assessment

The enterprise involves a complex network of interfaces between the corporation and all of its supply networks, customers, stakeholders, competitors, strategic partners, and various parties in related industries and the infrastructure. Improvements anywhere in the system mean enhancements in the SBD of the corporation. Reducing impacts increases quality, eco-efficiency, economic viability, social acceptance, environmental consciousness, and long-term survivability. The following are some of the tangible and intangible benefits of impact improvement:

- Improved value proposition through lower costs, enhanced economics, and reduced liabilities, defects, and burdens.
- Enhanced public perceptions of corporation through the mitigation of impacts. Impacts negatively affect people, other species, or objects in the business environment. In the case of water pollution, a corporation that fails to treat its water effluents negatively affects society.
- Preemption of environmental regulations and requirements eases the burdens on the corporation. With less waste and fewer liabilities to worry about, management can spend time on more productive investments.
- Enhanced information can then be communicated to customers.
- There are savings in time and money as problems are corrected.

- Prevention programs can be easily incorporated into the management system using design and development methodologies rather than corrective actions.
- Discovery of hidden defects and burdens before they become apparent in the marketplace. Taking preventive action can enhance reputation and avoid reputation-damaging corrective actions.

The most profound benefit of improvement assessment is that decisions are based on objective information and data. The corollary is that uncertainty about potential problems and difficulties is significantly reduced. The objective proof of the pluses and minuses of products and processes can be used to convince customers about the benefits and value they receive. The use of LCA details may even change the paradigm in marketing. Credible evidence from LCA may force competitors to follow suit on improvements. Certainly, the facts provided by one producer/marketer make it more difficult for competitors to use subjective information.

LCA and program evaluation

Revisiting the value proposition

In today's world of high-tech products that are designed and produced using six-sigma methods, the ability to enhance the value proposition of a new product is becoming increasingly more difficult. Historically, corporations focused on the positive side of the value equation. However, the value proposition is a function of both the positive and the negative effects. If the positive side of the equation has had significant improvements, it becomes difficult to continue to make additional meaningful gains. For example, Intel continues to make its microprocessor more beneficial to users, even though many users employ only a fraction of the power available in their PCs. In this situation, the real opportunity for improving products lies in eliminating defects and burdens. Given the impacts of waste streams, toxic substances, inefficiencies, liabilities, disposal problems, resource and energy consumption, and others, there are numerous ways in which the value proposition can be enriched.

Minimizing uncertainties and risks

Uncertainty is an inherent part of business. While the greatest uncertainty usually pertains to the business environment, uncertainty about products and processes have plagued corporations over the years as well. Many major disasters, such as the *Exxon Valdez* oil spill and the toxic emission at Bhopal, were due to defects in the operating system and not just caused by shifts in the conditions and trends in the business environment. Similarly, products such as cigarettes, asbestos, and lead-based paints were known to have negative effects. Yet the companies involved did not aggressively examine the implications of their products, or seek solutions to these defects. They remained uncertain about the ramifications, including the social and legal aspects. Their short-sightedness ultimately threatened the survivability of their enterprises.

Although LCA takes time, effort, and money, the information it provides reduces uncertainties and improves confidence in decision-making and ultimately makes investing in products and processes easier. One of the greatest challenges in business is selecting the right new products for commercializing or redesigning existing ones. By reducing uncertainty, the full benefits of each option can be seen and compared.

Risks are the natural consequences of doing business: they are ever-present. If there were no risks, rewards would be small, and the number of competitors would be large. Outstanding management must still seek to mitigate risks in order to direct operations as successfully as possible.

Risks can be divided into the following five key categories:
- Changing conditions and trends in the business environment (business and competition)
- Uncertainties and unknowns about existing technologies, products, and processes (technical)
- The latent effects of customer and stakeholder preferences (market)
- Uncertainties and unknowns in new technologies, products, and processes (innovation)
- The capabilities of the enterprise and its value networks to exceed expectations and perform in accordance with mandates, standards, and protocols on a global basis (strategic).

While investing money in new technologies, products, and processes was once viewed as risky failing to do so today carries its own significant risk. Risks are an inherent part of making decisions or failing to make decisions.

LCA, however, is an effective risk mitigation methodology that allows corporations to keep pace with the changing business environment. As it examines each stage of the life of a product or process, it does so in the light of the forces driving change in the business environment and the wants and needs of constituents. Inventory and impact assessment provide insights about how to create better solutions and improve the product delivery system. One of the most crucial aspects of LCA is its ability to discover the means to make improvements before customers and stakeholders demand them.

LCA is effective for new-to-the-world technologies and products as well. Given the huge investments normally required to commercialize new products, it is incumbent on the corporation to ensure that those investments will endure for the intended time horizon. Finding defects and burdens during the early phases of NPD allows management to take action to address them early, when it is easier and less costly, and thereby reduce the risk of the investment.

Protecting the reputation of the corporation, however, is perhaps the most important outcome of LCA, with the resultant mitigation of impacts and improvements in strategic position. While LCA is time-consuming and costly, the improvements in corporate image often justify the expense.

Performance evaluation and metrics

Evaluating technologies, products, and processes involves determining the impacts and comparing those impacts with established baselines. The standard comparison is with equivalent competitive products. Performance evaluation using LCA can be divided into sixteen environmental categories and uses selected performance measures or metrics to ascertain the relative merit. Each performance measure is further subdivided into subcategories or specific impact areas. This approach offers a balanced, multidimensional mechanism for evaluating performance so that progress toward achieving LCA objectives in one area is not made at the expense of performance in another.

Table 11.5 identifies the main categories and subcategories of performance measures across the enterprise.

The design and development of a performance evaluation system related to LCA can be linked directly to the assessment process, or it can be part of a separate system following corporation policies or international standards such as ISO 14031. Much of the data and information to support the performance evaluation process (emissions rates, waste stream flows, risk assessments, financial data, and input-output data) may already exist or may be derived from the LCA. Information and data of known and verifiable quality can provide a reasonable basis for evaluating performance. Appropriate quality assurance functions must be in place to ensure the validity of the data collection methodologies, modeling techniques, etc. This is particularly important if the information is used in the external reporting process.

Table 11.5. Selected performance measures across the enterprise

Primary category	Example impact areas	Selected indicators
Corporate management system	Equity/Stability/Insights	
Management system model	*Reputation and governance*	
Sustainable development leadership	Policies, principles and philosophies	Frequency of meetings with leadership
Business Integration	Objectives and guidelines	No. of related documents
Management commitment	Responsibility and accountability	% of management educated/ aligned
Strategies and direction	Technologies, products, and processes	% of strategies based on SBD
Resources and capabilities	Strategic programs	% of corporate resources committed
Corporate citizenship	Philanthropy	Amount of giving relative to ability
Corporate capabilities		
Knowledge and analytical skills	Education, training, and learning	No. of employees educated and trained
Health and safety considerations	Awareness, skills, and acceptance	% of processes with assured safety/health
Innovativeness	Creativity and solutions	No. of new solutions
SMS	Value creation/Eco-efficiency	
Customer satisfaction		
Value proposition	Customer perception of expectations	% of transactions that exceed value
Customer needs, wants, and expectations	Customer satisfaction	% of delighted customers
Reliability and longevity	Long-term satisfaction	% of products that are early failures
Customer involvement	Awareness and participation	No. of customers involved in meetings
Stakeholder management		
Social responsiveness	Community involvement/ participation	% of facilities with awareness program
Communications – disclosures/reporting	Annual reporting	No. of areas covered in report
Community relations	Communications	No. of releases per year
Stakeholder involvement	Awareness and participation	No. of stakeholders involved in programs
Emergency planning and response	Emergency preparedness	No. of employees trained/ response time
Improvements in impacts	Enhancements/corrective actions	No. of impacts mitigated per year
Compliance	Enforcement actions	No. of violations/amount of fines

Table 11.5. (cont.)

Primary category	Example impact areas	Selected indicators
Strategic programs		
Technological innovation	New business development programs	No. of new SBD businesses
Technology development	New technology development programs	No. of SBD technology developments
Product innovation	NPD programs	No. of SBD new products
Process innovation	New process development programs	No. of SBD new processes
LCA	Impact and improvement assessments	No. of LCAs performed
New technologies and products		
Clean technologies	New technology development programs	% of clean technologies
Zero-emissions products	Product innovations with zero defects	% of products with zero defects
Value networks		
Strategic partners	Integration of partners	No. of fully integrated partners
Social contracts	Value contribution	% of involvement/No. of contracts
Economic and financial		
Wealth creation	Investment level	No. of new initiatives/level of spending
Improvements	Improvement programs	Total money spent
Capital investment	Environmental costs	% of revenue on such costs
Cash flow and profitability	Capital investments	Rates of return
Product delivery system	"Logic-based" precautionary principles	
Supply networks		
Cradle-to-grave thinking	Linkages and frameworks	% of supply networks linked
Supply chain integration	Information flow	% of required information links available
LCT	Cradle-to-grave	No. of supply chains fully linked
Supplier development	Supplier and contractor management	No. of awareness and training programs
Existing products		
Safety and responsibility	Level of assurance and communications	No. of product recalls
Resource utilization	Reduction in material utilization	% of reduction in mass per product
Waste generation	Improvement in yields/toxicity	% of reduction in footprint
Reuse and recycling	Secondary applications	% of products recycled/% of content
Use of recycled materials	Material recycling	% of materials used that is recycled
Existing processes		
Toxic substances	Hazardous materials	No. of toxic substances
Resource efficiency	Resource conservation	% of material reduction
Energy consumption	Energy conservation	% of energy consumption reduction

Table 11.5. (cont.)

Primary category	Example impact areas	Selected indicators
Prevention and risk mitigation		
Pollution prevention	Pollution prevention program	No. of programs
Conservation and preservation	Corrective and preventive action	No. of actions
Waste minimization	Environmental impact minimized	% of total wastes reduced per year
Risk reduction, environmental	Responsibility demonstrated	No. of adverse events and incidents per year
Operations		
Air emissions	Air emissions identification	Total amount of emissions
Water effluents	Wastewater identification	% of water that is untreated
Solid residual waste programs	Process waste identification	Efficiency of programs
Hazardous wastes	Oil and hazardous waste spill prevention	Reliability of processes
Accidental releases (incidents)	Preparedness and prevention	No. of sites fully prepared
Environmental		
Ecology	Habitat	% of reduction in land use
Water quality	Water utilization	% of reduction in water use
Air quality	Air quality nonrenewable resources	% of reduction in air emissions

Each major category should have at least one metric or indicator to measure the catagory's performance. The performance evaluation system and the associated metrics or indicators should be linked to the most important issues and impacts. They should also be compatible with the elements included in the environmental audit system.

Assessing performance in each of the areas presents huge challenges since not all business units or products are comparable. Metrics or indicators may be characterized in a number of ways: (1) absolute values; (2) relative rating; (3) aggregate factors; (4) qualitative; and (5) indices. The more complicated the indicator, the more difficult it is to interpret. Metrics or indicators can be used to highlight the high-risk aspects of a category, or where impacts are expected to be severe.

The LCA framework is designed to provide a consistent format for an authoritative overview of performance. The approach enables performance to be measured:

• With respect to how well the corporation is meeting objectives, targets, standards, and mandates (ranked as "exceeds," "meets," "has some deficiencies," or "requires immediate corrective action")

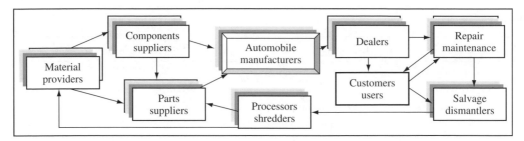

Figure 11.2   LCA framework of direct impacts in the automobile industry

- Relative to industry or global corporations that are peers (ranked as "best," "top 10%," "mid-range," or "below norm")
- Relative to other sites, facilities, and operations (ranked as "high," "medium," "low," or "bottom") and/or
- Relative to other defined benchmarks (ranked as "best," "equal," "below average," or "worst").

Most importantly, there are many external organizations that evaluate corporate performance and establish ranking systems to categorize corporations in terms of their SBD effectiveness. For instance, Innovest and the DJSI rank companies in terms of "best in class," "top tier," "middle tier," or "bottom tier."

Figure 11.2 shows the simplified LCA framework with only direct impacts. The primary entities are the automobile manufacturers, the customers, and the users. Their blocks are depicted differently to show their significance. Material and component suppliers, dealers, and repair entities support producers and customers. Dismantlers and processors support afterlife considerations.

Metrics are used to examine the absolute and relative differences between manufacturers at various points in the product and the relative efficiency of products and processes. They also allow practitioners to determine the most suitable options to pursue, the effectiveness of one product versus another, and changes in positions and waste streams over time. However, the most important metrics are those that relate to the principles of sustainable development. They include measures of value creation, eco-efficiency, use of the logic-based precautionary principle, equity, and stability. The following are examples of ten metrics that can help corporations understand the LCA implications for SBD:

- *Value creation across time*   The ratio of economic and social inputs to the longevity of the outputs. For example, houses built using quality materials, excellent construction methods, and proper insulation generally last longer and require fewer major repairs. In contrast, poorly constructed products often are damaged and discarded before the original human and economic investment is recovered through beneficial use. Relevant questions to consider include:

- What percentage of the material flow across all of the stages remains after a designated period of time?
- What percentage of the product fails prematurely?
- How is value determined? What are the key components to the value proposition?

- *Eco-efficiency across the supply network*   The ratio of a material contained in the final desired part, component, or product to the sum of the inputs for that material across a number of stages of the life cycle. For example, 4 lb of bauxite are required to produce 1 lb of aluminum. In producing an aluminum rotor blade out of a solid block of metal for a helicopter, more than 90 percent of the metal is milled away, leaving only 10 percent of the material in the final part. The key questions include:

  - What percentage of the material flow across all of the stages remains in the final product?
  - How much of the mass flow is converted to waste streams requiring abatement, treatment, and disposal?
  - How much energy is consumed in all of the subprocesses to create the product?
  - What stage has the worst efficiency in terms of inputs, outputs, and energy use?
  - What percentage of the inputs are recycled materials?

- *Eco-efficiency during applications*   The ratio of beneficial outputs to the mass or energy consumed during use. For example, the fuel efficiency of an automobile is a prime factor in both resource depletion and environmental degradation. The standard internal combustion engine automobile with all of its engine, aerodynamic drag, power train, rolling resistance, braking, and idle losses is approximately 12.5–15 percent efficient.[7] The key questions include:

  - What is the overall efficiency of the product or device, especially if it consumes large quantities of energy while in use?
  - What is the expected life of the product and the measure of resource utilization per unit of time?

- *Eco-efficiency at end of life*   The ratio of the parts of the product that are reused or recycled to the entire original product produced, in terms of either numbers or gross weight. For example, approximately 60 percent of the aluminum cans used in the United States are recycled. BMW's system has the capability to recycle approximately 85 percent of its cars. The key questions include:

- What percentage of the parts and components is reused?
- What percentage of the weight of the product is recycled? Is there a closed loop?

- *"Logic-based" precautionary principle*   The fraction of investments that are used to prevent problems from occurring or to ensure that negatives are mitigated as quickly as possible. For example, emergency preparedness is like buying insurance and hoping that it is never used. The money spent on exploring ways to handle climate change issues currently fits into this area. The key questions include:
  - How much of the corporation's investment portfolio is spent on mitigating impacts? Preventing pollution? Exploring open-ended global issues?
  - What investments are being made in minimizing accidental spills, accidents that affect health and safety, and unexpected negative events?

- *Equity from a customer's perspective*   The relative quality of the products and services from a customer perspective versus that of competitors' offerings. The fraction of product output that meets or exceeds goals and standards is a key metric. Questions to consider include:
  - What is the quality level of products versus that of the competition?
  - How many products fail to meet expectations?
  - How much money is spent correcting defects and problems? Fulfilling warranty claims?
  - How many customers' claims are not honored?

- *Equity from a stakeholders' perspective*   The fraction of products and operations (facilities) that are accepted by stakeholders as meeting or exceeding their requirements relative to that of peers in the industry or among global corporations. The following are the key areas:
  - What is the corporation's position in terms of customer satisfaction or image compared to its peers?
  - How many critical issues is the corporation managing?
  - Are the corporation's concerns and impacts transparent to stakeholders?
  - Does the corporation report and disclose both the positive and negative aspects of its technologies, products, processes, and facilities?

- *Equity from society's perspective*   The fraction of products and operations (facilities) that fully comply with regulatory mandates. The numerical ranking of the corporation, its products and processes in terms of social responsiveness and emergency planning. Questions to consider include:

- How quickly does the corporation respond to issues, negative events, or emergencies?
- How many noncompliance issues does the corporation have?
- Are permits obtained in an open process? Do all stakeholders have a voice?
- Are local citizens provided with opportunities to become involved with the corporation's operations?

- *Stability through SBD and enterprise thinking*   The fraction of new technologies, new products, and new processes that were developed using SBD principles and the percentage of programs that focus on enterprise thinking. The key questions are:
  - How do the corporation's SBD programs compare to those of the competition?
  - How many of the corporation's programs are in line with SBD goals?
- *Insights through SBD*   The fraction of concerns and impacts that have been mitigated through LCA and the percentage of products and processes that have been improved via LCA. Consider:
  - How does the corporation reduce impacts? Have the worst products and processes been eliminated?
  - How many impacts have been eliminated?

This list is intended to be edifying, not comprehensive. Improvement assessment involves integrating the value networks for the enterprise. It is also about capturing sustainable competitive advantages for the corporation, providing the best solutions possible for the business, and having outstanding brands and products for customers, stakeholders, and the product delivery system. These means provide above-average margins and excellent cash flow that result in improved equity for shareholders and outstanding value creation for everyone.

Improvement assessment depends on the intellectual capital of the organization and the integration of the management systems within and outside the organization. It also depends on the innovativeness of the participants and leadership of the senior management. In the long term, ongoing success requires solid relationships with customers, stakeholders, suppliers, distributors, and all of the other constituents. Success is built on providing total satisfaction and enhancing the organization's reputation for honest, ethical, balanced, and socially responsible behaviors. Ultimately, the long-term objective is to achieve sustainable success.

Summary

Business is a social structure that is intended to produce positive outcomes. Successful corporations make significant contributions to society, their customers, employees, and owners. SBD is a long-term journey toward sustainable success. Global corporations must lead others in this direction because they have the resources, capabilities, and the ethical responsibility to create solutions, not problems.

Great corporations understand the complexities of managing global businesses, sophisticated enterprises, and their management systems. Management recognizes that it must face and address all challenges, including those for which it has indirect involvement or responsibility. Moreover, there are certain issues, problems, or concerns that are global and require everyone's attention regardless of one's own culpability. For instance, climate change is an international issue legitimized by the 1992 Rio Conference and the 1997 Kyoto Conference. While there is significant debate about the causes, the issue remains at the forefront of social, political, and environmental agendas. Some of the proposed solutions will mean dramatic consequences for future generations, including economic and life style ramifications.

The "preemptive" corporation recognizes the importance of such issues and their role, as part of the international business environment, in addressing them. Leading corporations examine the basis for these concerns and their causes, obtaining valid scientific information about the phenomena. These leading corporations seek to resolve the issues or mitigate their consequences and create value for every participant.

LCA plays a vital role in understanding these kinds of situations and developing courses of action for managing the implications of business over time. It is one of the most significant constructs for achieving sustainable development. The very essence of LCA is to discover everything possible about the situation in order that corporations may exploit the positive, and mitigate the negative. Taking a holistic approach, LCA helps to frame the issues and determine the appropriate responses. Exploring causality is critical in formulating solutions.

In the world of global business enterprises, the business environment provides opportunities, challenges, and threats. It is imperative that management understand the factual realities. While management theory has many robust constructs for dealing with business opportunities, managing the challenges and threats in the business environment lacks the same level of sophistication. LCA is a balanced methodology for understanding all of the implications of the business environment: opportunities, threats, and challenges.

Impact assessment focuses on discovering and understanding the challenges and concerns in the business environment. It is a systematic method for determining what has to be done, and prioritizing the efforts. Improvement assessment involves initiating actions to create a sustainable future and to mitigate the risks and uncertainties in the business environment. Given the complexities of the problems around the business world, the approaches and methods described represent the beginning of a long journey toward a more sustainable future rather than a definitive solution to the existing challenges.

Supplementary material

Learning objectives

Chapter 11 has the following learning objectives that are intended to guide and support students and practitioners:
- Understanding the benefits and implications of LCA.
- Understanding the Impact phase, including computational models for analyzing, interpreting, and understanding data and information.
- Understanding the Improvement phase, including how to achieve long-term gains.
- Understanding the tools and techniques, including evaluation and metrics, risk mitigation, and quality methods.

Research questions

The following are questions related to SBD in order to facilitate learning and ongoing discussion and analysis of the main topics covered in the chapter:
- What is the most important aspect of impact and improvement assessments?
- How do executives and senior management evaluate results?
- What are the best applications of LCA?
- How do practitioners start the process?

NOTES

1. Under the provision of the US Comprehensive Environmental Response, Compensation, and Liability Act, there is special treatment for a potentially responsible party if its involvement represents a *de minimis* (extremely small) case.
2. Please note that the generation of the precursors to the acid rain is a direct effect. For example, the production of sulfur dioxide from a power plant is an immediate effect. The effects of the acid rain take some time to produce a negative impact because of the naturally occurring conditions.
3. Bjørn Lomborg, *Global Crises, Global Solutions* (Cambridge: Cambridge University Press, 2004), p. 14. The amount of carbon released to the atmosphere was estimated to be 6.9 billion tons in 2000.
4. *Ibid.*, p. 13.
5. Thomas Graedel, *Streamlined Life-Cycle Assessment* (Englewood Cliffs, NJ: Prentice Hall, 1998). See appendix A and B, pp. 235–264.
6. Peter Schwartz, *Inevitable Surprises: Thinking Ahead in a Time of Turbulence* (New York: Gotham Books, 2003), p. 215. The consequences of an asteroid hitting the Earth would be catastrophic, yet most people do not think about the potential problem because of the low probability of occurrence at a given period of time. However, scientists do suggest that it is only a matter of time: it has happened before, and it will happen again.
7. *Source*: US EPA and Department of Energy (DOE).

REFERENCES

Graedel, Thomas E. (1998) *Streamlined Life-Cycle Assessment*. Englewood Cliffs, NJ: Prentice Hall

Lomborg, Bjørn (2004) *Global Crises, Global Solutions*. Cambridge: Cambridge University Press

Schwartz, Peter (2003) *Inevitable Surprises: Thinking Ahead in a Time of Turbulence* New York: Gotham Books

12 Inventing the future through enterprise thinking and sustainable business development

Introduction

SBD and enterprise thinking provide the means for creating innovative solutions to social, economic, environmental, and business challenges. SBD invites corporations to create a better future through improved and enduring outcomes.

Business opportunities and challenges in the twenty-first century are expanding dramatically as the global business environment becomes more complex and dynamic. Large corporations have become global enterprises with sophisticated technologies, products, and services that depend on resources from far-flung suppliers, distributors, partners, and allies. Customers expect and demand innovative, high-quality and cost effective products and services. Forces such as globalization, technological change, increasing stakeholder power, the rapid transfer of information, knowledge, and technology, the outsourcing of operations, and increasingly intense market expectations and competitive responses define the new global business environment. In addition, the transformation to a digital world, shrinking product life cycles, fusion of technologies, customization of expectations, increased importance of partnerships and relationships, and proliferation of information place corporations in a new and unprecedented context, requiring innovative management constructs for achieving extraordinary results and sustainable success.

Corporations responded over the twentieth century by expanding the basis for decisions, making it more inclusive and more open to external participation. Listening to external constituents and understanding their requirements are the critical mechanisms for having a comprehensive perspective for determining strategic direction. By responding to a broader slice of the real world, corporations can discover new opportunities. The great challenge is strategically aligning and integrating the internal and external dimensions to satisfy the needs and expectations of all constituencies, not just customers and shareholders. The domain of customers and stakeholders contains hundreds, if not thousands, of critical requirements that must be successfully managed and fulfilled. For example, a new pharmaceutical product has to be safe, effective, and affordable from a customer's perspective. The producer has to satisfy all of the regulatory mandates and validate every aspect of its development, production, and distribution. The physicians who prescribe the product must have complete information and knowledge about its appropriate uses and any potential side effects or concerns. The list of requirements facing the producer is extensive. With the challenges of hidden problems and uncertainties, management must ensure that every aspect has been examined and that all appropriate precautions have been taken.

Historically, the management constructs for leading change were based on piecemeal approaches or partial solutions, attacking problems one at a time or prioritizing the requirements and dealing with the most pressing ones. Today, executive management must strategize how to establish a comprehensive business model for developing complete solutions and fulfilling the vision for the future.

The premises outlined in this book are based on the principles and precepts of SBD and enterprise thinking, interrelated constructs that have to be instituted in parallel. SBD focuses corporate executives, strategists, managers, and professionals on creating value, leading change, and satisfying every requirement. It encourages a balanced perspective on meeting the needs and expectations of the business environment and achieving the strategic objectives of the corporation. In concert with enterprise thinking, SBD reaches across space and time to invent a future that is advantageous to the corporation, its customers, constituents, shareholders, and society as a whole. Together, they incorporate the essential elements of the prevailing theories and practices of business management. The choice is not one of switching from TQM methods, six-sigma quality techniques, ISO 9000/ISO 14000 management systems and the other prevailing management constructs, but rather to create an overarching, holistic management system that represents the convergence of the best approaches and practices across the entire enterprise.

Theories and methods pertaining to SBD and enterprise thinking are still being developed and improved, and the development cycle may take decades to reach maturity. Similar to the development of TQM, the process is evolutionary as innovations and improvements are compounded over time. The promise of a more comprehensive perspective of the business environment and integrated corporate responses to its opportunities and challenges offers management, professionals, and practitioners the belief that truly outstanding and balanced outcomes are possible.

This chapter examines the following topics:

- Inventing the future through positive relationships with customers, stakeholders, and other constituencies that can actually preempt the forces driving change.
- Maximizing value for everyone in order to generate cash flow, sustain profits, realize growth, provide total satisfaction, and sustain the future through learning and knowledge.
- Examining the implications of, and future directions for, the integration of enterprise thinking and SBD.
- Exploring the insights provided by leading edge, global corporations.

Inventing the future through positive relationships

Global challenges of the twenty-first century

Throughout the 1990s, new technologies and business enterprises that affect how people live and behave developed in rapid succession. The digital revolution affected almost everything from computers, telecommunications, and the Internet to automobiles, TVs, and digital cameras. Digital technologies are generally smaller, requiring fewer resources per device and lower costs. They are more reliable and more affordable because of the large volume of high-quality, inexpensive components available. Many of the new technologies are based on software that can be replicated at minimal cost and provided in many forms. For example, the world of movie rentals is transitioning from the Blockbuster stores with thousands of DVDs and videotapes to the digital world of "pay per view" where the customer never takes possession of the product. Likewise, TV is transforming from prescribed network programming to highly interactive individually selected viewing. Such examples provide a glimpse of the world of tomorrow in which outstanding solutions are achieved with negligible effects on resource depletion, degradation, and residuals on a per-use basis. Digital technologies support this kind of change and the application of clean technologies.

Embedded within the digital world is the all-encompassing Internet. Its exponential growth since 1994 has radically changed the realms of information, communication, and business transactions, and has been a prime mechanism supporting globalization. Individuals, groups, and corporations can share information using web sites, have two-way communications, and conduct business transactions, all on a virtual basis. While these capabilities are not brand new, the full implications of the Internet are still becoming apparent. During the 1990s, corporations viewed the Internet as a means to get their message out to millions of people and make them aware of products and services. It seemed to be a cost effective way of selling products and services. Indeed, the "dot.com" phenomenon exploded on the scene based on the belief that the Internet provided a low-cost means of reaching potential customers and circumventing many costly activities, and would result in huge profits. The "dot.com" bubble burst a few years later because the underlying business models overly simplified the complexities of the business environment and the requirements for satisfying customers and stakeholders. As the number of web sites escalated into millions, and the hoped-for business relationships did not materialize instantaneously, the challenge became one of building awareness and acceptance: there were simply too many sites to gain a true competitive advantage via the Internet based solely on having a web presence.

Nonetheless, the widespread sharing of information that resulted transferred significant power from producers to users and stakeholders. Customers now have more knowledge about the products that they buy; they know the costs and quality parameters and can make informed decisions. Stakeholders can easily obtain the information they require to explore their concerns. In an information-rich world, the power now rests with those who understand the implications of the information and have formulated approaches for improving their situation and leading change.

The expanding power of stakeholders is one of the most profound changes since the mid-1970s. Stakeholders are more informed than ever before about products, by-products, and waste streams. Governments have enacted legislation and promulgated regulations and directives requiring disclosure of information on emissions, effluents, waste streams, spills, and other releases from manufacturing plants, processing facilities, or mining operations. This includes information concerning past practices and the impacts of current products and processes. Moreover, public interest groups, NGOs, and other social and political advocacy groups play powerful roles in promoting public awareness of the implications, impacts, and consequences of business operations.

The rapid transfer of knowledge, technologies, and information has also affected the competitive strategies of global corporations. Historically, the inventors, developers, and producers of innovative technologies enjoyed competitive advantages for years, if not decades, until the know-how and technologies became available to other entities through the public domain. The sharing of information and data among individuals and groups on a transactional basis was a slow process. Moreover, without a ubiquitous means of communication such as the Internet, technology transfer was often in "parts and parcels" that were usually insufficient to provide the complete picture or the proprietary secrets. Most of the information and data was in fragmented formats such as two-dimensional drawings using company-specific standards rather than the prevailing CAD/CAM systems of today that use standard software and universal protocols. The mechanical systems of the early twentieth century were often unique to the originator and would require significant effort and enormous expense to translate into another system. In the digital world, all that is changed. Information and design details are easily copied and translated – indeed, piracy of software, music, movies, and other digital forms is a global problem, costing the owners of the intellectual property billions of dollars per year.

Globalization is the ongoing phenomenon of connecting businesses and their constituents, wherever they may be. It may take decades to fully understand the implications of this global connectedness, but in the meantime globalization is leveling the playing field between large corporations and small ones, businesses and stakeholders, buyers and sellers, and suppliers and producers. The rapid transfer of technologies that globalization allows enables emerging companies and mid-size corporations to participate in business endeavors traditionally dominated by global corporations. Clearly, every emerging company does not have ready access to all the propriety technologies, intellectual capital, or confidential information it may desire, but now, with the time frame for the diffusion of technology, knowledge, and technical capabilities measured in years instead of decades, its chances of obtaining the necessary resources in time to be competitive are much improved.

Developing companies in countries such as China, India, Brazil, and South Korea do not just want commonplace technologies that are near obsolescence. They desire the latest and most advanced technologies available. They want to become global competitors, not subservient suppliers or second-tier competitors. For instance, Germany enjoyed a trade surplus with China because its machine tool industry has successfully sold sophisticated machine tools that provide Chinese manufacturers with state-of-the-art operations. The Chinese companies are becoming more capable as they exploit the technological and managerial know-how they acquire from their western partners.

This increased connectedness and opportunity-driven innovativeness has increased global wealth as markets for products and services have expanded dramatically. While equalization may not occur instantaneously, globalization is helping emerging companies to acquire knowledge, capabilities, and technologies in order to exploit the economic and social wealth being created.

Given the capabilities and sophistication of global corporations, products and services with enhanced value propositions have increased dramatically as well. Low-end products are disappearing as superior products and services are often the most competitive ones. Markets and customers expect the best, and are forcing producers to continue to make improvements just to stay competitive. Moreover, the underutilized production capacity in many industries means that customers have the power to buy what they demand at the price they are willing to pay. For example, the global automobile industry has millions of available units of production capacity that are unused because there is insufficient demand. Global competitors fight for every sale by offering incentives such as low-interest loans and deep discounts.

As competitors continuously replace their existing product portfolios with new and improved versions, and with the rapid development of new technologies and products, it is becoming increasingly difficult to obtain a truly competitive advantage. The rapidity of change makes it virtually impossible for any single corporation to have the resources and capabilities to manage the entire process associated with developing, producing, and delivering the requisite innovative products or services. Producers are becoming more dependent on external networks of suppliers and distributors. Outsourcing to low-cost providers, especially to suppliers in countries with low wages and minimal benefits, is a global phenomenon. Global corporations are outsourcing commodity products, standard parts and components, and repetitive services in order to reduce their costs and enhance the economics of their primary products. While there are benefits to the principals involved, such practices require greater scrutiny and assurances that appropriate safeguards are in place for people, society, and the natural environment.

Technological change is also a critical part of the transition to a richer future. New technologies generally have fewer inherent defects from social, economic, environmental, and market perspectives. Moreover, the development of new technologies provides opportunities to cure the defects and burdens of the past and to create new value streams without the negative impacts of previous technologies. Technology fusion allows producers from various industries to combine their capabilities to create innovative offerings that enhance the value proposition and meet customer and stakeholder expectations. While perfection is still a distant dream, technological changes are moving our world toward a more sustainable future.

Enterprise thinking and leading change: SBD, the new paradigm

Enterprise thinking and SBD are high-level management constructs that are interrelated and interdependent. SBD requires enterprise thinking and linkages to build the foundation for inventing the future. This is not just a linear extension of the environmental management concepts of pollution prevention and waste minimization; it is a paradigm change affecting the strategic thinking and management of the entire enterprise. It involves all of the people affected by the enterprise and ensures that the best outcomes are achieved. The challenges are enormous, but the potential rewards will reach the social, economic, and environmental dimensions. The essential ingredients include the integration of the corporate management systems with the external dimensions of the business environment, the innovation of new solutions, technologies, and products, and executive leadership that provides the vision, strategic thinking, and inspiration for people to excel.

Inventing the future requires a dynamic perspective of the global business environment. The world is ever-changing, and an innovative corporation must continuously evolve and improve ahead of expectations. It must be at the forefront of change and lead in the development of new businesses, technologies, products, methods, and techniques. Figure 12.1 depicts the essential links between SBD and enterprise thinking and the essential constructs of executive leadership, strategic thinking, and innovation.

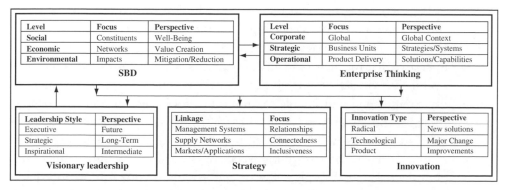

Figure 12.1   The essential links between SBD and enterprise thinking

Executive/visionary leadership drives the entire paradigm, and remains the fundamental challenge for most corporations. It isn't enough to simply embrace the principles of SBD. The corporation must reinvigorate the organization and all of its constituencies and motivate people to make the necessary investments of time, effort, and money to achieve a sustainable future. It takes exceptional vision and inspiration to unite all of the participants with a shared commitment for improving every facet of the external and internal dimensions of the enterprise.

The leadership of the corporation generally evolves over time as new executives replace their colleagues who retire or move on to other corporations. The commitment to SBD has to be robust so that the momentum continues despite such transitions. Many corporations have difficulties maintaining long-term programs when new leadership takes the helm.

Outstanding accomplishments and extraordinary gains are usually realized only if the efforts are compounded over time and if new initiatives are mindful of past experiences. In the world of science, the phenomenal gains made during the twentieth century in our understanding of the natural world and the universe are the result of cumulative knowledge from the past and our increasing understanding of what it means. Similarly, in business, successful outcomes usually derive from the integration of knowledge and what it means for the corporation. Insights and profound thoughts are often a synthesis of multiple facts. In isolation, or using a simplistic model, a certain phenomenon may seem to make sense and be worthy of the primary consideration; reality may, however, prove that many other important factors must also be considered.

For example, the simplistic model of "supply and demand" focuses on customer satisfaction as the prime motivating force. However, while customer satisfaction is important, there are many other important constituencies that have to be satisfied as well. The basic difficulty with such perspectives is not that they are wrong, but that the model under which they were derived is incomplete. Executive leadership defines and develops that model, and – most importantly – integrates all of the people and relationships. It is imperative that the view of reality be as inclusive and innovative as possible.

While it is virtually impossible for senior and operational management to fully comprehend and handle the multiplicity of relevant issues, concerns, problems, and impacts, especially on a global basis, it is possible to establish enterprise thinking and to initiate SBD for creating a more enticing future. Leading change is the reward for executive leadership that successfully integrates the business enterprise and its context and then continues to expand through innovation, achievements, and sustainable success.

Maximizing value for customers, stakeholders, and constituencies

The paradigm shift

Globalization, the increasing sophistication of technologies, the rapid pace of change, and many other profound changes are causing a dramatic shift in the management constructs used by leading corporations. While businesses have been making incremental improvements over the decades, they now must make even more dramatic improvements. In the early 1980s, business executives and management consultants were excited and enthralled with *In Search of Excellence*, as leaders tried to find a magic formula for outperforming their competitors and for achieving extraordinary results. *In Search of Excellence: Lessons from America's Best Run Companies*, the book written by Tom Peters and Robert H. Waterman, Jr., was a best seller, providing insights about new and effective management theories. Peters and Waterman provided eight principles for achieving outstanding results:[1]

- *A bias for action*   Excellent companies focus on getting results via decisive actions.
- *Close to the customer*   Excellent companies have close relationships with their customers, and understand customer needs.
- *Autonomy and entrepreneurship*   Entrepreneurial thinking leads to creativity, innovation, and wealth.
- *Productivity through people*   Excellent companies improve outcomes through people-oriented practices based on trust. High productivity lowers costs and enhances value.
- *Hands-on, values-driven*   Everyone in the organization understands, and is guided by, the corporate values. They must be guided by balanced principles.
- *Stick to the knitting*   Successful companies should follow their core competences and avoid outrageous diversification.
- *Simple form, lean staff*   Companies should keep the system as simple as possible and avoid building elaborate structures and procedural requirements. Lean methods reduce waste and inefficiencies.
- *Simultaneous loose–tight properties*   Excellent companies maintain control without stifling creativity and innovation.

Many of Peters and Waterman's principles still ring true today. Achieving excellence is a foundational underpinning of SBD. "Bias for action" is related to today's concept of preemptive actions. "Simple form, lean staff" is clearly an important and fundamental concept within SBD that focuses on eliminating economic and environmental waste that can compromise outcomes. However, "stick to the knitting" is more complicated to discuss because sometimes there are legitimate evolutionary as well as revolutionary changes that represent dramatic shifts in strategic direction, technological and product forms and focus. For example, Intel shifted from memory chips to microprocessors in the mid-1980s. IBM shifted from calculating machines to computers, and then later to services and "system solutions." SBD involves preemptive, value-driven changes that are ongoing and relentless in the pursuit of significant strategic improvements and superior performance.

During the early 1990s, Gary Hamel and C. K. Prahalad wrote an article, "Competing for the Future," and a book with the same title. Hamel and Prahalad challenged the prevailing management constructs with new notions about "creating the future." Their views on strategic direction were the start of a paradigm shift toward the philosophies of SBD. At the end of their *Harvard Business Review* article that summarized key perspectives taken from the book, the authors stated:[2]

Developing a point of view about the future should be an ongoing project sustained by continuous debate within the company, not a massive one-time effort. Unfortunately, most companies consider the need to regenerate their strategies and reinvent their industries only when restructuring and reengineering fail to halt the process of corporate decline. To get ahead of the industry curve, to have a chance of conducting a bloodless revolution, top managers must recognize that the real focus for their companies is the opportunity to compete for the future.

In "Competing for the Future," Hamel and Prahalad suggest that executives use imagination and foresight when challenging the status quo and exploring and exploiting opportunities that are on the leading edge of changes in the business environment.

Conceptually, James C. Collins and Jerry I. Porras' *Built to Last* published in 1994 could be considered a forerunner to the philosophies of SBD.[3] Many of the principles and premises of the enduring companies that the authors examine are clearly critical for achieving sustainable outcomes and long-term success. The title, *Built to Last*, connotes the very essence of what SBD is intended to achieve in the long term. Table 12.1 indicates the links between the main concepts contained in *Built to Last* and the principles of SBD.

The intent of the comparison is not to suggest a perfect alignment between philosophical perspectives, but to indicate that there are parallel views. *Built*

Table 12.1. Links between the main concepts of *Built to Last* and SBD

Built to Last concepts	SBD Constructs
Clock building, not time telling "Visionary companies stem from being outstanding organizations, not the other way around"[a]	**Enterprise thinking** The embedded enterprise management system involves building a solid foundation of relationships that are sustained over the generations. It involves linking all constituents from cradle-to-grave
No "tyranny of the OR" (embrace the genius of the and) "A visionary company doesn't seek a balance between the short term and the long term, for example. It seeks to do it very well in the short term and in the long term."[b]	**The solution matrix** The solution matrix examines the primary and secondary effects and focuses on maximizing positives and minimizing negatives. The construct avoids deciding between the options and focuses on achieving all of the necessary goals
More than profits "Profitability is a necessary condition for existence and a means to an important end, but it is not the end in itself for many of the visionary companies."[c] It is easy to be profitable in the short term, but often such gains are not translated into sustainable successes.	**Value creation** The value proposition that includes total satisfaction for all constituencies is the essence of sustainable outcomes, longevity and ongoing success. Customers and stakeholders (people) want complete satisfaction that translates into more than short-term profits. Success is a long-term venture
Preserve the core/stimulate progress "If an organization is to meet the challenges of a changing world, it must be prepared to change everything about itself except beliefs."[d]	**LCT** LCT must encompass the whole enterprise and every dimension and focus on satisfaction that meets all objectives
Big hairy audacious goals (BHAG) "A BHAG engages people. It is tangible, energizing, highly focused."[e]	**Total satisfaction** Satisfaction is the ultimate goal. It includes the market, social, economic, environmental, and business-related objectives
Cult-like culture "Because the visionary companies have such clarity about who they are, what they're all about, and what they're trying to achieve, they tend to not have much room for people unwilling or unsuited to their demanding standards."[f]	**Core capabilities** People achieve success. The adaptability and agility of the organization provide the means to embrace change and to create opportunities and positive outcomes. The capabilities of the organization and the enterprise participants are the strategic resources
Try a lot of stuff and keep what works "In examining the history of visionary companies we were struck by how often they made some of their best moves not by detailed strategic planning but rather by experimentation, trial and error and opportunism."[g]	**Sustainable innovation** Innovation depends on the willingness and capability to manage change and create improvement across the enterprise. Innovation is the relentless pursuit of making improvements through strategic, operational, and fundamental means and mechanisms, including good luck
Home-grown management "A visionary company absolutely does not need to hire top management from the outside in order to get change and fresh ideas."[h]	**Executive leadership** Crafting an SBD culture within the organization is based on critical thinking and envisioning solutions for the future. Such leadership is based on a continuity of effort and a deep understanding of organizational capabilities

Table 12.1. (cont.)

Built to Last concepts	SBD Constructs
Good enough never is "The critical Question is 'How can we do better tomorrow than we did today?' " [i]	**Inventing the future** The ultimate objectives are to eliminate all defects, burdens, impacts, and negative consequences and enhance the positives to the maximum degree It is to invent a better future

Notes:

[a] Collins and Porras, *Built to Last* (1994), p. 31.

[b] *Ibid.*, p. 44.

[c] *Ibid.*, p. 55.

[d] *Ibid.*, p. 81. The quote was taken from Thomas J. Watson, Jr.'s booklet, *A Business and Its Beliefs*, pertaining to IBM.

[e] *Ibid.*, p. 94.

[f] *Ibid.*, p. 121.

[g] *Ibid.*, p. 141.

[h] *Ibid.*, p. 182.

[i] *Ibid.*, p. 192.

to Last focuses on business principles. The constructs of SBD involve systems perspectives that cut across the entire enterprise: the social, economic, and environmental dimensions; the traditional focus on customers and markets; and the internal aspects of engineering, production, marketing, and finance. *Built to Last* discusses lessons from successful American companies. SBD, on the other hand, includes theoretical and practical solutions for ensuring success over time. Moreover, SBD is in the early stage of development. There are few examples of corporations who have fully invested in SBD with a fully articulated enterprise management. Even the corporations that have made commitments to SBD have only a few years of experience using the constructs and methods.

In 2000, Gary Hamel expanded upon his concepts for creating new wealth and competitive advantage in his book, *Leading the Revolution*. He articulated that in the nonlinear world of the twenty-first century companies must adopt a radical innovation agenda.[4] Hamel's work focuses on business concept innovation, radical innovation, and sustaining the revolution. Business concept innovation is related to enterprise management and its embedded subsystems. Hamel's model covers customer interface, core strategy, strategic resources, and value networks. In particular, value networks provide the opportunities and the means to achieve extraordinary results. These elements are the essential parts of the enterprise and warrant management's continued attention. Hamel's view of radical innovation is a perfect fit with the concept of preemptive strategic action and proactive initiatives to gain leading edge outcomes. Most importantly, Hamel articulates ways to sustain the revolution over time through insights, learning, and continuous commitment and action.

As articulated in the books, *In Search of Excellence, Competing for the Future, Built to Last,* and *Leading the Revolution*, pursuing improved management constructs, enhanced business performance, increased financial strengths, and sustainable outcomes are critical aspects of corporate leadership today. The evolutionary trend has been toward greater sophistication and understanding of the entire business environment and corporate management systems. Management concepts have also evolved from overarching principles and best practices to management frameworks, like Hamel's model, that focus on the total solution. Instead of simply offering lessons learned, the leading corporations and foremost authorities on management are developing sophisticated business models and integrated systems that allow solutions to be based on the whole, and not simply the parts. The "magic formula" has become an integrated system calling upon executive leadership and the innovative capabilities of the organization to discover, explore, and exploit new solutions that meet the full spectrum of needs, wants, and mandates. The most critical aspects of this systems thinking are the notions of inclusiveness, continuous innovation, and openness to the global communities.

With this shift in perspective, the whole system creates value and enhances outcomes. Improvements are achieved across both space and time. The process is dynamic and continuous, engaging the full leadership capabilities of the corporation from the top to the bottom. This search for excellence, this persistent drive toward perfection, characterizes sustainable development thinking in the early part of the twenty-first century. Table 12.2 provides a simplified view of the evolution of management thinking since the 1960s.

During the early to mid-part of the twentieth century, most of the management perspectives were based on "either/or" thinking. For example, quality control techniques attempted to determine whether the product was good or bad. If the products were deemed to be good, they were shipped to markets, and customers had to endure the consequences of any problems.

The basic approach to marketing was to assess whether customers would accept the product or not. If they would, the products would be designed and produced regardless of the inherent defects and burdens. In many cases, defects were well known, but neglected if the underlying assumption was

Table 12.2. Simplified perspectives relating to paradigm changes in management thinking, 1960s–present

Dimensions	Mid-twentieth-century	Late-twentieth-century	Early-twenty-first-century
Environmental	In compliance/Unknown	Waste management → Prevention	Eliminate degradation, depletion, impacts
Economic	Feasible/Not feasible	Supply/demand → Value delivery	Value creation across the enterprise
Social	Concerns/No concerns	Awareness → Involvement	Equity, social responsibility
Finance	Profitable/Not profitable	Cash flow → Long-term wealth	Value creation and sustainable performance
Markets	Acceptable/Unacceptable	Satisfied → Delighted	Total satisfaction
Products	Good quality/Poor quality	Three-Sigma quality → Six-Sigma quality	Zero defects and zero burdens
	Linear thinking (Either/or – binary)	**Distributed thinking** (Continuous improvements)	**SBD thinking** (Zero defects and radical improvements)

that the products would still be viable in the marketplace. Financial implications often formed the criteria for making such decisions. If the products generated profits, corporations would risk the liability issues, assuming that it would be difficult for plaintiffs to win in a court of law. The asbestos cases indicated the willingness of corporations to produce and sell products with known problems. Another example is the story of cigarettes. While concerns about the dangers of smoking have been at the forefront of medical discussions for more than fifty years, producers were seemingly unwilling to make major changes to their products and operations.

Social concerns were likewise often overlooked unless the consequences were so severe as to spur a political response. For example, during the late 1960s P&G was involved in a controversy over phosphates in its detergents. Phosphates tend to overstimulate the growth of algae that consume oxygen in water, causing eutrophication.[5] The public began to blame phosphates for the accelerated eutrophication of lakes and waterways, and many manufacturers switched to less powerful agents. P&G was slow to adapt, believing that there was no scientific evidence of causality. However, as government pressure increased and calls for banning phosphates were heard, P&G eventually spent over $130 million in search of a substitute.[6]

Corporations handled economic questions in a similar way. The main criteria were the feasibility of products and processes. Environmental issues usually were handled as tangential matters. If laws and regulations existed, the approach was to comply with the mandates but not to spend time and money doing more than was necessary. While these comments are an oversimplification, the general pattern was to make decisions on a linear basis.

Since the 1980s, management has shifted toward the more flexible approach of attempting to find distributed outcomes using continuous improvement methodologies. Distributed thinking is based on the notion that solutions are time-based and dependent on the prevailing situation. It recognizes that improvements are made over time and that what may be an acceptable solution today could be rejected as inferior tomorrow. Distributed thinking is typified by the TQM and six-sigma quality movements. The TQM efforts of Motorola and other corporations during the 1980s and early 1990s are an excellent example. Motorola executed a three-phase program that improved product quality from Three-Sigma to Six-Sigma levels over a more than twelve-year period. Constant improvements characterized its relentless efforts to become a "world-class" producer while most corporations simply began to examine the potential for incremental improvements and not to identify the details of what might be possible.

Similarly, the goals for customer satisfaction changed from simply fulfilling customer requirements to ensuring that customers were completely delighted with the total package of products and services. In a pivotal late-1980s study, AT&T realized that customers who indicated that their satisfaction was simply "good" instead of being "delighted" were not assured of being retained as customers. Indeed, 40 percent would seek alternatives.[7]

Yet one of the most profound changes in corporate thinking during this time was the move toward viewing cash flow as more critical than profits and the creation of economic value and wealth as pivotal. While there are still ongoing discussions about short-term versus long-term financial rewards, it is generally recognized that long-term rewards are essential for enduring success.

Perhaps the most philosophical modification in financial management thinking, however, was articulated in Robert Kaplan and David Norton's *The Balanced Scorecard*.[8] Kaplan and Norton asserted that financial success depends on more than just making money. In their view, financial success is derived from a balanced management system that focuses on long-term investments in customers and employees (people), product innovation, and the system. Their perspective links distributed thinking about making money with enterprise thinking about creating value for all the internal and external participants and stakeholders.

The social, economic, and environmental aspects of corporate strategy have evolved as well. The social perspective changed from one of first

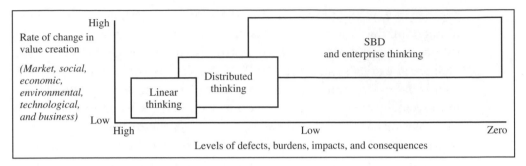

Figure 12.2   The evolution of management perspectives

ignoring and later managing problems to one in which corporations seek to enable stakeholders to understand and participate in shaping products, processes, and operations. Corporations no longer simply provide information in response to "right-to-know" mandates. The economic equation has shifted from the simplistic views of "supply and demand" to the more complex, balanced, and ultimately more sustainable value proposition of creating value for all constituents.

The view of environmental management has similarly evolved from the recognition that waste management is critical for reducing the intensity of environmental concerns to the understanding that pollution prevention and waste minimization are absolutely necessary. The avoidance of problems saves money, time, and energy in both environmental remediation and in corporate image repair.

Enterprise thinking and SBD represent the next advancement in future-focused management constructs. They incorporate the prevailing trend of continuous improvement and focus on the full integration of the management systems with the external business environment. The challenges are enormous. SBD requires a shift from focusing on incremental improvements to focusing on radical improvements system-wide.

Figure 12.2 provides a graphical representation of the evolution of management perspectives that has occurred since the 1980s. Linear and distributed thinking are broad concepts embodying numerous methodologies that have coexisted over time and still persist today. SBD and enterprise thinking represent a radical shift in the strategic logic of leading and managing an enterprise.

SBD is a convergence of thought and action toward improving all aspects of the enterprise. Its ultimate goals include zero defects, burdens and impacts, regardless of the prevailing conditions and trends. It presumes that developing new technological and product solutions are important ways to mitigate or eliminate the negative. It is an optimistic, yet realistic, belief that total satisfaction, not just customer satisfaction, is possible, that sustainable performance (strategic and financial) is the strategic aim of the corporation, and that the most important social responsibility is to all constituencies.

Corporations are social organizations chartered to meet the social–economic needs of the people involved, directly and indirectly. In reality, SBD and enterprise management are a manifestation of this original purpose.

Moving toward more ideal solutions

The transformations of business constructs and strategies over the decades have been incremental, yet profound. Technologies and products have always played significant roles in defining the opportunities and challenges in the business environment. During the early twentieth century, manufacturing processes and capabilities defined the essence of the competitive landscape. For example, "Fordism," Henry Ford's assembly line methodology employing mass production, provided the solution for creating automobiles that were affordable and durable enough for the rural population of the 1920s. While the Model T was a great product success, the underlying value creation was its production processes.

During the latter part of the twentieth century, the product became the principal source of value creation as technological and product innovations added features, functions, and variations. While process technologies were still critical for providing solutions, the focus had shifted toward product designs and market approaches, and the benefits they provided to customers and stakeholders. The PC, the wireless telephone, and the TV are other examples of products where the focus is on the product attributes, not the manufacturing processes. Selecting and delivering products that exceeded the needs and expectations of customers and stakeholders drove their development.

However, both products and processes are critical to success, and the systems approach allows gains made in one area to be shared across the enterprise. It offers the means to leverage insights and improvements in one product line with other product groups. This dissemination of improvements enriches every aspect of the enterprise, allowing it to become more capable of reaching the next level of sophistication with its concomitant opportunities and challenges. The underlying system and resources, including the relationships with customers, stakeholders, and supply networks, become stronger. The challenges increase as well, however, because as the impacts decrease, the ability of the system to continuously improve is stretched. Similarly, as the corporation expands its capabilities and reaches higher levels of accomplishments, the challenges increase nonlinearly. For example, if a producer has ten suppliers and each supplier has ten suppliers, then as the producer expands its reach into the supply chain and adds additional tiers to its assessments of products and processes, the numbers involved become far greater. The depth of knowledge and understanding increases, but so does the complexity.

As the system improves and the solutions move toward ideality, the following five trends become apparent:

- *Low versus high percentage improvement*   It becomes increasingly difficult to make significant improvements as the prevailing outcomes approach the ideal. For instance, it is easy to quadruple the amount of material that is recycled when one starts with a rate of only 5 percent being recycled. Conversely, it is difficult and costly to make further improvement if the rate is 99 percent.

- *Internal versus external impacts and improvements*   Corporations usually have excellent understanding and control of their own products, processes, and operations, but not of the impacts of suppliers, distributors, and customers. For instance, most corporations using reporting mechanisms such as GRI can account for their own waste streams and impacts. However, they usually lack detailed information about the processes and operations of their suppliers, or the applications of their customers.

- *Narrow to broad perspectives*   Most corporations have an understanding of the impacts of their operations and processes and can articulate appropriate strategies for making improvements. However, as the impacts reach outside the traditional domain of the corporation, the situation becomes fuzzy and the solution mechanisms clouded. For instance, many corporations have well-thought-out wastewater treatment strategies employing technologies that meet or exceed regulatory mandates. However, the same corporations are often not fully equipped to participate in improving the waterways affected by the outflow from their facilities. It is relatively easy to understand and manage the specific, but extremely difficult to contemplate and handle the broader implications, especially if they are downstream or upstream impacts.

- *Local to global reach*   It is easier to understand and manage local or regional issues than those that have global implications. For instance, corporations are usually more effective in handling the effects and impacts of sulfur dioxide emissions than understanding and managing the effects of climate change. It is easier to identify the causes and effects and formulate mitigation strategies for the former than to try to affect the combined efforts of government, NGOs, corporations, and the entire population of the world.

- *Short-term versus long-term efforts*   Most corporations are structured to manage short-term programs of seven years or less. The difficulties of sustaining leadership and organizational commitment make it rare to find improvement programs that have time frames of more than twenty years. The methodologies for managing such endeavors are often lacking. The major pharmaceutical companies and their programs to develop new breakthrough products come closest to such long-term development. However, the management techniques for effective decision-making are often lacking.

There are many other insights that could be added. However, enterprise management is the critical factor. Working to make the system more integrated and innovative is the best investment. The crux of an integrated system is executive leadership that explores opportunities for achieving balanced solutions over space and time. Lasting solutions depend on people, their capabilities and willingness to improve, and their understanding of the explicit and implicit nature of the corporation and its overarching objectives. While value creation is the underlying objective of the internal and external participants, creating value requires an extraordinary perspective on the responsibilities of the corporation itself. It is easy to measure business performance on the simple basis of making money and increasing shareholder wealth. It is a greater challenge to assess the true accomplishments of a corporation over time as it improves not only its money-making capabilities, but its ability to create new capabilities for the future, truly satisfy customers and stakeholders, exceed mandates, lead positive change, and make dramatic long-term improvements. Figure 12.3 depicts the strategic architecture of SBD and enterprise management.

While figure 12.3 depicts only the essential elements, the implications are profound. The ultimate goal is perfection. However, the realities of the world paint a more sobering picture. While most people would like to have a perfect world without degradation, depletion, destruction, and disruption, they realize that it will take decades to move closer to that ideal. The path will unfold as a solid foundation of achievable outcomes over time.

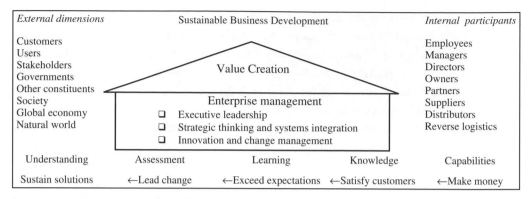

Figure 12.3   Strategic architecture of SBD and enterprise management

Leading change

Fortunately, SBD is not about achieving instantaneous perfection. Rather, the time horizon is long, and the improvements can build on previous ones over many generations. Improvements are made systematically using the corporate management system as the framework for achieving the desired results. For example, it may be impossible to deal with the potentially thousands of entities in the supply networks if they are treated as individual entities that have to be assessed and managed. However, if they become partners of the enterprise and follow the corporation's systematic approach for fulfilling requirements and transactions, the complexities are reduced significantly, and the end-results will tend to meet expectations. To use an old saying, everyone is on the same page!

Toyota is renowned for its supplier development program in which it spends a considerable amount of time and effort to educate suppliers about quality, lean production, and effective management skills. While such programs are expensive, they provide Toyota with direct feedback about the strengths and weaknesses of an essential part of its production capabilities. Moreover, Toyota is able to help its suppliers make immediate corrections and improvements, or prevent problems and even catastrophes.

Making suppliers and distributors partners of the corporation enriches the enterprise without creating a rigid structure. Creating enterprise management that integrates the corporation with its customers and other downstream entities on the application side and the supply networks many tiers deep on the upstream side provides a solid framework for understanding reality, predicting future needs, and leading change over several generations. Such a fully articulated system enables executive leadership to think in terms of business model platforms similar to the constructs of technology and product platforms.

Kim Clark and Steven Wheelwright, in *Revolutionizing Product Development*, defined the construct of the "platform or next generation" as a system solution for developing new products and processes using a family approach for making changes based on adaptable and expandable aspects of the underlying parameters.[9] Marc M. Meyers and James Utterback provided additional insights about product platforms in their *Sloan Management Review* article, "The product family and the dynamics of core capability."[10] They explored leveraging technology and product development over many generations, linking the new platform with the underpinnings of the old, and creating innovative outcomes based on the creative capabilities of the organization. The essential element is the platform that provides the means for enhancements and improvements that will lead to the next generation. Such changes depend upon the embedded knowledge of the organization, its understanding of the need for change, and its ability to transform its strengths and positions seamlessly into a higher level of new technologies, products, processes, and capabilities.

Such thinking can be applied to the SBUs and the business models used by the corporation in the context of SBD. As Gary Hamel discussed in *Leading the Revolution*, business concept innovation is the next level for creating new possibilities and opportunities. Hamel describes business concept innovation thus:[11]

In the new economy, the unit of analysis for innovation is not a product or a technology – it's a business concept. The building blocks of a business concept and a business model are the same – a business model is simply a business concept that has been put into practice. *Business concept innovation* is the capacity to imagine dramatically different business concepts or dramatically new ways of differentiating existing business concepts. (Emphasis added)

Hamel believes that business concept innovation is a rare occurrence within organizations, but one that offers exciting opportunities for outpacing the competition and creating new space. His view is that "unless you and your company become adept at business concept innovation, more imaginative minds will capture tomorrow's wealth."[12]

An effective business model is critical for leveraging capabilities and resources and meeting the needs of the business environment. It provides executives, management, and professionals with an understanding of the strategies and objectives of the whole system, the relationships that exist across space and time, and the dynamics of change. Enterprise management based on the principles and methods of SBD provides a robust business model for leading corporations into the future.

Business models of the past were stagnant constructs that were slow to respond to the pressures of the business environment and the needs of the organization. Historically, most business models were based on the organizational structure, defining roles and responsibilities without fully articulating scope, linkages, and management constructs. Such approaches were difficult to alter, requiring enormous pressure from external forces to demonstrate the need for change. While not all organizations were bureaucratic, there were tendencies to protect executive power, management positions, and the inner workings of the organization. Change was often viewed as a threat.

Today the next level of sophistication of innovation pertains to making the business model more capable of leading change and managing the change process. The business model platform or generation is a nascent concept that offers a dynamic mechanism for keeping the overarching perspective of the corporation on the leading edge of change. Just as Intel's technology platforms and next generation products provide a strategic means for linking its technologies and products over time and space, the notion of platforms and generations of business models offers executives a highly sophisticated way to outpace and outperform both competitors and peers.

The essence of the concept is to link integration and innovation at the highest level. Indeed, enterprise management and SBD do just that. The former considers space, positions, knowledge, and relationships. The latter involves time, change, improvements, learning, and future capabilities. Their marriage applies both of these innovative frameworks to the same end: achieving positive outcomes, putting the dynamics of innovation to work across the entire enterprise, and refining the business model itself, as well as technologies, products, and processes.

Inventing the future depends on having a robust and dynamic framework that can initiate change for the positive across the full enterprise, and eliminate the negatives wherever they exist. It also depends on relentless innovation that represents a continuum of thought, opportunities, and outcomes.

Dynamic management construct for leading change in the twenty-first century

The primary considerations in managing change in the twenty-first century are leadership, core capabilities, and intellectual capital. The future lies with the willing and able. They are the ones who will invent solutions before they are required. SBD requires courage and conviction. Without the initial commitments and investments in creating a new paradigm for the corporation, the principles, strategies, and actions that are necessary to lead the way to a sustainable future will never happen.

In 2001, Jim Collins, co-author of *Built to Last*, received acclaim with his book *Good to Great*. In the new book, Collins identifies the process that successful companies go through to evolve into a "great company." While it is always difficult to describe what a "great company" is, and it often depends on the criteria used in making the selection, Collins suggests that success involves disciplined people, disciplined thoughts, and disciplined actions.[13] His first element is possibly the most crucial. He describes "Level 5 Leadership" as the starting point in the process to becoming great.[14]

Level 5 leaders channel their ego needs away from themselves and into the larger goal of building a great company. It's not that Level 5 leaders have no ego or self-interest. Indeed they are incredibly ambitious – but their ambition is first and foremost for the institution, not themselves.

Leadership means actively engaging and energizing people into realizing extraordinary results on an ongoing basis. It occurs throughout the organization, not just at the executive levels, and it is both the trigger mechanism and the means for achieving lasting success. Engaging every manager, professional, and individual contributor to become a leader in preempting mandates and requirements and fulfilling total satisfaction is the ultimate mechanism for sustained success.

This kind of leadership and success necessitate an integrated system. Integration of the whole ensures that relationships are inclusive. It also means that the participants and actions across the enterprise are consistent. For instance, if the corporation has six-sigma quality processes, but its suppliers are still at Three-Sigma quality, the inconsistencies will undermine the gains of the corporation's processes. It is the capabilities of the whole that really matter.

The corporation must also be dynamic in order to successfully lead change. It is the ability to change and meet new requirements that allows the corporation to invent its own future. The system that is rigid and incapable of change is doomed to failure. Innovation provides the means to exceed expectations as changes occur in the business environment. Figure 12.4 is a graphical representation of the triad of leadership, strategy, and innovation.

Creating value and improving outcomes in ways that can be sustained over generations can link the external world with the internal workings of the

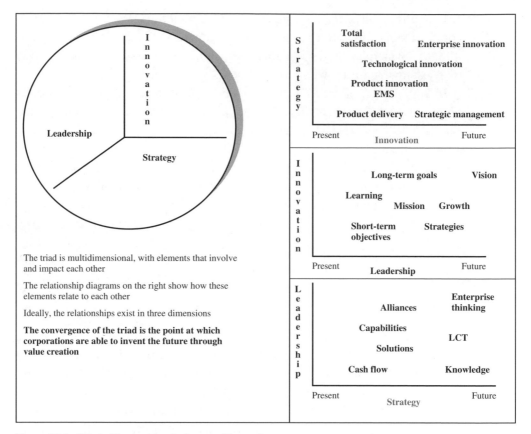

Figure 12.4   Triad of leadership, strategy, and innovation

enterprise. While many may say this ideal is but a dream, most of the technologies and products of the present would have seemed impossible fifty years ago. The power of enterprise management and SBD lies in the compounding effect of ongoing efforts.

The implications of enterprise thinking and SBD

Business model innovation

The last frontier of innovation methodologies is business model innovation. From the days of Alfred Chandler's work on *Strategy and Structure* in 1964, organizational business models have evolved slowly. Historically, most models were based on the organizational structure and the reporting relationships between the levels of management and supervision. During the 1980s these models were replaced with horizontal models at the product delivery (operations) system level and methodologies began to focus on processes rather than relationships.

During the late 1980s and early 1990s, reengineering and other related concepts attempted to make corporations leaner and more responsive to the needs of the external business environment. The successes of such approaches were viewed as radical changes in organizational thinking and were often touted by the investment communities as strategic answers to questions about corporate direction, competitive advantage, and organizational capabilities. In reality, many of the initiatives were cost reduction programs that cut headcount and the associated overhead costs without regard to long-term capabilities and consequences. While many believed that reengineering involved innovative methods for improving performance, many of the improvements were not sustained. However, there was recognition that the management system was the appropriate construct for tailoring the organization to better understand and exploit the opportunities and realities of the business environment. It is easier to change and improve the management system than it is to change the organizational structure. Flexibility and agility are crucial for the future.

With the rapidity of change and the need to make dramatic improvements quickly, the enterprise has to be as capable of developing the next business model as it is developing the next new product or technology. While there are credible methodologies for developing new products and for technological innovation, there are limited constructs for developing and validating new business models. This weakness is most likely due to the fact that such changes have been rare, incremental, and very slow. However, just as the life cycle of products and technologies has significantly declined over the last several decades, the life cycle of the business models/management systems has also declined. Since SBD requires an enterprise view of reality, it is imperative that corporations reinvigorate their business models as their reality changes.

The notion of a platform for the management system that evolves over time to the next generation is a construct that requires further development. Similar to the technology and product platforms, a management system platform would be reviewed periodically and the next generation introduced when necessary. Figure 12.5 portrays a conceptual view of the business model platform evolution.

There are many examples of business model platforms evolving over the course of history, but the process for making such changes is not fully

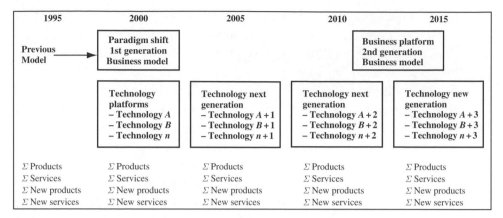

Figure 12.5 Conceptual view of the business model platform evolution

articulated. It has tended to be more of an ad hoc, reactive occurrence where such changes were forced by the business environment or a competitive situation. In many cases, the new business models were invented because of acquisitions or mergers that required the integration of new business units and new ways of managing the corporation.

For example, P&G created an organizational structure in 1931 that continually tracked products during their life cycle to keep them up to date. Its brand management concept was established to provide each brand with the resources and management attention necessary for success and to force P&G product managers to outperform each other. The brand management system ensured that communications flowed to the proper levels. By design, the vertical flow of information was excellent, but the cross-product line flow was limited. The brand management system promoted internal competition and was structured to create independent business units. In the mid-1980s, P&G restructured its organization because of declining profitability and growing dissension among distributors and retailers. As the number of related products grew, internal competition led to inefficiencies and confusion. P&G management realized it had to change. It realized that being satisfied with the status quo was as risky as making bold strategic changes.

In 1987, John Smale, the then CEO, developed the category management system. He divided the company into thirty-nine product categories and named twenty-six category managers; individual brand managers reported to the category managers. The category manager concept was designed to give the category manager spending power and decision-making authority to respond to fast-changing market conditions. These changes in the business model made P&G more responsive to external conditions and pressures.

Enterprise thinking does not provide a business model platform *per se*, but it helps strategists frame the proper questions. By having an inclusive view of the corporation's business environment, management has a more complete understanding of the social, economic, environmental, and business forces that it has to consider when designing the business model and formulating and implementing strategies and corporate direction. While business design innovation is not commonplace, it is nevertheless periodically required to ensure that the corporation's business model is in sync with the real world. Often the new business models are created by new players or by an outlier in the industry. The following are several examples of innovative companies that turned their industries inside out:

- *Wal-Mart* was a small regional retailer between 1945 and 1985 that few competitors noticed. Later, Wal-Mart's integrated information and distribution systems, among many other innovations, allowed it to outperform its rivals and become the largest retailer in the world.
- *Toyota Motor Corporation* has exploited its lean production system with its relationships with supply networks to outperform competitors and has expanded from a competent home market producer to a global powerhouse. As Toyota built plants in the United States, its business model evolved from one that tried to maximize Japanese content to one that sought to provide the best combination of inputs and outputs.
- *Siemens AG* has moved from a highly competent and innovative European electronics provider to a global developer of advanced technologies and products using virtual design and development processes. Siemens focuses on leveraging its leading knowledge and patented technologies to occupy highly advantageous positions.
- *ABB* created a flexible management system with highly distributed capabilities focusing on market demand. ABB does not have a strong national origin in many of its business units. It is a global entity that uses its strengths to develop leading edge technologies and exploit those technologies on a global basis.

Each of these companies has a dynamic business model that has evolved to stay on the leading edge of management thinking.

Today, corporations face intense market expectations, stiff competition, demanding government regulations and directives, and a myriad of stakeholder concerns and issues. They invest billions to fund the development of new technologies, products, and processes. Occasionally, the same corporations fail to think about the adequacy of their business models. It is critical to have effective business model development processes as well as effective

R&D capabilities and NPD programs. While the management constructs for business model innovation are still being developed, they are likely to be based on the EMM. Likewise, platforms and derivatives will evolve over time.

The future of enterprise management

Enterprise management is still in its infancy: many corporations have only just begun contemplating the implications of enterprise thinking. However, there are numerous examples of corporations that have taken action to begin building some form of framework for managing on an enterprise basis. Some of the near-term actions that are being developed and implemented include:

- Expanding the reach of the corporation to include suppliers and the suppliers of the suppliers. The Mercedes-Benz plant in Stuttgart is linking all of the suppliers, seven tiers deep, in an automated information technology system that tracks inventory throughout the system.
- Creating a product retirement system that provides effective solutions for post-customer handling, recycling, and disposal of residuals. The aluminum industry has an effective reverse logistics system that collects, processes, and recovers used aluminum-form can stock for use in aircraft parts.
- Linking stakeholders and other constituencies with information flow and an awareness of impacts and consequences. Many global corporations, such as BP plc (see box 6.1), provide annual sustainability reports using the GRI guidelines to disclose much of their social, economic, and environmental impacts and consequences.
- Expanding networking concepts to include all of the value-creating relationships from the beginning of the supply networks to the end of the product life cycle. Toyota reaches out to its suppliers and customers to ensure that they are part of the solution.
- Partnering with related industries to provide a complete solution when products combine two or more technologies and/or products. Sony works with software developers to ensure that there are games for its hardware.
- Building or renewing infrastructure assets to ensure that products and processes can be used in the most effective manner and to mitigate negative impacts to the greatest extent possible. Fuel-cell manufacturers are working with Shell Hydrogen to create a hydrogen fuel infrastructure.
- Deploying LCT and accepting cradle-to-grave responsibilities to improve design considerations and decisions. Corporations are also using LCT to examine the costs of designing, producing, and using products and

processes and to establish the proper timing for replacement and/or developing the next platform or derivative. These are in the early stages of development.

The overarching trend is the globalization of the business model to include all of the customers (present and future), stakeholders, social and economic implications, environmental impacts and their implications, and value networks for the nth-tier suppliers to the EoL solution provider. Enterprise management focuses on the total solution.

Future of SBD

SBD is also in its infancy. While the concept is well understood, the principles, methods, and techniques are still evolving as various governmental agencies and numerous NGOs from international groups such as the ISO and the WBCSD help to define and articulate standards and generally accepted approaches. It may take decades to fully develop and implement the explicit and implicit constructs of SBD. Moreover, as the leading global corporations, many of whom are mentioned in this book, refine their SBD practices, the state of the art will dramatically improve and will be shared with other corporations through the transfer and diffusion of knowledge and capabilities.

SBD is inherently positive even though much of the focus is on eliminating the negative. There are tremendous opportunities to make improvements through the reduction of degradation, the better use of resources, the eradication of destructive behaviors, and the avoidance of disruptive outcomes. There is also still room to converge the social, economic, and environmental agendas within and outside the business communities with ongoing business efforts to improve quality, instill lean behaviors, reduce risks and liabilities, and employ many other fundamentally sound business initiatives. And there is yet more opportunity to combine leadership, enterprise thinking, and innovation management to improve the future. These, too, are SBD.

The future direction of SBD will focus on total satisfaction, not just customer satisfaction. Total satisfaction provides more of the desired outcomes and less of the undesirable effects and impacts. World-class products and processes of the twenty-first century will have incredible advantages over their competitive counterparts, enjoying superior performance, features, and benefits, and imposing significantly fewer negative impacts, including costs. The notion of holistic management will expand into the full realm of the downstream side.

Table 12.3. Sales improvement, Wal-Mart and its competitors, 1990–2003

Company	Wal-Mart	Sears	Kmart	Target
1999 sales ($ billion)	165	41	36	34
2003 sales ($ billion)	246	41	31	44
2003/1990 sales ratio (2003 sales $ billion)	7.7	1.3	0.99	1.3

If business management of the later twentieth century was based on strategic and operational positions, and speed of action and innovation, then most outstanding corporations of the early twenty-first century will focus on the acceleration of strategizing, actions, learning, and innovation. They will improve everything on both sides of the value equation, taking multifaceted initiatives to make radical improvements to every aspect of the enterprise. In a multidimensional world of SBD, needs and expectations are high and the time frame to achieve them is short. There are enormous opportunities for corporations who can meet these expectations; those that fail to respect the realities of the future will suffer the consequences. For example, in 1990, Wal-Mart, Kmart, and Sears were essentially equals, with approximately $32 billion in sales each. Today, Wal-Mart has accelerated well beyond the others. Table 12.3 depicts the sales acceleration for four major retail competitors over 1990–2003.

Wal-Mart improved its annual sales by a factor of 7.7 between 1990 and 2003. Sears improved by a factor of 1.3 during the same time frame. While this is a simple view of a complex situation, and there are other factors that affect the competitive arena, it is clear that Wal-Mart is improving at rates the competition cannot duplicate. Kmart and Sears have announced that they are merging to improve their strategic position.

SBD is based on preemptive constructs that seek to outperform expectation, peers, and competitors. The compounding effects of planning, developing, implementing and sustaining system, technological, product, and process initiatives to achieve extraordinary outcomes and total satisfaction effectively accelerate the corporation toward its envisioned future. A corporation such as Wal-Mart can then differentiate itself by its rate of improvement and by competing to achieve a higher rate of improvement than its competitors.

Table 12.4 provides a summary of how management perspectives have changed over the last sixty years.

Management perspectives have moved toward a broader view of reality and greater inclusiveness. The most significant changes for global

Table 12.4. Changing management perspectives, 1960s–present

Time frame	Mid-twentieth-century	Late-twentieth-century	Early-twenty-first-century
Innovation paradigm	R&D	Integrated development	SBD
Business model	Organizational structure	SMS	EMS
Core strategy	Industry position	Product/market leadership	Strategy, innovation, and leadership
Strategic resources	Capital and assets	Core capabilities and processes	Intellectual capital and learning
Value networks	Suppliers and markets	Supply networks and customers	Relationships and linkages (people)
Essential perspective	Vertical integration	Horizontal integration	Total integration
Business perspective	Owner satisfaction	Customer satisfaction	Total satisfaction
Management focus	Market position (static)	Speed (dynamic)	Acceleration
Bottom line	Profits (making money)	Cash flow and growth	Value creation (triple bottom line)

corporations have been the move from vertical integration and oligopolistic conditions during the early twentieth century to horizontal integration and hypercompetitive markets during the later twentieth century. SBD is the next phase in the ongoing evolutionary process. While it is still too early to prove the premises about SBD, there is evidence that corporations such as Toyota, Siemens, and ABB are more concerned about the *total business environment* than they are about competitors. These highly capable organizations are shifting their emphasis toward total satisfaction rather than the narrower perspective of beating the competition. The preemptive corporation theoretically renders its competitors irrelevant when analyzing the business environment, because it is moving aggressively to fully meet all expectations – and, by default, outperform everyone else. The transformation process for corporations to fully articulate sustainable development may take several decades.

Learning from leading edge, global corporations

From theory to reality

This book has examined the theories, methods, techniques, and practices associated with SBD and provided strategic and technical perspectives within the context of the business environment. Given the broad characteristics of the subject matter and the fact that most global corporations are in the early stages of SBD formulation and implementation, it is not possible to use conventional statistical analysis to prove or disprove the theories or premises. The focus here has been on potential business applications, and on the initiatives of global corporations. The examples used throughout the book were taken from the *Global Fortune 500* because of the public availability of information and the global reach of those corporations. Moreover, the largest corporations have more complex business models and have broader influences and impacts on the business environment: they have the most to gain or lose. They also have the intellectual capital and resources to invest in developing leading edge constructs for improving their business situations. It can be argued that some of the global corporations are engaged in creating social benefits by leading the pursuit of sustainable development and providing the methodologies for others to follow.

The company examples used here have highlighted some of the current methods, techniques, and practices of various global corporations. The pathway to the future is still very wide, brimming with opportunity and challenge.

The proof that SBD is the necessary paradigm change lies in the future. Based on the débâcles of Enron, Tyco, WorldCom, and the disasters of the *Exxon Valdez*, Shell Oil's Brent Spar incident, and numerous other problems around the world, it is clear that corporations must have a more inclusive perspective of their business environment and shoulder greater responsibility for protecting and improving the social, economic, environmental, and market aspects of business enterprises. Today, lapses in proper governance, ethics, social responsibility, and action are quickly disseminated to stakeholders, markets, and competitors. While the risks and threats associated with these failures can be devastating, the principles for sustainable growth, "triple bottom line," and LCT, among many others, provide new ways of achieving business, social, economic, and environmental objectives without compromise. The twenty-first-century business ethic must champion balanced and holistic solutions that provide total satisfaction.

Inventing the future

Management across the world is engaged in the relentless struggle to keep pace with technological, social, economic, and environmental changes that seem to accelerate as time moves on. Great strides in competitive advantages are marginalized by the gains of peers and competitors, and the changing business environment. Where past breakthroughs led to competitive advantages that lasted for decades, the effects of such achievements today are often measured in months. However, with all of the challenges, there are also enormous opportunities – opportunities to lead change and move beyond social, economic, and environmental mandates. Across the world, people want solutions to the problems they face. The opportunities for providing these solutions range from finding ways to expand health care and obliterate hunger to protecting natural resources and eliminating waste streams. While management constructs have to become more sophisticated and comprehensive to effect solutions, executive leadership and management capabilities can provide dynamic strategic direction through preemptive strategies. Corporate leaders can lead change by working to create value for all and thereby building an enduring corporation that becomes more capable and sustainable over time.

In *Good to Great*, Jim Collins suggests that one of the keys to success is "Level 5 Leadership." The Level 5 executive "builds enduring greatness through a paradoxical blend of personal humility and professional will."[15] Most importantly, Collins adds:[16]

Level 5 leaders are fanatically driven, infected with an incurable need to produce *sustained* results. They are resolved to do whatever it takes to make a company great, no matter how big or hard the decisions. (Emphasis added)

While the companies that Collins identifies as having transformed from "Good to Great" were selected based mostly on financial criteria, the notion of becoming a great corporation in terms of the social, economic, environmental, and business requirements and mandates is also useful. Though it is difficult, if not impossible, to define "great," the *quest for greatness* is what resonates within the construct of SBD.[17] Leading change requires vision, insights, conviction, and fortitude. SBD requires all of these, as it sets corporations on a mission to find enduring solutions for future generations.

The penultimate objective is the quest for greatness, the quest for perfection, not perfection itself. It is akin to the building of the great cathedrals of Europe. The architects and builders recognized the daunting nature of such projects; they knew that it would take many generations of skilled and dedicated people to realize the dreams. Nevertheless, they were willing to invest their time and effort in the process because they believed in the vision. They understood that laying the foundation and building solid walls would provide the means for others to continue building. Moreover, they realized that the succeeding generations of their relatives and compatriots would enjoy the fruits of their labor and that the structures would provide human-kind with a lasting testimonial of their contributions and achievements.

The central force for creating and supporting a paradigm shift toward SBD is committed, capable, and enthusiastic leadership from the highest level of the corporation to the managers of the operating system. It is leadership that integrates the whole system into an effective mechanism for leading change and realizing value creation. Change without improvements and enhanced value is meaningless or worse. Transparency allows peer review and an airing of ideas, expectations, actions, and accomplishments. Each of the key components interacts with one another.

The examples of award-winning performance and achievement contained in this book are provided to demonstrate the principles, philosophies, systems, processes, and practices that have been employed by these leading corporations. Each provides noteworthy insights about what sustainable development is and can be. Table 12.5 provides selected examples of global corporate initiatives. The selected examples are not intended to serve as benchmarks for the specific element, nor do the selected corporations' strengths lie only in the highlighted area.

Concluding comments

Ultimately, SBD is an idea. It is a dream. It is the transition from the self-interested and confrontational business philosophies of the twentieth century to more inclusive, transparent, innovative, and rewarding management constructs that focus on creating value and sustaining total satisfaction for all parties. The central idea is similar to the philosophy behind democracy. It does not have to be proven because it is inherently logical. It is based on fundamental rights, expectations, and obligations. The same is true for SBD. It is an ideal that sets the stage for immediate actions and initiatives and provides guiding principles for making decisions that will create the desired future, a future that meets the expectations of the external business environment and fulfills the balanced objectives of the corporation. The dream focuses on moving toward solutions with maximum benefits and minimum negative impacts. Value creation and total satisfaction create a unifying management construct for leading the enterprise.

Most importantly, SBD pertains to the present and the future. Corporations have to explore, assess, and exploit sustainable solutions in

Table 12.5. Selected examples of initiatives of global corporations

Corporation	Driving forces	Insights
Proctor & Gamble (P&G) *Value creation* Over the last several decades P&G realized that people want solutions that are free of problems	– As customers demand better value on a global basis, problems with products anywhere affect overall success – The greater the diversity of the operations from a geographical point of view, the more dependent the organization is on the effectiveness of the whole system – Negative events or incidents can radically change the public's perceptions about products – Recognizing the costly effects of negative publicity, P&G began to study the environmental impacts of all of its products in 1985	– P&G's EMS has evolved from a simple construct focusing on compliance with laws and regulations and cleaning up wastes to a sophisticated construct, focusing on the sustainability of environmental, social, and economic objectives – In 1999, sustainability became the mantra – The company created a Corporate Sustainable Development Organization – One of the most important initiatives was the conversion of the annual Environmental Progress Report to the Sustainability Report – The strategic focus shifted from quality management to sustainability. – In March 1999, P&G elected to use GRI to standardize its disclosures to the public and provide transparency to its corporate information – Sustainability is about creating value for customers, employees, stakeholders, shareholders, and communities on a regional, national and global basis
Royal Dutch/Shell Group (Shell) *Transparency* Shell recognized that it had to improve the whole system, not just its image	– The market reacted against Shell's plan to remove the Brent Spar oil platform using deepwater disposal in the North Sea rather than properly dismantling it at a recovery facility and recycling or disposing of the residuals – Greenpeace challenged the plan because it feared it would set a precedent – Shell had to change the plan because of boycotts – Shell had massive problems in Nigeria through spills and other problems	– In 1997, Shell introduced its sustainable development initiatives by including environmental and social metrics in measuring business performance – Shell began publishing a sustainable development progress report – Rather than simply using a marketing campaign to overcome the negative perceptions caused by Brent Spar and other situations, Shell shifted its entire approach toward such difficulties and attempted to improve the entire system – In 2003, Shell transformed itself into a diversified energy company with a holistic view of the entire energy value chain

Table 12.5. (cont.)

Corporation	Driving forces	Insights
Toyota Motor Corporation (TMC) *Innovativeness* Toyota knows that success in the present can be fleeting and that long-term success depends on developing solutions ahead of the demand for them	– The automobile industry is undergoing significant changes – Globalization is causing the industry structure to be less stable and more turbulent – Research with Japanese consumers indicated that 88% of car owners wanted to buy low-polluting cars, and 72% said that they would buy green cars even if they cost more[a] – The government predicted that gasoline prices would rise as millions of first-time car owners took to the roads in China, India, and other developing countries	– In the 1990s, Toyota began to truly globalize its production and purchasing operations – It also modified its car platforms to accommodate the needs of the different regional markets – In 1996, Hiroshi Okuda, President of TMC, mapped out the company's strategy for sustainable growth in the twenty-first century – It included balancing the needs of people, society, and the global environment – Toyota articulated its position in Vision 2005, providing direction for achieving the dual goals of protecting the environment and offering consumers a wide range of environmentally friendly vehicles – Toyota's technology development strategy is a three-pronged approach including *incremental innovations of existing product technologies* (improving conventional engine technology using lean-burn methods that increase fuel efficiency while reducing emissions), *hybrid technological innovation* (developing vehicle technology that exploits the benefits of electric power with the support of lean-burn conventional technology), and *radical technological innovation* (exploiting electric vehicle technology and developing fuel-cell technology for future automobile applications)
Siemens AG *Inclusiveness* Siemens has an outstanding enterprise management system	– Siemens is engaged in the fast-paced electronics industry with changes occurring in months rather than years – Siemens is driven by its global social responsibility initiatives – It creates knowledge though linkages with strategic partners	– Siemens takes an integrated view of environmental protection that spans the whole product life cycle – The integrated product policy also takes the entire product life cycle into account during product planning – The company's corporate principles involve linking with both customers and stakeholders

Source: [a] "The greening of Japan," *Japan Automobile Trends*, September 1998, p. 1; see http://www.jama.org./autoTrends/detail.cfm?id.

Box 12.1 Alcoa and its vision to be the best company in the world!

Alcoa is the leading aluminum producer in the world. It is also recognized as one of the world's leaders in SBD. Corporate Knights and Innovest Strategic Value Advisors named Alcoa as one of the top three most sustainable corporations in the world by in 2005, and the DJSI ranks Alcoa No.1 in the metals industry.[1] While such recognition is important and helps building corporate image and admiration, Alcoa's vision, short-term and long-term goals, and performance, and management controls drive sustainable success. Moreover, corporate values and principles provide the underpinnings for articulating how sustainable development provides the foundation for building a solid future.[2]

Integration is a fundamental perspective that Alcoa focuses on to link the corporation with its customers, stakeholders, employees, shareholders, and society. In 2004, Alcoa established a Sustainability Team, sponsored by the Executive Council. The team developed a plan to integrate sustainability in Alcoa's businesses. The Alcoa Business Sustainability Model focuses on three strategies:[3]

- *People*   involve stakeholders in the development and delivery of our sustainability strategies.
- *Processes*   integrate sustainability fully into all of our processes and systems.
- *Products*   produce more sustainable products that contribute to people's quality of life.

The Model links stakeholders with the vision and the governance of the corporation. The Model incorporates the Alcoa Business System (ABS) with all of the business units. ABS provides a framework for connecting all of the businesses across the corporation and all of their partners and constituencies. In Alcoa's *2002 Environment, Health and Safety Progress Report*, Alcoa states its commitment to sustainability:[4]

> Sustainability requires environmental excellence, economic success, and social responsibility. This is the Alcoa Business System at work. We have developed a strategic framework that allows each of our businesses worldwide to develop its own goals and actions plans. This set of goals will be milestones along the way to the ultimate vision of a company where all wastes have been eliminated, where all products are designed for the environment, where the environment is fully integrated into manufacturing, where the workplace is free of injuries and leaks, where protecting the environment is a core value of every employee, and where all stakeholders recognize Alcoa as a leader in sustainable development.

In 2000, Alcoa established a Strategic Framework for Sustainability that provides well-articulated targets for determining its pathways toward its vision for 2020. The strategic framework provides the basis for integrating sustainability into decision-making processes. The following are the main initiatives:[5]

- Supporting the growth of customer businesses.
- Standing among the industrial companies in the first quartile of return on capital among Standard and Poor's Industrials Index.
- Elimination of all injuries and work-related illnesses and elimination of wastes.
- Integration of environment, health, and safety with manufacturing.
- Products designed for the environment.
- Environment, health, and safety as a core value.
- An incident-free workplace. Increased transparency and closer collaboration in community-based environment, health, and safety initiatives.

Engagement with stakeholders is central for ensuring that integration is real and based on a partner-type relationship rather than the more traditional "buyer–seller" approaches. Alcoa focuses on the whole picture and thinks about the success of its customers and partners as well as its own. Alcoa's perspective gives a concrete view of what a total solution is, what total satisfaction means, and how to define sustainable success. Moreover, transparency underpins Alcoa's values and principles. Such openness reinforces integrity, the pursuit of excellence, and accountability.

Leading change and achieving extraordinary goals depend on *innovation*. Innovation is at the heart of creating value and improving the value proposition. Alcoa is planning to build state-of-the-art, low-emission aluminum smelters in Iceland, Trinidad, and China. These new plants will provide improved life cycle inventory profiles with reduced impacts. Alcoa uses LCA on a number of its product lines (automotive, beverage containers, and building components) to explore opportunities to improve products and processes. Examples of Alcoa's technology and product developments include designing aluminum alloys for the automobile companies to resist corrosion without coatings, recycling used products and production materials, improving health, safety, and ergonomics, protecting wild life and their habitats, and eliminating wastes.[6]

Leading change and innovation are among the hottest topics in the corporate world. Alcoa is at the forefront of developing new technologies to eliminate many of the problems of the past. Alcoa is a global corporation with sophisticated technologies, products, and services that depend on global resources from far-flung suppliers, distributors, partners, and customers. Leading change through innovation is critical for achieving sustainable success.

Ultimately, it is *leadership* that makes the difference. CEO Alan Belda and his leadership team are committed to the company's vision, values, and principles. The strategic leadership of Alcoa is dedicated to the social, economic, and environmental underpinnings of sustainable development. They are integrating the corporation with its business environment to enjoy a consistent mindset to exceed expectations. That mindset includes leading change and becoming the best in the world in all endeavors. It includes creating extraordinary value for all constituents and inventing the future rather than merely fighting for the prevailing competitive positions, exploiting current resources and capabilities, and generating revenues and profits. While the latter perspectives are important, creating extraordinary value and providing total satisfaction are critical for achieving sustainable success.

Alcoa's leaders focus on the formulating and implementing preemptive, creative, and innovative strategies, involving people, integrating sustainability into processes and systems, and creating sustainable products and services. Its strategic leadership ensures the proper governance of the corporation, and determines how to create value and wealth for all of its constituents, including customers, shareholders, employees, stakeholders, and society. The focus is on what Alcoa must become to realize its vision to enjoy a sustainable future.

Notes:

1. Alcoa, *Sustainability Report, 2004*, p. 70; *Fortune Magazine* lists Alcoa as the most admired company in the metals category and ranks it second in social responsibility. *Forbes Magazine* recognizes Alcoa as the best-managed company in the materials category.
2. *Ibid.*, p. 3.
3. *Ibid.*

4. Alcoa, *Environment, Health and Safety Progress Report, 2002,* "A Decade of Reporting Commitment," p. 1.
5. Alcoa, *Sustainability Report, 2004*, p. 9.
6. Alcoa, *Environment, Health and Safety Progress Report, 2002,* "A Decade of Reporting Commitment." The report cites examples of numerous initiatives based on technology and product developments.

the present in order to move toward the ultimate solutions of the future. While it would be ideal to simply find the ultimate solutions that eliminate all problems and maximize all benefits, such outcomes are not possible in the immediate term. In most cases, radical improvements and outcomes are made through sustained efforts that arrive at revolutionary results through the compounding of continuous improvements.

Equally important is the notion that the management system provides the means and mechanisms to achieve success. While superior products and technologies were once viewed as the key to success, the demanding business environment of the twenty-first century requires leading edge management systems as well as superior technologies and products. Today, a robust and agile management system steeped in the philosophical principles of SBD provides the integrating force for ensuring ongoing success.

Within the myriad initiatives and accomplishments in the realm of SBD, some commonalities are evolving. The most profound initiatives involve developments that serve to lay a foundation for future improvements. These initiatives are demonstrating the increasing value being placed on inclusiveness, openness, value creation, innovativeness, and leadership.

Inclusiveness is one of the fundamental aspects of SBD. It is crucial for ensuring that decision-making includes all dimensions, all constituencies, and all effects and impacts, both positive and negative. Today, innovative global corporations are expanding their view of the enterprise to include cradle-to-grave participants, partners, stakeholders, and customers. They are also incorporating enterprise management thinking with its holistic view of reality.

Creating an open dialog with all of the constituencies of the corporation is an essential element in moving toward sustainable development. The concepts of **openness** and transparency are pivotal in reaching out to the world and building trust-based relationships with all constituencies. Corporations are building awareness and understanding among customers and stakeholders through open and effective disclosure of critical information and data pertaining to social, economic, and environmental considerations. This openness also creates linkages. Pamela Passman, Deputy General Counsel and Managing Director of Global Corporate Affairs at Microsoft Corporation said "Microsoft wants to build a glass house that no one will throw stones at."[18] The idea is that people operating in the open will make good decisions and not fear the ramifications of their actions.

Innovation bridges thinking and action. Improvements and enhancements are realized through creative thinking, engagement and investment of time, money, and effort. Inventing the future is about creating new solutions that are superior to the old ones using a platform for continuous improvement. It is the relentless pursuit of perfection through real action.

Redefining corporate purpose and objectives from making money to creating value for all constituents is a critical step on the path to SBD. Corporate leadership must seek to balance the scorecard. And, most importantly, value creation must assume both a short-term and a long-term perspective. Maximizing short-term gains at the expense of long-term sustainability is not only foolish, it consumes valuable resources and capabilities in less than fully productive outcomes.

Leadership is proving to be a powerful expression of management's willingness to invest in SBD and lead positive change. SBD is not just about new programs, products, or processes; it is a new way of thinking, strategizing, behaving, and achieving. It requires total commitment and dedication to SBD principles, not for one year or ten years, but for 100 years and more.

Committed, capable, and enthusiastic leadership from the highest level of the corporation down through to the managers of the operating system is the central force for creating and supporting a paradigm shift toward sustainable development. It is leadership that integrates the whole system into an effective mechanism for leading change and realizing value creation. Changes without improvements and enhanced value are meaningless, or worse. Each of the key components is linked and interacts with the others. In an effective enterprise, executive and managers lead people to desirable achievements that are sustained over time through ongoing dedication and commitment.

Finally, from an enterprise and strategic management perspective, leading change may be the greatest opportunity of the twenty-first century. While the most significant management constructs of the twentieth century – including strategic thinking, technological innovation, IPD, TQM, mass customization, and lean business management – are still prevalent and gaining significance, many corporations have found that the best way to keep up is to actually outpace changes in the business environment and become an agent of change.

In today's complex and turbulent world, setting the pace of change and influencing the standards of the future are prime avenues for achieving competitive advantages and sustainable success. The old notions of reacting to change or anticipating changes are defensive, and may lead to significant vulnerabilities as conditions and trends change quickly. Just keeping pace with fast-moving currents is difficult when the forces of change are global and the time horizons are short.

Strategic leadership integrates the organization with the business environment and provides a consistent mindset to exceed expectations, lead change, and become the best in the world in all endeavors. The goal becomes creating extraordinary value for all constituents and inventing the future rather than merely fighting for the prevailing competitive positions, exploiting current resources and capabilities, and producing revenues and profits. While the latter perspectives are important, creating extraordinary value and providing total satisfaction are critical for achieving sustainable success.

NOTES

1. Tom Peters and Robert H. Waterman, Jr., *In Search of Excellence: Lessons from America's Best Run Companies* (New York: Harper & Row, 1982), pp. 13–16.
2. Gary Hamel and C. K. Prahalad, "Competing for the future," *Harvard Business Review*, July–August 1994, p. 128.
3. Jim Collins and Jerry I. Porras, *Built to Last: Successful Habits of Visionary Companies* (New York: Harper Business Essentials, 1994), pp. 23–200. The book has an American focus, since most of the companies discussed in the book are headquartered in the United States. Nevertheless, the notion of enduring success of more than fifty years is directly related to the objectives of sustainable development.
4. Gary Hamel, *Leading the Revolution* (Boston, MA: Harvard Business School Press, 2000), pp. 13–29.
5. Oscar Schisgall, *Eyes on Tomorrow – The Evolution of Proctor & Gamble* (Chicago: J. G. Ferguson Publishing Co., 1981), p. 251. P&G tried a substitute called sodium nitrilotriacetate (NTA), which offered the same product performance features as phosphate. During the product introduction, government scientists found some health hazards pertaining to NTA, causing P&G to voluntarily redraw the product in December 1970. The company steadfastly maintained its product position with phosphates as an essential ingredient. However, many of its competitors reformulated their products to be phosphate-free. By holding its position, P&G lost market share and profits even though its detergents, which used phosphate as a builder, were more effective cleaning agents.
6. *Ibid.*

7. Bradley Gale, *Managing Customer Value: Creating Quality & Service That Customers Can See* (New York: Free Press, 1994), p. 78. The data were taken from R. Kordupleski and W. Vogel, "The Right Choice – What Does It Mean?," AT&T, 1988.

8. Robert Kaplan and David Norton, *The Balanced Scorecard: Translating Strategy into Action* (Boston, MA: Harvard Business School Press, 1996), pp. 4–19. The authors argued that a balanced perspective that includes financial, customer, internal business process, and learning and growth aspects is critical for linking measures to strategy.

9. Steven Wheelwright and Kim Clark, *Revolutionizing Product Development: Quantum Leaps in Speed, Efficiency, and Quality* (New York: Free Press, 1992), pp. 92–96.

10. Marc M. Meyers and James Utterback, "The product family and the dynamics of core capability," *Sloan Management Review*, 29, 1993, pp. 29–47.

11. Gary Hamel, *Leading the Revolution*, pp. 65–66.

12. *Ibid.*, pp. 62–63.

13. Jim Collins, *Good to Great: Why Some Companies Make the Leap ... and Others Don't* (New York: Harper Business, 2001), p. 142.

14. *Ibid.*, p. 21. While some of the concepts discussed in *Good to Great* fit the constructs of sustainable development, the premise of success using Collins' methods depended on meeting financial objectives rather than achieving multifaceted outcomes.

15. *Ibid.*, p. 20.

16. *Ibid.*, p. 39.

17. It is my view that many of the leading global corporations that have embraced the principles and precepts of SBD are moving along the pathway that can be characterized using the notion of the "Quest to Greatness." It is difficult to prove that corporations will set a proper course or that they will ultimately be successful. In addition, not only is "Great" difficult to define and achieve, it is difficult to sustain. There are many companies during the twentieth century that may have been great at certain periods of time, but who then failed to sustain being great. RCA and Pan Am were leaders in technology and their industries, yet they failed to survive.

18. Pamela Passman was the keynote speaker at the 2004 Leadership Conference on Global Corporate Citizenship conducted by The Conference Board on February 26 and 27, 2004 in New York City.

REFERENCES

Chandler, Jr., Alfred (1962) *Strategy and Structure: Chapters in the History of the American Industrial Enterprise*. Cambridge, MA: MIT Press

Collins, Jim (2001) *Good to Great: Why Some Companies Make the Leap ... and Others Don't*. New York: Harper Business

Collins, James C. and Jerry I. Porras (1994) *Built to Last: Successful Habits of Visionary Companies*. New York: Harper Business Essentials

Gale, Bradley (1994) *Managing Customer Value: Creating Quality & Service That Customers Can See*. New York: Free Press

Hamel, Gary (2000) *Leading the Revolution.* Boston, MA: Harvard Business School Press

Hamel, Gary and C. K. Prahalad (1994) "Competing for the future," *Harvard Business Review,* July–August

Hamel, Gary and C. K. Prahalad (1994) *Competing for the future.* Boston, MA: Harvard Business School Press

Kaplan, Robert and David Norton (1996) *The Balanced Scorecard: Translating Strategy into Action.* Boston, MA: Harvard Business School Press

Meyers, Marc and James Utterback (1993) "The product family and the dynamics of core capability," *Sloan Management Review,* 29

Peters, Tom and Robert H. Waterman, Jr. (1982) *In Search of Excellence: Lessons from America's Best Run Companies.* New York: Harper & Row

Schisgall, Oscar, (1981) *Eyes on Tomorrow – The Evolution of Proctor & Gamble.* Chicago: J. G. Ferguson Publishing Company

Wheelwright, Steven and Kim Clark (1992) *Revolutionizing Product Development: Quantum Leaps in Speed, Efficiency, and Quality.* New York: Free Press

Glossary

The page number where the term is first discussed in the text is shown in parentheses after the definition.

Term/concept	Definition or use of the term or concept
afterlife (253)	The afterlife of a product relates to how products, components, parts, materials, and all residuals (*q.v.*) are handled, documented, controlled, and ultimately eliminated after their original economic purposes have been fulfilled and owners no longer wish to own or use them.
Agenda 21: Earth's Action Plan (1)	Agenda 21 includes action plans and specifications for a wide array of government organizations and NGO (*q.v.*), businesses, workers and trade unions, and many other groups with concerns such as poverty and promoting human health. Agenda 21 formed the underpinnings of sustainable development as developed during the United Nations Conference on Environment and Development at the Rio Earth Summit in 1992. The Rio Conference and the subsequent World Summit on Sustainable Development in Johannesburg in August 2002 laid out the principles and proposed action plans, but did not reach consensus on how to implement the initiatives.
Agility (283)	Agility is the ability to move quickly in new directions. It also means being able to transform existing core capabilities (*q.v.*) into new ones that are in sync with new realities.
Attributes (102)	The sum of the benefits, features, and functions of a product deployed to meet the needs of customers.
Axioms (55)	Axioms are fundamental truths that are embedded in the design process. The underpinnings of axioms are based on scientific thinking pertaining to superior designs.

Backcasting (352)   Backcasting involves a fundamental change in the mind-set of strategic thinking. It starts with the desired future business conditions, organizational capabilities, and strategic positions and then explores the strategic options available to achieve those targeted outcomes. Backcasting examines future needs and expectations and determines what has to be accomplished over a predetermined time horizon. The premise is based on "what must be accomplished" instead of on "what can be achieved."

Balanced scorecard (23)   According to Robert Kaplan and David Norton, an organization must use what they call a "Balanced Scorecard" when making decisions. They suggest that business organizations balance their objectives by including in them financial considerations, customer satisfaction, organizational learning, and internal business improvement.

Benefit-cost (B/C) analysis or equation (102)   B/C analysis or the B/C equation depicts the sum of the benefits divided by the sum of the costs. It is a ratio of expected outcomes to expected costs (investments). The equation can be expressed as: $B/C = \Sigma$ benefits $(B) \div \Sigma$ costs (C).

Brainstorming (413)   Brainstorming is an open exchange of ideas without negative feedback or adverse consequences, attempting to create "out-of-the-box" thinking.

Brand (143)   Brand is the term used for creating awareness and acceptance of the company's product as a "unique" position with its own attributes and value proposition.

Breakthrough technologies (486)   Breakthrough technologies are new-to-the-world technologies that change the nature of competition and provide the ability to create new types of products. It often requires the development of an infrastructure (*q.v.*) and support/related industries.

Business environment (11)   The business environment includes the external forces impinging upon the corporation. They can include the social, economic, political, technological, environmental, and market forces. It includes the external dimensions of markets, stakeholders (*q.v.*), competition, related industries, supply networks (*q.v.*), and infrastructure (*q.v.*).

Business integration (3)	Business integration links all of the essential elements into a comprehensive management system. This includes being connected with all supply networks (*q.v.*), customers (*q.v.*), stakeholders (*q.v.*), and other constituents.
Business strategy (165)	Business strategy is the determination of how a company will compete in a given business and position itself to serve customers (*q.v.*) and compete among its competitors (*q.v.*).
Capabilities (89)	Capabilities are the strategic assets (people and resources) that translate objectives and strategies into realities. They are the means for crafting strategies, effecting solutions (*q.v.*), and sustaining them in the future.
"Circle for Inventing the Future" (109)	The "Circle for Inventing the Future" is a high-level process dedicated to exploring the business environment (*q.v.*) for innovative ways to enrich the opportunities of the corporation and for assessing the best approach for leading change. A strategic analysis (*q.v.*) of the business environment includes not only the primary constituents of the enterprise (*q.v.*) (stakeholders (*q.v.*), customers (*q.v.*), suppliers, distributors, related industries, and competitors) but other corporations who are initiating innovative processes and practices to improve outcomes and mitigate defects and burdens.
Clean technology (630)	Advanced state-of-the-art technology designed and employed to maximize the positive benefits and minimize the negative defects, burdens, and impacts. It is an often-used but ill-defined term that includes systems, processes, equipment, and know-how that eliminates, reduces, or controls pollution and waste streams better than the available alternatives.
Closed-loop recycling system (327)	A closed-loop recycling system generally involves a complete solution (*q.v.*) for managing EoL requirements through a comprehensive system of collection, processing, reuse (*q.v.*), remanufacturing (*q.v.*), and recycling (*q.v.*) of products and materials.
Computer-aided design (CAD) (351)	CAD is IT incorporating software and hardware into a computerized design system that links all of the participants and design elements and integrates the design and the work flow.

Computer-aided manufacturing (CAM) (351)	CAM links the design elements to the manufacturing requirements and production processes, eliminating the steps to convert information on drawings into details used for producing a prototype or manufacturing the product.
Concept (10)	A concept is a new product candidate that is fully articulated into a defined opportunity and expressed in terms of the targeted product/market and described in terms of its technical design aspects, marketability, producibility, and feasibility perspectives.
Construct (94)	Constructs are the theoretical frameworks (models) used to analyze and determine strategies, systems, structures, and solutions. The concept of a construct is relatively new. A construct is intended to be a representation of the dimensions and elements of business situations. It combines information, data, and experience with theoretical thinking about how to view the corporation in the light of its opportunities, challenges, and constraints.
Context (157)	Context provides the basis for analysis and understanding. It includes the business environment (*q.v.*) and the management systems (*q.v.*) of the organization. Context is based on defining the scope of the analysis and the inclusion or exclusion of variables. The context includes both time and space considerations, enterprise thinking (*q.v.*) and LCT (*q.v.*), in order to provide a comprehensive and inclusive basis for decision-making.
Continuous improvement (36)	Continuous improvement is a broad concept that implies products and processes are never perfect and require ongoing improvements.
Core capabilities (113)	Core capabilities are the fundamental strengths and intellectual capital (*q.v.*) that an organization enjoys, but they are not necessarily unique to the organization.
Core competencies (328)	Core competencies are the capabilities of the organization that it uniquely possesses and are difficult for others to emulate. C. K. Prahalad and Gary Hamel define core competencies as "the collective learning in the organization."

Corporate management system (3)   The corporate management is responsible for the embedded management systems (*q.v.*) related to enterprise thinking (*q.v.*), strategic direction, innovation (*q.v.*), and product delivery. Its aim is to create value for the enterprise (*q.v.*) and to ensure sustainable success. It involves creating a sophisticated business model that provides proper strategic direction and governance (*q.v.*) and guides the strategic and operating actions of the corporation. It is a fundamental responsibility of executives.

Corporate Social Responsibility (CSR) (214)   CSR implies that corporations have a fiduciary duty to meet the needs and wants of customers and stakeholders (*q.v.*) and protect the health and safety of both humankind and the natural environment. More specifically, it means taking corporate responsibility for the decisions and actions of the whole enterprise (*q.v.*), not just those of the corporation.

Corporate strategy (152)   Corporate strategy is the pattern of decisions in a company that determines and reveals its objectives, purposes, or goals, produces the principal policies and plans for achieving those goals, and defines the range of businesses the company is to pursue, the kind of economic and human organization it is or intends to be, and the nature of the economic and noneconomic contributions it intends to make for its shareholders, employees, customers (*q.v.*), and communities.

Cost/benefit (C/B) analysis (101)   C/B analysis is the calculation of the present value (PV) of the benefits in terms of cost associated with a product, program, project, or action. It is a simplistic technique that views only the quantifiable benefits and measures their value-based monetary aspects on a discounted basis.

Creative strategies (403)   Creative strategies are the most radical and difficult to articulate. They involve starting or creating whole new business approaches, reinventing the whole business model or a significant part of it, or creating new opportunities, technologies, and products.

Cross-company integration (CCI) (363)   CCI involve linking all of the players in the enterprise (*q.v.*) together and connecting them into an effective team structure so the information, actions, and decision-making

Cross-functional team (362)
flow seamlessly from suppliers to producers, distributors, and customers (*q.v.*) as well in the reverse direction. A group (team) of individuals from various disciplines who are organized into a temporary work arrangement to perform selected tasks concurrently. Cross-functional teams are often organized to develop new products.

Customers (16)
Customers are the buyers and/or users of the products and services provided by businesses. They are the direct recipients of the economic benefits of the corporation.

Degradation (214)
Degradation involves the effects and impacts of pollution, waste streams and the accumulation of nonnatural substances that can threaten human health and safety and the natural world.

Depletion (214)
Depletion involves the loss of natural resources or the consumption of resources at rates greater than can be naturally restored or regenerated.

Derivative (400)
A variation to a technology platform that results in a product form that is different from its predecessors. It offers different or alternative attributes.

Design for the Environment (DFE) (473)
DFE is a systematic process for evaluating the effects of products and processes, and their impacts on human health, safety, and the natural environment. DFE is an environmental management construct based on cradle-to-grave assessments that focuses on developing new products that have improved attributes.

Design for Six Sigma (DFSS) (465)
DFSS provides a development process to achieve higher-quality and world-class performance with a high degree of customer (*q.v.*) and stakeholder (*q.v.*) satisfaction.

Design for Sustainability (DFS) (34)
DFS is built on the philosophy that LCT (*q.v.*) and LCA have to be fully integrated into new product concepts (*q.v.*) and designs during the NPD (*q.v.*) process and not after the new product has been commercialized.

Destruction (214)
Destruction includes potential or actual impacts that have severe and potentially irreversible consequences. It includes environmental impacts such as climate change, eutrophication (*q.v.*), acidification, ozone layer depletion, toxic contamination, habitat loss, and catastrophic illnesses.

Development (144)	Development involves the increased capabilities to make incremental and radical improvements and changes that contribute to value creation (*q.v.*), wealth, and social, economic, and environmental well-being. Development may include the concepts of economic growth; however, growth is does not always mean development.
Differentiation (182)	A strategic position with one or more attributes that are significantly different from those offered by others. Differentiation is used to obtain an advantage over competitors.
Disruption (214)	Disruption includes the relatively simple impacts of noise and odors, concerns about the balance of nature, and the compounding effects of such issues as deforestation and ocean contamination. It involves anything that has a negative effect on the natural order.
Distribution channels (90)	The distribution channel provides a means to reach potential customers (*q.v.*). It consists of intermediaries, wholesalers, retailers, and/or agents who link the organization with the ultimate customer and provide the flow of information and physical products.
Dual-sided marketing (298)	The concept is similar to green marketing (*q.v.*). It involves communicating the entire message about products and services, including both the positive attributes and the negative impacts.
Eco-efficiency (526)	Eco-efficiency involves the production and application of goods and services that satisfy human needs and provide quality of life at the same time reducing the ecological impacts and material and energy intensity across the life cycle. According to WBCSD, eco-efficiency is achieved through business taking the following actions: (1) reduce the material intensity of goods and services; (2) reduce the energy intensity of goods and services; (3) reduce toxic dispersion; (4) enhance material recyclability; (5) maximize sustainable use of renewable resources; (6) extend product durability; and (7) increase the service intensity of goods and services.
Eco-Management and Audit Scheme (EMAS) (195)	EMAS is an EU voluntary EMS (*q.v.*) focusing on environmental protection and continuous improvement of environmental performance. It includes periodic auditing and standardized environmental reporting.

Eco-system (78)	The eco-system is the interconnected system of living organisms and their biological, physical, and chemical support structures in the environment. It links the material and energy flows.
Effectiveness (86)	Effectiveness involves selecting the right programs to investigate, analyze, and implement, allocating the appropriate resources to achieve the desired results, and leading the proper change mechanisms in the right direction. It is about discovering opportunities for leading change and creating solutions that eliminate underlying problems and impacts.
Effects (76)	Effects result in impacts or consequences on the downstream processes operations or customers (*q.v.*) if the failure mode is not prevented or corrected. They are also the outcomes of upstream actions at some time in the future.
End-of-life (EoL) considerations (2)	EoL considerations involve producers assuming the responsibility for providing solutions for mitigating negative impacts and disposal of their products at the end of their useful life. Most importantly, producers are expected to build in solutions to EoL disposal problems through creating a "take-back" system, reuse (*q.v.*), recycling (*q.v.*), remanufacturing (*q.v.*), and other related initiatives.
End-of-pipe treatment (74)	The processes and/or technologies used to reduce, abate, or capture emissions, effluents, or wastes after they have been created in a process or system, or by a product or service.
Enhancements (400)	Enhancements are incremental changes to existing products and processes that improve one or more of its features, functions, and benefits.
Enterprise (75)	The enterprise is the entire organization (corporation) with all of its external relationships and linkages. It is a high-level SMS (*q.v.*) of the corporation and all of its SBUs and their product delivery systems (*q.v.*), along with all of the direct and indirect relationships with supply networks (*q.v.*), partnerships, alliances, and other value networks (*q.v.*).
Enterprise management (17)	The full integration of the internal operational areas and strategic position of the organization with all of the external factors influencing the business.

Enterprise Management Model (EMM) (88)

EMM presents a holistic, multidimensional view of the business environment (*q.v.*), including all customers (*q.v.*), stakeholders (*q.v.*), supply networks (*q.v.*), strategic partners, related industries, competition, and infrastructure (*q.v.*). It is an embedded management system (*q.v.*) that includes the SMSs (*q.v.*) and the product delivery systems (*q.v.*). EMM provides a framework for ensuring that all of the essential dimensions and elements are covered in the analysis of the business environment and is part of the solution matrix. EMM sets the stage for a descriptive, analytical, and structural understanding of the needs, opportunities, challenges, requirements, specifications, strategies, and action plans.

Enterprise thinking (2)

Enterprise thinking is a mindset of examining the whole business environment (*q.v.*) and its context (*q.v.*). It includes examining the implications and impacts on both the social and the natural world. This includes being inclusive and open with all constituents.

Entrepreneur (434)

A business person who creates or takes advantage of opportunities and acquires and builds the capabilities (*q.v.*), resources, systems, processes, and methods necessary to formulate and implement business strategies (*q.v.*) and achieve positive outcomes.

Environmental management system (EMS) (22)

EMS is a formal management system (*q.v.*) that focuses on managing the environmental aspects of the business. It is often a subset of the product delivery system (*q.v.*) and/or SMS (*q.v.*). EMS can be based on ISO 14000 (*q.v.*) Standards and/or company-developed methods.

Equity (98)

Equity encompasses the human side of the value equation and the social implications of corporate responsibilities. There are always many stakeholders (*q.v.*) involved within the business environment (*q.v.*), and their needs are important considerations in decision-making. Equity can be divided into categories: the "must do" (laws and regulations), "should do" (social norms and expectations), "may decide to do" (logic and fit), and "would like to do" (philanthropy). The first category is mandatory and usually well defined.

Eutrophication (259)   Eutrophication involves negative change in the state of an aquatic eco-systems, usually due to excessive amounts of nutrients from industrial, commercial, agricultural, and/or household sources that stimulate plant and algae growth, causing oxygen depletion and a decline or destruction of other species.

Evolutionary innovation (404)   Evolutionary innovation focuses on incremental improvements to existing products and processes to enhance their value for existing markets and customers (*q.v.*). It is generally a response to short-term pressures by customers, stakeholders (*q.v.*), and competitors, or a concerted effort to stay ahead of the driving forces of change.

Externalities (external costs) (243)   External costs are related to the effects and impacts of pollution and residuals from operations, products, and processes, and are borne by stakeholders (*q.v.*), communities, and society. Externalities also include benefits not captured by the producer.

Feedback mechanisms (162)   These are the tools and techniques needed to evaluate performance and communicate outcomes to internal managers, professional people, practitioners, and external shareholders, stakeholders (*q.v.*), and other constituents. The objective is to improve performance in the future and to make positive improvements to enhance sustainable success.

Financial risk (462)   Financial risk includes the failure to achieve an acceptable financial reward, the damage to the corporate reputation and its ability to generate future cash flow, and the costs to mitigate defective products and/or deficiencies of the NPD (*q.v.*) program.

Focus (182)   The approach that concentrates time, effort, and money on a given geographical area or group of customers (*q.v.*) where a competitive advantage can be achieved, or on selected problems where effective solutions (*q.v.*) can be realized.

Framework (151)   A management system (*q.v.*) that includes the interrelated dimensions and the elements and defines the boundaries and scope of the system from a spatial and temporal perspective.

Fusion (433)   Fusion involves two or more technologies that are combined to create a new product having enhanced attributes and expanded potential.

Global enterprise management (125)   Global enterprise management has three levels: the corporate management level, the strategic management (*q.v.*) level, and the operating management level. Corporate management concentrates on the corporate vision (*q.v.*), the desired strategic competitive advantages relative to the global business environment, and the creation of sustainable success. Strategic business management involves assessing, developing, and implementing business strategies and initiatives for leading changes that facilitate the strategic transformation to a richer existence. Operating (product delivery) management addresses near-term goals and related activities to ensure superior performance and exceptional results.

Globalization (10)   The notion that the world's economies are shifting toward a borderless economic structure in which nation states are less relevant and global corporations vie to satisfy customer (*q.v.*) demand based on standardized ("globalized") products and more homogenized approaches. Space and time are compressed and geography is not a critical factor.

Governance (131)   Traditionally, governance involved management control but it is in fact a much more powerful perspective on leading and managing change to achieve positive outcomes. It means that senior management must ensure that management systems (*q.v.*) are functioning properly, that all compliance requirements are understood and met, and that product delivery systems (*q.v.*) are appropriate and effective. Governance means managing change and directing integration and innovation (*q.v.*). It also includes the board of directors' fulfillment of its fiduciary responsibilities to protect intellectual capital (*q.v.*), corporate assets, and the interests of shareholders, society, customers (*q.v.*), stakeholders (*q.v.*), employees, partners, and all other constituents. It means that the structure of the corporation – in particular, its high-level management – is sufficient for managing all potential outcomes, whether they are normal expectations or the most unlikely scenarios.

Green marketing (296) Green marketing, also known as environmentally conscious marketing, was developed in parallel with pollution prevention (P2) (*q.v.*) and Product Stewardship. It has many definitions, depending on the applications and theoretical framework used. It examines the positives attributes and negative impacts of products and services, and attempts to minimize the negatives or turn the negatives into positives.

Green products (283) Green products are designed based on a more balanced perspective of incorporating social, economic, and environmental considerations into product attributes (*q.v.*). It also involves minimizing any negative impacts.

Idea (475) An idea is simply a new product possibility that requires further definition before it can be converted into an opportunity.

Impact assessment (556) Impact assessment is the process of determining the severity and significance of defects and burdens and any related implications. It evaluates the waste and energy flows to determine the impacts and consequences of resource utilization, waste generation (*q.v.*), and disruptive and destructive activities.

Improvement assessment (559) Improvement assessment determines the gains that can be realized through strategic and tactical actions. It involves responding to impact assessments (*q.v.*) and the prioritization of necessary initiatives.

Inclusiveness (37) Inclusiveness is one of the fundamental aspects of SBD (*q.v.*). It is crucial for ensuring that decision-making includes all dimensions, all constituencies, and all effects and impacts – both positive and negative. Today, innovative global corporations are expanding their view of the enterprise (*q.v.*) to include cradle-to-grave participants, partners, stakeholders (*q.v.*), and customers (*q.v.*).

Incremental change (438) Incremental change focuses on proportional improvements in products and technologies, typically measured in terms of 5–20 percent improvement. It is also viewed as evolutionary change.

Industry dimensions (industry structure) (93)
The industry dimensions include the producer, its competitors, and related industries. These dimensions represent the industry structure from an economic perspective. The industry supports customers with the additional product and service choices needed for making purchase decisions, for supporting product applications, and/or for managing the implications of the product.

Infrastructure (92)
The external infrastructure includes Internet communications, telecommunications, energy systems, airways, roads, waterways, atmosphere, etc. These networks and resources add value that facilitates the movement of goods, information, data, waste, and energy to and from the supply networks (*q.v.*). The infrastructure provides logistical support for the flow of products to customers.

Innovation (4)
A change or improvement that has a positive outcome(s) with respect to customers (*q.v.*), stakeholders (*q.v.*), and the organization.

Innovative strategies (403)
Innovative strategies are based on technological innovation (*q.v.*) and creating new technologies that eliminate the deficiencies of earlier versions. The intent is to discover the means and mechanisms to improve the positive side of the value equation and minimize the negative side.

Insights (73)
Insights are the perspectives and/or lessons gleaned from an assessment of the business environment (*q.v.*), or a portion of it, that lead to a broader understanding of reality and how to manage the situation and make appropriate decisions.

Intangibles (102)
Intangibles include the psychological and the other less apparent aspects that may be important to customers (*q.v.*) and stakeholders (*q.v.*).

Integrated product development (IPD) (438)
IPD is the concurrent development of new products using cross-functional teams (*q.v.*) that are aligned strategically and tactically. It is the prevailing form of product innovation (*q.v.*). IPD is a powerful management construct that systematically links the external business environment (*q.v.*) and its needs, wants, opportunities,

and challenges with the internal dimensions of the organization and its capabilities (*q.v.*) and resources to create innovative solutions (*q.v.*) based on improved products and services.

Intellectual capital (350) The intellectual capital of a corporation includes its knowledge, learning, and experience, its intellectual property (patents, trade secrets, protocols, databases), and the creative talents of the people within the organization.

Inventory assessment (535) The inventory assessment is the in-depth identification of the material and energy flows within the product delivery system (*q.v.*) and the quantification of inputs and outputs at each step of the processes used to design and produce the products.

ISO 14000 (22) The International Organization for Standardization (ISO) developed the ISO 14000 family of Environmental Management Standards to provide a framework and guidance for EMSs (*q.v.*), environmental auditing, environmental labeling, environmental performance evaluation, and LCAs.

Lean production (12) A manufacturing system that minimizes inventory and other resources and produces exactly what is required from a customer (*q.v.*) perspective when it is required.

License to operate (285) The term *license to operate* refers to the legal standing of corporations as regulated by governments in their home country and wherever their operations are located. Duly organized corporations have to be registered or sanctioned by each of the countries, states, and/or provinces in which they do business in order to be recognized as legal entities.

Life cycle assessment (LCA) (6) LCA is a systematic methodology used to identify and evaluate the environmental impacts and burdens associated with a product, its related processes, supply and distribution requirements, and applications. LCA uses scientific principles and technical rigor to ensure the validity of the assessments and the appropriateness of the steps taken to make improvements. LCA is a multi-stage input-output model that examines and analyzes all of the inputs and outputs, their consequences and impacts (including materials, products, wastes, and emissions), and the possible options for improving the value creation and the value proposition of products and processes. LCA examines the existing situation and explores the possibilities for systematic improvements through product design, development, and deployment.

Life cycle costing (249)   Life cycle costing is a culmination of all costs from the cradle-to-grave, direct and indirect, private and external, short-term and long-term. It includes all of the costs to acquire the means of production, to produce, store, transport, and manage the product, process, or service, and to use, maintain, improve, and dispose of it, accounting for recycling (*q.v.*), disposal, and residuals (*q.v.*).

Life cycle framework (508)   A life cycle framework provides a systematic view of all the participants and stages in production. It is useful for discovering and understanding opportunities to dramatically improve products and processes, enhancing the linkages and communications between the entities, and improving value creation (*q.v.*) by the entire system.

Life cycle thinking (LCT) (2)   LCT is an inclusive, intellectual methodology for examining, analyzing, and improving products and processes. It includes a "cradle-to-grave" evaluation of the upstream supply network (*q.v.*) management and manufacturing, the downstream aspects of product sale, use and EoL considerations (*q.v.*), and all of the entities related to the production and applications of the products and processes. The use of LCT for reducing environmental impacts, improving economics, and enhancing the social dimensions is based on strategic thinking and an analysis of product requirements, and the selection of the most economic, technical, and environmentally conscious approaches.

Management system (167)   The management system is the integration of all of the processes and activities, the relationships and people, and the leadership and organizational capabilities (*q.v.*), knowledge, skills, and methods. It is the modern platform for translating strategies into the structure of the organization and for implementing initiatives and action plans.

Mass-balance equation (582)	The mass-balance equation is the sum of all of the direct inputs of mass plus the air, water, and secondary materials (such as packaging) which then must equal the sum of the outputs of product(s), by-products, and waste streams.
Mass customization (272)	Mass customization involves creating product platforms that allow the producer to change product configurations to meet the unique specifications of selected customers (*q.v.*) or market segments. Products are tailored to the cultural, environmental, and/or application requirements of selected customers and markets.
Methodology (439)	The processes, procedures, practices, and guidelines used by practitioners and management to formulate and execute strategies, programs, and action plans. It includes the methods, techniques, and analysis to understand the prevailing situation and to determine appropriate actions.
Mission (483)	The mission defines the long-term direction of the organization and how opportunities fit the strategic direction. The mission fuels the passion for achieving outstanding performance and results.
Monitoring (221)	Monitoring involves following specific driving forces and understanding the key issues, concerns, impacts, and implications, and their patterns.
New product development (NPD) (4)	The overarching term used to describe the processes, programs, and practices to identify, conceptualize, design, develop, validate, and commercialize new products and services. It includes the methods, techniques, and processes for making incremental changes (*q.v.*) to the products and product lines employing the prevailing technologies and organizational capabilities (*q.v.*).
New-to-the-world products (439)	Products that are new creations not based on previous product lines or technology platforms. They are normally the results of technology development and new technologies derived from technological innovation (*q.v.*).
Non-governmental Organizations (NGOs) (1)	NGOs are usually voluntary, nonprofit organizations that focus on enhancing the public good or a specific subset of it, including protecting the environment, promoting social justice, developing economic opportunities for the disadvantaged, and working on climate change concerns.

Openness (37)   Openness involves creating an open dialog with all of the constituencies. Openness and transparency (*q.v.*) also involve reaching out to the business environment (*q.v.*) and building trust-based relationships through creating awareness and understanding among customers (*q.v.*) and stakeholders (*q.v.*). It includes open and effective disclosure of critical information and data pertaining to social, economic, and environmental considerations.

Outsourcing (364)   Outsourcing is the set of outside suppliers to provide services or products, frequently offering a cost competitive alternative to performing the required activities in-house.

Pathway (173)   A notion taken from organic chemistry that represents one of several ways to achieve an end result(s). It has the connotation of being a defined route with built-in flexibility.

Performance evaluation system (196)   The performance evaluation system validates decision-making and provides confidence that the strategic analysis (*q.v.*) and direction are on track. It also offers insights about the actions required for meeting targets and objectives, or for taking corrective actions. The performance evaluation system measures the corporation's actual performance against the expectations of customers (*q.v.*), stakeholders (*q.v.*), the community, regulatory agencies, and other constituencies.

Platform (399)   The technology base that a series of products are built upon. The platform is the basic architecture of the technology.

Polluter pays principle (PPP) (245)   PPP is used by governments to establish direct links with the sources of pollution, and make those responsible for the pollution to pay for the costs of managing and abating it.

Pollution prevention (P2) (21)   P2 represents the "second generation" of environmental management that focused on creating EMSs (*q.v.*) to systematically deal with environmental laws and regulations and attempt to prevent pollution and waste problems before they became significant. P2 focused on pollution reduction at source, and reuse (*q.v.*), recycling (*q.v.*), and proper disposal of wastes.

Precautionary principle (PP) (88)	PP involves taking preventive measures when there is good reason to believe that potential danger, harm, or an impact(s) exists even before there is conclusive evidence about causes (causality) and effects and that the most reasonable course of action is to err on the side of safety and human health considerations, and protection of the natural environment.
Preemptive strategies (403)	Preemptive strategies are intended to gain a competitive advantage by significantly improving products and processes; such actions are generally an extension of corporate programs for product innovation, compliance, pollution prevention (P2) (*q.v.*), stewardship, and beyond. The focus is primarily on the product delivery system (*q.v.*) and its portfolio of products and services.
Pre-launch (485)	Pre-launch includes all of the activities required to prepare for the launch of the new product. It includes initiating the marketing campaign, building production facility(s) and/or inventory, and distributing the product.
Primary dimensions (90)	The primary dimensions include the producer, its suppliers and all of their suppliers, the distribution channels, the customers (*q.v.*), their customers and the tertiary users, and all those engaged in the retirement (*q.v.*) and disposal of the products and the residual effects. Michael Porter called this construct the "value system" (*q.v.*).
Principles (118)	Principles can be viewed as links between the vision (*q.v.*), strategies, and objectives of the corporation. They help to provide an understanding of SBD (*q.v.*) and how professionals and practitioners within the SMSs (*q.v.*) and operating management systems should respond to situations. They are intended to provide decision-makers with the means to make effective decisions and balance the competing objectives of the enterprise (*q.v.*).
Private costs (243)	Private costs are the direct and indirect costs associated with the operations of the producer, and typically include the costs of acquiring the materials, production, distribution, and selling.

Process flow diagram (580)	A process flow diagram provides a graphical representation of how parts and materials flow through the process, and depicts the overall behavior of the operating system. Tasks are represented as small rectangles, flows (both physical as well as informational) are represented using arrows, inverted triangles represent inventory storage (incoming material as well as work-in-process), and circles represent the storage of information.
Process management (174)	Process management is a horizontal construct that links activities and actions for converting inputs into outputs in a systematic way.
Product delivery system (79)	The operating system includes the marketing and production of existing products and related services. It includes the contributions of supply networks (*q.v.*) to meet the needs and expectations of customers (*q.v.*) and stakeholders (*q.v.*). It also includes managing EoL considerations (*q.v.*). It focuses on near-term results and the operational requirements to meet expectations.
Product development (18)	The overarching term used to describe the processes, program, and practices to identify, conceptualize, design, develop, validate, and commercialize new products and services.
Product innovation (417)	A broad management construct that includes the initiatives, methods, techniques, and processes for making incremental changes (*q.v.*) and improvements to existing products and services. It involves making evolutionary changes to the products and product lines employing the prevailing technologies and organizational capabilities. It represents superior improvements for meeting the needs of both customers (*q.v.*) and stakeholders (*q.v.*).
Product life cycle thinking (519)	Product life cycle thinking includes planning for the requirements necessary to assure the success of the product after launch and during its life in the market(s).
Product portfolio (565)	The product portfolio includes the core products, related products, services, aftermarket products and services, and their relationship to new products.
Profit maximization (87)	An unproven theory that suggests that the sole purpose of a for-profit corporation is to maximize profits.

Project management (479)	A management construct (*q.v.*) that is used to manage one-of-a-kind programs, especially those involving technological innovation (*q.v.*).
Quantum change (404)	Quantum change represents stepwise improvements that have significant consequences for the value equation, typically measured in terms of factors (200 percent or more) of improvement.
Radical change (84)	Radical change focuses on creating a new reality. It is difficult to articulate the implications precisely, but often the results lead to improvements that are $10 \times$ to $100 \times$ or more. It also involves eliminating significant barriers or burdens associated with the prevailing technologies.
Radical (technological) innovation (62)	Radical (technological) innovation involves creating new-to-the-world technology that brings about revolutionary changes and often creates a brand new industry or market structures, or involves dramatic changes to existing ones. It may involve starting a whole new business unit or subset of it, or making substantial changes to the existing SMS (*q.v.*), including developing new customers (*q.v.*), new markets, new supply networks (*q.v.*), and other related entities.
Recycling (91)	The purpose of recycling is to salvage as much value as possible from retired products and their inherent materials. This includes reusing parts and components, recovering materials, and capturing some beneficial value.
Reductionism (157)	An analytical method used to examine complex products, processes, operations, or systems by dividing the whole into components or parts, and trying to understand the whole through the parts.
Refurbishment (324)	Refurbishment involves restoring the product back to the original specifications. The intent is to provide additional useful life for primary or secondary users. Refurbished products often have reduced capabilities and limited service life.
Regulatory milieu (235)	The regulatory milieu consists of the laws and regulations that mandate specific protocols to be followed during the conduct of business operations. There are four broad

categories of regulation: (1) mandated policies and practices within an industry; (2) standards for performance and outcomes; (3) reporting and information disclosure requirements; and (4) incentives and disincentives.

Related industries (93)   Related industries provide complementary and support products and services that make a new product more valuable or even feasible.

Reliability (4)   Reliability is defined as the probability that the product will perform its specified functions under the anticipated conditions of the design for a specified length of time.

Remanufacturing (325)   The purpose of remanufacturing is to upgrade the product and improve its quality and performance.

Research and development (R&D) (59)   R&D involves basic and applied research in the fundamentals of science and technology to discover new technologies, methods, and applications.

Residuals (76)   Residuals are the unwanted by-products of processes, pollution, discards, wastes, and EoL products that require collection, processing, and disposal.

Retirement (325)   Retirement is a broad term used to characterize the activities involving the afterlife (*q.v.*) treatment of residuals and/or disposal.

Reuse (91)   Reuse involves the secondary and tertiary use of products in similar or unrelated applications. It extends the life of the products through alternative uses.

Reverse logistics (324)   Reverse logistics usually involves collecting discarded products, transporting the waste streams to processing facilities, remanufacturing (*q.v.*) those products that can be refurbished, and processing the residual materials into their elemental roots – thus paving the way for the recovered materials to reenter the value chain as raw materials.

Scanning (110)   Scanning is the sweeping surveillance of the critical social, political, economic, environmental, and market conditions undertaken to find important concerns and issues that may be related to the activities and actions of the corporation and to discover early signals of changes that may have direct and indirect implications for the corporation.

Secondary dimensions (91)	The secondary dimensions include stakeholders (*q.v.*) and the external infrastructure. From an enterprise (*q.v.*) perspective, stakeholders (*q.v.*) and the infrastructure are critical external dimensions that warrant significant consideration. Stakeholders are the supporting, challenging, confronting, and/or controlling entities that influence the life cycle of products, from their development to applications and beyond. The external infrastructure includes Internet communications, telecommunications, energy systems, airways, roads, waterways, atmosphere, etc.
Six-Sigma thinking (183)	Six-Sigma thinking is more than a quality methodology: it is a business philosophy and a way of managing processes for production, operations, or product development (*q.v.*). It focuses on achieving "world-class" performance and distinction by eliminating defects and problems.
Solution (177)	A solution is a multifaceted concept that includes the product, the service, the underlying technology(ies), and all of the tangible and intangible elements of the system that accompany it. It is temporal as well as physical and psychological.
Specifications (382)	The requirements that customers (*q.v.*) seek in the product and what the producer has to provide as attributes (*q.v.*).
Stakeholder (4)	Any individual or group that is directly or indirectly affected by the products, programs, processes, and/or systems, but does not directly benefit as an economic participant such as a customer (*q.v.*) or supplier. Stakeholders (*q.v.*) include government agencies, interest groups, communities, society in general, and other constituencies.
Stakeholder-based model (277)	A model that includes stakeholders (*q.v.*) as co-equal to customers (*q.v.*) and suppliers as participants in the system or process.
Strategic alignment (89)	Strategic alignment is the process to ensure that the internal dimensions are consistent with the strategies, are linked together, and are properly positioned with respect to the external dimensions.

Strategic analysis (153)
This provides an understanding of the current business situation in the light of opportunities and challenges and a determination of the most advantageous avenues for achieving sustainable success.

Strategic management (153)
Strategic management provides the direction and strategic logic for achieving sustainable success. It includes the upstream planning and analysis of strategic business issues, opportunities, and vulnerabilities, and the selection of a vision for the future, long-term objectives, and a grand strategy for the corporation.

Strategic management framework (14)
This involves defining the scope of the business environment (*q.v.*) to be examined, and establishing the essential internal and external dimensions to be included in the strategic analysis (*q.v.*) of opportunities, challenges, and vulnerabilities.

Strategic management system (SMS) (3)
The SMS focuses on the strategic logic of the organization and its mission (*q.v.*). It connects the core operating units at the base of the corporation with the global view of the entire enterprise (*q.v.*). It integrates the objectives, strategies, concerns, and directives of the corporate executives with the management of operations. SMS integrates the organization's processes and resources into a comprehensive framework for managing and directing business strategies (*q.v.*), including those related to technology and NPD (*q.v.*).

Strategic marketing (3)
Strategic marketing places the customer (*q.v.*) at the center of attention, and concentrates the organization's marketing programs and resources on gaining customer awareness, interest, trial, and acceptance.

Strategic technology management (386)
Strategic technology management is the management of technological solutions. It involves planning and analysis, formulating and implementing strategies, selecting and executing development programs, and evaluating results. It includes managing all of the knowledge, technological capabilities, technologies, technological innovation (*q.v.*), and the development processes for managing change and creating new technologies, products, and processes. It provides the architecture for integrating and managing

knowledge and technologies and for being creative and leading change through technological innovation, product innovation (*q.v.*), and the related development processes.

Streamlined life cycle assessment (SLCA) (564)

SLCA examines the essential elements of the system using a predetermined logic for choosing what elements to include or exclude. It uses selected product characteristics or life cycle implications to concentrate on either the product side or the application side of the value system (*q.v.*). The intent is to ascertain the most crucial concerns about the product and its applications and construct an LCA (*q.v.*) framework that addresses the major issues systematically without becoming overwhelmed with nonessential parts of the equation.

Supply networks (10)

Supply networks include the suppliers, suppliers of suppliers, distributors, and other entities that provide the flow of materials and finished goods, information, and relationships from the origins of the raw materials through distribution channels (*q.v.*) to customers (*q.v.*).

Sustainable business development (SBD) (1)

SBD is a holistic management construct (*q.v.*) that includes the entire business system from the origins of the raw materials to production processes and the customer applications and the EoL solution (*q.v.*). SBD involves making dramatic improvement and positive changes to the full scope of relationships and linkages of the supply networks, customers (*q.v.*) and stakeholders (*q.v.*), and support service providers for handling wastes, residuals (*q.v.*), and impacts. It also involves LCT (*q.v.*) and management thinking about all of the effects, impacts, and consequences from cradle-to-grave. It involves achieving sustainable outcomes that balance the performance objectives of the present with the needs and expectations of the future.

Sustainable development (1)

The notion of the sustainable development originated in the Brundtland Report entitled *Our Common Future* prepared by the WCED for the General Assembly of the United Nations. The report defined sustainable development as "[meeting] the needs of the present without compromising the ability of future generations to meet their own needs." Sustainable development inherently means creating a future that minimizes depletion of resources, eliminates impacts of pollution from waste streams, and builds longevity into solutions.

Sustainable product development (524)
Sustainable product development is the search, discovery, and cure for hidden defects that may seriously affect the viability of the new product. It focuses on creating products that are more capable and attractive from environmental management as well as from economic, social, technological, and legal perspectives. The construct focuses on minimizing the risks and liabilities and improving the longevity of the new product.

Sustainability (1)
Sustainability implies that all human and business activities are carried out at rates equal to or less than the Earth's natural carrying capacity to renew the resources used and naturally mitigate the waste streams generated.

Systems integration (509)
Systems integration involves integrating the entire system, from the depths of the supply chain to the far reaches of customers (*q.v.*) and secondary markets; linking the afterlife (*q.v.*) of products and material recovery to the product delivery system (*q.v.*).

Technological change (279)
Technological change involves the driving forces of change in the business environment (*q.v.*) caused by the discovery, invention, and development of new technologies, knowledge, and mechanisms for providing solutions to customers (*q.v.*), stakeholders (*q.v.*), and society, as well as the natural world.

Technological innovation (4)
Technological innovation is the systematic creation of new-to-the-world technologies that are superior to their predecessors and the improvement of existing technology portfolios. Technological innovation also occurs when improvements are made to the use and effectiveness of knowledge, or when technological sophistication and organizational learning are advanced.

Technology (18)
Technology is a complex term that includes art, science, engineering, devices, methods, and know-how that are applied in a beneficial manner.

Technology assessment (415)	Technology assessment is the act of interpreting the results of the scanning (*q.v.*), monitoring (*q.v.*), and forecasting in order to understand how the business environment (*q.v.*) and selected technologies can converge toward a solution.
Technology development (486)	R&D (*q.v.*) and/or related constructs (*q.v.*) for the invention, discovery, and development of new technology(ies). It also includes enhancing technology platforms, improving existing technologies and derivatives of them.
Technology life cycle (487)	The technology life cycle is a time-based theory of technological change that uses the "S" curve to depict the development and growth of a technology. The concept (*q.v.*) is based on biological life cycles, which include early development, rapid growth, maturity, and decline over the life of an organism.
Theoretical construct (161)	A management model that represents the real world situation or management system (*q.v.*) defining how the elements are linked together and how the responsibilities, relationships, and actions, are designed, and examining the spatial and temporal relationships with every constituent.
Total costs (243)	The total costs of any business activity are the sum of private (conventional) costs, public costs, hidden costs, applications costs, and external costs (externalities) (*q.v.*).
Total integration (15)	Total integration includes connecting the entire system, and all of its participants, into a cohesive and high-performance enterprise (*q.v.*) and ensuring that the system functions properly and meets all expectations. Total integration involves effective communications, building relationships and capabilities (*q.v.*), and linking the present with the future.
Total quality management (TQM) (30)	A widely accepted quality management system related to the product delivery system (*q.v.*) or operating system that incorporates the quality management practices and techniques necessary for meeting customer (*q.v.*) expectations in terms of quality, reliability, and responsiveness. The basic philosophy of TQM is to build quality into every product and process and to strive for continuous improvement.

Total satisfaction (137)	Total satisfaction is a complement to the total solution (*q.v.*). It includes ensuring compliance with laws and regulations and other external standards, eliminating external impacts through effective management, providing supporting entities with the proper information, direction, development, and integration, and closing the loop on every question, concern, or problem.
Total solution (137)	The total solution is the integrated contributions of those within the corporation and its support team. It includes excellence in design, superior product and service applications and benefits, waste minimization, pollution prevention (P2) (*q.v.*), EoL (*q.v.*) answers, ongoing support, longevity, and value.
Transparency (12)	Transparency means open disclosure and reporting of social, economic, and environmental performance, including information about products, processes, practices, and the underlying premises and scientific principles.
User pays principle (UPP) (245)	UPP invokes the responsibilities of consumers, users, and owners to pay a more accurate share of the costs of using products that create environmental impacts.
Value creation (37)	Value creation involves moving toward ideal solutions (*q.v.*) with greater benefits, fewer deficiencies, and reduced impacts. The objective is to create the best possible solutions for customers (*q.v.*), stakeholders (*q.v.*), and society; solutions that maximize gains and minimize losses. Such solutions are sustainable solutions.
Value maximization (97)	Value maximization is the underlying premise of a corporation that the main objective is to maximize value for all constituents, including customers (*q.v.*), stakeholders (*q.v.*), shareholders, etc.
Value networks (15)	Value networks are all of the interrelated entities in the enterprise (*q.v.*) that contribute to value creation (*q.v.*) and the sustainable success of the enterprise. They include all of the partnerships, alliances, supply networks, customer (*q.v.*) and stakeholder (*q.v.*) relationships used to create value.
Value proposition (73)	The value proposition examines all of the benefits, positive effects, and knowledge in terms of the investments

made by all of the constituents – and, similarly, all of the costs, defects, and burdens associated with the situation. Figure 2.7 (p. 102) depicts the general form of the value equation from an enterprise perspective.

Value system (162) Michael Porter's construct (*q.v.*) that includes the primary dimensions of the product delivery system (*q.v.*), supply networks (*q.v.*), and customers (*q.v.*).

Vision (82) Vision is the high-level perspective that encapsulates the desired translation of external forces, opportunities, challenges, and internal capabilities (*q.v.*) into a new reality for the enterprise (*q.v.*). It should describe how a sustainable entity can meet the needs of the present and the future. It is generally assumed that the vision may take years, even decades, to realize. Vision is "what the enterprise can be" rather than "what it is." It can be stated in terms of the theoretical instead of the practical, although it should be logical and achievable if it is to be effective. Vision guides the people within the organization as well as customers (*q.v.*), stakeholders (*q.v.*), shareholders, and other constituents, clearly stating for them why the organization exists and what it seeks to do to create an improved future.

Waste generation (298) Waste generation involves the production of unwanted residuals (*q.v.*) including air emissions (gaseous residues), water effluents (liquid residues), and solid waste.

Select Bibliography

GENERAL

Collins, Jim (2001) *Good to Great: Why Some Companies Make the Leap . . . and Others Don't.* New York: Harper Business

Fiksel, Joseph (1996) *Design for Environment: Creating Eco-Efficient Products and Processes.* New York: McGraw Hill

Graedel, Thomas (1998) *Streamlined Life-Cycle Assessment.* Englewood Cliffs, NJ: Prentice Hall

Hamel, Gary (2000) *Leading the Revolution.* Boston, MA: Harvard Business School Press

Kaplan, Robert and David Norton (1996) *The Balanced Scorecard: Translating Strategy into Action.* Boston, MA: Harvard Business School Press

Porter, Michael (1985) *Competitive Advantage: Creating and Sustaining Superior Performance.* New York: Free Press

Pursell, Jr., Carroll (1990) *Technology in America: A History of Individuals and Ideas*, 2nd edn. Cambridge, MA: MIT Press

Rainey, David L. (2005) *Product Innovation: Leading Change through Integrated Product Development.* Cambridge: Cambridge University Press

Senge, Peter M. (1990) *The Fifth Discipline: The Art and Practice of the Learning Organization.* New York: Currency/Doubleday

Weaver, Paul, Leo Jansen, Geert van Grootveld, Egbert van Spiegel, and Philip Vergragt (2000) *Sustainable Technology Development.* Sheffield: Greenleaf Publishing

Wheelwright, Steven and Kim Clark (1992) *Revolutionizing Product Development: Quantum Leaps in Speed, Efficiency, and Quality.* New York: Free Press

World Commission of Environment and Development (WCED) for the General Assembly of the United Nations (1987) *Our Common Future: The Brundtland Report.* Oxford: Oxford University Press

ENTERPRISE THINKING

Chandler, Jr., Alfred (1977) *The Visible Hand: The Managerial Revolution in American Business.* Cambridge, MA: Harvard University Press

Davenport, T. H. (2000) *Mission Critical: Realizing the Promise of the Enterprise Systems.* Boston, MA: HBS Press

Drucker, Peter (1946, 1972) *The Concept of the Corporation*, 1972 edn. New York: The John Jay Co.

Haeckel, S. H. (1999) *Adaptive Enterprise: Creating and Leading Sense-and-Respond Organizations.* Boston, MA: Harvard Business School Press

Hamel, Gary and C. K. Prahalad (1994) *Competing for the Future.* Boston, MA: Harvard Business School Press

Hammer, Michael and James Champy (1993) *Reengineering the Corporation: A Manifesto for Business Revolution.* New York: Harper Business

Lawrence, Paul R. and David Dyer (1983) *Renewing American Industry.* New York: Free Press

Murman, Earll, Thomas Allen, Kirkor Bozdogan, Joel Cutcher-Gershenfeld, Hugh McManus, Deborah Nightingale, Eric Rebentisch, Tom Shields, Fred Stahl, Myles Walton, Joyce Warmkessel, Stanley Weiss, and Shelia Widnall (2002) *Lean Enterprise Value: Insights from MIT's Lean Aerospace Initiative.* New York: Palgrave

Savory, Allan (1999) *Holistic Management: A New Framework for Decision Making.* Washington, DC: Island Press

Slywotzky, A. J. (1996) *Value Migration: How to Think Several Moves Ahead of Competition.* Boston, MA: Harvard Business School Press

Sullivan, P. H. (2000) *Value-Driven Intellectual Capital: How to Convert Intangible Corporate Assets into Market Value.* New York: John Wiley

ENVIRONMENTAL MANAGEMENT

Buchholz, Rogene (1993) *Principles of Environmental Management: The Greening of Business.* Englewood Cliffs, NJ: Prentice Hall

Dennison, Mark (1996) *Pollution Prevention: Strategies and Technologies.* Rockville, MD: Government Institutes, Inc.

Harris, Jonathan M., Timothy A. Wise, Kevin P. Gallagher, and Neva R. Goodwin (2001) *A Survey of Sustainable Development.* Washington, DC: Island Press

Fischer, Kurt and Johan Schot (1993) *Environmental Strategies for Industry: International Perspectives on Research Needs and Policy Implications.* Washington, DC: Island Press

Laszlo, Erwin (2001) *Macroshift: Navigating the Transformation to a Sustainable World.* San Francisco: Berrett-Koehler Publishing

Lesourd, Jean-Baptiste and Steven G. M. Schilizzi (2001) *The Environment in Corporate Management.* Cheltenham: Edward Elgar

Lomborg, Bjørn (2001) *The Skeptical Environmentalist: Measuring the Real State of the World.* Cambridge: Cambridge University Press

Makower, Joel (1993) *The e Factor: The Bottom Line to Environmentally Responsible Business.* New York: Times Books

Ryding, Sven-Olof (1994) *Environmental Management Handbook: The Holistic Approach – from Problems to Strategies.* Amsterdam: IOS Press

Schaltegger, Stefan, Roger Burritt, and Holger Peterson (2003) *An Introduction to Corporate Environmental Management: Striving for Sustainability*. Sheffield: Greenleaf Publishing

Tibor, Tom and Ira Feldman (1997) *Implementing ISO 14000: A Practical, Comprehensive Guide to the ISO 14000 Environmental Management Standards*. New York: McGraw-Hill

INNOVATION MANAGEMENT

Afuah, A. (1998) *Innovation Management: Strategies, Implementation, and Profits*. New York and Oxford: Oxford University Press

Betz, Frederick (2003) *Managing Technological Innovation: Competitive Advantage from Change*. New York: John Wiley

Boutellier, Roman, Oliver Gassmann, and Maximilian von Zedtwitz (2000) *Managing Global Innovation: Uncovering the Secrets of Future Competitiveness*. Berlin: Springer-Verlag

Christensen, C. (1997) *The Innovator's Dilemma: When New Technologies Cause Great Firms to Fail*. Boston, MA: Harvard Business School Press

Day, George and Paul Schoemaker (2000) *Wharton on Managing Emerging Technologies*. New York: John Wiley

Gulati, Ranjay, Mohanbir Sawhney, and Anthony Paoni (2002) *Kellogg on Technology and Innovation*. New York: John Wiley

Hargadon, Andrew (2003) *How Breakthroughs Happen: The Surprising Truth about How Companies Innovate*. Boston, MA: Harvard Business School Press

Janszen, F. (2000) *The Age of Innovation: Making Business Creativity a Competence, not a Coincidence*. London: Prentice Hall

Leifer, R., C. McDermontt, G. C. O'Connor, L. Peters, M. Rice, and R. Veryzer (2000) *Radical Innovation: How Mature Companies Can Outsmart Upstarts*. Boston, MA: Harvard Business School Press

Meyer, M. H. and A. P. Lehnerd (1997) *The Power of Product Platforms*. New York: Free Press

Miller, William and Langdon Morris (1999) *Fourth Generation R&D: Managing Knowledge, Technology, and Innovation*. New York: John Wiley

Phillips, Fred (2001) *Market-Oriented Technology Management: Innovating for Profit in Entrepreneurial Times*. Berlin: Springer-Verlag

Thomke, Stefan (2003) *Experimentation Matters: Unlocking the Potential of New Technologies for Innovation*. Boston, MA: Harvard Business School Press

STRATEGY MANAGEMENT

Day, G. S and D. J. Reibstein with R. Gunther (1997) *Wharton on Dynamic Competitive Strategy*. New York: John Wiley

Grayson, David and Adrian Hodge (2004) *Corporate Social Opportunity*. Sheffield: Greenleaf Publishing

Kaplan, Robert and David Norton (2001) *The Strategy-Focused Organization: How Balanced Scorecard Companies Thrive in the New Business Environment*. Boston, MA: Harvard Business School Press

Kaplan, Robert and David Norton (2004) *Strategy Maps: Converting Intangible Assets into Tangible Outcomes*. Boston, MA: Harvard Business School Press

Sterad, W. Edward and Jean Garner Stead (2004) *Sustainable Strategic Management*. Armonk: M. E. Sharpe

SUSTAINABLE DEVELOPMENT

Bennett, Martin and Peter James (1999) *Sustainable Measures: Evaluation and Reporting of Environmental and Social Performance*. Sheffield: Greenleaf Publishing

Charter, Martin and Michael Jay Polonsky (1999) *Green Marketing: A Global Perspective on Greening Marketing Practice*. Sheffield: Greenleaf Publishing

Charter, Martin and Ursula Tischner (2001) *Sustainable Solutions*. Sheffield: Greenleaf Publishing

Cooper, Phillip and Claudia Maria Vargas (2004) *Implementing Sustainable Development: From Global Policy to Local Action*. Oxford: Rowman & Littlefield

Dresner, Simon (2002) *The Principles of Sustainability*. London: Earthscan Publications

Doppelt, Bob (2003) *Leading Change Toward Sustainability: A Change-Management Guide for Business, Government and Civil Society*. Sheffield: Greenleaf Publishing

Galea, Chris (2004) *Teaching Business Sustainability*. Sheffield: Greenleaf Publishing

Seiler-Hausmann, Jan-Dirk, Christa Liedtke, and Ernst Ulrich von Weizsacker (2004) *Eco-efficiency and Beyond: Towards the Sustainable Enterprise*. Sheffield: Greenleaf Publishing

Index